MOTIVATION AND EMOTION

MOTIVATION
AND EMOTION
A SURVEY OF THE DETERMINANTS
OF HUMAN AND ANIMAL ACTIVITY

PAUL THOMAS YOUNG, University of Illinois

New York • London, John Wiley & Sons, Inc.

to the memory of
WILLIAM STEWART YOUNG
and
ADELE NICHOLS YOUNG

PREFACE

There is a growing recognition of the close relation between the topics of motivation and emotion. In elementary textbooks, the chapters on emotion are placed either within the broader context of motivation or immediately after the material on motivation. Psychologists have recognized that the best way to understand a specific emotion is to analyze the underlying dynamics.

The present book is an outgrowth of some thirty years of teaching university courses concerned with motivation and emotion. From 1929 to 1945, I offered two courses alternately: one entitled "Motivation," the other "Feeling and Emotion." Subsequently the two courses were merged into one entitled "Motivation and Emotion." Along with the teaching of these courses I published two textbooks: *Motivation of Behavior* (1936) and *Emotion in Man and Animal* (1943). Both books are out of print and in need of rewriting to take account of the wealth of new material that has become available. Instead of revising these books, however, it seemed wiser, in view of the current trend, to combine the two topics within a single textbook.

This book is in no sense a revision of the earlier ones. It is a new book, a new survey of the field. Some descriptive portions of this book have been borrowed from the earlier ones. For example, the account of patterns of emotional response in Chapter 9 has been drawn largely from *Emotion in Man and Animal* and the discussion of social incentives and motives in Chapter 11 has been borrowed from *Motivation of Behavior*. The great bulk of material in the present book, however, is entirely new and not contained in either of the previous ones.

One reason for writing this book has been to present the findings from our laboratory at the University of Illinois and to relate our work to that of others. A survey of our studies in experimental hedonism is presented in Chapters 5 and 6. In discussing this work I have gone beyond the doctrine of factual hedonism, as stated in *Motivation of Behavior,* and have presented an out-and-out hedonic theory of regulation, direction, and organization of behavior. While doing this I have also recognized that psychological hedonism is not a completely adequate theory of motivation, but only a part of the whole.

This book is intended for use as a college text in advanced courses on motivation and the affective processes. It can well be used as a collateral textbook or a reference work for courses on learning, adjustment, personality, and related topics. The book is intended for students who have had introductory courses in psychology and who also possess some background in physiology and general biology. A background knowledge of physiology is presupposed, particularly in Chapter 4, which deals with homeostasis, and in Chapter 9, which deals with the bodily mechanisms of emotion. The other parts of the book can be understood by students whose backgrounds are limited to introductory courses in psychology.

The area of psychology covered by this book is exceedingly wide and complex. There is a good deal of confusion within psychology concerning the definition of terms and concepts. Psychologists do not yet agree upon the definitions of basic terms like *drive, need, anxiety, attitude,* and *motive,* and I doubt whether it would be possible to give a definition of *emotion* that all psychologists would accept.

I have defined emotion as an acutely disturbed affective process of psychological origin, and extended this definition to include persistent states of disturbance within individuals. Emotional disturbances assuredly exist as facts of nature. If they did not exist, we could drop the word *emotion* from our psychological vocabulary and consider everything under the heading of motivation.

The present survey shows that there are many specific facts and principles within motivational psychology. In facing the complexity of the materials, the reader will discover that an attempt to structure the field of motivation and emotion is something like working a jigsaw puzzle. Many parts fit into the total picture, but there are obvious gaps and pieces that do not seem to belong. If the present book reveals some of these gaps in our knowledge, and if this revelation leads to further research, it will have served a useful purpose.

This book, as the subtitle indicates, is a survey of the literature upon motivation and emotion. Excellent symposia, handbooks, and reference works are available to anyone who wishes to investigate specific topics down to the grass roots. The advanced student who may wish to investigate a specific problem will be aided by the reading suggestions placed at the ends of the separate chapters. The suggested readings are selected as aids to advanced study, but, obviously, it has been necessary to omit many important works. Also a few questions and exercises have been appended as aids to study.

The general plan of the book is as follows: Certain chapters that deal with closely related topics belong together. The first two chapters are introductory. Chapter 1 treats the nature of causation and explanation, the various views concerning the nature of motivation, and the fundamental points of view towards the individual and his world. The chapter presents the doctrine of psychological relativity. Chapter 2 contains a preview of the principal forms of activity, both specific and general, that are of interest to a student of motivation. These forms include behavioral trends such as play, manipulation, exploration, curiosity, and general activity, as well as persistent goal-directed behavior. The problem of intrinsic motivation is also considered.

Chapters 3 and 4 belong together in that they deal with basic biological determinants: drive, homeostasis, organic need. Instinct is regarded as a descriptive label rather than a determinant of behavior. Instincts are innate patterns of behavior that are common to a species and elicited by environmental stimulus patterns under specific physiological conditions. Drive is a basic explanatory concept. Different views concerning the nature of drive are considered. Chapter 4 deals with two basic concepts: homeostasis and need. The maintaining of homeostasis is a basic principle that determines behavior. *Need* is a separate concept; it can be equated neither with disturbed homeostasis nor with drive. The concept of need is discussed in relation to drive, appetite, and habit; a few experiments upon the control of behavior through homeostatic needs (hunger and thirst) are examined. At the close of Chapter 4, the importance of the homeostatic doctrine is considered, and certain extensions and limitations are noted.

Chapters 5 and 6 belong together. They describe research on the role of affective processes in motivation and learning. Chapter 5 begins with a brief review of the historical background of hedonism in American psychology. It proceeds to a somewhat technical consideration of the hedonic hypothesis which is based, in good part, upon my own studies of food preference, appetite, palatability, and dietary habit. An attempt is made to relate hedonic determinants to the physiological processes of activation. Chapter 6 deals with affective processes in relation to incentive motivation. This chapter considers typical experiments upon positive and negative incentives. It examines the nature of reinforcement and extinction from the point of view of hedonic theory.

Chapters 7 and 8 belong together since they deal with the regulation and direction of activity as distinct from activation, or arousal. Chapter 7 considers purposive behavior, the regulation and direction of activity by determining set, the nature of tension and effort, and the role of feedback and of environmental factors in the regulation of behavior. Chapter 8 deals with the relation between cognition and motivation. The chapter considers the directive-state theory of perception, the role of feeling and evaluation in the determination of action, the nature of cognitive organization as related to motivation, and other topics.

Chapter 9, in a sense, stands alone, but it is related to almost everything in this book. It is the main chapter on emotion. This chapter takes up the difficult task of defining emotion. A basic definition and a proposed extension are given. The chapter considers the physiology as well as the psychology of the emotions. Among the topics discussed are the structure and function of the autonomic nervous system, the surface manifestations of emotion, typical patterns of response that appear in emotional behavior, visceral processes in emotion, and the role of central neural structures in emotional disorganization. The topic of emotion is elaborated upon in Chapters 10 and 12. Chapter 10 contains a discussion of emotional development, emotional maturity and control. Chapter 12 deals with the conflict theory of emotion, the relation of emotion to health and to dynamic processes generally. The topic of emotion is also related to the prior discussions of affectivity in Chapters 5 and 6. Emotion has *not* been identified with affectivity in general but with a specific form of affective process that is characterized by an acute disturbance of psychological origin.

Chapter 10, on the development of motives and emotions, extends the concepts of earlier chapters. Among the topics considered are the interrelation of motivation and learning, the physicochemical regulation of growth and behavior, the effects of early experience upon subsequent performance, the nature of emotional development, and the role of feeling and emotion in psychological growth. Emotional development is similar to all other aspects of psychological development. It is a progressive change within the individual which can be examined from the point of view of organization or from the point of view of disorganization and reorganization (adjustment).

In Chapter 11 the search for determinants is extended into the social and personal areas. Human behavior is determined by cultural patterns and by interpersonal and intergroup relations as well as by physiological determinants. Also social motives and incentives play a tremendously important part in the control and regulation of behavior. The study of determinants is carried into the field of personality. Dynamic concepts like need, interest, attitude, orientation, and value are viewed as hypothetical constructs—factors within personality. These are factors that can be tested and measured. The dynamic self-system is also considered. In any comprehensive survey of motivation one must examine self-knowledge, self-evaluation, ego-involvement, and related topics. In general, the search for determinants extends beyond the individual into the cultural, social, as well as into the physical, worlds; but the psychologist's interest in motivation centers around the *individual* who lives through his life cycle within a social order.

In Chapter 12, motivation and emotion are related to the dynamics of behavior. The relation of motivation and emotion to frustration, conflict, stress and neurosis, is examined. The practical bearing of motivation and emotion upon health and adjustment is considered. The general aim of the last chapter is to relate motivation and emotion to conflict, adjustment, and human welfare.

A general conclusion is added. It introduces no new content but is an evaluation and an overview of the whole. When one has made an excursion through a vast territory that is poorly mapped and has paused at various points along the way one looks back to gain an impression of the trip. Some general conclusions and suggestions to other explorers of the same land are given.

Motivation is a word that wears a halo. It is like *justice, democracy, freedom.* Everybody approves of it. Yet there is little agreement as to what it means. Furthermore, the whole field of motivational psychology is characterized by turmoil, confusion, and uncertainty. I have recommended a multifactor approach to the study of motivation, that the serious student restrict his aims, and that he remain tolerant. The unity of psychology will be found, I believe, not in the data, for they are diverse and observed from various points of view, but in the inferences and interpretations based upon the data.

PAUL THOMAS YOUNG

Urbana, Illinois
March, 1961

ACKNOWLEDGMENTS

My obligations are many. I am indebted to the hundreds of investigators whose work produced the body of material that is surveyed in this volume. In a real sense this book is a reflection of the labor of others. The field of motivation and emotion is rich—so rich, in fact, that a wholly different selection of illustrative materials could be made with little or no overlap. I must assume responsibility for the selection of illustrative materials as well as for the accuracy of presenting the work of others, but, obviously, I am not responsible for confusion and contradiction that presently exist within the broad field of motivational psychology.

The symposia upon motivation published by the University of Nebraska Press, under the editorship of Marshall R. Jones, have proved to be a gold mine of information. These papers contain useful points of view, suggestions and references; I have drawn extensively upon them in writing this book. The symposia indicate the wide range of topics commonly included under the rubric of motivation and the wealth of factual content available as well as differences in emphasis, point of view and interpretation among investigators.

I am indebted to a group of research assistants, graduate students and colleagues at the University of Illinois who, through the years, have assisted in various ways. Some of my colleagues have assisted by furnishing sound counsel in research, by letting me see and utilize their unpublished manuscripts, by reading and criticizing specific parts of the text and making constructive suggestions, by replying to inquiries, furnishing offprints, and helping in various other ways. Among those who have assisted are Doctors David Asdourian, Charles W. Eriksen, G. Robert Grice, Joseph McV. Hunt, William E. Kappauf,

Lawrence I. O'Kelly, and Ivan D. Steiner. I am indebted to Dr. Lyle H. Lanier for arranging a light teaching schedule for me so that I could give time and energy to research and writing.

The following psychologists furnished photographs or communicated materials that have been used in the text: Doctors Nancy Bayley, Ralph R. Brown, Elmer A. Culler, Harry F. Harlow, Donald W. Lauer, Donald B. Lindsley, Neal E. Miller, James Olds, Phil S. Shurrager, and B. F. Skinner. The photographs of an aquarium shown in Figure 2 were taken by the Photographic Department of Harvard University.

Credit for quotations and illustrations borrowed from the literature has been given at the place of citation. The following organizations have granted permission to reproduce figures and excerpts from copyrighted sources: *American Journal of Psychology*, American Psychological Association, Appleton-Century-Crofts, Cambridge University Press, Clarendon Press, Columbia University Press, Cornell University Press, Harcourt, Brace and World, Harper and Brothers, Holt, Rinehart and Winston, Houghton Mifflin Company, McGraw-Hill Book Company, The New York Academy of Sciences, W. W. Norton and Company, Oxford University Press, The Ronald Press, W. B. Saunders Company, University of Nebraska Press, John Wiley and Sons, Williams and Wilkins Company, Yale University Press.

In the early stages of writing this textbook my wife, Josephine K. Young, M.D., read and revised portions that have a medical aspect and helped with the manuscript in other ways. And during the process of publication Mrs. Roxana Keenan, Staff Editor of John Wiley and Sons, has greatly improved the readability and style.

To all of these individuals and organizations I acknowledge a debt of gratitude.

CONTENTS

1 ORIENTATION

The problem of motivation is far more complex than the Freudians would have us believe and its solution is to be sought in the investigation of many related fields: the analysis of specific instinctive responses, the neural basis of emotions, the mutual influence of habits, the total integration of all such systems of reaction.

K. S. LASHLEY

To the layman the analysis of motives is an attempt to answer the question "Why?" Why did Johnnie steal the apples? Why did Mary run away from school? Why did Mr. Jones decide upon teaching as a profession? Why did the criminal shoot his victim? Why . . . ? Such questions call for answers. They present a challenge to the psychologist.

The layman is aware that purposes, desires, and other motives, lead him to act. He imputes similar conscious processes to other individuals to help him understand their ways. He has read a little psychoanalysis and knows that unconscious motives influence human conduct. The reasons which an individual gives to justify his actions may be nothing but rationalizations—defense reactions which conceal some irrational determinant of conduct.

To understand human behavior better, to gain insight into and to explain the actions of people (including one's self), the student turns to psychology and, especially, to the study of motivation. Practical considerations also lead to this study. We desire to understand, to influence, and to control our own behavior and that of others.

1

THE PRACTICAL ORIENTATION

In applied psychology motivation is taken for granted. Investigators are more concerned with practical problems than with the nature and theory of motivation. An example of the practical orientation is found in a symposium on marketing (Cole, 1956) held at the University of Illinois.

A report of this symposium shows the breadth of views that investigators take. In the area of marketing, motivation research is concerned with practical problems such as: What makes the consumer buy what he does? What factors influence him? In the study of these problems investigators range widely over the fields of anthropology, sociology, psychology, psychoanalysis, and others. Any approach that throws light upon the determinants of consumer behavior appears to be of interest.

Much of the same can be said about motivational research as related to personnel problems, morale in the army, the applications of psychology to industry, education, social problems, engineering, health, and other areas. A broad and multifactor view of the determinants of human behavior is usually taken.

Experiments have been performed which show that motivational factors produce increments and decrements in human performance. A few examples are these: (1) With human subjects the speed of reaction depends upon knowledge of results (information about speed of reaction) and upon punishment (electric shock) for slow responses. (2) The amount of muscular work accomplished during a constant work period depends upon the presence or absence of a visible goal. (3) The score that a child makes on an intelligence test depends upon whether he is praised or reproved for his efforts. (4) In a factory the rate of production varies with the wage-incentive system employed. (5) In the laboratory the precision and coordination of muscular movements depends upon whether or not the subject is "razzed" during his test of performance. In these as in similar examples the level of performance has been found to vary with conditions defined as motivating.

Experiments with human and animal subjects have shown that the level of performance varies with the *degree* of motivation. For any task there is an optimal degree, or level, of motivation, i.e., a degree of motivation that yields maximal output. Many industrial workers are undermotivated; increased incentive would result in improved perform-

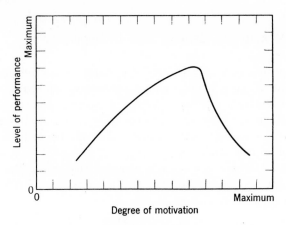

Figure 1. Representation of the general relation between level of performance and degree of motivation.

ance. But when the degree of motivation is above a critical level, there is disturbance of performance and lowered efficiency. The subject is overmotivated.

A representation of the general relation between degree of motivation and level of performance is given in Figure 1. This figure illustrates what is meant by undermotivation, optimal motivation, and overmotivation. If we think of motivation in terms of the degree of activation, then the base line represents degrees of activation, or motivation. The relationships pictured can be demonstrated in many specific experiments, but the present illustration is general. It implies that motivation is a *quantitative variable* and that the level of performance varies with the degree of motivation. Nothing is implied concerning the hypothetical nature of motivation as such.

In general, psychotechnologists have little concern for the theory of motivation. Their orientation is practical. The industrial psychologist, for example, seeks to find a wage-incentive system that yields optimal production and high morale. Again, the educational psychologist seeks a method of motivating Mary and Johnnie so that they will study their arithmetic lessons more effectively. To such practically minded men the study of motivation is important without regard to theoretical considerations.

CAUSATION AND THE SEARCH FOR DETERMINANTS

To the professional psychologist the study of motivation is much more than an attempt to untangle human motives and to reveal mental causation. Motivational psychology is a study of the conditions that determine the occurrence and patterns of human and animal activity. The scientific search for determinants goes far beyond the layman's view of mental causation.

Before we examine contemporary views concerning the nature of motivation, it will be well to consider the problem of causation and explanation within psychology.

Causation and "Free Will"

The layman believes that the events of nature are determined by causes, but the man of science is likely to say little about causation. He speaks in terms of correlation and covariation, in terms of dependent and independent variables, and in terms of conditions and determinants.

A primitive man thinks of spirits and animate forces as the causes of natural events, including human behavior. He thinks of his own spirit as an efficient cause of his actions. This manner of thought is known as animism.

The layman thinks of himself as a "free" moral agent. It is an ancient doctrine and a widespread belief that a man is a free agent capable of choosing between right and wrong courses of action. In important decisions, a man believes that he is free to choose between two courses of action. Will it be a career in law or in business? Will he propose marriage to Jane or to Helen? Will he invest money in common stocks or in bonds? A man deliberates. Decision may turn out to be wise or unwise but at the time of choice the man believes himself to be a free moral agent. Also in the most trivial matters a man believes himself to be free.

I sit at my desk with pencil in hand. I can lay it down at the right or at the left; I can pick it up and place it in the center or hold it in the air as I wish. Certainly I feel that I am free to do with the pencil as I will.

Physicists, chemists, and biologists, in contrast with the layman, explain behavior in mechanistic terms. The human body is a machine interacting with the physical environment and subject to physical laws. Behavior depends upon the organic structures and environmental factors that release energy within the tissues and that regulate the pattern of response. Most biologists object to the introduction of mentalistic and vitalistic forces to explain why we act as we do.

Freud assumed that all mental processes are causally determined. Slips of the tongue, breaking and losing objects, forgetting names, failures to keep appointments, and the other irregularities are not pure accidents but are dependent upon mental causes. Although fundamental motivations are frequently unconscious, all behavior is motivated in the sense of being causally determined.

The serious discussion of the problem of "free will" can safely be left to philosophers, but two points should be made before we drop the topic: First, the question of free will does not arise in the psychological laboratory. The experimenter can observe and analyze uniformities of behavior and experience. He can seek to discover the determinants of behavior, including the determinants of choice and preference, without raising the question of free will. Second, when we assume that decision is influenced by reasons, beliefs, attitudes, wishes, neural associations, habit structures, and similar factors, we are postulating a kind of psychological determinism. Motivational psychology has a great deal to say about the determinants of choice and action.

The postulate of free will does not really explain anything in a scientific sense. So for purposes of the present discussion, we will postulate that all behavior is dependent upon certain conditions and determinants. When a psychologist seeks to *explain* something, he looks for the essential conditions and determinants of the event. Our quest in this book will be a search for determinants.

Motivation as a Mental Determinant

Troland (1928), in an early work on *The Fundamentals of Human Motivation*, wrote that the problem of motivation presents a paradox. When we ask for motives, we demand a mental explanation for events that are physical. The problem of motivation, he wrote, is *psychophysiological* in that it involves conscious experience as well as overt behavior and physiological events that are hidden within the brain.

The layman does not worry about physiology. In a criminal court, for instance, the bodily processes of the suspect are of little concern, but motivation remains of paramount importance. The difference between murder and manslaughter is a difference of motivation. If a man is convicted of murder, he may go to the electric chair; if of manslaughter, he receives a lighter sentence. The court is not concerned with the neural mechanisms and glandular processes involved. An exact account of the physical processes in nerves, muscles, and glands would be regarded by the layman as boresome and also as an inadequate explanation of the act.

The word *mental* implies the existence of conscious experiences in the lives of individuals. To the layman and to many others a *motive* is, as Troland said, something mental. Let me take an example from everyday life:

A man who is lying down on a couch says, "I am going to the basement to fix the furnace and then I'm going to lie down again." Following this statement he arises, carries out a sequence of acts that can best be described by his own words—"going to the basement," "fix the furnace," "lie down." Now the verbal statement and the sequence of actions are all that we have actually observed. We postulate, however, a third factor in the situation—an inner determination, or motive, to carry out a specific sequence of acts as verbally stated. This inner determination is what we commonly designate as a *motive*.

The motive, please note, is postulated and not observed. Conceivably some neurologist of the future might observe the clicking and setting of neural machinery by means of some ultramodern electronic device; but if this were possible, it would provide just one more bit of material evidence. The layman would still postulate a motive.

There are many words to label this inner determination: *purpose, intent, aim, goal, decision.* We say, "my mind is made up," "I am set to act," "I intend to do this." To the psychologist this presents a problem or, better, a group of problems.

A postulated motive has various attributes. It persists in time. It directs and regulates behavior. It is terminated by the achievement of an end or goal. It energizes and arouses action in the individual. A motive, moreover, can be latent (inactive) for considerable periods of time. If, for example, I resolve to take a trip next week, the mental determination does not show itself continuously but only from time to time. I sleep and wake and carry out innumerable activities with this motive latent throughout.

Motives are described in words, and they may also be inferred from overt behavior. Of course, words can mislead. A man might lie about his motives, or distort them, or refuse to verbalize them, or deny that they exist; but words can, and often do, communicate motives correctly.

The layman commonly distinguishes between motives and habits.

The difference is this: A motive is properly described as a readiness to carry out some specific act. The motive is capable of building up tension or causing action. The motive, moreover, is removed by completion of an intended act, i.e., by a goal response. A habit, contrastingly, lacks these attributes. Habits are patterns of neural organization that make it possible for individuals to carry out innumerable acts of skill; but they do not instigate, sustain, and regulate action in a dynamic sense. Insofar as they do, they are motivating.

For example, the question, "How much is 8 times 9?" motivates the response, "72." The habit organization that made this possible was acquired years ago through drill and other experiences in the schoolroom. The habit organization was latent until the individual was motivated by a problem.

Causation and Covariation

In his classical analysis of causation, David Hume pointed out that causation implies a regular conjunction of cause and effect and, furthermore, the effect has a functional dependence upon the cause. All of us believe that the effect *necessarily* follows the cause but our belief in the necessary connection, Hume argued, is not based directly upon sensory experience. All we observe is a sequence of cause and effect.

In a careful study of the explanation of human behavior, Smith (1951) considered the nature of causation. In a somewhat negative statement he wrote: ". . . a cause of a phenomenon would be defined as *any condition or occurrence, which if it did not exist or had not existed, would result in the phenomenon not being precisely what it is observed to be."*

The explanation of a bit of human behavior involves the discovery of a whole network of causal relationships. If the complex web of relations is known and the causal status of these relations assured, the act is explained. Ordinarily, however, it is difficult or impossible to discover all of the causal determinants of a human act.

Some have argued that science can dispense with the concept of causation and simply describe covariations and functional relations. For example, it is known that the length of a metal rod increases as the temperature rises. One can plot a curve to show the relation between length of rod and temperature. One can determine the mathematical equation of the curve. The graph and the equation are useful to the engineer who wants to allow for expansion and contraction with changes of temperature; but the concept of causation is unnecessary. The graph shows covariation without causal sequence.

In an important theoretical paper, Ritchie (1954) argued that the science of psychology must abandon the common-sense notion of causation and substitute a study of functional relations. He pointed out that what we actually do in the laboratory is to investigate the relations between variables. For example, consider what we mean when we say, "The subject is thirsty." We may refer to an internal bodily state. Laboratory studies of thirst, however, express the facts by graphs and equations. The results from the Columbia obstruction apparatus (which requires a thirsty rat to cross an electrically charged grid in order to reach water) show a definite relation between the frequency with which a rat crosses the grid during a 20-minute period and the number of hours of water deprivation. Other studies show quite different relations, as that between the rate of drinking and the viscosity of the saliva.

Such relations can be generalized in this way: $(X) \phi (X)$. The formulation is symmetrical in the sense that it expresses a relation without implying temporal sequence. When we say, "The subject is thirsty," we predicate a state or disposition of the subject. When we attempt to describe the state or disposition, we do so with two-termed symmetrical statements of functional relation in the form $(X) \phi (X)$.

If we want to measure within psychology, Ritchie states, both terms in the statement $(X) \phi (X)$ must be expressed physically. Psychologists can and do operate, however, with derived magnitudes like the physical magnitude *density*. An example of a derived magnitude within psychology is *palatability*. Ritchie states that the palatability constant p has exactly the same logical, mathematical, and physical status as the constant R in Ohm's law, which is used to measure the resistance of various substances.

It is beyond doubt that quantitative relations within psychological phenomena can be expressed by graphs and equations precisely as Ritchie has claimed. These representations are descriptive. They show relationships of covariation and dependence.

A positivist would stop with the description of observed phenomena and the relations among them. He would see no need for postulating extrinsic motives and causes—no need for drives, forces, and other forms of impetus.

As Kelly (1958) has put it:

Perhaps we can condense the argument into three sentences. First we saw no need for a closet full of motives to explain the fact that man was active rather than inert; there was no sense in assuming that he was inert in the first place. And now we see no need to invoke a concept of motives to explain the directions that his actions take; the fact that he lives in anticipation automatically takes care of that. Result: no catalogue of motives to clutter up our system and, we hope, a much more coherent psychological theory about living man.

The Nature of Explanation within Psychology

How do psychologists explain? They explain in various ways:

Lewin (1927) distinguished three forms of explanation. The first form he called *conditional* explanation, or explanation in terms of underlying conditions. For example, water-seeking behavior is explained by a physiological account of the bodily mechanisms of thirst that underlie behavior. The second form he called *genetic* or *historical* explanation. This is explanation in terms of previous conditions. For example, a phobia can be explained by reference to a fright that occurred earlier in the life cycle of the subject. Since genetic explanation is an account of previous conditions, the two forms of explanation are really one. Lewin referred to this as *conditional-genetic* explanation, or explanation in terms of present and previous conditions. Opposed to conditional-genetic explanation is a third form that is something different; namely, *theoretical* explanation. When a chemist postulates the existence of atoms, he is giving a theoretical explanation. He is going beyond the facts of observation. Similarly, when a psychologist postulates associative bonds, neural sets, and dispositions, he is resorting to a theoretical form of explanation.

Lewin distinguished between the observed forms of behavior and the underlying motivation of behavior. Two bits of behavior may look alike but be differently motivated. A skilled actor, for example, may express anger on the stage so convincingly that the pattern is indistinguishable from genuine anger. The aim of the actor may be to put on a good performance; genuine anger is determined by the frustration of some purpose. Again, bits of behavior may be very unlike in appearance but, nevertheless may express a common motivating tension. For example, a man leaves the house with a letter to mail. He can drop the letter in a mail box, or hand it to a postman, or ask a friend to mail it. These bits of behavior are superficially very different, yet, according to Lewin, they stem from a common motivating tension. Borrowing terms from biology, Lewin called patterns of behavior that look alike *phenotypes,* regardless of their motivation. He used the term *genotype* to designate patterns of behavior that have a common motivation, regardless of their outward appearance.

Stanley Cobb (1948) is another who became interested in the nature of explanation. Within psychiatry he reduced the multiplicity of probable causes to four main categories: *"genogenic,* or hereditary; *histogenic,* or due to visible lesion of the tissue; *chemogenic,* or due to ultramicroscopical changes in structure; and *psychogenic,* or due to maladjustments in interpersonal relations." Psychiatrists, he said, explain by reference to heredity, or to bodily structures or to chemical agents, or to past experience—especially social experience.

Thus there are various ways in which men seek to explain human and animal activity. These ways can be integrated.

To the above I might add, finally, a sixfold reclassification of the forms of explanation within psychology. When a psychologist seeks to explain human and animal behavior, he takes one or more of these paths:

1. He turns to the genes and the mechanisms of heredity, possibly to the processes of organic evolution, and to ontogenetic development.

2. He explains in terms of hormones and other chemical factors that act directly upon neural centers and upon other bodily structures.

3. He turns to physical conditions and explains in terms of stimulus and response, distinguishing different forms of stimulation, and distinguishing between external and internal patterns of stimulation.

4. He explains in terms of the structure of the organism, especially in terms of the structure of the nervous system, depending upon the biological structure-function principle.

5. He turns to the sociocultural environment. The child, a biological organism growing up within a society, acquires the ways of his group and is influenced by interpersonal relations.

6. He explains in terms of the conscious experiences of individuals. Especially important for the student of human motivation are affective experiences (distress, relief, enjoyment, satisfaction), conscious meanings (perceptions, memories, fantasies), the awareness of aims (intentions), and expectations. In everyday life as well as in ethics, religion, law, and other areas, a motive is considered to be a *conscious* determinant of action; but psychologists also consider *unconscious* motivations.

Pseudo Explanations

Lewin's three forms of explanation—conditional, genetic, theoretical —have one thing in common. In each form something is added to the facts that are to be explained. The conditional type of explanation gives us additional information about conditions that underlie behavior. The genetic type tells us about previous conditions. The theoretical type tells us about hypothetical or imagined conditions.

If an explanation tells us nothing new, it is a pseudo explanation. If an explanation gives us no additional facts or hypotheses, we have no greater knowledge after the explanation than before.

A common form of pseudo explanation involves a fallacy known to logicians as *hypostatization*. This is the fallacy of naming something, then assuming that the name designates a reality. For example, a layman states that birds have an instinct to fly, spiders have an instinct to build webs, monkeys have a gregarious instinct, men have an instinct of workmanship. The term *instinct* is a useful label for patterns of behavior that are innate; but the word explains nothing. If we explain that birds fly because they have an instinct to fly, spiders build webs because they have a web-building instinct, etc., we have added nothing to the facts that are to be explained. We become guilty of hypostatization.

Genuine explanation is not so simple. Consider, for example, the explanation of the process of food ingestion. When an organism eats a bit of food the process looks very simple but there are actually a good many determinants. Food ingestion is determined by: (1) past experience that has resulted in formation of feeding habits and attitudes towards specific foodstuffs, (2) the organic state of hunger which in itself is complex, (3) the sense appeal (palatability level) of the foodstuff, and in man (4) by social customs and taboos which have influenced the formation of habits and attitudes. Each determinant can be broken down further into many specific factors that influence the process of food ingestion. To postulate a single instinct or drive or motive to ingest food is quite inadequate.

The nature of pseudo explanation can be illustrated by a song that we used to sing to the tune of *Auld Lang Syne:*

> We're here because we're here
> Because we're here because we're here.
> We're here because we're here
> Because we're here because we're here.

After the song there is still an unanswered question: "Why are we here?"

The Search for Determinants

If we eliminate the concept of causation as scientifically useless, and substitute concepts of covariation, correlation, and factor analysis, what happens to the psychology of motivation?

My answer is that we still need to search for the conditions that determine the occurrence of such phenomena as food seeking, sexual behavior, exploratory and manipulative behavior, play, and other forms of activity. We still need to account for goal direction and for the interplay of the determinants of human and animal activity. We still need to search for the *determinants* of activity.

There is need for a sound descriptive psychology of experience and behavior—for a psychology that does not become involved in questions about causation and motivation—but there is also need for an explanatory and theoretical psychology.

Representations by graphs and equations bypass temporal sequences and in this way eliminate causation from the picture. Such representations give the impression of static relationships. But a temporal and developmental view is necessary in studying many problems of motivation and emotion. To illustrate: The concept of motivation implies that an event occurring at one time (e.g., decision) influences subsequent activities. Since a temporal sequence is fundamental in motivational psychology, any static or purely descriptive view is bound to be inadequate. After the graphs have been drawn and the equations formulated there still remains the problem of explaining the sequences of behavior. This problem lies at the heart of motivational psychology.

After the determinants have been described there still remains the problem of investigating the dynamic interaction of determining factors in frustration, conflict, stress, problem-solving behavior, the making of adjustments, and the relation of these determinants to health.

A search for the determinants of human and animal activity goes beyond descriptive analysis to a study of the conditions—present and past—that influence activity. These conditions may be physiological, as with the bodily mechanisms that regulate homeostasis, or they may lie outside the organism within the physical or social worlds. They may lie in previous experiences of individuals. In any event, a search for determinants goes far beyond the purely descriptive account of phenomena in terms of covariation, correlation, and factor analysis.

Kinds of Determinants

The main aim of this book is to survey the determinants of human and animal activity. A search for determinants is complicated by the fact that there are several kinds of determining factors. At least these four categories of determination must be considered.

1. *Activating* determinants are those that arouse, evoke, stimulate, instigate, and initiate action through energy transformations within the tissues. They change a relatively passive state of the organism or a latent neural structure into an active state. Forms of activation are sensory stimulation, chemical excitation of neural centers, neural activation by brain cells, and activation through perception of a situation, or through the building up of proprioceptive tension.

2. *Regulating* and *directing* determinants are those that orient, steer, channel, limit, or restrict the course of action without activating behavior. There are passive and active forms of regulation. The curves in a railway track passively regulate the path that the locomotive takes through space without energizing the machine.

Some physical conditions *support* behavior without regulating it, and perhaps they should be called *supporting conditions*. For example, speech is supported by the surrounding air, for without this, sound waves and communication would be impossible. Again, when a man takes a step forward, the floor supports his weight and makes walking possible, but the floor does not activate behavior.

In contrast with conditions which support and passively regulate behavior, there are factors which actively regulate and direct the course of action. A postural set, a goal orientation, and an intent to carry out some act, are examples.

3. *Predisposing* determinants are those that bias, prepare, make ready, set, or sensitize the organism in a particular way. For example, the instructions to a laboratory subject predispose him to react in a specific way. Again, when Grandmother is searching for her glasses she is predisposed to find them.

Predisposing conditions are also regulating and directing, and they may be activating determinants of behavior.

4. *Organizing* determinants are those that create new patterns of action. For example, affective processes organize patterns of approach

or avoidance; they regulate the development of preferences and habitual discriminations.

The organizing function is not the same as learning through exercise, but the organizing function determines what patterns are likely to be learned. Analysis of the organizing of behavioral patterns takes us into the very heart of developmental psychology, for *organizing* is a process of forming neurobehavioral patterns.

If we make an honest search for all kinds of determinants of human and animal activity, we must take account of habit strength along with the organizing principle. We must take account of learning and other factors in the development of behavior.

VIEWS CONCERNING THE NATURE OF MOTIVATION

When we turn to technical psychology, a diversity of opinion is apparent. Psychologists do not agree upon the basic concepts, and there is little indication that they are approaching agreement. Littman (1958) considered the problem of motivation and found it exceedingly complex. He found that different definitions of motivation have little in common except, perhaps, an ancient distinction between "active" and "passive."

In the following sections some of the main views concerning the nature of motivation are briefly considered.

Broad and Narrow Views of Motivation

Is all behavior motivated? Most of us would answer "Yes," meaning that all behavior is causally determined. We might point out that everything has a cause and that motivation is just the cause of behavior. Some psychologists, however, would reply "No." They would distinguish between "motivated" and "unmotivated" behavior.

McDougall (1923) is one who takes the narrow view. He distinguishes between behavior and physiological processes. Behavior is always purposive—characterized by striving towards a goal. Reflexes are not behavior; they are physiological processes. Reflexes: (1) lack the spontaneity of behavior, (2) lack the persistence of behavior, (3) are stereotyped and fixed, (4) do not present the appearance of seeking a goal, (5) do not show preparation for an oncoming event or situation, and (6) are not improved by repetition as are the movements of behavior. The study of motivation, according to Mc-

Dougall, is limited to purposive behavior. Reflexes are causally determined, according to McDougall, but not motivated. Most psychologists, however, would regard a reflex as a bit of behavior, and all would agree with McDougall that the reflex is causally determined.

Another psychologist who has given a restricted definition of motivation is Maier (1949). He is concerned with an important distinction between behavior that is goal-oriented and behavior that is caused by frustration and that lacks a goal. "Motivated" behavior, Maier states, is goal-directed activity; but frustration leads to abnormal forms of behavior that are not oriented towards goals.

As a matter of fact, Maier operates with three main categories of behavior: (1) motivated behavior that is characterized by persistent goal orientation, (2) frustration-instigated behavior or behavior without a goal, and (3) reflexes and automatic behavior that are determined only be neural connections. For Maier, the reflex is neither motivated nor frustration-instigated; it is regulated mechanically by neural structure. (See pages 535–538.)

Maslow (1954) is another psychologist who states that some behavior, but not all, is motivated. For him motivated behavior is need-related. Maslow has described a hierarchy of human needs extending from the basic physiological needs to the need for self-actualization. (See pages 588–590.) Motivated behavior is related to these needs. Mechanical associations are not motivated. For example, if the stimulus word *table* elicits the response word *chair*, the response is determined by associative mechanisms and is not need-related; hence the response is not motivated.

Such views of motivation are narrow in the sense that they restrict the concept of motivation to behavior which is purposive or goal-oriented or need-related. They exclude reflexes and other physiological processes, abnormal patterns, and mechanical associations from the study of motivation.

This writer has consistently argued for a broad and multifactor view of motivation, asserting that all behavior is motivated (causally determined). The task of a student of motivation becomes that of seeking out the determinants of activity whether the behavior is goal-directed or not.

The argument for a broad view of motivation runs something like this: Behavior is a form of physical movement, and, like all physical movement, it is causally determined in the sense that it depends upon conditions. It is not necessary to assume, of course, that all forms of physical movement are behavior. When an apple falls to the earth, there is physical movement but no true behavior. When a man falls out of a window, his fall through space is physically determined, as with the falling apple, but falling to earth is a purely physical movement. The man may struggle as he falls, but there is an inexorable force of gravitation. Thus, all physical movement is causally determined, and behavior is one form of physical movement.

This broad view makes it possible to study all psychological activity within the framework of physical science. The broad view permits one to study all the determinants of all forms of behavior. One can study the development of purposive activity and its dissolution when an organism is frustrated. One can study reflexes, stereotyped patterns, and automatic responses, as well as goal-directed activities, under the broad heading of *determinants*.

Of course, one must distinguish between physical and psychological determinants. If a man jumps out of a window in an attempt to commit suicide, his behavior is motivated. But his fall is physically determined even though he waves his arms, grasps at objects, and shows other behavior during the fall. The search for determinants is broader in scope than the study of narrowly-defined motives.

Energizing and Regulating Functions

We have seen that some psychologists restrict the definition of motivation to behavior that is purposive or goal-oriented or need-related. There is another way in which the scope of motivational psychology has been restricted.

Fryer (1931), in a book upon the measurement of interests, distinguished between motivation and interest. Motivation, he stated, is the *energy* aspect of experience and reaction; a basic motivational principle is that varying degrees of stimulation liberate different quantities of energy. Interest, contrastingly, refers to the *acceptance-rejection* aspect of reaction and to the qualitative patterns of behavior. The measurement of motivation and the measurement of interest, Fryer stated, should be kept separate to avoid confusion.

A somewhat similar distinction was drawn by Brown (1953) and by Farber (1955). They defined motivation as an energizing, dynamogenic function, and they defined learning as an associative, regulative function. (See pages 104–106 and 418–420.) The directive and regulative aspects of behavior are attributed to learning—to the formation of habits and associations. Motivation is entirely a matter of the energetics of activity.

In one sense, the view shared by Brown and Farber is broad. If motivation is the process of arousing behavior through energy transformations within the tissues, then all behavior—whether learned or innate—is motivated, for behavior is completely dependent upon such energy transformations. In another sense, the view of Brown and Farber is narrow. It attributes the regulative function, including the development of goal-directed behavior, to the process of learning and thus distinguishes sharply between learning and motivation.

Bindra (1959) defines motivation so as to include both energizing and regulating functions. He regards purpose and goal direction as one of the central problems in motivational psychology but he does not restrict the study of motivation to goal-directed activities. Bindra argues that the traditional problem of the strength of motivation is essentially a problem of *the roles of different factors that determine the occurrence of a given response.* He considers four relevant sets of variables: habit strength, sensory cues, level of arousal, and blood chemistry. These are the variables that determine the occurrence of the various activities that exist in an animal's repertoire and that are commonly described as motivational phenomena: general activity, exploration, play, withdrawal, aggression, eating, drinking, and sexual, maternal, and similar activities. Bindra admits that the problems of motivation are as extensive as psychology itself.

Bindra's view is closely related to that of this writer. I have argued that the study of motivation is a search for the determinants of human and animal activity. These determinants include both energizing and regulating factors. They include more than purposive sets or intentions.

Motivation as a Physical Process

The word *motivation* is derived from the Latin *movere* which means "to move." Taken literally, motivation is the process of arousing movement; but the term ordinarily applies to the arousal of one kind of movement—behavior.

The study of motivation, however, is not restricted to the process of *evoking* behavior; it includes an analysis of the conditions which sustain activity and which regulate and direct its patterning. An important problem, in the study of motivation, is accounting for the purposiveness of behavior.

Physically viewed, motivation is the process by which movement is produced and regulated through the release of energy within the tissues. To the physiologist, energy transformations appear as movement—movement of muscles, blood, lymph, and various other organic movements—and as body heat. The source of this energy is the oxidation of substances stored in the body. Thus, within the body, energy is chemically bound, and the release of this potential energy makes it possible to do muscular work. The liver, for example, stores potential energy, to be drawn upon continuously to meet bodily needs, in the form of glycogen. In times of stress, the bodily reserves of energy are drawn upon more extensively than under normal resting conditions, and vigorous, prolonged activity ensues.

The arousal of behavior through stimulation is a complex process of energy transformation. When a stimulus excites a receptor cell it releases energy within that cell. Receptor cells release energy in neurons; neurons release energy stored in other neurons (for the propagation of a nerve impulse involves expenditure of at least a small amount of energy); and, finally, energy is released in the gland and muscle cells. When an individual muscle fiber contracts, doing work, it utilizes energy stored within itself, but oxygen, glucose, and other substances are taken constantly from the blood. The entire bodily process, from the simplest response of a cell to the most prolonged and vigorous activity of the whole organism, can be viewed as one of energy transformation within the tissues.

What *does* motivate us? Is it the energy stored in the tissues? Or the stimuli and other conditions which release energy? Or the kinetic energy itself after it has been released?

The answer to these fundamental questions is much the same as in the classical example of the billiard ball. What motivates it in its course across the table? Is it the mechanical energy transferred through the cue from the muscles of the player? Or is it the kinetic energy in the moving ball, which is gradually reduced by friction? The question, "What makes the billiard ball move?" raises one of those ultimate problems which seem to extend beyond the realm of science. Perhaps the best one can do is to describe the motion carefully and to study all the conditions upon which it depends.

Similarly, the question, "What motivates a man?" is an ultimate one to the physicist. In considering this question from the physical point of view, the following points are important: First, the immediate energy source of behavior and of all muscular work is certain chemical substances stored in the body. Second, stimuli, both environmental and internal, release this energy which is stored within. Third, in the energy transformations, heat and work are produced. Finally, energy expenditure is regulated and directed so as to produce certain results in behavior.

As seen by a physicist: *Motivation is the process of arousing, sustaining, and regulating behavior through energy transformations within the tissues of an organism.* When a physicist thinks of a *dynamic* process he thinks in terms of the *energetics* of activity.

Motivation as a Physiological Process

According to a view that is no longer tenable, an organism is a passive structure that is activated by stimuli. Modern investigations in the field of electroencephalography have shown that brain cells are continuously active, even during sleep, and that brain activity can initiate movement apart from external stimulation. We must learn, therefore, to think of an organism as a self-determining creature.

To the physiologist, motivation is fundamentally a process of stimulation or excitation. External and internal stimuli excite receptor cells and thus initiate a complex process that is outwardly observable as behavior. Chemical agents in the blood sensitize or activate neural centers. Hormones and other chemical factors are known to be important determinants of specific food hungers, air hunger, fatigue, sexual and maternal behavior, the excited emotions, and other physiological states. Also the behavior of drug addicts is known to have a biochemical basis.

The physiologist is concerned with conditions that regulate and direct behavior as well as with those that arouse activity. The pattern of a reflex, for example, is determined by bodily structures as well as by the stimuli that release energy. Goal-directed activities are regulated by postural sets and neural adjustments. The pattern of a total act, as Sherrington pointed out, reflects the integrative action of the nervous system.

In general, the physiologist's account of motivation is an extension of the physicochemical view to events that occur inside the body. *The physiologist aims to give an account of the underlying bodily processes that arouse, sustain, and regulate behavior.*

Motivation as Hypothetical Construct

Some psychologists who have approached the theory of behavior from a strictly physical point of view have avoided physiological details. Hull (1943), Spence (1956), and others, have constructed non-physiological theories of motivation. Instead of using the nervous system as a model for explanatory purposes they have represented the organism as a rectangle or other figure and placed therein various symbols of determinants: H (habit strength), D (drive), K (incentive motivation), and others. These symbols represent hypothetical constructs. They are postulated to explain the facts of behavior, but are not identified with specific physiological events. Motivation thus enters the picture as an inference, a hypothetical construct. It is an inference based upon the facts of behavior and anchored solidly to the physical world.

Hebb (1949) has interpreted the phenomena of perception, learning, and motivation in terms of hypothetical constructs but his "neurologizing" is based upon and made to agree with contemporary neurology. He speculates that the neural integrations underlying behavior consist of spatially distinct organized units, called *cell assemblies,* and temporally organized sequences of cell assemblies functioning in *phase sequences.* Hebb's work tends to integrate the psychology and the physiology of motivation.

Skinner (1938) pointed out that it is possible to investigate behavior for its own sake without becoming involved in physiological speculations. He has sought to establish psychology as a pure science of behavior which is independent of neurology. He points out that it is possible to describe the dependence of behavior upon environmental conditions by means of graphs and equations. It is possible to avoid concepts like *drive* and *emotion;* but these concepts are often found to be useful. Skinner's position has been described as a "psychology of the empty organism" to contrast it with physiological psychology.

Motives and Social Determinants

Sociologists and anthropologists have taught us that a man's behavior, to a high degree, is determined by the social and cultural environment into which he happens to be born and within which he develops. Thus Sorokin (1947), who thinks in terms of a superorganic world, pointed out that the individual is born into a social and cultural environment which determines his actions, his states of conflict, and traits of personality. The individual, Sorokin argued, has several selves that depend upon the groups and strata of society to which he belongs. This fact is recognized when we describe a man by his occupation as a musician, a philosopher, a plumber, a baker, a sportsman, etc., or when we refer to a man's role and status by describing him as a slave, a manager, a laborer, a president, etc. The diversity of roles is bound up with the fact that the normal individual belongs to a plurality of groups.

The groups to which an individual belongs determine the person's actions, duties, thoughts, attitudes, and conflicts. If an individual belongs to groups that are radically different, he may find himself in conflict. The sociocultural basis of conflict is well illustrated by an example from Kluckhohn (1949):

A young man arrived in New York City from China. He could not speak a word of English and was obviously bewildered by American ways. By "blood" he was American for his parents had gone from Indiana to China as missionaries. Orphaned in infancy, he was reared by a Chinese family in a remote village. All who met him found him more Chinese than American. He had blue eyes and light hair but this was less impressive than a Chinese style of gait, Chinese arm and hand movements, Chinese facial expressions, Chinese modes of thought. His biological heritage was American, but his cultural heritage and background were Chinese. He later returned to China, being unable to adjust to American ways.

An example of conflict which depends upon the fact that an individual belongs to different groups is the following:

During World War I, Madame Schumann-Heinck, the eminent contralto, had some sons fighting in the German Army and other sons fighting in the American Army. Her cultural background was both German and American. This fact made an inner conflict inevitable. Since she kept in close contact with both national groups, she was suspected of being a spy.

Social and cultural determinants of behavior have objective existences as truly as does the physical world. An individual happens to be born into a sociocultural environment that determines the language he speaks, the religious beliefs he professes, and the attitudes, personality traits, and goals he develops.

It is obvious from the above illustrations that the concept of social causation is very broad. The sociocultural determinants of action and personality traits cannot be called *motives* in the usual sense of the word. They are more akin to physical determinants of behavior that exist within the physical environment.

If a psychologist is making a search for *all* the determinants of human action, he cannot ignore the social and cultural environments any more than he can ignore the physical world. The search for determinants of human behavior, therefore, is a broader task than the analysis of motives.

Motivation and Personality

Although the analysis of social determinants of human behavior belongs strictly within sociology and anthropology, it is obvious that social conditions profoundly influence behavior and modify the development and action of persons who grow up within a given society. Social determinants influence the formation of traits of personality, attitudes, interests, motor habits, and goals.

Students of personality, when considering motivation, usually refer to specific kinds of determinants: attitudes, interests, motives, sentiments, traits, habit structures, and the like. Each specific kind of determinant is regarded as having some influence upon the pattern of behavior. It is probable that these concepts refer to different aspects of motivation, rather than to numerically distinct determinants that exist within persons.

Each individual organism begins its life cycle as a fertilized ovum. Within the life cycle, after birth, the human organism becomes socialized. He acquires the ways of his group. He learn to observe, to think, feel, and act, like other persons in his society. This obvious fact means that he acquires from the social environment determinants that regulate and direct his actions. It is these structural organizations (dispositions) to which the terms *attitude, interest, motive, sentiment, trait, habit,* and the like, refer.

When a student of personality approaches a group of persons, he may administer psychological tests and make psychological measurements. Typically he proceeds to analyze results statistically using such methods as correlation and factor analysis. He comes out with factors that are not anchored to physiological processes and hence are culture-bound artifacts. These "discovered" factors may be practically useful but they are not related to physiological mechanisms.

It is possible, however, to approach the study of personality with physiologically sound concepts of motivation and to relate these concepts to the social and cultural determinants of behavior. This approach is the difficult road of objective science, and progress along the road has been slow.

Dynamic Psychology

The current psychology of motivation is bifurcated. It has a dual origin and a dual nature. On the one hand, there is an elaborate dynamic psychology that has grown out of the work of Freud, Adler, Jung, and other psychoanalysts. On the other hand, there is a psychology of motivation that is scientifically grounded upon research in comparative, physiological, and experimental human psychology.

The one kind of psychology is practically useful but some of it is of questionable scientific status. It rests upon the insights and inspirations of Freud and other talented men. The other is unquestionably sound, for the most part, but not always of practical value. If a student comes naïvely to the study of motivation expecting to learn techniques for unraveling the intricacies and complexities of human motives, he may get more help from current dynamic psychology than from laboratory studies of animal behavior.

The phrase *dynamic psychology* is widely used to designate the psychology of human motivation—normal and abnormal. In dealing with the complexities of human motives psychologists and laymen employ terms and concepts drawn from the Freudian type of psychology, such as: *unconscious motivation, conflict, repression, projection, sublimation, fixation, identification, rationalization, compensation,* etc. The commonplaceness of these terms is a witness to the fact that Freud has exerted a profound influence upon the psychology of human motivation. Freudian concepts have worked their way into current thought and into experimental research. They have suggested problems for the laboratory.

The two types of motivational psychology are merging, but they have not yet become integrated into a single system.

Concluding Statement

It is hardly necessary to comment that the above views concerning the nature of motivation diverge widely and differ among themselves. The different views, however, are compatible to a high degree and are supplementary. Not all of them are mutually exclusive.

From these different views one might generalize: *Motivation is the process of arousing action, sustaining the activity in progress, and regulating the pattern of activity.*

The process is complex. It can be viewed from different angles as something mental, physical, physiological or as a hypothetical construct. There are many factors that determine activity.

The concept of motivation is exceedingly broad—so broad, in fact, that psychologists have attempted to narrow it. In narrowing the concept some psychologists have singled out one aspect or another of the complex processes of determination. The two most important aspects are the *energetic* aspect and the aspect of *regulation and direction.* Some would restrict the concept of motivation to the energetics of activity; others would restrict the concept to the analysis of behavior that is goal-directed, or need-related, or purposive. Still others, including the present writer, would define the study of motivation broadly as *a search for the determinants (all determinants) of human and animal activity.*

POINTS OF VIEW AND PSYCHOLOGICAL RELATIVITY*

The following sections reveal the complexity of the situation that confronts a student of psychology and, in particular, a student of motivation and emotion. Various points of view must be distinguished. Facts of observation are relative to points of view. It is essential that we understand the nature of this psychological relativity.

Views of the Individual and the World

In everyday life, various words are used to designate the human individual. The physician, concerned with matters of health, refers to the individual as a *patient.* The lawer, trying to help a man write a will, refers to his *client.* The business man speaks of the individual as a *customer;* the clergyman, as a *parishioner;* the teacher, as a *pupil;* and so on. Academic people have other words. We read about the *economic man,* the *political man,* the *religious man,* etc. Students of biology, according to the context, refer to the individual as a *mammal,* a *primate,* or an example of *Homo sapiens.*

---

*The material in this final section presents the writer's views concerning the definition of psychology in relation to the study of motivation and emotion. Study of these pages could be omitted or postponed without disturbing the development of the main topic.

The basic sciences have different views of the individual and the world in which he lives.

1. From the *physical* point of view, a man is regarded as a *body* surrounded by other bodies in the physical world. All physical bodies are characterized by their properties—mass, volume, motion, chemical constitution, electrical potential, and the like. If a man jumps out of a plane, he falls to earth; when a parachute checks his fall he still moves in accordance with physical laws. He behaves as other physical bodies. His falling through space is a kind of movement that is different from the autogenous activity that a psychologist calls behavior.

2. From the *biological* point of view, a man is an *organism* living within a physical environment. Like other organisms the human individual grows, reproduces, responds to stimulation, ingests and assimilates food, eliminates wastes, moves about within his environment, and adapts himself to changing conditions.

Angyal (1941) recognized that the line of distinction between organism and environment is artifical; the line is drawn for convenience only. He proposed that the realm within which the total biological process takes place be called the *biosphere,* that is, the sphere of life. "The biosphere includes both the individual and the environment, not as interacting parts, not as constituents which have independent existence, but as aspects of a single reality which can be separated only by abstraction."

3. From the point of view of *subjective psychology,* an individual is a *conscious subject,* aware of the world about him as well as of memories, thoughts, emotions and desires. The psychological individual *knows* about the world within which he lives, *reasons* about problems, and *dreams, loves, hates,* and *strives* to reach goals and to carry out intentions.

The world within which the psychological individual lives is described as a world of experience. The individual himself is part of his experienced world. He perceives himself, evaluates himself, builds concepts concerning his nature and existence. An individual's direct experience is sometimes called *phenomenal experience,* and the study of conscious phenomena is called the *phenomenological* approach.

4. From the *social* point of view, a man is a *person* living within a sociocultural environment. At birth the individual enters a world containing other persons—mother, father, nurse, siblings, playmates. He interacts with these persons and gradually develops traits of *personality.* From his society he acquires attitudes, ways of speaking,

of acting, of thinking, and of expressing feelings and emotions. He learns to manipulate tools, to draw, to read.

The cultural environment is more permanent than any person. Culture contains: (1) artifacts—buildings, clothing, tools, weapons, and other physical products of human activity; (2) symbols that preserve ideas from generation to generation—printed words, painted pictures and signs, carving, and the like; (3) manners, styles, attitudes, and ways of acting that are transmitted directly from person to person. The patterns of culture can and do exist independently of behavior.

The above four views of the individual and his world are summarized in the following tabulation:

Point of View	Individual Is Named:	World Is Named:
Physical	Body	Physical world
Biological	Organism	Environment
Psychological	Subject	Experience
Social	Person	Sociocultural world

These fundamental points of view are frequently combined. Thus there are such compound terms as *psychophysical, biosocial, biochemical, psychophysiological, psychobiological, sociopsychological,* etc. We do not need to choose among the views for they supplement each other. They are not contradictory and all are valid.

With all points of view there are two factors. There is always an individual factor (I) and a world factor (W). The individual is part of the world within which he moves, lives, and has his being.

The Relativity of Fact to Point of View

Different views of the world are not incompatible. A classical example is found in astronomy. If one plots the paths of the planets as they are seen from the earth, one finds that each planet moves in a curve known as an epicycle. If one imagines himself standing on the sun and plots the motion of the planets as seen from this point in space, as Copernicus did, the planetary orbits are elliptical. Since astronomers know that the sun, and not the earth, is the center of the planetary system, it is correct to say that the planets move about the sun in elliptical orbits but that the epicycles are apparent orbits as seen from the earth. The two views of planetary motion are not incompatible although at first they may seem so. What one sees is dependent upon one's position in space.

Another illustration is the following: My son has an aquarium containing a single goldfish. If the eye or camera is placed at the side of the aquarium, a single fish is seen. (See Figure 2a.) If the eye is raised above the upper edge of the aquarium, two fishes appear. (See Figure 2b.) If the eye is moved to the corner of the aquarium, three fishes are seen. (See Figure 2c.) Whether the observer sees one or two or three fishes is dependent upon the position of his eyes. Moreover, the shape of the fish varies somewhat with the observer's point of view.

This illustration raises an interesting question which can safely be left to philosophers: Which of the fishes that appears in the photographs is, or corresponds to, the *real* one? Probably no one of the observed fishes is physically real. A physicist can explain the facts in terms of the refraction of light; but a physicist insists that there is *only one real fish* in the aquarium.

Consider another illustration: A botanist, a geologist, an artist, and a real estate agent take a trip together. Each man attends to what interests him. The botanist observes the flora; the geologist attends to the rock formations; the artist is impressed by the beauty of the scene; the real estate agent considers the possibility of opening up a tract of land and subdividing it. What one sees depends upon what one is interested in seeing.

In the sphere of social psychology the concept of attitude plays a major role. If a newcomer enters the group, he is treated as friend or foe depending upon the attitudes of the people. There are attitudes of acceptance and rejection, of hostility, fear, disgust, love, hate, amusement, and the like. Such predispositions are clearly regulative of the experience and behavior of people.

Now the above illustrations show that the facts of experience are dependent upon the position of the observer, upon his interest and attitude. In other words, facts are relative to some point of view. This principle was also illustrated in the foregoing section in which distinctions were drawn among the physical, biological, psychological, and social points of view.

Subjective and Objective Points of View

The whole of physical science is relative to the assumption that an objective world exists independently of the observer. Objects of perception are viewed *as if* they were external to the observer, physically independent of perception, existing in their own right. If certain objects—after-images, dream objects, hallucinations, thoughts, feelings, desires, etc.—do not agree with this assumption, they are called illusions, delusions, conscious phenomena, or subjective experiences.

The whole system of physical science is evidence for the validity and utility of the objective way of regard. Within psychology, also, there is an objective approach which is unquestionably sound and definitely allied to the other objective sciences, especially to the biological sciences.

Traditionally, however, psychology has been concerned with the conscious experiences of individuals. After-images, dreams, hallucinations, memories and thoughts, feelings, desires, and other aspects of experience (which the physical scientist must ignore), are of great psychological interest. These conscious experiences, along with the whole of objective experience, depend for their existence upon processes within the brain of the experiencing individual. The subjective point of view regards the whole of experience as dependent upon processes within the psychological organism.

There is a large literature dealing with subjectivism, the method of introspection, mentalism, and related topics. This is no place to review it. But it must be noted that many psychologists reject subjective data and regard the "introspective" method as invalid, and they abhor "mentalism."

In agreement with the *Zeitgeist,* Bindra (1959) rejects subjectivism. He puts it this way:

...the various activities must be defined without any reference to subjective states, such as "feelings of anger or anxiety," "desire for affiliation," and "emotion of rivalry." The verbal reports of experiential states are, of course, activities that must be studied like other activities, but such subjective experiences cannot be considered as representing psychologically valid categories for the analysis of behavior.

If we reject the subjective, or individual, point of view, however, we are closing the eyes to a world of fact. But if anyone wishes to close his eyes, there is nothing to stop him.

There are obviously different points of view within psychology. The

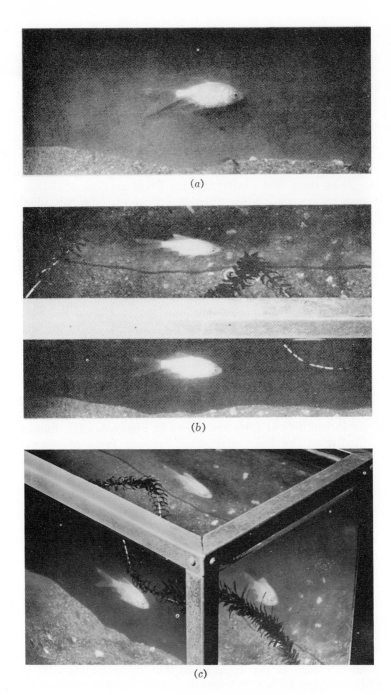

(a)

(b)

(c)

Figure 2. Three views of a goldfish in an aquarium.

relativist is tolerant. His motto is: Live and let live. He admits the relativity of facts of experience to points of view. And he is aware of the multiplicity of points of view.

Facts and Inferences within Psychology

The events directly observed by psychologists can be classified as: (1) facts of human experience, (2) facts of behavior, (3) physiological facts. From these facts, inferences are drawn.

Human experience is always the experience of some individual. It includes a man's perception, memories, feelings, desires, beliefs, and the like. Behavior is observed as a change in the dynamic relation between an organism and the environment. Behavior includes gross movements, such as running, and the movements of speech mechanisms. In non-human organisms, behavior includes changes like the production of light or electric shock or a change in pigmentation or color pattern, etc.; but human behavior is based upon two kinds of bodily changes—movement of muscles and secretion of glands. Certain facts of physiology are intimately related to experience and behavior. The psychologist must know about them and take account of them. What is outwardly observed as behavior may be inwardly described as a process in the nerves, sense organs, muscles, and supporting tissues.

These three kinds of facts are shown in Figure 3. The line in this figure indicates the basic distinction between facts of observation and inferences. The facts are above the line and the inferences below. Although the psychologist may deal with facts other than the three kinds shown, these three are the most important to him.

Below the line is a circle that represents the psychologist's organism. The arrows connecting the organism with the facts of observation indicate a two-way relation: hypotheses about the organism are based upon three main kinds of facts, and these hypotheses are tested by further observation. This organism has characteristics attributed to it in order to explain the three kinds of facts above the line. It is assumed that the organism provides a fully adequate basis for explaining behavior and physiological facts as well as a basis for explaining the facts of conscious experience.

Please note that the postulate of a *single* organism is an inference. It is an inference in the same sense that the postulate of a single goldfish, in Figure 2c, is an inference.

Philosophers and psychologists have sometimes postulated two

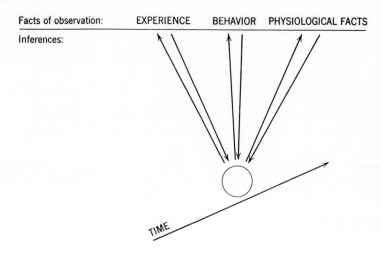

Figure 3. Representation of the facts and inferences with which the psychologist deals.

individuals—a mind and a body—but the doctine of biological monism postulates only one individual—the psychologist's organism. This organism wakes and sleeps, perceives, remembers, imagines, thinks, feels, desires, and acts, i.e., it is the subject of conscious experience. Moreover, psychologists attribute to the organism certain abilities, traits of personality, interests, attitudes, and motives, as well as conflict states, neuroses, good and bad adjustments, and the like. These characteristics of the organism are attributed to it on the basis of the facts of human experience, the facts of behavior, and physiological facts.

Dynamic processes like repression, dissociation, unconscious motivation, and the like, are also inferred; but whether or not these inferences are sound is another problem.

The concept of a single psychological organism needs to be extended to take account of developmental changes that occur in the course of time. The organism lives through a life cycle extending from conception to death. During this life cycle the organism matures, learns, solves problems, acquires traits of personality, attitudes, motives, interests, motor skills, information, etc., as well as conflicts and neuroses. A temporal dimension must be added to the illustration to take account of these changes. An arrow below the organism symbolizes the temporal dimension.

A Fixed Point of View versus Eclecticism

A student of psychology when confronted with so many points of view may be at a loss not knowing what to do.

One way out of the difficulty is to hold rigidly to some fixed and well-defined point of view. This was Titchener's way out. He defined psychology as the science of experience; by experience he meant something that exists, that is observable or reportable, that depends upon neural processes. Watson, the radical behaviorist, held to a fixed objective point of view. He defined psychology as an objective science of behavior of man and brute.

Skinner, Spence, Snygg and Combs, and others, have met the complex situation differently, but all have done so by defining and holding to a fixed point of view. A good case can be made for this procedure. It can be argued that holding to a fixed point of view is necessary to make progress in this age of scientific specialization.

A fixed view, however, necessarily restricts the scope of a science and makes it difficult to appreciate the merits of other viewpoints.

The eclectic, within psychology, frankly faces this situation and shifts his point of view according to his immediate interest or aim. The eclectic, as Boring pointed out, is not wedded to any fixed point of view but changes readily from one view to another as a matter of convenience. The eclectic, within psychology, develops facility in changing from one view to another as a musician, in playing a piece, shifts from one key to another.

An Alternative to Eclecticism

Eclecticism may lead to despair in the face of complexity. It is unsatisfactory to persons who hope to find unity within psychology. One alternative to eclecticism, as we have seen, is to hold firmly to a fixed point of view. But there is another way to escape from the complexity of the situation. This way begins by frankly recognizing the relativity of facts to points of view. It is recognized, moreover, that man is the kind of creature that can readily shift from one point of view to another. He can change his orientation. In fact, the human being does constantly change his orientation and is very capable of looking at the diverse aspects of the world of experience. This is a remarkable fact.

In the area of social behavior a frank recognition of the relativity of facts to points of view has important consequences. If a man *believes* something to be true, that makes it true for him. A man's belief influences his perception of the world, his remarks, his overt actions.

The doctrine of psychological relativity is important in the area of religion: Many a man takes his religious faith seriously. Wars have been fought to defend a faith. Yet a calm study of comparative religion reveals the upsetting truth that there are many faiths, many systems of religious belief that differ, sometimes radically, from each other. That means that one's most cherished faith is just one specimen of religious belief.

Much the same can be said about political and moral beliefs. There is a high degree of relativity among beliefs and among attitudes. It is not surprising, therefore, to find different views of psychology and different views concerning the nature of motivation. The question a student of motivation must ask is: What should I do in the face of such complexity?

An alternative to embracing eclecticism is to study the psychological nature of points of view, attitudes, orientations, beliefs, and the like, and to observe the way these work as determinants of behavior and experience. One can ask about origins: How did this particular orientation arise? How does it influence behavior and experience? How can it be changed? These are questions of central psychological importance in the study of motivation. They are questions that admit psychological relativity and yet move beyond this doctrine into the realm of determinants.

Psychological relativity is recognized by the propagandist and advertiser. The quest of a propagandist is for *psychological* truth. The propagandist does not ask, "Is this objectively true?" He asks: "Is this believed and believable?" "Will this appeal, evoke the kind of action I want?" "How does this item make people feel and act?" Such questions go to the heart of motivational psychology. They presuppose psychological relativity of fact to orientation. They recognize, in fact, that every word that is uttered is motivated and also motivating.

The concept of stable dispositions—including attitudes, interests, motives, conflict states, and the like—is at the center of psychodynamics. An approach to psychology through the study of dispositions might be called a *dispositional* or *attitudinal* approach. Such an approach frankly recognizes the relativity of facts to points of view, or orientations, and it centers psychological interest on determinants. Psychological relativity is essential to any final integration of psychological principles, especially in the broad and complex field of motivation.

The Individual and the Self

Since the facts of observation are diverse, the unity within psychology must be sought in some kind of theoretical system. The physical model for such a system must be the organism-within-an-environment, for no other structure can adequately account for all the facts of physiology, behavior, and conscious experience. But the organism-within-an-environment, as postulated by the psychologist, must be *fully adequate* as a basis for explaining *all* psychological facts. The psychologist's organism has abilities, traits of personality, habits, attitudes, motives, and other attributes, that are imputed to it to explain the facts.

The unity within psychological science must arise from the development of a fully adequate conception of the organism. *The true unit for psychological study is an individual living throughout a life cycle from conception to death.* This individual has both physical and psychological attributes.

The facts of psychology must be anchored to reality in some way. They can be anchored to the physical world or to the conscious experience of individuals or to the behavior of organisms or to the social environment or to the process of organic development. Perhaps a psychology that has many anchors is more secure than a psychology with only one. But a common center for all psychological theories is the psychological individual. This individual has attributes fully adequate to the interpretation of all pertinent facts.

The psychologist's individual is not identical with the self. The perception of one's self is a product of development as is the perception of other persons, animals, inanimate objects, etc. The beliefs concerning one's self are the product of experience as are other beliefs about earth, sky, water, and air. The attitudes towards the self change with age and experience as do other attitudes. Self-regarding attitudes are based upon appraisal of one's abilities, the views of other persons, successes and failures, and other factors.

The development of perceptions and beliefs and attitudes relating to one's self is comparable to the growth of other system of perception, belief and attitude. Self-systems are functional parts of the individual, but they cannot be equated with the total psychological individual.

CONCLUSION

When a layman looks for motives, he asks the question "Why?" He thinks in terms of mentalism, free will, and causation. He wants to understand the reasons for human activity.

It is important to ask: What is meant by explanation, causation, will, when problems of motivation are viewed scientifically? There is a contrast between the views of the layman and the views of the psychologist concerning the nature of motivation. For psychology, as for other sciences, a genuine explanation always adds something (more than a word) to the facts that are to be explained. The "something added" may be an account of present conditions or previous conditions or some hypothetical determinants of behavior.

Within psychology there are different views concerning the nature of motivation. The process of motivation may be restricted to the *energizing* aspect of activity or it may be restricted to the aspect of *regulation and direction.*. Some psychologists would limit the definition of motivation to behavior that is goal-directed or need-related or purposive. Motivation may be viewed, from different angles, as a physical process, a physiological process, a theoretical construct, a social determinant, a determinant within personality, and in other ways. Fortunately, the psychologist is not compelled to choose among these different views. He can try to understand them and gain something of value from each. The study of different views should make one tolerant and give a comprehensive understanding of the complexity of the problem.

There are different views—physical, biological, psychological, social—concerning the nature of the individual and the world. Again, it is not necessary to choose among these different views; one can gain some understanding from each view.

The facts of psychology are relative to points of view. One can hold arbitrarily to a fixed point of view or shift points of view, with facility, as does the eclectic. One can escape from eclecticism by recognizing psychological relativity and centering one's study upon the nature, development, and function of dispositions and attitudes (points of view).

The unit for psychological study is the individual living within a physical and social world. Processes of development occur within the life cycle of individuals—the cycle commencing at conception and

terminating at death. The organism-within-an-environment has physical, biological, social, and mental attributes.

The aim of the present book is a survey of the determinants of human
and animal activity. The concept of *determinant* is broader than the
common-sense notion of motive. Our aim might be characterized as
a quest for the determinants of human and animal activity.

Reading Suggestions

The Nebraska symposia on motivation, under the editorship of M. R. Jones
(1953–   ), reveal a wide variety of research projects, a diversity of opinions, a
complexity of problems, and an enormity of details, covered by the single concept
of motivation. The series of studies, with bibliographies, constitutes an excellent
source for advanced study of motivation.

Bindra (1959) gives a useful survey of research in the comparative and physiological psychology of motivation. His work contains a valuable list of references.

Woodworth (1958) examines the relation of motivation to perception, learning,
thinking, and other processes. He presents a "behavior primacy" theory—his
latest view upon motivation. For clear discussions and selected references, see
Woodworth and Schlosberg (1954); Chapters 5, 6, and 7 deal with emotion, and
Chapter 22 with motivation in learning and performance.

Atkinson (1958) presents a series of investigations on the assessment of human
motives through analysis of content by a thematic apperceptive technique. The
volume contains material by many authors upon various aspects of human motivation. Atkinson's work is closely related to that of McClelland (1951), who
describes motive as a personality variable. In *Studies in Motivation,* McClelland
(1955) presents a useful collection of readings on the main aspects and topics of
motivation, with selections from the works of various authors.

Symonds (1946) gives an encyclopedic treatment of the dynamics of human
adjustment with many references to the literature. In a briefer textbook, Symonds
(1949) restates the dynamic principles preserving his psychoanalytical bias.

For discussions and references to the earlier experimental literature of motivation, see Young (1936), and for an examination of problems of motivation within
comparative psychology, see Young (1951).

For an historical and critical introduction to problems of motivation see the first
four chapters in Troland (1928).

Atkinson, J. W. *Motives in fantasy, action, and society: a method of assess-
ment and study.* Princeton, N. J.: Van Nostrand, 1958.
Bindra, D. *Motivation, a systematic reinterpretation.* New York: Ronald,
1959.
Jones, M. R. (Ed.) *Nebraska symposia on motivation.* Lincoln: University of
Nebraska Press, 1953–   .
McClelland, D. C. *Personality.* New York: William Sloane Associates, 1951.
——— *Studies in motivation.* New York: Appleton-Century-Crofts, 1955.
Symonds, P. M. *The dynamics of human adjustment.* New York: Appleton-
Century-Crofts, 1946.

Symonds, P. M. *Dynamic psychology.* New York: Appleton-Century-Crofts, 1949.
Troland, L. T. *The fundamentals of human motivation.* Princeton, N. J.: Van Nostrand, 1928.
Woodworth, R. S. *Dynamics of behavior.* New York: Holt, 1958.
—— and Schlosberg, H. *Experimental psychology.* New York: Holt, 1954.
Young, P. T. *Motivation of behavior: the fundamental determinants of human and animal activity.* New York: Wiley, 1936.
—— *Motivation of animal behavior.* In C. P. Stone (Ed.), *Comparative Psychology,* (3rd ed.) Englewood Cliffs, N. J.: Prentice-Hall, 1951.

2 FORMS AND DETERMINANTS OF ACTIVITY

One of the most important lessons of experience is learning to distinguish between the facts of observation and the inferences drawn from those facts.

W. B. CANNON

The wisdom of Cannon's remark will appear as we consider, in this chapter, the main forms of behavior and the problem of searching for determinants.

The aim of the present chapter is to survey the main forms, patterns, and trends of behavior, and to consider the problems of describing and explaining them. A central problem in motivational psychology is the analyzing of goal-directed behavior—its development, nature and explanation. Another central problem relates to the nature of intrinsic motivation.

SPECIFIC AND GENERAL ACTIVITIES

The total activity of an organism can be regarded as a complex pattern built out of many separate segments of behavior. In the white rat, for example, it contains such segments of behavior as walking, running, climbing, sniffing, biting, gnawing, eating, drinking, urinating, defecating, preening, copulating, and fighting. These and many other bits of behavior can be recognized easily in the total stream of ongoing activity.

Some of these distinguishable activities appear rhythmically when an animal is observed under constant conditions; others appear sporadically. For example, eating and drinking have a characteristic periodicity when the physical environment is constant and there is an unlimited supply of food and water. Similarly, the eliminative processes, female sexual behavior, sleeping, and breathing (respiratory cycle) all have a periodicity. But no such cycles are known for gnawing, burrowing, climbing, preening, fighting, etc.

Several types of laboratory apparatus have been devised for measuring the level of general activity without analyzing behavior into specific acts or patterns. In the rotating-drum type of activity cage a record of running is obtained. The apparatus is similar to the running wheels that are used in zoos for exercising squirrels and other small animals. In the laboratory a counter is attached to the central axis of the drum so that the number of revolutions per hour or per day can be measured. Rats sometimes run in the activity wheel for hours at a time with relatively few pauses. There are several types of stabilimeter. In one type the animal is placed in a cage that is delicately balanced on a central pivot. Every movement of the animal tilts the cage in one direction or another. These tilts are recorded by microswitches. In another type—the triangular activity cage—the weight of the apparatus is supported on tambours at the three corners. Every movement the animal makes changes the pressure within a pneumatic system; these pressure changes are recorded. The record shows amount of activity without analyzing gross behavior into its components. In another type of stabilimeter the cage is supported from above by a spiral spring. Every movement of the animal jiggles the cage and the movements are recorded.

Experiments with activity cages have demonstrated that the level of activity varies with such conditions as temperature, illumination, age of the subject, stage of the estrous cycle, sleep and waking, the surgical removal of endocrine glands, and other conditions.

Cycles of Specific Activities and of General Activity

Two illustrations of activity cycles are described below: (1) The running cycle of the female rat, and (2) the diurnal drinking cycle.

The mature female rat, when not pregnant or lactating, exhibits regular periodic variations in the level of running activity as recorded by the rotating drum apparatus. This estrous rhythm is absent with the immature female. Figure 4 shows the onset of the activity cycle at puberty. The cycle persists from puberty throughout the reproductive period of the rat; it is suspended during pregnancy and lactation. It can be eliminated by ovariectomy and restored by transplantation of ovarian tissue or by the administration of ovarian hormones. The periods of heightened activity coincide with the periodic liberation of quantities of follicular hormone into the blood of the animal. The peaks of high activity for the average adult female rat occur with a periodicity of about 4.7 days.

The second illustration of an activity rhythm is the diurnal drinking

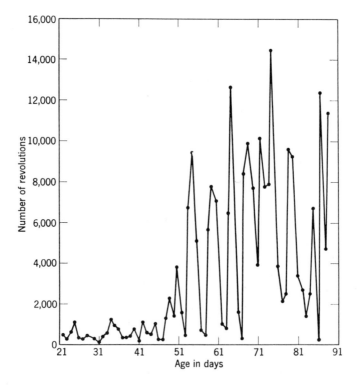

Figure 4. Record showing the burst of activity and appearance of the estrous activity cycle at the time of puberty. *From* Richter (1927), *after* Wang (1923).

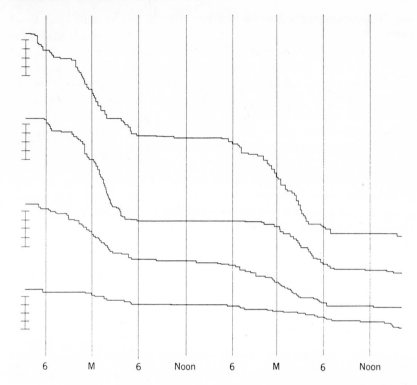

6   M   6   Noon   6   M   6   Noon

Figure 5. Diurnal drinking curves of the rat. The graph shows periods of drinking and non-drinking of distilled water. The records were obtained from four rats recording simultaneously. Scales at the left indicate quantity of water consumed in units of 10 grams. *From* Young and Richey (1952).

cycle of the rat. A continuous record of fluid intake can be readily obtained (Young, 1957).

If laboratory rats are maintained upon an unlimited supply of food and water, they become increasingly nocturnal in their habits of ingestion. In the writer's laboratory continuous recordings of the intake of solid food and water showed well-defined diurnal rhythms. In one experiment (Young and Richey, 1952), distilled water was continuously exposed for 48 hours.

Figure 5 shows the intake of distilled water for four rats during the 2-day exposure. For each curve a horizontal line indicates no drinking; a vertical drop indicates a fall in the water level of the drinking tube.

due to ingestion of water by the rat. If the reader will scan these curves, he will observe a characteristic diurnal pattern of intake for each animal. There is relatively little drinking between 6 A.M. and noon. The rate of drinking increases during the late afternoon and night, reaching a maximum around midnight. The curves reveal marked individual differences in the pattern of intake, but all rats show a clear diurnal cycle of drinking.

Incidentally, this finding has a bearing upon the common practice of measuring the degree of thirst in terms of the number of hours of water deprivation. If the water bottles were removed from 6 A.M. till 12 noon, this would make little difference to the rats since they do relatively little drinking during this time of day; but a 6-hour deprivation between midnight and 6 A.M. would markedly disturb their habitual rhythm. Obviously, if the degree of thirst is to be measured in terms of the number of hours of water deprivation, the drinking habits of the subjects must be considered. To meet this difficulty it is common laboratory practice to habituate rats to a predetermined schedule of feeding or drinking before testing them.

Sleep and Wakefulness

According to Kleitman (1939), sleep and wakefulness are complementary rather than opposed states; they complete each other as the trough of a wave completes the crest.

The human cycle of sleeping and waking is normally completed in 24 hours, but the cycle can be changed. In experiments at the Mammoth Caves of Kentucky, Kleitman demonstrated that if the alternations of light and darkness are artificially speeded up or slowed down, the habits of sleeping and waking readily adjust themselves to the shortened or lengthened day. Presumably we have to *learn* to adjust our habits of sleeping and waking to the 24-hour cycle of light and darkness.

The newborn infant spends most of his time in sleep; he wakens when hungry, cold, wet, in pain, or in other discomfort. The periods of wakefulness are characterized by crying and other signs of distress. When distress has been relieved the infant lapses quickly into sleep. Since brief periods of wakefulness are necessary for vegetative existence, this periodic wakefulness has been called a "wakefulness of necessity."

The newborn wakens and sleeps with a regular rhythm throughout the day and night. As the infant grows older the periods of wakefulness become gradually consolidated into one prolonged period of waking; the periods of sleep, likewise, become consolidated into one prolonged period of sleep. The child of 1 to 4 years takes occasional naps during the day. The 10-year-old, in good health, omits these naps. The adult has learned to sleep at night and to cut down the duration of sleep to 8 hours or less.

With the adult there is a "wakefulness of choice." Kleitman believes that this voluntary wakefulness depends upon man's highly evolved cerebral cortex and distance receptors and upon the effects of experience. Man's cortical development permits a large number and variety of impulses to reach the cortex from the sense organs. With this comes an increased capacity to profit from experience, to discriminate, and to maintain voluntary wakefulness.

What causes the "wakefulness of choice" to abate? With continued wakeful activity the skeletal muscles become fatigued. The eye muscles, in particular, are constantly active and ocular symptoms of fatigue are among the earliest marks of sleepiness. Closing the eyes cuts off visual stimuli and decreases cortical activity. Similarly, lying down and relaxing groups of muscles reduces proprioceptive impulses to the cortex and this favors sleep. Cutting off sound stimulation by seeking a quiet place favors sleep. Popularly it is said that we sleep because the brain needs a rest, and that is why we cut off sensory stimulations when we want to sleep.

There is a subcortical neural center whose continuous activity is necessary to maintain wakefulness. If there is a lesion in this subcortical center, produced surgically or through sickness, the individual remains asleep indefinitely—he does not wake.

Kleitman observed the sleeping and waking of decorticate dogs. Decorticate animals showed only the primitive "wakefulness of necessity" produced by stimulations from the vegetative organs, the skin and other receptors. The wakefulness center could be thrown into activity at any time by appropriate auditory or cutaneous stimulation. When the dogs were awake they showed no signs of pleasure. Only when being fed could they be touched without eliciting a growl or snarl. Wakefulness appeared to be an unpleasant disturbance of primitive quiescence. When left alone the dogs lapsed quickly into deep sleep.

When human subjects are experimentally deprived of sleep they are able to maintain mental and muscular performances at normal levels provided the tests are of short duration, but sustained effort becomes impossible. Deprivation of sleep brings increased sensitivity to pain, impairment of disposition, tendency to hallucination, and other symptoms. These signs point to fatigue at the higher levels of cerebral activity.

Kleitman has argued, from an evolutionary point of view, that it is not sleep that needs to be explained but wakefulness. Wakefulness represents an addition of activities to the sleeping organism. The basic question is not "Why do we sleep?" but "Why do we wake?" Plants never wake or sleep since they have no organ of consciousness. Through roots and leaves they obtain the necessary materials for vegetative existence. Animals, however, must wake to continue their existence. They move about in their environments and have constantly changing relations with the objects and other organisms in their world. In order to survive, animals must avoid enemies; they must find food and mates. To regulate behavior, they have evolved a complex nervous system, distance receptors, and effectors. Wakefulness is a *necessity* of animal existence. Vegetative activities—circulation, respiration, metabolism, excretion—are manifestations of life that persist during sleep when animalistic activities are absent or present in low degree.

Viewed objectively, sleep appears as a low level of general activity. During sleep the heart rate is reduced, blood pressure is low, volume of blood in the brain increases, respiration is slow and deep, body temperature drops slightly, and there are marked changes in the electroencephalogram. Gastric contractions, however, go on during sleep, sometimes with a vigor that is greater than that during waking. The thresholds of reflexes are raised. There is loss of consciousness.

Sleep differs from coma and from unconscious states produced by drugs in one respect: the sleeping organism can be aroused by intense stimulation but it is not possible to arouse a patient in coma or in deep anesthesia by sensory stimulation.

Activity and the Endocrine Glands

Richter (1932, 1933) has shown that the surgical removal of the hypophysis, adrenals, gonads, or thyroid is followed by a marked lowering of the activity level. After hypophysectomy the animals became almost totally inactive. The effect of adrenalectomy was less marked, that of gonadectomy still less, and that of thyroidectomy the

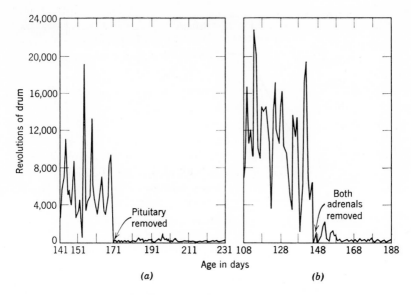

Figure 6. (a) Graph showing the effect produced upon running activity by hypophysectomy. (b) Graph showing the effect produced upon running activity by adrenalectomy. *From* Richter (1932).

least of the four, although it, too, produced a not inconsiderable reduction of activity.

Figure 6 shows the effect upon running activity of removal of the pituitary in one animal and the adrenals in another. The subjects were female rats. After the operations the amount of general activity suddenly and markedly dropped to a very low level, and remained at this level indefinitely.

The effect of gonadectomy upon running activity is presented in Figure 7. The curves show clearly that the activity level is exceedingly low in the absence of the gonadal secretions. Despite the marked lowering of activity level, however, the relative variations dependent upon age are still appreciable.

One surprising result which sometimes occurred after surgical removal of these glands was the production or accentuation of activity rhythms. The graphs in Figure 8 display them well. Precisely what bodily mechanisms are responsible for the appearance of these activity rhythms is not known. In this connection, it is important to note that a number of glands can be removed without affecting activity in any

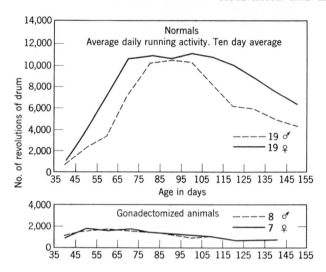

Figure 7. *Top:* 10-day averages of running activity of nineteen normal males and nineteen normal females. *Bottom:* 10-day averages for eight castrated males and seven spayed females. *From* Richter (1933).

way. These include the pineal gland, the thymus, and the posterior lobe of the pituitary body.

Levels of Activity

The concept of *activity levels* is based upon observation and experience. It is an empirical, rather than a theoretical, construct.

Differences in the observed levels of general activity can be represented by positions upon a continuum. At the top of the continuum is the highest possible level of activity. Then, coming down on the continuum, are the levels described as: strong excited emotion, alert attentiveness, relaxed wakefulness, drowsiness, light sleep, deep sleep, coma, and death. See Figure 9.

The concept of levels of activity can be applied to human performance as well as to the behavior of laboratory animals. Numerous experiments with human subjects have demonstrated that the level of performance varies with such factors as: the condition of fatigue, effort expended, presence or absence of distraction, music, value of the incentive, and the like. The level of performance varies with age, sex, previous practice, attitude towards the task, etc.

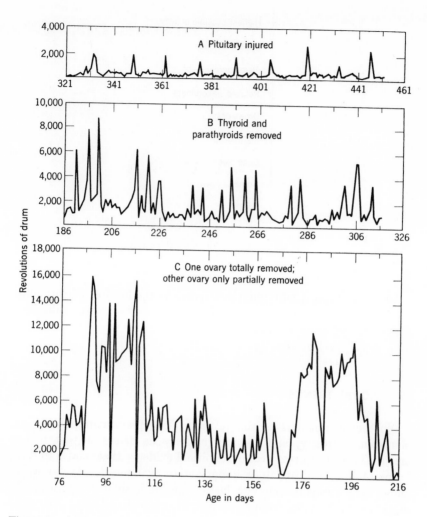

Figure 8. A. Graph showing rhythm of activity in a 12- to 16-day cycle produced by pituitary injury. B. Graph showing rhythm of activity in a 25- to 35-day cycle produced by thyroidectomy. C. Graph showing rhythm of activity in a 90- to 100-day cycle produced by total removal of one ovary, and partial removal of the other, leaving only a very small remnant. *From* Richter (1932).

— Highest possible activity

— Excited emotion

— Alert attentiveness

— Relaxed wakefulness

— Drowsiness

— Light sleep

— Deep sleep

— Coma

— Death

Figure 9. Levels of general activity.

There are typical individual differences in the level of performance. Some persons are temperamentally hyperkinetic—active, talkative; others are hypokinetic—slow, lethargic. Everyone varies from time to time in the level of activity.

BEHAVIORAL TRENDS

Whether or not it is legitimate to speak of play, manipulation, exploration, curiosity, and running activity as *drives* doesn't matter much. There is a great deal of empirical evidence that relates to these forms of behavior, and it is important to examine it. As far as we know, these forms of behavior lack a specific basis in the tissues. In this respect they differ from forms of behavior with endogenous motivation like hunger, thirst, air hunger, fatigue, sleep, the eliminative urges, and other so-called *primary* motivations.

The forms of behavior described below depend upon environmental circumstances. They can be described as behavioral trends regardless of how they are explained.

The descriptive analysis of behavioral trends should not be confused with theoretical explanation. If we postulate drives and motives to explain behavior, we have left facts for theory. It is possible, of course, to hold to a descriptive point of view and to forget causation and the complex determinants of behavior.

It is also possible that a *physiological* explanation of curiosity, exploration, manipulation, and related behavior will some day be given since these forms of activity depend upon exteroceptive stimulation. But a *physiological* explanation must also take account of environmental determinants.

Playful Behavior

There has been much discussion and speculation about the nature and function of play but very little objective research upon playful behavior. The analysis of play has lagged behind the analysis of other fundamental forms of behavior.

One reason for this gap in our knowledge is that playful behavior cannot easily be interpreted in terms of the prevailing homeostatic and drive-reduction paradigms of motivation. There is no gland or hormone that regulates play. Moreover, playful behavior does not consist of any specific pattern of responses that can be analyzed in terms of stimulus and response (S-R) psychology. The forms of play differ widely from species to species and from age to age. Thus the playful kitten pounces upon a moving leaf, utilizing built-in reflexive mechanisms; the playful puppy romps around the yard and barks; the playful colt kicks up his heels in the field. The playful child engages in innumerable activities—running, jumping, laughing, dancing, dressing a doll, etc. What do all forms of play have in common? Obviously nothing in terms of specific patterns of behavior.

If, however, we look at play from the point of view of affective psychology, we are impressed by the fact that playful behavior is typically pleasing. The playful child is obviously "having fun." The games and sports of the adolescent are "for fun." The less turbulent interests of the adult yield enjoyment—listening to music, painting, observing works of art, playing a game of golf, etc. Such interests and hobbies are carried on for their own sake. It is reasonable to assume that playful behavior is generally enjoyable, hedonically positive. It is difficult to imagine a persistent form of play that is unpleasant.

The main current beliefs concerning the nature of play have been summarized by Beach (1945) under five headings: (1) It is commonly assumed that playful behavior, in animals as well as in man, is a pleasant, enjoyable activity. (2) Play is usually regarded as characteristic of the immature animal rather than the adult. The child plays more frequently than the grown up. (3) It is often supposed that playful behavior lacks biological utility. In other words, play has no immediately useful result. (4) As noted above, play has diverse forms.

Dogs, horses, apes, children, and other creatures, play in different ways. (5) In the higher organisms play is more frequent and more variable than in the lower forms. In the higher forms, moreover, playful behavior occupies a relatively longer period of the life span.

It is obvious that play depends upon the state of health of an organism since an animal that is sick plays little or not at all. Further, an environment that is strange does not induce play; the play-inducing environment is one with which the organism is familiar, "at home," secure. Conditions that produce negative affectivity are incompatible with play.

The above comments, of course, do not explain playful behavior. Before we can explain, there must be a lot of specific observations and experimentation upon diverse forms of playful behavior. There is every reason to believe that the problems of analyzing play can be solved through objective observation and experiment, just as problems in the study of maternal behavior, courtship and mating, food selection, territory defense, social dominance, learning, and many others have yielded to the application of experimental and comparative methods.

Manipulative Behavior

Harlow, Harlow, and Meyer (1950) have reported that monkeys persist in manipulating gadgets that resemble puzzles. The animals learn to solve problems without extrinsic reward. Manipulation of the gadgets does not yield food, water, sexual gratification, or relief from pain. Nevertheless, monkeys work persistently upon the solving of certain puzzles.

Figure 10 pictures a monkey at work on a puzzle. The apparatus consists of an unpainted wooden base to which are attached a series of hasps and hooks. When the apparatus is set for presentation, the hasps are closed and hooked as shown at the top of the illustration. Each hook is restrained by a metal peg placed in the board and attached to a chain. The task for the monkey is first to remove the peg, then to unhook and open the hasp.

Harlow proposed the hypothesis that such manipulative behavior is elicited by the environmental situation and provides its own reward. He wrote of a manipulative drive which does not fit into the traditional pattern of homeostatic drives. The manipulative drive is non-homeostatic.

Figure 10. Monkey working on mechanical puzzles. *Courtesy* H. F. Harlow.

Manipulative behavior in the monkey is somewhat akin to human solving of mechanical puzzles. Why do human beings work persistently to solve puzzles? Is it "curiosity"? Is it a form of play? Whence comes the motivation? We cannot accept mere words for an answer.

Nissen (1954) has argued that there is a biogenic drive to explore, to perceive, to know. The capacity to know carries with it the motivation for expression. "Capacity is its own motivation. A function or capacity of the sense organs and brain is to perceive and to know, and this is one of the more important drives of all organisms."

The organism does anything that it can do, Nissen stated. It is so constructed that if its bones, tendons, and muscular and nervous structures permit it to walk or to fly, it *will* walk or fly. The chimpanzee shows considerable inclination to climb trees and to brachiate, a performance for which he has considerable talent, thanks to his bodily proportions and leverage systems. Similarly, the sense organs, nerves, and muscles of the monkey have a capacity to manipulate objects. Manipulative behavior is simply the functioning of a bodily structure.

Exploratory Behavior

It is common knowledge among laboratory workers that when a rat is placed in a new piece of apparatus his first response (if not paralyzed by fear) is to run about, looking, sniffing, touching objects. If a rat is hungry when placed in a novel apparatus, he will explore before eating; if thirsty, he will explore before drinking; if sexually excited, he will explore before copulating. In other words, exploratory behavior dominates the animal's activities in a novel environment.

It is sometimes assumed that the amount of exploratory activity is a positive function of the strength of a primary drive such as hunger or thirst. Such a relationship, if it existed, would have obvious survival value: if hunger makes animals more exploratory, it also enhances their chance of finding food. Montgomery (1953), however, has shown that exploratory behavior is present with satiated as well as with hungry rats. Contrary to general belief, the deprivation of food significantly *reduces* the amount of exploratory behavior, the maximal decrement occurring after 24 hours of food deprivation.

Montgomery described the exploratory drive as a primary drive, aroused by external stimuli, which undergoes a decrement in strength when another primary drive, such as hunger or thirst, is present. The conditions which determine the strength of the exploratory drive are different from but related to the conditions that determine hunger or thirst.

That the exploratory drive is an independent motivation is shown by the fact that rats will select the path of a maze that leads to an opportunity to explore. Montgomery (1954) offered rats 48 free-choice trials in a Y-maze, one alley of which was blind and the other led to a large Dashiell-type maze. This type of maze provides ample opportunity for exploration and apparently invites exploratory behavior of the rat. On the first 24 trials the D-maze was attached to one arm of the Y; on the second 24 trials the D-maze was moved to

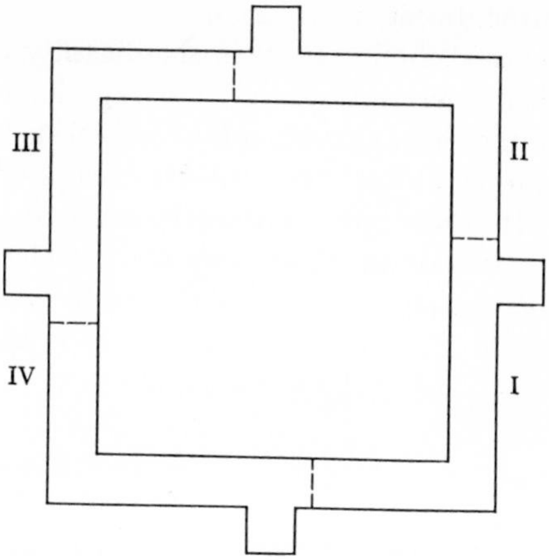

Figure 11. Apparatus for study of environmental motivation. *After* Harlow (1953).

the other arm. Results showed that during the first 24 trials the animals learned to enter the arm leading to the D-maze and that they reversed their choices during the second 24 trials. In other words, they learned to take the path that led to an opportunity to explore.

Another example of learning which appears to depend upon the impulse to explore has been described by Harlow (1953). He used a continuous runway similar to that pictured in Figure 11. The apparatus consisted of four sections (I, II, III, and IV) separated by doors. In front of each door was a blind or cul. In an experimental group the door was promptly opened when a rat poked his nose into a blind; the animal could then proceed to the next section. In the control group the rat was not required to poke his nose into the blind; his forward running was unimpeded since the door ahead was always open. For both experimental and control groups retracing was prevented by closing the door behind the rat after he had cleared one of the sections of the apparatus and entered the next.

For 6 days the only motivation for running was the novelty of the apparatus itself. This novelty elicited exploratory behavior in all of the rats. Then conditions were changed. All rats were made thirsty and a water incentive was placed in section IV of the apparatus. Further, the animals in *both* groups were now required to poke their noses into the blinds before the doors ahead would be opened.

During the runs prior to the introduction of a thirst drive, the experimental animals showed a steady gain in cul entries, and the controls showed a decrease in the frequency of cul entries. On the first trial after thirst motivation was introduced, the experimental animals reached the incentive in significantly less time than the controls. This fact demonstrates that the experimental animals had learned a pattern of behavior when the motivation was the impulse to explore. This learned pattern was utilized when a thirst drive was introduced.

It seems possible that the motivation may have included something more than an exploratory drive. The rules of running were something like the rules of a game played between the experimenter and the rats. Could there be an element of playfulness in the motivation over and above the exploratory impulse?

Curiosity

A novel situation may or may not produce fear. With many animals a novel object or situation induces observant, manipulative, and exploratory behavior. Such activity results in acquaintance with the environment.

Berlyne (1950) reviewed theories of curiosity and proposed a view that agrees with common observation. He postulated that when a novel stimulus affects the receptors of an organism, a curiosity drive is aroused. Further, when the stimulus that arouses curiosity continues to affect the receptors, the curiosity diminishes. Berlyne related these postulates to the Hullian system and made several predictions that he confirmed experimentally.

In one experiment, rats were first allowed to explore the apparatus to become acquainted with it. Then they were given cubes or rings to examine in accordance with an experimental design. Berlyne demonstrated that rats spent more time exploring a novel object than an object they had previously explored. Further, they spent less time exploring an object the second time they encountered it. In other words, curiosity was reduced when familiarity replaced novelty. Berlyne (1960), in a recent book, has developed and extended his work on exploratory behavior.

This work agrees with the experience of laboratory workers generally. Novelty does excite observant, manipulative, and exploratory behavior. Repetition of the situation leads to reduction in the amount of such behavior.

With primates there is a wealth of data that show the great importance of what we commonly call curiosity. Manipulating, exploring, examining with the hands or mouth, looking or feeling or listening, destroying, and similar actions play tremendously important roles in primate behavior. Such behavior has biological utility in that it acquaints the organism with its environment, provides knowledge of its surroundings.

The youth sets out to see the world, the man of science to understand it. There is a wish for new experience, as W. I. Thomas called it, a seeking of new experience as an end in itself. Scientific curiosity has been described as a desire to know, to understand.

The Activity Drive

It is normal for organisms to be active. When an organism is immobilized a need for activity develops.

Hill (1956) confined rats, individually, in cages so small that they could not be active. An animal could stand or lie at full length but he could not stand on his hind legs or walk except by circling in the small circular cage. Each cage contained food and water but deprived the subject of activity.

Forty rats were tested, each after four degrees of confinement: 0, 5, 24, and 46½ hours. After the rats had been deprived of activity, they were tested in an activity wheel. The number of revolutions during the test period (1½ hours) was counted.

The data show that there was greater activity following the longer periods of activity deprivation. The level of running in the activity wheel was a monotonic increasing function of the number of hours of confinement, except that in one group there was slightly less running after 5 hours of confinement than after 0 hours. Hill concluded that the differences in running activity are explicable only by postulating a genuine activity drive that is built up by the deprivation of activity.

Earlier, Kagan and Berkun (1954) had concluded that the opportunity to run in an activity wheel is rewarding and can reinforce an instrumental act such as bar pressing.

Primary and Secondary Drives

In this section we have considered playful behavior, manipulative and exploratory behavior, curiosity, and the activity drive. These behavioral trends raise a question concerning the nature of the distinction between primary and secondary drives.

To most psychologists, the distinction between primary and secondary drives refers to the difference between innate and learned determinants of activity. Innate drives are primary determinants; learned or acquired determinants are secondary. In this sense one might argue that play, manipulation, exploration, curiosity, activity, and similar trends are *primary* since they appear under suitable conditions apart from learning.

To other psychologists (including the present writer) the distinction between primary and secondary refers to the source of motivation. Primary drives, like hunger and thirst, have internal, organic origins; they rest upon observable tissue conditions. Secondary drives, by contrast, originate externally; they are environmental determinants. Viewed from this angle, play, manipulation, exploration, curiosity, activity, and similar forms of behavior are *secondary* until they have been shown to have observable bases or origins within the tissues.

Still other psychologists regard primary drives as important motivations and secondary drives as less important. When these behavioral trends are viewed in this light, I believe we would all agree that they are important—but this is a matter of evaluation.

To avoid confusion we must state what we mean if we talk about primary and secondary drives. One point is clear: The behavioral trends we have considered in the present section depend upon the total situation, involving organism and environment, and they seem to lack specific bases in the tissues.

GOAL DIRECTION

The analysis of goal direction, as it appears and develops in behavior, is perhaps the most central problem in the psychology of motivation. Almost every topic in this book has a direct or indirect bearing upon goal-directed behavior.

Behavioral Trends and Terminal States

Some behavioral trends have a terminal state. There is a final response—a consummatory or goal reaction—that brings the trend of activity to a close. For example, the finding and ingesting of food bring food-seeking behavior to a close. The drinking of water brings water-seeking activity to an end. The eliminative acts bring to a close the search for a suitable place to urinate or defecate. When an organism lapses into deep sleep, this state terminates various forms of behavior that are present in a drowsy creature. A state of complete rest terminates the behavioral signs of fatigue. All of these trends are determined by endogenous conditions.

There are other behavioral trends, however, that lack a clear organic basis but that still move towards a terminus. Thus exploratory behavior is terminated by continued exploration which brings familiarity, instead of novelty, to the subject. High levels of general activity are reduced as boredom sets in. Kurt Lewin pointed out that almost any activity in which we are interested becomes boresome if sufficiently repeated. For example, a youth enjoys playing a piece on the piano; but if he plays the piece over and over again, he comes to a point where he has had enough piano playing; he terminates and does something other than playing the piano. There is a *psychological* satiation.

Various forms of emotional behavior move towards a terminal state. The emotion of fear is terminated by successful flight to a secure place. Anger is terminated by aggressive behavior which removes or destroys the source of frustration. Lust is terminated by copulation and a state of sexual exhaustion.

In the sphere of everyday life there are innumerable examples of activity that moves along to a terminal state. A man intends to find a screw driver; when he finds the tool his searching is terminated. He intends to see a show; when he is seated in the theater his activity trend (going to the theater) is terminated. He wishes to make a remark; when he has made the remark the tendency to speak is temporarily ended. Such behavior is obviously goal-directed.

Problems of goal-directed behavior arise because behavioral trends move along towards terminal states. Terminal states, including the goal reaction, have a definite bearing upon goal-oriented activity.

Goal-directed Behavior—Facts and Inferences

There is a difference between observing behavior and interpreting the observed facts. Behavior can be interpreted *teleologically* in terms of its use, value, or purpose. Thus, the obvious utility of the wink reflex is to protect the eyes from damage by foreign bodies; the utility of the sucking reflex in an infant is to obtain nourishment; the utility of a sneeze is to clear the air passages, etc. But behavior can also be interpreted *mechanistically*. There are bodily mechanisms that regulate reflexive patterns. The structural organization of a neural arc and the external stimulus determine the pattern of the reflexive response. The value of mechanistic explanation is apparent in explaining certain reflexes that lack utility, like the knee-jerk reflex in man. Again, the moth's phototaxis of flying into the flame can be explained mechanistically but it has no utility.

It is necessary to distinguish between the facts of observation (which are the same regardless of interpretation) and the explanation of those facts. The facts are the same whether one interprets them teleologically or mechanistically. One can avoid the difficulty of interpretation by holding to the facts, by analyzing and describing them without interpretation.

Now, persistent, goal-directed behavior is a fact of observation and not an inference. In the laboratory, for example, one can observe a rat persisting in his course through the maze until he comes at last to the goal. With repeated runs, his entrance into blind alleys becomes less frequent until the animal finally runs in a smooth, direct path from starting box to goal. Hundreds of experiments have been carried out upon goal-directed behavior of rats in mazes.

It is futile to speculate whether a rat is aware of the goal when he runs a maze. But persistent, goal-directed behavior, as Tolman pointed out, is an objective fact of observation. It is something to be explained. We must ask: How does goal direction arise? What regulates and directs persistent goal-oriented activities? These are straightforward questions and they deserve straightforward answers.

In studying these questions one soon discovers that *instrumental* acts occur. Instrumental acts are learned activities that lead to a consummatory, or terminal reaction. Many examples of instrumental acts could be cited, but we return to the familiar rat in the maze. A rat learns to wind his way through a maze and to avoid blind alleys. Finally he takes the most direct path to the food in the goal box. His behavior is *instrumental* in obtaining food. This is shown by the fact that if he is allowed to eat to satiation, his maze running slows down and "errors" reappear.

On the human level, a laborer persistently works for his pay check. The pay check is a means to an end. It has utility in obtaining food and other satisfactions. Working for money is, therefore, an *instrumental* act.

Bindra (1959) formulated, tentatively, two generalizations that relate to the acquisition of goal direction in behavior:

1. *Some degree of repeated or continued exposure to a situation is a necessary condition for the development of activities that are goal-directed with respect to some feature of that situation.*

2. *Behavior becomes goal-directed by virtue of the fact that certain movements or component responses (occurring in a matrix of general activity) that are accompanied by a given goal are selectively strengthened or reinforced. This selective reinforcement leads to an increase in the frequency of reinforced movements, so that they appear to constitute an integrated, goal-directed response.*

Bindra's second generalization leaves open the question as to the nature of reinforcement. These generalizations affirm, quite correctly, that all persistent goal-directed behavior is learned.

A human being who displays persistent goal-directed activity is aware of his goal. He has conscious aims, intents, purposes, ideals, values, interests and attitudes. He is aware of himself as moving towards certain goals, of striving to reach ends, of his aims and purposes. These are *facts* of conscious experience. They are data for psychology. They are something to be explained. The student of human motivation has a duty to examine the facts and to do his best in interpreting them and their relation to human activity.

INTRINSIC MOTIVATIONS

The behavioral trends which were described above can be analyzed without imputing to them any drive, motive, cause, or conscious intent. Indeed, it may needlessly confuse the picture to explain by imputing motives.

In the following sections some views are considered which recognize that behavior is self-sustaining, autonomous, and intrinsically motivated.

Woodworth's Behavior-Primacy Theory of Motivation

Objecting to the view that all behavior is motivated by needs, Woodworth (1958) formulated a behavior-primacy theory. His view is that the motivation to deal with the environment is primary and does not require extrinsic drives to support it. Organisms are born with specific capacities. When the capacities of a species are known, their behavior in dealing with the environment can be predicted. For example, from the bird's capacity to fly we can predict that the bird will fly and will prefer flying to walking. The young bird makes considerable progress in mastering its mode of locomotion before it begins to use this skill in hunting for food. The creature exercises its capacity to fly for its own sake at first, and only later in the service of organic needs. Woodworth wrote:

The main contention of this book—seemingly a perfectly obvious and innocent view—is that behavior consists in active give and take between the organism and the objective environment. This interrelationship may be called "dealing with the environment." To deal with the environment the organism must do more than merely receive stimuli and make muscular responses; it must use the stimuli as indicators of objects in space, and use the muscles for movements adapted to the objects; that is exactly what the organism does. A dog's ears receive a certain shrill tone; he turns his head in the direction of the source of the tone which is issuing from the lips of his master; immediately the dog's leg muscles begin a series of contractions which carry him over the ground to his master. Evidently the dog has done much more than receive an auditory stimulus and make a series of muscular contractions. The whole performance is geared to the objective environment—to the master as a known object, to the location of the master, to the more-or-less level ground and its unevenness, and to other demands of the situation.

Instead of saying that behavior is motivated by organic needs or other great motives, Woodworth insists that dealing with the environment is the primary drive and that large-scale purposive activities are based on this primary drive. In order to motivate food-seeking behavior, the hunger drive has to break into the ongoing behavior and give it a special direction.

According to Woodworth, the tendency to deal with the environment is *the* primary drive in behavior. An organism's capacities for dealing with the environment afford outlets for the general behavioral drive and give it various forms in different situations.

This theory predicts that if an individual has a capacity for dealing with the environment, the individual will develop a specific interest. We know that musical capacity shows itself early, given a favorable environment. The potential musician is attracted to the piano and does much more than pound on the keys. He does not need an adult to stand over him continually to tell him when he is striking the right notes; he can tell himself, from the sound. The musical effects reinforce the performance. If an individual has a capacity, he will show this in behavior; he will become absorbed in his activity, interested in it and motivated to bring it to conclusion.

Competence and Effectance

A view closely related to Woodworth's has been expressed by White (1959). White points to the general discontent with motivational theories that are based exclusively upon organic drives and instincts. Something important is left out when drives are made the main operating forces in human and animal behavior. White introduces the term *competence* to designate an organism's developed capacity to deal effectively with its environment. The motivation to attain competence is not derived wholly from sources of energy currently conceptualized as drives or instincts.

There is a tendency in current psychology to emphasize forms of behavior that cannot be explained in terms of drives or instincts: observant behavior, curiosity, exploration, manipulation, play, and similar trends. Such behavioral trends are present when an organism is not occupied with hunger, thirst, and sex.

It is only occasionally that an organism's transactions with its environment are disturbed by homeostatic drives. Only occasionally is behavior oriented towards biologically basic goals. For most of the time an organism is actively observing, manipulating, exploring, playing, with environmental surroundings. This non-homeostatic activity leads to development of skill, to knowledge, i.e., to *competence* in dealing with the environment. Continued practice leads to increasing competence.

These behavioral trends are not aroused and sustained by tissue conditions that are external to the nervous system. There is a truly *neurogenic* motivation. Work upon the reticular activating system has shown that nerve cells are continuously active even during sleep. No longer can we think of the nervous system as a passive structure awaiting excitation from environmental and organic stimuli. Activity rather than passivity is the normal state of neural tissue.

It seems likely that nervous tissue requires excitation for normal growth and health. Moreover, an organism goes out actively to seek stimulation. A man takes rides on a roller coaster, engages in dangerous sports like skiing, plays games that involve risk and suspense, and works endlessly to solve puzzles. The search for stimulation, for exciting forms of activity, is not motivated by tissue needs that underlie the homeostatic drives.

Some psychologists designate exploration, manipulation, curiosity, observant behavior, play, problem solving activity, and the like, as "secondary" drives. The designation usually implies that behavioral trends rest upon primary homeostatic motivations. But, as White pointed out, if we admit exploration to the category of drive, we are committing ourselves to the view that drives may have no extraneural sources in tissue deficits or visceral tensions, that driven behavior is not necessarily aroused by strong or persistent stimuli, that consummatory responses are not required for learning, and that an increase of drive as well as drive reduction can sometimes be reinforcing.

Underlying the tendencies to deal with the environment is a form of motivation which White calls *effectance*. The "energies" of effectance are neurogenic, being simply those of living cells that make up the nervous system. External stimuli play an important but secondary role. Effectance motivation is persistent. It occupies the spare waking time between episodes of homeostatic crises. Referring to the neural basis of effectance motivation, White writes:

> In our present state of relative ignorance about the workings of the nervous system it is impossible to form a satisfactory idea of the neural basis of effectance motivation, but it should at least be clear that the concept does not refer to any and every kind of neural action. It refers to a particular kind of activity, as inferred from particular kinds of behavior. We can say that it does not include reflexes and other kinds of automatic response. It does not include well-learned, automatized patterns, even those that are complex and highly organized. It does not include behavior in the service of effectively aroused drives. It does not even include activity that is highly random and discontinuous, though such behavior may be its most direct forerunner. The urge toward competence is inferred specifically from behavior that shows a lasting focalization and that has the characteristics of exploration and experimentation, a kind of variation within the focus. When this particular sort of activity is aroused in the nervous system, effectance motivation is being aroused, for it is characteristic of this particular sort of activity that it is selective, directed, and persistent, and that instrumental acts will be learned for the sole reward of engaging in it.

The Autonomy of Behavior

Woodworth's behavior-primacy theory of motivation suggests similar views expressed by other psychologists: Gordon Allport (see pages 423–424) developed a doctrine of the functional autonomy of motives which, in a sense, was a protest against the necessity of postulating extrinsic drives in explaining adult social behavior. The activities of mature individuals, he wrote, are self-sustaining, self-motivating. Nissen (see pages 95–97) argued that bodily processes can function autonomously without external motivation; instinctive behavior often occurs in response to environmental stimulations quite apart from the chemical sensitization of internal mechanisms. An organism's structure and capacity are sufficient explanation of its function. Koch (see pages 171–172) stated that much human activity is intrinsically motivated. There is no point, he wrote, in looking for extrinsic motivation.

Again, Jersild (see pages 587–588) pointed out that the child is not a passive creature that responds only when stimulated or driven; he shows a positive impulse to be active. Child development shows an indigenous motivation. Hill (see page 55), and others, have postulated an autonomous activity drive. The healthy organism *needs* activity even when other needs are met.

Work with the EEG has demonstrated that the brain is self-active, even in sleep. We cannot think of the human brain as a passive machine that responds only when it is stimulated. The brain may initiate activity which shows up as autonomous behavior. This work with the EEG suggests that the normal state of an organism is one of activity— just as it is normal for planets to move around the sun. The organism is not a passive structure that must be aroused to activity any more than the planets are passive bodies that must be moved by external forces.

There are thus a good many protests against the view that we must seek some extrinsic drive or motive in explaining behavior. Reflexes, instinctive and emotional patterns, tropisms, habits and associations, are simply *released* by environmental stimulations quite apart from external drives and motives.

Philosophers, psychologists, and others, however, have often postulated drives, motives, forces, urges, and other forms of impetus, to explain behavior. For example, there is McDougall's "hormic force," Bergson's *"élan vital,"* Schopenhauer's "will-to-live," Driesch's "entelechy," Freud's "libido." A question can be raised as to whether such extrinsic motivations are necessary.

Bindra (1959) wrote as follows:

...Such end-determining systems have been called desires, motives, urges, wishes, wants, needs, instincts, demands, drives, and so on. These postulated entities have then been defined in terms of certain functional properties and elaborated upon by linking them to certain real or presumed biological processes such as homeostasis, tension reduction, pleasure, and pain. As we have seen, the main shortcomings of this approach lie in the *ad hoc* way in which the end-determining entities (e.g., instincts) are postulated, and in the tenuous line of arguments with which the exceptions to any specific interpretations are handled.

The main feature of the point of view adopted in this book is that it is unnecessary and futile to postulate drives, motives, instincts, or any other end-determining systems in order to account for the various motivational phenomena. From this point of view, it becomes pointless to define terms such as "motive" and "drive," and no attempt will be made to do so here, except in referring to their usage in the works of other authors.

In the light of the above points one can see the strength of Woodworth's behavior-primacy principle. It implies that the primary datum for psychology is behavior—which, for Woodworth, is an organism's activity in dealing with the environment. Hunger, thirst, and other organic states, do motivate behavior and lead to the development of instrumental acts; but these motivations are unnecessary for behavior to occur and they may actually interfere with an organism's activity in dealing with the environment.

In agreement with the *Zeitgeist*, Woodworth's theory emphasizes behavior. But why not an "experience-primacy" theory that places the main emphasis upon the conscious experiences of individuals? Or why not an "individual-life-cycle-primacy" theory that emphasizes the developing individual as the main subject matter of psychology? Other emphases are possible.

One final comment on Woodworth's formulation might be added: The behavior-primacy theory is an empirical formulation. We need both empirical and theoretical approaches to psychology.

The Structure-Function Relation

I do not believe that Woodworth's behavior-primacy theory is a true theory of motivation; but rather it is a broad generalization about behavior that provides a kind of background principle for the study of motivation. The behavior-primacy doctrine does not provide answers for questions like these: What conditions in the environment and in the organism release specific behavioral patterns? What conditions produce changes in the pattern of behavior? What directs behavior towards a goal? The bare assertion that behavior is the primary datum does not answer these questions. So further study becomes necessary.

The behavior-primacy view recognizes that the capacities of an organism—the kind of things it can do and will do—are dependent upon the structural organization of the creature. This sounds like the familiar structure-function relation of the biologist.

The structure-function relation is well illustrated by any simple reflex. The prevailing view is that the neural structure (neural arc) determines the pattern of reflexive response. The receptors, effectors, and supporting structures, of course, are part of the physical mechanism that is actuated when a stimulus produces a reflexive response.

But the structure-function relation has a much broader biological significance: It is a remarkable fact that organisms develop structures well suited to their modes of existence. Birds develop wings and a boney structure that permits flight. Squirrels develop neuromuscular mechanisms well suited to life in the trees—climbing, jumping, gnawing, etc. Human beings develop mechanisms that permit observant behavior, manipulation of objects, speech.

These diverse structures develop according to the laws of heredity and growth. A series of fertilized eggs may look alike to an observer yet one will develop into a kitten, one into a rat, one into a monkey, and one into an infant! A mechanism that regulates growth determines the structural organization that is characteristic of a species.

Moreover, in the course of growth there are instances where structure anticipates function. For example, in the human fetus the eye is well developed at the time of birth but it has no function in the uterus. Similarly, the mechanisms for breathing are well developed but functionless before birth. Further, the mechanisms for sucking, elimination, temperature regulation, and the like are well developed in the neonate but these mechanisms are not actuated in the prenatal environment. There are thus many instances in which a growing structure anticipates post-natal function.

Structural development extends, also, to the internal organs including the gross structures of the nervous system. There are built-in mechanisms that regulate reflexive and instinctive patterns. Environmental stimulus-patterns simply release the inner mechanisms and evoke patterns of behavior.

Thus structure determines function. This is a broad principle that relates to all behavior. Neural organization is a structural determinant of behavior and experience—of its pattern and organization. The basic forms of behavior, at least, can be interpreted in terms of the structure-function relation.

The facts suggest questions that lie beyond the scope of this book. These questions relate to the nature of biological adaptation and evolution, the nature of heredity and the regulation of growth, the physical nature of bodily processes, and the relation of all these to the behavior of organisms. These are profound questions that arise when we seriously consider the structure-function relation.

Within the psychology of motivation the structure-function relation is of basic importance. A fundamental distinction is repeatedly drawn between activity and passivity. For example, a neural structure may persist indefinitely in a relatively passive state but from time to time this structure is activated. Thus, the neural arc persists but when the appropriate environmental stimulus is present this structure is activated and the reflexive movement occurs. Both the structure and the stimulus *determine* the response.

The Hedonic Factor

White's view recalls an early statement by Herrick (1915) regarding the neural basis of pleasure:

The simplest view seems to the writer to be that the normal activity of the body within physiological limits is intrinsically pleasurable, so far as it comes into consciousness at all. There is a simple joy of living for its own sake, and the more productive the life is, within well-defined physiological limits of fatigue, good health, and diversified types of reaction, the greater the happiness. The expenditure of energy within these physiological limits is pleasurable *per se* except in so far as various psychological factors enter to disturb the simple natural physiological expression of bodily activity. Such disturbing factors are anxiety, want, rebellion against compulsory service, and unrelieved routine. The expenditure of intelligently directed nervous energy along lines of fruitful endeavor is probably the highest type of pleasure known to mankind.

Herrick may be correct in recognizing that a great deal of human activity is subjectively pleasant. This fact in itself, however, does not *explain* self-sufficient, autonomous activities.

CONCLUSION

In this chapter we have considered some of the forms, or patterns, of activity that are of interest to students of motivation and the problem of searching for determinants.

There are simple reflexes, tropisms, instinctive patterns; and there is general (unanalyzed) activity. Levels of general activity can be observed and measured directly without breaking down complex behavior into its components. There are behavioral trends—play, exploration, manipulation—which depend mainly upon environmental conditions. There are other trends—food-seeking, water-seeking—which depend upon internal organic conditions and which move to a terminal state. Organisms learn goal-directed behavior and instrumental acts that lead to terminal states. Goal-directed activities can be objectively observed, described, analyzed, and measured, without imputing to them any conscious purpose.

Behavior can truly be analyzed without benefit of drives, motives, or other forms of impetus. Hence a serious question must be raised: Do we need a concept of motivation? Some would say "No," we do not need concepts like drive, motive, and force. A good defense for this position can be made. If the position revealed the whole truth, nothing would be gained by going further than this with the study of motivation.

I believe, however, that we need both a descriptive and an explanatory (theoretical) psychology. Motivation is a *theoretical* concept; it goes beyond descriptive generalizations. After the complete description of a bit of behavior there remains a need to search for conditions —present, past, hypothetical—that determine it. The central aim of this book is to search for the *determinants* of human and animal activities.

Reading Suggestions

Bindra (1959), in Chapter 2, entitled "Motivational phenomena," gives a survey of the kinds of behavior that are typically studied under the heading of "motivation." Young (1936), in Chapter 2, considers and gives references to some of the earlier studies on conditions that determine the activity level. For a discussion of the physiology of sleep and waking, see Chapter 17 in Morgan and Stellar (1950). Woodworth (1958) has presented his "behavior-primacy" doctrine and related studies in an important book. See especially his Chapter 4 on "Outgoing motivation." White (1959) has stated his concept of "competence" and given many references to the literature.

Bindra, D. *Motivation, a systematic reinterpretation.* New York: Ronald, 1959.

Morgan, C. T. and Stellar, E. *Physiological psychology.* New York: McGraw-Hill, 1950.

White, R. W. Motivation reconsidered: the concept of competence. *Psychol. Rev.,* 1959, 66, 297-333.

Woodworth, R. S. *Dynamics of behavior.* New York: Holt, 1958.

Young, P. T. *Motivation of behavior; the fundamental determinants of human and animal activity.* New York: Wiley, 1936.

3 INSTINCTIVE BEHAVIOR AND DRIVE

Once the point of view of a dynamic psychology is gained, two general problems come into sight, which may be named the problem of "mechanism" and the problem of "drive."

R. S. WOODWORTH

For Woodworth the *drive* of a machine is the energy that puts it in motion. A machine is a mechanism, but without energy transformation it remains inert, motionless.

Some machines have separate structures for propelling and steering. A steamship, for example, is driven through the water by the propellers. The energy that moves the ship comes, in the last analysis, from the heat of combustion which is transformed into motion. The steering mechanism—the rudder and wheel—is controlled by a pilot who takes account of sailing orders, visibility, and other conditions. The cues that determine the actions of the pilot are derived from the environment.

With an organism, as with a man-made machine, structure regulates function. The gross structure as well as the minute structural organization within the nervous system determines the form of behavior. Neural organization and the associated bodily structures may remain relatively inert, quiescent, for long periods of time until they are activated in some way. With man-made machines, separate structures exist for propelling and steering. With organisms, contrastingly, a single structure may serve to regulate the pattern of behavior. A latent, passive structure determines the behavioral pattern when activated in some way.

In this chapter we shall consider instinctive behavior. This is behavior in which innate structure plays a dominant role. Activation typically comes from environmental conditions combined with internal physiological factors. Instinct is a basic descriptive concept.

The concept of drive, by contrast, is explanatory. Drive is a basic dynamic concept. There are diverse views concerning the nature of drive, as we shall see, and this fact presents a difficult problem to the student of motivation. What is the nature of drive?

INSTINCTIVE BEHAVIOR

In approaching the analysis of reflexive and instinctive behavior it is well to keep in mind several interrelated questions. What bodily mechanisms underlie reflexive and instinctive behavior? What activates these mechanisms thus producing the characteristic patterns of activity? What environmental stimulus patterns release the energy? How are the patterns of behavior regulated? Can we distinguish the drive from the releasing and steering mechanisms?

The following sections have a bearing upon these questions.

Reflex Patterns

The modern concept of reflex action originated with Descartes, who argued that animals are automata behaving in a machine-like manner. Just as a ball hits the wall and bounces back, or a beam of light strikes a mirror and is reflected, so the stimulation of receptors, Descartes believed, starts a mechanical process that travels along the nerves and is reflected back to the periphery as a pattern of response.

A reflex is a relatively simple pattern of response that follows the stimulation of receptors. For example, the pupil constricts when a bright light enters the eye; this is reflex action. In the infant, examples of reflex patterns are sneezing, yawning, coughing, sucking, swallowing, sitting up, standing, balancing. For each of these patterns there is: (1) a characteristic pattern of stimulation that elicits and sustains the response, and (2) a structural organization within the nervous system that regulates the form of the pattern.

With man there are two kinds of response—movements and secretions. Since human effectors are either muscles or glands, man is limited in the kinds of response he can produce. Other organisms, however, can respond in different ways. The firefly emits light reflexively during a brief upward flight; the electric eel carries around with him a storage battery through which he can produce electric shocks; the chameleon is able to change color; some fishes can change the pattern of pigmentation so that they become well camouflaged against a rocky floor. Man is not so gifted!

Reflex patterns are constantly modified during the course of development. Coghill (1929) has traced out the development of certain patterns in the behavior of the embryo salamander, *Amblystoma*.

In early developmental stages of the feeding reaction the trunk component—a short quick jump forward—becomes functional before snapping with the mouth appears. This characteristic, forward jump can be elicited by a light touch of a limb or adjacent part before there is any evidence of a true response to visual stimulation. At a later stage of development, the jumping response appears when a bristle or similar object is moved back and forth at a distance of 2 or 3 millimeters in front of the young salamander's eyes. With this stimulation the animal jumps toward the moving object but without making perceptible jaw movements. Still later, the pattern includes snapping at an object that is moving in the visual field. In a word, the gross trunk movements of the feeding response develop first, then there is response to movement within the visual field, and finally there appears a coordinated pattern of snapping at an object that is moving in the visual field and catching it in the mouth.

The adult reflex pattern thus matures through characteristic stages; it does not suddenly appear as a unit in behavior.

It is of great interest that development of behavior in the embryo anticipates function. The separate components of the snapping pattern are meaningless as they appear in the embryo but the completed pattern has functional significance in the life of the salamander. Another example of this principle is the development of the eye. The structural development of the human eye in embryo and fetus, in one sense, anticipates a function that appears after birth.

As development proceeds, activity modifies the pattern of response. Every student of psychology is familiar with the work of Pavlov upon conditioned reflexes. A conditioned reflex is a *learned* response but, if it is thoroughly learned, it has a superficial resemblance to an unconditioned reflex.

Reflex patterns are thus modified by learning as well as by maturing, or natural growth. At every stage of development, function and structural change go hand in hand.

Instinctive Behavior

Beach (1951) has argued that the distinction between instinctive behavior and learned behavior is not helpful in the experimental analysis of animal activities. Various patterns of response have been grouped together under the rubric of instinct, not because they share any positive characteristics, but because they have been arbitrarily excluded from a rather narrowly conceived category called learned behavior.

It is certain, according to Beach, that the so-called instincts do not belong together in a single class of behavior. After a review of the literature upon reproductive behavior he writes:

We have seen that sexual behavior develops in various ways in different animals and may be controlled by different external and internal correlates in males and females of the same species. Parental behavior appears to be affected by a variety of factors ranging from the female's diet during immaturity to her previous experience in rearing young. Species differences are pronounced, and in any one species the behavior is governed by a complex combination of processes. This kind of evidence contraindicates categorization of mating and maternal behavior as unlearned or instinctive.

Indeed, Beach states, the term *instinct* might profitably be dropped from the scientific vocabulary. Instead of explaining by words we could better study concrete instances of behavior and examine the various determinants of behavior.

Examples of Instinctive Patterns

If we drop the term *instinct*, we must then find another word to label those remarkably complex patterns of behavior that develop uniformly in the members of a species. The term is useful as a descriptive label but it does not explain anything.

There was a day when students of social psychology, following the lead of McDougall, "explained" behavior by reducing it to a pattern of instinctive forces. Then there was an anti-instinct movement, associated with the names of Kuo and Dunlap, that resulted in rejection of the concept of instinct. Psychologists were cautious about using the word *instinct* for fear that they might be accused of being pseudo-scientific. Now that the anti-instinct movement is safely past, a question arises as to the utility of the concept.

This writer believes that the term is useful as a descriptive label. It designates complex patterns of behavior that are common to a species and that typically have obvious biological significance. Instinctive patterns regulate biologically important processes such as: locomotion (walking and running, flying of birds, swimming of fish, spatial orientation of bats, etc.), feeding (primary acceptance and rejection), reproduction (mating, incubation of eggs, nursing and care of young), protection against natural enemies (flight, fighting, protective patterns), adjustments to such environmental conditions as temperature, currents of air or of water.

At this point it will be well to have before us several concrete examples of instinctive patterns of behavior.

Interlocking behavior in fertilization. Tinbergen (1951) has carefully observed the mating behavior of a small fish—the three-spined stickleback. The fertilization of eggs in the stickleback consists of a series of reactions in which the male responds to the female and she, in turn, to the male. The sequence of events is represented in Figure 12. Arrows indicate the normal course of events.

When the female appears, the male executes a zigzag dance, Figure 13. At low intensities of excitement the zigzag dance consists of two or three leaps; at higher intensities it consists of up to twenty leaps in quick succession. At low intensities the fish moves in a slow

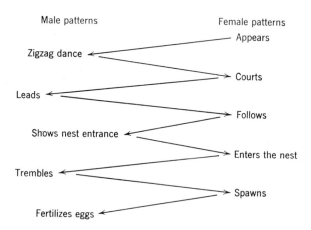

Figure 12. Schematic representation of the interbehavioral relations of male and female three-spined stickleback. *Modified from* Tinbergen (1951).

Figure 13. Zigzag dance of male three-spined stickleback; left at high intensity and right at low intensity. *After* Tinbergen (1951).

gradual curve; at higher intensities the movements are quick and the turns are sharp.

The female responds to the zigzag dance by courting behavior. She swims directly towards the male. This courting induces the male to turn around and swim rapidly to the nest he had previously built. Swimming to the nest entices the female to follow and this stimulates the male to point his head into the entrance of the nest. This is a signal for the female to enter the nest. Entrance of the female into the nest induces a trembling or quivering reaction of the male. His head in contact with the female induces spawning. The presence of fresh eggs in the nest causes the male to enter the nest and fertilize them.

The process of fertilization in the three-spined stickleback thus consists of a series of reactions in which the behavior of the male is interlocked with the behavior of the female. The reaction of one animal excites a response of the partner.

Gaping response of the nestling. The thrush nestling responds to the return of the parent by gaping, i.e., widely opening the mouth to receive food. When the birds are very young and their eyes are closed the gaping response is evoked by tactile stimulation. In response to contact the young birds stretch their necks vertically with their beaks widely opened. At about 8 days after hatching, the nestlings open their eyes and then direct their gaping towards the head of the returning parent. The gaping thus becomes directed at a certain stage of maturation.

Tinbergen (1951) studied the gaping response of the young thrush by bringing different models to the nest. Dummies were prepared with a large part (corresponding to the body of the parent) and a small part (corresponding to the head). It was found that the gaping was directed towards the small part even though its shape varied considerably. Figure 14 shows directed and undirected responses.

It thus appears that the gaping pattern can be aroused either by tactile or by visual stimulations and that the direction of the pattern is dependent upon visual form. There are, in fact, different mechanisms for *releasing* the gaping response and for *directing* it.

In general, Tinbergen was able to show that this instinctive feeding reaction is dependent upon three kinds of determinant: (1) the internal organic state of hunger or satiety; (2) the pattern of environmental stimulation; (3) the level of maturation of the bird.

Retrieving the young. Wiesner and Sheard (1933) have made extensive studies of maternal behavior in the rat. Maternal behavior is complex, being composed of separate activities: parturition (the act of giving birth to young), removal of fetal membranes, cleansing the newborn, retrieving the young when they wander away from the nest, building and repairing the nest, hovering over the young, nursing, licking the young and licking oneself, defense of young upon occasion, etc. These patterns of behavior are present at and following the birth of the first and successive litters. Virgin rats do not display these reactions toward young of their own species.

Retrieving the young when they are out of the nest is observable soon after parturition, but the tendency to retrieve diminishes as the young grow bigger. How long retrieving persists depends upon the organic state of the mother and upon the presence of small young. If the young are beyond a certain age, the mother rat does not retrieve them. She brings *small* young back to the nest while at the same

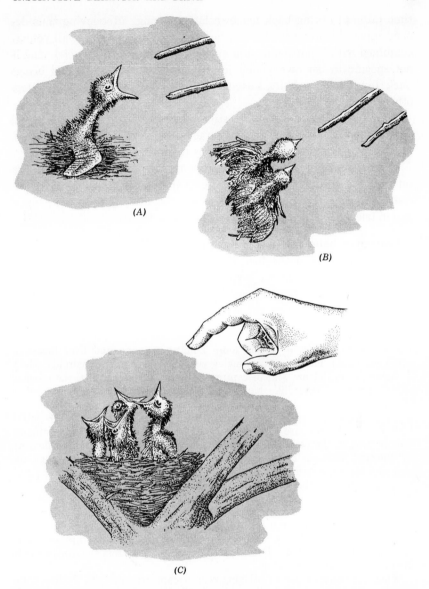

(A)

(B)

(C)

Figure 14. Directed and undirected gaping of the thrush nestling. A. Gaping at the higher of two identical sticks. B. Gaping at the nearer of two identical sticks. C. Gaping that is elicited by visual stimulation but not directed by it. *After* Tinbergen (1951).

time failing to bring back her own larger young. Retrieving thus depends upon the presence of a satisfactory maternal object (small young) combined with a particular organic state. The pattern of retrieving is not specific to her own young for the mother rat when tested brings back young mice, rabbits, kittens, chicks, as well as young from litters other than her own.

If young rats are painfully stimulated, they squeal. The sound elicits marked agitation and hyperactivity of the lactating mother. She searches for the young and returns them to the nest.

If the young of meadow mice fall out of the nest, they utter a series of shrill squeaks. In response to these squeaks the mother becomes highly active and continues to search until the young are found and retrieved.

Instinctive behavior in a microorganism. We have illustrated instinctive patterns in the fish, the bird, the mammal. The following example is drawn from the behavior of microorganisms.

In an important paper upon instinctive behavior Lashley (1938), basing his account upon the work of Kepner, gave a description of the behavior of Microstoma:

> This creature, related to the more familiar planaria and liver flukes, is equipped with nematocysts or stinging cells like those of the hydroids, which it discharges in defense and in capture of prey. In discharging, the stinging cell evaginates a threadlike barbed tube through which a poison is ejected. The striking fact about the creature is that it does not grow its own weapons, but captures them from another microscopic animal, the fresh water polyp, Hydra. The Hydras are eaten and digested until their undischarged stinging cells lie free in the stomach of Microstoma. The nettles are then picked up by ameboid processes of the cells lining the stomach and passed through the wall into the mesoderm. Here they are again picked up by wandering tissue cells and carried to the skin. The stinging cells are elliptical sacks with elastic walls, which are turned in at one end as a long coiled tube. In discharging, the wall of the sack contracts and forces out the barbed poison tube, from one end of the sack. The nettle cell can therefore only fire in one direction. When the mesodermal cell carries the nettle to the surface, it turns around so as to aim the poison tube outward. It then grows a trigger, and sets the apparatus to fire on appropriate stimulation.
>
> When Microstoma has no stinging cells it captures and eats Hydras voraciously. When it gets a small supply of cells these are distributed uniformly over the surface of the body. As more cells are obtained they are interpolated at uniform intervals between those already present. When a certain concentration of the cells is reached, the worm loses its appetite for Hydras and, in fact, will starve to death rather than eat any more of the polyps, which are apparently not a food but only a source of weapons.

Lashley comments that here, in the length of half a millimeter, are encompassed all of the major problems of dynamic psychology. There is a specific appetite that leads Microstoma to seek and ingest Hydras. This appetite is satisfied when there is a certain concentration of nettles in the skin, but the satisfaction is dependent upon a very indirect series of activities.

There is recognition and selection of a specific object, through the sensorimotor activities of the animal. Later there is recognition of the undischarged stinging cells by the wandering tissue cells. And there is something akin to form-perception because the nettle cells are aimed in an outward direction. The uniform distribution of the nematocysts over the surface of the body is a splendid illustration of a Gestalt.

Innate Perceptual Organization

There is considerable evidence that animals are able to discriminate visual forms on the basis of innate bodily organization. Here are a few examples:

Female flickers invite males to copulate by uttering a specific call and assuming the coital position. Under normal conditions the male mates with a bird that shows these reactions. He attacks an intruding male, however, apparently recognizing him by a black "moustache" that is worn by all males but not by females. If an artificial "moustache" is attached to a female, the male will attack her despite her uttering of sex calls and adopting the copulatory posture. A visual stimulus pattern is the basis of the discrimination.

Other examples of discrimination based upon innate perceptual organization are given by Lashley (1938). If sooty terns are given eggs of a related species to hatch, they invariably reject the foster children within a short time after hatching, throwing the chicks out of the nest and sometimes killing them. Strange chicks of their own species, however, are accepted during the first few days of brooding. The chicks of the two species do not differ greatly in appearance, yet the discrimination is certain. The sensory basis of this discrimination is unknown, but it is probably not wholly visual.

Again, sea gulls retrieve eggs that are moved some distance from the nest. They also retrieve objects of various sizes, weights, textures, and specific heats, ranging from small pebbles to potatoes and billiard balls. But if there is a marked departure from a rounded or oval

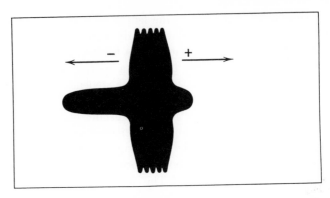

Figure 15. Silhouette of a form that resembles a hawk when moved to the right and a harmless goose when moved to the left. *After* Tinbergen (1948).

shape, the object is not retrieved. The gulls reject cubes, angular stones, mudballs, and the like. In retrieving and incubating eggs, certain perceptual requirements are necessary to elicit the appropriate behavior. The adequate stimulus of an egg may be defined as a rounded object of certain limited size and texture. This object, in the setting of a nest, elicits retrieving, cleaning, and brooding behavior. Objects that depart appreciably from this form are rejected.

Lorenz and Tinbergen have reported some instructive experiments upon innate perceptual dispositions. By cutting cardboard forms, they prepared the silhouette of a flying bird that resembles a swift-moving predatory hawk when moved to the right and a slow-moving harmless goose or other water bird when moved to the left. See Figure 15. This figure, appropriately suspended on wires, caused fear in certain species of birds (such as ptarmigan) when it moved in the hawklike direction but it elicited little more than passive attention when moving in the gooselike direction.

The discrimination appeared in several species of birds reared in captivity. It depends upon a combination of two visual characters, outline and movement. The facts suggest that an innate perceptual disposition underlies the discrimination. The biological utility of the discrimination is obvious enough.

The above examples (and there are many more like them) suggest that behavior is regulated to some extent by innate perceptual organization within the bodily structures, especially the nervous system.

Studies of the honey dance of the bee, the nest building of the oriole, the web building of the spider, and other instinctive patterns, have ended with a familiar conclusion: It is the *end attained*—the hive, the nest, the web—that is fairly constant and characteristic of the species but the series of acts through which it is constructed varies with every new element in the environment. The web of a spider, for example, may be fitted into a corner of the barn or into the limbs of a shrub or attached to rocks. Each web has individuality and is different from all other webs; yet all have a common pattern which is characteristic of the species. Behavior moves towards an end result but the specific responses which accomplish the final result vary with environmental conditions. As Koffka put it, the bird builds a nest until there is "closure" or completion of the final form.

This working towards a goal, which the animal does not foresee, is difficult to express in terms of motor mechanisms since motor activities are highly variable and, therefore, cannot be interpreted as predetermined sequences that run off automatically like serial habits. The investigator must search, rather, for controlling factors that are characteristic of the animal's perceptual organization. Perhaps the oriole continues to build the nest until it "feels right" or "looks right." What this statement means in terms of bodily structure, especially neural organization, is a problem that must be raised but cannot yet be answered.

Reflex, Instinct, Tropism

The terms *reflex, instinct* and *tropism* are in common use. They are interrelated in that all refer to basic aspects of behavior that are mechanically determined and little modified (if at all) through learning. It will be worth while to consider briefly these concepts.

The reflex is a relatively simple pattern of response that is determined: (1) by a characteristic pattern of stimulation and (2) by a preorganized bodily structure. From the point of view of stimulus-response psychology we can say that the stimulus activates (motivates) the response and that the neural organization determines its pattern.

The instinct, in general, differs from the reflex in several respects:

1. Instinctive patterns are more complex than reflexes. According to an older theory (now abandoned) instincts are viewed as concatenations of reflexes.

2. Instinctive patterns are typically more persistent than reflexes. Activities such as the building of a nest, the incubation of eggs, the

care of the young, extend over considerable periods of time. Reflexes, by contrast, are often completed in a fraction of a second.

3. Instinctive behavior is more plastic, variable, adaptable to environmental conditions than reflexes. The typical reflex has a pattern that is rigidly determined by a neural arc.

4. Finally, the determination of instinctive behavior is more complex. Instinctive acts are commonly determined by hormones from the ductless glands but a sustained chemical excitant is not characteristic of reflex action. Further, instinctive activity is elicited by a complex environmental situation and the reflex by a more simple stimulus.

The term *tropism* has long been employed by biologists to designate a persistent orientation of the total organism to a field of force. For example, the moth maintains a fixed orientation towards the candle flame and, with this orientation, flies directly into it. The salmon, at the migrating season, heads persistently up-stream rather than down. Several varieties of caterpillars climb up the tree trunk and out the limbs, against gravity, to the green leaves. Paramecia, if placed in a container with an even temperature of 19°C, distribute themselves uniformly throughout the field; but if one end of the container is warmed to 25°C, the paramecia migrate to the warm end; also they move away from temperatures as high as 38°C.

Tropisms are thus orientations of the total organism to fields of force. They are reactions to fields of light, gravity, currents of water or air, gradients of temperature, persisting chemical stimulations, and the like. Tropisms depend upon stable conditions within the physical environment. They are more or less mechanical adjustments to environmental field forces.

A tropism is said to be positive if the organism turns toward the persistent field of force and negative if it turns away from it. A tropism, literally, is a turning towards or away from a persistent force, a constant orienting within a physical field.

From the point of view of causation the concept of tropism introduces a distinctive factor—the factor of a relatively stable, persisting physical force in relation to which the organism orients itself.

A distinction is sometimes drawn between *tropism* and *taxis*. *Tropism* refers to an orientation to light, gravity, or other force, and is found in both plants and animals. *Taxis* refers to progressive movement relative to some orientation. Thus the moth's orientation towards the light can be described as a phototropism but the progressive flight into the flame is a phototaxis. The term *taxis*, obviously, is appropriate in describing animal behavior that is determined in part by a fixed orientation to a field of force.

The Evolutionary Setting

To understand reflexes, instincts, and tropisms, we must consider them within the setting of untold ages of biological evolution. These terms are descriptive only; the problem of explanation extends into the broad field of biology.

We all know that many structures of the organism are remarkably well adapted to the functions they serve. The wings are adapted to flight, the fins to swimming, the legs to locomotion, the eyes to seeing, the reproductive mechanisms to the perpetuation of the species, etc.

This process of adaptation of structure to function extends to the internal organs. There are built-in mechanisms of the body well suited to the functions they perform in the interests of survival. The structural organization of the nervous system, different from species to species, is the end product of eons of evolution. Each type of nervous system is suited to the type of life the creature leads.

The individual develops the body form, the internal structure, the type of nervous system, that is characteristic of his species. The genes and later the endocrine glands regulate the structural development of the individual.

This evolutionary setting must be taken into account when we consider the utility of many instincts and reflexes. But useless acts also exist; the end result of evolution has not been perfection. The positive phototaxis of the moth flying into the flame terminates the creature's life. The knee-jerk reflex has no obvious service to the organism. Some vestigial patterns may have been useful at an earlier stage of evolution. For example, when a dog lies down on a hard wood floor he may turn around several times before lying down. This pattern, according to Darwin, is a vestige of an evolutionary stage when the wolf had to trample down the grass to make a place to lie in. The neural organization persists when the behavior is useless.

An interpretation in terms of biological utility, however, is not necessary. We can simply describe the built-in mechanisms and study the way they are activated. We can rely upon the structure-function principle and start from the bodily structures as we find them at the present time.

SEXUAL MOTIVATION IN ANIMALS

An important area of instinctive behavior is that concerned with reproduction—with the process of mating, the birth, and the subsequent care of the young. In the following sections we will consider some of the determinants of sexual behavior. What determines the sexual patterns of behavior?

It is not enough to state that sexual behavior is instinctive. *Instinct,* as we have seen, is not an explanatory concept but rather a descriptive label for patterns of behavior that are determined by the genes and that appear at a certain stage of maturation. Thus when we use the label *instinct* we are still left with the problem of explanation.

Environmental Determinants of Mating

Beach (1951), from the point of view of comparative psychology, has reviewed many biological and psychological studies of sexual, parental and filial behavior. His survey contains a wealth of detail. Even a superficial glance at the evidence shows that patterns of sexual behavior differ widely from species to species and that, in all species, environmental stimuli have important influences upon mating.

The environmental stimuli that influence sexual behavior can be divided arbitrarily into three categories.

1. There are *predisposing conditions within the physical environment.* It is well known that for many animals there are mating seasons, i.e., the readiness of organisms to respond sexually varies with the season of the year. Such environmental conditions as illumination, temperature, the presence of other animals, markedly affect the readiness to mate.

2. There are *critical features of the immediate surroundings* that predispose the sexually ready individual to respond appropriately to the stimuli afforded by a potential mate. For example, the presence of water is necessary for reproduction of certain forms, such as amphibians, which live a terrestrial existence but mate only in the water. Again, some male fish and birds prepare nests before engaging females in courtship.

The following account, based upon the work of several observers, describes the reproductive behavior of the fur seal and the elephant seal. It shows that one specific condition of mating is the claiming and defending of a territory:

Bulls arrive at the rookery several weeks in advance of the cows, and with a great deal of fighting each male chooses and protects his particular area on the beach. Old and large individuals claim locations near the water's edge, and younger bulls are forced to settle down in less desirable regions. When a cow arrives and climbs out on the beach, she enters the territory of some male and he forcefully prevents her departure.

By permitting females to join his harem and then holding them there, the bull accumulates from three or four to as many as 50 or 75 cows. Pups conceived the previous years are born shortly after the female's arrival, and then copulation takes place. Cows are not allowed to leave the territory of their mate until they have been impregnated. Thereafter they are free to enter the ocean and feed, later returning to suckle the pups. In these cetaceans sexual and territorial behavior are interdependent.

3. There are *stimuli afforded by the sexual partner* that induce mating. The critical stimuli might be chemical or auditory or visual.

Chemical stimulation is well illustrated by the reproductive behavior of the gypsy moth. The male gypsy moth is attracted by a glandular secretion of the female. Concentrated extracts have been prepared that are specific for the species. Such extracts attract male gypsy moths from distances of more than two miles but are ineffective with other kinds of moths!

The role of auditory stimulation is illustrated by the behavior of the cricket. Sexually active male field crickets produce chirping sounds by rubbing their wing covers together. Females that are ready to mate move toward the sources of these sounds. In one experiment the males and females were placed in separate cages that were connected by a sound system. The females clustered around the speaker from which the chirping of the males issued. When male crickets in a glass container were placed in the females' cage, the visual stimulation did not produce orientation on the part of the females.

Visual stimulation is known to play an important role in the courtship and mating of some fish. The three-spined stickleback will court the model of a female if the abdomen is swollen but will not court any model without a swollen abdomen.

Orientation and movement toward a potential mate, as we have seen, may be elicited by chemical or auditory or visual stimulation. In all or nearly all animals, however, sexual excitement and mating are elicited by the activation of several senses. Any or all of the sense modalities may be involved in exciting and guiding the bodily reactions of male and female during precoital courtship. The final stages of the copulatory relation are almost universally dependent upon somatic excitations of touch and pressure.

Sexual Appetite and Organic Need

We are accustomed to think of a drive as produced by a state of need, frequently by a deprivation of some sort. The sex drive is commonly grouped, with hunger and thirst, as a primary motivation, but it differs from them in at least one important respect. Sexual deprivation does not result in death. If an individual is deprived of a sexual outlet, he does not perish, no matter how long the time involved. Sexual abstinence fails to create a genuine tissue need.

When an animal is deprived of food, a catabolic process occurs. The bodily stores of energy-producing substances, such as sugars and fats, are gradually depleted to maintain normal metabolism. If the bodily reserves are not built up through substances derived from the breakdown of newly ingested foodstuffs, depletion and loss of efficiency become inevitable. When the period of deprivation is pro- longed indefinitely, death is certain. Survival, in fact, depends upon the meeting of metabolic needs. The effects of water deprivation are comparable but they appear in a much briefer time-span. The deadly effects of oxygen deprivation appear in a matter of minutes.

There is a further difference between such drives as hunger or thirst and the sexual drive. A food-deprived animal removes the depleted state by ingesting foodstuffs which relieve the tissue need. Feeding permits an *anabolic* process that returns the organism to an optimal physiological condition. A sexually deprived male, contrastingly, who engages in unlimited sexual activity, experiences a depletion of energy that continues, in *catabolic* fashion, until a state of exhaustion is reached.

The sequel to food satiation is a gradual reinstatement of tissue need and a recurrence of hunger. The sequel to sexual satiation, or exhaustion, is a gradual return to the rested condition, a recovery from fatigue. In other words, the period following satiation upon food is one during which a need develops but the period following sexual satiation is one of recovery from exhaustion.

Beach (1956) has pointed out that after ejaculation the male rat is sexually unresponsive to the receptive female. The duration of the refractory period varies from individual to individual. In one experiment, males were placed with receptive females until the males became sexually exhausted. The criterion of exhaustion was that the male did not mount the female for a period of 30 minutes. Following exhaustion the males were retested after 1, 3, 6, or 15 days of rest. On the retest, individual differences in behavior were apparent. Some rats reached the criterion of exhaustion after five ejaculations, whereas others ejaculated ten times before becoming inactive.

A very sensitive index of recovery from sexual exhaustion is the latency of response. Thus, in retests after one day of rest, the median number of seconds preceding the first intromission was 3600. Comparable scores were 623 seconds for tests after 3 days of rest, 135 seconds for the 6-day rest, and 18 seconds for tests following a 15-day rest period. These data for the male rat indicate that the curve of recovery from sexual exhaustion is asymptotic with negative acceleration. That is to say, recovery is most rapid during the days immediately following exhaustion, and the process of recovery approaches a limit or stable condition.

According to an older theory of sexual motivation, the secretions gradually accumulating within the accessory sex glands and the nerve impulses from distended receptacles generate sexual tension. According to this view the male sexual drive was regarded as analogous to the eliminative urges that depend upon distended bladder or rectum.

This hypothesis concerning the nature of sexual motivation is negated by the experimental facts. Beach has shown that male animals that have been surgically deprived of the glands in question continue to display unmistakable signs of sexual arousal and potency. Further, homologous structures are undeveloped in the female; yet the female exhibits a sexual drive as truly as the male.

To the present writer it seems that sexual motivation is more akin to certain food appetites than to biological hungers for air, water or food. An individual may develop an appetite for sweets, for example, when there is no metabolic need for carbohydrate. Such an appetite may be satiated or oversatiated (so that the individual is negative), and then the appetite gradually develops again. The eating of candy is not necessary for survival but the craving develops and persists. The appetite can be aroused by environmental stimulations such as presence of candy, and, as we said, it can be satiated.

Beach has stated that the adolescent boy's preoccupation with sexual matters is traceable to psychological stimuli, external and phantasied, more than to his recently matured reproductive glands. Human erotic urges arise from sociocultural influences more than from strictly organic sources. Sexual behavior, therefore, depends upon external stimulation to a much greater extent than does hunger and thirst.

The comparison of the human sexual appetite with the seasonal behavior of animals is misleading. Accounts of the rutting stag actively seeking a mate are inaccurate. When the stag encounters a receptive female he may or may not become sexually excited. It is unlikely, therefore, that when erotic stimuli are lacking he exists in a state of undischarged sexual tension. Moreover, the human male differs from the stag in that he carries around with him a complexly organized nervous system that makes possible patterns of thought and desire.

We conclude that the human sexual appetite is acquired and that to a large extent it is aroused by environmental influences which include, of course, the behavior of the human female.

Neural Basis of Sexual Behavior

The neurological evidence indicates that sexual behavior in all animals includes a number of reflexes that are controlled by primitive neural circuits. From the frog to man, Beach (1951) points out, we find proof that elements in the normal mating pattern can be mediated by spinal mechanisms that lack any connection with the brain. At the same time it is clear, as we go up the phylogenetic scale, that integrated sexual patterns become increasingly dependent upon the forebrain.

Among insects the neural mechanisms that regulate mating are built into the nervous system. Grosch amputated the posterior segments of the male wasp and observed that such preparations displayed typical courtship reactions and repeatedly tried to mount the female. The sensory and motor mechanisms of the anterior part of the body, therefore, were capable of carrying out a large part of the sexual pattern even though the body segments containing the reproductive organs were missing.

With mammals it has been shown that genital reflexes survive complete transection of the spinal cord in the lumbar region. Erection and ejaculation in male rodents, rabbits, and dogs occur in response to electrical stimulation of the sacral cord.

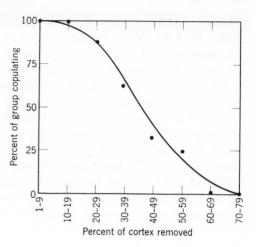

Figure 16. Effect of cerebral injury on mating behavior in male rats. The proportion of different groups continuing to copulate after operation varies according to the amount of cortex removed. *After* Beach (1940, 1951).

The cerebral cortex is not directly involved in the organization of primary sexual responses of the male rat but the cortex serves to maintain the excitability of lower centers that are essential to the integration of mating behavior. Figure 16, from Beach (1940), shows the effects of cortical lesions upon the copulatory behavior of male rats. The graph gives the proportion of different groups that continue to copulate after surgical removal of different amounts of the cerebral cortex.

Hormonal Factors in Sexual Activation

It is commonly known that hormones from the reproductive glands activate the neural mechanisms that regulate mating. Two experiments that illustrate this point for the male sexual drive are considered below. In both experiments it was demonstrated that castration weakened or removed the sexual drive of male rats and that subsequent injection of the male hormone restored the sexual drive.

Beach and Holz-Tucker (1949) gave male rats a mating test. The male was placed in a circular observation cage and three minutes later a receptive female was quietly placed in the center of the cage. The behavior of the male was scored in terms of whether or not he mated and in terms of the frequency of copulation during the ten-minute test. After preliminary tests the males were castrated.

With castrated males the frequency of copulation per test decreased markedly, and the latency of sexual responses markedly increased. Removal of the testicular hormones from the blood by the surgical operation resulted in a marked diminution of sexual drive.

The castrated animals were next given regular and graded injections of the male hormone. A direct relationship was demonstrated between the number of micrograms of hormone injected per day and the objective measure of sexual potency. The amount of hormone necessary to maintain sexual performance at or near the preoperative level varied somewhat with the behavioral criterion selected as a measure. Generally, 50 to 75 micrograms per day maintained a rat at his preoperative level. When the castrated males were given daily injections of 100 to 500 micrograms of hormone per day they exhibited sexual performance equal or superior to that shown prior to the operation. The work indicates clearly a quantitative relation between the measure of sexual performance and the number of micrograms of testosterone propionate injected per day in the castrates.

Another experiment, similar to the above, has been reported by Beach (1956). In this study male rats were trained to traverse a runway to a goal box containing a receptive female. After copulating once, the male was returned to the starting box and given another run. The day's testing concluded with the trial on which ejaculation occurred.

A positive relation was found between the male's speed of running and the intensity of his sexual reactions to the estrous female in the goal box.

In this experiment the males that had been running rapidly and mating promptly were castrated. Following the operation there was a gradual loss of sexual ability, shown by decrease in the intensity, completeness, and frequency of mating responses in the goal box. When the copulatory responses began to weaken and disappear, the time required to traverse the runway steadily lengthened. Finally, when copulatory responses were abolished many males remained in the starting box, failing to enter the runway.

The inactive animals were then given daily injections of testosterone propionate. When the injections were given there was an increase in the sexual reactions to the estrous female and a steady decrease in the time required by the male to reach the goal box.

These two experiments confirm the results of many previous studies. They show the importance of hormonal factors in maintaining sexual responsiveness. Sexual activation, therefore, depends upon hormonal factors and not merely upon environmental stimulations.

Two Mechanisms in Sexual Activation

Beach (1956) assumes that there are two mechanisms in sexual activation—the one is general, the other specific. The assumption of two mechanisms is necessary in the interpretation of an experiment by Jordan and Beach.

They observed, during a series of tests with male rats, that successive ejaculations were achieved with fewer and fewer intromissions. Ordinarily, male rats must achieve intromission from eight to fifteen times before ejaculation occurs; but with repeated copulations the number of intromissions required to reach the threshold of ejaculation is steadily reduced. This fact suggests that repeated copulations lower the threshold of ejaculation, i.e., produce a state of increased sexual excitement. A fact that appears to contradict this interpretation, however, is that the time required to recover sexual responsiveness increases progressively with succeeding ejaculations. The lengthening of recovery time suggests a gradual weakening of sexual motivation.

Beach has explained the seeming paradox by assuming that there are two regulatory mechanisms. First, there is a mechanism that regulates the thresholds of sexual arousal. This is shown by the fact that the male rat, after exhaustion, is refractory to sexual stimulation and requires a period of recovery before he can be sexually aroused; and, further, the period of unresponsiveness is increased by successive ejaculations. Second, there are specific bodily mechanisms that regulate the genital patterns of intromission and ejaculation. There are built-in reflexive mechanisms.

The postulate of two regulatory mechanisms agrees with the facts of sexual behavior in other mammals, including man. The principal difference between man and lower mammals lies in the extent to which the mechanism of sexual arousal is controlled by symbolic factors. Sexual play, or contrectation, leads to the establishment of bodily contact and general physical stimulation; but there is a second specifically genital mechanism that leads to intromission and ejaculation. Both mechanisms—the one general, the other specific—are aroused in sexual behavior.

Human Sexual Motivation

The two mechanisms in sexual activation, described by Beach, agree quite well with the two processes that are described in the pre-experimental literature upon sexual motivation.

According to Havelock Ellis (1920), human sexual motivation has two phases. There is an impulse of tumescence and an impulse of detumescence. Tumescence occurs during amorous behavior, sexual play; it builds up sexual tension with erection of the genital organs in preparation for coitus. Detumescence is the release of tumescence at the time of and following the sexual orgasm.

Caressing or petting (contrectation) builds up a tension or appetite which is the normal preparation for sexual union. The sexual tension is released, the appetite satisfied, by sexual union culminating in detumescence. Following intercourse there is a relaxed, pleasant mood known as sexual analepsis. If the orgasm is incomplete, analepsis may not follow. This failure to reach an orgasm is more frequent with the female than the male. Instead of sexual satisfaction and relaxation there is then a state of dissatisfaction, tension, and excitement. If there is frequent failure of sexual satisfaction, a wife may develop negative attitudes of hatred and resentment towards her husband. This is a major source of maladjustment and divorce.

Closely associated with tumescence and detumescence are two other impulses: domination (masculine) and yielding (feminine). These impulses are also found in the behavior of non-human animals.

Males frequently fight for possession of a female. In the animal world mating is associated with struggle, bloodshed, and pain. Copulation itself appears to involve violence. A sexually excited yet frustrated male fights for a mate with the same vigor and abandon that he displays in fighting for defense of territory or food.

The daily newspapers frequently carry stories of a sadist whose rape was followed by murder or associated with some form of mutilation or torture. Normal persons read such stories with horror but some are fascinated by them.

Brutality, cruelty, and the inflicting of pain, when associated with the sexual act, is known as *sadism*. The term was derived from Marquis De Sade, who was born in 1740, in Paris. De Sade obtained satisfaction from whipping a young woman forcibly and from imagining scenes of torture, in which the infliction of pain was associated with sex. The complementary impulse is called *masochism*. This term was derived from Leopold von Sacher-Masoch who was born in 1836 at Lemberg in Galacia. Masochism is the obtaining of sexual enjoyment from having pain inflicted upon one's self. Although sensory pain is characteristically unpleasant, it may be pleasant when associated with sex. Both sadism and masochism, in extreme forms, are regarded as pathological.

The sexual appetite may or may not be accompanied by tender feelings. Tenderness is not a *necessary* component of sexual desire. Tender feelings are characteristically associated with parental behavior, with care and protection of the young and other helpless and dependent creatures. In romantic love, tender feelings are associated with sexual behavior, but tenderness and the sexual impulse are not necessarily found together.

It would be misleading to assume that the desire to reproduce is necessarily a part of the sexual impulse. Although civilized man knows the relation between the sexual act and the subsequent birth of young, there are primitive peoples who do not understand this relationship. According to Malinowski (1927), the Trobriand Islanders are ignorant of the relation between the sexual act and paternity. Among them kinship is reckoned through the mother. The mother's brother exercises an authority over her child that, with us, is assumed by the father. Ignorance of the physical basis of paternity implies lack of moral responsibility for the procreation of children. Sexual impulses, from infancy to maturity, are relatively uninhibited as they are with nonhuman animals. The development of sexuality is free from censure and moral reprobation, and there is less sexual frustration with the Trobrianders than with more civilized people, and fewer nervous breakdowns.

Since the Trobrianders are ignorant of the biological facts of life, it cannot be that a desire for children drives them to sexual union or that the desire for children is part of their sexual motivation. Sexual behavior among these primitives is much as it is with other animals who do not foresee the birth of young following sexual union. Sexual motivation, whether in man or other animals, is an impulsive, nonrational, highly affective, process.

NATURE OF THE DRIVE

In the above discussion I have used the term *instinct* as a descriptive label for complex innate patterns of behavior. The term explains nothing.

Under attacks from the anti-instinctivists, during the 1920s and 1930s, the concept of instinct fell into disrepute. At about this time the concept of drive became increasingly popular. One of the main objections to the instinct doctrine was that it offered a pseudo explanation of behavior. Anything we do might be explained by postulating an instinct that caused it!

Drive is mainly an explanatory concept although there are descriptive (behavioral) meanings. The concept is central in motivational psychology.

There are a good many shades of meaning. Earlier (Young, 1936) I listed six meanings of the term *drive*. These were as follows: (1) Drive is the energy which moves the body. (2) Drive is the stimulus or else the internal tissue condition which releases energy and leads to activity. (3) Drive is general activity. For example, in the activity cage the female rat shows rhythmical variations in "drive." (4) Drive is any behavioral tendency, whether goal-directed or not, such as playfulness, sociability, laziness, exploratory trend, restlessness, etc. (5) A drive is a specific, goal-directed activity such as food-seeking or mate-seeking. (6) Finally, in human psychology, drive is a motivating factor within the personality—an interest, a purpose, or a wish.

These meanings have persisted, but they have been amplified somewhat, and other meanings have been added. In the following sections we will consider the main views concerning the nature of the drive.

Drive as Physical Energy

When Woodworth (1918) introduced the term *drive* to American psychology he meant the physical energy that makes the machine go. He distinguished between the mechanism that regulates and directs the pattern of behavior and the drive, or energy, that puts the machine in motion and keeps it going. A mechanism remains inert until physical energy transformations activate it.

Holt (1931), however, pointed out that there are two basic meanings to the energetic concept of drive: (1) Drive is the physical energy which does work—chemical energy derived from the breakdown of substances stored or bound within the tissues. (2) Drive is an agency that releases stored energy. In the second sense, stimuli that impinge upon sense organs and release energy are drives.

The second of these meanings has dominated theoretical discussion. For Hull, Spence, Neal Miller, Guthrie, and others, *drive* is essentially a persisting stimulus—a stimulus that releases stored-up energy and thus initiates behavior. Guthrie (1938), for example, states that what we call "drive" is a pattern of persisting and disturbing stimuli. A problem—whether the problem of a cat in a puzzle-box or of a child confronted by an unyielding parent—is essentially a persisting stimulus-situation of such a nature that the subject is disturbed and excited until some act is hit upon that removes the maintaining stimuli and allows the excitement to subside. Guthrie (1944) elsewhere questions whether two concepts—drive and stimulus—are needed. The persistent excitation from a distended bladder, he writes, is quite effectively described as a stimulus and there is little point in describing it as a drive. Drive is stimulus and stimulus is physical energy that releases energy in receptor cells.

Following Woodworth's introduction of the term, Moss (1924) published an experimental study of animal drives. Although Woodworth had referred to *drive* (in the singular) as the energy that motivates behavior, Moss wrote of *drives* (in the plural) such as the hunger drive, the thirst drive, the sex drive, and also he wrote about external *resistances*. This plural usage of the term was taken up by Dashiell, Tolman, Richter, Warden, Stone, and others, and from these psychologists the concept came into widespread and general use in comparative and physiological psychology.

If we speak of *drives* (in the plural) we at once raise a question as to how many different drives there are and how they can be recognized and distinguished from each other. It is obvious that differences in goal-orientation and differences in the pattern of consummatory response provide a means of differentiation. Physiological psychologists, however, have consistently sought to differentiate drives in terms of internal bodily mechanisms. On the basis of anatomy and physiology one can distinguish and describe the mechanisms for hunger, thirst, sexual and maternal behavior, sleep, urination, defecation, respiration, and a few other organic conditions that motivate behavior. *Drives* (in the plural) are not different kinds of energy; they are different bodily mechanisms that determine behavior.

Duffy (1951) pointed out that the concept of motivation includes two distinct factors. A motive is said to *energize* behavior and to *direct* it. The same two factors appeared in the older concept of instinct: in instinctive behavior, energy was *released* and *guided* in a particular direction. These are different concepts, she said, and it would be better to treat the energetics of behavior and the regulation of behavior separately.

The degree of energy mobilization is the extent of release of stored energy of the organism through metabolic activity in the tissues. This appears to occur in a continuum, from a low point during deep sleep to a high point during frantic effort or excitement. The energetic aspect of behavior has basic significance.

Duffy supports her argument by several propositions which rest upon empirical data:

1. Every activity, overt or covert, in which the individual engages requires the release of energy.

2. The extent of the energy release is determined by the degree of *effort* required by the situation *as interpreted by the individual*. Difficult tasks, for example, require more energy expenditure than easy.

3. The extent of energy release is determined also by physiological factors, such as endocrine secretions, food, and drugs.

4. The extent of energy release varies with the type of situation under which it is measured, and it varies from individual to individual under the same situation.

5. Variations in energy release determine the variance of performance as shown in measurements of reaction, sensitivity, coordination of responses and in the general quality of performance.

6. The relation between energy intake and storage, on the one hand, and energy expenditure, on the other, are important factors in the health and well-being of the individual.

All things considered, Duffy argues, we should treat the level of energy mobilization as a single, basic variable in behavior, apart from the directive aspect. Energy release is a common factor in all motives and emotions.

Duffy's point is well taken and seems to bring us back to Woodworth's original concept of drive as the energy that makes the machine go. Duffy's concept of a continuum that represents different degrees or levels of energy release and mobilization, agrees with Lindsley's concept of levels of activation, which is described in Chapter 5.

If we accept the *energetic* concept of drive, we must always remember that energy transformations occur within the cells, organs and tissues of the body; and that bodily structures determine the pattern and course of behavior. In Woodworth's terms, we must distinguish between the drive and the mechanism.

Drive as Activation of Specific Built-in Mechanisms

Lashley (1938) proposed the view that instinctive behavior depends upon specific chemical activation of neural centers. Physiologically viewed, all drives are nothing more than the activities of specific built-in mechanisms. There is no general drive, or libido, Lashley assumes, and there is no disturbed organic equilibrium underlying instinctive behavior. Instead, there is partial excitation of specific sensorimotor mechanisms within the body.

In the sex and maternal drives, hormones act directly upon the central nervous system to increase the excitability of the specific sensorimotor mechanisms that underlie instinctive activities such as mating and nursing the young. The bodily mechanisms of instinctive behavior are mature, in the developing organism, long before the hormones from reproductive glands activate them.

Thus, for Lashley, drive is specific chemical activation of preformed bodily mechanisms through excitation of neural centers. He believes that the same kind of selective activation occurs when the organism reacts to specific dietary deficits.

Chemical Sensitization of Bodily Mechanisms

Nissen (1954) elaborated and extended the earlier view of Lashley. For Nissen, *drive* is a specific chemical factor that sensitizes a bodily mechanism and thus elicits a fairly specific pattern of behavior.

Nissen rejected certain other views concerning the nature of drive. Drive is not a persisting stimulus. The concept of stimulus is required to explain brief and relatively simple responses such as reflexes, but if we equate drive and stimulus, we have stripped *drive* of its distinctive and useful meaning. The term *drive* refers typically to a persisting determinant of goal-directed, purposeful behavior. The determinant is chemical in nature.

Nissen rejected the distinction between "learned" and "unlearned" drives. The concept of "acquired drive" or "learnable drive" does not make sense, for all drives are innate. All are biogenic. All are primary. Of course, organisms acquire new subgoals and new patterns of behavior but they do not acquire drives *as such*. By taking this stand Nissen avoided a good deal of the confusion that was aired by Judson Brown (1953) in his study of the concepts of habit and drive.

In addition to chemical drives, Nissen continued, we must take account of the fact that many bodily mechanisms function autonomously. We do not need to invoke chemical sensitizers to explain their activity. There are many unitary patterns of behavior that are autonomously motivated and that exist independently of the sensitizing factors which we call *drives*. For example, there is a biogenic drive to explore, to perceive, to know, that does not depend upon chemical sensitization. Apropos of this drive, Nissen quotes Woodworth (1947):

The present thesis . . . is that perception is always driven by a direct, inherent motive which might be called the will to perceive. . . . To see, to hear—to see clearly, to hear distinctly—to make out what it is one is seeing or hearing—moment by moment, such concrete, immediate motives dominate the life of relation with the environment.

We do not need to assume that the nervous system is the servant of other organs of the body. The nervous system is part of the body and as such it has homeostatic requirements of its own that are comparable to those of other organs. There is a primary drive for the brain to perform its functions of perceiving and knowing that exists quite apart from other drives.

Nissen questioned the validity of the distinction between homeostatic and non-homeostatic drives. He argued that all bodily organs play a part in maintaining homeostasis; each organ has its special function. It is the function of the sense organs and the nervous system to perceive and to know. Observant behavior, exploration and manipulation, are thus "homeostatic" patterns in the sense that they favor survival of the individual and the species and thus tend to preserve the *milieu intérieur*. There is no superbiological force underlying curiosity and other alleged "non-homeostatic" drives.

The activities of some animals serve nutritional needs but they have no direct and obvious relation to a *present* disturbance of homeostasis. Thus: the bee constructs a hive and fills it with honey; the spider weaves an elaborate web; the beaver fells trees and builds a dam. The external situation calls out the pattern of activity. These activities are biologically basic but they are not motivated by disturbed homeostasis. They are elicited by environmental conditions.

In an earlier review Nissen (1951) pointed out that many forms of instinctive behavior are elicited (sensitized and regulated) by environmental conditions. For example, *Daphnia* rise to the surface when carbon dioxide is added to the water of their aquarium; but if the aquarium is lighted from below, the addition of carbon dioxide results in movement to the bottom of the tank. The light serves as a directive factor, but only in the presence of carbon dioxide. In the absence of carbon dioxide there is no orientation, no movement, to the light. Such behavior is purely a tropism, regulated by external conditions, and has no apparent relation to the regulation of homeostasis.

Underlying Nissen's clear and cogent analysis are several basic motivational concepts. First, there is the well-substantiated view that hormones and other chemical factors sensitize neural centers and thus arouse specific patterns of behavior by sensitizing the mechanisms.

Second, there is the concept of environmental stimulation that releases patterns of behavior quite apart from the internal chemical sensitization of bodily mechanisms. And, finally, there is the view that bodily structures can function autonomously without the need of any extrinsic motivation.

Drive as the Lowering of Thresholds for Response Patterns

A view expressed by Ausubel (1956), and others, is that the primary drives are central states that facilitate specific patterns of behavior by lowering the thresholds of the effector mechanisms rather than by exciting these mechanisms. According to this view the thresholds of different groups of responses are differentially lowered in accordance with their acquired drive-reducing capacity. Thus, if thirst is the drive state, there is a lowering of the thresholds for a group of learned water-seeking responses.

Ausubel distinguished between the drive state, as such, and the determinants of this state. Drive determinants are conditions—sensory, humoral, cognitive—which selectively facilitate behavior by lowering the thresholds of control mechanisms thus increasing the probability that an appropriate drive-reducing response will occur.

An experiment by Campbell and Sheffield (1953) appears to support this view. They started from a common observation that hungry animals are more active than satiated. Most workers have assumed that the increased activity of the animals is an expression of their hunger state; but the activity level of animals is known to depend upon a good many conditions, including environmental stimulation. In experiments upon hunger and the level of activity the environmental conditions have rarely been controlled.

Campbell and Sheffield controlled environmental stimulations when rats were hungry and non-hungry. They housed rats in activity cages that were installed within a soundproof cabinet. Each activity cage was mounted to control four microswitches, arranged to record all gross movements of the subjects. The apparatus gave a quantitative index of the level of activity during the observation period.

Activity was recorded at noon for two 10-minute periods daily. When the first activity record was taken the environment remained unchanged. When the second record was taken the environmental conditions were altered—the change being produced by turning off the ventilating fan and turning on the lights.

The level of activity was recorded on 7 days, first with a constant

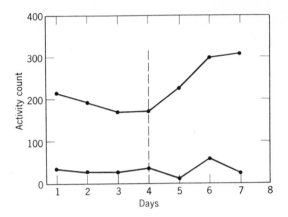

Figure 17. The effect of deprivation on the activity response to an environmental change. (For explanation of the figure, see the text.) *After* Campbell and Sheffield (1953).

environment and then with changed environmental conditions. During the first 4 days, the rats were free from hunger; during the last 3 days food was removed from the cages and there was a gradually increasing hunger. Water was continuously present.

Figure 17 presents the results of the experiment graphically. The graph shows the mean activity count for the 7 days of the experiment. The lower curve presents the activity count based upon the 10-minute periods with a constant environment. The upper curve presents the activity count based upon the 10-minute periods with environmental stimulations from changed conditions. It will be seen at a glance that the rats were more active when environmental conditions were changed than when they remained constant. This finding agrees with the view that a change of environment elicits increased activity—presumably of an attentive, exploratory nature.

The important comparison in Figure 17 is that between the first 4 and the last 3 days. The graph shows that when environmental conditions are held constant the presence or absence of hunger made little or no difference in the level of general activity. When environmental conditions were changed (upper curve) the hungry animals were found to be increasingly and significantly more active than the non-hungry.

The total data suggest that hunger is not expressed by a rise in the level of general activity when environmental conditions are constant but hunger involves a lowering of the thresholds of response to external stimuli. Simply stated: starvation does not instigate activity; it lowers the thresholds for external stimuli so that the animal is observed to be more active when hungry than when non-hungry.

In view of this bit of evidence a question should be raised as to how far hunger serves to *elicit* increased activity and how far hunger merely *sensitizes* the animal, lowering thresholds, as Ausubel assumes, so that the animal responds more readily to external stimulus cues. Lashley, Nissen, Beach, and others, have emphasized the chemical basis for drive; but the question remains as to how far chemical conditions *excite* and how far they *sensitize*, i.e., lower thresholds. It may be that the chemical agent merely lowers the thresholds for certain response patterns but does not elicit them. Environmental stimuli elicit responses and chemical factors sensitize selectively. The matter, of course, needs further study.

Theory of the Central Motive State (CMS)

Morgan (1957, 1959) has recalled and elaborated his theory of the Central Motive State (CMS) that was formulated, in 1943, in his *Physiological Psychology.*

The CMS is hypothetical; it does not have a precise bodily locus. The locus might be the reticular formation (Lindsley) or the hypothalamus (Stellar), or it might include both of these structures and also the medulla, midbrain, and diencephalon. Who can say? The CMS is a concept and not an anatomical structure or a precise physiological state.

The CMS takes account of three main stages in the motivational process: (1) the arousal of behavior; (2) the maintenance of such behavior; (3) the satiation or termination of such behavior.

The arousal of behavior may come either from a stimulus or a chemical condition. Stimulation of exteroceptors or receptors within the body can motivate behavior. Persisting stimulation from the contracting stomach or from the dry throat can motivate; pain and cold stimulation from the environment can also arouse behavior. There is plenty of evidence that chemical and hormonal conditions in the blood may arouse motive states.

When a CMS has been aroused, it tends to persist without outside support from sensory inputs or excitants. The CMS does not continue indefinitely, but it has a certain inertia. In addition to persistence, the CMS has several other characteristics. General activity accompanies a CMS and is an integral part of its expression. Again, a CMS may emit certain patterns of behavior that are characteristic of the state without specific stimulation of receptors. The CMS acts selectively in that it predisposes the organism to react in certain ways to particular stimuli and not to react to others.

The satiation or termination of behavior, once aroused, can come about in several ways: (1) by the elimination of the stimulus or humoral factor which originally gave rise to the behavior; (2) by the liberation of some humoral agent different from that arousing the drive but capable of reducing the CMS; (3) by stimulation of receptors during the course of behavior emitted by the CMS; and (4) by the behavior *per se* resulting from the CMS.

This is Morgan's theory in barest outline. It is a central physiological theory of drive. It opens the door to research leading to the more exact description of conditions that arouse, maintain and terminate specific patterns of behavior.

Drive as a Hypothesis and as Observed Behavior

Skinner (1938) was among the first to point out that drive is a hypothetical construct. The problem of drive arises, writes Skinner, because much of the behavior of an organism shows variability. For example, eating in the presence of food is not inevitable, but the acceptance of food varies with past interactions between organism and environment. Because an animal does not invariably eat when in the presence of food, we must make the hypothesis of an internal state to which we can assign this variability.

Skinner argues that we are not forced to turn to physiology for an explanation of behavior. We can study the functional relations between environmental conditions and behavior without entering the field of speculative neurology. *Drive* is a logical construct based upon the facts of behavior. It should be possible, Skinner has argued, to dispense with the concept of drive entirely and to limit ourselves to empirically observed relations.

For others, *drive* is an inferred variable intervening between stimulus conditions and response. Thus Hull regards *drive* (*D*) as an intervening variable. Although Hull tends to think in physiological terms, *drive* is nonetheless a hypothetical construct.

For most of the views considered above, drive is a hypothetical factor. Morgan's CMS is inferred and not observed. The view that *drive* is a lowering of thresholds for groups of responses in a hypothesis. Even the view that *drive* is physical energy or the release of energy, is a hypothesis. Energy is not directly observed by the physicist, but it is a logical construct. For the physicist, energy equals $MV^2/2$; in which M is a capacity factor and $V^2/2$ an intensity factor. Physical energy is a logical or mathematical concept and not a fact of observation.

If we agree with Skinner that *drive* is a hypothetical construct and then turn to behavior to discover what empirically observed relations indicate the presence or absence of a drive, what do we find?

On the level of behavior there are two main types of activity that have been identified with drive. First, the level of general activity as recorded by activity cages has been taken as a measure of drive. Activity cages do not analyze behavior into specific components, but they give an over-all rating of the quantity of movement of the subject during a fixed period of time. The level of activity is known to depend upon glandular secretions, deprivations of food or water, temperature of the environment, and other factors. A high level of general activity has been identified with high drive and a low level with low drive. Second, drive has been identified with persistent goal orientation observed in behavior.

Warden (1931) gave a behavioral definition of drive. He wrote: "By a *drive* we mean an aroused reaction tendency which is characterized primarily by the fact that the activity of the organism is directed towards or away from some *specific incentive*, such as food, water, animal of opposite sex, etc." For Warden *drive* does not refer to an internal bodily state such as hunger but to the persistent goal-directed behavior itself. When an animal persists in crossing a charged grill to reach the goal object he reveals a drive. The strength of drive can be controlled by manipulating environmental conditions, e.g., by removing food from the cages, but the drive itself is directly observed as behavior. On the basis of behavior one can distinguish the hunger drive, the thirst drive, the sex drive, the maternal drive, the exploratory drive, and others.

The majority of psychologists, however, think of drive not as behavior *per se* but as an organic state that motivates behavior. Behavior is *driven* and the impetus comes from some bodily or hypothetical factor that is assumed to exist outside of the *driven* behavior.

The Arousal Function and the Cue Function

In his book upon *The Organization of Behavior*, Hebb (1949) argued that motivation is not a distinctive process, and that the principles of cell-assembly and phase sequence apply to it as much as they do to learning. "The term motivation then refers (1) to the existence of an organized phase sequence, (2) to its direction or content, and (3) to its persistence in a given direction, or stability of content." The term *drive* did not appear in the table of contents of Hebb's exciting book.

In the light of recent physiological developments, however, Hebb (1955) revised his view. He now takes what might be called the *energetic* view of drive and holds to his former position in accounting for the regulation and direction of behavior. His change of view is based upon developments within the field of brain physiology.

Prior to 1930 it was accepted that the neuron fired with maximal energy or not at all; but the all-or-none principle has been challenged. Current neurology recognizes that the dendrite has a "slow-burning" activity that does not follow the all-or-none principle, and that the brain is self-active and not merely a passive machine that responds to external stimulation, and that there is a true *neural* fatigue lasting minutes instead of milliseconds. These and other factual discoveries have changed Hebb's basic concept of motivation.

Again, the experiments of Moruzzi and Magoun, Lindsley, and others, upon the activating system of the brain stem, force us to revise the concepts of both motivation and emotion. This work revealed two kinds of pathway from the receptors to the brain. There is thus a changed view of sensory function:

> In the classical conception of sensory function, input to the cortex was via the great projection systems only: from sensory nerve to sensory tract, thence to the corresponding sensory nucleus of the thalamus, and thence directly to one of the sensory projection areas of the cortex. These are still the direct sensory routes, the quick efficient transmitters of information. The second pathway is slow and inefficient; the excitation, as it were, trickles through a tangled thicket of fibers and synapses, there is a mixing up of messages, and the scrambled messages are delivered indiscriminately to wide cortical areas. In short, they are messages no longer. They serve, instead, to tone up the cortex, with a background supporting action that is completely necessary if the messages proper are to have their effect. Without the arousal system, the sensory impulses by the direct route reach the sensory cortex, but go no farther; the rest of the cortex is unaffected, and thus learned stimulus-response relations are lost.

Lindsley has stated, and Hebb agrees, that the diffuse excitation of the cortex provides a physiological basis for the concept of arousal or energizing that is essential in most studies of motivation and emotion. There are, Hebb points out, two functions: One is a *cue function* related to the guiding or steering of behavior. The other, less obvious but no less important, is an *arousal* or *vigilance function*. Without a foundation of arousal, the cue function cannot exist.

Arousal, in this sense, is synonymous with general drive. Drive, as *energizing*, can now be identified anatomically and physiologically. Drive is an energizer, not a guide; an engine, not a steering gear; a propeller, not a rudder. Drive gives impetus to behavior but it is always related to the cue (directive) function.

The recognition of a general drive state clarifies a number of points that would be difficult to explain without it. For example, perceptual processes have a drive value which may be described in terms of alertness and anxiety. Hebb, in agreement with Nissen, finds it unnecessary to postulate extrinsic motivation to explain observant and manipulative behavior. Again, some organisms appear to seek excitement that has no apparent relation to satisfaction of the primary drives. A man will go to considerable trouble to get into more trouble at the bridge table or on a golf course. There is a taste for excitement. People welcome the risk of a roller coaster or mountain climbing or a problem to be solved. Many such facts make sense if we think of the arousal function in terms of diffuse cortical excitation.

Hebb's view has an important bearing upon the concept of emotion as well as drive. A high level of arousal produced by intense stimulation, great pain, anxiety tension, or other condition is associated with reduction in the level of cue function. That is to say, emotional disturbance is associated with high levels of activation.

Drive and Affective Arousal

Hebb's distinction between a cue function and an arousal function is sound and important. The cue function is dependent upon sensory discrimination, and it is expressed in motor performance. The arousal function is dependent upon activation; it is related to energy mobilization rather than to the transmission of information to the brain. This is a distinction between cognitive and motor aspects of the psychological process, on the one hand, and motivation, on the other.

Hebb's view of motivation, however, needs to be modified to take account adequately of the affective processes especially the distinction between positive and negative affective arousals. Since this is the main topic in Chapter 5, the discussion will be resumed there after we have examined the relation between affective arousals and activation.

Drives, Habits and Motives

In a critical study of problems presented by the concept of "acquired drives," Judson Brown (1953) denied that drives, as such, have a steering function. He listed three main properties of drives as follows: (1) Drives have an energizing, activating property. (2) Drives have a property of reinforcing responses that lead to drive reduction. (3) Responses that are followed by pain tend to be abandoned.

Brown intentionally omitted a guiding and directing function from his list of the properties of drives. Bodily mechanisms that guide and direct behavior, he states, are acquired through a process of learning and they are more appropriately called habits. His view is summarized as follows: "Because drives, as such, are regarded as incapable of steering or directing behavior, it is necessary to deny that the individuals can acquire drives for any specific goal object or situation whatsoever. What individuals do acquire are numerous habits or modes of reacting to complex situations made up of both external and internal stimulus components."

Brown is mainly concerned with the distinction between *drive* and *habit*. He states that habits are acquired or learned. Habits guide and direct behavior but drives lack a steering function. To avoid confusion he would abandon such phrases as "acquired drive" and "learnable drive."

The author is quite sympathetic with Brown's position but would state matters a little differently. On the one hand, it is sound to think of drive in terms of unlearned physiological conditions. There are chemical sensitizers that lower the thresholds of responses or that activate neural mechanisms. There are persistent stimuli from the pain receptors and from tissues-in-need that release energy and thus evoke behavior. There are built-in mechanisms that are excited by environmental conditions such as the taste of sweet. These and other conditions that might be mentioned are independent of learning. On the other hand, it is safe to assume that all persistent goal-oriented behavior is learned. All instrumental acts and goal-directed responses (CRs) are acquired through learning.

A question can be raised, however, as to whether organic drives do not have a property of direction and regulation. The chemical states present in hunger, thirst, pain, sexual excitement, fatigue, fear, and other conditions, differ among themselves. They predispose the organism to different kinds of behavior—and what is this but a kind of chemical regulation and direction?

The main difficulty appears to be one of definition and concept. If we hold to the energetic concept of drive, we can readily distinguish between drive and habit—but where do motives come into the picture? And shall we distinguish between habits and motives?

In everyday life a motive is a determination to act in some specific way, to carry out an intention, to arrive at a goal. We usually distinguish between *motive* and *habit*.

Motives are definitely acquired in the sense that they are products of experience and learning. They are, actually or potentially, energizing. They are regulating and directing. They have the properties that Brown ascribes to drives and also the properties of habits. They energize, steer, regulate.

In the writer's opinion the concepts of motive and habit are both necessary for clear and consistent thinking about problems of motivation. Neural organization may be latent, inert. There are countless neural structures that are quiescent—potential skills and memories that can be called into action when a need arises. Such neural organization, if not exercised occasionally, may be forgotten; it may disappear with the lapse of time.

In sharp contrast with latent neural organization is a latent motive or a specific determination to act. The latent motive is a readiness to carry out a specific course of action. It is capable of producing tension and overt action. It can select and utilize the bits of habit organization that are relevant to carrying out its aim.

When we speak of a *motive* we refer to an acquired determination to act. When we speak of a *habit* we emphasize the fact that a neurobehavioral pattern has been learned. Both concepts are required by the facts.

There is another difference between habits and motives that is fairly obvious. A motive can be satisfied by a goal response. After satisfaction it ceases to exist as a specific determinant of behavior. The neural organization that underlies an habitual act, contrastingly, continues to exist indefinitely. It does not make sense to talk about the satisfaction or consummation of habit structure by removal or accomplishment of its end.

Therefore, I believe we must retain both concepts—habit and motive. This does not mean that there are two kinds of neural mechanism. Rather there is only one neural mechanism but when we consider this mechanism from one point of view we refer to *habit* and from another point of view to *motive*.

Status of the Drive Concept

If we review the above discussions of the nature of drive, we find it difficult to define the drive concept precisely. The views, however, are inter-related and emphasize different aspects of a common process.

What is drive? Drive is a chemical sensitizing of a built-in bodily mechanism. Drive is the chemical activation of neuromuscular centers. Drive is a lowering of the threshold of response for a group of specific patterns. Drive is a persisting stimulus, especially one from the visceral organs. Drive is something assumed to exist: an intervening variable or a central motivating state of physiological nature. Drive is an arousal function with different degrees or gradations or an arousal function that is frequently characterized by positive or negative affectivity.

These views supplement each other emphasizing different aspects or phases of a central physiological state. If we disregard the behavioral (descriptive) views of drive, there remains a general agreement upon the following points: Drive is an *organic* motivation rather than something environmental. Drive is a *persisting* motivation rather than a brief stimulation. Drive is an *activating*, energizing process.

The functions of drive have been described as follows: Drive instigates, sustains, regulates, and organizes behavior.

Although the concept of drive is fairly broad, it cannot be equated with motivation. Other motivational concepts are: incentive, stimulus, set, and tension. Drive is usually regarded as an *innate* determinant and distinguished from acquired determinants designated as motives, habits, attitudes, and traits.

CONCLUSION

The concept of instinct was dropped from respectable psychology because it offered a pseudo explanation of behavior but it proved necessary to retain the term *instinct* (*instinctive behavior*) as a descriptive label for complex acts that are common to the species, innate, and elicited by environmental patterns of stimulation. It is recommended that the term *instinct* be retained as a descriptive label but not as an explanatory concept.

While instincts were being abandoned, by psychologists and social scientists, drives became popular. *Drive* is primarily an explanatory concept; the *drive* concept took over the explanatory functions of *instinct*. Some psychologists would now abandon the term *drive;* but there is need for explanatory concepts.

Instinctive behavior is elicited by environmental stimulus patterns. Some instinctive behavior, e.g., sexual behavior, has a persistent chemical motivation. *The instinctive patterns are driven and sustained by hormones as well as released by environmental conditions.*

Instinctive behavior is often contrasted with habit. *Habit* emphasizes the fact that a neurobehavioral pattern is learned; but a *motive*, which directs and regulates behavior persistently towards a terminus, is also learned.

Drives arouse, sustain, and, to some extent, regulate the pattern of behavior. They lead to organization of acts that are instrumental in reducing the drive state.

Physiological drives are organic states that lead to the development of goal-directed behavior and that regulate its occurrence. A drive is here conceived as a physiological determinant of behavior and not as a behavioral trend. The *driven behavior* is not to be confused with the drive which motivates it. Certain behavioral trends (to explore, to manipulate, to play, to fight, to flee, etc.) have been called *drives*, but these trends depend mainly upon environmental conditions and are more akin to instincts than to organic drives. A trend which depends entirely upon environmental conditions is certainly *not* an autogenous physiological drive.

Drive is a broad and general concept. When one takes up the analysis of specific physiological drives (thirst, hunger, sex, etc.) it becomes necessary to deal with bodily mechanisms in detail. This leads directly to the study of physiology and related biological sciences. The concept of *drive* is useful when a general explanation is required in terms of organic conditions.

Reading Suggestions

Beach (1951) has published a comprehensive review of the literature upon instinctive behavior, with many references. The work of Tinbergen (1951) and other ethologists is highly important. Tinbergen has published a brief statement of principles in McClelland (1955). The two reports by Kinsey et al. (1948, 1953) are mines of factual information concerning human sexual behavior. Although the approach is statistical rather than dynamic, any student of sexual motivation will find in these volumes a world of important material and extensive bibliographies. The chapter by Morgan (1959) is an excellent introduction to the physiology of drive.

Beach, F. A. *Instinctive behavior; reproductive activities.* Chap. 12 in: S. S. Stevens (Ed.), *Handbook of experimental psychology.* New York: Wiley, 1951.

Kinsey, A. C., Pomeroy, W. B. and Martin, C. E. *Sexual behavior in the human male.* Philadelphia: Saunders, 1948.

Kinsey, A. C., Pomeroy, W. B., Martin, C. E. and Gebhard, P. H. *Sexual behavior in the human female.* Philadelphia: Saunders, 1953.

McClelland, D. C. (Ed.) *Studies in motivation.* New York: Appleton-Century-Crofts, 1955. Pp. 113–124.

Morgan, C. T. Physiological theory of drive. In S. Koch (Ed.), *Psychology: a study of a science,* Vol. 1. New York: McGraw-Hill, 1959.

Tinbergen, N. *The study of instinct.* Oxford, England: Clarendon Press, 1951.

4 HOMEOSTASIS, NEED, AND BEHAVIOR

La fixité du milieu intérieur est la condition de la vie libre, indépendente: *le mécanisme qui la permet est celui qui assure dans le* milieu intérieur *le maintien de toutes les conditions nécessaires à la vie des éléments.**

CLAUDE BERNARD

Claude Bernard (1859, 1878), the great French physiologist, distinguished between the internal environment (*milieu intérieur*) consisting mainly of the fluids within which the cells of the body live, and the external environment (*milieu extérieur*) which surrounds the organism as a whole. In a series of brilliant lectures upon the fluids of the body, he pointed out that the internal environment varies within narrow limits and that variation outside of these limits endangers the existence of the cells and hence of life itself.

Cannon (1932), physiologist at the Harvard Medical School, crediting the concept of internal stability to Bernard, discovered further instances of physiological constancy. He coined the word *homeostasis* to designate an internal physicochemical state of relative stability and constancy. Cannon wrote:

* Stability of the internal environment is the necessary condition of free and independent life. The mechanism which permits this also guarantees the maintenance of conditions within the internal environment which are necessary for survival of the cells.

109

The constant conditions which are maintained in the body might be termed *equilibria*. That word, however, has come to have a fairly exact meaning as applied to relatively simple physico-chemical states, in closed systems, where known forces are balanced. The coordinated physiological processes which maintain most of the steady states in the organism are so complex and so peculiar to living beings—involving, as they may, the brain and nerves, the heart, lungs, kidneys and spleen, all working cooperatively—that I have suggested a special designation for these states, *homeostasis*. The word does not imply something set and immobile, a stagnation. It means a condition—a condition which may vary, but which is relatively constant.

The concept of homeostasis is definitely physiological. The principle is important, however, for an understanding of bodily needs, self-regulatory mechanisms, and those primary physiological drives that lead to the development of goal-directed behavior.

In this chapter we will consider two distinct models or concepts of motivation. The first—homeostasis—refers to a condition of physical and chemical stability within the organism. The second—the concept of need—refers to a lack or want. Although needs can be defined in terms of privations that disturb homeostasis, the *need* concept is much broader than this and more inclusive. Hence the concepts of homeostasis and need must be regarded as distinct ways of conceiving motivation; but the two are related as we will see when we examine some experiments upon the control of behavior by deprivation and satiation.

HOMEOSTASIS

It is a remarkable fact that organisms, composed of materials which are characterized as inconstant and unsteady, are able to maintain steady physicochemical states in the presence of changing environmental conditions. This is the more remarkable when we consider that the organism is an *open* physical system.

A *closed* physical system may be illustrated by a hot water heating plant. The same water circulates from the furnace to the radiators and back to the furnace. If there are no leaks in the system, the same water can circulate indefinitely; it does not have to be replaced. But the human organism is an *open* system. Water is lost through the urine, through evaporation at the skin, and through respiration. Unless the organism repeatedly obtains water from the environment, the tissues become dehydrated.

Examples of Homeostasis

Specific examples of homeostasis are the following:

1. The internal temperature of the body remains relatively constant despite wide variations in external temperature. A man can go to the arctic regions with temperatures 30°F, or more, below zero and survive there. Men have been exposed to dry heat at temperatures as high as 240°F without an appreciable increase of their body temperatures above the normal level. Despite such wide variations of external temperature, the internal temperature remains close to 98.6°F. So constant is this temperature that departure by a few degrees above or below the normal level is regarded by the physician as a symptom of disorder. The bodies of warm-blooded animals contain mechanisms for keeping the internal temperature within the limits required for survival of the cells and hence for survival of the total organism. The temperature of cold-blooded animals, however, varies with that of the environment.

2. Bernard was impressed by the relative constancy of blood sugar despite changing external and internal conditions. The concentration of glucose in the blood is regulated by storage of glycogen in the liver and intermittent release of the glycogen from the liver to the blood in the form of glucose. If the regulatory mechanism is overwhelmed by excessive sugar, the excess is wasted through excretion of the kidneys. If, because of some failure of the regulatory mechanisms, the concentration of blood sugar falls to a low level, convulsions and coma ensue. For normal existence it is necessary that the level of blood sugar vary within a narrow and fixed range of concentrations.

3. The acidity of the blood is held remarkably constant at a point near to neutrality. A slight shift towards acidity results in coma and death. A shift towards alkalinity produces convulsions. The maintaining of a relatively constant pH in the blood is one of the conditions of life.

4. The water content of the blood and lymph must be maintained at a relatively fixed level as one of the conditions of survival. Failure of the organism to obtain and ingest water results in dehydration of the tissues and increased concentration of mineral salts within the blood and lymph. Thirst is experienced when there is a water deficit; this organic state leads to the intake of water and to the removal of the water deficit.

5. The oxygen content of the blood is maintained at a relatively constant level through elaborate bodily mechanisms. Air-breathing organisms have evolved respiratory mechanisms that keep the blood oxygenated. Red blood corpuscles carry oxygen from the lungs to tissues throughout the body. In times of stress the concentration of red blood corpuscles is increased through mechanical action of the spleen; this facilitates the process of oxygenation. In drowning, the oxygen supply is cut off at its source; carbon dioxide accumulates in the blood with fatal result.

Similarly, there are homeostases of blood sodium, blood calcium, and other minerals, of blood fat, protein, and other dietary elements.

The internal conditions, as Cannon said, are not rigidly fixed, but they vary within limits according to the demands of the external environment. Thus if the existence of the total organism is threatened by an encounter with an enemy, there are prompt alterations within the internal fluid matrix that tend to assist the organism in a struggle for existence. For example, if a cat is threatened by a barking dog, there is a rise in the level of blood sugar, thus providing a source for increased energy during vigorous muscular exertion; the circulation of blood in muscles and brain is speeded up; the processes of digestion are temporarily checked; adrenin is poured into the blood stream by the adrenal glands thus stimulating the heart and producing other adaptive changes; oxygenation is accelerated through action of the spleen, etc. All such changes prepare the cat for a life-and-death struggle in the face of a crisis. Thus internal changes meet the demands of external conditions.

Homeostasis and Behavior

Richter (1942) extended the principle of homeostasis to show how behavior aids an organism in maintaining physicochemical steady states. If homeostasis is disturbed, behavior compensates for the disturbance and tends to restore the steady state. The principle is shown most clearly in experiments that involve the surgical removal of ductless glands.

If the pituitary gland is removed, rats suffer from inability to produce adequate amounts of heat; as a result they are threatened with a fatal reduction of body temperature. The operated animals compensate for the loss of heat by increased nest-building activity. They build larger nests than normal animals, utilizing more paper strip in an attempt to conserve their body heat.

Self-regulatory behavior appears, again, in the selection of food. If the adrenal glands of rats are surgically removed, the adrenalectomized animals normally die in from 10 to 15 days as a result of the loss of sodium chloride through the urine. In one experiment, Richter (1936) found that when the operated rats were given free access to a 3 percent sodium chloride solution they ingested several times the normal amount of salty fluid and kept themselves alive indefinitely in seemingly good health. With some rats the salt intake was increased tenfold by adrenalectomy! The increased appetite for salt thus served to maintain homeostasis and life itself.

In another experiment, Richter (1939) found that the preferential taste threshold for salt was lowered by adrenalectomy. For normal rats the preferential taste threshold averaged 0.055 percent or about 1 part of salt in 2,000 parts of water. For adrenalectomized rats the preferential taste threshold averaged 0.003 percent or 1 part of salt in 33,000 parts of water. They preferred salty solutions so weak that the NaCl they contained could not possibly have any beneficial effect.

In another experiment, Richter and Eckert (1939) removed the parathyroid glands of rats. This operation is ordinarily followed by loss of weight, tetany, and death. When the operated animals, however, were given free access to calcium solutions (lactate, acetate, gluconate, and nitrate) they greatly increased their intake of calcium. The loss of weight was checked; the tetany improved; and mortality was reduced to zero.

Other examples of self-regulatory behavior are found in the avoidance of poisons. If rats are offered a choice between distilled water and a solution of mercuric chloride, they reject the toxic substance and select the water. Even at concentrations that are too low to harm the animal there is a preference for water.

Through these and other examples Richter demonstrated that behavior serves to maintain homeostasis. He concluded that: "in human beings and animals the effort to maintain a constant internal environment or homeostasis constitutes one of the most universal and powerful of all behavior urges or drives."

It is obvious that the drives leading to food seeking, water seeking, and air seeking (when an organism is deprived of certain substances), and the drives to avoid extremes of heat and cold, are "homeostatic" in that they aid the organism in maintaining a constant internal en-

vironment. Also the eliminative urges—to urinate and to defecate—
are related to the necessity of maintaining constant internal conditions.
Such primary physiological motivations are essential to the life of the
cells and hence to the survival of the total organism and the species.

The physiological principle of homeostasis, therefore, provides a basis
for analyzing the most fundamental drives and needs of the organism.
The primary function of physiological drives is to maintain an internal
balance, or homeostasis.

The Energetics of Homeostatic Behavior

An organism has two main kinds of relation with its environment:
a metabolic and a behavioral relation. The metabolic processes go on
inside the body and include the digestion of food, the general distribution of nutritive substances by the circulatory system, assimilation,
elimination of waste products, and related functions. Important segments of behavior are directly concerned with these metabolic processes: the seeking of nutrients, the selection and ingestion of foodstuffs.
Other segments are not so obviously related to metabolism.

The physical energy that underlies behavior and makes behavior
possible is derived from the food input. The organism, as we noted
above, is an *open* energy system. It does not run down nor burn up;
but this is only because the organism constantly obtains food, water,
and oxygen, from its environment. The obtaining of these substances
is clearly essential to maintaining homeostasis and to life itself.

The energy that is obtained from the input of food is physical energy.
Physical science does not recognize psychic energies such as the *libido*
of Freud and the field forces of Lewin. The energy that makes the
human organism move is located inside the skin and bound to the
tissues. Methods for measuring and testing energy transformations
include: calorimetry, measurement of oxygen consumption through
determination of the basic metabolic rate, measurement of the loss or
gain of weight, palmar skin resistance (GSR), measures of blood pressure and of muscular tension, and chemical tests of blood and urine.

The behavioral relation between an organism and its environment
is regulated by the neuromuscular system. This system regulates the
release of energy but does not furnish the sources of energy. The interlocking relation between the two main energy systems of an organism
is represented schematically in Figure 18, which is borrowed from G. L.
Freeman (1948).

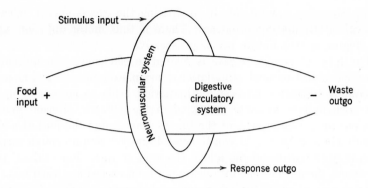

Figure 18. Interlocking of the two main energy systems of an organism. *After* G. L. Freeman (1948).

Freeman argues that underlying all kinds of behavior is a basic level of energy transformation which he calls the level of postural tension. Every stimulus which excites a receptor and elicits a response releases some energy and changes the basic level of postural tension. Any stimulation—from a light, a sound, a contact, or an odor, from bladder pressure, or from the bodily set of attention—forces the organism above a basal level of energy expenditure. The increments of tonic activity from sensory stimulation are superimposed upon the existing level of postural tension. Psychologists sometimes ignore this background level of energy expenditure and attempt to explain behavior in terms of stimulus and response alone; but to ignore the basal level of tonic activity and the physiology of energetics can only lead to an inadequate understanding of motivation.

When an activity-in-progress is blocked through some form of frustration there is mobilization of additional energy. The energy reinforcement serves to carry the blocked activity to completion—if possible—thereby attaining an equilibratory effect through behavior. This compensatory energy mobilization has been demonstrated in experiments upon work and fatigue, loss of sleep, distraction, and the like. In everyday experience we are aware of exerting extra effort when a path to the goal is blocked; this extra effort is motivating.

Over-stimulation, Freeman points out, is revealed in excitement which spreads to many organs unless there are organized motor outlets available and ready. Motor automatisms, tics, nervous mannerisms, and accessory reactions such as gum chewing, smoking, pacing the floor, may play a vital role in dissipating the excess energy released through a stimulating situation. There is thus motor diffusion when the degree of stimulation becomes excessive.

The level of energy release is related to efficiency. An individual can tolerate just so much stimulation, tension, excitement—and no more —without collapse. Excessive stimulation leads to emotional upset. For each individual there is a kind of "psychiatric plimsoll mark." The phrase is reminiscent of the line placed around the hull of a ship to indicate how heavily it can be loaded and yet retain enough surplus bouyancy to withstand the added stress of storms. For optimal performance, the level of energy release must not exceed a critical point.

Freeman's view of the energetics of behavior is definitely physiological and physical. There is a homeostasis within the cells of an organism. There is a homeostasis maintained by the coöperative action of organs and tissues. Also the behavior of the total organism, as Richter pointed out, is driven by the necessity of maintaining homeostasis. Freeman has extended the concept of homeostasis to include the neuromuscular system and its role in the regulation of energy expenditure. The neuromuscular system regulates energy release in the interests of maintaining homeostasis. Behavior is the outer aspect of the energetic process.

Freeman believes that stimulations from the internal environment dominate those from the outside. His view reminds one of Kempf's claim that the functions of the autonomic nervous system have priority and dominance over the functions regulated by the cerebrospinal system. Kempf argued that the cerebrospinal system is the servant of the autonomic, and that "segmental cravings" control the behavior of an organism in meeting its basic needs.

Biological Evolution of the Homeostatic Mechanisms

It is a remarkable fact that the body fluids (blood and lymph) of present-day vertebrates are similar despite gross differences of body form. The bloods of different animals are alike in ionic composition, in glucose concentration, and in acidity; and the temperature in all warm-blooded animals permits little internal variation. Indeed, the facts suggest that the conditions under which the cells of warm-blooded animals can exist are narrowly restricted. These conditions cannot have changed substantially since life on the earth began.

The concentrations of salts in blood sera today are similar to the ionic concentrations of salts in tropical oceans. For this reason it is commonly believed that life began in the Archean seas. In these ancient seas the original forms of life existed in habitats that were reasonably stable and that were favorable to survival.

Dempsey (1951) has discussed the gradual evolution of bodily mechanisms for regulating homeostasis: At the dawn of life homeostatic mechanisms were unnecessary because the environment provided for regulation of water content and electrolytes. Temperature fluctuations were within a range that permitted life to continue. To free themselves from their original marine habitat, the early organisms had to develop means for maintaining an internal fluid environment with ionic concentrations that would permit cellular life to exist. Once this feat had been accomplished the marine forms could invade fresh water.

Later when lungs for gaseous exchanges put in their appearance, organisms for the first time could creep out upon dry land. The conquest of terrestrial environments was limited, at first, to diurnal or seasonal forays until temperature regulating mechanisms were established. The external variations of temperature were so great that internal temperatures compatible with life could not be maintained. When the living forms at length developed heat-conserving mechanisms it became possible to withstand cold environments and hence to migrate into temperate and arctic regions. Similarly, the evolution of heat dissipating mechanisms permitted the conquest of tropical habitats.

The elaborate bodily mechanisms for maintaining homeostasis, that exist today, did not arise full-fledged. Doubtless a few simple devices were gradually evolved, and these were replaced by more complex and efficient mechanisms. The increasing effectiveness of these internal self-regulatory mechanisms is an essential condition of evolutionary advance.

The many forms of organisms on the earth today are the final products of millions of years or organic evolution along widely divergent paths. These varied forms are alike in that they have evolved means for maintaining similar internal environments.

The forms of organisms differ and the patterns of behavior differ but all necessarily maintain similar conditions within the body fluids. Arctic animals have protected themselves against extremes of cold by growing an extensive insulating pelt. Water-dwelling forms have achieved the same result with thick pads of fatty blubber. Birds have developed patterns of migration through which they escape the approaching cold of winter. Hibernating mammals have learned how to find protected places where they can lapse into a state of suspended animation and thus conserve their energies through the long winter season. The higher mammals, including man, have built protective devices. Man has developed clothing and techniques for heating his dwellings so that the rigors of climate do not destroy him. In all of these ways homeostasis is maintained.

In conclusion, homeostatic mechanisms have developed through a long course of biological evolution. The maintaining of homeostasis, in modern organisms, is a complex physiological process regulated by bodily mechanisms.

Thirst as an Example of Homeostatic Regulation*

Thirst is an organic state of dehydration that leads adult organisms to seek and ingest water. Water is lost, normally, via the kidneys in urine, via the lungs in respiration, and via the sweat glands through sensible and insensible sweating. To make up for this loss fluids are taken into the body by mouth. Water is absorbed by the small and large intestine and circulated through the body to the cells.

Some 70 percent of the body weight of a human adult is water. Of this quantity about 50 percent of the body weight is within the cells (intracellular fluid) and about 20 percent outside of the cells (extracellular fluid). Of the extracellular fluid, about three-fourths circulates in the blood and lymphatic vessels (intravascular fluid) and one-fourth resides in spaces between the cells (interstitial fluid).

The cells of the body, as pointed out above, live within a fluid matrix which must remain relatively constant if life is to continue. This fluid matrix, in its physical and chemical properties, resembles the marine environment where, we may suppose, life began. Man, in fact, is a marine animal! His skin is a kind of sac containing the extracellular fluids as well as the cells which compose the various organs and tissues of the body.

There is constant passage of water across cell membranes from

---

* This rather detailed and somewhat technical discussion of thirst in the next few pages can be omitted, if desired, without disturbing the main line of argument. This section illustrates the fact that any discussion of the bodily mechanisms for maintaining homeostasis inevitably leads into a labyrinth of specific physiological details. The main aim of this book is to survey the whole range of determinants of behavior and not to delve deeply into the details of physiology.

intracellular to extracellular fluids and vice versa. This passage is regulated by hydrostatic and osmotic pressure. An important factor which regulates the passage of water across cell membranes is the concentration of sodium which, in the blood of man, is about 0.90 percent. When a man is deprived of water the concentration of sodium in the extracellular fluid rises and water flows out of the cells. This results in dehydration within the cells.

When the extracellular fluids are depleted of water there is an increased concentration of sodium (and other minerals) within the blood. This hypertonicity of the extracellular fluids excites the posterior portion of the pituitary gland to secret a hormone (antidiuretic hormone or ADH) which checks the loss of water through the kidneys. The hormone leads to increased reabsorption of water in the kidney tubules and is thus self-regulatory in conserving body fluid. The production of ADH is inhibited by the drinking of water in sufficient quantity to return the concentration of sodium to its normal level.

The organic state of thirst has been described as a general dehydration within the cells which motivates drinking behavior; but the physiological mechanisms of homeostatic regulation are complex. To study the matter further and to see how internal conditions regulate behavior so as to maintain homeostasis we will examine some of the facts in more detail.

Factors that regulate the intake of water and salt solutions. The intake of water and salt (NaCl) solutions is controlled by three factors that are complexly interrelated, as Stellar, Hyman and Samet (1954) have demonstrated. First, there is regulation by taste and other sensory mechanisms located in the mouth. Second, there is regulation by gastric distention. Third, there is regulation by dehydration of the cells.

The taste mechanism alone can regulate the quantity of saline beverage ingested. This was demonstrated by placing a fistula in the rat, so that fluids taken by mouth pass out of the fistula, and do not reach the stomach. With such a device it was found that the greatest quantities of solution were ingested when the concentration of NaCl was the same as that in the blood (0.87 percent). The quantity was regulated by the taste mechanism.

When fluid was placed by fistula directly into the stomach, by-passing the taste receptors, it was found that the drinking of the rat was such as to maintain a relatively constant concentration of NaCl in the extracellular fluids. When the stomach was loaded with hypertonic salt solution the rats subsequently ingested more water than without the load and with a less hypertonic saline solution. When comparable loads of water were introduced this depressed the ingestion of water but elevated the drinking of hypertonic salt solutions. In other words, the drinking behavior of these rats was such as to maintain a relatively constant salt concentration in the extracellular fluids.

Further studies upon loading the stomach demonstrated two internal factors that regulate intake. First, the *volume* of fluid in the stomach acts mechanically to check ingestion when the volume of stomach contents reaches a critical point. Second, the *osmotic pressure* of the fluid contents of the stomach regulates ingestion. If the stomach of a rat is loaded with about ten cubic centimeters of water, there is cessation of drinking; but if the stomach is loaded with the same quantity of 3 percent NaCl, the intake of water is dramatically elevated. The NaCl concentration and the volume, therefore, are independent determinants of drinking behavior. The NaCl solution draws water from the cells, through osmosis, and this dehydration is an independent factor regulating the intake of water.

Gastric preloads as related to drinking. The internal factors that regulate drinking were studied further by O'Kelly and Falk (1958) with normal rats. They were interested especially in the volume of stomach contents and the NaCl concentration as related to drinking behavior.

The technique employed was that of loading the stomach by stomach tube just before a test of drinking. The content of the preload was varied either in volume or in NaCl concentration with volume held constant.

Water-seeking behavior was recorded automatically by a bar-pressing apparatus. The apparatus was constructed so that the nozzle of a drinking tube moved into the cage whenever the rat pressed a bar. After a 3-second exposure—during which time the animal was free to drink—the drinking tube was automatically withdrawn. Pressure upon the bar brought the water tube into the cage for another 3-second period. Thus, repeated bar pressing was necessary for the rat to continue drinking. The cumulative frequency of bar pressing was automatically recorded by the apparatus.

Before any preloading of the stomach, the rats were habituated to a daily schedule of 23½ hours of water deprivation followed by ½ hour for drinking in the apparatus. At the time of the experiment

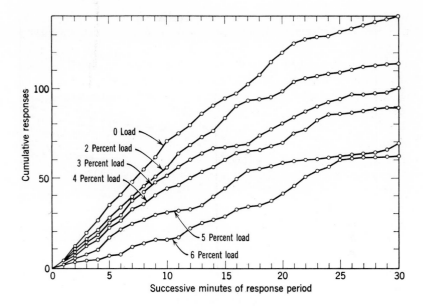

Figure 19. Mean cumulative bar-pressing responses as a function of the volume of gastric preload. *From* O'Kelly and Falk (1958).

the rats were accustomed to obtaining their drinking water by the instrumental act of bar pressing.

In one experiment the volume of water preloaded into the stomach was varied. The rats were weighed 15 minutes before the test and preloads were measured to equal 0, 2, 3, 4, 5, and 6 percent of the body weight of the subject. A gastric preload of water lessens the water deficit since water leaves the stomach and is promptly absorbed in the intestine. Larger preloads reduce the water deficit to a greater extent than smaller. Hence rats with larger preloads required less water to reach satiation than those with smaller preloads.

Figure 19 shows the mean cumulative frequency of bar-pressing responses when the gastric preload of water is equal to 0, 2, 3, 4, 5, or 6 percent of the subject's body weight.

In another experiment the volume of the preload was held constant and the NaCl concentration was varied. Results of this experiment are shown graphically in Figure 20.

When the NaCl concentration was 3.00 percent, the rate of bar pressing and amount of drinking was markedly increased above the

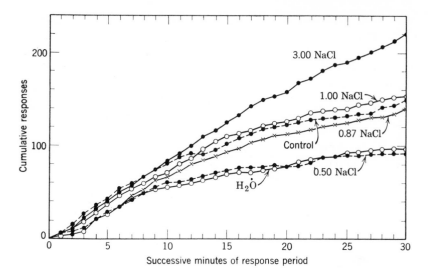

Figure 20. Mean cumulative bar-pressing responses as a function of the NaCl concentration of preload. *From* O'Kelly and Falk (1958).

control level (with no preload). When the concentration of the pre-loaded fluid was 0.87 percent (isotonic for the rat) or 1.00 percent (slightly above isotonicity) the behavior was about the same as that without any preload (control condition). Preloads of water and of 0.50 NaCl were equal in their effect. Both of them lowered the water deficit and consequently reduced the frequency of bar pressing.

The significance of these findings is clear. Bar pressing is an instrumental act that enables the animal to obtain water. The rate of bar pressing is dependent upon internal conditions. This rate is increased by conditions that produce dehydration of the cells and decreased by conditions that remove such dehydration. The regulation of fluid intake, therefore, is such that water homeostasis *within the cells* is maintained.

CRITIQUE OF THE CONCEPT OF ORGANIC NEED

We turn now to the second main concept considered in this chapter—the concept of need. As stated above, the organism has needs that are related to disturbances of homeostasis; but the concept of need includes more than homeostatic needs. There are social needs, personality needs, and other varieties.

The concept of need is firmly embedded within motivational psychology but it is, nevertheless, a source of confusion. Some of the difficulties with this concept are considered below.

One difficulty is that *need* has both dynamic and non-dynamic meanings. The dynamic meaning of *need* is synonymous with *drive* or *motive* and hence is superfluous. The non-dynamic meaning of *need*, however useful it may be, is not a motivational concept. Another difficulty is that the concept of *need* is evaluative. When we speak of a *need* we imply some standard of appraisal or judgment. Evaluations in terms of *need* are practically useful; but the science of psychology could get along nicely without evaluations in terms of *need*. Science deals with facts and not with values.

Despite these difficulties it is important to understand the nature of the concept of *need* and to see how it is related to motivational psychology. The following sections deal with the problem.

Dynamic and Non-dynamic Definitions of Need

The view that need is a *tension* or *force* is commonly met in contemporary psychology. Murray (1938) defined need as a construct which stands for a *force* in the brain region. His concept is definitely dynamic.

MacKinnon (1948), in an excellent textbook chapter on motivation, made *need* the central concept. He began by referring to need as a want or lack, but he gave a dynamic definition: *"A need is a tension within an organism which tends to organize the field of the organism with respect to certain incentives or goals and to incite activity directed toward their attainment."*

Again, Cameron and Magaret (1951) have defined *need* as *"a condition of unstable or disturbed equilibrium in an organism's behavior, appearing typically as increased or protracted activity and tension."* They go on to describe in detail the physiological indicators of protracted tension from which the investigator may infer disequilibrium and unsatisfied need.

Klein (1954) writes: "Needs push, but as with any force, there must be limits."

These definitions illustrate the view that *need* is a tension, force, or push. It is something dynamic. The dynamic definition clearly overlaps the meanings of *drive* and *motive*.

In order to think clearly about needs, one must recognize that the concept is also defined in a non-dynamic sense. When so defined, a need is not a tension or a force or a drive; a need may exist independently of motivation. A need is simply a want or a lack, looked at from some evaluative point of view.

For example, if a rat has a dietary deficiency of vitamin D, he develops rickets. The nutritionist knows that the animal *needs* vitamin D for normal bone growth. The rat is ignorant of the facts and does nothing to correct the disorder. The rachitic rat has no drive to go out and seek the needed vitamin.

Again, a small child fails to develop normal speech and motor habits; medical examination leads to the diagnosis of cretinism. The physician knows the child *needs* thyroxine and that the sooner the treatments begin the better from the point of view of normal development. The child does not know that he needs anything. He has no motive to change his condition.

Sometimes a child's motives are opposed to his needs. Suppose a small child is attempting to reach some dangerous object—a bottle of poison, his father's razor, a box of matches. The parents frustrate him by keeping the dangerous object out of reach. From a dynamic point of view it can be said that the child's needs are blocked; he is unable to get what he desires. The parents, thinking in terms of the child's welfare, are convinced that he does not *need* these dangerous objects.

In general, therefore, the concept of need has both dynamic and non-dynamic meanings. Some psychologists regard *need* as a motivational concept; others, including the present writer, do not.

Need Is an Evaluation Relative to Some Criterion

In everyday life the concept of *need* is evaluative. When we say that the child needs a spanking we mean that the spanking would be good for him. When we say that a man needs a new coat we mean that the garment would improve his appearance and comfort. Need implies a value judgment—either an absolute or relative judgment of value.

In some scientific work a relativistic concept of need may be useful. A *need* is relative to a criterion. For men to agree about the needs of organisms they must first agree upon the criterion. A need is a requirement *of* something *for* something.

Various criteria are possible for defining the physical needs of organisms. The principle of homeostasis provides an excellent criterion for an objective analysis of organic needs. To maintain homeostasis the organism *needs* (requires) oxygen, water, protein, carbohydrate, fat, certain minerals, vitamins, a certain range of temperatures, etc. If these needs fail to be met, homeostasis is impossible and the cells die.

Survival of the individual is another criterion closely associated with maintaining homeostasis but a somewhat broader criterion. To survive an organism must not only maintain homeostasis; he must successfully fight enemies and avoid physical dangers. He *needs* adequate means of defense and offense.

Reproduction of the species is still another possible criterion. For example, it can be said that chicks, mice, and other laboratory animals, *need* vitamin E since a deficiency of this vitamin impedes reproduction. Also from this point of view it can be said that sexual behavior is needed.

Another possible criterion for defining needs is normal growth and function. If normal growth and function are known, then there is a criterion for specifying organic needs.

Possibly health is a criterion. The state of health has many aspects but if one can state objectively what is meant by "being in sound health," one can then specify the needs of organisms to remain healthy.

In general, a *need* is an evaluation that is made by reference to some criterion. The needs of an organism are the requirements for maintaining homeostasis, surviving, reproducing, growing and functioning normally, or keeping healthy.

Visual Sensitivity as Measure of a Need

Since the non-dynamic concept of need is evaluative, and not factual, it is possible to dispense with the concept. To illustrate this possibility consider an experiment by Russell and Younger (1943) upon the relation between the differential threshold for visual intensity and a vitamin A deficiency in the diet.

It is well known that vitamin A plays an essential role in the photochemical processes of vision. Vitamin A is a precursor of visual purple (a photosensitive substance) as well as a product of its decomposition.

On the basis of available evidence, Russell and Younger predicted that avitaminosis-A would raise the differential threshold for visual intensity and that restoration of vitamin A to the diet would lead to recovery of normal visual discrimination. In laboratory tests it was found, as predicted, that the differential threshold for visual intensity increased to three or four times its original level when rats were maintained upon a diet deficient in vitamin A. When the rats were returned to a complete diet the threshold decreased to its normal level. Only 4 or 5 days were required for the threshold to return to normal.

In reporting this work the investigators did not mention the concept of need. They simply described the functional relation between two variables: (1) the duration of dietary depletion of vitamin A, and (2) the differential threshold for visual intensity. It would be easy, however, to introduce as a criterion of need: "the ability of the rat to discriminate visual brightnesses." With this criterion one can readily demonstrate a need for vitamin A by the depleted rats.

There is a large and growing literature that deals with the impact of diet upon behavior. Many examples can be found of relationships between behavior and specific dietary deficiencies. But all such relationships can be described in a matter of fact way without introducing the concept of need, as in the above example.

Need and Drive

Yamaguchi (1951) made a careful study of the relation between hunger drive and the number of hours of food deprivation. He trained rats to obtain food by pressing a Skinner bar and later extinguished this instrumental act by letting the animals press the bar without any food pellets for reward. Five groups of rats were trained and extinguished, each group at one of five deprivation intervals: 3, 12, 24, 48, or 72 hours. There were eighty-eight training trials in the Skinner box and then massed extinction trials. Each group was extinguished at its training level of hunger and the number of reactions required to extinguish the pattern was taken as an index of the strength of hunger drive.

From the data, Yamaguchi computed the absolute reaction potential, using one of Hull's equations. He then plotted absolute reaction potential against the number of hours of food deprivation with the result shown in Figure 21.

This curve rises with concave upward sweep between 3 and approximately 24 hours. Beyond 24 hours it rises with convex curvature. Although the maximal number of reactions to extinction was obtained with an interval of 48 hours, the curve shows a maximal reaction potential at approximately 60 hours of deprivation. After 60 hours

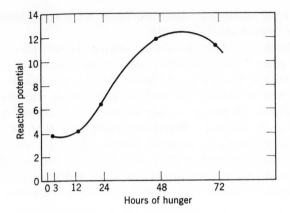

Figure 21. Relation between hours of food deprivation and reaction potential. *After* Yamaguchi (1951).

there is a drop in the curve. Yamaguchi estimated that the curve would reach absolute zero at a deprivation period of 101 hours.

Other investigators have found that the maximal strength of drive occurs at 36 hours or at 96 hours—depending upon the method of measuring the strength of drive. But all investigators agree on one point: When the interval of deprivation is longer than 60 hours, the animal becomes enfeebled as it approaches death by starvation. A starving animal not only loses weight but he expends very little energy in behavior. He is weak and inactive.

Yamaguchi distinguished two factors to account for the curve: a *drive* factor and a factor of *enfeeblement* that is closely related to inanition. When the period of deprivation is increased beyond 60 hours, the enfeeblement factor becomes increasingly important. The drive factor is related to the energy or vigor shown in behavior.

It is obvious that the *need* for food increases steadily with the duration of deprivation up to the point of death through starvation. The *need* for food is one thing; the *drive,* as shown by the vigor of behavior, is something else.

Need and Appetite

In some instances a metabolic need is associated with a craving, or appetite, for the substance needed. An example of this is found in the case of the small boy, described by Wilkins and Richter (1940), who had an intense appetite for salt.

When about a year old, he started licking the salt off crackers and asking for more. He would chew soda crackers until he got the salt off and then spit them out. Although he didn't speak at this time, he had a way of letting his parents know what was wanted. At eighteen months, he started to say a few words, and *salt* was among the first that he learned. Practically everything that he liked very well was salty: crackers, pretzels, potato chips, salt mackerel. His foods were all very much saltier than those of his parents and, in addition, he ate about a teaspoonful of table salt per day. He drank large amounts of water and showed a marked preference of water to milk.

At the age of three and a half this boy was admitted to the Harriett Lane Home for Children and placed upon the regular diet of the ward, which contained only a normal amount of salt. As a result of salt deprivation, 7 days after admission he suddenly died. Post mortem examination revealed deficient tissue in the cortex of the adrenal glands.

This finding is significant because it is known from laboratory experiments that, if the adrenal glands of rats are surgically removed, the animals die within 10 to 15 days when maintained on the ordinary stock of laboratory diets. Death occurs largely because of excessive loss of salt through the urine. But the survival time of these adrenalectomized rats can be increased by adding sodium chloride to the diet until it approximates the amount of salt lost in the urine. Further, it has been shown that, if adrenalectomized rats are given free access to a salt solution, they ingest large amounts of it. As a consequence, they keep themselves alive indefinitely and free from the symptoms of insufficiency. Apparently the boy with deficient adrenal glands had kept himself alive by ingesting great quantities of salt. The boy's appetite was an accurate index of his bodily need.

Such examples are interesting but it would be misleading to generalize them and to claim that appetite is an infallible guide to organic needs.

Food Acceptance and Organic Needs

Richter (1943) reviewed the evidence from agricultural stations and laboratories of nutrition to show that animals and human beings have the ability to select foods that meet their metabolic needs. They also avoid toxic substances. Moreover, rats are able to make beneficial selections from a group of purified food substances. Richter argued that the food selections of animals are in accord with Claude Bernard's principle of maintaining a constant internal environment. Food appetites, he believed, are dependable guides to nutrition.

The editors of *Nutrition Reviews* (1944), however, after considering available evidence, published a blast against the view that appetites are dependable guides to sound nutrition. In view of this blast no one today would have the temerity to claim that the food choices of animals are infallible guides to correct nutrition. Nor would any one be so rash as to claim that the food selections of animals have no relation to organic needs. The question to be answered is this: To what extent do animals accept foodstuffs which meet metabolic needs? This is a question of fact and the answer must be on the basis of observation and experiment.

This question is complicated by two factors, other than organic needs, that regulate food acceptance. First, there is the factor of affectivity. It is known, for example, that rats prefer water sweetened with saccharin to plain water. The saccharin has no nutritive value; it passes through the body unaltered and its main effect is to stimulate the taste receptors producing a sweet taste. An explanation of this preference in terms of organic need would be superfluous and misleading. Second, animals form stable dietary habits that regulate food acceptance independently of organic needs. These factors will be considered below.

Appetite, Need, and Habit

According to a traditional view, an appetite is a conscious craving that is based upon an organic need or tension. The term *appetite* is often applied to the desire for food or sex but there are also appetites to drink, to inhale air after holding the breath, to sleep, to relax, to be active, to urinate, to defecate, etc. There are various tensions that determine conscious cravings.

Appetites differ from aversions in three main respects.

1. Appetites go through a series of stages that constitute a cycle. The cycle tends to recur. Aversions, by contrast, occur sporadically and unpredictably with environmental circumstances.

In the first stage of the appetitive cycle there is restlessness and uneasiness coupled with a seeking for the objects or conditions that satisfy the appetite or reduce the tension. This stage is accompanied by discomfort and, in developed organisms, by purposive behavior. In the second stage the appetite is satisfied by consummatory activity. Typically, a state of agitation is followed by quiescence. With some appetites there may be a third stage of negativity. For example, one can overeat to such a degree that the sight of food produces nausea or revulsion. Oversatiation, if it occurs, is followed by a stage of indifference with relative freedom from the appetite. In a final stage the appetite gradually increases and the cycle is repeated. Thus there are appetitive stages of arousal, satisfaction, possibly overindulgence, and freedom from the appetite.

2. Appetites depend upon organic conditions but aversions typically depend upon environmental conditions like a bitter taste, a foul odor, a painful stimulation. These conditions produce reactions of avoidance or withdrawal which are typical of aversions. Under some conditions, as noted above, organic states may generate aversions.

3. Appetites are expressed by seeking and approach behavior; aversions by patterns of avoidance and escape. This does not mean that appetites are hedonically positive and aversions hedonically negative. On the contrary, appetitive states, such as intense hunger, may be felt as intensely unpleasant. The ingestion of food relieves the unpleasantness and the craving.

In general, appetites and aversions cannot be identified with states of need nor with habits.

The nutritionist can describe innumerable states of need produced by specific dietary deprivations. For some of these need states, such as depletion of thiamine or riboflavin or pyridoxine, rats develop appetites. For other states of need, however, the animals fail to develop appropriate appetites. For example, a mineral deficiency of magnesium leads to development of an aversion for the needed element. Again, animals develop appetitive behavior for substances, like saccharin, which meet no known metabolic need. Therefore, appetite and need must be distinguished.

Cannon distinguished between appetite and hunger. Hunger, he said, is a need state characterized by contractions of the empty stomach which are correlated with hunger pangs. Appetite is something different. We eat sweets and dainties from "appetite" at the close of a meal when hunger no longer exists. We develop "appetites" for specific kinds of foods. In this sense an "appetite" is a specific craving or desire that develops on the basis of an hedonic change in the positive direction (enjoyment or relief).

Hebb (1949) identified hunger with habits of food ingestion. He pointed out that lack of food tends to disrupt behavior producing restlessness, discomfort, irritability and, in extreme degrees, emotional apathy. The disruptive effect can be well observed in the behavior of young infants. The hungry infant becomes restless; he moves, cries and, in great hunger, kicks and screams. These patterns mark an acute emotional disturbance.

When the hungry infant finds the nipple he stops crying and starts to suck. Ingestion of milk produces quiescence. As satiation approaches, he stops sucking and goes to sleep. The basic physiological processes are all reflexive: moving restlessly, kicking, crying, screaming; sucking, swallowing, relaxing, sleeping, digesting.

These primitive responses, Hebb pointed out, are transformed through experience into the food-seeking habits of adults. The infant learns to recognize the milk bottle, to reach out for it, and, to bring it to his lips. Later, as a schoolboy, he learns to go to the drinking fountain and to turn it on when he is thirsty. As an adult he learns refined techniques to meet bodily needs such as ordering a meal from a menu card. Thus, at different levels of development and complexity, the individual learns how and where to satisfy his needs.

Hebb regards hunger as a *learned* tendency to eat. He asks: What controls the initiation and termination of eating? Hunger, as the adult knows it, is not a simple and direct product of need but rather the excitation of a neural mechanism that controls eating. Learning how and where to obtain food and water are similar to other forms of learning in that they involve a change of relationships between cortical phase sequences.

Hebb's description of hunger as a habit is clear-cut and definite but his account is too restricted. Dietary habits cannot be identified with nor confused with appetites. Habits play a tremendously important role in the regulation of ingestion but their role is different from that of appetites.

Again, Hebb does not adequately consider the role of affective processes in the regulation of ingestion. No matter how thoroughly an organism has *learned* an instrumental act that leads to food, there is still an affective element—distress, relief, enjoyment, satisfaction —in the feeding process.

Factors that regulate the selection and ingestion of foods can be categorized under four main headings:

1. *Stimulus and receptor conditions.* The term *palatability* refers mainly to an affective arousal determined by peripheral conditions.

2. *The organic state.* The terms *need, hunger, appetite, satiation,*

over-satiation, relief, etc., refer to internal or organic conditions that regulate food selection.

3. *History of the organism.* This category includes two main factors that are important in the organization of behavior: affective arousals and exercise (practice, drill, training). Together these two factors result in the formation of specific habits.

4. *Constitution.* This category recognizes individual and species differences in food preferences. Little is known positively about them except that they exist.

THE CONTROL OF BEHAVIOR BY DEPRIVATION AND SATIATION

If an organism is deprived of one of the substances required for maintaining homeostasis—oxygen, water, food, or some specific dietary element—a *need* for this substance develops. As we have seen, a homeostatic need may affect growth, reproduction, or the functioning of an organ, with little direct influence upon behavior. Some needs, however, have a profound effect upon the behavior of organisms. The depletion builds up a tissue condition which stimulates the nerves and produces negative affectivity. When needs influence behavior they do so through specific bodily mechanisms.

In the laboratory, homeostatic needs can be manipulated. Organisms can be deprived of water or food or some specific dietary element for controlled periods of time and the effect of this deprivation observed. Organisms can be satiated and the need thus reduced to zero.

How far do homeostatic needs influence behavior? Can a rat, for example, learn to take one path to food when hungry and another path to water when thirsty? How far is there internal control? The following sections bear on these questions.

The Experiments of Hull and Leeper

Experiments by Hull (1933) and Leeper (1935) demonstrated that the rat, in a constant environment, can learn to take one path to food when hungry and another path to water when thirsty, selecting the appropriate path on the basis of his organic state.

Hull employed an apparatus that contained a pathway resembling that of a T-maze. At the point of choice the rat could turn to the right and traverse a path to food, or he could turn left and traverse a path to water. Since the food and water were beyond the range of the animal's head receptors, the choice would have to be made (appropriately or inappropriately) on the basis of the organic state of need. Hull found that the rats could learn to turn to food when hungry and to turn to water when thirsty. In other words, they could learn to react differentially *in a constant physical environment* on the basis of their organic state just as a man can learn to go to the refrigerator for a snack when hungry and to the faucet for a drink when thirsty. But the rats were exceedingly slow to learn this discrimination. Even after 9 months of training, Hull's rats did not attain the limit of 100 percent correctness in their first choices. Although learning was slow, the result was certain: The rats did learn to make one turn when hungry and another when thirsty.

Hull explained the facts in terms of drive stimuli. Persisting drive stimuli either from the contracting empty stomach (hunger) or from the tissues of the mouth (thirst) were associated with all of the reactions that led to the goal response and the reduction of the drive. The animals learned two patterns of response, and the discrimination was based upon a difference in the drive stimuli.

Leeper's work also demonstrated that rats can discriminate between hunger and thirst. His mazes were somewhat different from that used by Hull but they involved the same principle, namely, that the point of choice was distant from the incentive objects (food or water) and the animals were required, in a constant environment, to discriminate on the basis of their organic state.

Leeper found that after a rat had acquired the habit of turning in one direction for food and in the opposite direction for water, the organic state could and did control the pattern of behavior which was evoked in the situation. He distinguished between the *acquisition* and the *utilization* of habit organization. After the two habits— turning in one direction to food and in another to water—had been acquired the organic state determined which of the habit organizations was utilized in behavior.

In an unpublished experiment (personal communication), Leeper demonstrated differential control of behavior by specific appetites. Corn meal was placed in one goal box and lettuce in the other; water was continuously present with both test foods. On certain days the rats were prefed to satiation upon corn meal and on alternate days they were prefed to satiation upon lettuce. After a few weeks of training the percentage of appropriate choices was about 75 percent on first runs. Thus the choice of a route through the maze was governed by specific appetites dependent upon short-term qualitative changes in the diet.

The net result of these studies is that the rat can learn to discriminate between organic states controlled through the techniques of deprivation and satiation. The learning, however, is slow and difficult. Once the animal has learned the discrimination, the organic state can and does control behavior.

The Externalization of Drive

In a series of papers, Anderson (1941a, 1941b, 1941c, 1941d) presented his theory of the externalization of drive. He argued that a primary drive like hunger is originally an organic state of need which controls behavior. As behavior develops, however, the control is increasingly taken over by environmental conditions. This increasing dominance of environmental controls of behavior he called the *externalization* of drive.

On the basis of the principle of externalization, Anderson made 29 predictions which he tested in a series of experiments with the rat and the maze. For example, he predicted that during the early stages of learning, when drive is more influential than external situation in control of behavior, a change in the environment would be less disturbing to performance than a change in drive. To be specific, removal of food from the goal box would be less disturbing during the early stages of learning (and more disturbing during the late stages of learning) than removal of the hunger drive through satiation. In other words, organic controls are more important during early stages of learning and environmental controls more important during later stages. On the whole, Anderson's experimental results confirmed his theoretical predictions.

Anderson's basic assumption is that a neural mechanism regulates persistent food-seeking activity. This neural mechanism is aroused to action both by physiological changes, produced by deprivation, and by environmental stimulus conditions. As the process of learning continues, the external situation becomes increasingly efficient in arousing the directive mechanism.

The theory of externalization squares with the facts of human experience. In the neonate, hunger is almost entirely an internal state. When deprived of food, the infant cries, moves restlessly, kicks, and screams; in this emotional display there is little or no purposive behavior. An adult, contrastingly, is governed more largely by external situations. He has become habituated to three meals a day and his feeding is controlled by the time of day and environmental circumstances. His behavior, to a high degree, is externalized.

The process of externalization, as Anderson described it, relates to increasing environmental control of behavior through instrumental acts that are learned such as the running of a maze by a rat.

Internal and External Controls of Ingestion

The topic of externalization of drive raises a question: To what extent is external control of ingestion present at the start of learning?

In one experiment (Young, 1945a) I naïvely assumed that the total deprivation of food or water would produce two drives—hunger or thirst—and that the relative dominance of these drives could be studied by offering the animals a choice between a dry solid food and water. Total deprivation periods (in hours) were enforced as follows: 5, 11, 16, 24, 48, 96, 120, and 144. After a given period of deprivation the rats were allowed to recover before another test was commenced. Twenty-two rats were given a test between dry solid food (Purina powder) and distilled water. The standard preference tester was used with the test foods close together and the positions alternated from trial to trial.

On the first tests, with the shorter periods of total deprivation, the rats selected the dry food in preference to water. The food was selected in more than 70 percent of the initial choices when a chance result would be 50 percent. As the period of total deprivation was steadily increased the percentage of food choices rose from about 70 to 97 percent. There was obviously an initial preference for the dry food. The preferential discrimination developed steadily with practice despite gradually increasing periods of total deprivation.

The experiment showed the great importance of external controls of ingestion. To the human observer, the Purina powder has a marked odor and distilled water has none. It seems very likely that the sensory properties of the test foods determined the preference rather than any supposed balance between hunger and thirst.

In another experiment the states of hunger and thirst were varied independently through the deprivation-satiation technique and a different method of testing preferences was used. The dry food and the water were in fixed and widely separated positions as in a Y-maze. Various degrees of hunger (with water satiation) and of thirst (with food satiation) were tested. Under these conditions the hungry rats developed a preference for food; the thirsty animals developed a preference for water. This experiment, therefore, confirmed the finding of Hull and Leeper that organic states can and do control behavior. But the total experiment also showed the great importance of sensory factors in the control of ingestion.

Further Experiments upon the Control of Behavior through Hunger and Thirst

In an instructive experiment, Kendler (1947) found that hunger and thirst did not effectively control behavior when the organic states were opposed by pre-existing habits. Kendler utilized a simple T-maze with water at the left and food at the right. To aid the rat in discrimination, visual cues were provided: one alley was painted black and the other was left unpainted.

During the training period, the rats in one group were thirsty, being deprived of water but satiated upon food. The animals in another group were hungry, being deprived of food but satiated upon water. All animals were given equal opportunity to experience the contents of both goal boxes. This was accomplished by alternate free-choice and forced-choice runs. During this training the thirsty rats sipped the water but ignored the food; the hungry animals nibbled the food but ignored the water.

After training, the need states were reversed. The once-thirsty rats were now satiated upon water but made hungry through food deprivation. The once-hungry animals were now satiated upon food but made thirsty through water deprivation.

Kendler found that, during the test series, the rats *inappropriately* followed the path they had learned during the training period. The once-hungry-but-now-thirsty rats *inappropriately* turned to the food. The once-thirsty-but-now-hungry animals *inappropriately* turned to the water. In other words, the established habit, rather than the metabolic need, dominated behavior. This underscores the importance of dietary habit in the regulation of the feeding process.

In another experiment Kendler (1946) gave the rats preliminary training under total deprivation; the animals were both hungry and thirsty. Food was in one goal box of the T-maze and water in the other. The animals were allowed to nibble the food and sip the water. Equal experience with food and water was controlled by alternate free-choice and forced-choice runs.

During a test series the animals were alternately made thirsty (with food satiation) and hungry (with water satiation). The problem, of course, was to discover whether the organic need state could control the animal's selection of an appropriate path on the maze.

The results showed convincingly that rats can and do select an appropriate path on the basis of their organic state of need. Hungry rats selected a path to food; thirsty animals selected a path to water. The results again confirm the finding of Hull and Leeper that rats are able to react differentially on the basis of the organic states of hunger and thirst. It should be noted, however, that organic states controlled behavior *after* the animals had already formed habits of eating food in one place (not merely looking at it) and drinking water in another place (not merely seeing it there).

A closely related experiment by Spence and Lippitt (1946) should be considered in the present context. These investigators trained thirsty rats in a Y-maze. One path led to water—an appropriate reward for thirsty animals. The other path, for half of the rats, led to food—an inappropriate reward. For the other half it led to an empty goal box—no reward at all.

During the test series all animals were made hungry and satiated upon water. The problem was to discover whether organic motivation could control behavior and whether "knowledge that food was in the goal box" would be utilized appropriately when thirst was changed to hunger.

Spence and Lippitt found that "knowledge" was not utilized. All the hungry animals *inappropriately* ran down the water alley to water. Further, as the rats learned to take the appropriate path to food there was no difference between the animals that had been trained with food in the goal box and those that had been trained with the goal box empty. The sight of (untouched) food in the goal box did not facilitate learning. Actual reinforcement by contact with the food-stuff appeared to be necessary.

Summary

An attempt to summarize the complicated findings of the above experiments must recognize that the principles involved are concerned with the relation between need, on the one hand, and habit (or motive), on the other.

The experiments agree that states of hunger and thirst can and do regulate behavior when the goal objects are out of range of the head receptors and the paths to food and water have been previously learned.

Leeper's distinction between *acquisition* and *utilization* of habit organization is right to the point. An organic state can utilize neural organization that already exists but if an animal has never learned the paths to food and water, hunger and thirst are impotent to instruct him and to guide him to the appropriate goal. It appears that animals respond on the basis of neural organization they already possess whether or not this organization is appropriate to their need state.

Actual contact with food or water is necessary for animals to learn paths of approach to the incentive substances. When a need-free rat merely looks at food he does not obtain information that is utilized subsequently when he is hungry. A prerequisite for the control of behavior by hunger and thirst is the prior development of food-seeking and water-seeking habits through actual contact with the incentive substances. In the experiments of Hull and Leeper such contact occurred during the gradual process of learning.

There is much evidence that environmental stimulus cues can regulate food ingestion independently of organic needs. Food preferences develop on the basis of taste regardless of needs.

Externalization is a process of learning through which environmental stimulus cues increasingly determine behavior. Anderson's account does not imply that need states cease to exist as determinants of behavior. Need states can and do develop from time to time in both experienced and naïve organisms.

The acquired neural organization that directs an animal towards his goal has been called *habit* and *motive*. The term *habit* emphasizes the fact that a bit of neural organization has been learned. The term *motive* emphasizes the fact that acquired neural organization orients an organism to a goal, regulates and directs his behavior as he approaches a goal, and is activated in some way by excitations from the environment and from a state of organic need. Finally, whether we use the term *habit* or *motive* we must admit that the acquired neural organization is not equivalent to the need state produced by deprivation and removed by satiation.

EVALUATION OF THE HOMEOSTATIC DOCTRINE

In the following sections we will consider both the importance and the limitations of the homeostatic doctrine.

Importance of the Homeostatic Doctrine

The principle of homeostasis is importantly related to three main psychological concepts: need, drive, instinct.

1. The principle of homeostasis, as we have seen, provides an objective basis for defining metabolic needs. In order to maintain homeostasis an organism *needs* (must find) certain nutritive substances in its environment: oxygen, water, protein, fat, carbohydrate, minerals and vitamins. Moreover, an organism *needs* to maintain itself within a limited range of external temperatures as an aid to keeping a stable internal temperature. Further, an organism *needs* to protect itself from attacks of enemies in order to survive. The requirements for survival are also requirements for maintaining homeostasis. *Needs* can thus be defined objectively in terms of the requirements for existence.

2. The principle of homeostasis is related to physiological drive. Homeostatic mechanisms generate drives that underlie the development of goal-seeking behavior. For example, the bodily mechanisms of thirst lead to the development of water-seeking behavior. In fact, the bodily mechanisms of thirst can be described as homeostatic mechanisms.

3. The principle of homeostasis is related to instinctive and reflexive behavior. The relation becomes clear when we consider the evolution of homeostatic mechanisms. Instinctive patterns, typically, have utility in the struggle for existence, in obtaining food, in reproduction, in protection against enemies. The evolution of instinctive mechanisms is the evolution of conditions essential to life itself, essential to the maintaining of homeostasis.

Extensions of the Homeostatic Doctrine

It is not surprising that a principle so basic as homeostasis should be extended beyond its physiological bounds. There have been attempts to extend the doctrine to the maintaining of stability within the social order, to the perceptual constancies within the psychological environment, to the maintaining of stability within our perceptions of the social world, to constancies in personality and in psychophysical judgments. All such attempts have departed widely from the physiological concepts of Bernard and Cannon. I prefer to preserve the original physicochemical meaning of the term *homeostasis*.

Other terms, like *adjustment* and *adaptation*, are more appropriate in considering complex social and behavioral processes.

Limitations of Homeostatic Theory

Some forms of behavior are motivated by hedonic processes that have no obvious relation to the reduction of homeostatic needs and drives. Experiments with saccharin (a sweet-tasting substance that meets no bodily need) may illustrate the point.

Carper (1953) compared the reinforcing values of glucose (an adequate food) and saccharin (which passes through the body unaltered and provides no calories). Both the glucose (7%) and the saccharin (0.13%) are hedonically positive.

In the study, general hunger was produced by habituating rats to a 12-hour deprivation schedule. One group (hungry) was tested before feeding and another group (satiated) was tested after feeding. In addition to the general hunger a specific hunger for calories was produced. Groups of rats were fed a diet deficient in calories so that a specific caloric hunger was superimposed upon the general hunger. The caloric deficiency was present in rats that were satiated upon the inadequate diet as well as in those that were deprived of it.

Carper used a bar-pressing technique to compare the performance of eight groups in a $2 \times 2 \times 2$ factorial design. The groups can be described in terms of: (1) presence or absence of general hunger, (2) presence or absence of a specific caloric deficiency in the total diet, (3) reinforcement with glucose or with saccharin.

The experiment showed, among other things, that saccharin reinforced bar-pressing responses with both satiated and hungry animals. In other words, something about the saccharin reinforced bar-pressing apart from meeting bodily needs and maintaining homeostasis.

Carper's study confirms an earlier finding of Sheffield and Roby (1950) that saccharin has reward value even though the sweet-tasting substance is non-nutritive.

Carper also found that there was no difference in resistance to extinction when reinforcements were by glucose and by saccharin. In agreement with Sheffield and Roby it can be said that no homeostatic need factor is involved in either extinction or reinforcement since saccharin meets no need.

The facts can be readily interpreted from the point of view of experimental hedonism; but this point of view implies that the homeostatic doctrine is inadequate as a complete theory of motivation. Something more than the maintaining of homeostasis must be considered in a fully adequate account of the determinants of behavior.

Non-homeostatic Motivations

In addition to the hedonic determinants of behavior there are other non-homeostatic motivations that should be considered in the present context.

In Chapter 2, I discussed certain behavioral trends including play, manipulation, exploration, curiosity, and the general activity drive. Some psychologists refer to these trends as "drives" but this is little more than the postulate of some underlying and poorly defined motivation. The fact of the matter is that these behavioral trends are determined mainly by environmental conditions. They do not originate in any known tissue conditions nor in disturbances of homeostasis. The motivation of play, manipulation, exploration, curiosity, and related forms of behavior, is non-homeostatic.

When we turn to human motivation we find innumerable examples of non-homeostatic determinants. Relative to this matter Harlow (1953) has written:

> If we are to understand human motivation, it is of paramount importance that we keep in mind the characteristics of human motivation and, particularly, the relationships between human motives and learning, for we are giving special emphasis to this aspect of motivational theory. (1) Man's motivation may be independent of, or far detached from, the homeostatic drives. Many people live and learn even though they have no memory of true hunger or thirst. They learn in spite of, not because of, sex, temperature, elimination, respiration, anxiety, and pain drives. (2) Man's motivation is extremely strong and persisting. Man may continue to learn or to carry out previously learned performances over long periods of time. The existence or demands of physiological drives may be unnoticed or ignored during the course of these motivated performances. (3) Man attempts with a haunted zeal to solve problems whose solution has no apparent utility and may even produce personal pain or harm. The problem, even though difficult or impossible of solution, appears to provide its own motivation. (4) Most, if not all, of man's complex learning is motivated by nonemotional or mildly pleasurable stimuli and is disrupted or inhibited by intense affective states.

In view of the above considerations we are justified in concluding that the homeostatic doctrine does not provide a complete and fully adequate basis for the analysis of motivation. Despite its strong points, one must recognize determinants of human and animal behavior other than the maintaining of homeostasis.

Adjustment and Homeostasis

The topic of adjustment will be considered in another chapter but it should be pointed out here that adjustment and homeostasis are different concepts.

Discussions of adjustment frequently refer to motivational changes in a given direction. For example:

Drive → drive reduction
Motive → motive satisfaction
Goal-set → goal reaction
Anxiety → anxiety reduction
Unclosed pattern → closure
Problem → solution
Frustration → relief
Dissonance → consonance
Distress → relief
Tension → tension reduction
Disequilibrium → equilibrium

All such processes imply changes from imbalance to balance, from inadequate adjustment to adjustment. A disturbance of homeostasis, in the physiological sense, may or may not underlie these changes. In any event, the physiological processes of homeostasis must be distinguished from the psychological processes of adjustment.

Adjustment will be considered again in Chapter 12. Adjustment implies a change in the relation of an organism to its environment. Homeostasis is a steady physicochemical state within an organism.

CONCLUSION

Homeostasis is a physicochemical steady state of the organism. This steady state defines the conditions necessary for survival of the cells and hence for survival of the total organism.

When there is a disturbance of homeostasis a need arises to restore the steady state. It is possible objectively to define the needs of an organism by reference to homeostasis as well as by other criteria such as growth, reproduction and health.

Needs are not motives. If *need* is regarded as a dynamic concept, *need* is equivalent to *drive* or *motive*. There is a non-dynamic concept of need that is useful in studies of nutrition, growth, reproduction, health, etc., as well as in researches upon motivation. The student of motivation should be warned that the concept of *need* is commonly used in a dynamic as well as a non-dynamic sense.

A question arises as to how disturbances of homeostasis affect behavior. Experiments upon the control of behavior through deprivation and satiation have shown that organisms can and do learn to regulate their behavior to meet homeostatic needs. In other words, animals can learn to take a path that leads to food when hungry and a path that leads to water when thirsty. Organic states, to a certain extent, are determinants of selective behavior. But environmental stimulations also instigate and regulate behavior and these must be considered in their own right.

The homeostatic doctrine, though of basic importance in the study of growth and metabolism, is limited as a general explanation of all behavior. Other principles of explanation are required.

Reading Suggestions

The following works are pertinent to the doctrine of homeostasis and its relation to behavior. *The wisdom of the body*, by Cannon (1932), is the basic work. Dempsey (1951) has examined the evolutionary and biological aspects of homeostasis. Richter (1942) has related the doctrine to behavior. Bindra (1959), in Chapter 2 entitled "The role of blood chemistry," has presented materials and references on the chemical determinants of behavior.

The system of needs devised by Murray (1938) is discussed in Chapter 11 of this book.

Bindra, D. *Motivation, a systematic reinterpretation.* New York: Ronald, 1959.

Cannon, W. B. *The wisdom of the body.* New York: Norton, 1932.

Dempsey, E. W. Homeostasis. Chap. 6 in S. S. Stevens (Ed.), *Handbook of experimental psychology.* New York: Wiley, 1951.

Murray, H. A. *Explorations in personality, a clinical and experimental study of fifty men of college age.* New York: Oxford University Press, 1938.

Richter, C. P. Total self regulatory functions in animals and human beings. *Harvey Lectures Series,* 1942, **38**, 63–103.

5 AFFECTIVE AROUSAL AND ACTIVATION

Of several responses made to the same situation, those which are accompanied or closely followed by satisfaction to the animal will, other things being equal, be more firmly connected with the situation, so that, when it recurs, they will be more likely to recur; those which are accompanied or closely followed by discomfort to the animal will, other things being equal, have their connections with that situation weakened, so that, when it recurs, they will be less likely to occur.

E. L. THORNDIKE

When Thorndike (1898) first described his well known experiments upon cats, dogs, and chicks, there was no clear formulation of the much discussed law of effect. There were, however, repeated statements that pleasure "stamps in" an association between situation and response, and that non-successful impulses are "stamped out."

Thorndike's experiments were carried out at a time when the anecdotal method was widely used in animal psychology and scientific methods for the objective study of behavior had not been established. There was much anthropomorphism and little real objectivity. Animal psychology was a study of the animal mind—of what the animal sees and feels. Today the early writings of Thorndike seem naïve and near to the level of common sense.

Thorndike recognized, however, that his hedonistic view implied a

144

mind-body interactionism. He wrote: "I have spoken all along of the connection between the situation and a certain impulse and act being stamped in when pleasure results from the act and stamped out when it doesn't. In this fact, which is undeniable, lies a problem which Lloyd Morgan has frequently emphasized. *How are pleasurable results able to burn in and render predominant the association which led to them?* This is perhaps the greatest problem of both human and animal psychology."

Later, Thorndike (1911) republished his earlier papers and formulated his two basic laws of learning: the law of effect and the law of exercise. The law of effect, which is quoted in its original form at the head of this chapter, affirms that satisfaction strengthens an associative bond between situation and response, and discomfort weakens a bond. The law of exercise makes no reference to the affective aspect of response but refers only to the number of connections between situation and response. The law of exercise will be disregarded here but not the law of effect. Most psychologists recognize the validity of some form of the law of effect.

In this chapter we will first take a brief look at the historical background of hedonism in American psychology. After that we will consider the logical construct of affective processes and show that on a strictly objective basis it is necessary to distinguish between sensory and affective processes. Then we will describe studies of palatability, appetite, and food preference—all of which point to the necessity of an objective postulate of affectivity. After this we will consider the affective processes as related to motivation, learning, and performance, touching upon problems of value, intrinsic and extrinsic motivation, and habit. Then some of the psychophysiological investigations of activation and affective arousal will be examined. And, in a final section, objective principles and postulates of an experimental hedonism will be stated.

HISTORICAL BACKGROUND OF HEDONISM IN AMERICAN PSYCHOLOGY

The Empirical Law of Effect

In his review of research upon the fixation and elimination of responses, McGeoch (1942) adopted a phrase, suggested by Carr: *the empirical law of effect.*

The law has been stated in different ways but *effect* always refers to something that happens as a consequence of an act—usually something that happens within a very few seconds after the act. In its simplest form, the statement is that *acts are fixated or eliminated as functions of their effects*. If an act produces one kind of effect, it is fixated; if another, it is eliminated.

Thorndike stated the kinds of consequences that fixate a response and the kinds that do not: *Acts followed by a state of affairs which the individual does not avoid, and which he often tries to preserve or attain, are selected and fixated, while acts followed by states of affairs which the individual avoids or attempts to change are eliminated.*

Another formulation, on a slightly more inferential level, takes account of the concept of motivation. McGeoch's formulation was as follows: *Other things being equal, acts leading to consequences which satisfy a motivating condition are selected and strengthened, while those leading to consequences which do not satisfy a motivating condition are eliminated.*

When the empirical law of effect is stated as a broad generalization of the facts it is not open to argument. It simply summarizes what is observed. Everyone is bound to accept it. For example, if a child is offered a plate containing pebbles and pieces of candy of similar size, he will learn to put the candy in his mouth more frequently than the pebbles. If we ask *why* the preference for candy develops, differences of opinion can arise; but there is no room for argument over the empirical generalization.

McGeoch pointed out, in considering objections to the law of effect, that criticisms usually turn out to mean that some particular theoretical explanation of how effect acts to promote fixation is regarded as unacceptable. The objection is not to the empirical law, but to a hypothesis about the law. Thus the hypothesis that subjective feelings of pleasantness and unpleasantness influence brain processes to produce lasting effects may be rejected; but the empirical law still stands. The empirical law simply states that acts are fixated and eliminated as a function of, or in correlation with, their consequences, regardless of the psychological classification of these consequences and regardless of one's theory of the mind-body relation.

In current psychology the *effect* is commonly thought of in terms of success and failure relative to the achievement of a goal. As Thorndike's later work showed: The words *right* or *wrong*, spoken by the experimenter, or the "OK" reaction of the subject, are effects that influence performance and learning.

There are differences of interpretation but no real argument over the empirical law of effect and, as Meehl (1950) has pointed out, there is no real circularity in the law of effect when properly stated and understood.

Beneception and Nociception

Postman (1947) pointed out that Thorndike's formulation of the law of effect reflected the impact on psychology of three major trends in the history of thought: associationism, hedonism, and the theory of evolution. The last two of these trends concern us here.

The doctrine of hedonism is almost as old as human thought. Philosophical hedonism was well developed before Thorndike formulated his law of effect. To a hedonist of the Bentham type, "pleasure and pain" are the governing principles of behavior. The search for "pleasure" and the avoidance of "pain" are the mainsprings of conduct, individual and social, and are the bases of social interaction and organization.

The theory of evolution, since the time of Darwin, has been concerned with the adaptiveness of behavior. Some responses to environmental situations are superior and lead to "survival of the fittest." Other responses are inferior and organisms making them risk biological extinction. The biologist has been concerned with the problem of how superior responses evolve. To thinkers like Spencer and Bain the "pleasure-pain" principle provided a means for the selection, fixation, and perpetuation of adaptive behavior. The Spencerian principle is clearly recognized by Troland in his formulation of the concepts of beneception and nociception.

Basing his theory on the biological doctrine of weal and woe, Troland (1928) coined the following terms:

Beneception—A process in a sense-organ or afferent nerve channel which is indicative of conditions or events that are typically beneficial to the individual or species.

Nociception—A process in a sense-organ or afferent nerve channel which is indicative of conditions or events which are typically injurious to the individual or species.

Neutroception—Any kind of sensory process which is neither beneceptive nor nociceptive.

As examples of beneception Troland lists: erotic excitation which leads to reproduction; gustatory stimulations from sugars which lead to the detection of carbohydrates that are sources of energy; afferent stimulations from fruits and vegetables that have food value and that yield ethereal, aromatic, and balsamic odors; the tactual excitation that produces feelings of warmth, indicative of the proximity of heat energy needed in cold environments to restore the temperature equilibrium of the body.

As examples of nociception Troland lists: pain excitation from damage to the tissues; organic stimulations from such bodily conditions as hunger, excessive heat and cold, deprivation of air or water, and the need to urinate, defecate, etc. These stimulations indicate bodily conditions that are detrimental to the integrity of the organism or the species. A bitter taste frequently bespeaks the presence of toxic, alkaloidal materials that are dangerous to life. The alliaceous, caprillic, nauseating, and other repugnant odors identify substances that are unwholesome or injurious if used as foods.

Finally, examples of neutroception can be found in the many excitations from our surroundings—lights, noises, odors, etc.—that are neither harmful nor beneficial in a direct biological sense.

Troland gives no physiological criterion for distinguishing between beneception and nociception. The distinction is based upon extrinsic considerations of biological utility. Nevertheless he regards beneceptors and nociceptors as anatomical structures that lead to excitations in the brain. The action of nociceptors upon the nervous system is to inhibit cortical processes, whereas beneceptors have a facilitative effect. Troland's basic proposition is stated in these words: *"Nociception is accompanied by a decreasing of the conductances of operating cortical adjustors; whereas beneception is accompanied by an increasing of the conductance of operating cortical adjustors."*

The process of changing cortical conductances is designated *retroflex* action. This concept implies a facilitative or inhibitory feed-back into the cortex, as indicated by the following quotation from Troland:

The cortex, by its principle of trial and error or random activity, initiates a certain line of response. This, in turn, produces certain actual or incipient organic changes which are reported back to the cortex via the beneceptive or nociceptive channels, and the excitations of these channels modify the cortical tendency. If the "report" is beneceptive or favorable, the tendency in question in enhanced, whereas if it is nociceptive or unfavorable, the tendency is reduced. These actions can be regarded as being determined quite mechanistically, without reference to any accompanying pleasantness or unpleasantness, or any "intelligence" on the part of the cortical process. Facilitative retroflex action, based upon beneception, may be characterized as *positive* because it increases the given cortical conductance; while the nociceptive consequences may be characterized as *negative*.

Troland writes that the important point about retroflex action, so far as learning is concerned, lies not in the immediate effect of the nociceptive excitation upon cortically controlled behavior but in the fact that a permanent alteration has been made in the tendencies of cortical adjustment.

In general, Troland proposed a hedonistic theory of human motivation. He recognized the distinction between positive and negative affectivity and the concept of general facilitation and inhibition. He operated with a physiological model, even though an inadequate one. If he were writing today, he would doubtless locate the beneceptive and nociceptive processes in the subcortical regions of the brain rather than in the afferent nerve channels.

It may well be, as Troland and others have argued, that the long course of biological evolution explains why it is that sweet-tasting substances are acceptable and bitter substances rejected. The details of behavioral evolution, however, are out of sight—lost far beyond our present horizon. What we have today is the concept of built-in adaptive mechanisms however they may have developed. These mechanisms can be studied *as such* regardless of their origin.

Pleasantness and Unpleasantness

Another influence upon the development of hedonism was the traditional psychology of affective processes.

Towards the close of the nineteenth century Wundt proposed his tridimensional theory of feeling. Human feelings, he said, change within a space that can be defined by three mutually perpendicular dimensions intersecting at indifference. The first dimension extends between the extremes of pleasantness and unpleasantness; the second between the extremes of excitement and quiescence; the third between the extremes of strain and relaxation. At any given time, Wundt declared, a feeling can be located somewhere within this tridimensional system and changes of feeling can be described by reference to the three dimensions.

Titchener (1921), on the basis of introspective experiments, criticized Wundt's tridimensional theory. He reduced the system of feeling to a single affective dimension extending between the extremes of pleasantness and unpleasantness. Subsequently, under the influence of a doctoral dissertation by Nafe (1924), Titchener went over to a complete sensationism. He identified pleasantness with a bright, diffuse, pressure-like, experience that is thoracically localized, and unpleasantness with a dull, less diffuse, pressure-like experience, abdominally localized. The affective experiences are palpable, in some sense observable.

In the meantime Watson (1914) launched his polemic against introspectionism and mentalism. He denied that pleasant and unpleasant feelings are fit subjects for investigation. Psychology is an objective science of behavior having nothing to do with states of consciousness, as such.

Watson took a stand against hedonism: "It is our aim to combat the idea that pleasure or pain has anything to do with habit formation or that harmfulness or harmlessness has anything more to do with the situation. It is perfectly natural in unreflective minds that the idea of good or bad or harmful or harmless should be called in to explain the habits we force upon animals and children. It is a bit strange that scientifically minded men should have employed it in an explanatory way. . . ."

Watson's views about subjectivism and introspection have been influential. A number of contemporary theorists hold to the objective and physical view of behavior as the only scientifically sound view for psychology. It would not be profitable, however, to delve into the controversy over the merits of behaviorism. Instead, I will state simply my own bias:

I believe that the facts of conscious experience can be reliably reported and that a *complete* psychology must take account of them. As a single example, consider a study by Kniep, Morgan, and Young (1931). The study dealt with affective reactions to odors. Fourteen organic substances were presented for affective ratings to three groups of subjects: (1) fifty children, ages 7 to 9; (2) fifty children, ages 11 to 13; (3) one hundred college students. The odors were presented one at a time under standard conditions and each subject was asked to report whether he liked or disliked the odor. The frequency of the report 'I like it' ranged from about 10 to 90 percent. When the odors were arranged in sequence from the least to the most frequently liked, the rank order correlations among the age groups ranged from 0.91 to 0.98. In other words, there were marked uniformities among the different age groups in affective reactions to odors. Since most of the odors were unfamiliar to the subjects, this uniformity must be explained in terms of underlying bodily conditions.

I believe that the affective reports were based upon a primary hedonic experience. The facts of experience imply the point of view of the experiencing individual. If a subject reports "I see a black cat," he is describing his phenomenal experience. Let us not confuse the muscle twitch of the speech mechanisms with the object of experience that is clearly seen and described. Similarly, when a subject reports pleasantness and unpleasantness he is reporting one aspect of his conscious experience.

The concept of affective processes had its origin within a psychology that dealt primarily with the facts of conscious experience. A *complete* psychology must take account of the facts of experience and give a fully adequate analysis of them.

Beebe-Center (1932) regards pleasantness and unpleasantness as concepts characterizing experience. They are quantitative variables so related to each other that they may be represented respectively by the positive and negative values of a single algebraic variable. This variable he called *hedonic tone*. Beebe-Center described an hedonic continuum which is identical with the one described below on the basis of strictly objective data. The hedonic continuum, therefore, is an example of a theoretical construct that can be formulated on the basis of the reports of felt experience or on the basis of objective data obtained from laboratory animals.

In the following sections, however, my aim will be to show that the construct of affective processes can be based solely upon objective data. Studies of food preferences force us to postulate the objective existence of affective arousals. Experiments upon the physiology of "reward" and "punishment" are in line with the objective approach to the study of affectivity.

THE CONSTRUCT OF AFFECTIVE PROCESSES

Let us begin by postulating that affective processes have objective existences within the organism and that their nature and functions can be discovered.

Definition of the Affective Processes by Their Attributes

The affective processes can be defined objectively in terms of three attributes: sign, intensity, and duration.

1. *Sign.* In laboratory situations, one observes that naïve animals develop approach-maintaining or avoidance-terminating patterns of behavior. If they develop the approach-maintaining pattern, I would assume that the underlying affective process is positive in sign. If they

develop the avoidance-terminating pattern, I would assume that the affective process is negative in sign. If neither positive nor negative behavior develops, I would make no assumption concerning the sign of affective arousal.

It is important to note that the bare existence of adient or abient behavior is not a sufficient ground for inferring affective processes. Approach-maintaining and avoidance-terminating behavior may be habitual, automatic and affectively indifferent; but the *development* of approach-maintaining or avoidance-terminating patterns *by naïve animals* is the criterion for the sign of affective processes.

2. *Intensity.* In addition to sign, affective processes differ in intensity, or degree. Affective processes vary along a bipolar continuum between the extremes of maximal negative and maximal positive intensity.

One way to demonstrate the relative intensity of affective processes is to give animals a brief-exposure preference test with foods. A brief-exposure test is recommended because with prolonged exposures the level of acceptability of test foods declines as the terminal state of satiation is approached.

In the brief-exposure test the animal is offered a series of choices between two test foods (A and B). The series of choices reveals whether a preference develops for one food (A) or the other (B). There is no way to force an animal to show a preference. Either a preference develops, with repeated choices, or it does not develop. Weak preferences, strong preferences, alternating preferences, and no preferences at all, have been observed. In some tests the preference is obvious but, in others, statistical methods are needed to determine whether or not a particular body of data indicates a significant preference or a mutation of preference.

If both test foods are accepted, I would assume that the preferred food arouses a higher intensity of positive affectivity than the non-preferred. This is what is meant, objectively, by the statement that the preferred food is the more palatable. Again, it must be emphasized that the *development* of a preference *in naïve animals* indicates relative hedonic intensity and not the bare existence of a preference, since a preferential discrimination can be purely habitual and automatic.

3. *Duration.* In addition to sign and intensity, affective processes differ in duration and temporal course. Insofar as affective processes are induced by taste solutions, the duration of stimulation can be used to control the duration of affective arousal. The number of seconds that an animal is in contact with a food can be controlled or the num-

ber of individual licks of a fluid can be counted by an electronic device. The frequency and schedule of affective processes can thus be controlled.

With painful stimulations, it is also possible to control precisely the intensity, frequency, and schedule of presentations. In addition to direct stimulation, negative affectivity can be produced by frustration and conflict; but these conditions can be controlled less precisely than the conditions of sensory stimulation.

The Hedonic Continuum

The sign, intensity, and temporal changes of affective processes can be represented upon the hedonic continuum. Figure 22 shows this continuum extending from the extreme of negative affectivity (distress) to the extreme of positive affectivity (delight). Different intensities of affective arousal are represented by arbitrary units marked off upon the continuum. Midway between negative and positive affectivity is the range of indifferent, neutral processes and others that are weakly affective.

The arrows represent two opposed directions of hedonic change. The upper arrow, pointing away from the negative end and towards the positive end of the continuum, represents a kind of hedonic change that is of great importance in the organization of behavior. According to the hedonic hypothesis, neurobehavioral patterns are organized that minimize negative affectivity (distress) and maximize positive affectivity (delight). That is to say, organization is dependent upon hedonic change in the positive direction. Changes in the negative direction necessarily and frequently occur, and the lower arrow represents such changes. The total figure implies a principle of affective opposition or antagonism: There can be a change towards either pole but not a change in opposite directions at the same moment of time.

Although there are two opposed directions of change, there are, logically and psychologically, four main kinds of affective change that

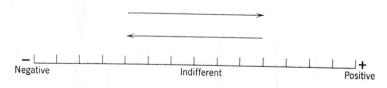

Figure 22. The hedonic continuum.

need to be considered: (1) increasing positive affectivity, (2) decreasing positive affectivity, (3) increasing negative affectivity, (4) decreasing negative affectivity. The first kind of hedonic change (increasing positive affectivity) is present when an animal tastes a sugar solution and organizes an approach-maintaining pattern of behavior. The fourth kind of change (decreasing negative affectivity) is present when an animal succeeds in relieving the "distress" associated with an electric shock or reducing a need produced by dietary depletion. "Distress reduction" is the hedonic equivalent of "drive reduction" in the organization of instrumental behavior.

Changes in the negative direction occur under various circumstances. When an organism continues eating an acceptable food, the level of acceptability gradually declines as the final state of satiation is approached. Hedonic changes in the negative direction are also produced by shocks, burns, cuts, shrill sounds, and similar conditions. When negative affectivity is present the organism tries to reduce it. The very attempt to escape from inducing conditions is the earmark of negative affectivity.

The Distinction between Sensory and Affective Processes

To a psychology that is limited by the concepts of stimulus and response the postulate of central affective processes may appear superfluous. I believe, however, that any theory of behavior which ignores the concept of affectivity will be found inadequate as an explanation of the total facts. There are facts which are difficult, if not impossible, to explain in strictly S-R terms.

Sensory processes convey specific information to the brain centers that make it possible for an organism to discriminate differences in spatial position, differences in time, quality, and perceptual configuration. Affective processes convey little or no information. In so far as they convey any information that relates to the organism's orientation, affective processes are primitive evaluations. A positive response indicates *good, pleasant, "green light"* and a negative response indicates *bad, unpleasant, "red light."* Relative preferences indicate evaluations—*"better than"* or *"worse than."*

The sophisticated evaluations of the artist are far removed from the primitive affective arousals. His affective processes depend markedly upon knowledge, information, training, and past experience. The appreciative judgments of an artist may be largely cognitive; yet at all levels of sophistication some degree of central affective process may be present.

The distinction between sensory and affective processes is seen clearly in the contrast between sensory and hedonic intensity.

If pairs of sucrose solutions are presented to rats briefly for choice, the animals select the higher of two concentrations in preference to the lower. Scale values based upon preference tests show that the level of acceptability is directly proportional to the logarithm of the concentration. Young and Greene (1953) found that this relation held all the way up the scale of concentrations.

From the facts about sucrose solutions one might be tempted to argue that *sensory* intensity or physical concentration of solution is the critical determinant of behavior. But difficulty with a purely sensory interpretation appears when one considers the relative palatability of solutions of sodium chloride.

Young and Falk (1956a) ran a series of preference tests between distilled water and sodium chloride solutions of different concentrations, and between pairs of sodium chloride solutions. They found that need-free rats revealed an optimal concentration for sodium chloride within the range of 0.75 to 1.5 percent. When concentrations were below this range, need-free rats preferred the higher concentration; when above this optimal range, they preferred the lower concentration. Within the optimal range there were marked individual differences in preference and there was much indiscriminate behavior. The experimenters concluded that there is a *range of acceptance* within which acceptability rises with increasing concentration of NaCl and a *range of rejection* within which acceptability falls as concentration rises. A similar result was obtained by Bare (1949), and others, who relied upon an intake method of studying acceptability of NaCl solutions.

It is clear, therefore, that with solutions of sodium chloride, hedonic intensity does not have a one-to-one relation with sensory intensity. *Sensory* intensity is an increasing monotonic function of concentration of solution; *hedonic* intensity is a discontinuous function of concentration.

In another experiment, Young and Asdourian (1957) selected a 1 percent sodium chloride solution as representative of the optimal range of NaCl solutions. This near-optimal concentration was tested for preference against distilled water and four concentrations of sucrose solutions. The 1 percent sodium chloride solution was preferred to distilled water by need-free rats; but *all* the sucrose solutions were preferred to the near-optimal NaCl solution. It was found that all concentrations of sucrose are hedonically positive and high concentrations of sodium chloride are hedonically negative. Hence *sensory* intensity and *hedonic* intensity must be distinguished.

And, of course, the basic distinction between *positive sign* and *negative sign* is meaningless if we limit consideration to sensory processes and their underlying stimulus conditions.

It is not possible, therefore, to accept the complete generality of a principle formulated by Schneirla (1959) that weak stimuli have positive valences and lead to approach behavior while intense stimuli have negative valences and lead to withdrawal. This principle is not invariably true.

PALATABILITY, APPETITE, AND FOOD PREFERENCES

The postulate that affective processes have an objective existence has great utility in the field of food acceptance. In fact, the experimental findings in studies upon the acceptance of food practically demand such a postulate.

The following sections illustrate the practical utility of the construct.

Kind and Amount of Food Accepted versus Affective Processes

When an objective psychologist takes a look at food objects, he probably sees them as physical things. He observes that food objects differ in *kind* and that the *amount* presented to an animal as a reward or consumed by him is a quantitative variable.

In my early studies of food preference, I utilized different kinds of common foodstuffs, such as milk, butterfat, sugar, flour, and whole-wheat powder. To the human sensorium, as doubtless to that of the rodent, these foods differ in taste, smell, texture, appearance, and other sensory attributes. Several writers have commented that this work demonstrated how performance depends upon the *kind* of food offered as a reward. The statement is doubtless correct but the sensory character of a foodstuff must not be confused with its hedonic value.

I have repeatedly found that, when dietary conditions are held constant, common foods arrange themselves into a preferential hierarchy or transitive series from low to high palatability. The *kind* of food (defined by its physical properties) has no obvious relation to palatability (defined by preference tests). Foods that differ markedly in

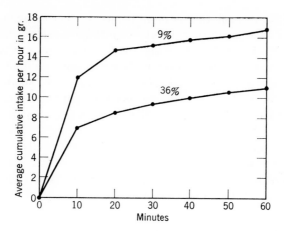

Figure 23. Average cumulative intake, in grams of fluid, of two sucrose solutions presented singly for a 60-minute test. *From* Young and Greene (1953).

kind may be isohedonic. Also, one and the same *kind* of food can vary widely in acceptability with such conditions as deprivation and satiation.

The amount or quantity of food ingested has been frequently used as a measure of acceptability. Innumerable studies in the fields of nutrition, physiology, and psychology have recorded the amount of food accepted per day by laboratory animals. The quantity accepted per unit of time is certainly a useful measure when related to body weight, growth, reproduction, state of health, and other variables.

The quantity of food accepted, however, depends upon a number of physiological conditions and for this reason it is an ambiguous measure of behavior. The nature of the difficulty came to light clearly in an experiment by Young and Greene (1953). They gave a group of five rats a 60-minute drinking test with a 9 percent sucrose solution and another group of five rats a 60-minute drinking test with a 36 percent sucrose solution. Intake of fluid was recorded graphically.

Figure 23 shows the average cumulative intake, in grams of fluid, of the two sucrose solutions presented singly. Measurements of the original graphs were made at 10-minute intervals and the values averaged.

The illustration shows clearly that greater quantities of the 9 percent solution were ingested consistently throughout the 60-minute test. On the basis of these results with single stimuli, one might well predict that the 9 percent solution is more palatable (better liked) than the 36 percent solution and that, if rats were given a choice, the 9 percent solution would be preferred. This prediction, however, turned out to be contrary to fact. In a 60-minute test with the two fluids presented simultaneously for choice, the rats ingested greater quantities of the 36 percent solution. Also, when given a brief-exposure preference test they selected the 36 percent solution in preference to the 9 percent solution.

The nature of the difficulty is clear. Intake depends upon at least two kinds of determinants—palatability and appetite. Hence intake does not measure any single motivational factor. And a critical factor in the situation is the possibility of choice.

The Distinction Between Palatability and Appetite

The term *palatability* refers to the hedonic value of a foodstuff that depends upon taste, aroma, texture, temperature, appearance, and other sensory properties, and upon the surroundings of a foodstuff (environmental setting). In need-free organisms a preference between two taste solutions reveals a difference in palatability.

The term *appetite* refers to internal determinants of food acceptance and preference. In so far as a preference is determined by deprivation or satiation, by surgical operation, by special organic conditions such as pregnancy and lactation, diseases, etc., it is appropriate to speak of appetite. When an animal eats a food continuously there are appetitive changes. The eating of salted nuts and other titbits before a meal is said to whet the appetite. The French have expressed it in an aphorism: "L'appétit vient en mangeant." And with continued eating there is the inevitable approach to satiation or sating of the appetite. This is experienced subjectively as a reduction of the desire to eat.

The distinction between palatability and appetite does not imply that there are two kinds of affective processes. I would postulate only one kind of affective process, with positive and negative signs, but a variety of conditions that influence affectivity.

An experiment by Shuford (1959) will be considered in some detail because it illustrates the validity of the distinction between palatability and appetite as objective concepts.

Shuford studied the relative acceptance of sucrose and glucose solutions by need-free rats. He arbitrarily selected for study three concentrations of glucose solutions, namely, 5, 15 and 35 percent. For each of these solutions he computed, on the basis of preference tests of the intake type, the concentrations of sucrose solutions that would be equally acceptable. The three sucrose concentrations, respectively, turned out to be: 2, 9.6 and 27.6 percent.

During the main experiment thirty animals were given, individually, a 20-minute drinking test with each of the six sugar solutions (three of glucose and three of sucrose) presented singly. Each rat was given one test per day. The six solutions were presented according to a counterbalanced latin square design.

The curves presented in Figure 24 show the cumulative mean intake for each of the six solutions as a function of drinking time. It is obvious at a glance that the six solutions do *not* yield identical curves of intake. The greatest quantities of fluid consumed during the 20-minute test were for the 9.6 percent sucrose solution (9.6 S) and the 15 percent glucose solution (15 G). The lowest fluid intake was for the pair of solutions with the highest concentrations (27.6 S and 35 G).

A careful study of these three pairs of curves reveals an interesting fact. The *initial* rate of acceptance is practically the same for the two fluids in each pair of equally palatable solutions. Compare the curves for 5 G and 2 S during the first 12 minutes; and the curves for 9.6 S and 15 G during the first 5 minutes; and the curves for 27.6 S and 35 G during the first 1 or 2 minutes. If the initial slopes of these pairs of curves are studied by noting the angle of a curve to the vertical, it will be seen that the highest rate of acceptance was for the pair with highest concentrations; an intermediate rate was obtained for the pair with intermediate concentrations; and the lowest initial rate was for the pair with the lowest concentrations.

In an earlier study, McCleary (1953) failed to find a positive relation between initial rate of acceptance and concentration of solution. His rats, however, were thirsty and doubtless drank at a maximal rate of acceptance throughout the tests. Shuford's rats, by contrast, were not thirsty, hungry, or deprived in any known way. With the need-free animals the initial rate of ingestion was positively related to the concentration of solution.

McCleary recognized a distinction between two groups of factors that regulate intake; taste factors and postingestion factors. The postingestion factors serve to check ingestion. He demonstrated the importance of postingestion factors by introducing solutions through a small tube directly into the stomach of the rat—thus bypassing the taste receptors. McCleary found that preloading the stomach with glucose depressed the ingestion of glucose after the stomach tube had been removed. He showed that the depression of intake is related to

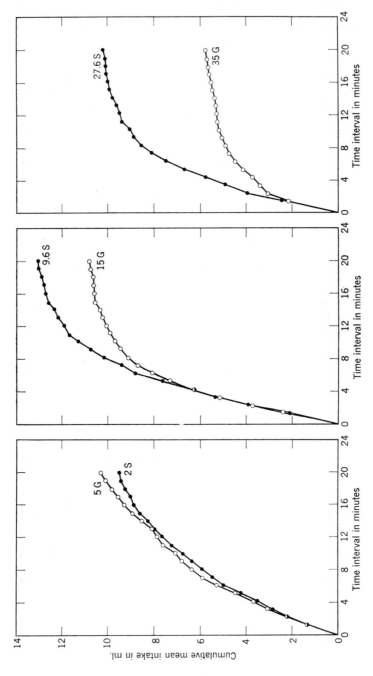

Figure 24. Intake curves for pairs of isohedonic solutions of glucose (G) and sucrose (S) with need-free rats. *From* Shuford (1959).

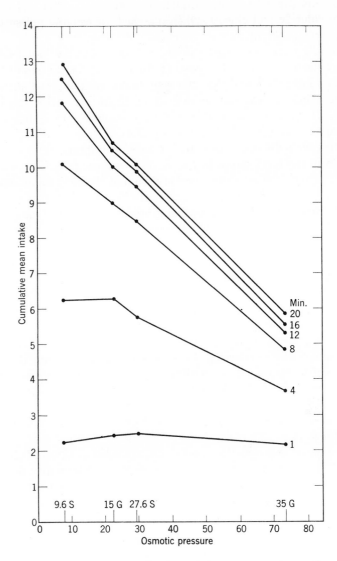

Figure 25. Cumulative mean intake of sucrose (S) and glucose (G) solutions as a function of osmotic pressure and drinking time. *From* Shuford (1959).

the osmotic pressure of the fluid in the stomach. Preloads of urea, sodium chloride and glucose, when matched for osmotic pressure, produced equivalent amounts of depression of ingestion.

Shuford's work confirmed the distinction, drawn by McCleary, between a taste factor and a postingestion factor in the regulation of intake. Shuford showed that the taste factor regulates the initial rate of acceptance; but sooner or later a postingestion factor checks the intake. It is the postingestion factor that accounts for the difference in Shuford's curves after the first few minutes.

To test the influence of osmotic pressure upon intake Shuford plotted his data in the form shown in Figure 25. Osmotic pressure (in atmospheres) is represented along the baseline and the four sugar solutions that are hypertonic are placed upon the baseline according to their osmotic pressures. The illustration gives the cumulative mean intake (in milliliters) for the four hypertonic solutions, plotted after 1, 4, 8, 12, 16, and 20 minutes of drinking.

It is obvious from this illustration that the quantity of fluid ingested during a fixed period of time is a decreasing function of osmotic pressure of the solution as well as an increasing function of the drinking time. If drinking time is held constant, at 4, 8, or 20 minutes, the quantity of fluid ingested decreases as the osmotic pressure increases.

In general, these experiments demonstrate the validity of a distinction between the peripheral (sensory) and internal (organic) determinants of ingestion. Since both sets of determinants regulate intake, it would be confusing, as I pointed out above, to interpret the amount of fluid ingested as an index of either appetite or palatability. There are at least these two determinants that operate jointly in the regulation of ingestion. They can be experimentally distinguished.

Palatability and appetite can be distinguished in terms of the complex sets of conditions that regulate ingestion. Palatability is a variable that depends upon processes within the head receptors. Appetite is a variable that depends upon internal, organic conditions.

The Experimental Control of Food Preferences

The methods employed for the experimental control of food preferences and some of the main results obtained are summarized below under five headings:

1. *Reversal of a preference through satiation upon the preferred food.* In an experiment by Young (1940), it was first determined that the maintenance diet for rats supported a stable preference of sucrose

to whole-wheat powder. Then the animals were prefed upon sucrose, for controlled periods of time, immediately before tests of preference. Prefeeding to the extent of 100-400 contact-seconds did not change the preference but, when the animals were satiated (900 contact-seconds or less), all of them developed a preference for whole-wheat powder.

The original preference did not change immediately, but it changed gradually through a series of choices. When the prefeeding of sucrose was discontinued the original sugar preference did not immediately return, but there was a gradual and unmistakable trend in the direction of the original preference.

2. *Reversal of a preference through creating a metabolic need for the non-preferred food.* In an experiment by Young and Chaplin (1945), groups of rats were maintained in cafeteria cages upon a self-selected diet, i.e., the animals were given unlimited access to the components of an adequate diet, presented in separate containers. Repeated preference tests were made between two of the dietary components: sucrose and casein. The need-free rats developed a consistent preference for sucrose. After the preference had developed, protein starvation was commenced by removing casein from the diet.

As protein starvation steadily increased, the animals continued to select the sucrose (which they did not need) in preference to the casein (which they obviously did need). Then a new technique of preference testing was introduced. The rats were placed in an apparatus that resembled a Y-maze with test foods far apart and in fixed, familiar positions. In this apparatus all animals promptly developed a preference for casein. For a while there were two incompatible preferences. On the standard apparatus the rats showed a preference for sucrose: on the Y-maze apparatus they showed a preference for casein.

A series of control experiments (Young, 1945b) demonstrated that if naïve rats are first depleted of protein and then tested with both kinds of apparatus, they develop the same preference—a preference for casein. This preference agrees completely with metabolic needs.

The total investigation demonstrated these principles: (1) Need-free rats prefer sucrose to casein and the difference is one of palatability. (2) Protein-starved rats develop a preference of casein to sucrose, in agreement with their metabolic needs. (3) Established habits of preference tend to persist as regulators of food selection even when the selections are out of line with metabolic needs and out of line with previous relations of palatability. A general principle can be stated this way: *Preferential food habits tend to form in agreement with metabolic needs but established habits regulate food selections regardless of needs.*

3. *Control of preference by changing palatability.* An obvious method for controlling food preference is to alter the palatability of one of the test foods. Humans alter palatability whenever they add sugar or salt or vinegar to a food or change its temperature to make it taste better. Actually this is a change in the character or kind of food.

Some unpublished observations by Kent Christensen, and others, have made it clear that the addition of sodium chloride to a sucrose solution may either raise or lower the level of palatability depending upon the concentrations of both components of the compound solutions. Also, if compound solutions contain both sucrose and quinine, the palatability level can be raised by increasing the concentration of sucrose and lowered by increasing the concentration of quinine.

4. *Control of preference by associating a flavor with organic relief.* During the early years of vitamin research Harris et al. (1933) studied the acquisition of preferential food habits by laboratory rats. They found that when rats were depleted of the vitamin B complex, they were unable to select a food containing a small but sufficient amount of the vitamin. If, however, the animals suffering from avitaminosis were isolated and fed a vitamin-adequate food with a distinctive flavor, so that they could associate a specific flavor with relief from the distressing symptoms of vitamin deficiency, they continued to select this food when it was placed among other foods. The rats continued to select this food (labeled by a flavor) even after the vitamin was withdrawn and the diet again made inadequate.

This pioneer experiment indicates that preferential food habits can be altered by associating sensory qualities with organic relief from distress. It also supports the above principle that food habits, once they are established, take over the function of regulating food selections independently of metabolic needs and affective processes.

5. *Control of preference through habituation and training.* Experiments upon the control of food preferences through training, when palatability and metabolic need are held constant, have thus far given negative or indecisive results. In one study rats were forced to accept casein (an unpalatable food) for one thousand runs without choice. Periodically during their training they were given brief preference tests between casein and sucrose. The forced acceptance of an unpalatable food only made the preference for sucrose stand out with increasing clarity and certainty.

In general, the methods that have proved successful in the experimental control of food preferences have consistently involved an hedonic change in the positive direction. And there is much evidence that, once a food habit has taken over the regulation of the feeding process, this habit tends to persist as a stable determinant of food selections regardless of metabolic needs and prior relations of palatability.

An Electronic Preference Tester

Figure 26 shows an electronic preference tester used for observing preferences of rats between pairs of test fluids. The illustration pictures a series of six individual boxes employed in testing squads of six rats simultaneously.

The two graduated burettes clamped to the front of each box contain test fluids—in this instance, for example, a simple sucrose solution and a compound solution containing both sucrose and quinine. The

Figure 26. Electronic preference tester. Apparatus used at the University of Illinois for testing preferences of squads of six rats simultaneously. Animals are given a continuous choice between a pair of simple or compound taste solutions.

burettes are provided with standard nozzles that project through lucite windows into the testing boxes. Each nozzle has a platinum wire, fused through the glass, which is in contact with the fluid inside.

When the tongue of the rat touches the fluid at the tip of a nozzle a circuit is made through the animal's body and the floor of the apparatus. Each box is provided with a system that permits voltage and power amplification of the pair of circuits. The circuit for each unit is similar to that described by Hill and Stellar (1951).

The current that passes through the body of the rat is of such low voltage that it has no physiological effect. But when amplified the current from each unit controls a relay that activates a counter or a cumulative recorder. From the numerical count of separate tongue contacts or the graphic record, the preference that develops can be readily observed.

MOTIVATION AND THE AFFECTIVE PROCESSES

From every point of view the affective processes must be regarded as motivational in nature. First, affective processes are intimately related to the activation of neurobehavioral patterns. Second, affective processes regulate and direct behavior according to the principle of maximizing the positive and minimizing the negative. Third, affective processes have a specific role of organizing neurobehavioral patterns. They lead to the development of motives and evaluative dispositions that become relatively stable and permanent determinants of behavior.

The following sections will treat some of the ways in which the affective processes are related to the regulation and organization of behavior.

The Regulative Role of Affective Processes

Affective processes regulate the neurobehavioral patterns that organisms develop. If a rat, on the preference tester, develops a preference of A>B, I would assume that A is more palatable than B; if he develops a preference of B>A, I would assume that B is more palatable. If no preference develops, there is no basis for assuming a difference of palatability; the two test foods may be isohedonic or the animal may be dominated by position of the food, color of the container, or another factor that is not directly related to the foodstuff.

A preference test does not reveal the *absolute* level of affective intensity but only the *relative* levels associatd with two incentives. This fact will be illustrated by data obtained in an experiment by Young (1947).

Preference tests were run with three pairs of test foods: (1) sucrose and casein, (2) wheat powder and casein, (3) sucrose and wheat powder. The percentages that indicate preference changed from test to test as the animals gained practice in the discrimination. These percentages are shown graphically in Figure 27.

The percentages indicating preference were consistently highest for the first pair (sucrose and casein) where the *difference* in palatability is known to be the greatest. The percentages for the second pair (wheat powder and casein) were almost as high; and this agrees with the fact that wheat powder is just slightly below sucrose in level of palatability. The percentages were lowest for the third pair (sucrose and wheat powder) where the *difference* in palatability was relatively

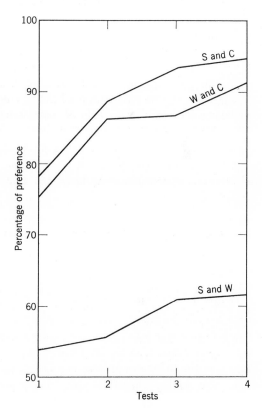

Figure 27. Curves of preferential learning for three pairs of test-foods. The top curve shows percentage of choices of sucrose in a test between sucrose (S) and casein (C). The middle curve shows percentage of choices of wheat powder in a test between wheat powder (W) and casein (C). The bottom curve shows percentage of choices of sucrose in a test between sucrose (S) and wheat powder (W). Each point plotted is based upon 360 choices— 12 rats, 30 choices per animal. *From* Young (1947).

slight but the incentives themselves were of high palatability. A preference test, therefore, reveals only the *relative* affective intensities.

In the light of many such sets of curves, I make the assumption that affective processes have a regulative and organizing role. The relative intensities of affective arousals that are associated with two stimuli determine whether the animal will develop one preference or its opposite or no preference at all. Also, the *relative* hedonic intensities determine the rate of growth of a preferential discrimination when the frequency of repeating an affective response is held constant.

On the negative side of affectivity it is equally obvious that hedonic processes have a regulative role. The role is frequently that of inhibiting or blocking neurobehavioral patterns. To illustrate this point consider a bit of evidence in an experiment reported by Neal Miller (1956).

Miller was interested in measuring degrees of hunger by adding, progressively, different amounts of quinine to an acceptable food. He described the method as follows:

A series of bottle caps are countersunk on the periphery of a metal disc that is driven by a slipping clutch and escapement mechanism. The bottle caps appear immediately below an opening in the floor of a small cage that is arranged so that the rat can reach only 1 cap at a time. After a hungry rat has learned to drink a few drops of milk from each bottle cap as soon as it appears, it is presented at 30-second intervals with a series of 10 bottle caps, each cap containing 3 drops of milk, and each solution being adulterated with progressively increasing amounts of quinine hydrochloride ranging from concentrations of 0, 0.004 per cent, 0.008 per cent, to 1 per cent. For each cup that he cleans up, the rat receives 2 points; for each one started without finishing, 1 point; and for cups not touched, zero. The cumulative score has been found to be a sensitive and reliable measure of hunger.

The argument underlying this method is that the bitter taste of quinine hydrochloride inhibits ingestion and the degree of inhibition varies with the concentration of quinine in the solution. Consequently an acceptable food (milk) can be made unacceptable by addition of quinine; and the degree of hunger, Miller argued, can be measured in terms of the strength of the inhibiting agent.

Hence negative as well as positive affective processes have a regulative role in behavior. Affective processes determine what neurobehavioral patterns a naïve animal will organize and exercise, whether or not he will learn a particular pattern or preference, how many trials it will take him to learn a pattern up to some specified criterion of performance, how well a learned act will be performed and how frequently it will occur, what behavioral patterns he will inhibit, etc. But despite all this, I know of no evidence that affective processes *cause* learning. They have a regulative and organizing function and hence influence the neurobehavioral patterns that are learned. And, of course, we know that affective processes are not essential for human learning. Their main role is regulatory.

Incentive Value and Affective Processes

I pointed out above that affective processes are contemporary events going on within the tissues of an organism. That is to say, they are *events* that occur here and now; they are not substances that can be measured in grams or cubic centimeters. Affective processes differ in sign (positive or negative), in intensity (or degree), and in duration and temporal course.

Affective processes, however, must be distinguished from the stable conditions in the nervous system that are organized on hedonic (and other) principles. Through affective experience an animal develops stable organizations within his nervous system. He learns to run to places where sugar solutions can be found and to avoid places that yield electric shocks. He learns preferential discriminations—accepting one food and rejecting another. Through affective experience he builds up attitudes of liking and disliking, emotional dispositions, motives, and stable systems of value.

If a rat develops a positive orientation toward a sugar cup, this orientation can be taken as a mark of positive evaluation. If he develops a negative orientation toward a charged grill, this orientation can be taken as negative evaluation. Similarly, if repeated preference tests are given with the foods of a group, the animal will develop a *value system.* For example, if well nourished rats are tested with sucrose and wheat powder and casein, they develop a stable hierarchy of preferential values: sucrose is the most palatable, wheat powder is almost as palatable, and casein is the least palatable.

Such a value system is based upon affective processes. It has a stability and permanence (dependent upon the nervous system) that is independent of current affective arousals. The sign of an evaluative disposition is based upon the sign of the affective process aroused by the object. The degree of incentive value is related to the intensity of the primary affective arousal.

If an affectively neutral stimulus object, like an auditory click, is presented to an animal at the same time as acceptable food, the click acquires a positive incentive value. If this same physical click is presented to other animals with a painful electric shock, the click acquires a negative incentive value. If the click is presented without any hedonic accompaniment, it will be disregarded and become indifferent.

The facts indicate that almost any indifferent stimulation can become associated with an affective arousal. After an association has been firmly established, the erstwhile indifferent stimulation arouses or re-arouses an affective process. The general principle is this: *Any stimulus which occurs consistently, repeatedly, and contiguously with a primary affective arousal will tend to elicit a similar affective arousal.*

This principle applies not only to the gross difference between positive and negative affective processes but it applies also to hedonic intensity. For example, an object associated with a very sweet taste will elicit a stronger affective process than an object associated with a weakly sweet taste.

Affective arousals are conditioned to the stimulus-situations within which they occur but the stimulus situations acquire incentive value by virtue of their association with affective arousals. This is essentially the mechanism of "secondary reinforcement" or "acquired reward." It is not necessary to assume two kinds of conditioning—sensory and hedonic—but it is necessary to assume that stimulation evokes an affective process.

The incentive values shown in behavior can be changed by deprivation and satiation. For example, an unpalatable food, like casein, can become more highly valued than sucrose if rats are starved for protein. Again, the incentive value of water is low when animals are satiated but is greatly raised by deprivation of water. When incentive values are changed in these ways a stable value system may be disturbed and readjustments within the system are gradually made. A value system that has been well learned is more resistant to change than one in the process of formation.

When an evaluative disposition has been well learned it regulates the pattern of behavior even if there is no direct contact with the incentive object. For example, Schlosberg and Pratt (1956) baited one side of a T-maze with food which could be smelled and seen by rats but not touched; the food was covered with a mesh screen so that it was definitely inaccessible. Hungry rats learned to run the maze to the familiar but inaccessible food object. Satiated rats did not learn it. In this experiment there was no consummatory response, no drive reduction, no affective arousal through contact with food. The inaccessible food object had incentive value to the hungry animals; it was interesting and exciting.

This experiment recalls an earlier study by Grindley in which hungry chicks ran down a runway to grains of rice which they ate; other chicks ran down the same runway to a plate glass through which they could see, but not touch, the rice grains. The sight of food was temporarily effective as an incentive but after the first four or five trials the inaccessible food reward began to lose its motivational effectiveness.

The value systems of laboratory animals have an obvious dependence upon affective processes. Human systems of value are more complex than those of the rat. Human evaluations are made in terms of standards, goals, anticipated satisfactions. To a high degree they depend upon cognitive, rational processes. Koch (1956) regards the study of value as a central problem in human motivational psychology; but value, he argues, rests upon bases other than affectivity. There is no reason to question this view provided the role of affectivity in the organization of value systems is properly recognized and appraised.

Intrinsic and Extrinsic Motivation

A distinction that is commonly met in educational psychology is that between intrinsic and extrinsic motivation. When a school child is interested in an activity such as riding a bicycle or readng, the activity goes along smoothly with no added incentive. If the child is bored by a task or indifferent towards it, some external incentive is required. The teacher may motivate the pupil by offering a prize for good work or placing a gold star beside the child's name or praising him or getting him to compete against his previous record, etc.

Intrinsic motivation is present in activities that are valued for their own sake and that appear to be self-sustained. Koch (1956) has illustrated the distinction and the problem involved as follows:

X looks at a painting for five minutes, and we ask, "Why?" The grammar of extrinsic determination will generate a lush supply of answers. X looks in order to satisfy a need for aesthetic experience. X looks in order to derive pleasure. X looks because the picture happens to contain Napoleon and because he has a strong drive to dominate. X looks because "paintings" are learned reducers of anxiety. X looks in order to satisfy a need based on the association of the color of his mother's dress with the ground-color of the painting. Answers of this order have only two common properties: They all refer the behavior to an extrinsic, end-determining system, *and* they contain very little, if *any*, information. Anyone who has looked at paintings knows that if X is *really* responding to the painting, then any one of the above statements, which may happen to be true, appears trivial.

The fundamental problems centering around intrinsic motivation are problems of value and interest. The problems of extrinsic motivation are related to incentives and the way they influence performance.

Affective Intensity and the Strength of Motives

In earlier studies I wrote about "food-seeking drives" but this terminology can be confusing and has been abandoned. Food-seeking behavior is purposive and is always *learned* and drives, if we follow Nissen, are always innate. According to Nissen, it is nonsense to talk about "acquired drives." Judson Brown (1953) deserves the credit for pointing out the ambiguity in the concept of "acquired drives."

Animals acquire patterns of behavior that are instrumental in arriving at goals. Rats learn to run a maze, to press a bar, to shuttle back and forth on the preference tester, to swim over a pathway, etc., in order to arrive at a goal. What they learn is not a drive; it is sometimes called a *habit* and sometimes a *motive*.

Motives are acquired determinations that regulate the pattern of action and that arouse or activate behavior. By common consent it is proper to speak of the acquisition of motives. Motives, by definition, are *learned* determinants of behavior.

The strength of motives depends upon the intensity of the affective processes that organized them. This proposition is supported by the following three experiments:

1. Young (1947) timed rats as they shuttled back and forth on the preference tester to obtain nibbles of food from a single cup. Each rat made thirty runs (round trips) for a sucrose incentive, thirty for wheat powder, and thirty for casein. These ninety runs constituted a cycle, and each animal went through the cycle five times.

Preference tests, in another part of the experiment, established the fact that sucrose was the most palatable of the three incentives; wheat powder was almost as palatable as sucrose; casein was very low in palatability relative to the other two incentives.

The data showed that the rate of running was directly proportional to the palatability level of the incentive. The animals ran fastest for a sucrose incentive, almost as fast for wheat powder as for sucrose, and the slowest running was for casein. The rate of running, therefore, correlated perfectly with the level of palatability as determined by preference tests.

The rate of running, for all incentives, increased steadily with practice. But at any given stage of practice the rats *ran* faster for the more palatable incentive. *Running* is performance that depends upon the amount of practice, the intensity of affective arousal, and other factors such as glandular balance, state of health, environmental temperature, etc. Rate of *running* is not to be confused with rate of *learning*.

In the above experiment, practice and other determinants of performance were controlled and balanced. It appeared that the rate of running was proportional to the palatability level of the incentive. We concluded that the strength of the motive determining the shuttle pattern is proportional to the affective intensity of the food incentive.

2. The strength of a motive depends not only upon affective intensity but also upon the duration of an affective arousal, upon the frequency of occurrence of the affective process, and probably also upon its recency. The dependence of strength of motives upon hedonic intensity, duration, and repetition, was studied in an experiment by Young and Shuford (1954). To control hedonic intensity they varied the concentration of sucrose solutions (54, 18, 6, or 2 percent); to control hedonic duration they varied the number of seconds of contact with a solution per trial (1, 4, or 16 contact-seconds); to control repetition or frequency of affective arousal they gave the animals one run per day for 18 days.

The apparatus used in this experiment is diagrammed in Figure 28. It consists of a starting box (B), a guillotine-type door (D), a single food cup (F) in an open field, and an observation window (W). This is essentially a preference tester provided with one instead of two cups.

Before the experimental tests, each rat was allowed to explore the apparatus thoroughly, the door (D) being open and the food cup (F) empty. After this exploration the door (D) was closed and the food cup (F) filled with a sucrose solution. Each rat was allowed to accumulate 60 seconds of preliminary contact with his specific sucrose incentive, prior to Trial 1.

On Trial 1 the approach time from starting box to test fluid was measured. It was found that the rats ran faster in approaching a sucrose solution of 54 or 18 percent than one of 6 or 2 percent. The median running times for the four groups are shown graphically in Figure 29. It will be seen that the rats *ran* faster to the higher concentrations than to the lower, on Trial 1.

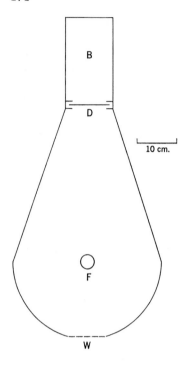

Figure 28. Ground plan of food-incentive apparatus.

All animals speeded up markedly with practice. After 14 to 18 daily
runs the rats in all incentive groups approached the sucrose solution
with near-maximal speed. The lower curve in the graph shows the
median running time for Trials 14 through 18, inclusive. The initial
differences in speed of running (dependent upon palatability) were obscured by practice which had the effect of accelerating all animals and
of reducing the group differences in performance.

This finding suggests that positive affective processes have the role
of *organizing* approach motives. After an approach motive has been
organized it tends, with practice, to become automatic and habitual.
Habit strength depends upon the amount of practice. Motive strength
also depends upon hedonic intensity.

In this experiment a positive relation was found between approach
behavior and the duration of affective processes. The experiment was
so designed that one-third of the animals in each incentive group received daily 1 contact-second with the sucrose solution; another third
received 4 contact-seconds; another third received 16 contact-seconds.
After practice, the *latency* (time required for a rat to leave the starting

box) was inversely related (.05 confidence level) to the duration of contact with the sucrose solution.

3. In another study, Mason (1956) controlled the duration of contact with a sucrose solution by varying the number of separate licks. He found that fifty licks of sucrose solution were more effective than ten licks as an incentive to rats running down a 5-foot runway. He also found, in agreement with Young and Shuford, that the concentration of sucrose solution and the frequency of contact (which he described as the ratio of reinforced trials) were highly significant determinants of performance.

The above three investigations agree completely in the main points. All of them show that the *intensity* of affective arousal (controlled by kind of food incentive or by concentration of sucrose solution), the *duration* of affective arousal (controlled by number of contact-seconds or number of licks), and the *frequency* of affective arousal (controlled by number of contacts with the food) are significant determinants of the rate of running for a food incentive.

Figure 29. Median running times on Trial 1 (upper curve) and Trials 14 through 18 (lower curve) as related to concentration of solution. There were twelve rats in each of the four groups. *From* Young and Shuford (1954).

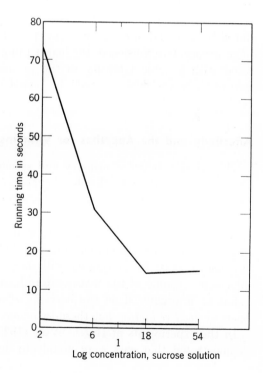

The data justify the postulate that the *strength* of a motive to approach, as shown by speed of locomotion and latency, is directly related to the intensity, duration, and frequency of affective arousals. We might add that the recency of affective arousal is probably also a factor.

It should be pointed out that in the experiment by Young and Shuford the rats had only one brief contact with the sucrose solution per day and that the strength of the approach motive was measured 24 hours after this brief contact. This means that there are at least two factors in the motivation: the primary affective arousal and the learned neural organization that orients the animal toward the goal and regulates the pattern of his approach. The learned orientation is an approach motive. Its strength is correlated with hedonic intensity, duration, frequency of occurrence, and probably recency.

It is obvious that we must distinguish between the primary hedonic motivation and the secondary motivation that is based upon it. I would postulate that, after initial contact with the sucrose solution, the environmental stimulus cues from the apparatus redintegrate the animal's goal orientation and that the strength of this secondary motivation is dependent upon the intensity of proprioceptive tension produced by the goal orientation. This postulate implies that the degree of proprioceptive tension in the learned motivation is positively correlated with hedonic intensity in the primary motivation. This is a matter, however, which should be tested in the laboratory and not settled by words.

Affectivity and the Appetites for Vitamins and Minerals

The relation between primary and secondary motivation is critical in problems relating to the development of appetitive behavior. In these problems it is important to distinguish between affectivity and states of need.

In experiments upon the acquisition of appetites for vitamins and minerals there are indications the metabolic needs, produced by deprivations, may be associated with negative or neutral or positive affectivity. Some of the investigators have suggested that appetitive behavior is organized on the basis of *affectivity* rather than on the basis of *need reduction* but these two concepts are interrelated.

In the experiments of Harris et al. (1933), cited above, it was first demonstrated that rats were unable to detect a small but sufficient quantity of the vitamin B complex when mixed with other dietary components. The animals were offered, in separate containers, a choice among six or more foods only one of which contained the vitamin. Under these conditions vitamin-depleted rats were unable to detect and select the food that contained the vitamin.

After this inability was demonstrated the rats were given a period of dietary education. This consisted of feeding them exclusively, for 2 or more days, the vitamin-containing diet marked with an artificial flavor. During this "education" the rats regained lost weight and general food appetite. They were able to experience curative and beneficial effects and associate them with the characteristic flavor of the food.

Following this period of "education" the rats were again given a choice among a variety of foods of different flavors. This time they were able to select the vitamin-containing food, presumably identifying it by the flavor. The vitamin was then withdrawn from the preferred food and placed in a food with a different flavor. For example, if the vitamin-containing food was flavored with cocoa, the vitamin was removed from this food and placed in one flavored with Bovril. The "educated" rats, however, did not change their preference. They continued to select the cocoa-flavored food which had been made deficient; they began to lose weight and show other signs of avitaminosis.

The vitamin-depleted rats were now "re-educated." They were placed upon the Bovril-flavored diet until they could experience relief from the distressing symptoms of avitaminosis. After "re-education" they were again given a choice. This time they selected the Bovril-flavored food in preference to the others. Harris et al. assumed that, for the rats to form a habit of selecting the adequate diet, they must associate relief from the distressing symptoms of avitaminosis with some distinctive flavor or sensory characteristic of the foodstuff.

The picture is different, however, when the vitamin is presented in crystalline form or in a solution. Richter, Holt, and Barelare (1937) reported that rats deficient in vitamin B showed an "overwhelming appetite" for the vitamin B complex when it was presented in pure crystalline form, either as B_1 or riboflavin. Also when vitamin B_1 was presented in an aqueous solution of synthetic thiamine chloride the rats showed a great craving for it: "The odor of the vitamin as well as its taste aroused great interest. This is shown by the fact that the rats found the bottles at once, even when as many as twelve other containers filled with different foods or solutions were present in the cage at the same time. It was difficult to stop the animals from drinking the substance, once they had tasted it. Efforts to remove the bottle were met with fierce resistance. The bottle was held tightly with both paws and even with the teeth. By reaching far up into the bottles the rats made an effort to obtain every remaining drop of the vitamin."

A further study of the appetite for B vitamins was made by Scott and Quint (1946). They used a technique that bypassed the head receptors and produced specific vitamin deficiencies without complications from taste and smell. They trained rats to swallow daily a pill that contained vitamins in accurately controlled amounts. By removing from the pills a specific vitamin (thiamine or riboflavin or pyridoxine or pantothenate) they could produce a specific vitamin deficiency.

Each cage contained two cups—one filled with the standard diet and the other filled with the same diet plus the vitamin being tested. During a 3-week control period the diet was supplemented by the vitamins in the pills. During the experimental period the pill technique was continued but a single vitamin was removed and added to one of the two test foods. Under the experimental conditions a specific vitamin deficiency would develop unless the rats could learn to select the vitamin-containing diet in preference to the control diet.

Scott and Quint found that when rats were depleted of thiamine, riboflavin, or pyridoxine, they developed an appetite for the food that contained the needed vitamin. These investigators believe that the preferential selection of the vitamin-containing diet was learned since the preference developed gradually. But, importantly, the preference developed only under conditions of need. When there was no vitamin deficiency in the diet the rats failed to develop a preference for the test food that contained the vitamin.

Pantothenate was different from the other three vitamins in that a specific appetite for it developed only when the vitamin-containing diet was labeled with an odor. Even then some pantothenate-deficient rats failed to acquire an appetite for the food that contained this vitamin.

These experiments, interesting as they are, leave us uncertain as to the precise basis upon which appetites are organized. In a further study Scott and Verney (1947) suggested two possible explanations of the acquisition of specific appetites for vitamins: (1) A preferential habit is set up on the basis of an association between the feeling of well-being and some characteristic of the foodstuff. (2) There is an increased stimulus to eat, presumably derived from a persisting feeling of well-being. Both suggestions imply an affective basis for the organization of appetitive behavior.

Some dietary needs, however, may be associated with positive affectivity. In an experiment upon magnesium deficiency Scott, Verney, and Morissey (1950) reported that rats maintained upon a magnesium-deficient diet *avoided* foods that contained magnesium despite the fact that this mineral was essential to their health and ultimate survival. We cannot, therefore, think of behavior as always instrumental in the meeting of nutritive needs.

In an attempt to explain their findings with magnesium deficiency Scott et al. commented as follows:

> The most plausible explanation of these results is that the avoidance of magnesium is learned. It is well-known that a feeling of well-being is not always associated with the best possible physical status nor the ultimate welfare of an individual. Examples that may be cited are those of alcoholism, narcotism, and the euphoria that may occur in high altitude anoxia. Magnesium-deficient animals are nervous, highly excitable, and likely to go into convulsions on slight stimulation, while magnesium is a nervous system depressant. It is possible that the highly excitable stage of magnesium deficiency is pleasurable to the rat, and that he learns to avoid a diet that represses this pleasurable state. . . .

This speculation concerning pleasure may or may not be correct, but at least it can warn us against assuming that every need state is hedonically negative. The total evidence suggests that affective processes, rather than states of need, organize appetitive and aversive patterns.

The hypothesis I would defend is that the organization of appetitive behavior is dependent upon the association of sensory characteristics of a needed food and its surroundings with an hedonic change in the positive direction. When the ingestion of a food is followed by relief from distress or by positive comfort and sense of well-being the animal is likely to repeat those acts that are instrumental in producing relief or comfort. When the ingestion of a food is followed by distress (green apple effect) which becomes associated with the sensory properties of the foodstuff, the animal will learn to avoid that food. The hypothesis is nothing more than an extension of the hedonic principle from the periphery to the internal regions of the body.

Hedonic Effects of Deprivation

One of the commonest techniques for controlling the degree of motivation is to deprive an animal of food or water for a specified period of time. Thus, one reads about a 24-hour hunger drive or a 12-hour thirst drive. Well-starved animals are the rule rather than the exception!

One limitation of the starvation technique is that with prolonged deprivation an enfeeblement develops which lowers the level of drive. Although *drive* is low, the *need* for nutrient increases steadily up to the point of death through inanition.

States of deprivation raise the value of incentives. Hungry animals are more interested in food than satiated; thirsty animals are more interested in water. Human subjects report that hunger and thirst are unpleasant states and that ingestion brings relief and comfort. There are thus hedonic changes associated with states of depletion and satisfaction.

For several years I have experimented with need-free rats, i.e., rats that have an unlimited supply of adequate diet and water in their cages at all times up to the moment of testing. There can be no doubt that such need-free animals respond positively to food incentives that are supplementary to their maintenance diet just as a child responds positively to candy which he does not need.

I have controlled degree of motivation by manipulating incentive conditions rather than by deprivations. When solutions are employed as incentives, a precise quantitative control over motivation is possible and, incidentally, it is possible to scale incentives with a precision far exceeding that obtainable from the starvation methods.

In two experiments a 24-hour thirst was introduced for experimental purposes. The thirst produced two interesting side effects which were discovered more or less accidentally. Since they have a bearing upon the effects of deprivation, they will be considered.

1. Young and Falk (1956b) found that thirst made rats less ready to discriminate between two kinds of drinking water. The non-thirsty animals that had previously been trained to run upon the preference tester, were given a choice between local tap water and distilled water. All twelve animals selected tap water in preference to distilled; five of the twelve revealed a preference significant at the .01 confidence level or better; no rat preferred distilled water. When the rats were made thirsty this preferential discrimination vanished completely.

Although the rate of running the shuttle pattern on the apparatus was markedly increased by thirst, the rats were completely indiscriminate. Our interpretation of this finding was that thirst raised the appetitive level (incentive value) for all kinds of drinking water. The appetitive increment masked a small but consistent difference in palatability which was readily demonstrated under the need-free conditions. The result is what we might expect if the Weber-Fechner principle applies to incentive values.

2. In a related experiment Young and Falk (1956a) studied the relative acceptability of sodium chloride solutions. It was found that need-free rats occasionally accepted sodium chloride solutions with concentrations as high as 3 or 6 percent. We hoped that, by making the animals thirsty, we could force them to show preferences between hypertonic solutions of NaCl. Actually, we found that the thirsty rats would not touch such salty fluids. Moreover, thirst markedly inhibited their running activity on the apparatus.

This inhibition of the shuttle pattern remained on the following days when thirst was removed and a more palatable solution was substituted for one of the hypertonic fluids. Some of the animals eventually recovered normal running but the way they recovered it is of interest. They made sporadic bursts of running at a highly practiced rate of activity and selected the more palatable fluid. The high level of activity indicates that the shuttle pattern had been *inhibited* by thirst. This inhibition is different from *extinction* which occurs, for example, when sucrose is withdrawn from an incentive solution.

In general: (1) Deprivation may obscure a small but consistent difference in palatability that is obvious under conditions of non-deprivation. (2) Deprivation may inhibit running activity if the starvation technique is used as a means of forcing animals to discriminate between two hedonically negative test fluids.

PSYCHOPHYSIOLOGY OF ACTIVATION AND AFFECTIVE PROCESSES

At the turn of the century a great deal of work was being done with the so-called expressive methods of studying human feelings. Subjects reported their conscious feelings of pleasantness and unpleasantness and their reports were correlated with bodily changes in pulse rate, pulse strength, respiratory rate and depth, blood volume in some part of the body, the galvanic skin response, and other peripheral changes that were objectively recorded. The expressive methods failed to find any perfect correlation between the affective processes and peripheral changes. There were associations, as between pleasantness and vasodilation and unpleasantness and vasoconstriction, but there were no one-to-one correlations.

The difficulty was blamed, in part, upon the introspective methods. It is possible, however, that no peripheral process is invariably present when pleasantness is felt and no peripheral process invariably present when unpleasantness is felt. It may well be that the ultimate correlates of *felt* pleasantness and unpleasantness are neural processes deeply hidden within subcortial brain centers. If this guess is correct, the psychophysiology of the affective processes must await discoveries of the neuropsychologist.

In the following sections we will consider some of the physiological work upon activation and some of the studies of the physiology of "reward" and "punishment." This work holds a hope that the psychophysiology of the affective processes will some day be known.

Activation as Shown by the Electroencephalogram

Lindsley (1951) formulated an activation theory of emotion based largely upon his researches in the field of electroencephalography. The theory takes account of strong excited emotional states such as rage, terror, pain, and great excitement; it does not adequately consider calm and depressed moods. The theory, moreover, takes account of drowsiness, sleep, and coma—which are not regarded as emotional states. Therefore, Lindsley's theory of emotion is more accurately described as a theory of activation.

Activation is a central neural process that can be localized in the reticular formation including the brain stem network and the diffuse corticothalamic projection system. Patterns of activation can be detected in the intact organism by changes in brain waves. When the subject is calm his brain waves, recorded in the electroencephalogram (EEG), reveal a smooth, rhythmic pattern, of about ten oscillations per second, known as the alpha rhythm. When the subject is highly excited, as by the bang of a gun or painful stimulation or by anxiety, the alpha rhythm is inhibited and instead there are fast waves of low amplitude. This change is known as the activation pattern. If the subject relaxes, as in sleep or lethargy or hypokinesis, there is a shift from the desynchronized activation pattern to increased synchrony and rhythmic alpha waves. In deep sleep there are still larger, slower waves and great synchronization.

Figure 30. Equipment for recording the electroencephalogram. *Courtesy* Dr. D. B. Lindsley.

The facts may be understood better by reference to Figures 30 and 31. Figure 30 shows the electroencephalograph—a rather complicated apparatus for recording brain waves. Ordinarily the subject is isolated in an electrically shielded room which may be darkened or partly soundproofed. For illustrative purposes, however, the subject is shown seated beside the apparatus. Electrodes are attached to the subject's scalp at fixed points. Changes in electrical potential between adjacent electrodes are recorded. The action currents produced by brain currents are exceedingly small but these currents can be greatly amplified and a graphic record of them obtained. The two black boxes located on either side of the experimenter are voltage and power amplifiers. The illustration shows the experimenter adjusting the inkwriting oscillograph which leaves its record on a moving paper tape.

Figure 31 presents a record of brain waves obtained from the frontal, motor, parietal, and occiputal lobes. The lower set of curves reveals relatively large and rhythmic alpha waves obtained from all lobes but especially from the parietal and occiputal lobes of the normal subject. The upper set of curves shows the shorter and less regular pattern of waves obtained during a state of anxiety.

According to Lindsley, the EEGs show different degrees or levels of activation. These levels can be arranged along a continuum as indicated in Figure 32. The different levels can be described in several ways: (1) in terms of the activation pattern of brain waves, (2) in terms of awareness, (3) in terms of the level of general activity, and (4) in terms of the efficiency of performance.

In terms of brain waves: The highest levels of activation are characterized by desynchronized waves of low to moderate amplitude with high mixed frequencies. Lower levels, like the level of relaxed wakefulness, are characterized by synchronized waves with an optimal alpha rhythm. At the level of drowsiness and sleep the alpha rhythm is reduced and larger, slower waves appear. In deep sleep there is great synchrony. In coma there are irregular large, slow waves; sometimes the brain is completely inactive electrically as it is in death.

In terms of awareness: On the level of strong excited emotion, awareness is restricted or it may be divided or there may be confusion and haziness. Alert attentiveness is characterized by a controlling set or

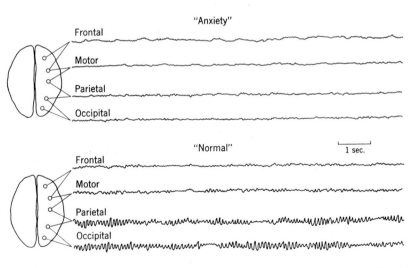

Figure 31. Electroencephalograms illustrating absence of alpha waves in the records during an anxiety state and the well-regulated alpha rhythms of a normal state. *Courtesy* Dr. D. B. Lindsley.

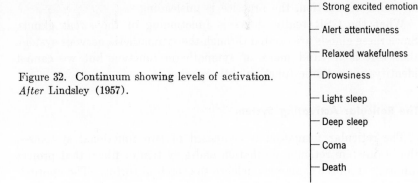

Figure 32. Continuum showing levels of activation. *After* Lindsley (1957).

— Strong excited emotion

— Alert attentiveness

— Relaxed wakefulness

— Drowsiness

— Light sleep

— Deep sleep

— Coma

— Death

concentration. In states of relaxed wakefulness, attention wanders; this state favors free associations. Drowsiness is a borderline condition with partial awareness; there is reverie and dream-like consciousness. In light sleep there is reduced consciousness and some loss of consciousness; but dreams occur and may be remembered. In deep sleep, coma, and death, there is complete loss of awareness.

In terms of the activity level: The continuum agrees well with observed differences in the level of general activity from the highest levels of emotional excitement down to the lowest levels of deep sleep and coma. It should be remembered, however, that activation is an internal physiological process and differences in the level of general activity are observed as behavior or performance.

In terms of efficiency of performance: The level of strong excited emotion is characterized by lack of control, freezing up, or disorganized behavior. Efficiency of performance is poor at the highest level of activation. Efficiency is maximal at the levels of alert attentiveness and relaxed wakefulness. Efficiency is very poor at the level of drowsiness. And it doesn't make sense to talk about the efficiency of performance during deep sleep and coma because these are purely vegetative states.

The GSR as an Index of Activation

In a clear and informing account of research with the galvanic skin response (GSR), Woodworth and Schlosberg (1954) stated that the GSR is an index of activation rather than an index of emotion (in the traditional sense). Although the GSR has been used extensively as an index of emotion, the practice is misleading.

What the GSR really shows is functioning of the sweat glands. Since these glands are excited through the sympathetic nervous system, the GSR is a valid index of sympathetic function but we cannot identify sympathetic function with emotion.

The Reticular Activating System

The reticular formation is composed of two functional systems— the brain stem reticular formation and a system of fibers that project diffusely from the thalamic nuclei to the cerebral cortex. The approximate location of the brain stem reticular formation is indicated by crosshatched markings in Figure 33. The structures are located at the

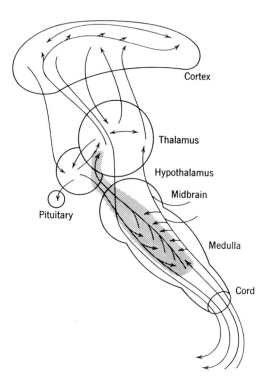

Figure 33. A schematic representation to show location of neural structures and probable pathways in the reticular formation. *After* Lindsley (1951).

levels of the medulla, midbrain, hypothalamus, and subthalamus. Arrows indicate the direction of conduction of neural impulses into the brain stem reticular formation and upward, through diffuse projection tracts, to the cortex. Other arrows indicate that there is a downward conduction from the cortex to the reticular formation.

The functional relations between the reticular activating system and the cerebral cortex can be better understood from Figure 34, which has been borrowed from Bindra (1959).

It is known that sensory pathways from all sense organs send off collaterals into the reticular activating system. The activating system is a network that contains many synapses and many smaller neural systems. Through the thalamic nuclei and diffuse projection fibers the system sends impulses to all parts of the cerebral cortex—sensory and non-sensory. This is indicated in the figure by arrows. The excitations over the diffuse projection system serve to alert or activate the cortex as a whole.

The reticular activating system is not limited to one-way conduction from sensory nerves to the cortex. The system is excited by cerebral action which, in turn, produces further effects via motor or efferent pathways. It is likely, for example, that when we anticipate pain or injury the cerebral action arouses the reticulum. This possibility is indicated by downward arrows in Figure 34. There is thus a two-way interaction between cortical and subcortical mechanisms.

The system is sensitive to drugs and chemical factors. Certain hypnotic drugs and anesthetics markedly affect the level of arousal.

The primary sensory systems conduct nerve impulses from the various sense organs to the thalamus and from there over direct projection pathways to the sensory areas of the cortex. Conduction through the primary sensory systems is direct, fast, and specific. The inputs into the system convey information; they are sensory cues or messages. The direct pathways have a discriminative or cognitive function.

Every sense-organ stimulation, however, initiates two kinds of sensory processes. Impulses, as noted above, are sent directly to specific cortical areas where they provide cues for discriminative responses. And impulses from the same stimulations are fed by collaterals into the reticular activating system where they serve to tone up or alert the total cortical area. Impulses in the reticulum are conducted over devious multisynaptic pathways and are transmitted diffusely to all parts of the cortex. This system has been called the

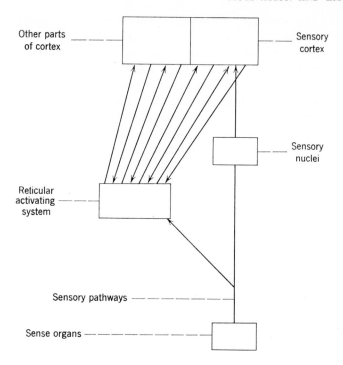

Figure 34. The reticular activating system. *After* Bindra (1959).

non-specific sensory system to distinguish it from the specific sensory system.

The non-specific sensory system furnishes a diffuse background of cortical activity which profoundly influences the way incoming primary sensory impulses are dealt with. Low levels of activation are correlated with sleep. Moderate levels are related to relaxed or alert wakefulness. The highest levels are present in emotional excitement; they are accompanied by lowered efficiency of performance.

The reticular activating system also influences lower neural centers and the outflow to various motor organs. Here again its effect upon motor function is non-specific—affecting the level of tonus rather than specific patterns of response. And, of course, the feedback from all reactions has a dual effect: it conveys specific information in the form of sensory cues, and it changes the level of arousal via the reticular activating system.

Activation and the Hedonic Continuum

Lindsley's activation continuum shows different levels of arousal within the brain. Degrees of activation exist within the reticular activating system and in the cerebral cortex. The subcortical and cortical processes occur within a single activating mechanism.

The continuum of activation is a theoretical representation. It must not be confused with representations of empirical differences in the level of general activity. Differences in activity level can be observed with the aid of activity cages, stabilimeters, and by other means. If one uses the rotating activity drum, for example, one can rate activity in terms of revolutions per hour or per day. This is an empirical measure of activity and not a measure of brain activation. The observed level of activity and the level of brain activation are related but they are different concepts.

An obvious limitation of the activation continuum is that it disregards the distinction between positive and negative affectivity. We have above presented the hedonic continuum—a bipolar continuum extending from intense negative affectivity, through indifference, to intense positive affectivity.

In Figure 35 the hedonic continuum is combined with the continuum of activation by placing the continuum of activation at the point of hedonic indifference. Both continua are hypothetical dimensions intended to represent differences in psychological processes. They do not refer to specific physiological events.

What are the implications of this figure?

The figure implies that in addition to differences in the degree of activation there are hedonic differences among positive, negative, and indifferent arousals. There are two dimensions of arousal rather than one.

The two dimensions form a frame of reference within which affective arousals and hedonic changes can be plotted. Arrows beside the hedonic continuum indicate two important directions of change but they disregard associated changes in the *level* of activation. Everyday experience reveals that there are exciting pleasures and calm pleasures. Consider, for example, the contrast between sexual excitement and sexual analepsis; or the contrast between the pleasant excitement of boy anticipating a trip to the circus and his relaxed, happy mood at some time after the circus; or the contrast between the excitement at a cocktail party and the relaxed glow of satisfaction after a fine

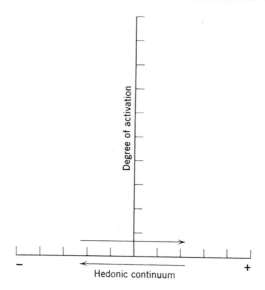

Figure 35. Activation and the hedonic continuum.

banquet. On the negative side, there are exciting displeasures such as
in great pain or agony; and there are calm displeasures as in bereavement and depressed moods generally. It would seem, then, that at
least two dimensions are needed to represent the facts of everyday
experience adequately.

In the laboratory, changes are observed in the level of activation
that occur with learning and experience. For example, when a rat
first tastes a sugar solution he does not appear to be particularly
excited by it. He may desert the cup at first and wander around
the apparatus. His speed of approach to the cup, however, increases
with practice and behavior shows increasing excitement during successive runs. Possibly the increased speed of running is dependent upon
increased proprioceptive feedback from the muscles that maintain an
orientation towards the goal. Again, animals show exploratory activity
when placed upon a strange apparatus. Exploratory behavior is
observed as an increase in the level of activity. Some animals, however "freeze up." Both types of behavior are modified by practice and
repeated experience. It is usually assumed that a strange environment elicits a negative hedonic response and that habituation changes
this to affective indifference.

The following sections describing the work of Olds, Delgado, Miller, and others, will show that there is sound evidence for an objective distinction between the physiological processes of "reward" and "punishment." It makes sense today to speak objectively about the central physiology of the affective processes.

Electrical Stimulation within the Limbic System as "Reward"

In the fall of 1953, Dr. James Olds was experimenting with electrodes implanted in the brains of healthy, normal rats. He was interested in stimulating the brain within the reticular formation to discover whether such stimulation would increase the alterness of the animals and thus facilitate learning.

Quite by accident, an electrode was implanted in the region of the anterior commissure. When the rat's brain was stimulated at this point the animal acted as if he liked it. If the brain was electrically stimulated when the rat was at a specific place in an open field, he would, sooner or later, return and sniff around that area. Repeated brain stimulations caused him to spend more and more time at the place where the internal brain stimulations were received.

Later Olds found that the rat could be trained to go to any spot in a maze if his brain was consistently stimulated when he arrived at that spot. In a T-maze, for example, the animal could be trained to turn consistently to the left or to the right if he was "rewarded" by brain stimulations. A hungry rat with food at both ends of the T-maze would stop at a point where he was "rewarded" by electrical brain stimulation. It became apparent that stimulation alone at certain points in the rat's brain is "rewarding" or "reinforcing."

Olds (1955) has described the technique he employed: A bipolar electrode was constructed by cementing two enameled silver wires into a plastic block. The wires were insulated from each other by the coat of enamel except at the tip where the stimulating parts were separated by about 3/1000 inch (the width of the enamel coatings on the two wires).

During an operation, the skin of the scalp is pulled back to expose the skull. A small hole is drilled through the skull of the anesthetized rat. A stereotaxic instrument is used to implant the electrode at the desired point. The precise location of the tip can be controlled by varying the place where the hole is drilled, the length of the stimulating wires, and the angle of the needle to the base of the plastic block. After insertion of the electrodes the plastic block is firmly

Figure 36. Photograph of a rat pressing a bar which stimulates a point in the septal area of the brain. The rat is "plugged in" to a light flexible cord that is suspended from the ceiling and is free to move about the apparatus. Through the implanted electrodes points in the brain are stimulated directly. *Courtesy* Dr. J. Olds.

attached to the skull with jeweler's screws. The scalp wound is closed with silk stitches, and the animal given time to recover from the operation.

The animal can now be connected to a light and flexible cord that is suspended from the ceiling so that the animal can move about freely in the apparatus. See Figure 36. Olds writes that the rat soon gets accustomed to the cord and it bothers him less than a leash troubles a dog. Through this cord and implanted electrode a fixed brain point can be stimulated. Alternating currents of low voltage are used. The illustration shows a rat pressing a bar which closes a circuit and delivers an alternating current through the electrodes to a point in the brain. One technical detail should be mentioned: A delay relay is incorporated into the circuit so that if the rat holds the

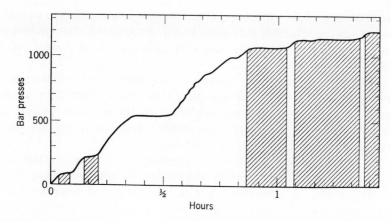

Figure 37. Unsmoothed response curve for a single rat showing cumulative bar presses. Shaded areas indicate extinction when the circuit was broken. *From* Olds and Milner (1954).

lever down for a second, the current is automatically turned off and the rat must release the lever and press it again to get more brain stimulation.

A typical graph based upon self-stimulation of a "reward" center is shown in Figure 37. This is an unsmoothed cumulative response curve obtained in an investigation by Olds and Milner (1954). The curve shows the cumulative number of bar pressings of a single rat during a period of 1½ hours. Shaded areas beneath the curve indicate periods of extinction when bar pressing produced no result. Unshaded areas indicate periods of time when bar pressing yielded electrical stimulation in the septal region. About ¾ hour was given to acquisition and ¾ hour to extinction. After extinction, a single stimulation of the "reward" center was given by the experimenter as a signal that the current was turned on. After receiving the signal the rat ordinarily resumed bar-pressing activity.

The curve shows that there is a very quick cessation of bar pressing when the circuit is broken; but a single stimulation given by the experimenter is sufficient to cause the rat to return to the bar and continue with sustained bar pressing.

The curve reveals a negative acceleration with plateaus of inactivity. One might think that this negative acceleration indicates learning; but against the learning hypothesis it can be argued that bar pressing is relatively simple and quickly learned to the asymptote of performance. More probably the shape of the curve indicates affective adaptation. Olds remarks that rats seem to become satiated after prolonged brain stimulation. Humans and rats alike can have enough of a delightful experience!

Subsequent observations, however, have shown that adaptation is lacking when the electrodes are placed at points other than in the septal area. If electrodes are implanted in the posterior portion of the hypothalamus, no adaptation occurs. Rats press the bar until exhausted. Then they collapse and sleep.

The index of the amount of bar pressing relied upon by Olds was the percentage of time spent by the rat in bar pressing during three 2-hour periods. A normal rat, left to himself in a Skinner box for 2 hours, will touch the lever enough to score from 2 to 10 percent. This is the "operant level" of bar pressing with no electrical brain stimulation.

The scores for stimulation in different parts of the limbic system, summarized from the data of Olds, are as follows:

Stimulation in *septal area*, 5 cases, average bar pressing   73%
Stimulation of *amygdaloid complex*, 5 cases, average bar pressing   52%
Stimulation of *hypothalamus:*
    Upper front part, 4 cases, average bar pressing   51%
    Lower front part, 3 cases, average bar pressing   80%

It will be seen that stimulations in these parts of the limbic system are highly "rewarding" in that the animal spends more than 50 percent of the 2-hour periods in self-stimulation by bar pressing.

The septal area of the limbic system (also called the rhinencephalon or the olfactory brain) was the first large structure of the rat's brain found to give consistently "rewarding" results. The septal area is a subcortical structure in the middle of the brain just in front of the thalamus.

Other limbic structures that give scores for bar pressing between 20 and 50 percent are the following:

In *tracts connecting structures of the limbic system*, 8 cases, average
    bar pressing   46%
Anterior nucleus of the thalamus, 4 cases, average bar pressing   45%
Cingulate cortex, 3 cases, average bar pressing   32%
Hippocampus, 6 cases, average bar pressing   31%
Hypothalamus:
    Back part, 2 cases, average bar pressing   36%
    Lower part, 1 case, average bar pressing   4%

The over-all average for all structures within the limbic system is 48 percent of the total time (during 2-hour test periods) spent by the subject in bar pressing that produces electrical brain stimulation. The over-all average for electrodes that are placed to stimulate outside the limbic system is 7 percent.

It is obvious that electrical stimulation of points within the limbic system of the rat's brain causes the animal to continue bar pressing as if he "enjoyed" the experience. In other words, such stimulation is "rewarding" or "reinforcing." Such stimulation is hedonically positive.

Electrical Stimulation of Subcortical Centers as "Punishment"

Olds also found negative "reinforcement" when stimulations were at points outside the limbic system. With electrodes implanted in the *medial lemniscus* (which is believed to fire into the reticular formation) the rats did not press the bar. A normal rat, with no electrical brain stimulation, will press the bar in about 2 to 10 percent of the total time during a 2-hour test. With self-stimulation in the *medial lemniscus,* however, his score will be 0 percent. Stimulation in this area appears to hurt the animal and he keeps away from the lever.

Delgado, Roberts and Miller (1954) implanted electrodes in the brains of cats and were thus able to provide electrical stimulation at specific points. In one experiment five cats were trained, before the operation, to rotate a wheel at the end of the cage in order to turn off an electric shock administered through a floor grid. A buzzer anticipated the shock by 5 seconds. The cats learned to rotate the wheel thus turning off both the frightening buzzer and the painful shock; if the cat turned the wheel within 5 seconds he avoided the shock. Training continued till all animals responded promptly to the buzzer and thus avoided the shock.

After this training, the electrodes were implanted and the cats allowed to recover from the operation. When the animals recovered from the operation they were healthy and normally active. Then they were tested with electrical brain stimulations. Some experimental animals turned the wheel immediately at the first stimulation of the brain. Others appeared to be confused by the motor side effects, but learned in a very few trials to turn the wheel and thus avoid the "punishment." The habit of turning the wheel transferred readily from the external "punishment" to the internal "punishment." The central brain stimulation could thus activate a learned pain-avoiding mechanism.

After this demonstration four of the cats were tested for conditioning. For three animals the conditional stimulus was a flicker produced by the rotation of a toothed wheel in front of an overhead light. For the other animal the conditional stimulus was a tone of 2,000 cycles per second. Preliminary tests showed that neither of these stimuli elicited wheel turning. The stimuli were then paired with the central stimulation just as the buzzer had been paired with the electric shock through the feet. After sixteen to ninety-two pairings, the new stimuli elicited wheel turning. In other words, the cats learned to respond to the flickering light or the tone by turning the wheel and thus removing or preventing the electrical brain stimulation.

A cat that was conditioned to tone also had a needle electrode in the motor area of the brain. Stimulation through this electrode elicited vigorous licking movements but no wheel turning. Conditioning was tried by stimulating first the motor area and then the "punishment" center. After a number of such paired stimulations a conditioned response was demonstrated. To the stimulation of the motor area alone the animal responded first by licking, then by turning the wheel.

In another experiment all five experimental animals were trained to eat fish from a dish. On the second day immediately after touching the food they were "punished" by electrical stimulation in the thalamic, mesencephalic or rhinencephalic structures. In one to four trials the hungry cats learned to avoid the food. Stimulation of the "punishment" centers inhibited the feeding of hungry animals.

These results were elicited with electrodes implanted in three specific regions: (1) the superior part of the tectal area in the neighborhood of the spinothalamic tract; (2) the lateral nuclear mass of the thalamus; and (3) the inferomedial part of the hippocampal gyrus. Stimulation of certain other regions of the brain, including the sensorimotor areas, did not elicit the "punishment" phenomena.

"Reward" and "Punishment" from the Same Neural Points

It is tempting to assume that there are positive and negative hedonic centers within the subcortical regions and that these centers have different locations. Do erotic excitations and sensory stimulations from sugars and flowers feed into a common "pleasure" center?

Do painful excitations and stimulations from bitter and sour substances feed into a common center for "displeasure"?

It is likely that this simple concept of separate locations for positive and negative affectivity is in error. A bit of evidence indicates this.

Miller (1957) reported some observations by Roberts on cats and rats, indicating that both "rewarding" and "punishing" effects can be elicited from stimulations of the same neural points. A rat, for example, would press a bar to produce electrical stimulation at a point in his brain; then go to the other end of the apparatus and rotate a wheel to turn off the current. The sequence of turning the current on and off was repeated over and over again.

Obviously we must know more about this phenomenon factually before venturing an interpretation. But if "reward" and "punishment" can be elicited by stimulating the same neural points, it is likely that temporal and intensive aspects of stimulation have an important relation to affective arousals and that there are no fixed centers for "reward" and "punishment."

Changes of Temperament Following Removal of the Limbic System

Another unsolved problem is raised by observations following the surgical removal of the limbic system in cats.

Observations reported by Bard (1950), in a study of anger, raise a question as to whether the limbic system can be regarded as an *excitatory* center of positive affectivity. Bard and Mountcastle removed the limbic cortex from three cats. Following the operation there was for each animal a *lowering* of the threshold for the rage pattern. This hypersensitivity to rage vanished within 2 weeks, and the animals became markedly friendly. A cat that had been shy before the operation became very friendly and exhibited pleasure on slight provocation. The change of temperament lasted through long survival periods and the friendly, pleasant behavior was not changed by repeated tests of the effect of roughing and painful stimulation. Examination of the brains of these animals showed that all limbic cortex had been removed from both sides.

The operation was repeated on two more cats. These animals, like the other three, became friendly and actively sought petting even at the hands of those who from time to time had subjected them to noxious stimulation (to which they responded with normal feline displays of anger).

Further, the surgical removal of the hippocampus had an effect similar to that produced by removal of the limbic cortex. One cat with hippocampus removed demonstrated a very low threshold for pleasure reactions, was most affectionate, and took advantage of every opportunity to be petted. She did not display anger unless definitely noxious stimuli were applied. Another cat was an undemonstrative male in whom, before the operation, it had been impossible to evoke what are commonly regarded as signs of feline pleasure. While not at all ill-tempered, he was readily induced to display anger. The operation rendered the cat friendly and demonstrative. There was a change of temperament through brain surgery.

If surgical removal of the limbic system can make cats more friendly and expressive of pleasure, how can we regard this system as an *excitatory* center for pleasure?

Olds found that after prolonged periods of electrical self-stimulation in the septal area of the limbic system, rats were very readily aroused to fierce fighting and explosive startle. And Bard found, in the above studies with cats, that surgical removal of the limbic cortex was followed by fighting and startle so pronounced that the animals were dangerous and had to be handled with care. The immediate effect, however, wore off and was followed by increased friendliness. These facts suggest that the reactions of fighting and startle are normally inhibited by excitations from the limbic system and that prolonged septal stimulations and surgical operations may serve to disinhibit the responses of anger and startle. This is only a suggestion, and the problem awaits further experimental evidence for a solution.

OBJECTIVE PRINCIPLES OF EXPERIMENTAL HEDONISM

At this point it is well to state some of the objective principles of experimental hedonism.

Statement of Principles

The following statements should be regarded as tentative formulations and as a basis for experimental studies:

1. *Stimulation has affective as well as sensory consequences.* Along with gustatory stimulation by sugar solutions, for example, there is a positive affective arousal which, by its very nature, is something to be prolonged and intensified. Along with painful stimulation there is a

negative affective arousal which, by its very nature, is something to be terminated.

2. *An affective arousal orients the organism toward or against the stimulus-object.* This goal orientation can be readily observed. For example, when a rat, in the course of exploratory activity, makes contact with a sugar solution he may pause for a moment, then continue to explore. Sooner or later, however, he returns to the solution and takes more. After repeated sips he becomes oriented toward the solution. If an experienced animal is forcibly delayed in his approach to the sugar cup, he shows a postural orientation toward the cup and approaches it quickly when released. He acts as if he expected or anticipated something. I would postulate a cognitive expectancy along with the affective arousal.

If an animal is offered a quinine solution, he fails to develop a positive orientation or an existing positive orientation is inhibited.

3. *Affective processes lead to the development of motives.* An orientation toward the goal object instigates and regulates behavior and hence is a motive. The sign of an affective arousal determines whether an approach-maintaining motive or an avoidance-terminating motive will develop. This principle can be illustrated by numerous runway experiments in which animals acquire, through affective arousals, motives that lead to approach or to avoidance.

4. *The strength of a recently acquired motive is correlated with the intensity, duration, frequency, and recency of previous affective arousals.* On the positive side, at least, the speed with which need-free rats approach a sucrose solution is related to the concentration, and to the duration, frequency, and recency of contact. With practice in running, however, the animals speed up as they approach their physiological limit. This speeding up with practice may level off and hence obscure initial differences due to affective arousals.

5. *The growth of motives is dependent upon learning as well as upon affective arousals.* Learning of a simple pattern such as running down a straight alley or running back and forth upon the preference tester is dependent directly on exercise (practice, drill, training); but affective arousals play an essential role in organizing, activating, regulating, and sustaining the neurobehavioral patterns that are learned.

It is necessary, therefore, to distinguish between learning through exercise (practice, drill, training) and the hedonic regulation of behavior. Affective processes regulate and organize neurobehavioral patterns in the sense that they determine what will be learned and what not; but such hedonic regulation and organization are not to be confused with learning through practice. Learning may be narrowly defined as a change in neurobehavioral pattern that depends upon exercise.

It should be pointed out that affective arousal is not necessary for human learning. To illustrate the point consider a subject who is instructed to memorize a series of nonsense syllables presented on a memory drum. The subject has an intent to learn. His instructional set furnishes adequate motivation for the task of memorizing. The learning proceeds whether the subject finds the task interesting, boresome, or affectively neutral. What appears necessary for learning to occur is the simultaneous excitation of contiguous neurons.

6. *The laws of conditioning apply to affective processes.* Psychologists ordinarily describe conditioning in terms of S-R bonds, but this view is inadequate unless it can be made to include central affective processes.

An environmental situation, through conditioning, comes to arouse affective processes directly. To illustrate: If a rat is placed upon a piece of apparatus, he learns to respond to the stimulus pattern of his surroundings; but, in addition to the usual S-R patterns, the stimulus situation produces an affective arousal. If there is a positive affective arousal, the whole situation becomes hedonically positive so that the animal comes to react positively to environmental stimulus cues. If the situation is hedonically negative, the environmental stimulus cues come to arouse negative affectivity—call it distress, anxiety, fear, or whatever you will.

There is an internal conditioning of affective processes along with the usual conditioning described in S-R terms. By human analogy it can be said that the animal learns how to *feel* in the situation as well as what cognitive discriminations to make and what acts to perform.

I would postulate that affective conditioning is a contemporary event. Affective arousal does not act retroactively to influence, in some mysterious way, previous acts. The primary affective process is evoked directly, e.g., by the stimulation of pain nerves. Conditioned affective arousals develop according to the principles of frequency and spatiotemporal contiguity.

7. *Affective processes regulate behavior by influencing choice.* Numerous experiments upon the development of food preferences show that the sign and intensity of affective processes influence choice. The development of a food preference between two acceptable foods indicates which food stimulus arouses the more intense affective process.

The acquisition of a preferential discrimination is not an instance of pure learning because affective processes determine whether one preference or its opposite will develop and, further, the relative hedonic intensities associated with two stimuli determine the rate of growth of a preferential pattern.

8. *Neurobehavioral patterns are organized according to the hedonic principle of maximizing the positive and minimizing the negative affective arousal.* This principle has a very wide range of application. It is seen most clearly in situations that involve choice. The stimulus associated with the more intense affective arousal dominates the preferential discrimination.

Functions of Affective Processes

In general, the affective processes have several important functions:

1. Affective processes have *activating* (energizing, driving) functions in that they provoke action. They lead the organism to do something.

Activation is dependent upon sensory stimulation (peripheral) and affective arousal (central). It is difficult to estimate the contributions of the peripheral and central factors. If an organism is painfully stimulated, the activation is dependent upon both the sensory (peripheral) and affective (central) processes. When a naïve rat for the first time tastes a sugar solution he does not appear to be greatly excited by it; but he does come back for more. When an experienced animal is placed in a situation that has repeatedly yielded sweet tastes, he moves promptly to the sugar solution and shows excitement if delayed. The facts suggest that activation comes from proprioceptive tension that is associatively aroused by the stimulus situation and the animal's goal set. Activation thus has a sensory as well as an affective basis.

2. Affective processes have *sustaining and terminating* functions. If the arousal is hedonically positive (like sexual excitement or the appetitive state produced by tasting honey), the induced patterns of behavior are sustained and repeated. If the arousal is hedonically negative (like that produced by electric shock, shrill tones, cold, bright lights, etc.), the induced patterns of behavior terminate the stimulation if possible.

3. Affective processes have *regulative* functions. At least they determine whether appetitive or aversive behavior will develop. They give a primitive kind of evaluation without providing specific information. They act like stop-go lights in traffic control.

4. Affective processes have *organizing* functions in that they lead

to the formation of neurobehavioral patterns which tend to become learned. This organizing of neurobehavioral patterns through subcortical affective arousals is perhaps the chief function of affectivity.

Positive affective arousals tend to facilitate and negative to inhibit activities that were instrumental in producing them. Through a kind of primitive evaluation ("good" or "bad") the organism is oriented towards or against certain kinds and intensities of stimulation. This organizing process is something very basic and widespread throughout nature.

Development of Approach and Withdrawal Behavior

In discussing Pavlov's principle of conditioning and the reflex-circle of Bok, Holt (1931) considered the origin of approach and avoidance patterns. He pointed out that certain reflex responses, e.g., reaching, go out to meet the stimulus, to get more of it. Adopting the terminology of the late Professor Warren, Holt designated these reflexes as *adient*. Adient behavior includes more than simple reflexes that maintain a pattern. Inquiring, examining, grasping, forward pressing, even predatory patterns, are *adient* in the sense that an organism goes out to get more of the stimulus, to approach it. The term *abient* designates reflexes the immediate effect of which is to give the organism less of the exciting stimulus. Behavior patterns that lead to escape, avoidance, removal of the stimulus, are *abient*. The term *abient* literally means turning away from the object and *adient* turning towards the object.

In making his argument, Holt was strictly objective. He deplored terms with subjective implications such as "pleasure" and "pain"—terms found frequently in the works of J. M. Baldwin, Alexander Bain, Herbert Spencer, and other psychologists. Such terms, he wrote, are remnants of the ghost-soul type of psychology, and they have no place in a radical empiricism; they tend only to obscure the basic problems.

Although Holt refused to talk about pleasantness and unpleasantness, he was forced to take account of adience and abience because they are objective facts of observation. Holt pointed out that adient and abient reflexes are organized in the fetus and that they appear later in the infant as reflexes. A moot question in this connection is whether some reactions of approach and withdrawal are dependent upon built-in or truly innate mechanisms. There is considerable evidence that they are.

Schneirla (1959), in a comprehensive review of the problem within comparative psychology, pointed out that there is a biphasic process of approach and withdrawal in all organisms from amoeba to man. He believes that stimulus-intensity is the controlling factor. All organisms, he wrote, tend to react positively to weak stimulation and negatively to intense stimulation.

While there is a good deal of evidence for Schneirla's thesis, I believe that *quality* as well as *intensity* of stimulation must be considered. The stimulus-quality producing a sweet taste, for example, leads to the development of approach *at all intensities*. Also the stimulus-pattern may be important in releasing instinctive acts, as the work of Lorenz, Tinbergen, and other ethologists, has shown. Schneirla, however, would interpret responses to stimulus-pattern in terms of intensity or change of intensity.

Going back now to Holt's view, I think that some principle of behavioral organization, other than Pavlov's principle of conditioning and Bok's principle of the reflex-circle, must be postulated to explain why an organism ever begins to respond so as to receive more of one kind of stimulation and less of another. The built-in bodily mechanisms are such that the taste of sweet leads to development of adient behavior and the taste of bitter to abient. Pain, when intense, leads to development of abience but in all sense departments there are many neutral stimulations that do not lead to approach or withdrawal.

Current research offers hope that some day we may be able to describe the neural mechanisms that regulate growth of adience and abience. In the meantime the growth of adient and abient patterns is a fact of observation. This fact would seem to imply some principle of organization related to affectivity.

CONCLUSION

The construct of affective arousal is supported by facts of human experience and by laboratory observations upon animal behavior. The affective processes can be represented as varying along a bipolar continuum extending from negative, through indifferent, to positive values. Affective processes vary in sign, intensity, and duration.

Affective arousals are motivating in the sense that they evoke action, regulate the course of behavior, and organize patterns of approach and withdrawal. They engender relatively stable systems of value within the organism.

The view that there are two dimensions of arousal—an activating and an hedonic dimension—is supported by physiological studies in electroencephalography and studies upon the physiology of "reward" and "punishment." There are degrees or levels of activation and also degrees of positive and negative hedonic intensity.

Affective processes can be studied objectively and their functions determined. Affective processes have functions of activating behavior, sustaining or terminating activities, regulating the pattern of behavior, and facilitating or inhibiting instrumental acts. The main function of affective processes, however, is that of organizing neurobehavioral patterns of approach and withdrawal or organizing the bodily mechanisms that lead to positive and negative forms of activity.

Reading Suggestions

The older literature on pleasantness and unpleasantness has been reviewed by Beebe-Center (1932). Much of the material in the present chapter on the objective approach to affectivity has been borrowed from a paper by Young (1959). An evolutionary and developmental theory of approach and withdrawal has been presented by Schneirla (1959).

Bindra (1959), in Chapter 8 entitled "Arousal and Behavior," discusses physiological indices of arousal and concludes that the term *arousal* can be usefully employed "only as an abstract label for a variety of measures of physiological functioning." Woodworth and Schlosberg (1954), in Chapter 6, give an excellent account of research with the GSR, along with technical discussion and references.

There is such a wealth of material upon the physiology of activation that a complete bibliography is out of the question. Anyone desiring an introduction to this area of research should see Olds (1955), Lindsley (1957), and a review of the literature on reticular mechanisms and behavior by Samuels (1959).

Beebe-Center, J. G. *The psychology of pleasantness and unpleasantness.* Princeton, N. J.: Van Nostrand, 1932.

Bindra, D. *Motivation, a systematic reinterpretation.* New York: Ronald, 1959.

Lindsley, D. B. Psychophysiology and motivation. In M. R. Jones (Ed.), *Nebraska symposium on motivation 1957.* Lincoln: University of Nebraska Press, 1957.

Olds, J. Physiological mechanisms of reward. In M. R. Jones (Ed.), *Nebraska symposium on motivation 1955.* Lincoln: University of Nebraska Press, 1955.

Samuels, I. Reticular mechanisms and behavior. *Psychol. Bull.,* 1959, **56,** 1–25.

Schneirla, T. C. An evolutionary and developmental theory of biphasic processes underlying approach and withdrawal. In M. R. Jones (Ed.), *Nebraska symposium on motivation 1959.* Lincoln: University of Nebraska Press, 1959.

Woodworth, R. S. and Schlosberg, H. *Experimental psychology.* New York: Holt, 1954.

Young, P. T. The role of affective processes in learning and motivation. *Psychol. Rev.,* 1959, **66,** 104–125.

6 INCENTIVE MOTIVATION

The problem of learning is extremely important, whether we are dealing with man or with insects, but it must not obscure or divert us from the even more fundamental and more general problem of the organizing factor in all behavior.

HENRY W. NISSEN

Within comparative psychology it is customary to distinguish between *drive* and *incentive.* Warden and collaborators regarded drive as an internal organic condition such as hunger or thirst or sexual tension, and incentive as an environmental condition such as the presence of food or water or mate. Drives and incentives, as Calvin Stone once said, are interlocking determinants of behavior. If an animal is satiated, the environmental goal object loses incentive value; but if the drive state is present the goal object furnishes incentive motivation.

It should be pointed out that some psychologists describe "drives" that lack any known organic basis—such as curiosity, exploratory and manipulative and play "drives." But with these "drives" there are environmental conditions that motivate behavior. It seems to me that in the analysis of these "drives" the role of affective processes has been neglected. A major interest in the present chapter is to reinterpret studies of incentive motivation in hedonic terms when this is possible.

Incentives are not always physical objects or things. Thus when a jockey uses the whip or spurs he speeds up the action of his horse. The painful stimulation, if not intense, is an incentive; it liberates energy and speeds up the animal. Again, if a schoolboy is slow in studying his arithmetic lesson, words of praise and rewards speed up perform- ance; they provide incentive motivation.

A distinction is commonly drawn in the literature of human motiva- tion between *intrinsic* and *extrinsic* motivation. If the schoolboy works with interest and zest, if he needs no prodding, he is said to be intrin- sically motivated. If rewards and punishments are required to make him work, these are extrinsic motivations.

The plan of this chapter is quite simple. First we will consider some experiments upon positive incentives and then some upon negative in- centives. After that we will consider the nature of reinforcement and extinction and the relation between incentive motivation and perform- ance. The discussion will show how difficult it is to draw a line of distinction between learning theory and the theory of motivation.

EXPERIMENTS UPON POSITIVE INCENTIVES

In *Motivation of Behavior* (Young, 1936) I reviewed some of the earlier experiments upon reward under the following headings: Appro- priateness of reward; Quantity of reward; Kind and quality of reward; Introduction of reward (latent learning); Removal of reward and the curve of "unlearning"; Symbolic reward; Inadequate reward (tran- sient learning); Delay of reward. These topics have been studied, some of them quite extensively, since 1936. Basic concepts have changed and our knowledge of incentive motivation has been extended.

In the following sections we will examine a few of the more recent developments in the area of "reward" or positive incentives.

The Drive-Incentive Relation

The drive-incentive relationship might be considered equally well under the headings of *drive* and *incentive motivation,* since both or- ganic and environmental factors are involved. It is obvious that for a given drive (such as thirst) a specific incentive (such as water) is ap- propriate and relevant. The relevant incentive is one that reduces or removes the drive state by meeting a need.

Two early studies by M. H. Elliott demonstrated the importance of the drive-incentive relation. In one experiment three groups of rats learned a multiple T-maze. The animals of one group were hungry;

those of another group were thirsty; those of a third group were both hungry and thirsty. For the first 9 days the incentive was food, and for 9 additional days the incentive was water. The shift from food to water changed the relevance of incentive to drive. The curves clearly showed that the performance of thirsty rats improved when the reward was shifted from food (an inappropriate reward) to water (an appropriate reward). The performance of the hungry rats was retarded, as we might expect, by a change from an appropriate reward (food) to an inappropriate one (water).

In another experiment Elliott shifted both the drive and the incentive, but kept the appropriate relationship between drive and incentive. The total shift of motivation produced only a temporary disturbance in the course of learning and performance. The experiment demonstrated that motivation can be shifted without appreciable disturbance in the course of learning if the incentive is kept relevant to the drive. The underlying principle is one which every school teacher knows: A pupil's learning, e.g., of arithmetic, may be continuous when motivating conditions are changed.

More recent studies of the drive-incentive relation have been made to test a postulate in Hull's theoretical system. Hull assumed that the strength of response is a multiplicative function of habit and drive; and that both relevant and irrelevant needs summate to determine the strength of drive (D). Thus if an animal has been deprived of both food and water for 22 hours, his drive state is stronger than if he had been deprived of either food or water alone for the same time. The summated drive state is stronger than the single drive state even though the incentive is irrelevant to one of the drives.

In an experiment by Braun, Wedekind and Smudski (1957) the relevant "drive" was the escape from water and the irrelevant drive was hunger. Rats learned to swim a modified Lashley maze with two temperatures of water. Cold water (15°C) provided a high level of motivation and a temperature approximately that of the body (35°C) provided a low level of motivation. For each temperature there were two groups of animals swimming the maze. One of these swam with 22 hours of food deprivation and the other with 0 hours of food deprivation. There was thus a high and low level of irrelevant drive.

It was found that the addition of a high level of irrelevant drive to both the high and low levels of relevant "drive" resulted in improved performance as measured by the time required to swim the maze and by the elimination of errors. The hungry rats were more highly motivated than the non-hungry and this difference was reflected in a performance that had nothing to do with obtaining food—swimming a maze to escape from the water.

The result suggests that activation is a general phenomenon and not bound up with any specific drive.

Performance and the Quantity of Incentive

After reviewing available evidence upon quantitative variations of incentive, Crespi (1942) carried out a series of well-controlled experiments. His method was to measure the time required for a rat to run down a 20-foot alley from starting box to goal box. By using treadle switches and a photo-cell relay Crespi recorded the time required by the rat to run each 5-foot section of the alley. The starting box was a 1-foot extension of the alley; the goal box was a square enclosure (14 x 14 inches) at the end of the straightaway.

The rats were rewarded for running by uniform pellets of Purina dog biscuit each weighing $\frac{1}{50}$ gram. Different groups of animals found 1, 4, 16, 64, or 256 pellets, respectively, in the goal box. At the time of running, the rats were hungry since they had been deprived of food for 22 hours prior to a test. After a test the animals were fed individually so that all received the same relative quantity per day. The rats receiving 256 pellets in the goal box obtained therefrom about 70 percent of their total daily food allowance; the other groups received correspondingly less of their food allowance in the goal box.

The results of Crespi's work show conclusively that runway performance is significantly related to the amount of food reward in the goal box. Figure 38 shows the average mean speed of running of three groups of rats receiving 256, 64, and 16 pellets, respectively, in the goal box. The graphs indicate that animals receiving the largest reward ran fastest at all stages of learning.

Figure 39 displays the average time in seconds required to run successive 5-foot sections of the alley by groups receiving 1, 4, 16, or 64 pellets of food. These speed-of-locomotion gradients were obtained after twenty practice trials, i.e., on runs 21 to 25. The curves clearly show that the speed-of-locomotion gradient, when animals are approaching their goal in space and time, is a function of the magnitude of reward. Crespi's findings are definite. There is, however, the question of interpretation.

In a subsequent paper Crespi (1944) was mainly concerned with interpretation. He criticized Hull's use of his data on several grounds, especially on the ground that the observed differences in speed of loco-

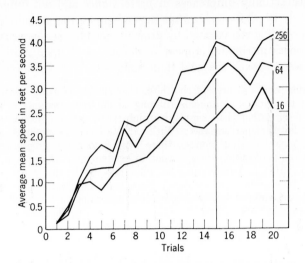

Figure 38. Average mean speed per trial of three groups of rats receiving 256, 64 and 16 pellets of food respectively. *After* Crespi (1942).

Figure 39. Locomotion-time graph, during trials 21–25, for groups of rats running to 1 (top curve) or 4 or 16 or 64 food pellets. *After* Crespi (1942).

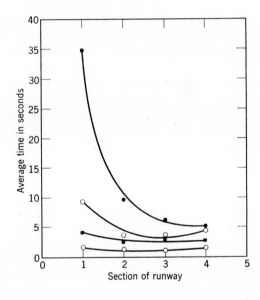

motion are actually differences in *performance* and not differences in *learning*. It is *performance* that depends upon the amount of incentive. *Learning* is represented by growing mastery of the situation but the differences in running appear to depend more upon motivation or an eagerness to reach the goal than upon learning. Crespi continues:

> The writer wishes to present the thesis that *emotional drive* has been varying among the groups of animals running to different amounts of incentive, and this factor rather than simply learning is the major determinant of differences in levels of performance. With varying incentive amounts, after they have been experienced of course, there arise among the groups of animals varying amounts of anticipatory tension or excitement at the prospect of their acquisition. This is a differential of what may be termed *eagerness*. This differential of eagerness, of emotional tension or anticipatory excitement for the various amounts of incentive generates, according to this hypothesis, the differences within each trial in the obtained curves of performance. The larger the incentive amount for which an animal is performing the more eager he is to attain it, i.e., the more emotional drive is summating with his hunger drive to motivate his response. Eagerness is related to learning only in the sense that the animal must find out how much incentive he is obtaining before he exhibits a corresponding amount of eagerness.

In other words, Crespi turns to an internal motivating factor—eagerness or expectancy—in explaining the observed differences in performance. A question can be raised whether this eagerness is related to perceived magnitude of the reward or to the satisfaction obtained from eating the reward. Obviously the "delight" of ingesting 256 pellets is of longer duration than that obtained from ingesting a single pellet! But how about the course of affectivity during continuous eating? With 256 pellets there may be a "warming up" effect in which the initial level of voracity rises, as with the human ingestion of salted nuts and other appetizers. Also with 256 pellets there is an undetermined degree of approach to satiation as the rat continues to eat. Not much is known about these matters but they are closely related to the psychological effects of ingesting different quantities of food reward.

In a minor experiment Crespi reported the effect of suddenly reducing the size of reward. With one group of rats the reward was reduced from 16 pellets to 1 pellet; with another group it was changed from 16 pellets to 4 pellets; with still another group from 16 pellets to 0 pellets. He found that when there was a shift down to 1 pellet the speed of locomotion was *slower* than when the shift was to 0 pellets. Crespi speculated that a single pellet whetted the appetite of the rat and then frustrated him by offering such a small amount. A reward of 0 did not whet the appetite and was, therefore, less frustrating.

It is reasonable to assume that the effect of frustration varies with the strength of the motive frustrated. Under some circumstances frustration may facilitate performance and under other circumstances it may inhibit. The effect of changing the magnitude of reward is a matter in need of further study.

Hull's Postulate about the Amount of Incentive and Stimulus Intensity

In the *Principles of Behavior,* Hull (1943) published a chapter entitled: *Habit Strength as a Function of the Nature and Amount of the Reinforcing Agent.* In this chapter he presented data from Gantt upon the amount of conditioned salivary secretion in dogs as related to the number of grams of food offered as reinforcing agent; and further data from Grindley upon the rate of running as related to the number of grains of boiled rice offered as an incentive. Both sets of data demonstrate that performance is an increasing function of the amount of reward presented to the subject. Hull concludes that *"habit strength at the limit of practice (m) will vary with the quality, as well as the quantity, of the reinforcing agent from a minimum of zero to a physi-. ological maximum of 100 habs, and that the rate of approach to that limit (F) will remain unchanged."*

In the *Essentials of Behavior,* Hull (1951) took account of the careful work of Crespi upon the quantitative variation of incentive as related to running performance in the white rat. He stated that reaction potential involves an incentive component, K. Hull arrived at the following postulate: "The incentive function (K) is a negatively accelerated increasing monotonic function of the weight (w) of food given as reinforcement, . . ." Thus, Hull expressed the incentive function in terms of the weight of food offered as a reward.

In the same work he introduced another factor (V), designated as *stimulus-intensity dynamism,* which factor is a component of the reaction potential. Hull arrived at this postulate: "Other things constant, the magnitude of the stimulus-intensity component (V) of reaction potential $(_sE_r)$ is a monotonic increasing logarithmic function of S (stimulus intensity or energy) . . . ."

In his *Principles of Behavior,* Hull stated that the reaction evocation potential is the product of a function of habit strength multiplied by a function of the strength of drive:

$$_sE_r = f(_sH_r) \times f(D)$$

In his most recent book, *A Behavior System*, Hull (1952) presented a modified equation:

$$_sE_r = D \times V_1 \times K \times {_sH_r}$$

The corresponding postulate upon the constitution of reaction potential became: "The reaction potential ($_sE_r$) of a bit of learned behavior at any given stage of learning, where conditions are constant throughout learning and response-evocation, is determined (1) by the drive (D) operating during the learning process multiplied (2) by the dynamism of the signaling stimulus trace (V_1), (3) by the incentive reinforcement (K) and (4) by the habit strength ($_sH_r$), ..."

Other modifications in Hull's postulational system need not concern us here. Our point is that Hull originally regarded the reaction potential as a multiplicative function of two factors: habit strength and drive. Later he introduced two other determinants of reaction potential: stimulus-intensity dynamism and incentive reinforcement. Thus there are *three* motivational determinants of reaction potential (D, V, K) along with habit strength ($_sH_r$).

A weakness of Hull's system is that it is limited by the framework of stimulus-response psychology and nowhere does it take account adequately of centrally aroused affective processes. An affective arousal cannot be identified either with a stimulus or with a response. Certainly, stimulus intensity and hedonic intensity cannot be equated. (See pages 154–156.) And it is unclear how Hull's postulated determinants relate to objective hedonic processes.

Again, Hull thinks of "amount of reinforcement" in terms of the weight of food presented or the number of grains of boiled rice offered or the number of food pellets in the goal box. Elsewhere I pointed out that the quantity of food presented (or ingested) is an inadequate measure of motivation. (See pages 156–158.) Physical measurements of the incentive objects are necessary to specify experimental conditions but such measurements are not a substitute for direct analysis of bodily processes, including affective arousals.

Perception of Size as a Determinant of Performance

In the light of Crespi's careful study no one can gainsay the fact that the level of performance varies with the physical quantity of reward presented. But it may be necessary to distinguish between the quantity of food *perceived* by the subject and the quantity *ingested*.

Dyal (1960) performed an experiment to test the hypothesis that the *perception* of magnitude is a determinant of performance. He trained hungry rats to run down a straightaway, timing their latency (delay before leaving the starting box) and their speed of locomotion down a 5-foot alley. On half of the trials the animals ran from a black starting box to a *large* reward (250 grams of food) in a black goal box; on the other half they ran from a white starting box to a *small* reward (5 grams of food) in a white goal box. Thus the large reward was associated with black and the small reward with white. For a control group these colors were reversed. The runway itself was always black.

A crucial point in the design of Dyal's experiment was that regardless of the quantity of food presented in the goal box during a given run all animals were confined to the goal box for the same time—30 seconds. Since 30 seconds does not allow sufficient time for a rat to consume even the small reward, the essential difference between the two experimental conditions must lie in the *perception* of the size of reward rather than in the *quantity of food consumed*.

Dyal found that after one hundred trials the latencies differed significantly with *perceived* size of reward. The rats left the starting box more promptly when running to a large reward than when running to a small reward. Also, on a test for extinction, there was a significant difference in latencies between runs to an empty "large-reward" box and runs to an empty "small-reward" box.

The findings suggest that perception of size may determine behavior independently of the quantity of food consumed. This means that the motive of running to a large reward is prepotent over the motive of running to a small reward when opportunity to ingest the food is held constant. In other words, the strength of a motive to approach may be, in part, determined by the *perceived* magnitude of the reward.

Frequency of Primary Reward and Secondary Reinforcement

One factor that has an obvious relation to behavior is the frequency of primary reward, or reinforcement. In an experiment by Hall (1951a) the frequency of primary reinforcement was the main variable. Primary reinforcement was studied in relation to the strength of secondary reinforcement.

During preliminary training rats learned to associate a color with satisfaction of the thirst drive and another color with absence of satisfaction. All animals were thirsty. They ran down a neutral gray straightaway to a goal box of distinctive color. Half of the rats were allowed to sip water for 20 seconds in a *white* goal box and the other half in a *black* goal box. In five out of eight runs the water-containing goal box with positive color was at the end of the straightaway; in three out of eight runs the rats entered an empty goal box of negative color.

Three groups of animals were run down the straightaway until they had been rewarded 25, 50, and 75 times, respectively. The frequency of reward was thus varied while other conditions were held constant.

After this training animals were tested in a T-maze. Each rat was given a choice between running to a *white* goal box or running to a *black* goal box. During the test the boxes remained in fixed positions. Since both goal boxes were empty, there was no primary reinforcement; but the color of the box provided secondary reinforcement. Each rat was given a series of fifteen runs in the T-maze with the same degree of thirst that was present during the training period. An animal's score was the number of choices of the goal box of positive color in the series of fifteen runs. It was recognized, of course, that the early runs to the empty goal box would lead to learning because of the secondary reinforcement from the color; and that later runs to the empty goal box would lead to extinction.

The score (mean number of runs to empty goal box in fixed position) indicates a marked dependence of performance upon the number of primary reinforcements. The data are presented graphically in Figure 40. Incidentally, the data show that the rats running to a black box made higher scores than those running to a white box; but our main concern is not with this fact. Regardless of the color of the box, the data indicate a positive relation between the number of primary reinforcements and performance when the box of a certain color is used as secondary reinforcement, or reward.

In a further experiment Hall (1951b) confirmed the above result under conditions of varying strength of drive. He trained and tested two groups of rats. One group was trained with a 6-hour thirst drive and the other with a 22-hour thirst drive. Both groups were tested with a 22-hour thirst drive.

The data confirmed the above result. The strength of secondary reinforcement varied directly with the number of primary reinforcements. Variation in the strength of thirst drive during the training period, therefore, made no significant difference in the strength of secondary reinforcement. The finding is in agreement with Hull's postulate that habit strength is independent of the strength of drive originally present during learning. It agrees with the view that learning is a function of practice alone.

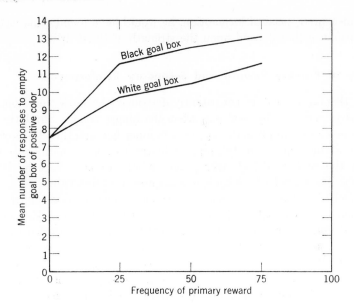

Figure 40. Empirical curves showing the strength of secondary reinforcement as a function of the number of primary reinforcements. The line extending from zero to 25 reinforcements is extrapolated. *Plotted from* data by Hall (1951a).

The results of these experiments can be readily interpreted from the point of view of hedonic theory. Two points are worthy of note:

First, it is doubtful whether sipping water in the goal box for 20 seconds would allow sufficient time for reduction of the thirst drive. If one assumes that the thirst drive was reduced during this 20-second period, then the hedonic change would be one of relief—a change away from negative affectivity. It is more likely that thirst raised the incentive value of the water reward. In this event the sipping of water would elicit a positive hedonic change instead of relief. The positive hedonic change would be immediate. In any event the hedonic change would organize an approach motive since it was a change in the positive direction.

Second, Hall's reliance upon the number of choices of white (or black) box in the T-maze gives a good measure of *learning* rather than *performance*. The rats learned to associate a particular color with hedonic change in the positive direction; the color acquired incentive value and functioned as a secondary reward, or reinforcement. If Hall had measured speed of locomotion, he would have found differences in performance that depend upon the strength of thirst drive.

Delay of Primary Reward and Secondary Reinforcement

If the family cat is consistently fed near the back doorstep, she learns to come to the food pan when the hinges creak. Similarly if a rat has learned to press the bar of a Skinner box and then to receive a pellet of food in the metal cup, he learns to approach the cup if he hears the click of the electromagnet and the rattle of a pellet in the chute. Thus incidental sounds can acquire incentive value.

Bugelski (1938) argued that the sounds which precede appearance of food are "subgoals"; they are secondary reinforcers. He demonstrated that the extinction of a bar-pressing habit is retarded by incidental sounds associated with food. In his experiment two groups of rats were given equivalent training in bar pressing. The bar-pressing habit was then extinguished under different conditions for the two groups. With one group, pressure upon the bar produced the usual click but no food. With the other group, pressure upon the bar produced neither click nor food. Bugelski found that the bar-pressing response was extinguished more slowly in animals that heard the click than in those that did not hear the click. Animals that heard the click made over 30 percent more responses than those that did not hear the click. The sounds, therefore, retarded extinction; they had an acquired, or secondary, incentive value.

This acquired incentive value depends upon the time interval between incidental sounds and contact with food. This was shown in an experiment by Jenkins (1950). He arranged Skinner boxes so that a small amount of food powder could be placed in the cup from outside the cage. During preliminary training a damped house buzzer was sounded for three seconds. The buzz was followed by a delay interval and then by presentation of a small amount of food powder in the cup. The interval of delay between buzz and primary reward was 1, 3, 9, 27, and 81 seconds, respectively, for five groups of rats. Each buzz-food pair was considered a trial. Trials were at the rate of ten per day, randomized in time, until seventy to a hundred eating responses had occurred following the buzz. Incomplete trials, when a rat failed to eat, were not counted.

The preliminary training associated buzz with food. After this training, a bar was introduced and the apparatus arranged so that when a rat pressed the bar a buzz was produced but the buzz was never fol-

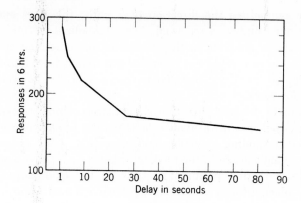

Figure 41. Mean number of bar-pressing responses to a buzz, in 6 hours, as a function of the delay in seconds between buzz and food during the training series. *Plotted from* data by Jenkins (1950).

lowed by food in the cup. Rats were tested individually for twelve ½-hour sessions, a total of 6 hours. Bar pressing was automatically recorded.

Qualitative observations of behavior revealed several overlapping stages. When the bar was introduced there was at first considerable exploration of the modified apparatus. This stage was followed by learning to press the bar and produce the buzz which had acquired incentive value. Then there was a stage of extinction since bar pressing never produced food. Finally, there was a stable but low level of bar pressing—a base line of behavior for each subject.

The mean frequency of bar pressing for the five groups of animals is shown in Figure 41. The graph reveals at a glance that the total frequency of bar pressing for the buzz alone was inversely related to the interval of delay of the primary reward.

The experiment is a good illustration of secondary reinforcement, or acquired incentive value. It shows that the effectiveness of a secondary reward is dependent upon the interval of delay between foresignal (buzz) and primary reward (food).

Symbolic Reward—Studies with Chimps and Chips

A symbol is a sign or object which stands for something else. The dinner bell symbolizes a forthcoming meal; a wooden hand with pointing finger symbolizes the direction of a path; the stars and stripes symbolize our country; a red traffic light symbolizes "STOP." A coin or pay check is symbolic in that it stands for something else that is valued. If the coin could not be exchanged for food or clothing or entertainment or something else that is valued, it would be useless as an incentive for work.

Wolfe (1936) demonstrated that chimpanzees can be trained to work for a token (poker chip) provided the token can be exchanged for food. He devised a vending machine, or "chimpomat," that automatically delivered a single grape to the food cup when a poker chip was inserted in the slot. During preliminary training the chimpanzees readily learned to place a token in the slot and receive a food reward. During the training period, the experimenter controlled the vending machine so that when the animal inserted a *brass* token, no food appeared, but a *white* token invariably produced a food reward. Under these conditions the animals learned to discriminate between brass and white tokens.

Wolfe also devised an apparatus that required the chimp to work for his pay! To obtain a reward the animal had to lift a weight. He could reach between two rods of his cage and grasp the handle of a lever. When the lever was moved from the horizontal to vertical position the reward was brought so near to the cage that the animal could reach it; but this required lifting a weight attached by cord to the lever. The reward might be a grape or a token that could be placed in the vending machine to produce a grape.

Wolfe found that three of his four chimps worked almost as well for the token as for the grape. He then carried out several experiments using token rewards. Several of these will be reviewed briefly because they throw light upon the nature of incentive motivation.

One experiment was concerned with the incentive value of different kinds of tokens. During the experiment Wolfe controlled the "chimpomat" so that if the animal inserted a dark blue chip in the slot, he was rewarded with *two* grapes; if he inserted a white chip, he was rewarded with *one* grape. All grapes were large and as uniform in size as possible.

The animals were offered a choice among three tokens: white, blue, brass. They had previously learned that brass tokens brought no reward and so they selected white. The next choice was between blue and brass. When it was found that a blue token produced two grapes a preference for blue tokens developed. The following tabulation shows the number of times blue tokens were selected in succcssive testing sessions of ten trials each:

Subject	Sessions of Ten Trials Each											
	1	2	3	4	5	6	7	8	9	10	11	12
Bon	0	0	3	8	10	10	10					
Velt	0	4	6	10	10	10						
Alpha	0	0	0	0	2	4	2	7	8	10	10	10

The initial preference for a white token was supplanted by a preference for a blue token as the animals learned that two grapes, instead of one, could be obtained regularly by inserting the blue chip into the vending machine. The symbolic rewards acquired a value proportional to the quantity of food they produced.

Another experiment was concerned with the relation between incentive value and organic state. Prior to the critical tests the chimps were trained to receive two peanuts when a *black* chip was placed in the slot and to receive a small quantity of water when a *yellow* chip was used. The apparatus was modified so that when the experimenter closed a switch a lid opened, making available a cup containing approximately ½ gill of water. The experimenter presented the water whenever the chimp inserted a yellow chip in the vending machine.

After the preliminary training the animals were deprived of food or water and again tested to discover the effect of hunger or thirst upon the preference. Wolfe found, in fact, that chimpanzees learned to select tokens appropriately; when hungry they selected black tokens and when thirsty, yellow. The incentive value of a token, therefore, can be varied by changing the organic state.

In other experiments Wolfe studied various methods of delaying the reward. He required the animals to work for a group of tokens before expending any of them. He found that the more tokens an animal had earned the fewer additional tokens he would work to secure! It was as if a human laborer quit the job when he had accumulated enough dollars to meet his immediate needs!

Wolfe also delayed the reward by forcing the chimp to wait for the food after he had deposited the chip in the vending machine. He found that the chips lost incentive value if the animal was forced to delay about 2 minutes between insertion of the token and reception of food. For a token to retain its effectiveness the food reward must appear promptly after the token has been placed in the slot. Any delay or irregularity in the appearance of the food lowered incentive value.

Incidentally, Wolfe found that the animals would compete for tokens as they compete to obtain food. One subject begged for tokens!

In short, Wolfe's study shows: (1) that tokens can function as surrogate rewards; (2) that in some situations tokens can motivate the animal almost as effectively as food rewards; (3) that chimpanzees show preferences among tokens according to their reward values; (4) that the value of a token can vary with the organic states of hunger and thirst.

Subsequently, Cowles (1937) verified Wolfe's findings and greatly extended the study of symbolic rewards. He confirmed Wolfe's finding that chimpanzees readily perform work for tokens that are exchangeable for food; and that they work not only for single tokens that are immediately exchangeable but they can be trained to work for ten to thirty tokens exchangeable as a group after they are obtained singly.

Cowles demonstrated that tokens can be used to maintain a high level of motivation in the day-to-day performance of laboratory tasks. He showed that chimpanzees will carry out a wide variety of tasks, that are of interest to psychologists, when the only reward is a token. He utilized token rewards in studies of learning—learning simple position habits, learning complex five-choice position habits, learning visual discriminations of size, learning visual discriminations of color patterns, and making delayed responses.

The uniqueness of the token, Cowles points out, lies in its object characteristics, its manipulability, its potentiality as a source of maintained motivation, and especially in the fact that it must be given up or exchanged for a primary goal. These properties give tokens great effectiveness in studies of acquisition and extinction.

A token can be used to motivate behavior not previously associated with it. The chimp will solve a new problem for a token reward just as the human subject will memorize a lot of nonsense syllables if he is paid for his time. For a token to be maximally effective the chimp must be able to exchange it for an immediate and invariable food reward.

The experiment has some bearing upon the theory of economic value. Does the value of money lie in the fact that it can be exchanged for some commodity that is wanted? The experiments with the "chimpomat" indicate an affirmative answer. A case in point, on the human level, is that of green stamps. Certain stores offer green stamps with purchases; others do not. The number of green stamps is related to the size of the purchase. The green stamps are saved and exchanged for various commodities. People tend to trade at the stores that offer the stamps. Why? It can be argued that the green stamps are valued because they can be exchanged for things that are wanted. If it were suddenly announced that green stamps could no longer be exchanged for anything, their value would disappear. The incentive value of the stamps rests upon the fact that they can be exchanged for something wanted.

The value of the stamps and of the token is within the organism. It rests upon past experience. Tokens that produce nothing lack incentive value.*

EXPERIMENTS UPON NEGATIVE INCENTIVES

The fundamental fact about "punishment" is a negative affective arousal that leads the animal to avoid or escape. Although there are many conditions that produce negative affective arousals, most laboratory research has relied upon the electric shock as a source of distress.

The following sections give only a sample of the rich experimental literature upon negative incentives. One interest in considering these studies is to discover how adequately the facts can be interpreted in terms of negative affective arousals.

Measuring the Strength of Negative Incentives

Techniques for the quantitative study of negative incentives have not been well worked out. The general plan seems to be one of working with drives and approach behavior and then of inhibiting the approach motive by a negative incentive. Two examples are the following:

1. Dr. Phil S. Shurrager (personal communication) tackled the practical problem of finding a repellent substance that would prevent wild rats from attacking cord, paper sacks, food containers, and other objects. Such repellents have obvious commercial value.

In solving this problem Dr. Shurrager developed an apparatus con-

* In this connection see the discussion of incentive value and affective processes on pages 169–171.

sisting of a series of compartments interconnected by doors. To open a door the rat had to gnaw through a piece of twine. When the twine broke the door automatically opened and the rat could enter the next compartment and obtain a bit of food. After eating the food the animal could gnaw through another piece of twine and open the door to the next compartment where there was a bit of food, and so on. The rats were hungry and readily learned to gnaw through twine to reach food.

After preliminary training, tests were run with twine that had been treated with various chemical substances. When a substance was repellent the rats showed this by aversive behavior. Upon making contact with the twine they did not gnaw and avoided it even though hungry. Many different repellent substances were discovered by this method. The time required for a rat to gnaw through the twine and open the door was automatically recorded and the strength of the negative incentive was measured by the latency between entrance to a compartment and completion of gnawing through the twine.

2. Another possible approach to the problem of measuring the strength of negative incentives is through combining negative and positive incentives and observing their interaction. For example, this writer has experimented with compound taste solutions that contain two solutes: sucrose and quinine hydrochloride. Simple solutions of sucrose at all concentrations are hedonically positive; simple solutions of quinine hydrochloride at moderate concentrations are negative. The combination of the two solutes gives a compound solution that may be either positive or negative depending upon the concentrations. By exploring the bittersweet area of taste sensation, with the preference method, it is possible to study the interaction of positive and negative incentives. The method may eventually be developed for measuring the strength of negative incentives.

The use of quinine to inhibit ingestion recalls the method employed by Neal Miller (1956) that was described on page 168.

Psychological Effects of the Electric Shock

In interpreting results from experiments employing electric shocks we should keep in mind the fact that a shock can have different psychological effects depending upon its intensity and whether or not it is associated with goal-oriented behavior. A weak shock can convey information, telling a subject that he is right or wrong; in this respect a weak shock is like any other sensory stimulation. A moderate shock

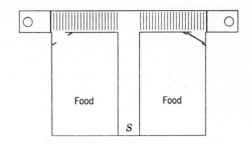

Figure 42. T-maze discrimination box. *After* Muenzinger
(1934).

can alert the organism and serve as a negative incentive; it is something to be avoided. An intense shock can disturb and even disrupt
purposive activity.

Some of these effects are illustrated by experiments of Muenzinger
(1934) and Muenzinger and Wood (1935) in which rats were shocked
for making *right* or *wrong* choices in a T-maze and in which rats were
shocked *before* and *after* making their choices.

A diagram of Muenzinger's apparatus is shown in Figure 42. It is
a simple T-maze with grid upon the floor of the right and left alleys.
At the end of both alleys are doors that open into food compartments.
The doors are so placed that a rat at the choice point cannot see
whether a door is closed or open. At the end of each alley is a ground
glass shield behind which is a light. The starting place is at *S*.

In the first experiment rats were trained to run to the lighted end of
the maze. The door to the food compartment was always open at the
lighted end and closed at the dark end. All animals were hungry and
there were crumbs of cheese present on the floors of both food compartments.

Three groups of rats (twenty-five in each group) learned to run the
maze under the following conditions. The rats of one group were
shocked when they made the correct choice of pathway (shock-right
group). The rats of a second group were shocked when they made an
incorrect choice (shock-wrong group). The rats of a third group
served as a control since their sole motivation consisted of hunger combined with an incentive of the cheese crumbs (no-shock group).

All the subjects were run to a criterion of two consecutive daily
series each of ten errorless trials.

The error scores for the three groups, plotted cumulatively, are
shown in Figure 43. The curves indicate that performance of the
no-shock group was inferior to that of the groups receiving shocks.
The best performance was from the shock-wrong group. The shock-

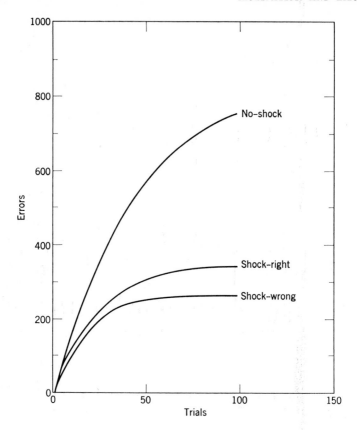

Figure 43. Cumulative error scores for shock-wrong, shock-right and no-shock groups of rats. *After* Muenzinger (1934).

wrong group, however, was only slightly superior to the shock-right group; and the difference between these two groups was not quite significant statistically.

In general, Muenzinger's experiment demonstrated that an electric shock, of the intensity used, facilitated maze performance; but it made little difference whether the shock was given for the right or the wrong choice. This result is impressive because the electric shocks were of moderate intensity and might have disrupted behavior. Instead they facilitated the goal-directed activity.

In a follow-up experiment a grid was placed in the central runway of the maze so that rats could be given a shock *before* selecting a path to the food. Two additional groups of twenty-five rats each were run

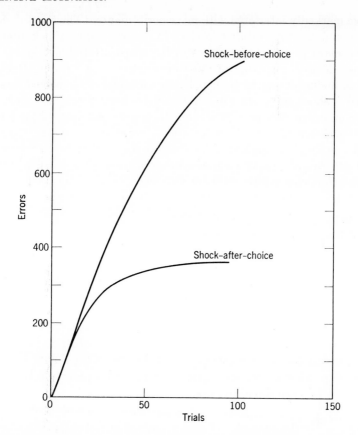

Figure 44. Cumulative error scores for shock-before-choice and shock-after-choice groups of rats. *After* Muenzinger and Wood (1935).

under the same conditions of motivation and training, i.e., all animals were hungry and were rewarded with cheese crumbs; all were trained to turn into the lighted alley.

The animals in one of the additional groups were given a shock before they selected the right or left alley (shock-before-choice group). There was no shock after the choice. The animals in the other group were given a shock after choice (shock-after-choice group). As a matter of fact, the grids in both right and left alleys were continuously charged so that animals were shocked in traversing the path whether they made a right or a wrong choice. They were shocked on every run.

The cumulative error scores for these two additional groups are given in Figure 44. One clear result is that a shock administered *before* choice markedly interfered with maze performance. The shock-before-choice animals were inferior to those in the original no-shock group.

The maze performance of rats in the shock-after-choice group was almost identical with that of those in the shock-right group. Relative to this finding it should be noted that the shock-after-choice rats received a shock on every run while the shock-right rats approached a shock on every trial as a limit since they were not shocked for errors. The shock-wrong rats, by contrast, received less and less frequent shocks as they approached the asymptote of errorless performance.

In general, Muenzinger's follow-up experiment demonstrated that a shock before choice disrupts maze performance and a shock after choice (when the rats are running to food) facilitates performance.

Acquisition of an Avoidance Motive

Numerous experiments have been made in which electric shock was used as a negative incentive. An example of this kind of work is the much discussed experiment of N. Miller (1948) in which rats learned to avoid a compartment in which they had been shocked.

Miller's apparatus is pictured in Figure 45. It consists of two compartments, one with a grill on the floor and the other with no grill. As an aid to the rat in distinguishing these compartments the one with a grill is painted white and the one with no grill is painted black. The compartments are separated by a doorway and the door has a distinctive black and white marking. The door can be opened by the experimenter or by the subject. If closed, the rat can open it by moving a roller above the door or by pressing a bar that projects from the wall at the left of the door. When the apparatus is properly adjusted one of these instrumental acts closes a circuit that drops the door.

In the first stage of the experiment a rat was placed in the apparatus, with open door, and allowed to explore. He explored both compartments without discernible preference between them.

In the second stage of the experiment a rat was placed on the grill of the white compartment and the door was closed. He was then given a shock and the experimenter opened the door. During a series of ten trials all animals learned to run into the black compartment. The door was then closed and after 30 seconds the rat was lifted out of the apparatus.

In the third stage of the experiment, for a series of five trials, a rat was placed on the grill with door closed. No shock was given.

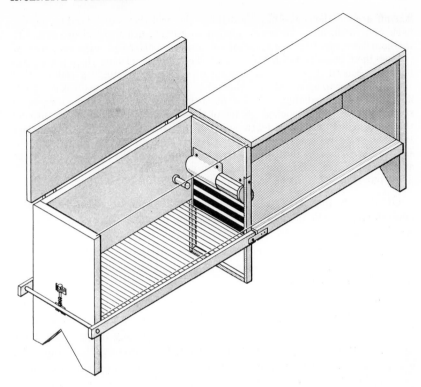

Figure 45. Apparatus for studying fear as an acquired drive. *Courtesy* Neal Miller.

The experimenter always opened the door before the rat reached it. In these non-shock trials the rats continued to run from the white to the black compartment. Each rat was left in the black compartment for 30 seconds, with door closed, and then removed.

In the fourth stage of the experiment a rat was placed in the white compartment and no shock was administered. The purpose of these non-shock trials was to discover whether the rat would learn to turn the roller above the door or to press the bar at the left of the door in order to escape from the white to the black compartment.

Miller described the behavior of the rats in this situation as follows:

When the procedure of the non-shock trials was changed so that the *E* no longer dropped the door and it could only be opened by moving the wheel, the animals displayed variable behavior which tended to be concentrated in the region of the door. They would stand up in front of it, place their paws upon it, sniff around the edges, bite the bars of the grid they were standing on, run back and forth, etc. They also tended to crouch, urinate, and defecate. In the course of this behavior some of the animals performed responses, such as poking their noses between the bars of the wheel or placing their paws upon it, which caused it to move a fraction of a turn and actuate a contact that caused the door to open. Most of them then ran through into the black compartment almost immediately. A few of them drew back with an exaggerated startle response and crouched. Some of these eventually learned to go through the door; a few seemed to learn to avoid it. Other animals abandoned their trial-and-error behavior before they happened to strike the wheel and persisted in crouching so that they had to be lifted out of the white compartment at the end of the 100-second period. In general, the animals that had to be lifted out seemed to crouch sooner and sooner on successive trials.

Of the twenty-five subjects, thirteen learned to turn the wheel enough to drop the door and thus to escape into the black compartment. After they had learned to turn the wheel, conditions were changed so that only pressing the bar would open the door. With this change of conditions the wheel-turning behavior extinguished and the bar-pressing pattern developed.

Miller argues that the fear of the white compartment is an acquired drive and that learning to turn the roller or to press the bar was caused by a reduction in the acquired fear drive. Obviously no primary drive (painful stimulation) was present during the course of learning. An escape from the grill compartment into the safe compartment reduces the acquired fear. This constitutes a reward which reinforces the instrumental acts leading to escape.

Critique of "fear as an acquired drive." No one can object to the factual findings of Miller's experiment; they are definite and clear cut. One can object, however, to the theoretical interpretations and to definition of terms.

The terms *fear* and *drive* are a source of confusion. There are several meanings of fear. According to one view, fear is an acute affective disturbance characterized by such responses as crouching, trembling, urinating, defecating, and internal visceral changes. Of Miller's twenty-five rats, only thirteen learned to turn the wheel; the others crouched or were so inhibited that they did not learn. It would seem that fear, in this sense of the word, was present in the situation that had previously produced pain. According to another view, fear is a highly activated pattern of organized behavior in which the animal avoids or escapes from a threatening situation. In the second stage of Miller's experiment about half of the rats learned instrumental acts that made it possible for them to escape from the white to the black compartment. According to still another view, which has been expressed by Mowrer and Miller, "fear" has an aspect of anticipation or expectancy. Perhaps *anxiety* would be a better word for this. A human subject who anticipates pain or failure or humiliation is said to have anxiety. Similarly, Miller's rats, during the non-shock trials, were "anxious" in a threatening situation.

Miller thinks of drive along Hullian lines, within the framework of a stimulus-response psychology. Elsewhere, Miller (1951) stated that learnable drives are strong stimuli produced by responses.

These views concerning the nature of drive and learning can be criticized on several counts:

In the first place, some psychologists think of drives as innate determinants of behavior. Drives may be chemical factors that activate the nervous system or that facilitate behavior by lowering response thresholds. With this definition of drive it is nonsense to talk about "acquired drives" and "learnable drives." Instrumental acts that lead to approach or avoidance, of course, are learned; but they are more appropriately called motives or, perhaps, habits.

In the second place, the concept of reinforcement through drive reduction is unsatisfactory for reasons which will be considered elsewhere. (See pages 246–248.) And the view that instrumental acts are reinforced by reduction of a fear drive is tenuous.

In the third place, Miller's S-R concept of drive disregards affective arousals. An electric shock on the feet of a rat produces pain (sensory) and also distress (affective). The distinction rests upon facts of experience and cannot safely be ignored.

In reinterpreting the facts I would assume that a painful shock on the feet produced a negative affective arousal of moderate (but unknown) intensity. Since this negative affective arousal occurred in the white compartment, many sensory cues from the walls, the floor, previous manipulations by the experimenter, etc., were associated with a primary affective process. The animal's responses to the shock— squealing, jumping, urinating, defecating, crouching, trembling, etc.— indicated an autonomic involvement characteristic of negative affective arousals. Through conditioning, these overt responses and associated negative hedonic processes became attached to the environmental stimulus cues. After conditioning, these external stimulus cues evoked the central affective processes and the associated responses in vegetative and skeletal systems.

Now whether the distress is produced directly by the shock or secondarily by associated stimulus cues it has certain properties. One of these properties is that an animal will organize or reorganize any pattern of behavior that reduces or avoids distress.

This explanation in terms of conditioned affective arousals substitutes "organization through distress reduction" for "reinforcement through drive reduction." The difference is more than verbal. For one thing, the hedonic hypothesis takes account of positive organization and reorganization that occurs in absence of any pre-existing drive. There is a positive *production* of motives which are not acquired through drive reduction.

In summary, Miller's facts of observation are interesting and important but I would reinterpret them. (1) The definition of fear is ambiguous and confusing. (2) The view that drive is a purposive determination that can be acquired through learning is out of line with the biochemical theory of drive. (3) The interpretation of behavior in terms of stimulus and response does not take account of central affective arousals. (4) The view that reinforcement through drive reduction leads to learning is inadequate and must be abandoned in favor of an hedonic interpretation.

Intensity of Distress and Speed of Bar Pressing

Miller (1951) described an experiment in which groups of rats were given different strengths of electric shock to establish "fear" of the compartment in which the shock was given. Following the initial shock there were two days of testing without shock. During these days the rats learned to escape from the compartment by pressing a bar.

The speed of bar pressing on successive non-shock trials is shown in Figure 46. The graph indicates that the rats previously shocked with 540 volts pressed the bar faster than those previously shocked with 180 volts. In other words, the speed of bar pressing—an instrumental act leading to escape—is related to the strength of shock originally used to establish "fear."

The interpretation of this fact in hedonic terms is quite simple. The intensity of distress produced by an electric shock is proportional to the voltage. Whether the negative affective process is produced primarily by the shock or secondarily by environmental cues associated with the shock this negative affective process organizes and facilitates behavior leading to escape from the distress-producing situation. The

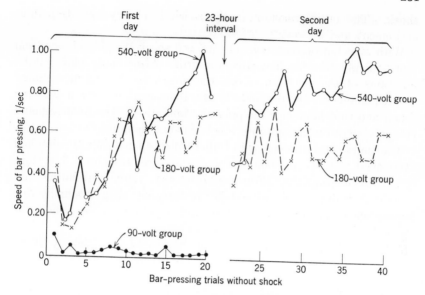

Figure 46. Speed of bar pressing without shock following previous stimulation with shocks of 540 and 180 volts. *After* Neal Miller (1951).

curves demonstate a quantitative relation between intensity of distress and speed of bar pressing.

Affective Arousal and Conditioning

In a motion-picture film, entitled *Motor Conditioning in Dogs,* Professor E. K. Culler has pictured the course of development of an adaptive response through conditioning.* The film shows a dog harnessed to a frame, of the Bechterev type, with front paw resting upon a grill. The animal is within a soundproof room.

Under laboratory conditions a tone is sounded and then a painful shock given to the foot. The dog's initial response to the shock is highly emotional. The animal yelps, makes diffuse movements as if struggling to escape from the situation, and occasionally urinates. During this emotional excitement the dog somehow manages to get his foot off the charged grill and thus to terminate the painful electric

* The film is distributed by the C. H. Stoelting Company, 424 North Homan Ave., Chicago 24, Illinois.

shock. The initial reaction to the shock is clearly one of painful excitement and distress.

With repeated presentations of tone and shock the animal more and more quickly lifts his foot from the grill. After many paired presentations of the tone and shock the dog lifts his foot in a calm, assured manner. He responds to the tone as if it were a warning signal and thus he avoids the painful stimulation. The final response is highly adaptive and entirely free from emotional upset.

The course of development in Culler's dog is from diffuse emotional excitement to a specific non-emotional, adaptive response. The signs of emotion—struggling, diffuse motor activity, yelping, urinating—are present only during the early stages of learning; these gradually disappear when the problem is solved and a pain-avoiding response is learned.

What would happen if the dog could not avoid the shock by lifting his foot? Suppose the animal invariably received a shock following an auditory signal and that no response of the animal could possibly avoid the painful stimulation. Would the emotional response continue indefinitely?

Laboratory tests made by Dr. Donald W. Lauer (personal communication) have shown that if the dog receives an auditory signal followed by a shock which he cannot escape, there are at first signs of emotional disturbance: yelping, struggling, and sometimes urination. If the situation is repeated, the animal eventually becomes non-emotional so far as outward appearances go. There may be internal changes in muscular tension or blood pressure when the warning signal is given but outwardly the dog appears to be calm when the signal and the shock are presented.

This result may indicate that when no adaptive response is possible there may be an affective adaptation. The animal learns simply to tolerate the shock—to take it in an outwardly calm manner.

In any event the emotional disturbance is characteristic of the early stages of learning and it tends gradually to disappear with repetition of the situation. There is affective adaptation whether or not an adaptive response can be learned.

Conditioned Affective Arousal

Solomon and Brush (1956) have made a critical review of the literature upon conditioning that is related to avoidance and escape.

Their discussion and bibliography constitute a useful introduction to this area of research.

They point out that although various kinds of aversive stimuli (bright lights, loud sounds, bitter tastes, extremes of temperature, etc.) are available, most research has employed electric shocks. The electric shock applied to the skin is a reliable aversive stimulus for mammalian species. In dogs, cats, rats, and other mammals, the onset of electric shock is usually accompanied by vigorous diffuse response or else by immobility. There are such accompaniments as high-pitched vocalization, piloerection, urination and defecation, gasping, drooling, trembling, pupillary dilation, and a host of internal bodily changes produced by an augmented autonomic discharge. These are the clear marks of a negative affective arousal.

Negative affective arousal constitutes primary motivation in the sense that the animal will act to reduce or eliminate the distress. If running away or jumping or clinging to the wall is successful in eliminating the distress, the subject will run or jump or cling.

If escape is impossible, as when an animal's paw is caught in a trap or an unavoidable shock is given in the laboratory, the animal will make varied responses but finally will endure the distress. Gibson (1952), in experiments with young goats, found that when shock was inevitable there were frequent shifts from one reaction to another, even after 25 days of training; but when shock could be avoided there was a definite trend toward a uniform avoidance reaction.

When an animal is given a shock, under laboratory condition, distress is produced within the specific setting. The floor and walls of an apparatus, the experimental room and the experimenter, and all surrounding sensory patterns, in fact, become associated with a centrally aroused distress. If, on a subsequent occasion, the animal is placed in the apparatus, distress will be evoked even though no further shock is given in the particular situation. When the animal is placed in the apparatus, one can observe that his heart beats more rapidly, he urinates or defecates, he explores cautiously or perhaps he freezes. Such responses can be explained according to classical principles of Pavlovian conditioning; but this is only part of the picture. The central affective arousal is associated also with the environmental situation.

Whether the affective arousal is produced primarily by electric shock or secondarily by environmental stimulus cues, it operates according to hedonic principles. That is to say, an animal will do what he can do to minimize distress. If shock is inevitable and trial-and-error activities turn out to be non-adaptive, these activities eventually drop out of behavior.

The simplest hypothesis is that a conditioned affective arousal operates in about the same manner as a primary (unconditioned) affective arousal. Conditioned affective arousal leads to the maximizing of enjoyment and the minimizing of distress.

In the experimental literature phrases are met like *conditioned emotional response, conditioned fear, anxiety*, etc. These terms imply that affective processes can be conditioned or associatively aroused through stimulus cues. A *noxious stimulus* or an *aversive stimulus* is one that evokes a negative affective process. The affective process has been conditioned to it.

Solomon and Brush have recognized a distinction between learning to *escape* the unconditioned stimulus and learning to *avoid* the conditioned stimulus. This distinction is valid but underlying both forms of learned behavior is the common principle of hedonic organization. The essential difference is that in learning to *escape* there is a *primary* affective arousal with negative sign while in learning to *avoid* there is a *conditioned* affective arousal with negative sign.

Solomon and Brush believe that there are two processes involved in avoidance learning, one of which obeys the Pavlovian laws of associative conditioning. The second principle, the present writer believes, is hedonic—a trend towards reduction of distress through the organization of instrumental acts.

In general: (1) primary affective arousals can be produced directly, as by shock, and conditioned affective arousals are produced by stimulus cues associated with the shock; (2) whether the affective arousal is evoked directly or through association, it operates according to the same hedonic principles; (3) affective arousals are associated with sensory excitations but are not identical with them.

THE NATURE OF REINFORCEMENT AND EXTINCTION

The concepts of reinforcement and extinction are thoroughly embedded in theoretical discussions of behavior. There is a good deal of confusion, however, about the exact nature of these processes.

In the following sections I will examine some of the current meanings of reinforcement and extinction in the hope that this will lead to the discovery of something sound and productive in this area of behavior theory.

Reinforcement Defined in Terms of Probability

What is reinforcement? According to the dictionary, "to reinforce" means "to strengthen by the addition of something new, as new material." Thus an army is reinforced by bringing up fresh troops, ammunition, and food; concrete is reinforced by addition of metal rods.

In psychology the term *reinforcement* has acquired several meanings and can be a source of confusion. Razran (1955) called attention to two distinct factors in reinforcement. First, there is the original formation of a connection between a stimulus situation (S) and a response (R). There is an initial organization of an S-R pattern. Second, there is the strengthening through repetition of an associative connection that has already been formed. This strengthening through repetition can be described in terms of the probability that a given S will evoke a specific R. The strengthening can also be described in terms of changing characteristics of the R: decrease in the latency of response, increase in the speed or rate of response, change in the smoothness or pattern of response, dropping out of random elements, etc. Razran's analysis indicates that in conditioning there is, first, an organizing principle and, second, a strengthening of associative bonds through repetition.

For a good many psychologists reinforcement is a kind of strengthening of associative bonds that is revealed by an increased probability that a given stimulus situation will elicit a specific response. Thus Spence (1956) writes:

Environmental events exhibiting this property of increasing the probability of occurrence of responses they accompany constitute a class of events known as *reinforcers* or *reinforcing events*. All environmental events not exhibiting this property fall into a different class that may be designated as *nonreinforcers*. . . . Responses accompanied or followed by certain kinds of events (namely, reinforcers) are more likely to occur on subsequent occasions, whereas responses followed by certain other kinds of events (namely, nonreinforcers) do not subsequently show a greater likelihood of occurrence.

Again, Ferster and Skinner (1957) write:

When an organism acts upon the environment in which it lives, it changes that environment in ways which often affect the organism itself. Some of these changes are what the layman calls rewards, or what are now generally referred to technically as reinforcers: when they follow behavior in this way, they increase the likelihood that the organism will behave in the same way again. Most events which function as reinforcers are related to biological processes important to survival of the organism. Thus, food is reinforcing to a hungry organism.

A definition of reinforcement in terms of probability is immune to criticism because it simply generalizes the empirical facts. This type of definition is theoretically safe. Its limitation is that it tells nothing concerning the nature of the reinforcing event. We would honestly like to know what goes on within the organism when reinforcement occurs and what goes on when a learned response becomes extinguished.

When learning is viewed in terms of probability one fact stands out clearly: Exercise (practice, drill, training) results in an increased probability that a given stimulus situation will elicit an associated response and the lack of exercise results in a decreased probability. Most psychologists, however, would distinguish between learning through exercise and reinforcement; and most would distinguish between extinction and forgetting.

To clarify the picture let us first regard reinforcement as a phenomenon of learning that is due to exercise and then consider some other views.

Reinforcement as Growth of Habit Strength through Practice

Hebb (1949), following Lorente de Nó, assumed that the physical basis of learning is a growth of synaptic knobs. When the axon of neuron A excites neuron B repeatedly and persistently, there is a growth process in one or both of the nerve cells such that A's efficiency in firing B is increased. This growth process appears as the development of synaptic knobs on one or both of the neurons at the locus of functional contact. The number and size of these knobs are dependent upon the frequency of joint excitation. Presumably the area of contact is the decisive factor in determining the likelihood that activity in one cell will fire another. The greater the area of contact, the lower the synaptic resistance. According to this view, learning is a physical growth process dependent upon simultaneous excitation of two or more contiguous nerve cells. Learning is a physical change in neural structure. A frequency-contiguity theory of learning appears sufficient to explain the facts of practice.

The view that practice reinforces an S-R bond and lack of practice extinguishes it, is unacceptable to most psychologists as a definition of reinforcement and extinction because it appears to miss the point. This view is out of line with Pavlov's original meaning. Pavlov demonstrated that for a conditional reflex to be organized and to persist it must be "reinforced." Everyone knows that if the bell is sounded repeatedly and the dog is never rewarded by meat powder, the

CR becomes "extinguished." For a CR to continue, it must occasionally be "reinforced" by the presentation of food.

The presentation of food, of course, is only one means of reinforcement. Some psychologists have confused the picture by identifying reinforcement with the food object that is offered as a kind of reward. In going over some current literature upon reinforcement I noted the following statements: Reinforcements are weighed in grams, measured in cubic centimeters, counted out in uniform pellets, controlled by drops of fluid. The concentration of sugar in a solution measures the *amount* of reinforcement. Some reinforcements are solid; others are fluid. One writer stated that the reinforcements were consumed by the rat! Reinforcements differ in amount and in quality; their presentation can be delayed, placed upon various kinds of schedules, etc. Now I submit that these statements make sense if, and only if, we assume that reinforcement is a food object offered to the animal as a kind of reward. There is thus a rather careless use of the term *reinforcement* and a tendency to ignore its nature as an internal, organic, process.

Reinforcement as Change in Performance Dependent upon Affective Processes

According to another view, reinforcement is a determinant that changes *performance* rather than *learning*. Performance is measured behavior. It depends upon learning, affective processes, and other conditions.

To illustrate the view that reinforcement is a change in performance dependent upon affective processes two experiments will be described.

1. Young and Asdourian (1957), in an experiment mentioned previously (see page 155), offered rats a choice between a 1 percent sodium chloride solution and a sucrose solution having a fixed concentration. For one group of animals the sucrose concentration was 54 percent (very sweet); for a second group the concentration was 18 percent (definitely sweet); for a third group the concentration was 6 percent (weakly sweet); for a fourth group the concentration was 2 percent (very weakly sweet). There were eight rats in each group. Every animal was given a total of one hundred choices between a sugar solution and the standard solution of 1 percent salt.

The thirty-two rats uniformly developed a preference for the sugar solution rather than the salt. The rate of growth of this preferential

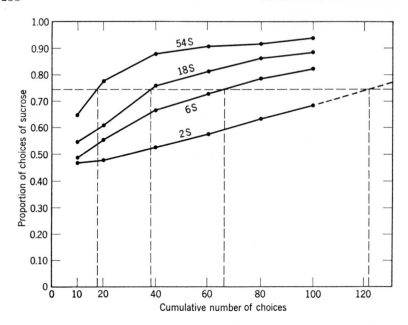

Figure 47. Proportion of choices of sucrose solutions, having the concentrations shown, when paired with a standard solution of 1 percent sodium chloride. *Plotted from* data obtained by Young and Asdourian (1957).

discrimination, however, depended upon concentration of the sugar solution.

Figure 47 shows the proportion of choices of sugar solution when tested against the standard salt solution. The proportions of choices for each sucrose solution have been computed on the basis of cumulative choices. To be specific: the first proportions are based upon the first ten choices per rat; the second set of proportions are based upon the first twenty choices per rat; the third upon the first forty choices per rat, and so on. The last proportions are based upon the total series of one hundred choices per rat (eight hundred for each experimental group).

Figure 47 shows that the proportion of choices of a sugar solution depends upon the total number of previous choices. This is because the animal steadily *learns* to make a preferential discrimination. The figure clearly shows that the growth of a preference is dependent upon two factors: (1) amount of previous practice, and (2) concentration of solution. Now, in terms of the probability doctrine, one must recognize that the probability that a rat will select a sugar solution in preference to a standard salt solution increases with both factors.

To illustrate the point further, consider a probability of 0.75—midway between chance (0.50) and invariable preference (1.00). In Figure 47, a line of dashes, parallel to the base, has been drawn at 0.75. Auxiliary dash lines have been drawn to indicate that a sugar solution will be selected in preference to a salt solution in 75 percent of the choices if:

1. A 54 percent sugar solution is offered for choice 17 times.
2. An 18 percent sugar solution is offered for choice 38 times.
3. A 6 percent sugar solution is offered for choice 66 times.
4. A 2 percent sugar solution is offered for choice 122 times.

This means that one can obtain a performance level of 75 percent of sugar choices for almost any concentration of sucrose simply by giving the animals sufficient practice in the preferential discrimination; but the lower the concentration of sugar, the greater the number of choices that are required to reach a specified level of performance.

The two factors that determine performance are independently variable and each can be expressed in equivalent terms of the other. It is possible, for example, to determine the *practice equivalent* of a 10 percent increase of sucrose concentration.

In general, it can be said that affective processes influence the course of learning. They determine whether an animal will develop one preference or its opposite. Hence they regulate and direct the course of behavior and development. They have an important influence on what we learn, how quickly we learn it, how well we perform. But affective processes are not a magic glue that makes associative bonds stick. It is *exercise* that modifiies neural structure. Exercise, presumably, has an influence that is independent of the kind of motivation underlying behavior. Certainly, with human subjects, an indifferent intent to learn—to carry out instructions in a memory experiment—can cause learning through exercise quite apart from hedonic processes. Affective processes, therefore, are not necessary for learning to occur but exercise is necessary.

Exercise can raise the level of performance independently of affective processes. For example, if rats are given a thousand runs to an unpalatable incentive (casein) without choice, their speed of running steadily increases with practice until they are running faster than less practiced rats run to a highly palatable food (sucrose). This exercise, however, does not change the preference of sucrose to casein. The exercise only makes the preference stand out with increasing clarity.

2. Another experiment that is closely related to the above has been described by Dufort and Kimble (1956). Their work clearly shows the relation between performance and the concentration of sucrose solution offered as a reward.

In their experiment rats ran down a straight 18-inch runway to a semicircular goal platform around the circumference of which were five cups (bottle caps) equally spaced. During pretraining, all animals received one drop of a 10 percent sucrose solution in each of the five cups. Then, during an original learning period of five trials, the animals learned to run to one of the cups that contained a single drop of sucrose solution, the other four cups being empty. Following the original learning, the forty animals were divided into four equivalent groups of ten rats each that were treated differently. The rats in one group learned to run to a cup containing a single drop of 20 percent sucrose solution. Those in a second group learned to run to a cup containing a single drop of 10 percent solution, i.e., there was no change of concentration. A third group learned to run to a cup containing a single drop of 5 percent solution. A fourth group was tested with a drop of distilled water (0 percent sucrose) in one of the cups.

The results are presently graphically in Figure 48. Dufort and Kimble plotted the mean percentage of correct responses under the different incentive conditions. It is clear from their data that the mean percentage of correct choices is a direct function of the concentration of sucrose within a single drop of incentive fluid. The 20 percent solution gave performance better than the 10 percent; the 10 percent was better than the 5; the distilled water (0 percent) led to extinction of the previously learned pattern. Dufort and Kimble correctly regard extinction as a limiting case in a series of tests with reduced concentrations of sucrose.

The extinction of a learned pattern when distilled water was substituted for a sucrose solution recalls Guttman's (1953) concept of the reinforcement threshold which can be specified in terms of concentration of solution.

This also recalls an unpublished study in which it was found that learning occurred intermittently when incentives of low hedonic value (2 and 6 percent sucrose solutions) were offered to need-free rats. The animals were timed as they made one run per day down a 5-foot

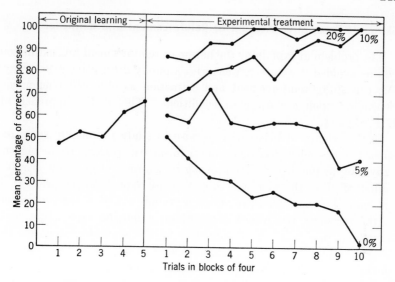

Figure 48. Mean percentage of correct responses as a function of practice and incentive value. *After* Dufort and Kimble (1956).

straightaway. Some animals showed learning for a series of days and then for a long series of days they continued to approach the sugar solution but with no indication of learning. They showed no improvement with practice; their performance was on a plateau. Animals running to higher concentrations, by contrast, produced the usual type of performance curve with negative acceleration.

It is clear from the above experiments that reinforcement may have either of two meanings: (1) reinforcement may be regarded as a phenomenon of learning—an increase of habit strength due to practice; or (2) reinforcement may be regarded as a motivational phenomenon —an increased level of performance dependent upon affective processes that are associated with sensory stimulations. These two meanings must be distinguished from each other.

Similarly, extinction may have either of two meanings: (1) extinction may be regarded as a phenomenon of learning—a decrease of habit strength due to lack of practice (forgetting); or (2) extinction may be regarded as a motivational phenomenon—the disintegration of a neurobehavioral pattern due to reduction of incentive value.

Skinner's Descriptive Account of Reinforcement and Extinction

The problem of explaining the nature of reinforcement and extinction can be avoided if we are content with a purely descriptive psychology. We can study reinforcement and extinction as observed phenomena depending upon a variety of conditions. This is the approach of B. F. Skinner.

In the science of behavior it is wise to study thoroughly some response that is characteristic of an organism, e.g., pecking in the pigeon, salivating in the dog, or bar pressing in the rat. Over a considerable period of time the characteristic response repeatedly occurs. If a mechanical device is used to obtain a graphic record of the occurrence of the response, the record obtained on a moving tape might look something like graph *a*, Figure 49. If the separate responses are added cumulatively by a mechanism that writes on a wide strip of moving paper, the record might look like graph *b*.

The cumulative curve shows the rate of responding during a period of time. The curve can serve as a base for analyzing the various conditions that affect the rate. For example, if the curve records the pecking behavior of a pigeon, it is possible to study variations in the

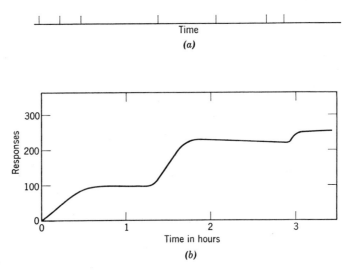

Figure 49. (*a*) Non-cumulative record of separate responses. (*b*) Cumulative record of responses.

rate of pecking that depend upon food deprivation, injection of drugs, light and dark, characteristics of the food incentive, and other conditions.

Skinner (1938) has done pioneer work in the development of objective methods for recording behavior. A commonly used device is the Skinner box for recording bar pressing in the rat. One of the models is pictured in Figure 50. The illustration gives an impression of the complexity of apparatus required for recording relatively simple components of behavior.

Without any special incentive a rat will occasionally press the bar; this may be incidental to the exploration and manipulation of the physical environment. If, however, the mechanism presents the rat with a food pellet every time he happens to press the bar, the rate of responding will increase above the normal level. There is *reinforcement,* or strengthening, of the response that is associated with the reward of food. After the animal has eaten a quantity of food the rate of responding will decrease; he may let the bar alone for a considerable period of time.

Let us suppose that a hungry rat has thoroughly learned to press the bar and received a food pellet. Let us suppose, further, that on a certain day the mechanism has been so arranged that bar pressing produces no food. Under these conditions the animal continues to press the bar for a while; but when no reward is forthcoming he slows down and eventually stops responding except for occasional incidental bar pressings. This disappearance of the response when reward is withheld is known as *extinction.*

Again, if rats are kept in darkness and the Skinner box arranged so that pressing the bar temporarily turns on a dim light, the animals learn to press the bar. The dim light is *reinforcing* when the rats are in darkness but under ordinary conditions of illumination the animals do not learn to press the bar even when it changes appreciably the level of illumination. If pressing the bar turns on a bright and dazzling light, the bar pressing response becomes extinguished.

As Skinner has shown, functional relations can be described without theorizing; but psychologists *have* resorted to theoretical explanations of reinforcement and extinction. Theoretical explanation goes beyond descriptive analysis.

Figure 50. Details of a Skinner box. The space occupied by the rat is the
screened box in the middle of the picture, one side of which has been removed.
The floor of the box consists of eight segments which move slightly when the
rat steps on them to operate microswitches which are visible at the bottom of
the box; these segments give a record of the location and extent of the rat's
activity. The bar, or lever, can be seen beyond a small piece of screen which
extends into the box; this screen prevents operation of the lever except when
the rat is immediately in front of it. The mechanism which drops pellets of
food into the cup can be seen at the right. It consists of a disc containing two
series of holes in which the pellets are placed. The disc is turned by a small
motor visible in the picture; the mechanism drops one pellet at a time. Above
the motor is a panel containing leads from cables which extend to the control
room. Other features of the apparatus are the following: At the left is a device which presents the rat with a single full daily ration. A loudspeaker for
auditory stimulation can be seen behind the box. General illumination is from
a dome above the box. Several of the units shown in the picture are kept in
a soundproofed room in which temperature and humidity are controlled. Each
box is soundproofed to prevent cross-cues between experiments. (The present
apparatus was constructed by Mr. Douglas Anger; the photograph and descriptive details were furnished by Dr. B. F. Skinner of Harvard University.)

The Drive-Reduction Theory of Reinforcement

According to Hull (1943), the primary reinforcement of S-R bonds is produced by diminution of a need and reduction of its associated drive.

Hull's theory rests upon a sound biological principle: The behavior of organisms tends to meet organic needs; animals learn acts that are instrumental in satisfying needs. Primary reinforcement is based upon need reduction. This is shown in Hull's statement of the law of reinforcement:

Whenever an effector activity occurs in temporal contiguity with the afferent impulse, or the perseverative trace of such an impulse, resulting from the impact of a stimulus energy upon a receptor, and this conjunction is closely associated in time with the diminution in the receptor discharge characteristic of a need or with a stimulus situation which has been closely and consistently associated with such a need diminution, there will result an increment to the tendency for that stimulus to evoke that reaction.

This theory of reinforcement through need reduction raises two problems which Hull himself considered. First, how does an internal need influence behavior? Hull postulated that each organic need has its own pattern of "drive stimuli." The "drive stimulus" persists as long as the need is present and this is a source of motivation. When the need has been met the "drive stimulus" is removed or reduced. Consequently *drive reduction* indicates the diminution of need.

Second, how can an animal learn an instrumental act that leads to the ingestion of food when the primary reinforcement comes after a considerable period of delay? When a bit of food is ingested this must be swallowed before the "drive stimuli" from the stomach can be reduced and the products of digestion must circulate before basic tissue needs can be met. This takes time. To solve this problem Hull postulated secondary reinforcement.

Drive reduction strengthens not only the immediately preceding S-R bonds but also those that are more remote in time. Thus the S-R sequence of tasting, chewing, swallowing, Hull believed, acquired reinforcing capacity because associated with the primary reduction of the hunger drive when food arrives in the stomach.

Hull, Livingston, Rouse, and Barker (1951) reported a few observations upon a single dog to test Hull's theory. The animal had an esophageal fistula so that when food was chewed and swallowed it came out of the fistula and thus was prevented from reaching the stomach and reducing the hunger drive. According to the report, the "habit" of eating was extinguished after eight sessions of "sham feeding." The experiment has obvious shortcomings, which need not be reviewed here, but it is important in that it shows the nature of Hull's thinking about primary and secondary reinforcement.

There are, Hull believed, primary and secondary gradients of reinforcement. Primary reinforcement diminishes in effectiveness as the time interval increases between a S-R bond and drive reduction. On the basis of results from experiments upon the delay of reward, Hull concluded that the gradient of primary reinforcement extended to about 30 seconds but not beyond. To explain the strengthening of S-R connections that precede primary drive reduction by more than 30 seconds, Hull postulated the existence of secondary gradients of reinforcement. Secondary reinforcement occurs when a S-R bond is closely associated, in space and time, with a S-R sequence that has the capacity to reduce a primary drive. Thus an experienced animal is excited by the sight of food because the sight of food is the beginning of a sequence of events that terminate in reduction of a primary need and its associated drive.

Critique of the drive-reduction theory of reinforcement. Hull's distinction between primary and secondary gradients of reinforcement has been criticized by Spence (1947) and Grice (1948) who argue that it is not necessary to postulate two gradients of reinforcement. A single gradient is sufficient. In the laboratory the problem of gradients takes the form of investigating the interval of delay between a discrimination to be learned and the event of primary reinforcement (drive reduction). If rats are required to make a discrimination and then forced to delay before obtaining a reward, the effectiveness of the incentive decreases as the interval of delay is increased.

Grice pointed out that in the usual T-maze situation, rats get spatial and proprioceptive cues from turning to the right or left. Such cues, when closely associated with reward, become reinforcing. To eliminate the spatial and proprioceptive cues Grice forced rats to discriminate between black and white. Positions of the black and white surfaces were randomized so that the animals were forced to rely solely upon the visual signals of reward. Under these conditions groups of hungry rats were delayed between black-white discrimination and food for periods of 0, 0.5, 1.2, 2, 5, and 10 seconds.

Grice found that there was a rapid decline in the reinforcement value of reward as the delay interval increased within the 10-second range. In the group with a 10-second delay, three of the five rats failed to learn. It appeared, therefore, that the elimination of spatial and proprioceptive cues reduced the effectiveness of a delayed reward well below the 30-second maximum mentioned by Hull on the basis of experiments by Perin (1943) and Wolfe (1936).

Secondary reinforcement was introduced by allowing rats to eat in a goal box of the same color as the positive stimulus (rather than a gray box). Under these conditions, Grice found, learning with delayed reward was greatly facilitated. He concluded that color of the goal box can become a secondary reward. Color cues can furnish secondary reinforcement.

The experimental results agree with a suggestion of Spence that it is unnecessary to postulate a *primary* gradient of reinforcement. All learning, when there is delay of reward, can be explained in terms of immediate reinforcement or secondary reinforcement. There is a gradient for secondary reinforcement but this can be explained by assuming that a trace of the visual stimulus persists after stimulation until time of primary reward.

There remains, however, a question concerning the nature of primary, or immediate, reinforcement. Hull postulated a unique pattern of drive stimuli for each organic need; but there are difficulties with this view. Estes (1949) established secondary reinforcement when a thirst drive was present and subsequently shifted the motivation from thirst to hunger. He discovered that secondary reinforcement based upon reduction of one drive was still effective when there was reduction of another drive. How, then, can Hull's view be maintained that acts instrumental in reduction of a specific drive are reinforced?

Estes abandoned the notion that secondary reinforcement depends upon reduction of a primary drive. He wrote:

> Unless new experimental developments force a distinction between conditioning by primary and secondary reinforcement, it will evidently be inaccurate to describe the process of reinforcement in terms of drive-reduction. While it is true that reduction of a drive is an event frequently associated with the operation of reinforcement, it is not necessarily the event responsible for conditioning. In fact the present results suggest that it is not. A stimulus which has been correlated with the presentation of water to thirsty animals clearly is effective as a reinforcer when the thirst drive has been eliminated by satiation.

The question of the nature of primary reinforcement, within the Hullian framework, remains a mystery. Hull, of course, operated within the postulates of a stimulus-response psychology and ignored the role of affective processes in learning and motivation.

It is common knowledge that many states of depletion (but not all) are hedonically negative. "Drive reduction" is typically a relief from general distress—"distress reduction." But it can be shown that positive affective arousal is also reinforcing in the absence of any initial distress. In simple words, neurobehavioral patterns are organized that produce hedonic changes in the positive direction whether such changes are relief from distress (as in drive reduction) or the arousal of a positive affective process (as in rewards with saccharin solution).

Any stimulus pattern whatsoever might become associated with affective change in the positive direction and thus acquire incentive value. This applies to peripheral stimuli—tastes, lights, sounds, etc. —and to internal stimuli associated with states of need.

The Consummatory-Response Hypothesis

To test Hull's drive-reduction theory of reinforcement, Sheffield and others performed two interesting experiments.

Sheffield, Wulff, and Backer (1951) utilized a peculiarity of the sexual behavior of the male rat. The copulatory pattern of the male consists of a series of discrete mountings with rapid pelvic thrusts ending in intromission and vigorous dismounting. This pattern is usually repeated a dozen times or more before the first ejaculation. It is possible, therefore, to allow the male to make a number of copulatory responses, as rewards for instrumental learning, and to remove the female before ejaculation and drive reduction occur.

Anecdotal evidence at the human level suggests that erotic stimulation is rewarding whether it terminates in orgasm or merely excites the sexual appetite. A question can be raised, therefore, as to whether sexual stimulation without drive reduction is in itself rewarding to laboratory rats.

Inexperienced males were employed as subjects. They were divided into groups on the basis of the strength of the copulatory tendency as shown by preliminary observations. The instrumental act to be learned was running down a runway and climbing a hurdle to reach the goal box. In the goal box was a reward consisting either of a female in heat or a male companion. Copulation, but without ejaculation, was permitted during a brief period of confinement after the male had reached the goal box. The time of approach was measured and the speed of approach computed as an index of performance.

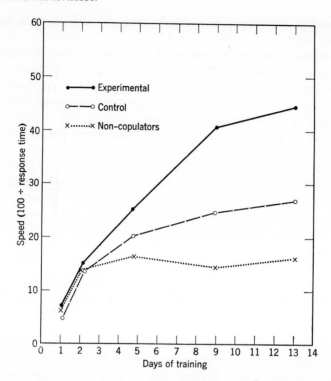

Figure 51. Reinforcing value of copulation without ejaculation. Experimental animals found a female in the goal box, control animals found a male, and non-copulators found one or the other but never attempted to copulate. *After* Sheffield, Wulff and Backer (1951).

Figure 51 shows the mean speed of approach to the goal box for three groups of rats. The data prove conclusively that copulation without ejaculation, and without a history of previous ejaculation, can function as an effective reward for performance of male rats. Also, the strength of the instrumental response is closely related to the strength of the copulatory tendency.

Sheffield et al. assume that elicitation of the dependable and pre-potent copulatory response is the critical factor in reinforcement rather than reduction of the sex drive.

A similar view was expressed in a study by Sheffield and Roby (1950) in which a solution of saccharin was offered as reward. Saccharin, in low concentrations, tastes sweet but it has no nutritive value;

the substance passes through the body unaltered and meets no known metabolic need.

Sheffield and Roby report that rats learned to run down the straight-away when their only reward was the sweet-tasting saccharin. The findings are at variance with the molar principle of reinforcement, as stated by Hull, which identifies primary reinforcement with need reduction. Also the facts do not agree with a view expressed by Miller and Dollard that reinforcement comes from reduction or removal of a drive stimulus.

Sheffield has argued that the eliciting of a consummatory * response, rather than reduction of need or drive, is the critically important factor in reinforcement. In the above experiments the consummatory response—whether copulatory or ingestive—leads to learning.

In a subsequent study Sheffield, Roby, and Campbell (1954) trained rats to run down a straightaway. As incentives they used a nourish-ing solution of dextrose, a solution of saccharin that lacks nourish-ment, and a solution containing both dextrose and saccharin. Intake was used as a measure of the amount or strength of ingestive activity and speed of running as a measure of the strength of instrumental response.

On the basis of results they concluded that the nourishment obtained from the dextrose is an irrelevant aspect of the reinforcing value of sweet-tasting solutions. Rather than nourishment it is the sweet stimulation that innately elicits ingestion. Reinforcement is in pro-portion to the strength of the ingestion response.

Mason's critique of the consummatory-response hypothesis. While Sheffield's work is a damaging blow to the drive-reduction theory of reinforcement, it does not disturb the hedonic hypothesis. I would argue that the affective arousal produced by a sweet taste or by sexual stimulation is the important factor in reinforcement rather than sensory stimulation or the consummatory response.

Sheffield's hypothesis was tested in a doctoral study by Mason (1956) who timed rats with a photoelectric cell as they ran down a 5-foot runway. Mason argued that if the consummatory response is the crucial factor in reinforcement, it should be possible to demon-strate this by varying the amount of consummatory activity.

Mason developed an electronic device that would automatically remove a sugar solution from the goal box after the rat had taken a

---

* *Consummatory* and *consumatory* should not be confused. The first term de-rives from *consummate* and the other from *consume*.

certain number of licks—ten licks for some animals and fifty for others. In the apparatus a subthreshold current was passed through the feet and tongue of the rat to the incentive fluid. This current was amplified and made to operate a rotary solenoid which removed the fluid from the goal box after a predetermined number of tongue contacts.

Now if the amount of consummatory activity is the crucial factor in reinforcement, fifty licks should be more effective than ten licks. If consummatory response were the sole factor in reinforcement, fifty licks of a 30 percent sucrose solution should be equally reinforcing to fifty licks of a 6 percent sucrose solution.

Predictions based upon the consummatory response hypothesis fell far short of statistical significance. The hedonic hypothesis, by contrast, would predict a faster approach to a 30 percent sucrose solution than to a 6 percent solution when the amount of consummatory activity was held constant. Predictions based upon the hedonic hypothesis were confirmed with a significance beyond the 0.001 level of confidence.

Incidentally, the number of licks of sugar solution does make a difference in the speed of locomotion, but this difference can be interpreted in terms of the duration of affective arousal as well as in terms of the amount of consummatory activity.

Reinforcement as Cognitive Feedback

A wholly different view of reinforcement is that of Thorndike (1935), who wrote about the *confirming* influence of rewards. In a series of experiments the word "Right," spoken by the experimenter, confirmed the correctness of a response and reinforced the S-R bond that was rewarded. The reinforcing effect, Thorndike believed, spread to connections preceding and following the rewarded connection. The word "Wrong" denied correctness and failed to confirm the connection.

Relative to the nature of reinforcement Thorndike wrote:

What sort of force acting through what sort of process or mechanism can be and do what the confirming reaction is and does? The answer which seems to me to fit all or nearly all the facts is that the force and mechanism of the confirming reaction are the force and mechanism of reinforcement, applied to a connection.

All explanations of reinforcement agree that one part of the brain can exert a force to intensify activities elsewhere in it and that processes or mechanisms exist whereby this force can be directed or attracted to one activity rather than promiscuously; and that is all that is required to explain the fundamental physiology of the confirming reaction. It is distinguished from other sorts of reinforcement by the fact that satisfaction sets the force in action and that the force acts on the connection which was just active in intimate functional association with the production of the satisfier, or on its near neighbors.

The spoken words "Right" and "Wrong" provide cognitive feedback to the subject. They convey information concerning the correctness or incorrectness of his responses. The word "Right" produces an "OK" reaction which has an informing, regulative and directive function.

The cognitive feedback can be by a prearranged signal instead of words. An example of feedback by a signal is found in the following neat experiment by Grant, Hake, and Hornseth (1951).

In the experiment the subject was seated before an upright board, painted in a flat black, with two 60-watt lamps—one at the left and one at the right. In an actual trial the lamp at the left was flashed for 3 seconds—at the close of which flash the right lamp was some-times actuated for 0.5 second. While the lamp at the left was lighted the subject was required to guess whether or not the second lamp would flash. He was instructed to note whether or not he had guessed correctly.

There were five groups of subjects. With one group the lamp at the right flashed in 100 percent of the trials. With other groups it flashed in 75, 50, 25, or 0 percent of the trials. Since the flashing of the lamp at the right was at random, the subject had no way of knowing in advance whether the lamp would or would not flash. He was forced to guess. If he guessed that the lamp would flash on, the response was designated as positive; if he guessed that it would not flash on, the response was designated as negative.

In the experiment there were one hundred and eighty-five subjects—thirty-seven in each of the five groups. Each subject was given sixty trials in the training series and then thirty trials, with the lamp never flashing, in the extinction series.

The trials were grouped in blocks of five successive trials. For each group of subjects the percentage of positive trials was then computed for the successive blocks. Results are presented in Figure 52.

The illustration shows that at the start of training all groups gave 50 to 70 percent of positive responses. Thereafter the rate of positive responses changed so as to approach the objective rate of positive trials as an asymptote. At the end of the training series, each group was emitting positive responses at about the same rate as it was receiving positive trials. In other words, the frequency of guessing

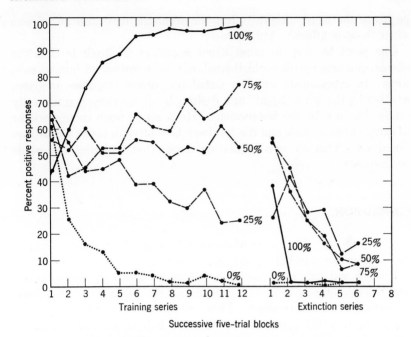

Figure 52. Percent frequency of positive responses plotted against trials during training and extinction for different percentages of positive training trials. *After* Grant, Hake, and Hornseth (1951).

that a lamp would flash approximated the objective frequency of flashing.

During the extinction series the lamp at the right was never flashed. The curves show that the rate of positive responses dropped off markedly. The drop was most rapid for the 100 percent group. The 25 percent group showed relatively little drop during the extinction series. The 50 to 75 percent groups were intermediate in the rate of extinction.

The experiment confirms the findings of L. G. Humphreys that there is greater resistance to extinction following 50 percent reinforcement than following 100 percent reinforcement; this was found for classical, operant, and verbal conditioning. Present interest, however, lies in the regulative function of cognitive feedback.

The feedback is *cognitive* whether or not it is accompanied by affective arousal. Of course, the subject might be pleased (affectively aroused) when he sees the lamp flash or, in Thorndike's studies, when he hears the word "Right." But the feedback may also be present when there is affective indifference.

One point to keep in mind about cognitive feedback is that the phenomena occur with sophisticated, carefully instructed human subjects. In experiments where a signal for correct responses is given, whether by the word "Right" or a flashing lamp, the subject is mentally set for his task by the instructions. He is set to learn or to guess or to carry out some task and the feedback is relative to his basic instructional set. This set is a regulating factor that underlies the whole performance.

CONCLUSION

The question "What is reinforcement?" was asked above. It may now be considered in light of the discussion.

First, I will eliminate the drive-reduction theory of reinforcement and the hypothesis that the consummatory response is of critical importance in reinforcement. These views are: (1) out of line with the facts, and (2) couched in peripheral, S-R terms rather than in terms of central neural processes. Second, I will disregard the probability concept of Spence, Skinner, and others, for the simple reason that it does not answer the question. Skinner's descriptive account of reinforcement and extinction, while scientifically sound, leaves open the question concerning the nature of reinforcement.

There remain three possible answers to the question.

1. There is a point mentioned by Razran and in the quotation from Nissen at the head of this chapter, that there is an organizing factor responsible for the initial organization of a conditioned response. One must keep in mind the importance of the initial organization of neurobehavioral patterns and their reorganization in repeated situations.

One of the main functions of affective processes is the organization and reorganization of patterns. Affectivity provides a steering principle that determines what neurobehavioral patterns will and will not become organized and reorganized. There is, moreover, a quantitative relation between the intensity of the affective arousal and the strength of motive organized.

2. Behavior is undoubtedly regulated through cognitive feedback. On the human level, at least, knowledge of results and information that is fed back to the subject regulate performance.

Regulation through cognitive feedback must be distinguished from hedonic regulation, although the two are most intimately related. The distinction between cognitive regulation and regulation through affective processes is one of basic importance for any analysis of the nature of reinforcement. One can argue that reinforcement is either: (1) the regulation of behavior through cognitive feedback, or (2) the regulation of behavior through affective arousals. Both influences are shown in the *development* or neurobehavioral patterns.

3. Exercise (practice, drill, training) leads to increase of habit strength and is thus a highly important determinant of behavior. According to the probability notion, it must be admitted that exercise is "reinforcing" since continued exercise increases the probability that a given S will elicit a given R.

Development through exercise is universally defined as learning; but most psychologists think of reinforcement as something different from the increase of habit strength through exercise. Reinforcement is a motivational phenomenon. It relates to the organization and development of neurobehavioral patterns through processes other than exercise.

Motivational processes determine what will be learned and what not, how well an organism will perform a learned act, etc., and hence are importantly related to learning. But one can give a strictly objective account of learning through exercise without appealing to drive reduction, consummatory responses, affective arousals, and other factors. Learning can be described in terms of the frequency and contiguity of responses.

If one views motivational psychology as the search for and analysis of the determinants of behavior, then *habit strength* must be regarded as one of the basic determinants. Learning is a developmental process that builds up habit strength. But in any event, learning through exercise must be distinguished from the organization and reorganization of patterns, from the regulation of behavior through affectivity, from regulation through cognitive feedback, and from the activation and sustaining of behavior. There are obviously several ways to define reinforcement and it will make for clarity to distinguish the different kinds of factors that determine behavior.

I believe that the study of incentives, whether positive or negative, can best be advanced by the frank recognition of the central role of affective processes in learning and motivation. The studies reviewed above can all be fitted into a framework which frankly recognizes the role of affectivity in behavior.

Reading Suggestions

The following works consider various studies of reinforcement in addition to those discussed in the present chapter. Bindra (1959), in Chapter 5, gives an analysis of reinforcers and, in Chapter 6, considers factors determining habit strength. Olds (1956), in Chapter 2, discusses the data relating to reinforcement. Spence (1956), in Chapter 5, examines the role of reinforcement in instrumental reward conditioning; his main concern is with experiments upon the magnitude and delay of reward. The present discussion of reinforcement is based largely upon a theoretical paper by Young (1959).

Bindra, D. *Motivation, a systematic reinterpretation.* New York: Ronald, 1959.

Olds, J. *The growth and structure of motives, psychological studies in the theory of action.* Glencoe, Illinois: Free Press, 1956.

Spence, K. W. *Behavior theory and conditioning.* New Haven: Yale University Press, 1956.

Young, P. T. The role of affective processes in learning and motivation. *Psychol. Rev.,* 1959, 66, 104–125.

7 DIRECTION AND REGULATION

Purposive action is the most fundamental category of psychology; *just as the motion of a material particle . . . has long been the fundamental category of physical science. Behavior is always purposive action, or a train or sequence of purposive actions.*

WILLIAM MC DOUGALL

For McDougall (1923) behavior is always purposive. He distinguishes between behavior and physiological processes. Reflexes, for example, are physiological processes and not bits of behavior. Reflexes are purely mechanical; they lack the attributes of purposive action.

Purposive behavior has certain characteristics that are lacking in reflex action. Purposive behavior is: (1) spontaneous, (2) persistent, (3) varied, (4) goal-oriented, and (5) terminated by a goal response. Moreover, purposive behavior (6) shows preparation for impending situations, (7) is improved by repetition, and (8) is a total reaction of the organism.

McDougall argues that the concept of motivation is not required to explain reflexes and very simple conditioned responses but all *behavior* is motivated.

Most psychologists, however, have not accepted McDougall's distinction between behavior and reflex action. The reflex, whether innate or conditioned, is commonly regarded as a bit of behavior. It is argued that the stimulus motivates (releases) the reflex response and that bodily structures, particularly neural arcs, regulate the pattern of reflexive action. (See pages 14–15.)

But whether we accept the narrow or the broad definition of motivation we are confronted with problems concerning the regulation and direction of behavior. These problems are fundamental in any search for the determinants of behavior.

The regulation and direction of behavior is the central theme of this and the following chapter. Here we will consider the basic processes of set, tension, effort, and feedback, in relation to regulation. In the following chapter we will consider the role of cognitive, affective, and evaluative processes in direction and regulation.

PURPOSIVE BEHAVIOR

It is necessary to distinguish between the facts of experience and the interpretations that rest upon those facts. If I view experience objectively, through the eyes of a physicist, I see that persistent goal-directed behavior is a fact of nature. If I view experience subjectively, from my own individual point of view, I observe the awareness of goals, the foresight of impending events, and the belief that conscious intentions influence my actions.

Goal-directed behavior and the awareness of goals are both facts of experience. If I leave these facts for interpretation, I can go along either of two paths: the facts may be interpreted teleologically or mechanistically. That is, I can read into them some purpose or other. I can, however, attempt to explain them physiologically in terms of bodily mechanisms and processes.

The interpretation—whether teleological or mechanistic—must not be confused with the facts themselves. Let us look now at some of the facts that relate to purposive behavior.

Goal-Directed Behavior

Persistent goal-directed behavior is a fact of observation and not an inference. Tolman (1925) has pointed that out in a discussion of purpose and cognition:

> When a rat runs a maze, it is to be observed that his running and searching activities *persist until food is reached*. And it appears that this persistence is the result of the physiological condition of hunger. We do not know whether

the rat, in so "persisting" is "conscious;" we do not know whether he "feels a purpose" (to use the terminology of the mentalists); but we do know that, given (1) the physiological condition of hunger and (2) the objective conditions of the maze, the rat thus *persists until the food is reached*. It is this purely *objective* fact of persistence until a certain specific type of goal-object is reached that we define as *goal-seeking*. And as thus defined, a goal-seeking is a wholly objective and a wholly behavioristic phenomenon. There is nothing "mentalistic" about it.

Tolman was writing at a time when psychologists were reacting vigorously against mentalism and attempting to establish psychology as a branch of objective science. He was concerned to establish goal-directed behavior as a fact of objective observation.

Bindra (1959) agrees with McDougall and Tolman that goal direction is a fundamental attribute of behavior. An analysis of the goal directedness of behavior is a central problem of motivational psychology. Bindra describes three distinctive features of behavior that is goal-directed: *appropriateness, persistence,* and *searching*.

Bindra defines *appropriateness* as the extent to which the organism adopts effective courses of action in response to variations in the stimuli connected with the goal. The statement needs clarification. There are a good many variations in the stimulus patterns that are associated with the goal object. The organism makes various responses to the stimulus patterns. Some of these responses are effective in leading the animal to the goal object and others are not. The degree of appropriateness of a bit of behavior is indicated by the number of effective responses. The appropriateness is indicated by the sequence of responses and not by a single response. Different sequences vary in the degree of appropriateness.

Bindra agrees with McDougall and Tolman that an important characteristic of goal direction is *persistence*. Persistence describes the rate or duration, or both, of the effective courses of action. The greater the rate or the duration of certain specified courses of action, the more persistent is the goal-directed activity.

Searching refers to the hyperactivity often shown by animals when they are exposed to the stimuli associated with a previously experienced goal. For example, if on a given trial a rat, previously trained in a Skinner box, finds no pedal in the box, it is likely repeatedly to go in the corner where the pedal used to be and, in general, to act as if it is reacting to the missing pedal. The frequency and duration of such responses defines what may be called *searching*.

Goal direction is thus a multidimensional concept. Appropriateness, persistence, and searching, as defined above, can be regarded as some of the dimensions that are involved in judging behavior as more or less goal-directed.

The Goal Gradient

The goal-gradient hypothesis can be stated in this way: *As an animal approaches the goal response, in space and time, his excitatory level rises.* The change in excitatory level can be measured in different ways.

Hull (1934) measured the goal gradient in terms of the speed of locomotion. He devised a straight 40-foot runway for timing the speed of locomotion as hungry rats ran from a starting place at one end of the pathway to a food reward at the other. The path of the apparatus was broken into eight 5-foot sections by valves of stiff cardboard which the rat lifted in running to the food. These valves prevented retracing of the path, and also made electrical contacts that were used in timing the running speed.

The results indicate that a hungry rat runs faster and faster as he approaches the food. Just before he reaches the goal, however, his speed of locomotion is slightly retarded. It is obvious that if he did not "put on the brakes" he would dash headlong into the food. With practice the speed of locomotion increases in all sections of the runway, but the practice effect is most pronounced in the first sections of the path. Practice tends to level off the initial speed-of-locomotion gradient.

After leveling through practice, the original steep gradient can readily be restored by creating conditions which render the motivation less effective. One of these conditions is frustration produced by removal of the reward. Another is removal of the drive by satiating the animal prior to a run. The effects of frustration and satiation are illustrated in Figures 53 and 54.

Compound gradients were produced by training the animals on 20 feet of the runway and then extending the runway to 40 feet. The contours of these compound gradients were rapidly obliterated by training.

The goal-gradient principle throws light upon a finding in several studies of maze learning by rats. Experiments by Spence, Tolman, Ruch, and others, showed that the blind alleys of a maze, on the average, are eliminated in a backward order from the goal to the

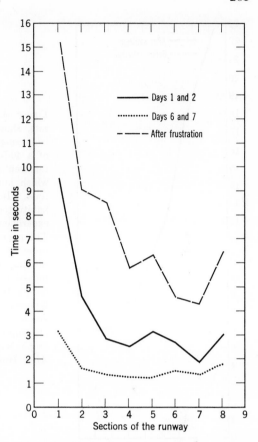

Figure 53. Composite graph for fourteen rats, showing mean time consumed in traversing each of eight 5-foot sections of a 40-foot runway. The solid line shows the speed-of-locomotion gradient on the first and second days. The dotted line shows the gradient on the sixth and seventh days, after practice. The dash line shows the restoration of a steep gradient by frustration, i.e., by removal of food after complete learning. Each point on the curve is the mean of 135 or 140 time measurements. *After* Hull (1934).

starting box. This is understandable if we assume that the animals are more highly motivated as they approach the goal in space and time.

Casual observations suggest that the goal-gradient principle operates in human behavior. If, for example, one has a definite objective such as sailing to Europe on June 16, one senses a general increase of excitement and activity as the time for departure draws nigh. If the goal is to attend a football game, the excitement grows markedly with the approach of the hour. If students are told that there will be several preliminary examinations and a final examination during the semester, their excitatory level rises as the fixed dates approach. Persons unconsciously act as if there were a logarithmic law in the activity gradient relative to a goal.

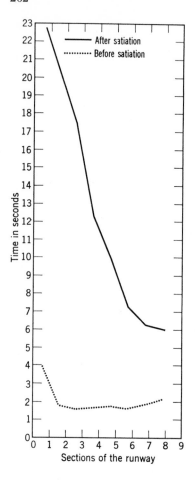

Figure 54. Composite graph for thirteen rats, showing mean time consumed in traversing each of eight 5-foot sections of a 40-foot runway. The lower curve represents the means from 3 days on which hungry rats were rewarded with food. Inasmuch as the animals were habituated to the apparatus before the experiment, the gradient is fairly level. The upper curve shows restoration of a pronounced gradient when the rats were satiated and the hunger drive thus removed before the runs. The days for tests with hunger and satiation were interspersed. Each point on the lower graph represents a mean of 200 time measurements; each point on the upper graph is a mean of 115 measurements. *After* Hull (1934).

Pregoal and Postgoal Behavior

The goal-gradient principle throws a light upon the contrast between pregoal and postgoal behavior. Activities that lead to a goal response are more quickly learned and more consistently performed than those irrelevant to the goal. This principle can be illustrated many times over from the behavior of children:

Mary, age 10, opens the refrigerator to find food but leaves the door open. She opens the back door to run into the yard but does not close it. She turns on the lights to read a book but when through reading leaves the lights burning. She opens the ink bottle to write a school lesson but leaves the bottle open. She turns on the radio but goes out to play with the radio booming. James, age 8, turns on the faucet to wash his hands but goes away without turning off the water. He uses the toilet but does not flush it. He fills the bath tub, takes a bath but leaves the dirty water in the tub. He opens a drawer to take out toys but does not close it. He plays with toys but when tired of playing runs to the yard with the toys still on the living room floor. He takes off his shoes and stockings but leaves them wherever they happen to fall.

In many such homely acts children are observed to do whatever is necessary to achieve an immediate goal. They readily acquire patterns of behavior that are instrumental in reaching a goal but omit postgoal responses that to them seem irrelevant or superfluous. Adults, too, often act in the same manner. They carry out and learn patterns of behavior that are relevant to some goal more readily than those that are not obviously and directly related to a goal response.

In training a child to close doors, turn out lights, pick up toys, etc., words are not very effective. When a child has achieved his immediate goal he proceeds to some other activity. The postgoal behavior can be justified on adult grounds of economy, neatness, esthetic fitness, conformity to social standards, approval of the neighbors, etc., but such considerations are not effective motivators of the child. He has to develop personality traits of economy, neatness, orderliness, conformity, and the like; these traits are not inborn. The child fails to conform to adult standards simply because he lacks the goals, personality traits, and evaluative dispositions of an adult.

The general principle is this: *Patterns of behavior that are instrumental in reaching a goal are quickly learned and consistently performed. Patterns that are irrelevant to an immediate goal—whether they occur before or after the goal response—tend to drop out of behavior.*

Awareness of Goal and Conscious Foresight

Everyone is clearly aware that at times his behavior moves towards a goal. Moreover, almost everyone believes that a conscious intention is effective as a determinant of behavior. John states that he is going to mail a letter. He acts according to his declared intention. He is constantly aware that actions agree with expressed purposes.

Concepts like expectancy, preparatory set, anticipation, and the like, clearly imply a reference to impending events. There is foreknowledge of what is about to happen. Conscious foresight is based upon past experience and upon the fact that the world in which we live is uniform. Regular sequences of events tend to occur. The physical world is dependable, and because of this fact we can learn dependable and consistent ways of reacting to it.

Gordon Allport (1947) distinguished among *intention, anticipatory goal reaction,* and *expectancy.* An *intention* is a guiding idea which may be in or outside of awareness. The term is not confined to reportable purpose, and sometimes the direction of an intention is understood by the subject; sometimes not. Allport writes: "Let us define intention simply as *what the individual is trying to do.* Naïve as this definition may sound it is in reality the product of decades of sophisticated wrestling with the problems of human motivation. In this concept influences as diversified as Brentano, Darwin, Freud, Cannon, and Wertheimer are brought into focus."

Conscious foresight is a fact of direct human experience. But if a psychologist imputes conscious foresight to an animal, he is promptly accused of being mentalistic and anthropomorphic. He can avoid this stigma by limiting his observations to the facts of behavior. Objectively viewed, persistent goal-oriented behavior is a fact of nature. Moreover, under laboratory conditions it is possible to observe the gradual development of goal-oriented behavior out of random, aimless activity.

I watch the cows walk slowly up the hill, across the field, into the barn where they are fed. Nobody knows whether the cow has a prophetic inkling of her goal when she starts the journey. It is idle to speculate about the matter.

I do know, however, that I am aware of certain goals, that to some extent I can foresee the consequences of my actions, and I believe that conscious purposes *as such* may have an influence upon my actions.

REGULATION AND DIRECTION BY SET

In a thorough review of the experimental studies of *set,* Gibson (1941) pointed out the divergent meanings in current usage of the term. The looseness of terminology is illustrated by the following list of variants, all of which occur in psychological articles: *mental set, motor set, neural set, voluntary set, unconscious set, postural set, organic set, preparatory set, task set, situation set, goal set, temporary set, permanent set, set to react, set to perceive, expectation, hypothesis, anticipation, foresight, intention, attitude, directing tendency, determining tendency, tension, vector, need, attention, perseveration,* and *preoccupation.*

The term *set* connotes different things to different psychologists. The term is used with various meanings in a large and heterogeneous literature of experimental studies. After reviewing this literature Gibson concluded that the divergent and overlapping meanings could be reduced to the following: (1) a prearoused expectation of stimulus objects, qualities or relations; (2) a conceptual schema, not expected, but aroused by the stimulus pattern; (3) an expectation of stimulus relationships, either prearoused or acquired during repeated stimulation; (4) an intention to react by making a specific movement, or not to react; (5) an intention to perform a familiar mental operation such as multiplying or giving a word of opposite meaning; (6) a mental operation or method, not intended, that is aroused by the problem or learned in the course of problem solving; (7) a tendency to complete or finish an activity; (8) a perseverative tendency to go on performing an activity after the occasion is over.

I have carefully considered Gibson's review and believe it is not necessary nor desirable to preserve all of the meanings of *set* under a single rubric. It seems to me that *set* is primarily a neural structure or organization which is regulative and directive. This neural structure may be called a *central set.* The term *expectation* refers to a central set to observe or experience something. The term *intention* refers to a central set to act. There are other meanings of *set* that will be considered below.

Neuromuscular and Neural Set

The central set may or may not have peripheral manifestations. If it is revealed in bodily posture, with tonic changes in the somatic musculature, it is a *neuromuscular* set; but there are *neural* sets that do not show themselves in muscular changes.

Animals and human beings frequently assume bodily postures which reveal a preparation to observe or to respond to stimulation in a specific way. Thus the cat remains crouched before a mouse hole. She is relatively motionless except for a slight quivering, which is scarcely observable, and her whole body is set to pounce upon the mouse when the victim is well out of the hole. Again, a deer on the mountain side is startled by some noise. He stands motionless with head in the air—looking, listening, sniffing—poised to run. An unexpected movement or noise starts a race up the mountain side and away from possible danger. Again, a man is set to run 100 yards. His toe is on the line; he crouches and maintains a stance while awaiting the gun. His neuromuscular machinery is temporarily integrated for starting the race. His muscles are tense so that he can spring forward the instant that the gun is fired. He may even "jump the gun." Such overt bodily postures are readily observed. They involve tonic changes in the muscles and also inner preparation of the viscera and nervous system.

A distinction must be drawn between an overt bodily posture (neuromuscular set) and an inner preparation for perception and action which is not outwardly observable (neural set). The need for this distinction came to light clearly in a classical study of delayed reaction.

Hunter (1913) demonstrated that if animals are trained to leave the apparatus (for food) by an exit that is signaled by a light, they are capable of delaying their reaction when the signal is given and then removed while the subjects are delayed in the starting box. In other words, animals are able to delay their responses, reacting correctly when there is a pause between signal and release from the starting box. How do they accomplish this feat? By what bodily mechanism are they able to delay their responses? Hunter found that a dog might delay his response by lying on the floor with head and eyes pointed towards the position where the light had flashed. When released he moved in a direction determined by his bodily posture. Other subjects, notably raccoons and children, were able to delay their responses to the signals without maintaining overt bodily postures. Raccoons could move about in the restraining compartment of the apparatus without maintaining any postural set and yet go to the exit that had previously been signaled. Obviously, some inner mechanism made it possible for the subjects to respond correctly after intervals of delay. There was a *neural* set.

Every intent to perceive, every intent to react in a specific way, has its corresponding neural preparation. The intent to take a trip, to visit a friend, to see a particular show, to make a purchase, etc., is a neural readiness that persists over a period of time. For example, when Paul Revere was set for his historic ride he awaited the appearance of one or two lights in the belfry of Old North Church. "One if by land, two if by sea." The perception of first one and then a second light released in him a pattern of behavior for which he was fully prepared. There was a prearranged signal, a preparatory set, an intent to act.

Experiments on the Organizing of a Central Set

In year number five of the Stanford-Binet test of intelligence is the following item: ". . . Here's a key. I want you to put it on that chair over there; then I want you to shut (or open) that door, and then bring me the box which you see over there. . . ." If the child understands the instructions and carries out the three commissions correctly, he passes the item. The verbal instruction builds up a temporary set which regulates the ensuing behavior.

In laboratory tests upon immediate memory and the span of attention the subject is typically presented with sensory material (letters, short words, dots, geometrical figures, etc.) and instructed to reproduce it immediately after presentation. In one experiment, for example, the subject was seated before a panel of miniature electric lights; several of these (three to ten) were flashed successively. The subject observed the positions and sequence of the flashes; then reproduced the pattern by pressing appropriate keys. In this experiment the verbal instruction *set* the subject for his task. As the lights were flashing he organized them into a pattern and responded immediately on the basis of his *set*. The difficulty of a task depended upon the number of lights and their spatiotemporal pattern.

In a series of experiments at the University of Illinois it was found that the ability of a subject to organize a temporary set depends upon such factors as age, previous practice, rate of presenting the material, and spatiotemporal relations. Trained subjects report that when a pattern of lights is presented there is subjectively experienced an organizing or binding together of the successive flashes into a pattern which determines the following response.

In one experiment (Compton and Young, 1933) the aim was to discover how the sensory mode of presentation of a pattern affects the performance of the subject in immediately reproducing that pattern. In this experiment the subject was seated at a table with his bare forearms resting lightly on a felt pad.

The apparatus is pictured in Figure 55. In front of the subject were five posts and five signal keys (1, 2, 3, 4, and 5). On the posts were miniature electric lamps (located at A, B, C, D, and E) and electric

Figure 55. Apparatus for controlling the sensory mode of presenting spatio-temporal patterns. (Description in the text.) *After* Compton and Young (1933).

buzzers (located at Q, R, S, T, and U). In the felt pad there were holes (located at I, J, K, L, and M) through each of which a cutaneous stimulator, actuated by an electromagnet, could make a sharp contact with the skin.

The same patterns of stimulation were presented in three sensory modes: by successive flashes of lights, by successive soundings of buzzers, or by successive point contacts with the skin. Mixed modes of presentation were also used. The task of the subject was to attend to the pattern presented by successive point stimulations and to reproduce it immediately by pressing the signal keys. The timing, the sequence of point stimulations, and the recording of subjects' responses were all controlled remotely.

An analysis of the data brought to light several important points. It was found that difficulty in reproducing a spatiotemporal pattern depends upon the sensory mode of presentation. The little-used tactual mode was the most difficult of all and the mixed modes of presentation, e.g., visual and tactual alternating, were more difficult than the simple modes, e.g., all points presented visually.

For present purposes we are interested in the following: If a pattern is difficult when presented visually, it is also difficult when presented auditorily, tactually, or in a mixed mode. When the patterns were ranked in order of difficulty, as determined by errors in reproducing them, rank-order coefficients of correlation across the different sensory modes of presentation were in the range of .81 to .96. These high values can only mean that the difficulty of organizing a central set and acting upon it immediately, is dependent to a high degree upon the spatiotemporal relations. Although difficulty does depend upon the sensory mode of presentation, the main factor in difficulty lies in the spatial pattern and the sequence of point stimulations. Difficulty arises in the *central organization* of a set.

Another experiment (Thomas and Young, 1942) was a complement of the foregoing in that it involved one mode of presentation and three modes of reproduction. The aim was to discover how the motor mode of reproducing a pattern affects performance.

The apparatus was somewhat similar to that used in the above experiment. See Figure 56. The subject was seated at a table upon which were six posts (1, 2, 3, 4, 5, and 6) holding miniature electric lamps for presenting flashes of lights in sequence. All patterns were presented visually by the successive flashing of these lights. The subject, however, was instructed to use three modes of reproducing a pattern. He could signal the pattern by touching six keys with his head (A, B, C, D, E, and F), by pressing six keys with his fingers (G, H, I, J, K, and L), or by using pedals (M, N, O, P, Q, and R) resembling the pedals of an organ. These modes of reproducing a pattern were employed singly and also in combination, e.g., by pressing alternately a hand key and a pedal. Before every trial and throughout the trial a sign (located at X) indicated to the subject the mode of reproduction to be used on that trial. As in the first experiment, the patterns and timing and recording of errors in reproduction were all controlled at a distance from the apparatus.

Results show that the motor mode of reproduction is a factor determining difficulty of the task. Single modes, e.g., the use of hand keys only or pedals only, were the easiest. Patterns of response that required a shifting from one motor mode to another were more difficult, e.g., alternately using the head keys and the pedals.

Importantly, however, it was found that when a pattern was difficult to reproduce with one group of muscles, this pattern was also difficult when reproduced with other muscle groups. When patterns were ranked in order of difficulty for the different modes of reproduction the coefficients of correlation were in the order of .85 to .89. These high values indicate that difficulty depends upon the spatiotemporal relations of point stimulations in a pattern.

The above experiments show that sensory and motor conditions are important determinants of difficulty. They also show that the main source of difficulty lies in the *central organizing* of point stimulations into a spatiotemporal pattern, i.e., in getting set for action. The process of organizing a set is a *central* process which is dependent upon and revealed in peripheral conditions.

Learning to Assume a Set

In the experiments described above no test was repeated. Although the same spatiotemporal patterns of point stimulations were presented to each subject several times over, the patterns were presented in different sensory modes or reproduced in different motor modes. In terms of the S-R bonds no test was repeated for any subject. Despite this fact there was unmistakable evidence of a learning effect. The subjects steadily improved in their ability to assume a set and to respond correctly on the basis of that set.

Learning to assume a set, therefore, cannot be described in terms of S-R connections. It is a central process. The process has been described by Harlow (1949) as *learning to learn* or as the *acquisition of learning sets*.

Harlow offered monkeys and young children a choice between two objects that differed in some respect. If the subject lifted the "correct" object, a food reward was disclosed; if he lifted the "incorrect" object, there was no reward. There was always some cue as to which object was "correct." The cue might be the shape or size or color or some other specific feature of the object. In a series of trials the subject had to learn to discriminate between the objects on the basis of the cue.

In this work the experimental unit was not the single trial but the problem to be solved. For example, a problem might be solved by lifting always the triangular object or by lifting the smaller of two objects. In some tests the cue was reversed, e.g., instead of lifting the smaller object the subject was required to lift the larger. The first trial gave the subject an opportunity to discover which choice was rewarded and which was not. Trial 2 and subsequent trials revealed the extent of learning to solve the problem on the basis of information previously received. A complete test consisted of a series of fourteen different problems to be solved.

The percentage of correct responses on trial 2 was used by Harlow as a measure of performance. Figure 57 shows the percentage of correct responses in successive blocks of fourteen problems each. The lower curve pictures the improvement in performance that is dependent upon previous experience in problem solving. The upper curve records the percentage of correct discriminations when the sensory cues were reversed. This shows that after a problem has been solved the reversal

Figure 56. Apparatus for studying the motor mode of reproducing spatiotemporal patterns. (Description in the text.) *After* Thomas and Young (1942).

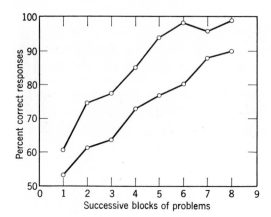

Figure 57. Acquisition of learning set based on trial-2 responses of monkeys. *After* Harlow (1949).

of cues leads to efficient relearning. Both curves indicate a *learning to learn,* or improvement in performance dependent upon previous experience in problem solving.

Figure 58 is similar. It shows the percentage of correct responses on trial 2 with children as subjects. Nine children, ages 3 to 5 years, were given four series of fourteen problems to solve. The curve shows that the percentage of problems solved correctly increased from block to block of trials. Further, the performance of the children was consistently superior to that of the monkeys.

Harlow has shown that antagonistic sets can develop together and coexist with a minimum of conflict. Thus monkeys were given a group

Figure 58. Acquisition of learning set based on trial-2 responses of young children. *After* Harlow (1949).

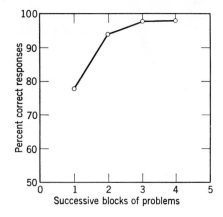

of fourteen problems that involved discrimination between the right and left positions; they were also given a group of fourteen problems that involved discrimination of object qualities. Blocks of fourteen object-quality problems and fourteen right-left discrimination problems were presented alternately. From block to block the percentage of correct responses for the right-left discrimination problems increased. The percentages of correct responses for the object-discrimination problems, however, remained about the same. By the end of the experiment two kinds of basically antagonistic sets had "learned" to live together.

Therefore, monkeys and men *learn to learn*. They acquire facility in learning to assume a set that leads to the solution of a certain kind of problem. Harlow has extended the principle into the field of personality.

Each contact of a monkey with a human being is a specific learning trial. When monkeys first come to the laboratory they are wild and intractable, but within a few years they acquire "good" traits of personality. They learn social-emotional sets. Each new person that the monkey encounters presents a separate problem. Learning to react favorably to one person is followed by more rapid learning of favorable reactions to the next person to whom the monkey is socially introduced. Eventually the monkey's favorable reactions to new people are acquired so rapidly that they appear almost instantaneously.

The Role of Response Set in Test Performance

Cronbach (1946, 1950) defined a *response set* as something that causes a person consistently to make different responses to test items from those he would have made had the same content been presented in a different form. Clear illustrations of response sets can be found in the marking, by the subjects, of standard psychological tests and examinations of the true-false variety. Subjects tend to use the same category repeatedly rather than to discriminate and judge.

In the Seashore test of pitch discrimination, for example, the subject is required to judge whether the second tone is higher or lower than the first. If the pitch difference is small, the subject may lapse into checking "H" (higher) consistently or "L" (lower) consistently. The score does not depend wholly upon the sensitivity to pitch differences but it depends in part upon a bias of reporting "H" or "L." Again, in a true-false examination the college student may have a bias to acquiesce which is shown by a tendency to answer "Yes" or "True" consistently for a series of items.

In some psychological tests there are three categories of response: "Yes," "?," and "No" or "Like," "Indifferent," and "Dislike." Here some subjects have a bias towards caution which leads them to check the neutral, or "can't say" category; others have a tendency to guess or gamble which leads them to avoid the neutral category.

In essay-type examinations some students have a bias toward expressing many ideas; others give only a skeletal outline. The wise student will not yield to his biases but try to find out what is desired by the teacher. When the form of question permits brief or extensive listing of items as "List the causes of . . ." or "Point out the differences between . . ." there are wide individual differences in the inclusiveness of the lists. The response set of the student is at least one factor regulating the inclusiveness of the list apart from the amount of information the student possesses.

Cronbach demonstrated the existence of response sets. He showed statistically that they affect the reliability and validity of test scores. Further, he made a number of practical suggestions for reduction of errors that depend upon response sets.

Laboratory rats commonly reveal response sets in tests of preference. An animal may consistently take the food at his left or that at his right without any preferential discrimination between the foods. Occasionally these position habits shift unaccountably. With rats a response bias is quite easy to observe; with human subjects the operation of a bias is more subtle and difficult to detect.

In general, the response set of the subject is a factor of considerable importance for it determines in part the response of the subject. It is a factor to be considered in any interpretation of test scores or laboratory data.

Neural Readiness without Intention

Typically the subject is not aware of his response set. The set is a determinant of behavior that operates without his knowledge. It is a neural readiness to react in a particular way.

Sometimes when a specific intent is frustrated a neural determination remains. Examples of this can be found in the experiences of everyday life. I recently wished to find and reread an article written by a colleague upon the history of educational psychology. I searched through several piles of offprints but failed to find the paper. The search was dropped and the matter put out of mind. Several weeks later, while I was looking for another article, the paper upon the history of educational psychology suddenly came to light. The paper was immediately recognized and removed from the pile. In this instance a neural readiness must have carried over from the frustrated search to the present discovery.

Another example of neural readiness is found in a common experience of trying, unsuccessfully, to recall some name or event. After futile attempts to recall, the matter is dropped but later, without warning, the sought-for memory suddenly appears.

Different from these examples are instances of perseveration. A catchy tune keeps running through one's head; one repeatedly hums or whistles it. Vivid images of an emotional experience recur; they are unwelcome but cannot be put out of mind. In such instances there is persistence without intention or persistence despite a wish to forget. Some neural readiness underlies the perseverative tendency.

Still different is the tendency to complete an unfinished act and the tendency to remember the incomplete act better than the completed act. These tendencies involve what Kurt Lewin would call a mental tension.

Some kinds of neural readiness may depend upon physicochemical sensitizing of bodily structures. For example, Craig (1918) reported that he could predict the behavior of doves by observing their incipient responses. If the birds were thirsty, they would become restless and make incipient drinking movements that persisted until water was found and taken. Again, during the nest-building season doves tend to pick up straws and build them into nests even when their behavior has no relation to the construction of a particular nest. The incipient behavior reveals a readiness or sensitization for a particular kind of activity.

It is doubtful whether the concept of *set* should be made to include instances of persistent behavior and behavioral trends such as the above. The concept is best limited to a central neural preparation or determination to act.

The Set of Attention and Will

The concept of *set* is of major importance in all discussions of attention and will.

Among writers of psychology textbooks the treatment of the topic of attention has varied widely according to the bias of the author. Some, like Titchener (1921), regard attention as a characteristic of experience and devote a separate chapter to the topic. Others, like

Newman (1948), treat attention within the context of perception. Others, like Cole (1939), prefer to consider attention within the framework of motivation. Still others, like Dashiell (1949), discuss attention in close conjunction with the concept of temporary set. Strict behaviorists do not use the term *attention* since it is said to have mentalistic implications. Despite this diversity, all psychology textbooks treat the topic of direction and regulation of activity.

Voluntary attention depends on a determining set to observe or to act. The set of attention may organize the perceptual field and the course of action. The set of attention may select out some part of experience for clear observation. The set of attention may sustain and regulate the activity in progress as when a student "attends" to the study of his lesson. The set of attention may give meaning to experience.

The concept of *set* is also of prime importance in the analysis of will. A person who continues without yielding in his determination to carry out some intended course of action is said to have a strong will. Columbus, for example, had a strong will when he kept his ships sailing westward into unknown waters despite the fears and protests of his men, the demand that he turn back, and the threat of mutiny. If we do not like the strong-willed man, we say he is stubborn! A weak-willed man, by contrast, is vacillating and uncertain. He is slow to make up his mind (to arrive at a determination) and easily changed.

A sympton of abnormal behavior known as *abulia* (no will) marks a condition in which the subject has great difficulty in deciding what to do and in holding to his decision.

Functional Properties of Determining Set

The above discussions have brought to light the functional properties of determining set. These properties are revealed in the conscious experiences of individuals and in their actions. The following list is a survey of the properties of set:

1. A set can *select* and *accentuate* some part of experience. Within the perceptual field an object may be singled out for attentive observation. A single tone within a musical chord may be selected for attentive observation; the tone is accentuated, emphasized.

2. A set can *selectively utilize the residues of experience*. If a subject is instructed to respond to a stimulus word by a word with opposite meaning, he can do so. If he is instructed to add, subtract, multiply

or divide, he can carry out the task. In all such instances the instructional set utilizes the residues of past experience

3. A set can *regulate* and *direct* the course of action. When a motorist signals a left turn by flashing his directional lights he is indicating a set to turn left; the set regulates his course of action. Again, in the reaction experiment the subject is instructed to press a key when a light is flashed; he is set for a very specific action.

An intent to act regulates behavior in relation to some goal. The set not only regulates the course of action but produces a motivating tension and thus energizes behavior.

4. A set can *sustain* activity. This property of set is especially prominent in voluntary action. A man says, "I'm going to close the window." He then walks across the room and closes it. His words express a determination that sustains and regulates action. In almost every sustained, purposive activity there is an underlying set that determines it.

5. A set can *organize* the pattern of experience. In the above experiments upon the organizing of a central set the subjects were instructed to reproduce a spatiotemporal pattern presented by point stimulations. They organized the successive point stimulations into a pattern which was immediately reproduced by movements.

If two stimulations are physically simultaneous, the impression for which the subject is attentively predisposed is the first to make its conscious effect. This is the so-called law of prior entry. For example, suppose that a sharp click is made at the ear and at the same instant an electrical stimulation of the skin. If the subject is expectantly set to hear something, he is likely to report the sequence click-touch. If he is expectantly set to feel something, he tends to report the sequence touch-click. Thus the time relations of conscious experience are to some extent dependent upon the subject's set.

The role of attentive set in organizing the pattern of conscious experience might be illustrated many times over from the literature of perception. This was shown by Floyd Allport (1955) in a scholarly review of contemporary literature upon perception. He emphasized the central and fundamental importance of the doctrine of determining set.

In general, it can be said that a determining set selects and accentuates experiences, utilizes the residues of experience selectively, regulates and directs the course of action, sustains activity, and organizes the pattern of experience. The concept of set is thus very broad. It is also basic.

TENSION AND EFFORT

When a man attends to a task under difficulties there is a sense of effort, strain, tension. Suppose one is studying a lesson while the radio is booming in the next room, or suppose one is driving a car at night and the glare from an oncoming auto makes it difficult to see the road. Immediately there is a feeling of strain or effort. Distractions, conflicts, and frustrations, are typically associated with tension.

Subjectively the feeling of effort has been described as a pattern of kinesthetic sensation. Objectively tension is measurable in terms of the action currents in the muscle fibers.

The following experiments relate to the factor of tension and effort as it exists in the subject while maintaining a determining set. There is also a discussion of the law of least effort which refers to the minimizing of effort or of work.

Induced Muscular Tension and Memorizing

It is widely known that both relaxation and a high degree of muscular tension interfere with the task of memorizing. A moderate degree of tension and alertness is conducive to efficient performance.

Under everyday conditions the subject feels a sense of effort when he undertakes to memorize a list of words. The sense of effort is based upon tension within groups of skeletal muscles. Under laboratory conditions the degree of muscular tension can be increased by requiring the subject to hold a weight or to squeeze a dynamometer while carrying out some task such as memorizing a list of nonsense syllables. The muscular tension produced in these ways augments the tension normally present when the subject is set to carry out the task.

In an experiment, which has served as a model of experimental method, Courts (1939) induced muscular tension by requiring his subjects to squeeze a dynamometer while learning three-letter syllables. On the first day of the experiment, sixty college men were instructed, individually, to squeeze as hard as possible upon the dynamometer for a period of 30 seconds. The maximal strength of grip was measured and in this way individual differences were determined. Then, for each individual, fractional tensions were computed equal to ⅛, ¼, ⅜, ½, and ¾ of the maximal squeeze. These tensions were utilized in the experiment.

The dynamometer was modified and adjusted so that a miniature light could be seen in peripheral vision so long as the strength of squeeze was kept at or near a constant level. If the squeeze was too weak or too strong, this light went out. It aided the subject in maintaining a constant tension while carrying out the experimental task of memorizing.

Each subject learned twelve lists of syllables. The syllables were exposed one at a time, at a constant rate, by means of a memory drum. There were pauses between the separate presentations of a list. After going through a list once there was a short rest period; then the list was repeated. This time the subject attempted to anticipate a syllable and spell it out before it appeared at the window. At the start of a retention test an X (the opening signal) appeared at the window; this served as a signal to spell out the first syllable. When the first syllable appeared the subject could verify his recall and attempt to spell out the next syllable on the list, and so on.

Each syllable consisted of three letters, such as BMT. The score for a given test was the number of letters correctly anticipated. The score is an index of efficiency in memorizing.

Figure 59 is a sample of the results obtained. The graph shows the relation between the mean number of letters correctly anticipated and

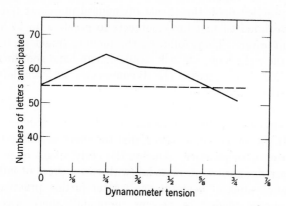

Figure 59. Relation between numbers of letters correctly anticipated and dynamometer tension. *Plotted from* data of Courts (1939).

the muscular tension as controlled by the dynamometer. The graph indicates that there is an optimal level of muscular tension for the task of memorizing this kind of material. The optimal tension is that produced by the effort of the subject in carrying out the task plus a tension induced by $\frac{1}{4}$ of the maximal squeeze on the dynamometer. Stronger or weaker tensions than this induce a suboptimal performance. When the induced tension was $\frac{3}{4}$ of the maximal grip the score for memorizing was lower than with no supplementary tension at all. This high level of tension was definitely disturbing to the subjects.

The result agrees with a well-known principle that in carrying out any task there is an optimal level of tension. G. L. Freeman (1938), for example, has offered data to support the thesis that each performance has an optimal level of muscular tension above which a further increase is disturbing. A tension load which is optimal for one type of performance may be detrimental to an activity of a different character. In general, the more complex the performance, the less the total tension that is required for optimal performance.

It may be assumed that for any given task there is an optimal level of tension. It is meaningful to speak of undermotivation, optimal motivation, overmotivation. In the above experiments by Courts the optimal muscular tension for memorizing three-letter syllables was experimentally demonstrated.

Induced Muscular Tension and Practice

In a follow-up experiment, Courts (1942a, 1942b) studied the influence of practice upon the effects of induced muscular tension. He required two hundred and forty subjects to practice up to fifty trials on a pursuit rotor. They followed the moving target of the pursuit rotor with the right hand—a task requiring eye-hand coordination. At the same time they squeezed the dynamometer with the left hand at the specified level of tension.

The data confirmed the above result that induced muscular tension may have either a facilitative or an inhibitory effect depending upon its level. It was observed, however, that the effect of induced muscular tension varied with practice. During the early stages of practice the curves of performance were bimodal, with two degrees of induced tension that gave superior performance. After further practice the performance curves tended to become unimodal; there was a single optimal tension.

Courts re-examined the data upon memorizing three-letter syllables with various degrees of induced muscular tension. He found that in the early stages of learning there was a bimodality in the curves of performance similar to that in the data obtained with the pursuit rotor. The curves were roughly M-shaped. With further practice, however, the curves of performance became unimodal.

To explain the facts Courts assumed that the net performance level is dependent upon two factors and is, in fact, the algebraic sum of these two determinants. The first factor is the influence of the proprioceptive tension itself. This can be either facilitative or inhibitory depending upon its degree. And this effect may change with practice independently of changes in the second factor. The second factor is an emotional disruption of behavior produced by (1) the pain from continuous pressure upon the dynamometer, and (2) the annoyance of having to attend to a bifurcated task—to following the target of the rotor and at the same time maintaining a constant pressure on the dynamometer. This pain-annoyance factor is greater at high levels of tension than at low.

Courts concluded that the detrimental influence of high degrees of induced muscular tension becomes more marked as learning continues. With degrees of tension that are above the optimal tension, the effect of practice is to accentuate the impairment of performance; and practice tends to impair performance at progressively lower levels of tension. With degrees of tension that are below the optimal tension, and hence facilitative, practice has a different effect. The facilitative influence of induced muscular tension increases, with practice, up to a maximum and then with further practice it decreases. Thus, Courts assumed, practice has different effects upon performances with super-optimal and sub-optimal tensions. Observed changes in performance are the result of these two hypothetical factors (inhibitory and facilitative) interacting.

Muscular Tension and Effort

In considering the optimal conditions for work the human engineer may take account of the effort that a worker devotes to his task. The worker may be lazy, over-relaxed, and not at all eager to accomplish anything or he may be over-zealous about his work. Somewhere between the extremes of minimal and maximal effort is a level of motivation that yields optimal performance.

The term *effort* has been widely used in daily life and in psychological writings but it has not been adequately defined in objective terms. More attention has been given to the study of fatigue than to effort during continuous work. It is probable that the psychological problems of fatigue are subsidiary to those of effort and that they can be more easily solved when a thorough study of effort has been made.

Ryan, Cottrell, and Bitterman (1950) made an experimental approach to the study of effort. First of all, they faced the problem of measurement. If one is to study effort in relation to the efficiency of performance, in the industrial situation or the school or the laboratory, a valid method for measuring effort must be found.

Effort obviously refers to a conscious experience of the worker. At times he feels he is doing all he can to perform well; at other times he feels that he is loafing on the job, just "coasting along." The worker experiences these differences in the intensity of his effort but there is no reliable method of scaling or measuring subjective feelings and evaluations. A physiological, objective method of measuring effort is, therefore, needed.

Ryan, Cottrell, and Bitterman write:

While effort is clearly related to energy consumption in the case of heavy muscular work, it is equally clear that energy consumption cannot be used as an index of effort in light or sedentary tasks. For example, very intense effort in solving arithmetic problems involves very low energy requirements even though the effort may be as great as that in lifting heavy weights. Here it would appear that it is not so much the amount of energy as the patterning of energy within the organism which is related to effort. Time-study engineers have developed procedures for evaluating effort in a worker by observing his performance, but these procedures have not been demonstrated to be reliable or valid even for tasks which involve overt patterns of movement, and they are not applicable at all to "mental" and sedentary tasks. Among the physiological indicators which correlate with effort, muscular tension holds much promise for the solution of a variety of practical problems of efficiency. Variations in muscular contraction which are too small to be reflected in the total energy consumption of the body can be measured electrically, and it appears likely that these small variations in level of muscular activity are related to effort in mental and sedentary tasks.

As an index of effort, Ryan, Cottrell, and Bitterman utilized muscular action potentials. They developed apparatus which permitted the continuous recording and totalization of electrical activity during periods of work. Simultaneous recordings of action potentials were made from four areas of the body—arm, leg, ears, and neck—that did not interfere with carrying out the experimental task.

The subjects were instructed to compare two groups of letters presented in a small window and to decide for each pair whether the two groups were the same or different. Glare was introduced to compel the subjects to exert effort in carrying out the task. The laboratory situation is analogous to that of an automobile driver who has to attend to road conditions at night while the glare from an oncoming car makes this difficult.

Results indicated that there were significant increments in muscular potential in all regions of the body when severe glare was introduced. There was no evidence of differential effects in the four areas of the body. A combination of the electrical changes occurring at several points in the body produced a more significant measure than changes in any single area.

Results demonstrate that effort in overcoming glare is indicated by activity of the muscles throughout the body. When the subject exerts an effort to carry out his task despite the glare there is a general increase of muscular tension. The exerting of effort, therefore, is an objective process that occurs in the muscles and nerves.

Distraction and Effort

In an early experiment Morgan (1916) studied the effects of distraction upon performance. His subjects worked upon a task that required constant attention while resisting a distraction.

The task consisted of pressing keys, one at a time, with the index finger. The keys in front of the subject were numbered: 1, 2, 3, 4, 5, 6, 7, 8, 9, and 0. At a window in front of the subject digits were exposed, one at a time, in a haphazard sequence. The task of the subject was to look at the window and see what number was exposed, then to press the corresponding key with the index finger of the right hand. When the key was pressed another number immediately appeared. Since the series of digits was haphazard, there was no way of predicting what the next figure would be. Continuous alertness was required.

The subjects worked singly in a room that was quiet except for the distractions introduced from time to time. Distractions consisted of phonograph music and various noises. Vocal and instrumental solos, conversation, and a monologue were played on the phonograph as distractions during the work period. Other distractions were a fire bell 8 feet behind the subject, an electric buzzer on the table, another buzzer on a tin box beneath the table, etc.

The subjects were not told the nature of the experiment and they were quite ignorant of the ways of experimental psychologists. They simply carried out the task of pressing the keys whether the room was quiet or noisy.

Several measures of performance were recorded. First, the reaction time (interval between exposure of digit and pressing of key) was measured. Second, erroneous responses were recorded. Third, respiration was recorded by means of a pneumograph. Fourth, the pressure of finger against key was measured.

Morgan found that the initial effect of distraction was to retard the speed of work. After an initial retardation, however, there was a compensatory increase in speed. In many instances the distracted subjects exceeded the speed attained before introduction of the distraction.

The subjects reported that they put forth an extra effort to overcome the distractions. The extra effort was registered objectively as increased pressure against the keys. During the noisy periods the pressure against the keys was increased and during periods of quiescence it was relaxed to a normal level. Some subjects resisted distraction by articulating the numbers; this technique showed up as a change in respiration. In general, the subjects reported that there was an increased tension associated with their efforts to overcome distraction.

The increased pressure against the keys turned out to be a better measure of resistance to distraction than the changes in reaction time.

It was found that a certain degree of auditory stimulation facilitates performance. The effort of maintaining an attentive set, despite distraction, builds up a tension that aids the worker. There is, however, an optimal level of tension. Very loud noises are disturbing or disrupting.

The Law of Least Effort

Zipf (1949) formulated a law of least effort which he regards as a primary principle governing the behavior of individuals and groups. He illustrated the principle in many contexts including the economy of speech, the development of language, the solving of problems, and gross physical work. Here is an example.

A man wishes to travel from one city to another. There is a straight road connecting the cities and he follows this road; it is the path of least distance, least time, least work. Suppose, however, that a range of mountains intervenes between the two cities. The path of least distance would be through a non-existent tunnel; but this is not considered for the work of digging a tunnel would be prohibitive. The least time might be achieved by a rapid climb over the mountain; but the muscular effort (as well as the risk of a climb) is so great that the possibility is abandoned. The path of least effort is to follow a tortuous road through the range of mountains. Men and pack animals take the long winding road because this is the path of least effort.

Zipf contends that human behavior is at all times determined by the necessity of economizing effort. He explains that by *least effort* he does not mean that the energy expended in work at a given moment is kept at a minimum, but he means that the average rate of energy expenditure over a period of time is minimized. A person is governed by a principle of *"least average rate of probable work."* The concept, Zipf points out, involves elements of foresight and "mentation," since the individual has to estimate what path requires the least effort.

Examples of the law of least effort can be found on every hand. Consider the relation between tools and jobs. A man uses a tool because his task can be accomplished with less effort than without it. The man who uses a team of oxen and a primitive plow to till the soil is accomplishing a large result with a minimum of energy expenditure. The modern farmer who operates a tractor is working with still greater economy of effort. Again, when a student walks across the campus from one building to another he tends to take the shortest path—across the lawn and through the hedge. A sign "Keep off the Grass" is a silent tribute to the law of least effort.

The principle has validity in physical science (least action) as well as in the science of human behavior (least effort, least work). As usually stated, the principle makes no reference to the bodily mechanisms that regulate behavior.

In a general way we can understand the biological utility of conserving energies. There is a limit to the amount of physical work an organism can accomplish. Long before that limit is reached processes of fatigue and pain set in to check further expenditure of energy in physical work. But in the normal activities of everyday life we tend to take the easier path, to follow the line of least resistance.

It should be emphasized that the selection of the path of least effort is dependent upon experience. An organism must discriminate between two paths to the goal to obtain some basis for estimating the relative energy expenditure (effort, work) involved in following the paths. Experience plays a major role in the discrimination between paths and in decision. If a man finds that a path in a labyrinth is a *cul de sac,* he learns to avoid it; entrance into a blind wastes time and energy. A man learns to avoid useless, energy-consuming, time-consuming movements and, in general, to follow the lines of least effort.

Laboratory animals learn to avoid blind alleys in a maze and to take the most direct route to the goal box. Useless and excessive movements tend to drop out of behavior and the shortest path is chosen. This fact has been generally recognized.

Tsai (1932) formulated two related principles which he called the laws of *minimum effort* and *maximum satisfaction*. He stated the principles as follows:

1. Among several alternatives of behavior leading to equivalent satisfaction of some potent organic need, the animal, within the limits of its discriminative ability, tends finally to select that which involves the least expenditure of energy (law of minimum effort).

2. Among several alternatives of behavior involving equivalent expenditure of energy, the animal, within the limits of its discriminative ability, tends finally to select that which leads to the greatest relief of organic needs (law of maximum satisfaction).

The first law (minimum effort) arises from objective experiments upon animal behavior. In one series of experiments rats were allowed to choose between two doors both of which opened to the food box. One door had a weight attached to it and the other had none. During a series of trials the rats learned to favor the door with no weight. When weights were attached to both doors the animals learned to favor the door with the lighter weight. In another series of experiments rats were offered a choice between two paths in each of which there was an obstacle to be climbed. During a series of choices they learned to select the path with the lower obstacle, i.e., the path that involved the least climbing. Again, there have been various experiments in which hungry rats have been offered a choice between a long and a short path to food. Generally they learn to select the short path. In these and related experiments the animal subjects have generally learned to select the path involving the least expenditure of energy. The choice, however, must be within the capacity of the animal to discriminate between weights, heights of obstacles, lengths of paths, and the like.

The second law (satisfaction) does not relate to the present topic so we will not elaborate upon it. Tsai illustrates the law of satisfaction by some experiments upon the choice of nutrients. When given a choice between food and water, hungry rats tend to select food and thirsty animals to select water. Animals that are both hungry and thirsty tend to select food and water combined in preference to either food or water. It is thus the kind of satisfaction that regulates performance rather than the level of energy expenditure.

Although Zipf regards the law of least effort as fundamental, it is clear that this is only one among other general principles. The principle can be obscured or opposed by other factors. For example, when a man makes a long and dangerous trip through the snow to rescue someone he is determined by something other than the law of least effort (which would require him to stay safely at home).

The man who takes the path of least effort may become a lazy bum, an object of charity. He may be socially condemned for acting according to Zipf's principle. This can only mean that there are other determinants of behavior than the exertion of effort.

THE FEEDBACK PRINCIPLE IN THE REGULATION OF BEHAVIOR

In any realistic explanation of behavior it must be recognized that the total pattern of excitation upon the sensorium is constantly changing. Every movement of the eye changes the pattern of the visual field. Every movement of the head changes the binaural pattern of stimulation. Every movement of a limb changes the pattern of stimulation from muscles, tendons, and joints. Every substance that is tasted or smelled produces a change in the total stimulus pattern.

These changes in the pattern of excitation are constantly fed into the central nervous system via the afferent nerves. The ever-changing patterns of information are utilized by the organism in solving problems, making adjustments to the external world.

Learning is possible when uniform sequences of excitation occur. For example, a man learns to follow the same path in walking from his home to his office. When he opens the front door he sees the same buildings and streets. When he turns left at the corner the same tree comes into view. When he puts his foot on the ground there is the same solidity and feeling of support—step after step. There is a uniformity within the physical world and a corresponding uniformity in the patterns and sequences of sensory stimulation. This basic fact underlies the learning of serial habits.

It is not possible here to go into the study of learning but the following sections will illustrate the nature and importance of the feedback principle in the regulation of behavior.

The principle of feedback is important in all self-regulating mechanisms. The governor of a steam engine, through a feedback mechanism, controls the speed. The thermostat, through a feedback mechanism, regulates the temperature of a room. The organism, by means of elaborate feedback mechanisms, maintains homeostasis within the body fluids. And in the carrying out of a complex act of will the self-regulatory behavior is possible only because there is an afferent backlash from every response that is made.

In play as well as in work there is constant feedback. A man plays a pinball machine. He makes a move and there are clicking sounds and flashing lights. This sensory feedback makes his task interesting. And the perceptual feedback is also regulative of his behavior.

Visual Feedback

A great many motor skills are dependent upon visual feedback for regulation and direction. When a man aims a gun his eye guides his hands. When he jumps a stream he first estimates the distance by eye. When a basketball player makes a free throw he keeps his eye on the basket and the perceived situation determines his stance and action. In typewriting, an error may be clearly seen so that behavior is regulated to some extent by visual feedback.

When a dog is chasing a rabbit across the field the behavior of the dog is regulated by the movements of the rabbit. If the rabbit runs under a fence, the dog jumps over it. If the rabbit runs down a hole, the dog approaches and starts to dig. Obviously the dog's behavior is regulated by a constantly changing visual pattern. Of course, the dog has an inner determination to pursue his prey.

Again, when a man drives an auto his behavior is regulated by the changing traffic situation as he sees it. His steering through traffic, stopping at a red light and starting at a green, sounding the horn when a child runs into the street—all his manipulations of the controls are regulated by the perceived situation.

An example of a motor skill that is dependent upon visual feedback is found in an experiment by Elwell and Grindley (1938). A sketch of their apparatus is shown in Figure 60. The subject stood in front of the apparatus and looked down upon a ground-glass target, *J-J*, which consisted of a bull's-eye and a series of concentric rings. Beneath the target was a torch, *T*, which threw a spot of light upon the target. The torch was attached to a system of steel arms, hinged

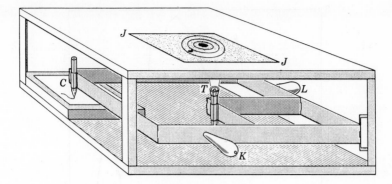

Figure 60. Two-hand motor coordination apparatus. *After* Elwell and Grindley (1938).

at every joint, which could be moved freely by two handles, K and L. The subject grasped K with the left hand and L with the right. By coordinated movements he could move the spot of light to any position upon the target. Before the experiment the torch remained switched on all the time, and the subject could study the effect of moving each arm of the apparatus. A pencil recorded movements on a paper which is shown at C.

In tests with knowledge of results the subject could see the initial position of the light before moving the handles. There was no light during actual movement. After setting the apparatus the subject could press a key to light the torch and thus he could see the direction and extent of his error. In tests without knowledge of results the torch was unlighted on all trials.

A score of 10 was given for a bull's eye, 9 for the next ring, and so on. The outermost ring scored 1 and a miss scored 0.

Figure 61 shows the average score for ten women in the two-hand coordination test. For the first two hundred trials there was knowledge of results; the subjects could turn on the light and see the direction and extent of their errors. After these trials, at a point marked B on the curve, there was no visual feedback. The subjects had no way of knowing how accurate their performance had been since the torch was not lighted on all trials beginning at B. When visual feedback was eliminated the motor skill showed a marked deterioration. The skill appears to depend upon visual feedback. The investigators concluded:

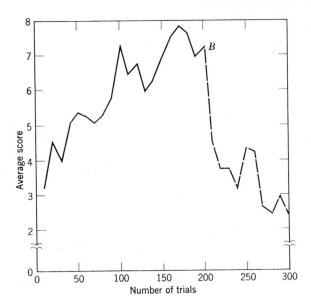

Figure 61. Scores on the motor coordination apparatus with and without visual feedback. *After* Elwell and Grindley (1938).

Knowledge of results appears to lead to improvement in performance, (a) by causing a tendency to repeat actions which have been successful, (b) by what may be called a "directive effect," i.e. by causing a tendency to correct, in the appropriate direction, any unsuccessful actions, and (c) by setting up a conscious attitude or mood which is conducive to accurate performance. Removal of knowledge of results produces, on the other hand, an attitude which is not conducive to accurate performance.

In the experiment of Elwell and Grindley the subjects reported that the task was boresome and unpleasant when knowledge of results was withheld; but it was interesting when there was the visual feedback. The affective changes have some relation to the accuracy of performance.

The experiment raises a question as to the nature of knowledge of results. In many of Thorndike's experiments the words "Right" or "Wrong," spoken by the experimenter, gave knowledge of results. These words were something like rewards or punishments in experiments upon animal learning and performance. The words "Right" or "Wrong" produced an hedonic effect. But in the present experiment of Elwell and Grindley the flashing of the torch after an adjustment of the apparatus gave visual feedback that was essential in the regulation and direction of behavior. The flashing of the light was *regulatory* in function more than incentive.

Two Examples of Spatial Orientation through Auditory Feedback

It has long been known that blind people can find their way about, perceiving and avoiding objects at a distance. How they do this has, until recently, been a matter of conjecture. Early investigators believed that the blind had a kind of "facial vision"—that they could avoid obstacles by perceiving air currents upon the face or through heightened sensitivity to pressure or temperature. Occult theories attempted to explain the facts by reference to magnetism, to ether vibrations, to the subconscious mind, or to vestigial sense organs!

The problem was brought into the laboratory by Supa, Cotzin, and Dallenbach (1944) who conducted experiments with blind and normal, blindfolded subjects. During the experiments various factors that might affect "facial vision" were systematically controlled. Vision was controlled by blindfolding normal subjects; tactile sensitivity through shielding the face; audition by plugging the ears.

The subjects were required to approach a solid wall from varying distances and to signal by raising the arm when they were near the obstacle. The blind subjects who successfully perceived and avoided the obstacle rarely could tell how they did it; they had different theories.

In these experiments, Dallenbach and his collaborators found that aural stimulation is a necessary and sufficient condition for the avoidance of obstacles by the blind. The ability was unimpaired by the elimination of cutaneous stimulation of facial nerves through air currents and sound waves. When the ears were plugged, however, and sound waves striking the ears were thus ruled out, obstacle avoidance could no longer be demonstrated. Finally, to clinch the point, it was shown that the ability to locate solid objects was retained when a microphone was moved near the object and the auditory cues were transmitted to a subject in a distant room.

Blind subjects, therefore, depend upon reflected sound waves, or an auditory feedback, to avoid collision with objects in their path. Frequently a blind person will aid himself by tapping with a cane, snapping his fingers, or shuffling his feet. The reflected sound waves enable him to maintain spatial orientation and avoid obstacles.

Another example of spatial orientation through auditory feedback is found in the flight of bats. It is commonly known that bats are practically blind; they do not depend upon vision for orientation during flight. They sleep during the day in caverns or deserted buildings, leaving at dusk to forage for food. Bats fly many miles in semidarkness, moving through forests without hitting the trees or branches; they return to their original sleeping places after a night of foraging. How do they find their way about?

Experiments by Griffin and Galambos (1941, 1942) have shown that bats avoid obstacles by emitting supersonic notes and reacting to sound waves reflected from the obstacles. The supersonic cries are above the human limit for hearing, having frequencies of 30,000 to 70,000 cycles per second. The supersonic cries are exceedingly brief in duration; in unobstructed space they are emitted at the rate of about thirty cries per second. The rate increases to about fifty per second when the bat approaches an obstacle and drops again to about thirty when the obstacle has been passed.

In the laboratory, bats were able to avoid. metal wires about 1 millimeter in diameter that were suspended vertically from the ceiling at intervals of about 30 centimeters. They avoided the wires when the walls and ceiling were padded to reduce reflection of sound to a minimum. If the eyes were covered with collodion, the performance was not impaired; but if both ears were covered, the bats were reluctant to fly and frequently bumped into walls and wires. Also when collodion was placed over the mouth, so that they could not emit supersonic sounds, the performance was greatly impaired.

The flight of bats thus illustrates how, through an auditory feedback mechanism, spatial orientation and the avoidance of obstacles are possible. Bats locate objects with reflected sound waves much as men locate underwater objects with sonar.

In some interesting experiments on the porpoise Kellogg (1958, 1959a, 1959b) demonstrated that this animal is able to avoid submerged objects by reflected sound. The porpoise has a natural sonar system for localizing objects by echo ranging and is able to discriminate between edible and non-edible objects on the basis of size. The regulation of behavior through auditory feedback thus exists in at least one marine animal.

Proprioceptive Feedback

When an animal assumes a bodily posture or makes a movement the sense organs in his muscles, tendons and joints are stimulated. The pattern of excitation from these proprioceptors is fed back into the central nervous system where it influences the ongoing neural activity. Every postural adjustment and every movement has its characteristic pattern of proprioceptive feedback.

In serial habits the proprioceptive feedback plays an essential role. Suppose, for example, that a subject is instructed to recite the alphabet. When he pronounces A there is a proprioceptive pattern that, through conditioning, arouses the response B; B arouses C, etc. Each verbal response has its own proprioceptive pattern that is associated with the next response in the series. Again, in typing by the touch system the striking of one key leads immediately to the striking of the next. The process becomes automatic so that we do not have to think about it. We think about a word or phrase and the fingers take care of themselves. One response, however, gives proprioceptive cues for the next response in the series.

Ordinarily proprioceptive feedback is bound up with other kinds of feedback. For example, consider a man who is riding a bicycle. He depends upon several senses for guidance: through vision he steers around a hole in the road; through audition he avoids a collision with an approaching vehicle; through proprioception he automatically works the pedals and controls the steering. He is scarcely aware of the role of proprioception in regulating his behavior.

Organic Feedback Systems

In emotional disturbances there are profound bodily changes in the smooth muscles and glands of the body. These changes are patterned by the joint action of the sympathetic and the parasympathetic divisions of the autonomic nervous system. The autonomic, however, is an efferent or motor system; it does not provide for the feeding back of information into the central nervous system.

There are two kinds of feedback from the bodily changes produced during emotional disturbance. The first is neural and the second is chemical.

There are afferent (sensory) nerves in the heart, esophagus, stomach, liver, spleen, colon, bladder, genitalia, and other structures that are excited by the autonomic fibers. These afferent nerves are technically a part of the cerebrospinal system rather than the autonomic. They return information to the central nervous system concerning the processes within the smooth muscles and glands. They feed impulses into the reticular formation and hypothalamic centers and thus influence cortical activity. They are definitely a system for organic feedback. William James described the conscious emotion as the awareness of bodily changes. Such awareness is based upon a feedback from the viscera and skeletal muscles that are involved in emotion. Sometimes the subject is aware of specific bodily changes such as the pounding heart. At other times he is aware of a diffuse dullness or brightness that is strongly affective.

In addition to the neural feedback there are chemical influences. Chemical changes in the blood stream are produced by the secretions of ductless glands and by the activity of muscles and other organs. These chemical changes may affect neural centers, especially those in the hypothalamic region. There is thus a chemical feedback from the bodily changes of emotion.

In general, it can be said that when the autonomic nervous system is thrown into action during emotional disturbances there is a diffuse feedback from the bodily changes produced by autonomic activation.

ENVIRONMENTAL REGULATION

In addition to the factors considered above—which for the most part control and direct behavior by internal mechanisms—there is a regulation by environmental conditions. Several examples of environmental regulation have come to light in our studies of food preferences. We have found, for example, that the food selections of rats depend upon such conditions as position and size of the food object, the color of the container, etc.

The importance of *position* of the food object is shown by the fact that in a preference test a rat will frequently accept the food at his left or that at his right regardless of quality of the food incentive. Such position habits typically develop when there is little or no difference in palatability between the food incentives.

The *size* of a food object is an important determinant of acceptance. When offered a choice, rats tend to select the larger of two seeds or grains. The perception of a large quantity of food appears to be more exciting than the perception of a small quantity when the amount consumed per trial is held constant. And Harlow reported that, with monkeys, the size of incentive determines choice and performance.

The *color* or *brightness* of the food container occasionally influences choice. In experiments with white and black cups, used to provide visual cues, some rats showed an initial preference for the white cup and others for the black—regardless of contents.

These factors influence food selections apart from the palatability of the food object itself. The term *palatability* refers to an affective arousal dependent upon the properties of a food incentive such as kind of food, texture, temperature, concentration of solution, etc. But conditions surrounding the food object also exert a regulative influence. The environmental regulation of feeding, then, includes more than the properties of the foodstuff.

With human subjects it is common knowledge that food acceptance varies with surrounding conditions. Flowers, music, good company, clean table linen—or the absence of these things—influence the acceptability of food. Environmental regulation thus includes more than incentive motivation.

In general, the human environment places innumerable limitations and restrictions upon behavior. In a very real sense it regulates behavior by limiting and restricting it. Also the environment provides the necessary physical supports for human activity.

CONCLUSION

The process of regulating and directing behavior is inseparable from the energetics of activity since energy transformations occur always in regulating structures. One form of regulation of special interest to the student of motivation is that which determines goal-directed behavior. Purposive behavior is regulated by sets and by other neural organizations which channel activity into specific patterns.

Regulatory mechanisms commonly build up tensions which energize the organism, especially if activity is distracted or blocked. These tensions underlie the sense of effort. The tension from frustration is a form of feedback. The feedback from all sources provides information and thus has a cognitive function as well as the function of energizing behavior.

It is necessary to distinguish between regulation and direction by organic factors such as set, attitude, motive, or the structure of a neural arc, and environmental regulators which include specific incentives as well as non-incentive surroundings and supports of behavior.

Problems of regulation and direction arise in all areas of psychology. These problems will be considered again when we examine the social determinants of activity—attitudes and orientations. Within social behavior, regulation and direction are achieved by attitudes, orientations, interests, needs, and related factors.

Reading Suggestions

For a comprehensive discussion of purposive behavior see the work by Tolman (1932). A brief account of goal direction is in Chapter 3 of Bindra (1959).

Reviews of the literature upon set and tension are available. Allport (1955), in Chapter 9, considers set and motor adjustment as related to perceptual theory. The experimental literature upon set has been reviewed by Gibson (1941); and the large and complex literature upon muscular tension has been reviewed by Davis (1942) and Courts (1942).

Allport, F. H. *Theories of perception and the concept of structure: a review and critical analysis with an introduction to a dynamic-structural theory of behavior.* New York: Wiley, 1955.

Bindra, D. *Motivation, a systematic reinterpretation.* New York: Ronald, 1959.

Courts, F. A. Relations between muscular tension and performance. *Psychol. Bull.,* 1942, **39**, 347–367.

Davis, R. C. Methods of measuring muscular tension. *Psychol. Bull.,* 1942, **39**, 329–346.

Gibson, J. J. A critical review of the concept of set in contemporary experimental psychology. *Psychol. Bull.,* 1941, **38**, 781–817.

Tolman, E. C. *Purposive behavior in animals and men.* New York: Century, 1932.

8 COGNITION AND MOTIVATION

*Denn Bindungen sind nie "Ursachen" von Geschehnissen,
wo und in welcher Form auch immer sie bestehen. . . .
Man wird also bei jedem seelischen Geschehen zu fragen
haben, wo die verursachenden Energien herstammen.**

KURT LEWIN

There is a passive form of regulation and direction which depends upon structural organization. The curves in a track and the setting of the switches regulate the path of the locomotive without furnishing impetus. Similarly, the associative bonds in the nervous system and the neural structures serve as passive determinants of the pattern of action. But connections, as Lewin wrote, are not dynamic causes. The student of motivation must seek out the energies that activate neural mechanisms. The problems of energetics and regulation by structure, however, are intimately related.

When we consider complex human behavior we find that regulation and direction are controlled by cognitive structures, just as the path of the locomotive is determined by the curvature of the track and the setting of the switches. Cognitive structures are based upon perception and depend also on learning through experience. Hence the study of these cognitive structures is essential if we would understand how patterns of human action are regulated and directed.

---

* *"For connections are never "causes" of events, wherever and in whatever form they may occur. . . . One must therefore inquire of every mental event whence the causal energies come."*

297

In classical discussions of human nature three inseparable aspects of the mind were described: cognition (knowing), affection (feeling), and conation (striving). The tripartite division of mentality has had a long and respectable history. It still has a considerable degree of validity and utility.

In the following sections we will consider the role of cognition, especially perception, in the regulation and direction of human action and the relation of cognition to motivation. We will also consider the role of affectivity. Cognition is closely related to feeling and desire which are of great importance as determinants of action.

PERCEPTION AND MOTIVATION

Perception is the primary and basic form of cognition. Remembering and thinking are also cognitive processes but they rest upon perception. It is important, therefore, to examine the nature of perceiving.

The Nature of Perceiving

In the simplest terms, to perceive is to observe through the senses. The paradigm for perceiving is as follows:

$$\text{To perceive} = \begin{cases} \text{to see} \\ \text{to hear} \\ \text{to touch} \\ \text{to taste} \\ \text{to smell} \\ \text{to sense} \\ \quad \text{internally} \end{cases} \text{some} \begin{cases} \text{thing} \\ \text{event} \\ \text{relation} \end{cases}$$

Innumerable illustrations of perceiving are found on every hand. Thus when a motorist reports "I see a red light," he is reporting something that he has observed, or perceived.

In every instance of perceiving there are several fundamental aspects. First, there is the *experiencing individual*. In the report "I see a red light" the "I" implies a subject of experience, an experiencing individual. Second, there is the *object* of perception—the thing, event, or relation which is perceived. The object of perception is technically designated the *percept*. The report "a red light" indicates a particular sensory quality which has form and meaning. The percept may be a physical body, a melody, a fragrance, an accident, or a relation such as "heavier than" or "to the left of." Third, perceiving is a *process*. It is a process that presents to the psychologist a number of fundamental and central problems.

Behind every act of perceiving is the individual's past history of experience. Previous experience has built up a relatively stable *cognitive organization* within the individual which determines the meaning of a particular percept.

To the psychologist the importance of perceiving lies in the fact that it is related to every aspect of mental activity. Perceiving is related to action as, for example, when a man sees a red light and steps on the brake pedal of his car. Perceiving is related to memory as, for example, when one recognizes the face of a friend in a crowd. Perceiving is related to emotion as when, for illustration, one understands through perception that a child is in danger but is unable to help him. Perceiving is related to thinking: If one reads a problem and starts to work out a solution, the reasoning was initiated by the perception of printed words. Perceiving is related to motivation. If a woman wants a hat and perceives one in the store window, she may enter the store and buy it. The want was there, and perception triggered the action.

Perceiving, in fact, must be considered in relation to all other aspects of mental life but our present interest is limited to perceiving as a determinant of behavior.

The Physical View of Perception

There are two main views of perception: (1) the objective, or physical, view and (2) the subjective, or mental, view.

Gibson (1950) recognized these views by his distinction between perception of the visual *field* and perception of the visual *world*. Although traditional studies of perception have been limited to a study of the visual *field*, Gibson asked: How can we account for the perception of the visual *world?*

The conception of a clear and accurate visual world as the end-product of perception is unorthodox. The science of vision, almost from its beginning, has emphasized the errors and inadequacies of vision whereas this conception of the visual world has emphasized just the opposite. It may strike the reader as naïve to assume that visual perception corresponds to its object when everybody knows how misleading perception can sometimes be. We may not legitimately *assume* the correspondence of perceptions to physical objects: that would indeed be naïve. But on the other hand, we may and should consider what correspondence there is, for this is what needs explanation. The discrepancies between percepts and objects are not difficult to understand; what we need to understand is why there are so *few* discrepancies. That is the real mystery and the really important problem.

The visual world appears to be external, extended, solid, ponderable. Yet the visual field, which includes all of our percepts of the visual world, comes and goes with the opening and closing of the eyes. Physical bodies have weight, extension, inertia, and other properties. But the *experience* of these objects is weightless.

In the enthusiasm of youth the present writer performed an experiment which was naïve and possibly wrongly conceived: Two subjects, one at a time, seated themselves upon the most sensitive large balance obtainable in the engineering laboratory at the University of Illinois. Each subject was weighed twenty times—ten times with eyes open and ten times with eyes closed; the two conditions were alternated. When eyes were open both subjects reported a visible world spread out before them with many physical objects in it. When eyes were closed both reported a gray field with no sharp boundaries. The weights with eyes open and eyes closed were exactly the same. From this fact a negative conclusion was drawn: there is no evidence that visual experience has physical weight. The sensitivity of the balance was such that the addition or subtraction of 4 grams to or from the weight of the subject could be consistently detected by the swinging-beam method; a difference less than 4 grams could sometimes be detected.

The *experiencing* of the physical world, therefore, is a process, or event. It is not a substance that comes and goes with opening and closing of the eyes.

In the strong trend towards physicalism within current psychology one basic fact must be kept in mind: a physical observation, whether under natural conditions or in the laboratory, is the sensory experience of an observer. The physicist may minimize the role of the observer and seek to eliminate errors of observation but in the last analysis the whole of physical science rests upon sense data.

Physical theories concerning the nature of the physical world are another matter. These theories are *concepts*—logical and mathematical constructs. Ultimately they rest upon perception and are tested by perception.

The Psychological View of Perception

If we view the matter broadly, every physical perception is also a psychological event. It is an observation by an individual who holds to a rather fixed objective point of view. The observation is interpreted within a strictly physical frame of reference.

But the psychologist analyzes the process of perceiving from the point of view of the experiencing individual. Perceiving is an event within the conscious experience of an individual. This point of view has been well expressed in a textbook by Combs and Snygg (1959):

> The concept of complete determination of behavior by the perceptual field is our basic postulate. It may be stated as follows: *All behavior, without exception, is completely determined by, and pertinent to the perceptual field of the behaving organism.* The perceptual field has also been called the personal field, the private world, the behavioral field, the psychological field, the individual's life space, and the phenomenal field. The last term is derived from a school of philosophy known as phenomenology which holds that reality lies not in the event but in the phenomenon, that is to say, in the individual's experience of the event. It will be recognized that this is essentially the position we have taken—that behavior is a function, not of the external event but of the individual's perception of it. Because it is similar to the early view of the phenomenologists, perceptual psychology is sometimes called phenomenological psychology, and the perceptual field is sometimes referred to as the phenomenal field . . .

From the individual point of view the whole of experience is dependent upon processes within the individual. This principle applies not only to perception but to memory, thought, imagination, and to feeling, emotion, attention, will, and desire.

What is the nature of those processes upon which experience depends? If we attempt to answer this question from the physical point of view, we find ourselves describing neural processes, especially processes in the brain. If we attempt to answer the question from the individual, or subjective, point of view, we find ourselves postulating perceptual dispositions, mental sets, habits, traits, abilities, and the like.

THE DIRECTIVE-STATE THEORY OF PERCEPTION

Classical theory of perception considered the stimulus, the effects of stimulation upon the receptors, the afferent neurons, and the functioning of sensory-cortical structures. To a considerable extent these factors are related to innate, or autochthonous, mechanisms.

In contrast to classical theory is what Floyd Allport (1955) has called the directive-state theory of perception. There is a great deal of evidence that perception is influenced by behavioral and central determinants such as needs, values, tensions, rewards and punishments, expectancies, emotions, and past experiences. Many of these are *motivational* factors that determine the organization and course of perceiving.

A sample of the experiments that show the influence of central motivational determinants, is given below. In general, the experiments cited are only a small part of the work available in this expanding field of research. But the whole field is in a state of turmoil!

Need as Related to Visual Brightness

In a well-controlled experiment, Gilchrist and Nesberg (1952) required subjects to match the brightness of pictures that were projected upon a screen. The general procedure was as follows: A picture was flashed upon the screen for 15 seconds. A few seconds after its removal it was presented again at a different level of brightness. The task of the subject was to adjust the level of brightness of the picture by turning a knob so that the repeated exposure matched the brightness of the previous exposure.

Some of the pictures projected upon the screen were definitely related to need states of the subjects; others were unrelated to need. Hunger and thirst were induced by instructing the subjects to abstain from food or water for various periods up to 20 hours. When the subjects were hungry, pictures of food objects were exposed: T-bone steaks, fried chicken, hamburgers, spaghetti. When the subjects were thirsty, there were pictures of a pitcher and a glass filled with ice water or orange juice or milk. As a control, objects unrelated to hunger and thirst were exposed. Since hunger and thirst might affect the visual function, homogeneous colored areas were projected upon the screen and the subjects were instructed to make a brightness match with the non-need-related colors.

Figure 62 is a sample of the findings. The illustration shows the average settings of the lamp voltage to match the original exposure as related to the period of water deprivation. Gilchrist and Nesberg consistently found that with increasing deprivation the subjects adjusted the dial so that the second exposure was objectively brighter than the first. That is to say, the need-related pictures were made brighter than those not related to need. In this experiment the need state was removed after 8 hours of deprivation by allowing the subjects to drink to satiation. The test was then repeated. The illustration shows clearly that the removal of thirst gave a result similar to that at the start with zero deprivation.

The subjects were not aware of any error in their settings of the

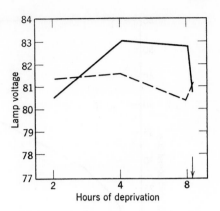

Figure 62. Mean lamp voltage settings for need-related (solid line) and non-need-related (broken line) objects as a function of hours of deprivation. Tests were made as the subjects became progressively more thirsty up to 8 hours of water deprivation. A final test was made with removal of thirst (indicated by arrow). *After* Gilchrist and Nesberg (1952).

apparatus when they adjusted the brightness of the second exposure to match that of the first. Nevertheless, a consistent error appeared with exposure of need-related objects but not when irrelevant colored surfaces were exposed.

The general result can be stated in these words: When there is a state of need the subjects unknowingly adjust the dial so that need-related objects are made objectively brighter than objects unrelated to need. The results suggest that the need state, in some way, interfered with and influenced the making of judgments of visual brightness.

Value and Need as Organizing Factors in Perception

In a hotly debated experiment Bruner and Goodman (1947) claimed to show that the apparent size of coins is related to their value. To poor children coins actually *look* larger than to rich.

Ten-year-old children served as subjects. In an actual test a child sat before a ground-glass screen upon which was a circle of light that could be varied in diameter. By turning a knob the child could regulate the size of the circle of light. He was told that this was a game; that he was to make the circle of light on the box the same size as various objects he would be shown or told about.

In one series he was asked to estimate the size of coins from memory. Each child made four adjustments for the size of a penny, a nickel, a dime, a quarter, or a half-dollar. In half of the trials the coins were mentioned in an order of ascending value; in the other half they were mentioned in an order of descending value. In half of the settings the child closed down the photographic diaphragm from

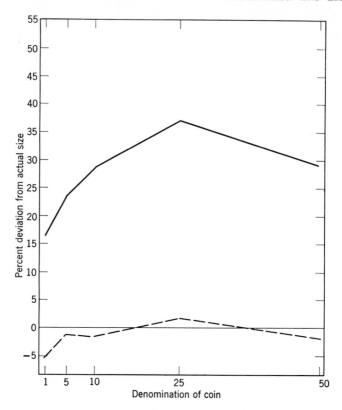

Figure 63. Errors of 10-year-old children in estimating the size of coins (solid line) and equivalent disks (broken line). *After* Bruner and Goodman (1947).

a wide-open size to the size of the coin; in the other half he opened up the diaphragm, increasing the spot of light from a small diameter to a diameter equal to that of the coin.

Following the memory series, the same adjustments of the spot of light were made with the coin actually present. The child held a coin in the palm of his left hand at the level of the light circle and about 6 inches to the left. He was given as much time as he needed to make the adjustment of the spot of light.

A control group made judgments of the size of cardboard disks. The disks were identical in size with the coins but there was no mention of money.

In the experiment with cardboard disks it was found that the coins were estimated to be larger than disks of the same objective diameter. See Figure 63. Further, the deviations of apparent size from physical size varied with the value of the coins. The size of a half-dollar, however, was less overestimated than the size of a quarter. Differences between estimates for coins and disks were statistically significant.

In a variation of the experiment the subjects were divided into groups of rich and poor. Well-to-do children were drawn from a progressive Boston school that catered to the sons and daughters of prosperous business and professional people. Poor subjects came from a settlement house in one of the Boston slum areas.

The data presented in Figure 64 show that the poor children, more than the rich, overestimated the size of coins. Differences between

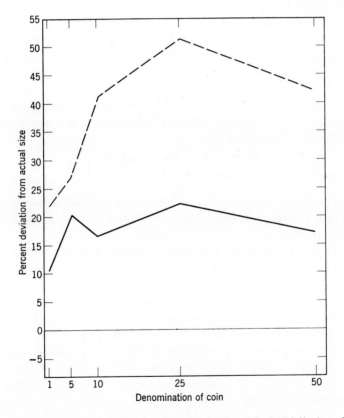

Figure 64. Errors in estimating the size of coins by rich (solid line) and poor (broken line) 10-year-old children. *After* Bruner and Goodman (1947).

the dial settings for rich and poor children were found to be statistically significant. Hence the coins actually *looked* larger to the poor children than to the rich!

In a follow-up study, Ashley et al. (1951) hypnotized adult subjects. Through suggestion the subjects were made to feel rich and again to feel poor. In the "poor" state the settings for coins were estimated at consistently larger sizes than in the normal state; in the "rich" state the settings were consistently smaller than normal. Further, hypnotized subjects were shown a slug from an electrical terminal box and told it was made of lead or silver or white gold or platinum. They adjusted the spot of light to equal the size of the slug, in both "poor" and "rich" states. The result was that the size of the spot which was judged equal to the size of the slug increased as the known value of the metal increased.

These and related experiments suggest that the phrase "a dollar looks big to him" may be more than a figure of speech. It should be said, however, that other experiments have failed to confirm the Bruner-Goodman results and that the matter is controversial. The evidence indicates that to obtain the result there must be an element of ambiguity in the sensory input; but when such ambiguity exists (as it did in the tests with memory for size of coins) apparent size *is* related to value and need.

Emotionality and Perceptual Defense

The phrase "perceptual defense" was used by McGinnies (1949) to refer to a certain resistance against the recognition of words that are socially taboo.

In an important study, McGinnies exposed single words in a tachistoscope with exposure times too brief to permit complete recognition. In preliminary trials he determined the threshold times for recognition by exposing stimulus words for 0.01 second, 0.02 second, etc., until complete recognition and correct verbal report occurred. He obtained the threshold recognition time for each subject.

In the main experiment eighteen words were presented one at a time. Eleven of these words were neutral and seven of them were critical, i.e., affectively loaded, taboo words. The list follows with critical words in italics:

1. Apple	10. *Kotex*
2. Dance	11. Broom
3. *Raped*	12. Stove
4. Child	13. *Penis*
5. *Belly*	14. Music
6. Glass	15. Trade
7. River	16. *Filth*
8. *Whore*	17. Clear
9. Sleep	18. *Bitch*

The subjects were told that they would be shown words which they might not be able to recognize at first. They were instructed to report whatever they saw or thought they saw on each exposure, regardless of what it was. They were asked to delay their report until a signal was given by the experimenter. The purpose of this delay was to allow about 6 seconds for the appearance and recording of the galvanic skin response (GSR).

Prior to exposures, electrodes were strapped to the palms of the hands for recording the GSR. The GSR is known to be a sensitive indicator of action in the autonomic nervous system.

McGinnies obtained two kinds of data for each exposed word. First, a record of the magnitude of the GSR and, second, a record of the subject's verbal response. There were, all together, sixteen subjects— eight male and eight female.

Average data for the group are presented in Figure 65 and 66.

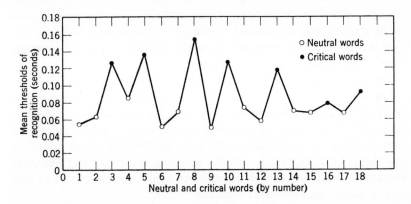

Figure 65. Mean thresholds of recognition (in seconds) for neutral and critical words. *After* McGinnies (1949).

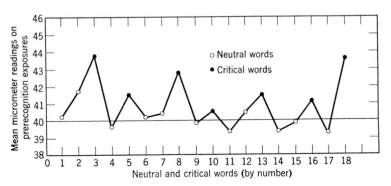

Figure 66. Magnitude of the galvanic skin response to neutral and critical words with exposure times too brief for recognition. *After* McGinnies (1949).

Fig. 65 shows the mean threshold time (in seconds) required for the recognition of neutral and critical (emotionally charged) words. The figure reveals that the recognition times are consistently longer for the critical (taboo) than for the neutral (non-taboo) words. The average difference between neutral and critical words is statistically significant.

Fig. 66 gives the mean micrometer readings on the instrument used to measure the GSR. These readings give an arbitrary index of the magnitude of the autonomic response. The readings were made with prerecognition exposures, i.e., with exposure times too brief to permit recognition of the word and verbal report. An interesting feature of these data is that the critical words evoked an affective response (GSR) with exposure times so brief that the words could not be recognized and correctly reported. This finding suggests that there is a resistance to recognition and/or reporting these taboo words. What is the nature of this resistance?

McGinnies calls this resistance to recognition "perceptual defense" and believes that the defense is a way of avoiding anxiety created by the briefly exposed taboo words. Early in life the child is taught that certain words are naughty and must not be used in polite society. A child is likely to be familiar with some of the bad words but if he uses them, he is reproved. Words referring to sexual and excretory functions are taboo; there is a resistance against using them and they tend to arouse an emotional response.

The facts indicate that there are two aspects to the response to a word. There is a cognitive, discriminatory aspect shown by recognition and verbal report of a word. There is also an affective aspect of the total response shown by the GSR and the delay of verbal report. Mc-Ginnies' study indicates that the affective arousal may be present when exposure times are too brief to permit clear recognition and report of the word.

Awareness and Consciousness

Eriksen (1958) proposed that the terms *conscious* and *unconscious* be employed to designate different physiological states of the organism. When an organism is conscious he is more alert and active than when unconscious. If we see a dog chasing a ball and retrieving it, we describe this alert and active state as conscious. If the same animal lies down, closes the eyes, breathes deeply and regularly, we describe the state as unconscious.

Eriksen proposed that the term *awareness* be employed to designate the subjective psychological quality of the conscious state. The only workable definition of awareness is one in terms of the verbal report of the subject. In perception, for example, the subject can describe verbally the experience of which he is aware. The verbal report is the only practical index of his perceptual awareness.

The distinction has importance in experiments upon discrimination without awareness. In the above experiment upon perceptual defense, for example, the GSR indicated discrimination between taboo and non-taboo words when there was no awareness of the briefly exposed words. That is to say, some word forms produced an emotional response and others did not, even when (presumably) the forms were not clearly perceived and named. There was a kind of discrimination without verbal response, i.e., without awareness.

The facts indicate that some discrimination is possible without an awareness that can be verbalized. Eriksen believes that such discrimination can be attributed to processes akin to attention.

If the stimulus energy is below the absolute threshold for sensory excitation, there is no evidence that discrimination can occur. Experiments upon conditioning subliminal stimuli have yielded a negative result. At best, the alleged evidence for subliminal conditioning is controversial. We cannot, therefore, speak of the "unconscious" as a super-sensitive discriminating mechanism.

Sensory and Affective Determinants of Report

McGinnies' finding that emotional and cognitive factors may function independently was confirmed in a study by Eriksen (1958). He exposed words with pleasant and unpleasant connotations in a tachistoscope. The exposure time was held constant at 0.01 second but the level of illumination was varied.

At the start of the experiment Eriksen instructed a group of subjects to rate a preselected list of sixty words on a seven-point scale for pleasantness (P) and unpleasantness (U). From these ratings he selected the ten words rated most frequently and highly as P and the ten words rated most frequently and highly as U.

Approximately 2 weeks after the ratings the subjects were presented tachistoscopically with a list of words containing the ten P and the ten U words. These twenty words were arranged in a random order and each word was exposed at a level of illumination well below the level required for recognition. The subject was asked to make a judgment whether the exposed material was P or U and to guess what the specific word was.

After the first presentation the twenty words were arranged in a new random order and again presented at a slightly higher level of illumination. This procedure was continued until a level of illumination was reached where 90 percent of the words were specifically identified.

It was found that at levels of illumination too low for the subjects to identify the stimulus words and to report them verbally, the subjects still reported the appropriate feeling (P or U) considerably better than by chance. For the seventeen subjects the results were statistically significant beyond the .001 level of confidence.

The finding indicates that with levels of illumination so low that visual recognition and report are not possible the subjects are somehow able to report the affective connotation. Here again, as with the McGinnies' experiment, there is an indication of two psychological bases for verbal report—the one sensory, the other affective. But Eriksen's experiment does not furnish any evidence for assuming that one basis is more fundamental than the other.

The problem comes up again in the following experiment.

Autonomic Response and Awareness

Lazarus and McCleary (1951) described an experiment in which the galvanic skin response (GSR) was conditioned to certain nonsense syllables and not to others. They found that when syllables were exposed too briefly for recognition and verbal report, the shock-conditioned syllables resulted in larger GSRs than the non-conditioned syllables.

The experiment was carried out in three stages or periods: the equation period, the conditioning period, and the final test period.

1. In the equation period the stimulus words were presented, by a projection tachistoscope, on a screen seven feet from the subject. The exposure times varied from $\frac{1}{150}$ second to 1 second. For each subject five speeds of presentation were used such that the slowest resulted in nearly 100 percent of accurate recognitions and the fastest resulted in a percentage of recognition near to the chance level.

Five-letter nonsense syllables were presented to minimize familiarity and to avoid any motive for withholding report (such as might occur if taboo words were exposed). Ten syllables were presented altogether. Samples are: YILIM, GEXAX, VECYD.

After practice in recognizing the syllables each subject was shown all ten syllables on the screen. The order of presentation and the exposure speeds were randomized. With exposures too brief for recognition the subjects were required to choose from the ten the one that had been exposed. After 100 presentations the experimenters divided the ten syllables into two groups of five each that were equivalent in accuracy of recognition.

2. During the conditioning period a 1-second exposure was consistently used. This gave all subjects ample time for recognition. Five syllables (experimental) were *sometimes* followed by a painful shock and the other five (control) were *never* followed by shock. A schedule of partial reinforcement was planned such that in one-third of the presentations the five experimental syllables were, at random, followed by shock. This procedure was continued until a consistent GSR had been established to each of the five experimental syllables. To maintain equal familiarity, however, all syllables were exposed with the same frequency during the conditioning period. In this stage of the experiment the subjects merely identified the syllables to themselves but made no verbal report.

3. In the final test period all ten syllables were presented tachisto-scopically in random order. No shock was paired with any syllable. Verbal report was delayed about five seconds after the tachistoscopic flash to provide time for a GSR to occur.

The data indicate that with exposure times too brief for the subjects to identify and report the syllables the GSR still differentiated between experimental and control syllables. Lazarus and McCleary referred to this as "autonomic discrimination without awareness" and they suggest that this unique form of discrimination be designated "sub-ception."

Eriksen (1956), however, analyzed the data of Lazarus and Mc-Cleary and questioned the necessity of interpreting them in terms of "subception." He pointed out that the experiment did not contain the necessary controls to permit the conclusion that discrimination had occurred without awareness. For such an interpretation to be per-missable, it must be demonstrated that the subjects had opportunity to show all the discrimination that they are capable of making; but, Eriksen argued, the limitation of the experiment to ten nonsense syllables did not permit any subjects to demonstrate all possible dis-crimination.

Further, Eriksen showed that the data of Lazarus and McCleary could be interpreted in terms of partial correlation. The so-called subception effect is a partial correlation between the GSR and the stimulus when the verbal response is held constant. Such a partial correlation will be obtained if the GSR and the verbal response are independently correlated with the stimulus. The correlation is not perfect for either the GSR or the verbal response. Both correlations are affected by unique sources of error.

One source of error that may affect the verbal response without affecting the GSR is the prompt forgetting of material that follows a brief exposure. An enforced delay of 5 seconds in the test period, while necessary to obtain a GSR, favors forgetting.

To the present writer it seems doubtful whether one can speak of "autonomic discrimination without awareness." Discrimination is a cognitive function and *conscious* discrimination rests upon some content of experience—sensory or affective. The autonomic nervous system is an efferent (motor) system that is markedly aroused in affective ex-periences but it does not serve a cognitive (discriminative) function. It is possible that if the subjects had been asked to report their feelings, they would have reported a dislike for the pain-conditioned nonsense syllables even though they were unable to identify them visually and to report them verbally after a 5-second delay. The GSR, in any event, indicated a conditioned affective arousal. It is at least possible, in the Lazarus and McCleary study, that there was an affective experience that might provide a basis for *conscious* discrimination.

AFFECTIVE AND EVALUATIVE DETERMINANTS OF ACTION

The main point in the following sections is that feeling and meaning are different aspects of conscious experience. Feeling and meaning may be fused and not easily distinguished. Nevertheless, the affective processes and evaluative judgments should be considered separately as independent determinants of action.

Importance of Feeling in Everyday Action

In a readable book entitled *Motivation in Advertising,* Pierre Martineau (1957), who is Research Director of the Chicago Tribune, argues on the basis of his vast experience in advertising that feeling is much more effective than argument in making people buy. People are not wholly rational. The *reason-why* type of advertisement is less effective than one which arouses feeling. In others word, feeling is more evocative of action than logic.

Martineau illustrates his thesis by many examples. For instance, in successful advertisements of Coca-Cola there is little or no argument. There may be a picture of happy, healthy people at the beach or in a mountain resort or in a home-like room. There may be a few words like *delicious* and *refreshing* but that is all. A person looking at the picture puts himself empathically into the situation and gets a comfortable, relaxed feeling. The positive feeling tone is associated with the product and that is enough to bias him favorably towards Coca-Cola. With such a feeling people are more likely to buy the product than if they were exposed to a *reason-why* type of advertisement.

Writers, musicians, actors, parents, politicians, and salesmen have understood for centuries the primary importance of feeling in shaping human judgments, beliefs, and actions. In political campaigns argument is less effective in winning votes than baby kissing and other emotional appeals. There are some, however, who do not admit this but argue that man is governed by reason and intellect; feelings are pushed out of sight. Today scientists and other thinkers recognize that man's complete rationality is a fiction. Write Martineau: "If we reconstruct our own lives for an hour or a day—our daydreams, our irrational actions, our behavior influenced by associations and attachments, our fondness for our children and pets, our escapes into hobbies and movies, our preference for pretty secretaries—we should be honest enough to realize that there is probably no mental action and no behavior in which feeling does not play a central role."

Again, the average motorist isn't sure what "octane" in gasoline actually is. He doesn't know whether there is peppermint octane or chocolate octane; but he does know vaguely that it is something good. So he orders "high-octane" gasoline because he wants this essential quality behind the meaningless surface of jargon.

Martineau tells this story about himself:

> I bought a Packard car. I wanted a Packard. It was my choice. When I tried some honest self-analysis for this choice, the only fact that turned up was that Packard began with the letter "P" and so did my first name. This is consistent with my other lifelong interests in things and places that begin with the letter "P," such as the Philadelphia Phillies.
>
> Now, obviously I couldn't make this explanation to other people. It was utterly irrational and would make me appear very silly in their eyes. So I groped for more acceptable causes, because I felt vaguely uncomfortable when my friends asked me how I liked the car and I was inarticulate about its mechanical qualities.
>
> Then I encountered in the advertising many proclamations about "torsion ride." I didn't have the slightest idea whether this was something on the antenna or the rear bumper. But this was my face saver. Now I could articulate to other people why I bought a Packard. I felt much better. My choice rested on logical foundations.

It has been found that people who have recently bought a Ford car read advertisements about that car more carefully than those who have not bought one. Perhaps they are looking for grounds to support their action which was largely non-rational. Conviction is inextricably bound up with feeling. Conviction depends upon feeling as much as upon logic.

Of course, emotive and esthetic appeals can be combined with sales logic but it is the affective arousal that makes people want to buy and that generates action. Sales logic, to be effective, must recognize the great complexity and changeability of human motivation. Martineau writes: "Most scientists today feel that there is no such thing as a single, pure motive for anything. There are many dominant motives and subordinate motives which may be involved in people's acts. There is a tremendous interpenetration of motives also. They influence one another in considerable degree. One motive can block out another motive entirely, as happens when a person becomes angry or frightened or thirsty. Mostly, however, they exist side by side."

And actually there is no complete stability of motives. What I feel impelled to do today may be changed tomorrow by circumstances. Moods are changeable and different. The advertiser needs to understand human motivation—conscious and unconscious, positive and negative, personal and social, dominant and subordinate. Through motivation research he should aim to get at hidden meanings and feelings.

In general, we must learn to recognize the importance of the emotional, non-rational determinants of human behavior, not only in advertising, but also in marketing, religion, propaganda and politics. Our interests and loyalties are matters of feeling, not reasoning. In any written or spoken communication there are two levels of symbolic language. First there are factual, logical symbols, that express meaning. Second, there are affective, evocative symbols that are non-rational. These symbols often arouse attitudes and cognitive dispositions below the level of conscious awareness. It is the *feeling* that matters in the determination of human behavior.

The Affective Processes and Memory

In a comprehensive study of the relation between emotions and memory, Rapaport (1950) reviewed the contributions of experimental psychology to the subject. He found a large and complex literature upon affective processes and memory. This literature gave him the impression of confusion. There was lack of agreement upon the definition of such fundamental concepts as emotion, affective process, and memory. Even when a clear distinction was drawn between the cognitive and affective aspects of experience there was confusion between evaluative judgments (cognitive) and hedonic processes (affective). Part of the trouble, Rapaport believed, was due to the large element of subjectivism in this literature.

Despite these difficulties the experiments tended to show that the more intensely something was liked or disliked the better it was retained. In other words, experiences rated as intensely pleasant or as intensely unpleasant tended to be remembered better than those rated as affectively indifferent. Pleasant experiences, in general, tended to be favored above unpleasant, in memory. This relation becomes more apparent as the meaningfulness and relevance of the learned material increases.

A good many of the experiments, Rapaport found, were based upon a false assumption that psychoanalytic theory taught a doctrine of "forgetting the unpleasant." Thus, the real psychoanalytic theory— *the avoidance of arousal of pain through memory*—was usually missed. The real theory makes allowance for manifold mechanisms that execute the avoidance of distress.

According to the true psychoanalytical theory we tend to inhibit the recall of experiences that would make us unhappy here and now. It is the *present* activity of remembering that is governed in part by the hedonic principle of avoiding unpleasantness. Troland would call this doctrine a "hedonism of the present."

It is necessary to distinguish between the hedonic regulation of recall, on the one hand, and the meaningful evaluation of past experiences, on the other.

The Affective Processes and Evaluation

In a textbook chapter upon affective and evaluative aspects of experience, Carr (1925), after considering several views of the nature of affective processes, stated his judgmental hypothesis:

The final view may be termed the *judgmental* conception. It assumes that pleasantness and unpleasantness are attributes which we ascribe to any stimulating situation in virtue of our normal reaction tendency toward it. We are so organized in respect to certain situations that we normally react so as to enhance, maintain, or repeat them. We catch sight of a certain picture and turn our eyes and walk nearer to it in order to see it better, and keep looking at it for some time in order to continue the experience. Such behavior is termed a positive reaction, and any situation that normally evokes such a response is judged to be pleasant. Other situations arouse negatively adaptive responses—responses which minimize or rid us of their stimuli and which we do not repeat. Because of our organization in reference to them, certain odors cause us to hold our breath or nostrils, flee their vicinity, and avoid them in the future. According to this conception, any situation that normally arouses such a response is judged to be unpleasant, while all situations that normally arouse neither type of adaptive response are regarded as lacking in affective tone.

According to Carr's hypothesis, an evaluative judgment expressed by the words "The perfume was very pleasant" is based upon a response tendency to continue smelling the perfume. The term "pleasant" simply means "I want more of this kind of experience."

There are, however, several difficulties with this view:

1. The words "The perfume was very pleasant" do not necessarily report a *felt* experience. The words do not indicate *when* an affective arousal occurred, *how intense* it was, *how long* it lasted, nor anything about the subjectively experienced pleasantness. The cognitive judgment evaluates the object of experience without directly reporting affective experience.

2. Carr argued that the judgments "pleasant" and "unpleasant" are based upon adient and abient response tendencies. This is not necessarily true. Some pleasant experiences are associated with relaxation rather than with active seeking. Some unpleasant experiences are simply endured; the subject does nothing (perhaps can do nothing) to avoid them. With a lack of adience or abience the subject still reports "pleasant" or "unpleasant."

3. An objective mark of pleasantness is the tendency to develop approach-maintaining patterns of behavior; and of unpleasantness the tendency to develop avoidance-terminating patterns. But affective processes cannot be identified with tendencies to approach or avoid. They (affective processes) are central in location and merely revealed by these developmental tendencies.

Therefore, a distinction should be drawn between affective processes and cognitive evaluations. Cognitive evaluations are meanings. Meanings are not identical with affective processes upon which they may or may not be based.

Affective Equilibrium and the Adaptation Level

The distinction between affective processes and cognitive evaluation comes up in various experiments upon affective value.

In an early study, Beebe-Center (1929) formulated a law of affective equilibrium which he stated as follows: *"The affective value of the experiential correlate of a stimulus varies conversely with the sum of the affective values of those experiences preceding this correlate which constitute with it a unitary temporal group."*

The law was demonstrated by shifts in the affective values of a set of odors. In the study twenty-one odors were presented to the observers. These odors were presented serially in successive pairs. Each odor was exposed for 5 seconds. The subject was instructed to make two kinds of judgments: (1) After two sniffs of each odor he was asked to judge which experience was the more pleasant. The judgment indicated *relative* affective value. (2) He was further instructed to make an *absolute* judgment, such as: "First pleasant, second unpleasant," "First indifferent, second pleasant," "Both pleasant," etc.

On the basis of previous experimental findings the twenty-one odors had been arranged for each subject in a rank order from maximally unpleasant to maximally pleasant.

In the main experiment there were two kinds of series: *determination* series and *test* series. In a *determination* series, the subjects were instructed to make affective judgments upon the ten most unpleasant odors of the total set. This was followed by a *test* series in which the entire set of twenty-one odors was presented. Similarly, in another *determination* series, the subjects were instructed to make affective judgments upon the ten most pleasant odors of the total set. And this was followed by a *test* series in which the entire set of twenty-one odors was presented for affective judgment.

The aim of the experiment was to discover the effect of habituation to the unpleasant odors upon the affective values of the total set; and, similarly, the effect of habituation to pleasant odors upon the affective values of the total set.

Results indicated that habituation to the unpleasant odors tended to shift *all* judgments in the total set of twenty-one odors towards the pleasant end of the affective continuum. Similarly, habituation to the pleasant odors tended to shift *all* judgments towards the unpleasant end. In other words, habituation to a group of ten odors, that constituted a temporal unity, influenced the evaluation of the total group of twenty-one odors.

Beebe-Center called this principle "affective equilibrium." But since his subjects were instructed to make *judgments*—relative and absolute—it is quite possible that the equilibrium is one of *judgment* and *cognition* rather than of affective processes. The finding, in fact, agrees closely with results of other experiments upon the adaptation of judgments to an order of magnitude. The work of Helson, and others, indicates that if the subject is adjusted to judgments of lifted weights in the range of 100 to 200 grams, for example, a weight of 400 grams will be judged "heavy," but if he is adjusted to judgments of lifted weights in the range of 600 to 1000 grams, a weight of 400 grams will be judged "light." Judgments are thus relative to the level of adaptation. This same principle can be invoked to explain Beebe-Center's law of affective equilibrium.

What is commonly called olfactory adaptation, however, includes several phenomena other than judgment. First, there is sensory adaptation which depends upon chemical changes in the receptor processes. Second, there is attentional adaptation which depends upon central neural processes. Third, there is affective adaptation which depends upon habituation. All of these phenomena may be involved in the usual illustrations of olfactory adaptation: A single whiff of perfume is pleasant but with repetition it becomes indifferent. Again, the odor of garbage is unpleasant but the garbage collector, after some days of work, ceases to notice offensive odors and to be disturbed by them.

In general, Beebe-Center's law of affective equilibrium, in so far as it depends upon judgments, is probably a law of *cognitive* adaptation.

Theory of Adaptation Level

Helson (1959) formulated a theory which has come to be known as adaptation-level (AL) theory. His work started with a study of sensory adaptation in vision but interpretation has been extended in several directions to include psychophysical judgments as well as personality and social dynamics.

Among the postulates that underlie AL theory, Helson lists the following:

1. All behavior centers about the adaptation level or equilibrium level of the organism. There is a behavioral homeostasis, or equilibrium, that parallels physiological homeostasis.

2. Behavioral equilibrium depends upon the interaction of all stimuli confronting the organism (simultaneous pooling), and between present and past stimulation (successive pooling).

3. The adaptation level is approximated as a weighted log mean of all stimuli affecting the organism.

4. All dimensions of present and residual stimuli are related to the AL. In some cases, only frequency, intensity, area, order, and spacing of stimulation need be taken into account in determining the AL; in others, properties such as difficulty, beauty, prestige, significance, quality, affective value, and so on, must be included.

5. The existence of an equilibrium level immediately indicates the bipolarity of behavior. Stimuli above AL elicit one kind of response,

stimuli near AL evoke indifferent responses, and stimuli below AL elicit opposite types of response.

6. The assumption that AL is the result of averaging mechanisms in the organism immediately implies that AL is the end result of integration since, mathematically, averaging operations are special cases of integration.

7. The behavior of groups, as well as of individuals, expresses group levels. Since it is not always possible to define group actions by reference to physical measures, it is necessary to resort to other criteria.

8. It is assumed that learning, acquisition of skilled acts, and all manifestations of capacity or ability represent ways in which the organism adjusts to the problems and tasks confronting it and that it is therefore meaningful to handle them within the structure of AL theory.

The above postulates do not state, in physiological terms, what an adaptation level is. The statements are vague concerning its bodily nature. It is clear, however, that the construct of AL is exceedingly broad and has many ramifications. Helson writes that both inner and outer factors must be considered in defining the AL. Inner determinants such as needs, values, drives, and traits can be studied and understood only as they interact with concrete situations. Such motivational factors have little meaning apart from situations.

Stevens (1958) suggests that we should distinguish between sensory adaptation and judgmental relativity. Both are real and basic processes, but the theory of "adaptation level" does not keep them separate. Adaptation has to do with alterations in excitability. Judgmental relativity has to do with the modulus of the scale of judgment.

If Stevens is correct, the adaptation level, in one sense, at least, is a function of judgment and cognition. The adaptation of judgments to a given context is essentially the same phenomenon as that which Beebe-Center described as "affective equilibrium."

Evaluation and Meaning

Osgood (1952) and Osgood and Suci (1955) have described the logic of their semantic differential—an instrument for the analysis of meaning. They make three main points:

1. The process of description or judgment can be conceived as the allocation of a concept to an experimental continuum, definable by a

pair of polar terms. For example, the meaning of *pacifist* can be indicated by a check upon the following continuum indicating the subject's judgment of where the term belongs:

kind ___:___:___:___:___:___:___ cruel

2. Many different experiential continua, or ways in which meanings vary, are essentially equivalent and hence may be represented by a single dimension. For example, ratings with the following pairs were found to correlate together .90 or better: fair-unfair, high-low, kind-cruel, valuable-worthless, Christian-anti-Christian, honest-dishonest. From this finding it follows that a few continua might give the fundamental dimensions of evaluation for all meanings.

3. A factor analysis shows that a limited number of such continua can be used to define a semantic space within which the meaning of any concept can be specified.

In the factor analytical study three main dimensions were found. The first is *evaluative*. It may be represented by bipolar continua such as: good-bad, beautiful-ugly, pleasant-unpleasant. The second and third factors represent *potency* and *activity*, respectively. *Potency* is represented by: strong-weak, large-small, heavy-light. *Activity* is represented by: sharp-dull, active-passive, fast-slow.

A tendency was found toward convergence of the scales into a single composite of evaluation: good-strong-active *versus* bad-weak-passive.

Osgood states that the semantic differential yields connotative meanings rather than specific denotative meanings. Denotative meanings are those that point to specific objects and events and relations. Connotative meanings are more general and related to what are commonly called feelings.

The semantic differential permits evaluations along many dimensions. Osgood's three major dimensions recall Wundt's classical tridimensional theory of feeling. Pleasantness-unpleasantness (Osgood's main evaluation dimension), strain-relaxation (Osgood's potency dimension), and excitement-calm (Osgood's activity dimension) are the three main dimensions. Of course, the correspondence between Wundt and Osgood is not exact. Wundt never heard of factor analysis and depended upon the introspective analysis of feelings and his own speculations. Wundt aimed to describe *feeling* and Osgood, *meaning*. In comparing the systems, however, a question is raised as to how one can distinguish between feeling and meaning.

I have argued that affectivity must be distinguished from cognitive meaning. Affective arousal is a central physiological process which is typically reflected in visceral changes. Evaluation is a discriminative and cognitive process. It is not to be confused with the report of affective arousals.

COGNITIVE ORGANIZATION AND MOTIVATION

Our actions are regulated both by knowledge (cognitive organization) and desire (motivation). The following illustration from everyday life was used by Olds (1956) to show the intimate relation between cognition and motivation.

The illustration gives the history of a specific motivation from inception to termination:

Stage 1: On a warm summer afternoon the subject is resting on the porch *not thinking* about anything in particular.

Stage 2: Someone suggests a picnic on the beach and the subject *wants* to have a picnic.

Stage 3: The want leads to *thoughts about various things* that would be needed—the sandwiches, the people, the car, etc.

Stage 4: The want leads to a *plan of action*—phoning, driving to get the things that are needed, buying.

Stage 5: The plan is converted into *action*. The plan elicits and regulates a variety of acts.

Stage 6: Next the people, the sandwiches, etc., which were merely thoughts are now actually present and perceived. The *perception* is dependent upon the previous thought, plan and action.

Stage 7: Finally, the picnic which was at first a thought and a want has become a reality. There is actual *enjoyment*.

These stages are not sharply marked off from each other. They blend and coalesce into a single event in which cognition and motivation are the main features. Cognition and motivation are intimately related but the illustration raises a number of questions:

First, it is necessary to distinguish different kinds of psychological existence. A subject is not likely to confuse the idea-of-a-picnic with the perception-of-a-picnic. One can eat a sandwich but not the idea of a sandwich! A subject is not likely to confuse the want-of-a-picnic with actual enjoyment-of-a-picnic. The lack is different from the realization! There is thus a relatively *autonomous state of existence* characterized by thoughts, wants, plans. There is also an *environmentally controlled event* characterized by perception, action, gratification.

In general, a plan for a picnic can remain latent, inert, passive; or it can be activated. When the plan is activated there are two levels of psychological existence: a covert level (thinking, planning, wanting) and an overt level (environmentally controlled perception, action and enjoyment). When the plan is latent it remains as a potential regulator of action.

Second, there is a similarity between cognition (idea) and motivation (want). Ordinarily we speak of ideas as if they were purely cognitive and wants as purely motivational; but the two can be interchanged without great violence. No one would be confused if we spoke about *ideas* of a picnic and the *want* for sandwiches.

Olds thinks that underlying such everyday events there is a single structure. He pictures this structure in terms of what Hebb called "cell assemblies." Some "cell assemblies" have an intrinsic motive force; these are the ones that are likely to be called *motives*. Other "cell assemblies" are relatively lacking in the dynamic factor, or so low in it that they are likely to be called *ideas*.

Olds argues that psychological processes are unitary and underlying them is a unitary neural mechanism. Since there are cognitive (associative) and motivational (dynamic) aspects to psychological processes, there must be similar aspects to neural functioning.

Sensory and Suprasensory Levels of Neural Organization

An infant must learn to perceive the simplest of objects. He must learn to perceive a cube by viewing it from various angles, manipulating it, mouthing it; gradually he develops the perception of the object as a cube. He must learn to perceive the cube on different occasions as the same cube, his mother as the same person, etc., by responding actively to his world.

When an adult looks at physical bodies and listens to spoken words he takes perception for granted. The percept of the adult is accepted without realizing that it is the product of past experience as well as present stimulation of the sense organs.

Superimposed upon the world of looks, sounds, tastes, smells, and feels, is a higher order of cognitive experience. On the higher level there exist: meaningful interpretations, thoughts, imagery. The complex life of association and thought is possible only after the human subject has learned to observe, discriminate, recognize, and manipulate, the simpler objects of his environment.

Hebb has described the neural basis of these two levels of cognitive organization. When the infant is learning to perceive simple objects he is building up neural organizations—"cell assemblies." After certain "cell assemblies" have developed a higher level of neural organization is possible. The more complex "phase sequences" are based upon and presuppose the prior organization of "cell assemblies."

A clear example of what is meant by the higher level of cognitive organization is found in a fascinating book, *Productive Thinking*, by Wax Wertheimer (1945).

Wertheimer relates a story about young Gauss, the mathematician. As a boy of 6, Gauss attended a grammer school in a small town. One day the teacher gave a test of arithmetic to the class and said: Which of you will be the first to get the sum of:

$$1 + 2 + 3 + 4 + 5 + 6 + 7 + 8 + 9 + 10?$$

While the children were busy figuring, young Gauss raised his hand and gave the answer: 55.

"How the devil did you get it so quickly?" exclaimed the surprised teacher.

Young Gauss answered something like this (of course, we don't know his exact words): "Had I done it by adding 1 and 2, and then 3 to the sum, then 4 to the new result, and so on, it would have taken very long; and, trying to do it quickly, I would very likely have made mistakes. But you see, 1 and 10 make 11; 2 and 9 are again— must be—11! And so on! There are 5 such pairs; and 5 times 11 makes 55."

The boy had discovered the gist of an important theorem. For most children the cognitive organization of the problem might be diagramed like this:

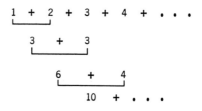

For Gauss, however, the problem was organized as follows:

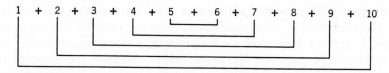

The difference between Gauss and the other pupils was in the manner of organizing the problem to be solved. This kind of organization is on a suprasensory level. Before such cognitive organization is possible the individual must have learned how to perceive numbers, arithmetical symbols, to understand spoken words, to add, and to think in terms of mathematical operations.

Cognitive Stability and Constancy

The world we perceive and know exhibits a stability and constancy which rests ultimately upon underlying physical constancy. Objects appear to be relatively constant in size and shape despite wide variations in their distance and position relative to the observer. Objects appear relatively constant in brightness and in color despite considerable variation in their physical illumination. The well-known constancies of size, shape, brightness and color have been developed through repeated experiences. The existence of these constancies points to a principle of maintaining stability, constancy, consistency and uniformity in the perceived world. Although psychologists have written much about illusions and the lack of dependability of the senses, the stability, constancy and uniformity of the visual world is a fact of major importance, as Gibson (1950) pointed out. The maintaining of perceptual constancy is, in fact, a condition of psychological existence for without some degree of constancy all would be confusion and disorder.

Within the social world, too, there is a great deal of stability and constancy. We recognize persons, social situations, patterns of social behavior, as identical or very similar on different occasions. We develop stereotypes for individuals, racial and other groups. Without these stereotypes the social world would be too complex for us to handle. We learn habitual ways of responding to the social order. To stabilize the social world and minimize its complexity we develop fixed beliefs, attitudes, habits. In other words, we develop a cognitive organization that maintains stability and constancy in both the physical and social orders.

Stagner (1951) pointed out that an essential condition for survival is the maintaining of a stable and constant external environment. This is just as important as maintaining internal homeostasis. In a textbook, Stagner and Karwoski (1952) extended the principle of homeostasis so that it would include the tendency to develop and maintain stability and constancy in the perceived world in both its physical and social aspects.

I think Stagner is entirely correct in emphasizing the tendency to maintain stability and constancy in the physical and social worlds as we perceive them and believe them to be. This, however, is a *cognitive* stability. But I question the advisability of designating the stabilizing tendency "homeostasis." This term already has a precise biochemical meaning that is lost when the meaning is extended to include cognition. (See pages 139–140.)

Cognitive Maps in the Rat

When a rat has learned to run a maze something like a field map has become established in the animal's brain. A cognitive map, Tolman (1948) believes, may be a narrow and strip-like map or a broad and comprehensive one. In the strip map the position of the rat is connected by a simple path to the goal. In the comprehensive map a wider segment of the environment is represented; the animal can select a path to the goal from various positions in the maze.

A cognitive map is carried within the brain of the rat as a bit of neural organization. It is learned organization that gives spatial orientation to behavior and enables the animal to respond appropriately to various parts of the maze.

Tolman's argument for the existence of cognitive maps rests upon five main lines of experimental evidence.

1. Experiments upon *latent learning* show that if rats have actively explored a maze without any food in the goal box, they learn the maze more quickly when a reward is placed in the goal box than rats that have not explored. During exploration the rats enter blind alleys, observe the spatial arrangement of doors and walls, gain familiarity with the entire apparatus. This knowledge of the environment, gained through exploration, is an advantage when rats have to run to the goal box.

2. Observations on what Professor Muenzinger called *vicarious*

trial and error (VTE) indicate that during the early stages of learning rats hesitate, look back and forth, make tentative movements at the choice points, as if vicariously running back and forth in the alleys. Such VTE occurs with greatest frequency when the animals are beginning to "catch on" to the correct response. The VTE indicates that the animals are responding selectively to their surroundings. They are beginning to build a cognitive map and to acquire response sets.

3. Rats often act as if they were searching for the stimulus object. This *search* is essential in the construction of a cognitive map. The importance of active searching is revealed by experiments that interfere with it.

Tolman reports a doctoral study by Bradford Hudson in which the search was disturbed by removal of important stimulus cues at the very instant a shock was given. Hudson observed that after rats had been given a shock they looked around as if to discover what had hit them. He thought that if the critical sensory pattern associated with the shock were made to disappear at the very instant the shock occurred, the rats would not be able to associate environmental cues with the shock. This, indeed, was what happened with many individuals. Hudson added electrical connections to his apparatus so that when a shock was received during eating, the lights went out; the food cup and surrounding visual pattern instantly dropped out of sight; within a second the lights came on again. The next day the response to the visual pattern was tested. Results indicated that when the visible object from which the shock had been received was removed at the moment of a shock, a significant number of rats failed to learn to avoid it. Some selected other features of the environment for avoidance; others avoided nothing. Thus the removal of the signal of a shock interfered with a search for the source, *after* the shock. In the absence of search, the avoidance learning failed to occur.

4. When rats are placed in an ambiguous situation they begin to form what Professor Krech has called *hypotheses*. For example, in a four-choice discrimination box the correct choice may be determined by the experimenter in terms of its being lighted or dark, left or right, or various combinations of these. If all possible cues are randomized, a solution becomes impossible. With a problem that can't be solved, Krech found, individual rats go through a succession of systematic choices. An animal might begin by choosing practically all doors at the right; then he might abandon this and select doors at the left; then dark doors, and so on. Such consistent and per-

sistent ways of responding are like human hypotheses, made and held during the solving of a complex problem. The tentative solutions correspond to central brain sets that play a role in the building up of cognitive maps.

5. In experiments upon spatial orientation it has been found that rats maintain a *general orientation* towards the position of the goal. If the accustomed path to the goal is blocked, rats still show an orientation that influences their selection of other paths. Results indicate that rats develop a comprehensive map so that they can move toward the goal from various positions. This may mean that stimulus cues from walls, windows, and other objects, keep the rat oriented towards the goal.

On the basis of the above five lines of evidence, Tolman concluded that rats develop cognitive maps of their surroundings. They acquire knowledge through exploration and manipulation, through VTE and through active searching. They form hypotheses and maintain spatial orientations which are in the nature of goal sets. Such cognitive organization is utilized in adaptive behavior.

Tolman's argument agrees with the proposition that the cognitive organization within the brain, of itself, does not activate the organism. A cognitive map has a regulative and directive function; it does not elicit behavior nor energize it. Something other than cognitive organization sets the goal and determines what neural structures will be learned and what will be utilized in adaptive behavior.

The Cyclical Structure of Events

Many natural events occur in cycles. This is obviously true with basic physiological and behavioral processes: Respiration is a cycle with successive phases of inspiration and expiration. There are cycles of sleeping and waking, eating, drinking, working and resting, accumulating and eliminating waste materials from the body. The reproductive cycle includes phases of mating, gestation, parturition, lactation, weaning, and care of the young. There are seasonal cycles for example, in the migration of birds.

In everyday life there are cycles of action and perception. In going to work and returning home we see the same landscape, day after day, and we come back to the place from which we started. In perceiving an object held in the hand we return, over and over again, to the same or nearly the same perceptual structure. Our eyes make excursions in viewing an object but the ocular movements return the eyes to the same or nearly the same fixation point.

Floyd Allport (1955) argued that the traditional S-R psychology of the Hullian type, is open-ended. Events are presumed to proceed in a linear fashion. The same linear sequence may be repeated—as it is in any habitual act—but the open-ended view, Allport believes, cannot yield a true picture of the structure of events as they are experienced.

Although the transmission of an excitation from receptor to brain is a one-way process (the impulse passing the synapse in one direction only), there is ample opportunity in the brain for cyclical, or circuital, action. Hebb, in fact, has made much of the concept of reverberating circuits that correspond to suprasensory organization in memory and thought. Referring to neural excitation, Allport writes:

> ...Instead of regarding its form in the traditionally familiar manner, as an open-ended, linear chain from receptor to cortex or from stimulus to response, we shall now take a different course. Let us follow the lead of certain theories which make use of *the principle of circularity*. Let us think of the series as *always coming back upon itself and completing a cycle*. The cycle of ongoings and events can be terminated at the region from which it starts, or it can be conceived as continuing, *repeating itself indefinitely in circular fashion*.

Allport distinguished between *ongoings* and *events*. An *ongoing* is a process, e.g., a wave of excitation in a neuron. An *event* occurs at the junction points of processes. For example, stimulation of receptors by external physical energy is an event, the excitation of one neuron by another or of a muscle fiber by a neuron is an event. Also the excitation of proprioceptors by an effector response is an event.

Events (X) and ongoings (—) may be organized in a circular fashion as follows:

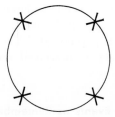

There is thus a cyclical structure to the sequence of events. The cycle may be repeated.

Further, two or more cycles may have events in comomn. The two cycles, in fact, may touch at several points:

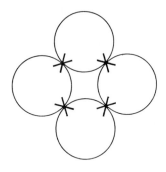

The most elementary ongoing, Allport states, is represented as a cycle and the points of tangency (X) are events within a closed system or cycle.

In comparing the traditional linear, open-ended way of conceiving events with the cyclic way, Allport writes:

> ...If, then, we do not bring the ongoing around to self-completion, as a cycle, we have to imagine that it is infinitely extended. But structures, if they are anything at all, must be finite. Moreover, they cannot close one another, as lines butting against one another enclose empty spaces; they must be *self-closed*; that is, they must have a cyclical, or circuital, format; and this must be true down to the smallest units of which a structure is composed. One cannot build a true structure out of linear, open-ended, or infinitely extended materials.

Starting with the cycle as the theoretical unit of psychoneural structure, Allport expands and elaborates the concept. He describes cycles of cycles and cycles within cycles. But we cannot here go into the details of Allport's theory.

For present purposes it is enough merely to note that he regards events are arranged in a cyclical format and he rejects the open-ended structure of the S-R psychology. The cyclical structure applies to all cognition—to events as perceived and events as remembered and thought about.

The Cyclical Structure of Events as Remembered

Allport's view of the cyclical structure of events can be applied to the recall of any complex system of experiences. Certain details and sequences of events stand out prominently in memory every time the system of experiences is recalled. Specific happenings are inter-related so that when the whole is recalled the memory experience has a definite structure. Within the structure there are relatively stable parts and sequences that are recognized upon repeated recalls.

If we represent the unit of structure as a closed curve (as Allport has done), then a remembered experience (such as the events sur-rounding the birth of my son) may be schematically represented about as follows:

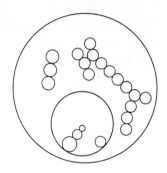

There are partial events within total events (circles within circles). There are sequences of events (series of tangent circles). There are interrelated patterns and series of events. And there may be isolated (dissociated) events.

When we recall an experience repeatedly we *re*-member the parts of the total structure or some part of it. The total structure constitutes a unit of experience within which there are interrelated parts. The *re*-membered experience is related to other experiences that preceded it, followed it, surrounded it in space and time. There is a complex nexus of structures.

From this point of view, the growth of one's experiences from birth till death can be compared to the growth of a tree. At any given time in the life cycle there is a structural organization that is the product of previous growth. In the structure there are collaterals that are products of independent developments. Thus for the growing child there is a system of events centering around the process of feeding, another system of events centering around the activities of dressing, another around relations with other children, with parents and teachers. Growth is organized around situations—the home, the play yard, the school, the church, etc.

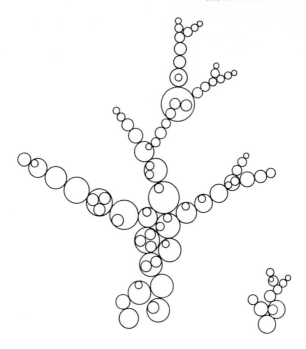

Figure 67. Schematic representation of the structure of events as remembered.

To a considerable extent experiences are systematized. They become organized around situations, places, times, people. The structure of experience *as remembered* is, therefore, more than a linear sequence. It cannot be adequately represented by a string of beads or by open lines but can better be represented by a tree-like structure with branches and collaterals spreading in many directions. The tree analogy, however, does not take account of isolated experiences that are not connected with the main structure. (See Figure 67.)

The remembered structure of events has a relative stability. When I attempt to recall a complex system of experiences I may "go back" and fill in details that were not at first recalled; or I can "go on" from one event to another that was not originally remembered. When I "go back" or "go on" or "turn to another feature" I am attempting to fill in or complete the structure of remembered events. I may be aware of a gap in memory, a hiatus.

When we take an objective view of the structure of remembered events we identify the psychological structure with neural structure.

The dynamic unit of complex neural organization is, we assume, a circuit or cycle of events within the cerebral cortex. This neural structure is latent for most of the time but it may be activated. When the structure is activated a circuit is excited. This, at least, is a fruitful way to picture the neural basis of cognitive structure.

The Organizing Mechanism in Cognition

The neural organization within a human brain is complex to a degree that stifles imagination. Although this bodily structure has developed through many days, months and years of experience, it remains, at any given moment, a complex whole.

Neural structure not only determines what lines of action are possible but it places restrictions upon behavior. Consider the analogy of a network of railway tracks throughout a region of the country. If a track leads to a certain city, a train can go there; if there is no track, the behavior of the train is limited. Similarly, if a man has learned to speak the Russian language, he can communicate with Russian people; but if he has not learned this language, his neural structure places limitations upon behavior. Without a particular language organization a man is unable to communicate verbally no matter how much he may *wish* to do so. Neural structures obviously limit and restrict behavior.

The above view of neural organization seems to imply that it is a passive structure. A striking feature of cognition, however, is that it is a dynamic, active process. There is a problem or task-set or some other motivator that acts selectively upon the associative machinery.

To illustrate the dynamic aspect of cognition consider selective recall and problem solving. Here and now I can relax and: (1) recall the events surrounding the birth of my first grandson; (2) Recall the names of cities in Illinois or the names of psychologists in the United States; (3) recall words of opposite meaning to such stimulus words as *white, heavy,* and *rich;* (4) recall the whole of an object when a part—such as *finger, page,* or *room*—is mentioned or mention a part when the whole is given; (5) give the sum or the product of two numbers such as 24 + 6 or 24 × 6. And so on, indefinitely. There are innumerable tasks and problems I can set for myself and that others can set for me. The task-set acts selectively in regulating the course of cognitive events.

Consider one more example. I can set for myself a rather lengthy

task of reciting the Greek alphabet or some part of it. Years ago
I memorized the letters of the Greek alphabet from Alpha to Omega.
I can now recite the entire series. When I have finished there is
closure in the sense of having completed a self-appointed task. The
entire cycle can be repeated many times over. The neural structure
that makes it possible for me to recite the alphabet is latent most
of the time; it remains inert, inactive. But the structure can be
activated when there is a need to do so.

Apart from a specific task which regulates the course of cognitive
activity there are certain general topics in which I am interested.
For example, segments of my life have been organized around music;
others around psychology; others around the southwestern regions of
United States, etc. If a conversation is started upon any one of
these topics, I participate actively because the topic arouses many
associations. There are systems of association, based upon experience, that remain inert for long periods of time but that can readily
be aroused by appropriate cues. When one of these cognitive systems
is activated it determines the course of my thought. There are thus
determining trends (*determinierende Tendenzen* as Ach called them).

There is obviously an organizing mechanism that selects, regulates,
and sustains the cognitive processes. This mechanism is operative in
thinking, creative imagination, planning and inventing, searching, as
well as in remembering. In fantasy one can imagine a mythical
creature—a mermaid or a centaur—by combining parts and features
of creatures one has perceived. The object is known to be unreal but
it is still possible in imagination.

CATHEXIS AND COGNITION

The term *cathexis* is used in psychoanalysis to mean a concentration or accumulation of mental energy on some particular idea or
object or along some particular channel. It implies both a dynamic
and a regulative factor. It recalls Newcomb's discussion of orientation which emphasized that there is always a cathectic as well as a
cognitive aspect to orientation. (See pages 516–519.) The cathectic
aspect refers to what has been called conation—striving, desiring,
willing.

Klein (1958) refers to *cognitive attitudes* and to the structural
arrangement of *cognitive attitudes* within the person as a *cognitive*

style. Cognitive attitudes, for him, are purposive without having the character of drives. They give direction to behavior without being committed to a search for particular objects or particular forms of satisfaction. Behavior, Klein states, must be provided not only with a motor but with a steering wheel and a map. Cognitive attitudes supply the map. They are regulative—giving direction to behavior —but they are not necessarily dynamic.

A question, therefore, arises, as to how goals, values, interests, desires, aims, and simliar cathectic factors, are related to cognition. If cognition is a purely passive form of regulation by structural organization, then cathectic, or motivational, factors can be separated sharply from it. Actually, however, motivation and cognition are inseparable. They are aspects of a single psychological process that has both directive and dynamic properties.

The following sections touch upon some phases of the relation between cathectic and cognitive factors.

Intrinsic Motivation as Related to Goals, Values, and Interests

A good deal of current research in animal behavior escapes the necessity of assuming extrinsic motivation by postulating exploratory and manipulative drives, a drive to play, a need to know (curiosity), exteroceptive drives, and the like. This work leaves a vacuum as to what intrinsic motivations support the activity. Koch (1956) believes that this vacuum can be filled by an empirical account of value.

Within human experience we are aware of ourselves as being interested in certain things, as acting in relation to ends and values. In practical life the ends are described in various ways to suggest: the production of pleasure, the increasing of goods and advantages, the removing of some irritant, the decreasing of pain, the increasing of comfort, the producing of rest, etc. When we act "in-order-to" accomplish something, the goal is extrinsic to the action. A great deal of human action, however, is intrinsically motivated. Human behavior is largely self-regulated, self-determined, self-energized, and, unfortunately, self-liquidated. It is not necessary to assume an external source of motivation for many of our actions.

Koch illustrates the contrast between intrinsic and extrinsic motivation by describing two states which he finds within his own experience:

1. In one psychological state activity is dominated by a problem or, better, by a direction that is defined by the context of the prob-

lem. There is a diffuse but absolutely compelling direction. Behavior is creative, integrated, efficient, pleasant; the motivation is high and is somehow built into the activity itself. Behavior is polarized. The individual does not merely work at or on a task. He has committed himself to the task and, in a sense, he *is* the task.

A remarkable property of this absorbed state is that thoughts relevant to the problem seem to well up with no apparent effort. They merely present themselves. There is a spontaneity, fluency of ideation, freedom from blockages that is similar in some respects to a dream state. Activity is effortless; there is no strain. Relevant ideas are generated easily and they are readily verbalized and communicated. Verbalization, writing, reading—all flow along smoothly and easily.

In sharp contrast to the above psychological state is another which is sometimes present:

2. The worker is distractable, flighty, self-prepossessed. He feels depressed, drowsy, guilty about his aimlessness and ineffectiveness. His responses to people are ineffective and rejective. He feels physically unattractive, devoid of color, wit and style. He moves through detours, meets resistances and pressures, before getting into the problem situation. He is impelled into the problem situation but not committed to it. Thinking is slow, disorganized, inelegant, inefficient, uncreative, unpleasant. Memory tends to be of the rote variety and is saturated with spotty amnesias. Writing is stilted, imprecise, unfluent. Reading is slow with much backtracking. The unhappy fact about this psychological state is that no manipulation of extrinsic conditions seems to improve matters.

The first state can be described as one with high or good intrinsic motivation. The second is one with low or poor intrinsic motivation.

Koch argues that intrinsic motivation is not tantamount to hedonism. Positive values are immanent within the processes that determine behavior but these values cannot be identified with pleasure and pain. A martyr, for example, may suffer pain but his experience has positive value to him. The value determinants are built into the activity system. We need not look further to find them. It is of little help, Koch declares, to state that the end state of behavior is tension release or drive reduction or restoration of equilibrium or removal of a strong stimulus.

All of us have experienced this difference in intrinsic motivation but psychologists know very little about it. Koch suggests that intrinsic motivation may be the primary and normal form of human motivation.

I believe that Koch is correct in distinguishing between interest and value. Interest is a feeling which is hedonically positive and much intrinsically motivated activity is described as interesting. The concept of value, however, relates to what we think is worth while, worth working for; and this is not the same as interest.

I think, further, that intrinsic motivation is often relative to a goal that is not continuously present in consciousness. Suppose, for example, that a man has decided to write a book or paint a portrait. He works steadily toward a remote goal; he becomes absorbed in the task. His mental economy is organized for the prolonged task. He works persistently, smoothly, efficiently, creatively, and in a highly integrated manner. His activity has value for himself and appears to be intrinsically motivated, autonomous, self-sustained. Actually the activity is relative to a goal that is not always conscious.

Determinants of Belief

In an investigation by Lund (1925–6) the subjects were instructed to rate propositions, first, in terms of their belief that the propositions were true and, second, in terms of their desire that they be true. Lund was primarily interested in the determinants of belief—what it is that makes people believe as they do.

After the subjects had rated the propositions in terms of belief-disbelief they were asked to indicate, so far as possible, the basis of their ratings. Lund listed eight possible determinants of belief (given below) and instructed his subjects as follows:

> We may take as a primary assumption that beliefs all have their antecedents, and are directly determined either by certain propensities inherent in the individual or by influences brought to bear upon him from without. With this in mind reconsider each proposition and along with its number state as briefly as possible—preferably in a word, phrase, or short sentence— what you think has been the main *determinant* for your rating of the proposition. The question is—what led you to rate it as you did? What (perhaps in your past experience) conditioned your rating? In some cases you may be able to think of no such condition or reason, in which event state that it is simply an opinion for which you can give no account.

The eight determinants of belief, as described by Lund, are given below in order from the one most frequently mentioned to the one least frequently mentioned. The frequencies are the total frequencies for thirty-five subjects after they had rated thirty propositions on a scale of belief-disbelief.

DETERMINANTS OF BELIEF

Frequency	Determinant	Description of determinant
317	Teaching and training	Belief conditioned by instruction received at home, through the church, school and similar institutions.
142	Personal experience	Acceptance engendered through sensory experience or observation.
116	Personal opinion	Beliefs for which no real account can be given except that one thinks it is so.
92	Personal reasoning	Acceptance determined by a rational process, a definite "thinking it out."
54	Desire and satisfyingness	Beliefs embraced because they satisfy or embody conditions that are desired.
46	Authoritative opinion	Acceptance determined by the prestige given through official or authoritative attestation.
44	Public opinion	Beliefs fostered through a general attitude of acceptance by people at large.
28	Axiomatic principle	Principles which cannot be doubted, being imperative in commanding belief.

After Lund (1925–1926).

The list indicates that the determinants of human belief are both rational and non-rational. Of the eight determinants, at least two or three can be described as rational: personal experience and observation, personal reasoning, and possibly axiomatic principle. But apart from these the remaining grounds for assent contain a large non-rational element. We have beliefs for which we can give no explanation. We assent because others do; we believe what we desire to be true, what satisfies us; we agree to what we are taught in the home, church, school; especially do we believe opinions which are expressed by persons of authority and prestige. Our beliefs are thus formed not only through the senses and through intellectual processes but by our wishes, feelings and other non-rational determinants such as hearsay, statements by other persons, and a desire to conform.

The most frequently mentioned determinant of belief is teaching and training at home, through the church, school, and similar institutions. Children tend to accept the religious, political and ethical beliefs of their parents. The things we are taught are rarely determined by a process of reasoning.

Long ago Alexander Bain used the phrase "primitive credulity." He argued that a child tends to accept whatever he is told until something in his experience gives him the shock of contradiction. Doubt, produced by contradiction, leads to thinking and to a critical attitude; but if contradiction is lacking, the child is primitively credulous. Small children, for example, readily accept the stories about Santa Claus.

An understanding of the determinants of belief is tremendously important for the educator, the politician, the propagandist, the psychiatrist, and others who are practically concerned with human relations. Man is only in part a rational animal.

The Fiction of Rationality

Aristotle said that man is a *rational* animal. The modern psychologist would be inclined to say that man is a *rationalizing* animal. Martineau (1957) wrote:

Most people accept the religion of their parents. But it doesn't sound very rational for an adult to admit this. So he sells himself on the proposition that his belief rests on completely logical grounds. He has examined, he says, numerous faiths, but his own is the one that makes the most sense to him. He would angrily deny the actual reason.

So would the attention getter deny heatedly that he was telling off-color jokes and serving vodka and wearing a back-yard chef's costume so that he could occupy the center of the stage. So does the social striver deny the true but not acceptable reasons why he has changed churches, changed friends, and changed neighborhoods.

The alleged reasons for our actions are not necessarily the true determinants. Freud made the point clearly in his emphasis upon unconscious motivations. What we say may be only an attempt to make ourselves appear reasonable and correct.

We have seen above that our beliefs rest upon both rational and non-rational grounds. The important point for a student of psychology is that beliefs regulate our actions and experiences. The point has been well stated by Britt (1949) in a chapter upon the psychology of irrationality: *"If people believe things to be true, then they are true for them and have social consequences."*

The propagandist aims to change beliefs and attitudes, starting with what people already accept. The unfortunate thing is that beliefs and attitudes can be changed by various techniques and without regard for objective truth and reality.

Belief and Desire

Human beliefs are determined to some degree by wishes or desires. The phrase *autistic thinking* refers to imagination, like that in day dreaming or building castles in the air, which is dominated by a wish rather than realistic logic.

The extent to which belief is dependent upon desire was investigated by Cronbach and Davis (1944) during World War II. In their work sixty-one college students were instructed to rate fifty statements about living conditions during wartime. The statements dealt with matters of importance to the subjects.

The statements were rated on a five-point scale, first as to the probability that an effect would occur and second as to the desirability of the effect. The instructions for the belief-disbelief ratings were as follows:

You are to indicate what effects you think the war will have on the United States as a whole. Each item in the test states an effect some people have said the war will cause. You are to show how likely you think each effect is by circling the proper key letter on the answer sheet. Circle:

CY (certainly yes) if you think the effect is *certain to happen.*
PY (probably yes) if you think the effect is *more likely to happen than not.*
E   (equally likely) if you think the effect is *equally likely to happen or not to happen.*
PN (probably no) if you think the effect *probably will not happen.*
CN (certainly no) if you think the effect is *certain not to happen.*

Four days after the belief-disbelief ratings the questions were again presented, without previous warning, and the students were instructed to indicate how desirable the effect was, using a similar five-point scale. In the scale for desire CY meant *certainly desirable,* PY meant *moderately desirable,* E meant *neither desirable nor undesirable,* PN meant *moderately undesirable,* CN meant *certainly undesirable.*

Cronbach and Davis found that for some statements there was a wide discrepancy between the ratings of belief and desire. For example, consider the statement: *Food will become so scarce after the war that civilians will go hungry.* Fifty-six of the sixty-one students believed this statement to be true, but not one of them desired it to be true. In general, however, there was a positive correlation between the ratings for belief and for desire. Lund had found a high positive correlation $(r = +.88)$. Cronbach and Davis found a lower but definitely positive correlation $(r = +.41)$. The reasons for the discrepancy need not be considered here.

Cronbach and Davis found marked individual differences in the extent to which persons are dominated by wishful thinking. For individual students the correlations between belief and desire ratings on the fifty propositions ranged from $+.74$ to $-.27$.

It was found that the degree of correspondence between belief and desire varied with the nature of the proposition rated. Several factors were demonstrated. (1) The *ambiguity* of a proposition leads to greater correspondence between belief and desire. If there is no ambiguity—if the objective facts are clear—even those with strong wishes are likely to believe what the facts imply. But if the facts are unknown or uncertain, desire is relatively more influential. (2) The *familiarity* of a statement affects judgment. If a statement that is unsupported by evidence has been frequently discussed, it is likely to be believed even if it is not desired. Familiarity breeds consent. The propagandist, as we know, may secure acceptance of a statement simply by reiteration. (3) If both ambiguity and novelty are present, the *plausibility* of a statement is a factor determining the agreement between belief and desire. A statement may be plausible that is not necessarily true; but if a statement is extreme, desire may be powerless to make one accept it. (4) The *importance* of a statement to the individual is likely to lead to correspondence between belief and desire only when there is no possibility of acquiring information on which to base a realistic judgment. If there is no basis of experience for making a judgment, the majority of persons tend to agree to a proposition. They show a tendency to acquiesce, to agree, to conform.

The tendency to believe what one desires is associated with optimism. Perhaps optimism can be defined as a tendency to believe what one desires. A person who is overoptimistic may refuse to face reality, being influenced largely by his wishes.

CONCLUSION

In the present chapter we have considered the interrelations of cognition, feeling and action. Cognitive processes—including perception, memory, evaluation, and reasoning—are intimately related to the pattern of human behavior. But man is only in part a rational creature since affective processes and desires play a dominant role as determinants of action.

Affective processes convey little, if any, information. Affective processes, as such, do not convey specific information about objects and events in the outer world. They constitute, rather, what is commonly called the *feeling tone* of experience—which is a kind of *connotative* meaning. The affective processes do not point to specific objects nor do they convey specific information; they lack *denotative* meaning.

Negative affectivity from frustration, pain, failure, and related conditions, however, gives a primitive kind of evaluation: *bad, terminate, escape,* etc. Similarly, positive affectivity from success, goal reactions, sweet tastes, fragrant odors, and certain other conditions, yields a primitive evaluation: *good, continue, more,* etc. In so far as these primitive evaluations convey any meaning it is an elementary kind of information about the state of the organism in a given situation.

Cognitive meanings are fused with affectivity. One cannot easily separate them in experience; yet the two are independent phases or aspects of human experience. Cognitive evaluations may rest upon affective processes or upon sensory processes or both. But evaluative judgments are *cognitive* events and affective processes are basically not judgments. Affective processes, subjectively considered, are conscious feelings.

Cognition is a central process in the regulation and direction of human behavior. Action can be adequately understood only in relation to perception, discrimination, judgment, memory, and related aspects of knowing. Affective processes, however, must also be considered since they lead to development of activating, sustaining, and controlling structures.

The search for *mental* determinants is merely an attempt to interpret the facts of experience and behavior from the point of view of the conscious individual. *Mental* causation is not logically opposed to physical causation. *Mental* concepts—perceptual dispositions, personality traits, social attitudes, personal goals, habit structures, abilities, skills, and the like—are supplementary to physical concepts.

Mental determinants, like physical, are inferred. Although dualists talk about the mind and body as if they were distinct entities, the present view of biological monism does not warrant a real dichotomy. Mind and body are one. There is a single individual underlying behavior and conscious experience. When this individual is studied from the point of view of conscious experience the term *mental* is used. This merely labels one line of approach to the study of determinants within the individual.

Reading Suggestions

A good critical introduction to the large and expanding literature that deals with motivation and perception may be found in Postman (1953). Selected readings upon motivation and perception are in Section 6 of Stacey and DeMartino (1958). The directive-state theory of perception is considered in Chapter 13 and following chapters of Allport (1955).

On the individual approach to psychology see the text by Combs and Snygg (1959) and a paper by Kelly (1958).

Allport, F. H. *Theories of perception and the concept of structure: a review and critical analysis with an introduction to a dynamic-structural theory of behavior.* New York: Wiley, 1955.

Combs, A. W. and Snygg, D. *Individual behavior, a perceptual approach to behavior.* New York: Harper, 1959.

Kelly, G. A. Man's construction of his alternatives. In G. Lindzey (Ed.), *Assessment of human motives.* New York: Rinehart, 1958.

Postman, L. The experimental analysis of motivational factors in perception. In *Current theory and research in motivation, 1953.* Lincoln: University of Nebraska Press, 1953.

Stacey, C. L. and DeMartino, M. F. *Understanding human motivation.* Cleveland: Howard Allen, 1958.

9 NATURE AND BODILY MECHANISMS OF EMOTION

Of points where physiology and psychology touch, the place of one lies at "emotion."

C. S. SHERRINGTON

If all behavior were well organized and directed towards a goal, there would be no need for a concept of emotion. The motivational concepts already considered—such as goal orientation, set, drive, incentive, activation, and affective arousal—would be fully adequate for purposes of descriptive analysis and explanation. It is because behavior does *not* always move smoothly towards a goal that the concept of disorganization becomes necessary. Frustration, the clash of motives, painful stimulations, stress, threats, problems, thwarted expectations, etc., are conditions that disturb smooth, goal-directed behavior.

In the present chapter we will first consider the nature and definition of emotion and then turn to the study of emotion as a *bodily* event. It is true, as the quotation at the head of this chapter suggests, that physiology and psychology meet in the study of emotion. This chapter has a definite physiological emphasis. We will examine the role of the autonomic nervous system in emotion and consider the objective manifestations of emotional processes at the surface of the body. We will describe some of the patterns of response that appear

344

in emotional behavior and, finally, we will consider the role of the central nervous system in emotional disturbances.

HOW EMOTIONS ARE RECOGNIZED, DISTINGUISHED, AND NAMED

Emotions are complex disturbances that are commonly recognized, distinguished, and named, in terms of the stimulus situation that induces them and the adjustments that an individual makes to this situation. Patterns of response—like weeping and laughing—also furnish cues for the recognition and naming of emotions; but these patterns do not furnish an adequate basis for distinguishing the nuances of human emotion.

Signs of Emotional Disturbance

Psychologists who have worked with rats know that when an animal is placed in a strange apparatus he shows emotional disturbance. Some animals actively explore the apparatus; others "freeze," remaining inactive. There is increased frequency of urination and defecation.

With human beings some emotions are exciting, as revealed by an increased level of activity, and others are quieting. If you tell a small boy that he is going to the circus, he is likely to jump up and down, clap his hands, talk rapidly, and show joyful excitement by other excessive activities. In adults, anger leads to heightened tension or activity; sorrow and grief lead to lowered activity levels.

Motor tests have shown that there is a loss of steadiness, lowered coordination and precision of movement, and a marked speeding up or slowing down of movement, during emotional excitement. There are gross changes in the efficiency of performance when an individual is emotionally disturbed. These can be measured in the laboratory but they are easily recognized in everyday life. Consider, for example, a student who is seated in the library, efficiently solving a mathematical problem; he glances up and sees his girl friend talking to another man; after that he is unable to hold himself to his task.

It is the activity in progress that is disrupted in emotion. But emotional disruption is different from a simple distraction of attention and from a simple change from one task to another. Emotional disruption is marked by visceralization of response—changes in glands and smooth muscles—and also by the appearance of reflexive patterns of response (laughing, weeping, rage, etc.) which are integrated at subcortical levels. In emotional disturbances there is a shift from cortical towards subcortical dominance.

Some affective states facilitate behavior. Mild anxiety, for example, may increase the efficiency of performance. But intense anxiety lowers efficiency. It is the *disturbance* of performance that is of interest to the student of emotion. Emotional disturbance is revealed by a variety of external signs.

The Psychological Origin of Emotion

Emotions originate in a psychological situation that always includes an environmental factor, present or past. Examples of psychological situations are: meeting a bear in the woods, receiving an insult, seeing one's sweetheart. There is an environmental factor in these kinds of situations and typically there is an environmental factor in the situations that induce emotions.

The psychological situation is not limited to present perception. One can become emotionally disturbed by remembering past events or imagining future or possible happenings. In memory, imagination, and thought, however, there are still two basic factors: organism and environment, individual and experience. These two factors interact within the total psychological situation.

Some situations are social, others non-social. Social situations involve persons or groups. Non-social situations involve the organism and the surrounding physical world.

Some situations are unreal. A man sees a movie, reads a book, hears a broadcast. He identifies himself with the situation presented through these different channels of communication. He puts himself in the place of some character or imagines, empathically, that he is in the situation. Genuine emotions are produced in this way. At the movie, for example, fear, anger, love, amusement, grief, and other emotions can be aroused by situations presented on the screen. Genuine emotions, therefore, can be produced by various substitutes for reality.

An emphasis upon the psychological situation in the origin of emotions is important because it is the *psychological* origin that distinguishes emotions from other affective states. Organic states of hunger, thirst, fatigue, sleepiness, and pain, as well as relief from these conditions, produce feelings. Appetites can be distinguished from emotions by the organic nature of their origin. We do not ordinarily speak of "emotions" of fatigue, sleepiness, hunger, and pain. We refer to such experiences as "feelings," indicating thereby that they are affective but not true emotions. It is the *psychological* origin, with an environmental factor (present, past, or imagined) that distinguishes emotions from appetites and organic feelings.

Perhaps some qualification of this statement is needed. It is true that injection of adrenin and other drugs can create affective states that predispose the organism. Such drugs may render the subject jittery or euphoric or anxious. This may or may not be an exception to the rule that emotions arise in a psychological situation. But it is still true, in general, that emotions typically originate in a psychological situation.

The psychological situation, of course, includes an individual's past experience, his present knowledge and beliefs. It includes his total world of experience.

How Emotions are Recognized and Named

A good many people believe that they are able to identify emotions on the basis of facial expressions. In an early experiment, Landis (1924) studied the ability of subjects to recognize and name emotions on the basis of facial expressions. He aroused genuine emotions in human subjects and then photographed the disturbed individual. To evoke emotion the following situations were employed: listening to music, reading the Bible, smelling ammonia, hearing a loud noise, writing out a *faux pas,* viewing pictures of skin diseases, pornographic material, art studies, reading sex case histories, handling live frogs, decapitating a rat, experiencing electric shocks, and, finally, relief from these various ordeals.

As an aid in the analysis of facial expressions dark marks were placed upon the subject's face. Measurement of the distances between these marks on the photographs revealed the degree to which different groups of facial muscles were contracted in emotional states and at rest. The subjects also gave verbal reports of their emotional experiences.

After measuring the photographs and studying the verbal reports, Landis made the following generalizations (his statements are not quoted literally):

1. For each experimental situation wide individual differences existed in the facial expressions evoked. For the total group of twenty-five subjects no fixed pattern of expression was common to any single situation.

2. Each individual tended to use some particular group of facial muscles

habitually, to the exclusion of others. This tendency gave certain character-istic facial patterns to each person.

3. With not one of the emotions reported did a muscle or group of muscles contract sufficiently to be considered as characteristic of the stated emotion.

4. When the subjects were instructed to imagine some emotion, no uniform relation could be found between the facial expression and the emotion which was imagined.

5. When the emotional expressions were ranked according to the gross amount of facial musculature involved, the rank order was found to be: pain, surprise, anger, exasperation, crying, disgust, sexual excitement, revulsion.

On the basis of these and other generalizations, Landis concluded that an emotion, as it is observed in the face, is not a true pattern of response as is, for example, the wink reflex. He suggested that the common names of emotions typically refer to *situations* which induce them rather than to the pattern of facial response. Also, he stated, the *degree of general disturbance* may be a factor which aids one in naming emotions, but *not* the facial pattern nor the subjectively experi-enced reaction.

This negative result is contrary to findings of other psychologists who have utilized photographs of facial expressions posed by skilled actors, instructing the subjects to name the emotions represented. Landis believes that *posed* expressions are conventional and that they are used in communication much as the spoken word is employed. The conventional expressions differ from culture to culture. Landis dis-tinguished between *social* and *emotional* expressions. The latter are reflexive patterns of response but, as pointed out above, the common names of emotions do not designate stable patterns of facial expression.

Tolman (1923) in describing the persistent purposive behavior which arises during emotion or out of emotion, has stressed the situation-response relationship. It is not the stimulus situation *as such,* he wrote, nor the response *as such* which defines emotion. Rather it is the response as affecting or calculated to affect the stimulus situation. Thus, in fear it is escape from the stimulus object, in anger the de-struction of it, and in love the encouragement or enticement of the stimulus object which objectively characterize the specific emotions. It is the "response-as-back-acting-upon-the-stimulus" which distin-guishes emotions as such. In other words, each emotional upset is characterized by a tendency toward its own particular type of adaptive behavior. The adaptive behavior appears as an adjustment to the emotional disturbance.

Hebb (1946a, 1946b) pointed out that a long-time acquaintance with chimpanzees is necessary to interpret their emotional behavior.

Animals have characteristic ways of responding emotionally and an observer must know the history of the animal, for example, to distinguish between *rage* and *hate*. Temperamental traits and specific emotions are recognized as deviations from the normal base of behavior but that base must be known before the momentary emotional states can be recognized and interpreted.

In general, then, the "emotions" that we recognize and name in everyday life are *interpretations* based upon experience. These interpretations involve a dynamic relation between an organism and its environment. There are specific forms of adaptive behavior that grow out of different forms of emotional upset and the "emotions" are recognized and named, in good part, by the adjustments that restore complacency.

How do we recognize and distinguish emotions? First, we rely upon our knowledge of the inducing situation and, second, upon our knowledge of the subject's history—his characteristic ways of responding to stimulus situations. We also rely upon the observation of adaptive behavior that appears in the disturbing situation as well as upon the objective signs of emotional disturbance—patterns of reflexive response and indications of visceralization.

The Evaluation of Emotion

In his classical work, *The Expression of the Emotions in Man and Animals,* Darwin (1872) formulated three principles for interpreting emotional manifestations. The first principle stressed the *utility* of the responses which appear during emotional excitement. For example, the hostile animal bares the canine teeth in preparation for biting; when an angry man curls his lip and shows the canine teeth he does not intend to bite but the expression is a vestige of a biologically useful act. The second principle emphasized the fact that certain emotional expressions are the *antithesis* of biologically useful acts. For example, the expression of friendliness in the dog and the cat is directly opposed to hostile patterns in these animals. (See pages 384–386.) The only way to interpret friendly behavior is as the antithesis of hostility. The animal, by his behavior, communicates the meaning: "My intentions are the opposite of hostile."

Darwin was unable to explain all emotional expressions in terms of their utility for survival of the individual or the species. Consequently he formulated a third principle which had no reference to utility. Some emotional expressions, he wrote, can be explained only by reference to the constitution of the nervous system. For example, in agony there are many useless movements—grinding of the teeth, staring of the eyes, perspiration, changes in circulation, in respiration, etc. Such bodily changes are useless, of no direct service to the animal. Their occurrence can best be explained in terms of the innate organization of the nervous system. When the nervous system is highly excited, excessive and useless bodily changes occur.

The principle of utility was extended by Cannon and others to include internal bodily changes that occur during the emergency emotions—rage, fear, excitement, pain. The visceral changes, Cannon stated, mobilize the energies of an organism in preparation for a vigorous fight or a race for one's life. (See pages 367–369.)

Now the words that are commonly used to describe emotional states —upset, disruption, emotional turbulence, disorganization, emotional outburst, disturbance, etc.—all suggest that emotions are useless and that we would be better off without them. Emotional development is described as the growth of adaptive behavior and the reduction of emotion. Emotion is regarded as something to be avoided, to be minimized.

But even disturbed states have utility. Emotional manifestations have social utility so far as they are signals to other members of a group. With animals, the erection of fur or feathers, drawing back (or erection) of the ears, vocalizations, and gross behavior, all serve to communicate to others the existence of danger. With man, smiling and laughing communicate friendliness and social acceptance when they may have no other meaning. Also, laughing and weeping may have a physiological utility in reducing tension.

The literature of emotion is permeated with references to the utility and inutility of emotional responses. It is said that the above words, used to describe emotional states, imply an element of negative evaluation. Other words, like adaptation and adjustment, imply positive evaluation.

If science deals with facts and not with values, a serious question must be raised as to whether a scientific definition of emotion is possible. It may not be possible but the question will be left open.

THE DEFINITION OF EMOTION

At best the definition of emotion presents a difficult problem. No single definition has proved acceptable to all psychologists. Several have suggested that the concept of emotion be dropped from technical psychology.

The difficulty seems to be that no single criterion has been found that clearly distinguishes emotional from non-emotional states. We must rely on several criteria and that, too, is not very satisfactory.

In the following sections I will consider some of the sources of confusion and difficulty in defining the psychological concept of emotion. And then, despite difficulties and objections, I will present a tentative definition.

Confusion about the Definition of Emotion

While everybody talks about emotion no one seems to know exactly what emotion is nor what to do about it. There is much confusion and uncertainty about fundamental concepts and definitions. The concept of emotion has been discussed by Leeper (1948), Duffy (1948), Webb (1948), Young (1949), and others.

Bentley asked: Is "emotion" more than a chapter heading in psychological textbooks? And Brown and Farber (1951) wrote: ". . . examination of current treatments of emotions reveals a discouraging state of confusion and uncertainty. Substantial advances have been made in recent years with respect to theories of learning and motivation, but the phenomena of emotion have not, as a rule, been considered in these formulations and remain a tangle of unrelated facts."

Duffy (1941) argued that the term *emotion* is superfluous; emotional behavior, she said, differs only in degree from other forms of behavior. The term does not refer to any distinguishable category of response. She wrote:

I am aware of no evidence for the existence of a special condition called "emotion" which follows different principles of action from other conditions of the organism. I can therefore see no reason for a pyschological study of "emotion" as such. Emotion has no distinguishing characteristics. It represents merely an *extreme* manifestation of characteristics found in some degree in all responses.

Emotional responses differ in *degree*. They can be ranged along continua. One such continuum represents the degree of energy mobilization within the organism. In emotional excitement the energy level is high; in depression it is low. A second characteristic of emotional behavior is disorganization. But, Duffy stated, disorganization is a function of any behavior at high and low level of energy expenditure and is not unique to "emotion." The third characteristic of "emotion" is the conscious quality of pleasantness and unpleasantness. Affectivity, however, characterizes all experiences and not merely "emotions." According to Duffy, there is no single and unique characteristic of behavior that can be used for defining the concept of emotion.

One might agree with Duffy and drop the whole problem of emotion. But instead of being a defeatist I prefer to look for the causes of the present confusion. I believe that part of the difficulty lies in the failure of psychologists to draw certain basic distinctions and to hold consistently to certain fundamental concepts.

Emotion and Other Affective Processes

One source of confusion lies in a failure to distinguish emotion from other varieties of affective processes.

The phrase *affective process*, historically considered, referred to conscious feelings of pleasantness and unpleasantness. Practically all psychologists who have classified emotions divide them into those that are pleasant (e.g., joy, love) and those that are unpleasant (e.g., sorrow, disgust). The classification suggests the primacy of pleasantness and unpleasantness.

There are, however, a good many varieties of affective processes. In technical psychology, the term *emotion* refers to one kind of affective process and not to all.

Among the varieties of affective processes are the following:

1. *Simple sensory feelings.* These are of two kinds: (*a*) *pleasantness*, induced by perfumes, sweet tastes, warm contacts, musical tones, colors, rhythmical movements, etc., and (*b*) *unpleasantness*, aroused by foul odors, bitter tastes, cutaneous pain, rasping sounds, dazzling lights, etc. These simple feelings induced by sensory presentations differ not only in sign (positive and negative) but in intensity, duration, and temporal course.

2. *Persistent organic feelings.* In this category are the aches and pains of disease, of hunger and thirst, of injury and other unpleasant conditions; and also the positive satisfactions that accompany food ingestion, sexual relief, and organic states of physical well-being.

3. *Emotions.* Emotions are acutely disturbed affective processes which originate in a psychological situation and which are revealed by marked bodily changes in the glands and smooth muscles. The following words designate emotional disturbances: *rage, horror, terror,*

agony, excitement, jealousy, shame, embarrassment, disgust, grief, joy, amusement, elation, etc.

4. *Moods*. The term *mood* refers to an affective state that is less disruptive than an emotion, of lower intensity and of longer duration. A mood may last for hours, days, or even weeks. There are moods of cheerfulness, depression, anxiety, resentment, amusement, excitement, and the like. A mood is a chronic condition; an emotion is an acute event.

Moods vary with the state of health, the weather, and other conditions, but it has been found that moods depend especially upon events in the social environment. Receipt of a check, invitation to a dance, failure in an examination, and loss of money are among the many conditions that induce moods.

5. *Affect*. The term *affect* is used in psychiatry and abnormal psychology for intense, pathological moods such as those of manic excitement, deep depression, persisting anxiety, euphoria, apathy, and similar conditions. In psychoanalysis an affect is regarded as an emotional state due to conflict or repression.

6. *Sentiments* are feelings which rest upon past experience or training and thus have a cognitive or intellectual basis. Under this heading are included the satisfactions and dissatisfactions with works of art—musical compositions, paintings, poetry, style of architecture, etc. There are sentiments of honor, of patriotism, and the like. There are moral, religious, esthetic, intellectual, and other kinds of sentiments.

7. *Interests* and *aversions*. Interests are activities that one likes, that one carries on "for their own sake." A man may be interested in baseball, stamp collecting, reading detective stories, playing the piano, etc. Aversions are activities that one dislikes and that one avoids if possible. A man may have an aversion to studying a particular subject, to keeping a social date, to eating parsnips, etc.

8. Finally, the term *temperament* refers to the affective aspect of personality as a whole. Temperaments are said to be apathetic, moody, phlegmatic, cheerful, vivacious, depressed, sanguine, etc.

Now the above terms overlap in meaning and may not all be necessary but one thing is clear: *An emotion is a variety of affective process distinguished from the others as an acute (brief and intense) affective disturbance.*

The distinction is ignored by psychologists who use the term *emotion* broadly to include all kinds of affective processes. Thus Hilgard (1953) wrote: "For literary and descriptive purposes we need a rich

vocabulary to describe emotional coloration. For psychological purposes, however, we shall group together the whole family of experiences, from mild satisfactions and annoyances at one end of the scale
through weak emotional states up to the most intense emotional states.
In so doing, we emphasize the continuities, rather than the discontinui-
ties, among these emotional states."

It should be noted that Hilgard's usage equates *emotion* with the
traditional *affective processes* and that the continuity underlying the
"emotional" states is a continuity determined by affectivity.

The Phenomena of Emotion and Underlying Dynamics

Rapaport (1950) wrote that a great deal of the confusion concerning
the definition of emotion has been due to failure of investigators to
distinguish between the *phenomena* of emotion and the underlying
dynamics. The phenomena of emotion are complex and can be analyzed from different points of view. The underlying dynamics are
postulated to explain the facts.

The phenomena of emotion present three main aspects. First, an
emotion is a conscious experience that is *felt* and directly reported.
All of us *feel* anger, fear, joy, sorrow, love, grief, shame, guilt, disgust,
amusement, and other affective experiences. Second, an emotion is a
bit of behavior. Everyone has observed *emotional behavior* in animals
and human beings: hostile excitement, friendly vocalizing, excited
jumping about, lustful approach, terrified flight, cries of fear and
pain, joyful behavior, and other patterns. Third, an emotion is a
physiological process. During emotion there is marked activity in the
autonomic nervous system and viscera, electrical and chemical changes
in cortical and subcortical centers. The physiological psychologist is
concerned with this vital aspect of the emotional event.

It is an article of scientific faith that these diverse aspects reveal
a single underlying emotional event. We believe that the different
facts, no matter how complex, can be fitted together into a single
account. Consider, by way of analogy, the event of a burning house.
The perception of the conflagration is different as seen from the north,
south, east, west, from the inside, and from an airplane. Yet we all
believe that the conflagration is a single event in nature and that
observations from all points of view can be fitted together into a
single, consistent story. Similarly, the diverse phenomena of emotion
belong together and the only question is a practical one: How can

the various facts be fitted together into a single congruent account? When we consider the dynamics underlying emotion we must take account of the clash of motives in conflict, repeated frustrations, expectations of success and failure, tensions and their release, painful stimulations, and other factors, that underlie the emotional phenomena.

Emotional Organization and Disorganization

By far the greatest amount of confusion arises from the definition of emotion as a disturbed state of the organism. Most psychological research is concerned with organized patterns of response that can be described in terms of stimulus and response.

The pattern-response definition of emotion implies that emotional responses are well integrated and resemble reflexes. Thus, Watson (1919), although he recognized at least three other formulations, stated explicitly in his major definition that : *"An emotion is an hereditary pattern-reaction involving profound changes of the bodily mechanism as a whole, but particularly of the visceral and glandular systems."* Also, Bard (1934a) in a review of research upon the neurohumoral basis of emotion emphasized that "in his experimental work the physiologist (as distinguished from the student of subjective experience) considers emotions as behavioral patterns."

One difficulty with the pattern-response definition of emotion is that it disregards the factor of disorganization that is present in all emotions. Hebb (1949) maintained that emotion is a disorganization at the cortical level but along with this there appear well-organized patterns of response that are integrated at subcortical levels. The disorganization at the cortical level is produced by intense stimulation, frustration and conflict, anticipation of harm, release from tension, and similar conditions. The cerebral disorganization releases the lower centers from cortical control.

Some psychologists, e.g., Leeper (1948), have objected to defining emotion as a disorganized and disorganizing response. But I believe that if it were not for the fact of disorganization, psychologists could dispense with the concept of emotion entirely. There are plenty of concepts within motivational psychology to describe well-integrated, goal-directed, purposive forms of behavior. It is because disorganization exists as a fact of nature, and for no other reason, that we need the concept of emotional disturbance.

An emotion is here defined as *an acutely disturbed affective state of the individual that is psychological in origin and revealed in behavior, conscious experience, and visceral functioning.*

Emotion as Facilitative

Opposed to this definition is a statement that emotion facilitates and furthers adaptive behavior. For example, Carl Rogers (1951) writes: *"Emotion accompanies and in general facilitates such goal-directed behavior, the kind of emotion being related to the seeking versus the consummatory aspects of behavior, and the intensity of the emotion being related to the perceived significance of the behavior for the maintenance and enhancement of the organism."*

The view that emotion facilitates goal-directed behavior is very different from the view that emotion is an acute affective disturbance. But there would be little room for argument if for "emotion" we substituted terms like *feeling, sentiment, interest, mood,* and the like. Some forms of affective processes *are* facilitative and organizing rather than disrupting. Feelings of self-confidence and assurance that come from success and achievement are not at all disruptive; they are facilitative.

The matter boils down to a question of terminology and definition. "Emotion," as Rogers, Hilgard, and others, have used the term, is equivalent to "affective process." We know that some affective processes are associated with facilitation and others with inhibition. Hence "emotion" may either facilitate or inhibit performance. But I have followed a tradition in defining emotion as a special form of affective process—a form that is described as an acute affective disturbance.

Emotion and Motivation

Bindra (1959), in considering the classification of motivational phenomena, wrote:

The term *emotional behavior* is used as a collective name for the behavior of anger, fear, joy, and the like, and *motivated behavior* as a general label for the phenomena such as hunger behavior (food seeking and eating), sex behavior and drug addiction behavior. Now, although emotional behavior and motivated behavior are often treated as if they were distinct classes of behavior, they are not so in fact. Over twenty years ago, Duffy . . . painstakingly started to examine the various criteria that had been suggested as the differentiating marks of emotional and motivated behavior . . . She found all such differentiating criteria to be inadequate, for they failed to set apart unequivocally the phenomena which, conventionally, are grouped together either as emotional behavior or as motivated behavior. . . .

Bindra argued that the distinction between emotional behavior and motivated behavior on the basis of degree of goal directedness is untenable. Emotional behavior is commonly regarded as disorganized, lacking goal direction. Motivated behavior, in contrast, is regarded as organized, goal-directed activity. But, Bindra argued, disorganized and organized behavior are different developmental stages. The same sequence of development appears (from disorganized to organized behavior) when we consider emotional behavior and motivated behavior. Lack of organization is an early stage of development; organization and goal direction, a later stage. We cannot distinguish between emotional and motivated behavior in terms of goal direction. That is because the degree-of-goal-direction dimension cuts across the traditional categories and cannot be employed as a differentiating criterion.

Again, Bindra argued, we cannot reliably distinguish between emotional and motivated behavior on the basis of external and internal origin. It is true that conditions that evoke motivated behavior appear to be mostly internal, whereas those that evoke emotional behavior seem mostly environmental. It can be shown, however, that both types of response patterns are determined by both internal and environmental conditions and can be controlled by manipulating either one of these sets of conditions.

The outcome of Bindra's argument is that there is no single criterion that can be used reliably for distinguishing between emotional behavior and motivated behavior. This view is unquestionably sound.

Emotion is an exceedingly complex event. Perhaps psychologists should study separately the very real differences between emotional and non-emotional forms of behavior. Five such differences are the following:

1. Emotional behavior is disturbed, disorganized. Non-emotional behavior is organized and frequently goal directed.

2. Emotional behavior typically originates within a psychological situation which always contains an environmental factor. Many forms of non-emotional behavior originate from internal tissue conditions.

3. Emotional behavior is characterized by visceral changes regulated by the autonomic nervous system. In non-emotional behavior there is a lower degree of visceralization and autonomic involvement.

4. Emotional behavior is characterized by a weakening or loss of cerebral control and the appearance of response patterns that are integrated at subcortical levels. Non-emotional behavior is characterized by a higher degree of cerebral control and dominance.

5. Emotional behavior, whether viewed subjectively or objectively, is characterized as intensely affective. Non-emotional behavior is more neutral, indifferent, affectively.

Now if Bindra, Duffy, and others are correct that no one of these contrasts can serve as an adequate criterion for distinguishing between emotional and non-emotional behavior, it may be necessary to replace the concept of emotion with five or more specific concepts. But if we can combine all of these contrasts, we arrive at a complex picture of emotion: *When an individual is affectively disturbed by the environmental situation to such an extent that his cerebral control is weakened or lost and subcortical patterns and visceral changes appear, that individual is emotional.* The emotional disturbance is a real, though complex, event.

A further point about Bindra's analysis is this: He regards "motivated behavior" and "emotional behavior" as separate classes, or categories, of activity. I would prefer to state that *all* behavior is motivated (causally determined) and that behavior is more or less emotional according to the degree of affective disturbance that is present in the arousal.

An Extension of the Definition of Emotion

The above definition of emotion affirms that an emotion is an acutely disturbed affective state that is psychological in origin and revealed in three aspects as: (1) behavior, (2) conscious experience, (3) bodily processes, especially visceral functioning. These three aspects include the total empirical evidence for the existence of emotion. The psychologist must deal with facts of behavior, conscious experience, and with physiological data.

When a psychologist goes beyond the empirical data he makes inferences. Psychological theory is concerned with postulates and logical constructs that rest upon empirical data. It is very important to distinguish between the facts of experience and the inferences based upon those facts.

In defining emotion as "an acutely disturbed affective state of the individual" we have already made certain inferences: (1) We have assumed that an emotion is an occurrence within a *single individual*. There are not two organisms—a body and a mind—but a single psychological individual. The organism that reveals emotion in behavior is one and the same as the organism that the physiologist studies when he is concerned with the bodily changes in emotion. Moreover, we have assumed that this organism is also the subject of conscious experience. (2) We have assumed that an emotion is a *single event*, or occurrence, within this individual. Although emotion is revealed in behavior (emotional behavior), experience (conscious emotion), and physiological processes (bodily emotion), these three are just aspects of a single natural event. (3) We have assumed, by definition, that an emotion is an acute affective disturbance. In other words, an emotion is a *contemporary event* of an affective nature. An emotional upset occurs here and now.

The view that an emotion is a *contemporary* event can be extended to take account of conditions that underlie and determine emotional upsets. The dynamic conditions that underlie emotional outbreaks are conceived as existing here and now but our understanding of these conditions is enhanced when we take a timewise view of the individual's past experience and development.

In psychosomatic medicine, clinical psychology, psychiatry, and related disciplines, an "emotion" is commonly described as a *persisting disturbance within the individual*. Emotional disturbances are regarded as chronic states rather than acute, contemporary processes. An extended view of emotional disturbance is implied whenever we describe a child or patient as *emotionally disturbed* and in need of help. The disturbance we are considering may last for weeks, months, or years. In the underlying disturbance is doubtless some conflict, traumatic experience, failure, frustration, injury, insult, thwarted expectation, or other cause of *emotional disturbance*.

To avoid confusion it is necessary to distinguish between emotion as a *contemporary event* and emotion as a *persisting state of disturbance* within the individual. The persisting state is conceived as a *condition* that underlies and determines acute emotional upsets.

This extension of the concept of emotion to include persisting states of disturbance does not contradict the above definition of emotion as a contemporary process. It supplements it by taking account of the temporal dimension. Such an extension is necessary when we consider emotional development and the dynamic factors underlying anxiety, hostile resentment, sorrow, depression, and other persisting affective states.

If the definition of emotion is extended to include persisting states of disturbance within the individual, a question immediately arises: How can one distinguish between emotional disturbances and other persisting disorders?

We will not attempt to answer the question here. We note only that it is unnecessary to identify emotion with all forms of persisting disturbance. The psychiatrist and clinical psychologist, in fact, make distinctions. For example, they do not identify emotion with neurosis and psychosis. These latter are broader concepts.

Emotion and Activation

When the concept of emotion has been extended to take account of persisting states of disturbance within the individual, a distinction can be made between latent and aroused emotion.

The term *activation* was used by Lindsley (1951) to describe a central neural process localized within the reticular formation and related neural structures. He investigated patterns of activation with the electroencephalograph. He described levels of arousal and identified the excited emotions—rage, terror, pain, great excitement—with high levels of activation. States of drowsiness, sleep, and coma, were related to relatively low levels of activation. Differences in the level of activation were described in terms of brain waves.

The term *activation*, however, as Duffy (1957) pointed out, has a wide range of applicability within psychology. In Lindsley's sense the term is closely related to *excitatory level, level of energy mobilization, intensity of motivation, degree of arousal, strength of drive,* and other dynamic concepts. According to the dictionary, however, the term *activate* means *to make active* or *to render capable of reacting or of promoting reaction.* Activation, in this sense, is almost synonymous with motivation.

In one sense of the word (which must not be confused with Lindsley's usage) an emotional conflict may be latent or activated. When an emotional conflict is activated it produces an acute affective upset —a manifest emotion. The popular phrase, "Let sleeping dogs lie," implies that emotional dispositions may remain dormant or they may be aroused. Psychologists know that music, words, odors, and other kinds of stimulation, may arouse memories that are emotionally disturbing.

Emotion Defined as an Intervening Variable

Within behavior theory an emotion is not regarded as a pattern of stimulation nor as a pattern of response; it is regarded as a hypothetical construct or as a variable intervening between stimulus and response. Thus, Brown and Farber (1951), operating within a Hullian frame of reference, conceptualized emotions as intervening variables.

The nature of emotion, they state, is well illustrated by frustration. As an intervening variable, frustration has two major effects: (1) Frustration produces an irrelevant drive that combines with a relevant drive (such as hunger or thirst) to produce an effective drive. For example, if a hungry animal is frustrated by a barrier so that he cannot reach food, the frustration produces a drive (irrelevant) that combines with the hunger drive (relevant) to produce an augmented effective drive. (2) Frustration generates specific frustration stimuli. These stimuli produce responses of their own as do other persisting stimuli. In both effects the emotion is driving and motivating.

The drive increment produced by frustration differs from the primary drive in that it depends upon the arousal of competitive tendencies rather than upon the conditions of deprivation. It also differs from other motivations with respect to events that result in its diminution.

The theory of Brown and Farber is admittedly incomplete. It does not take account of emotional states, such as joy and sorrow, that are produced by relief and relaxation of tension. Nor does it take account adequately of the physiology of emotion. Nevertheless the theory shows that it is possible to envisage emotion in logical and theoretical terms within the framework of motivational psychology.

EMOTION AND THE AUTONOMIC NERVOUS SYSTEM

The visceral components of emotion are regulated by the autonomic nervous system. It is important, therefore, to examine the structure and functions of the autonomic system and the way it regulates the bodily changes of emotion.

The Visceralization of Response

An organism's response (R) to a situation (S) is partly somatic, partly visceral. The two components of the total response can be represented in this way:

The total response is integrated, but there are degrees of visceralization.

What are the viscera? The term *viscus* (plural *viscera*) means a hollow structure such as the intestine, the tubes of the reproductive system, the blood vessels. The term is commonly used, however, to designate any soft organ located in the body cavities, such as the brain, heart, lungs, stomach, liver, etc.

Psychologists are agreed that emotional responses are highly visceralized. The blush of shame, the pallor of fear, the cold sweat of anxiety—these are visceral components of response which are outwardly observed and inwardly felt. The viscera are markedly aroused in emotional states such as rage, terror, horror, agony, laughing, and weeping.

Cameron and Magaret (1951) defined emotional reactions as: *"reactions whose non-specific visceral contribution dominates or determines them, or colors them distinctively."* This recognizes the central importance of visceral components of the emotional response. "Thus, climbing a fence in the course of a cross-country hike, and climbing it to escape a charging bull, may both involve visceral change; but in one the visceral participation is likely to be negligible, while in the other it is clearly dominant. The same distinction holds between dispassionate discussion and angry argument, between picking up one's valise on arriving at the railroad station and picking up one's child, between breaking up a radio for its parts and breaking it up as a reaction to what it says."

Cameron and Magaret emphasized the unity of the total emotional response of which the visceral component is just a part. If we try to think of some activity that is completely free from emotion, we will probably think of a routine, automatic action like knitting passively or twiddling one's thumbs. Possibly we will think of sleeping. In any event, non-emotional activity is relatively free from visceral changes; emotional activity is strongly visceralized. Thus, in the emotional displays of children we observe responses of the somatic muscles in crying, biting, striking, diffuse motor excitement, etc. We also observe the shedding of tears, the blush of anger, and other changes in glands and smooth muscles.

The patterns of response that appear during emotional disturbances contain both visceral and somatic components. In some patterns, such as the startle reflex, the somatic components appear first and constitute the pattern; visceral components may develop later and secondarily. In others, such as disgust, the visceral components are primary and the skeletal muscles adjust themselves to the primary anti-peristaltic pressures.

Dominance of the Autonomic Functions

Although there are differences of opinion concerning the proper definition of emotion, there is unanimity on one point: Emotional processes involve visceral changes that are regulated by the autonomic nervous system.

The autonomic and cerebrospinal nervous systems control different organs but are interdependent in function. Changes in one system rarely occur without producing effects in the other. The perception of a threatening or enticing situation is a function of the cerebrospinal system that produces visceral changes through the autonomic system. The visceral changes, once they are aroused, feed back excitations into the cerebrospinal system. At all times—during sleeping and waking, during calm activity and emotional disruption—the autonomic and cerebrospinal systems function interdependently.

The cerebrospinal system supplies innervation to the striped muscles of the head, trunk, and limbs; the autonomic system supplies innervation to the smooth muscles and glands of the gastrointestinal, circulatory, respiratory, and urogenital tracts. In general, the cerebrospinal system sends its nerves to the somatic system of skeletal muscles and receptors at the surface of the body while the autonomic nerves are connected with smooth muscles and glands and internal organs. The cerebrospinal system is directly concerned with adjustments of the organism to external reality; the autonomic with the essential processes of metabolism and reproduction.

From the point of view of development, the autonomic system is prior and dominant. In evolution, the autonomic system is of ancient origin. In the developing embryo the autonomic nervous system is comparatively well organized prior to a comparable organization within the cerebrospinal system. Dominance of the autonomic begins prior to birth and continues throughout life. If cerebral control is lost during an emotional crisis, the autonomic functions continue (perhaps with disturbance) despite disorganization at the cerebral level. If the brain is damaged, the vegetative processes (that are essential to life) continue.

Kempf (1920) argued that the autonomic functions are dominant over those of the cerebrospinal system. He wrote that we must learn to see the living body as a complex unity motivated by tensions that originate in the stomach, intestines, rectum, liver, salivary glands, bladder, diaphragm, heart, lungs, prostate gland, external genitals, kidneys, and other organs. These tensions from vegetative organs develop independently of each other and with different periodicities. When a tension exists in one of the vegetative organs the cerebrospinal system is compelled to make adjustments necessary to neutralize the disturbance. Even the tonus of skeletal muscles, as seen in posture and gait, is dependent upon autonomic tension.

Kempf's view is opposed to the notion that the esthetic, moral, religious, and intellectual life of man is of primary importance in motivation, while the vegetative functions are secondary. According to Kempf, this notion is the reverse of the natural order. The vegetative functions regulated by the autonomic nervous system are primary and the cerebrospinal system is the slave of the autonomic. Whether or not one accepts this evaluation it is clear that the two systems function interdependently during emotional and non-emotional activity.

Structural and Functional Divisions of the Autonomic Nervous System

The autonomic nervous system is an aggregation of ganglia, nerves, and plexuses, through which visceral organs (smooth muscles and glands) receive their innervation. The system is made up entirely of *efferent* neurons, i.e., nerve cells organized to conduct impulses away from the central nervous system toward the visceral structures. There are, however, visceral *afferent* fibers, in close association with the autonomic nervous system, which carry excitations from the viscera back into the central nervous system.

From the point of view of anatomy the autonomic nervous system is composed of three divisions: (1) The *cranial* division is composed of fibers making their exit from the central nervous system at the base of the brain in several of the cranial nerves. (2) The *thoracicolumbar* division is composed of fibers emerging from the spinal cord at the level of the thorax and in the lumbar region. (3) The *sacral* division is composed of fibers emerging from the central nervous system at the sacrum, or pelvic level.

Fibers from the central nervous system bring impulses to ganglia where synapses are made with other fibers that carry impulses outward to the visceral structures. Those fibers bringing impulses to the ganglia are called *preganglionic* fibers and those carrying impulses away from the ganglia to visceral structures are designated as *postganglionic* fibers. The fibers leading to the adrenal glands are different from the others in that they carry nerve impulses directly to the glands, without synapsing.

Although there are *three* structural divisions of the autonomic nervous system, there are *two* divisions when we consider the system from the point of view of function. The central division (thoracicolumbar), when considered from the physiological point of view, is commonly designated as the *sympathetic nervous system*. This system is a vast and complicated network related, in evolution, to a primitive network type of system. It functions as a unit. Neural excitations spread diffusely through the sympathetic network producing widespread and profound bodily changes in the smooth muscles and glands. The upper (cranial) and lower (sacral) divisions together constitute the *parasympathetic nervous system*. *Para* means "along the side of" or "beside." This designation is appropriate because the parasympathetic nerves are anatomically beside the sympathetic and, to a considerable extent, innervate the same effectors.

From the point of view of physiology, the sympathetic and parasympathetic nerves are functionally antagonistic. Where one kind of fiber excites, the other inhibits, and *vice versa*. See Table 1. The table shows, in the center column, some of the bodily structures that are excited by autonomic nerves. Effects produced by excitation of the sympathetic network are shown at the left. Effects of parasympathetic excitation are listed at the right. Some of the bodily structures are innervated only by sympathetic nerves; parasympathetic nerves have no effect upon them. This is true, for example, of the smooth muscles that erect the hair cells, the sweat glands, and the surface arteries.

A study of Table 1 shows that many of the bodily structures are innervated by both the sympathetic and the parasympathetic nerves.

TABLE 1

AUTONOMIC FUNCTIONS

Sympathetic Nerves	Bodily Structures	Parasympathetic Nerves
		Cranial
Dilates the pupil	Iris	Constricts the pupil
Inhibits secretion	Salivary glands	Facilitates secretion
Erects (pilomotor reflex)	Hair	
Augments secretion	Sweat glands	
Constricts	Surface arteries	
Accelerates	Heart	Inhibits
Dilates bronchioles	Lung	Contracts bronchioles
Secretes glucose	Liver	
Inhibits gastric secretion and pertistalsis	Stomach	Facilitates gastric secretion and peristalsis
Constricts, giving off erythrocytes	Spleen	
Secretes adrenin	Adrenal medulla	
Inhibits smooth muscle activity	Small intestine	Facilitates smooth muscle activity
Constricts	Visceral arteries	
		Sacral
Relaxes smooth muscle	Bladder	Contracts smooth muscle (empties)
Relaxes smooth muscle	Colon and rectum	Contracts smooth muscle (empties)
Constricts, counteracting erection	Arteries of external genitals	Dilates, causing erection
Contracts at orgasm	*Vasa deferentia*	
Contracts at orgasm	Seminal vesicles	
Contracts at orgasm	Uterus	

Where double innervation occurs the physiological actions of the two systems are opposed. Where the parasympathetic system facilitates, the sympathetic inhibits; where the parasympathetic system contracts, the sympathetic relaxes, etc. Both systems, however, function simultaneously in emotional processes and a visceral pattern results from the diffuse action of the sympathetic combined with some specific effect from a particular parasympathetic nerve.

It should be kept in mind that the sympathetic system acts diffusely to produce diverse and widespread effects. Excitations from the central nervous system spread through the central chains of ganglia and diffusely throughout the sympathetic system as a whole. The parasympathetic nerves, contrastingly, produce particular effects upon specific organs. The parasympathetic nerves send pre-ganglionic fibers directly to the organs that they innervate or, rather, to terminal ganglia close to or within these organs. Thus the third cranial nerve supplies the pupil; action through this nerve constricts the pupil, cutting down the amount of light that enters the eye. The seventh and ninth cranial nerves reach out to the salivary glands, to the mucous membranes and, through ganglia, to the lacrimal glands. The tenth cranial nerve (vagus) has a widespread distribution to heart, lungs, stomach, liver, pancreas, and intestine. The pelvic nerves supply the colon, rectum, bladder, and external genitals. By combining the diffuse action of the sympathetic system with the particular effects produced through the parasympathetic a variety of visceral patterns is possible.

Figure 68 is a schematic representation of the autonomic nervous system and the visceral afferent system. The figure shows, at the left, the central origin and peripheral termination of the sympathetic and parasympathetic nerves. It shows, at the right, the visceral afferent system that feeds back information about visceral changes into the central nervous system. Some of the more important visceral structures are listed in the illustration.

A detailed study of this chart is beyond our present concern. The reader interested in further details is referred to Lindsley (1951).

Cannon's Emergency Theory of Emotion

During a biological crisis, when an animal must fight or run for its life and when there is likelihood of bloodshed, profound and widespread bodily changes occur which mobilize the energies of the body for a vigorous and prolonged struggle. In fear, rage, pain, and emotional excitement, there is a diffuse discharge across the sympathetic network which produces a variety of bodily changes. There is also increased secretion from the medulla of the adrenal gland. The sympathetic discharge and the adrenal secretion combine to produce bodily changes that are *serviceable* to the organism in a struggle for existence.

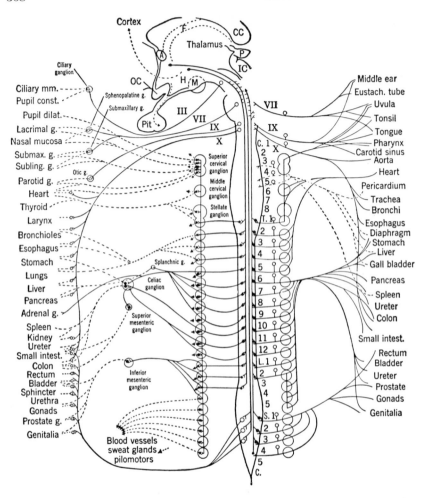

Figure 68. Schematic representation of the autonomic nervous system, showing the central origin and the peripheral termination of *sympathetic* and *parasympathetic efferent pathways* on the *left* and the origin of *visceral afferent pathways* on the *right*. Cell bodies of pre- and postganglionic neurons of the parasympathetic system are symbolized by open circles; those of the sympathetic system, by solid circles. Arrows projecting from sympathetic chain ganglia symbolize postganglionic fibers to blood vessels, sweat glands, and pilomotors. Dotted lines on left of figure represent efferent postganglionic fibers; those on right are nonautonomic fibers of the phrenic nerve. Key: A—anterior commissure; CC—corpus callosum; F—fornix; H—hypothalamus; IC—inferior colliculus; M—mammillary bodies; OC—optic chiasma; P—pineal body; Pit—pituitary or hypophysis. *From* Lindsley (1951).

Summarizing the detailed findings of many experiments, Cannon (1929) wrote:

Every one of the visceral changes that have been noted—the cessation of processes in the alimentary canal (thus freeing the energy supply for other parts); the shifting of blood from the abdominal organs to the organs immediately essential to muscular exertion; the increased vigor of contraction of the heart; the discharge of extra blood corpuscles from the spleen; the deeper respiration; the dilation of the bronchioles; the quick abolition of the effects of muscular fatigue; the mobilizing of sugar in the circulation—these changes are *directly serviceable in making the organism more effective in violent display of energy which fear or rage or pain may involve.*

The bodily changes produced by a discharge across the sympathetic network are supplemented and, to a considerable extent, supported by chemical changes. The sympathetic nerve endings control effectors by releasing a substance, *sympathin.* The medulla of the adrenal gland also releases, directly into the blood, a similar compound, *adrenin.* Adrenin is said to be *sympathetico-mimetic* in that it produces or supports, chemically, many of the changes also produced by action of the sympathetic nervous system, such as speeding up of the heart and the rate of breathing, and constricting the sympathetic blood vessels. Adrenin in the blood has effects of its own: it counteracts fatigue and speeds up the coagulation of the blood. Adrenin and the sympathetic nervous system cooperate in producing similar, though not identical, changes. Both effects—neural and chemical—have obvious utility in the struggle for existence. The bodily changes mobilize the energies of an organism and protect it against exhaustion and bleeding to death.

Cannon's emphasis upon the utility of the bodily changes in fear, rage, pain, and related emotions, agrees well with Darwin's claim that many of the outward expressions of emotion are signs of biologically serviceable acts. Cannon, in fact, carried Darwin's principle of utility inside the organism and thus supplemented and extended the Darwinian interpretation.

In a word, when an organism has to go on a wartime basis the sympathetic nervous system mobilizes the energy reserves of the body and prepares for the emergency. When there is no emergency—in times of peace—the parasympathetic nerves control the conservative and upbuilding processes of anabolism. The peacetime functions are incompatible with the emergency emotions. Because of this interpretation, Cannon's theory is known as the "emergency" theory of emotion.

Critique of Cannon's Theory and Reformulation

Cannon's emergency theory of emotion has been severely criticized and modified so that it can no longer be regarded as an adequate account of emotion. A review of some of these criticisms is illuminating and gives a more adequate view of emotion. We will, therefore, briefly examine three criticisms and then summarize the results.

1. Gellhorn (1943) demonstrated that the physiological basis of emotion lies in the simultaneous excitation of *both* divisions of the autonomic nervous system and not in sympathetic excitation alone. In emotion there is increased secretion of the glands controlled by *both* divisions of the autonomic nervous system.

There is much evidence for parasympathetic activity during emotion: It is common knowledge that under strong emotion the bladder and rectum are involuntarily evacuated. Although Cannon assumed this to be an exceptional case, there is additional evidence of parasympathetic action during excited emotions.

Since Pavlov's pioneer experiments, it has been known that pleasantness associated with the intake of food is accompanied by parasympathetic excitation. Thus the sight and smell of food causes "psychic secretion" of gastric juice. The effect is absent after severing the vagus nerve. Again, sexual excitement leads not only to secretory and vasodilator effects in the sexual organs but also to widespread parasympathetic effects in the gastrointestinal tract. One cannot assume, however, that pleasantness is associated with increased parasympathetic activity and unpleasantness with increased sympathetic activity. It is unfortunate that Cannon neglected the pleasant emotions with their parasympathetic effects and limited his investigations to pain, hunger, fear, rage, and related unpleasant emotions.

During fear and general excitement parasympathetic activity, rather than sympathetic, is predominant, Gellhorn argued. Parasympathetic dominance leads to spasticity of the sphincters, increase in peristalsis, diarrhea, hypersecretion of gastric juice. Even in mild excitement, such as that which may be produced by memory and imagination, the signs of parasympathetic excitation dominate sympathetic effects. The tears of grief, for example, are evoked by parasympathetic action.

Investigations of the circulatory changes accompanying emotional excitement have given evidence of both sympathetic and parasympathetic effects in emotion. The increased heart rate may be due to inhibition of tone in the vagus or to sympathetic impulses or to the secretion of adrenin or to all of these. There is multiple control.

Gellhorn concluded that various forms of emotional excitement (rage, "sham rage," fright) lead to excitation of the vago-insulin system as well as the sympathetico-adrenal system. Hormonal effects produced by nervous impulses include not only the secretion of the adrenal medulla but also the secretion of the pancreas and the pituitary glands.

2. Kling (1933), in agreement with Gellhorn, stated that Cannon's emergency theory of emotion is misleading. Cannon gave the impression that the sympathetic network alone is responsible for the major bodily changes in emotion and, further, that the parasympathetic nerves are concerned mainly with upbuilding and conservative functions of the body.

Cannon also gave the impression that emotion is an occasional event just as biological crises and emergencies occur from time to time. Actually, Kling pointed out, *both* divisions of the autonomic nervous system are on duty 24 hours a day. There are, of course, marked changes in autonomic function during an emotional crisis, but the sympathetic and parasympathetic nerves play equally important roles in these emotional responses. In most emotions there is a balanced action between the two divisions of the autonomic nervous system. This balanced action results in characteristic patterns of bodily changes. The patterns differ from emotion to emotion and are produced by reciprocal innervation of the two divisions of the autonomic. (See pages 398–399.)

In fear, parasympathetic symptoms are present as well as sympathetic. In sexual activity, both divisions of the autonomic system function together for, as we know, the sacral nerves lead to engorgement of erectile tissue and the sympathetic nerves lead to ejaculation. Further, the parasympathetic nerves become active during emotional states of depression and exhaustion as well as in excited states.

Kling stated that individuals tend to express all emotions by habitual patterns of facial and somatic expression. Along with these habitual patterns there are characteristic patterns of vagotonic disturbance that differ from individual to individual. The habits of emotional expression involve *autonomic* processes and not merely the sympathetic network.

3. Arnold (1945) is another critic of Cannon's emergency theory of emotion. She questioned Cannon's statements concerning: (1) the role of adrenin, and (2) the role of the sympathetic nervous system.

After surveying research upon adrenal function, Arnold affirmed
that cortin (the cortical hormone) rather than adrenin (the medullary
hormone) is instrumental in maintaining muscular strength. Adrenin,
in the intact organism, does *not* prevent fatigue, she stated. Adrenin
has a depressing rather than a stimulating effect. The secretion of
adrenin during fear or the injection of the drug adrenalin serves to
diminish muscular activity and reduce muscular contractions.

Physiologically, adrenin has diverse effects: (1) Adrenin produces
vasoconstriction and *reduced* blood flow. Actually the effect of adrenin
has to be overcome by muscular activity before an increased blood
flow can meet the augmented oxygen need of the skeletal muscles. (2)
Adrenin increases the heart rate but without increasing the stroke
volume and oxygen utilization. This would be a hindrance, rather than
a help, to forceful action.

Other effects of adrenin, to which Cannon referred, are probably due
to acetylcholine (the parasympathetic hormone) rather than to adrenin. The explanation of the energizing effect of adrenin after exhaustion can be found in Gellhorn's report that an increase in blood pressure
caused by adrenin or by sympathetic stimulation automatically produces parasympathetic action. The total physiological evidence, in
fact, gives little support to the view that adrenin has a dynamogenic
action and much support to the view that it has depressant effects.

Arnold goes on to consider the psychological effects of fear. In
every instance where the symptoms of fear are accurately described,
Arnold stated, the level of somatic activity is reduced rather than increased. This reaction is in sharp contrast to anger, where the activation level is definitely raised. Introspective evidence indicates that
extreme fear paralyzes action before the possibility of flight can be
explored. Laboratory workers know that when animals are placed in
an open field they show a lowered level of activity when neither flight
nor direct attack are possible. Timid rats in a strange situation don't
run; they explore cautiously or "freeze." The fact seems to be that in
mild fear muscular activity is reduced while in extreme fear it is prevented altogether.

The total evidence, Arnold stated, indicates that fear is enervating
rather than invigorating. Fear can be useful to the organism, indeed,
not because it prepares for action but because it forces caution. If
completely fearless, the human race, as well as its animal progenitors,
would have destroyed itself long ago. Fear came with the realization
of impending danger, caution, and, perhaps, the dawn of consciousness.
The penalty we pay for this increased awareness is retardation of ac-

tion. The emergency theory of emotion, therefore, is not valid for the emotion of fear. Nor can the effects of fear be explained as adaptive reactions. They are disturbing, disruptive.

Cannon's theory of homeostasis was a logical extension of the emergency theory of emotion. Cannon assumed that every reaction following some environmental interference (as when a dog barks at a cat) is adaptive and has survival value. This view, however, neglects the disruptive and disorganizing effects of fear and other emotions.

Arnold wrote: "Amending Cannon's theory of homeostasis we would suggest, therefore, that during overactivity of the sympathetic division of the autonomic nervous system (in fear or cold) the balance of the organism is restored by a cholinergic *reaction* in the form of activity; and during parasympathetic overactivity (in anger or during fear) by a secondary sympathetic *reaction* with its adrenergic effects. If such a reaction is delayed or insufficient or if the original stimulus is protracted too long, the primary effects of overstimulation may become irreversible."

Arnold identified fear with sympathetic action but claimed that fear has enervating rather than energizing effects. She suggested that anger is accompanied by dominant parasympathetic action and fear by dominant sympathetic action. According to this hypothesis, every parasympathetic excitation, e.g., in anger, produces a sympathetic reaction with a discharge of adrenin, though it does not necessarily produce fear.

Arnold concluded that there are at least three different physiological states corresponding to three different emotions: *fear,* with predominantly sympathetic excitation; *anger,* with strong parasympathetic activity; and *excitement* or elation, with moderate parasympathetic activity. In addition to these emotional states she noted two excitatory states which she hesitated to call emotions: (1) startle, and (2) an explosive or epileptoid reaction. Both of these reactions seem to represent a short circuiting which Darrow called "functional decortication."

The condition most favorable to efficient activity is found in a moderate stimulation of the cholinergic mechanism, resulting in facilitation of action by excitement without untoward secondary effects from adrenin. Neither anger nor fear can be shown to have an emergency function. Rather they are disruptive and represent obstacles to efficient action, the former by short-circuiting too large an amount of excitation into the parasympathetic and the latter by inundating the sympathetic system.

In summary, the above criticisms of Cannon's emergency theory of

emotion agree on several points: (1) Emotion is a function of autonomic activity and not a function of sympathetic action alone. Both
divisions of the autonomic system function simultaneously and reciprocally. In this reciprocal action different patterns of visceralization
are produced corresponding to fear, rage and "sham rage," general
excitement, sexual and other emotions. (2) In addition to adrenin
there are physiological effects produced, in emotion, by hormones from
the pancreas and the pituitary body. (3) The autonomic nervous
system is on continuous duty 24 hours a day. Changes produced by a
biological crisis correspond to departures from normal function. (4)
Cannon, like Darwin, has stressed the utility of the bodily changes in
emotion; but some of these bodily changes indicate disruption rather
than adaptation.

In a reformulation of Cannon's emergency theory of emotion we
should take account of the work of Selye (1956) upon the adjustments
of the organism to stress. This work will be considered in a later
chapter.

OBJECTIVE MANIFESTATIONS OF EMOTION

To assume that psychology is concerned only with the outwardly
observable manifestations of emotion, and physiology with the internal
mechanisms, is quite misleading. The true relation between outwardly
observable changes and internal changes may be illustrated by a concrete example borrowed from Cannon.

During emotional excitement the number of red blood corpuscles
(erythrocytes) per cubic millimeter of blood markedly increases. If
samples of blood are taken every few minutes from a laboratory cat,
it is found that the red blood count is greatly augmented shortly after
the cat has been confronted by a barking dog. When the dog is removed, the cat quiets down, and the red blood count, after 10 to 25
minutes, returns to its normal level. This marked increase in the number of erythrocytes is known as *emotional polycythemia*, a condition
attributed directly to the action of the spleen.

The spleen, a muscular organ which contracts and expands, is a res-
ervoir for erythrocytes. It renders the organism the service of quickly
increasing the number of erythrocytes circulating in the blood stream
and later of storing them away again. Contraction of the spleen occurs
in carbon-monoxide poisoning, in hemorrhage, in the lessening of the
oxygen content in the blood as during asphyxia and muscular exercise

and following injections of adrenin and pituitrin, as well as in emotional excitement.

Cannon has interpreted this fact: Erythrocytes carry oxygen from lungs to the heart, brain, active muscles; in a biological emergency which might involve a vigorous struggle or a race for one's life, this process is serviceable in that it facilitates energy liberation within the organism. It is part of a general preparation of the body for strenuous activity.

In this example it is seen that an external event (barking of a dog) produced an internal effect (increase in erythrocytes). The internal changes are interpreted in terms of their functional significance for behavior.

The manifestations of emotion which are observable at the surface of the body are only one aspect of the total process. The inner physiological changes are another aspect and these must be considered in relation to the outer changes. Still another aspect is the conscious emotion which the subject feels as an experience.

Peripheral Signs of Emotional Disturbance

Many of the somatic and visceral changes that occur during emotional disturbance are observable at the surface of the body. Changes in respiration, heart beat, sweat secretion, erection of the hair, etc., are apparent without the aid of instruments; but instrumental techniques have been extensively employed in experiments upon the peripheral manifestations of emotion.

The literature upon the bodily changes of emotion is voluminous and highly technical. Lindsley (1951), after a survey of the literature, listed the main bodily changes that have been studied and described the techniques for recording them. The following list is based largely upon Lindsley's summary.

1. *Electrical phenomena of the skin.* The phenomenon variously known as the galvanic skin response (GSR), psychogalvanic reflex, skin resistance, palmar resistance, palmar conductance, electrodermal response, and skin potential, is related to *sweating.* The effector mechanism for this response is the sweat gland membranes, activated by the sympathetic nervous system.

The activity of the sweat glands is augmented by a sudden noise, by a painful shock, by an odor, and by a word that is emotionally loaded through its associations. In some of the early studies the GSR was regarded as a dependable index of emotion. It has been shown, however, that the electrical conductance of the body is lowered during activities that require effort and controlled attention as well as emotion. Just analyzing a geometrical puzzle or turning impulsively from a problem in multiplication to one in division is sufficient to evoke a temporary GSR. The GSR is an index of activation. It does not distinguish pleasant from unpleasant arousals.

2. *Blood pressure and volume.* Changes in blood pressure and the GSR are probably the best indicators of facilitative and preparatory functions that are mediated mainly by the sympathetic nervous system. These changes occur also during the emergency emotions of rage, fear, pain, and excitement. There are two measures of blood pressure: the *systolic* pressure is the maximal pressure reached during contraction of the heart muscle and the *diastolic* pressure is the minimal pressure during expansion. The difference between them is known as the *pulse pressure.*

Blood pressure is usually measured by a *sphygmomanometer* which consists of a cuff placed about the arm of the subject and inflated. When it is necessary to record continuous changes in blood pressure, the pressure in the cuff is raised to a point above the diastolic level but not to a point where it occludes the circulation. With this mid-pressure it is possible to measure changes in blood pressure but not, of course, the absolute level.

The volume of blood in some part of the body is regulated by vaso-constriction and vasodilation. If the finger, hand, or foot is enclosed in a rigid apparatus, which is then filled with water, changes in the volume of the body part can be recorded in terms of pressure changes produced by rise or fall in the water level. The *plethysmograph* is an instrument for recording such changes in the volume of blood in a specific part of the body.

3. *Electrocardiogram and heart rate.* The usual method of determining the rate of heart beat is simply to count the pulse with watch in hand. The *electrocardiograph* is an instrument for recording the heart beat. Electrodes from the instrument are attached to the two arms of the subject or to either arm and the left leg or to the body wall near the heart. The electrodes pick up electrical potentials that accompany the cycle of the heart beat. The record obtained from the instrument is known as an electrocardiogram (EKG).

4. *Respiration.* Changes in the respiratory cycle are prominent in emotional conditions such as startle, fright, attempts at deception, states of conflict and anxiety.

The apparatus for recording respiration is a *pneumograph*—a flexible, air-filled tube that is placed around the thorax or abdomen of the subject and connected to a sensitive diaphragm that moves a stylus on a recording paper. The principal variables of respiration are rate, depth, pattern. The ratio of inspiration to expiration is commonly expressed as the I/E ratio and sometimes (more meaningfully) as the I-fraction. The I-fraction expresses the ratio between the duration of inspiration and the duration of the total respiratory cycle $(I/I + E)$.

5. *Skin temperature.* The temperature of the skin depends upon local vasoconstriction but also upon temperature of the blood and upon that of the body generally. Hence, indirectly, it depends upon a large variety of factors. It has been reported that emotional stress and persisting conflict are associated with a fall in skin temperature.

6. *Pupillary response.* In fear, rage, pain, and great excitement, the pupil dilates, indicating a response of the sympathetic nervous system. We all know, however, that the pupil has non-emotional functions. Constriction and dilation regulate reflexly the amount of light that is admitted into the eye.

7. *Salivary secretion.* The secretion of the salivary glands has been extensively studied by Pavlov and his associates in relation to conditioned reflexes but salivary secretion has been little studied in relation to emotion. The salivary glands and their blood vessels, however, are supplied by both sympathetic and parasympathetic nerves and their function is known to vary with emotional states. During the emergency emotions there is dryness in the mouth due to inhibition of the salivary secretion.

8. *Pilomotor response.* In various species, as Darwin has shown, emotional excitement is associated with erection of dermal appendages. When the cat is frightened her hair stands on end; when the porcupine is excited his spines erect; when the hen senses danger the feathers bristle. In man, the hair-raising reflex is vestigial but the hair-raising mechanism is still present. The "goose flesh" we experience when chilly is a pilomotor response. The wave of feeling sometimes experienced when a piece of chalk or the finger nail scrapes the blackboard is dependent upon a pilomotor response.

9. *Dermographia.* If a firm stroke with a dull rounded instrument and a constant pressure is made on the arm of the subject, the stroked area immediately appears blanched. In a few seconds it turns red and the redness then gradually disappears. The total duration of the response until the redness disappears is measured. The response may require 3 to 30 minutes or more. This measure, Lindsley writes, is

probably a better index of autonomic balance or stability than of emotional susceptibility.

10. *Skin sweating.* The galvanic skin response is an index of palmar sweating but in addition to this there are several types of chemical applications that reveal the distribution of sweating on the surface of the body. These chemical methods have a value in clinical diagnosis and possibly in future studies of emotional patterns of response in which both the sympathetic and the parasympathetic systems are activated.

11. *Analysis of blood, saliva, and urine.* Studies of the chemical constituents of the blood have shown that during emotion there are changes in the blood sugar level, adrenin content, acid-base balance, red cell count, and other factors. Changes in the acid-base balance of saliva, and in the sugar excreted in the urine, have been noted when samples are taken before and after emotional excitement.

12. *Gastrointestinal motility.* Studies of the motility of the stomach and intestine under emotional conditions have been made with animals and human subjects. Cannon demonstrated that the activities of the gastrointestinal tract of cats are inhibited during fear and anger. With human subjects the motility of the stomach and intestine has been investigated by having the subject swallow a tube containing a small bag which can then be inflated through the tube. Variations in pressure upon this bag, made by contractions and relaxations of the stomach wall, are transmitted mechanically to a recorder.

13. *Metabolic rate.* Basic metabolic rate (BMR) has been defined as the minimum heat or energy production required to keep the individual alive—to maintain respiration, circulation, digestion, muscular tonus, body temperature, glandular secretions, and other vital functions. One method of determining the BMR is to measure, by means of a *calorimeter*, the bodily heat produced. A more widely used method is to determine oxygen consumption through a test of respiration. Heat is produced by oxidation. The consumption of oxygen can be determined from the O/CO_2 ratio of inhaled and exhaled air.

The rate of oxygen consumption (BMR) generally increases during emotional excitement and during mobilization of the energies of the body for action.

14. *Muscle tension.* It is well known that anxiety is associated with an increased tension in the skeletal muscles. Muscle tension can be recorded mechanically or indirectly by recording muscle potentials. Muscle tension is an important determinant of performance and regu-

lates efficiency of action. It has been extensively studied in both emotional and non-emotional behavior.

15. *Tremor.* When antagonistic muscle groups are pitted against each other it is normal for a tremor to develop. In maintaining a posture, as in holding out an extended finger, a tremor of about ten to twelve oscillations per second develops. Muscle tremor is accentuated during emotional excitement, anger, fear, and grief. Luria recorded tremor mechanically by a pneumatic system; he studied tremor in relation to emotional conflict. In subsequent work more sensitive *tremographs* have been developed.

16. *Eye blink and eye movement.* Eye blinking suggests a kind of nervousness. It has been observed during anxiety and emotional tension. Movements of the lid and movements of the eyes can be recorded

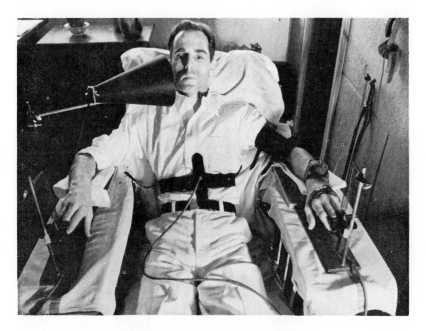

Figure 69. Subject adjusted for simultaneous recording of vocal response, involuntary movement of both right and left hands, respiration, galvanic skin reflex, pulse rate, and blood pressure. (The person shown in this figure is a normal subject who was an employee at the U. S. Public Health Service Hospital, Lexington, Kentucky, at the time the picture was taken; the photograph is reproduced with his permission.) *Courtesy* Dr. Ralph R. Brown.

by placing electrodes appropriately in the region of the eyes and registering changes of potential. There has been little systematic study of blinking as related to emotion.

Simultaneous Recording of Bodily Changes in Emotion

In some investigations of emotion a great deal of information is gained from recording simultaneously several forms of bodily changes. Figure 69 shows a subject seated in an easy chair with various kinds of recording apparatus attached. The view shows an arrangement for recording simultaneously the vocal response to a stimulus word, abdominal respiration, the galvanic skin response (GSR), pulse rate, changes in blood pressure, and two forms of response of the skeletal muscles (right and left hands respectively).

Figure 70 shows Darrow's *photopolygraph,* in an adjoining room, arranged for the simultaneous recording of bodily changes. The various bodily changes are recorded photographically on a moving film.

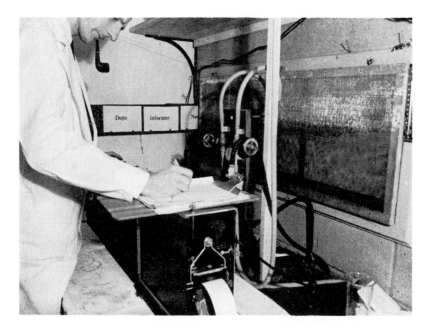

Figure 70. View showing Darrow's photopolygraph, one-way observation screen, and other details. *Courtesy* Dr. Ralph R. Brown.

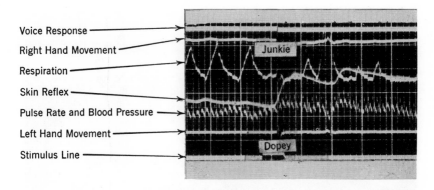

Voice Response

Right Hand Movement

Respiration

Skin Reflex

Pulse Rate and Blood Pressure

Left Hand Movement

Stimulus Line

Junkie

Dopey

Figure 71. Photograph of record from Darrow's photopolygraph showing the response of a male adult to the word "Dopey" in voice, respiration, skin reflex, pulse and blood pressure, and hand movement. *Courtesy* Dr. Ralph R. Brown.

In front of the experimenter is a one-way screen for direct observation of the subject's behavior. Stimulus words, presented to the subject, one at a time, can be seen upon the wall.

In work of this kind it is necessary to have a normal, or control, period as a base before stimulations are given. Figure 71 shows part of a photographic record. The vertical cross lines in the photograph indicate successive units of time.

The Art of Lie Detecting

The art of lie detecting is a practical application of the experimental psychology of emotion. The art rests upon a sound principle: If a man has knowledge of guilt which he wishes to conceal, he will be emotionally disturbed when questioned about his criminal or immoral act. A guilty person may control facial expression and tell lies with little outward emotion but the lie detector records *involuntary* changes in pulse and blood pressure, respiration, and electrodermal response. When we say that these changes are *involuntary* we mean that they cannot be suppressed by the wish of the subject to hide them.

The lie detector is really an *emotion* detector. The difference between truth and falsehood is not a *psychological* difference but rather one related to logic and morals. What the instruments really detect is the presence or absence of emotional disturbance. If the subject feels embarrassed or ashamed or guilty while making a true statement, the

Figure 72. Subject taking a lie-detecting test. The desk contains two three-channel polygraphs. A sheet contains a previously prepared and numbered list of questions, and the examiner is shown writing on the chart the number assigned to the question she has just asked. The cuff on the subject's right upper arm is connected by a rubber tube to the instrument for recording relative changes in systolic and diastolic blood pressure, pulse pressure, and heart rate. The distendable, corrugated pneumograph tube about the chest is attached to the instrument for recording respiration rate and depth. The electrodes attached to the left hand and to the recording galvanometer of the polygraph serve to register on the chart the electrodermal responses—variations in the resistance of the skin to minute electrical currents introduced through the electrodes. *Courtesy* Russell B. Chatham, Oak Ridge, Tennessee.

involuntary changes in blood pressure, pulse, respiration, and the GSR, still occur. Again, if a subject can deliberately make a false statement with composure, the lie detector records no emotional disturbance.

The first lie detector, historically, was a pneumograph—an instrument for recording respiration. The sphygmograph—an instrument for registering changes in blood pressure and pulse—was introduced later; it is now commonly employed alone or with the pneumograph in lie detecting. The galvanometer is sometimes used alone. Any one of these instruments can be used as a lie detector but a combination gives added checks upon the involuntary changes of emotion. These instruments automatically write their curves on a moving tape with ink pens. See Figure 72.

In questioning a suspect, the examiner asks a number of control questions and intersperses the critical items. For example, a farmer is suspected of arson; it is believed that he burned the barn of a neighbor and competitor. Control questions might include such items as: How long have you lived in Blanktown? How many children do you have? Critical items might be: Did you burn the barn? How did the fire start? If the lie detector consistently registers changes in blood pressure, pulse, respiration, GSR, for the key items and not for the controls, the subject is suspected of concealing knowledge of guilt. It is the *difference* between key and control items that is relied upon in the art of lie detecting.

The courts are generally unwilling to admit lie detector findings as evidence; but the result of a test may be so convincing that it leads to a confession. The test may be useful in helping detectives look for further evidence.

The methods of lie detecting, as discussed by Larson (1932) and Inbau (1942), are somewhat similar to those employed by psychiatrists to detect emotional complexes. The patient is made to relax and respond to selected stimulus words. If the words arouse emotion, involuntary bodily changes occur and can be recorded. The involuntary bodily changes are considered in conjunction with the meaning of the stimulus words.

PATTERNS OF RESPONSE IN EMOTIONAL BEHAVIOR

The view that emotion is a pattern of response makes a strong appeal to physiological psychologists and physiologists. There are a number of reasons for this: (1) Patterns of response are prominent components of emotional behavior. (2) Temporospatial patterns can be observed and conditions of their occurrence controlled. (3) Like reflexes, emotional patterns can be conditioned and the conditioned responses extinguished. (4) Patterns can be described in terms of stimulus and response. The pattern-response concept of emotion fits smoothly into the S-R paradigm. (5) The neural mechanisms that integrate some of the emotional patterns have been localized in subcortical regions of the nervous system and many of them have been described accurately.

These are sound advantages for an objective pattern-response concept of emotion. It is clear why Watson (1914), Bard (1934a, 1934b, 1950), and others, defined emotion as a pattern of response.

The following sections describe some of the patterns of response that occur during different forms of emotional disturbance.

Hostile and Friendly Behavior

Darwin (1872) argued that many of the expressions of emotion in animals, including man, are best understood in terms of their biological utility.   Other expressions can be understood only as the direct antitheses of biologically serviceable patterns. Thus the expression of hostility in mammals is a partial or complete integration for attack. The baring of the teeth, the growl, the bristling fur—are part of the animal's preparation for a fight. Patterns of attack and defense have obvious survival value in the struggle for existence. Animals that are able to fight and to defend themselves when attacked and in the capture of food are able to survive and leave offspring; the weaklings are eliminated.

Friendliness—the antithesis of hostility—also has survival value, especially in domesticated animals which are dependent upon man for food, shelter and protection. Friendly behavior might be described as the negative after-image of hostility for the friendly acts are directly opposite those of the hostile pattern.

Darwin's principles of biological utility and antithesis are illustrated in Figure 73.

View number 1 shows a dog approaching an enemy with hostile intent. The animal walks with a stiff gait; his head is slightly raised; the tail is erect and rigid; the hairs, especially along the neck and back, bristle; the ears are pricked up and directed forward; the eyes are widely opened and have a fixed stare; the animal growls. A human being is not likely to mistake the hostile intent of an animal approaching in this manner. Non-human animals immediately understand the meaning.

Now let us suppose that the situation abruptly changes. The dog perceives that the stranger he was approaching is not an enemy but his beloved master. There is a complete and almost instantaneous reversal of his whole bearing, as shown in view number 2. Instead of walking upright with a stiff gait, the body sinks downward or even crouches; the animal's movements are flexuous and supple; his tail, instead of being stiff and upright, is lowered and wagging from side

Figure 73. Hostility and friendliness in animals. (1) Hostility in the dog. (2) Friendliness in the dog. (3) Hostility in the cat. (4) Friendliness in the cat.

to side; his hair is smooth; his ears are depressed and relaxed backwards; his lips hang loosely and he salivates; the eyelids become elongated and the eyes no longer appear round and staring. The behavior of the friendly dog is just the opposite, the antithesis, of hostility. Friendly behavior tells this more clearly than words: I am not hostile; I have no intent to harm you.

Now consider view number 3, which pictures hostility in the cat. In many ways the hostile cat is similar to the hostile dog but there are differences. The cat, prepared for attack, is crouched and set to spring; her body is extended; the tail, or just the tip of it, is lashed or curled from side to side. The hair, especially that on the tail, bristles; the ears are pressed backward into a position that protects them during a fight; the mouth is partly open, baring the teeth; the forefeet occasionally strike out with protruding claws; the animal utters a fierce growl.

View number 4 portrays friendly behavior in the cat. The friendly animal stands upright with her back slightly arched—the antithesis of the posture for springing on an enemy. The hair, instead of bristling, is smooth; the tail is rigid and stands straight up; the ears are erect and pointed; the mouth is closed. She rubs against her master with a purr instead of a growl. The friendly behavior is thus the direct opposite of hostility.

The Pattern of Rage and "Sham Rage"

The pattern of rage appears during hostile attack. It appears also, in cats and dogs, after surgical removal of the cerebral cortex and is then called "sham rage" on the assumption that no conscious emotion can be experienced with the cerebral cortex removed. "Sham rage" is identical in appearance with rage as pictured by Darwin in the intact animal. Who can say whether or not the decorticate animal *feels* any conscious anger when the rage pattern is elicited? This is a matter for speculation!

In the decorticate cat stimulation of the skin produces a remarkable display of rage. The pattern includes lashing of the tail, arching of the trunk, protrusion of the claws, clawing movements, snarling or growling, spitting, turning of the head from side to side with attempts to bite, rapid panting with mouth open, movements of the tongue to and fro, and numerous signs of discharge across the sympathetic network. The indications of sympathetic discharge include: erection of the hair on the back and tail, sweating of the toe pads, dilation of the

Figure 74. The pattern of rage in a decorticate dog. (From a film, by Dr. E. A. Culler, depicting the behavior of a decorticate dog.)

pupils, increased arterial pressure and heart rate, secretion of adrenin and an increased level of blood sugar.

A similar pattern is elicited in the decorticate dog by mild rubbing of the fur. See Figure 74. In the dog there are such signs of rage as baring of the teeth, vicious biting and snapping, snarling or growling, struggling. When the animal is quiescent his behavior is mechanical and stereotyped. He walks monotonously around a circular path or remains in an awkward posture. If the fur is rubbed, the animal snaps and bites viciously at the stimulated area. There is obvious danger in handling such a preparation!

In the intact animal, fighting is regulated by the external situation. A normal animal distinguishes between friend and foe. He keeps a constant orientation towards his enemy. His movements are well coordinated and he retreats if the occasion demands it. The decorticate animal, contrastingly, snaps, bites, and growls indiscriminately and reflexively. He does not maintain a fixed orientation towards the enemy and in a bout he never retreats. Further, rage is more easily elicited in the decorticate animal than in the normal. A violent display of rage can be produced in a decorticate dog by mild stimulations that would not disturb a normal animal.

The components of the rage pattern such as baring of the teeth, biting, growling, pressing back of the ears, etc., are reflexive in character as truly as sneezing, coughing, sucking, yawning, and postural reflexes. These components are integrated into a temporospatial pattern at the brain stem and diencephalic level. The pattern has obvious utility during a fight.

It is reasonable to assume that man, like other mammals, carries around with him built-in subcortical mechanisms that are activated during vicious attack. Under quiet, peaceful conditions the rage pattern is latent. In man, its appearance is regulated by the cerebral cortex which may inhibit or facilitate the hostile expressions.

Terror in the Cat

In many respects the pattern of terror is similar to that of rage but there is a difference in bodily posture and somatic behavior. The terrified cat, for example, is poised either to run or, if necessary, to attack her enemy. Figure 75 portrays the attitude of a cat terrified by a barking dog.

The emotional arousal is complete. What happens next will depend upon the external situation. The animal might attack her enemy or run for a tree or remain momentarily in a state of terror.

Figure 75. Cat terrified by a barking dog. *After* Darwin (1872).

Patterns of Escape and Defense

Nature provides many kinds of protective and defensive patterns. An obvious reaction to danger is flight: birds take to wing; fish dart away; four-footed animals run to places of safety; insects move under cover or fly away or become immobilized. There are innumerable defensive patterns: the mollusk simply closes its shell when there is a disturbance; the turtle draws in its head, legs, and tail beneath a protective sheath; the porcupine erects its spines; the skunk ejects an offensive secretion.

A rather unusual escape reaction, found in the behavior of certain crustaceans and insects, has been described by the French psychologist, Piéron (1928). Certain creatures will amputate a leg or claw, when necessary to escape, rather than be devoured by an enemy, but the power of self-amputation is present only during immediate danger. Suppose, for example, that a crab has been tied to a stick with a piece of wire that is attached to one of its claws. If left alone, with food near by but out of reach, the crab will die on the spot, being unable to free itself. But when an octopus—the most dangerous of its enemies—is released, the crab snaps off its claw and escapes. This response, known as *autotomy,* is induced by the visible presence of a deadly enemy. Species of crabs differ in their readiness to sacrifice a limb. In one species (*Grapsidae*) a sudden seizure of the animal is sufficient to cause the abandonment of its claws, and even a quick movement of the hand, as though to seize it, brings immediate autotomy; whereas with another species (*Carcinus*) only the actual sight of an octopus produces autotomy. Self-amputation has been observed in various Orthoptera (an order of insects comprising the grasshoppers, locusts, crickets, and similar forms) when the situation requires immediate escape. If one of these creatures is tied by the tibia, it will die without freeing itself, but it amputates its leg immediately and takes to flight when a dangerous enemy approaches.

Organic Patterns of Sexual Response

An objective account of sexual behavior in animals includes a description of male and female patterns of response. These patterns are reflexive in nature even though in man they may become modified through social learning. The reflexive sexual patterns are clearly revealed in animal behavior.

Female Patterns. When a normal female cat is in estrus, as indicated by a swollen, congested condition of the genital organs and by the fact that males are strongly attracted to her, she behaves in a characteristic manner. This behavior has been described by Bard (1934b) as follows:

> Resting on forearms and chest with pelvis elevated and tail raised the animal executes alternate treading movements of the hindlegs and emits a curious low sound not heard at other times. This posture and this action are maintained for hours at a time even when the cat is left entirely alone. It can be said of such animals that they are bound by this pattern of behavior, for it is difficult, short of some excessive or unusual disturbance, to induce them to act in any other way. If now the vulval region be gently tapped or rubbed the treading is accentuated, and the pelvis is further elevated and the tail is raised until it is perpendicular to the vertebral axis. If a male be present and does not at once approach, the female is likely to go to him and roll playfully before him. When the male is aroused he attempts to hold the female by the loose skin of the back of the neck, and this usually induces a certain amount of spitting and growling.

In the decorticate cat, essentially the same behavior can be evoked. Bard reports that on the twenty-ninth day after the final cerebral removal an animal came into heat.

Insertion of a thermometer into the vagina immediately induced loud growling, lowering of head and chest, elevation of pelvis and tail, and treading movements of the hind legs. Except for the growling, the pattern is identical with that shown spontaneously by normal cats in estrus. The behavior was maintained for the few moments during which the thermometer remained in contact with the genitalia. On removal of the instrument the cat rolled over onto her side and, with face upward, playfully rubbed the back of her head and neck against the floor. This sequence of events was repeated on again inserting the thermometer. Furthermore, the typical posture of estrus was assumed and the treading occurred whenever the vulval region was tapped gently or rubbed. Stimulation of other parts of the body failed to produce this behavior; it is significant that insertion of a thermometer into the rectum never evoked the sexual response pattern.

Fulton (1938) has stated that the patterns of sexual behavior are laid down in the spinal cord. While experimenting with spinal dogs he found that a gentle manipulation of the external genitalia of the female elicits contractions of the uterus and probably also increased vaginal secretions. Sherrington and Goltz reported that a spinal bitch was artificially impregnated and delivered a litter of normal puppies after the usual period of gestation.

Male Patterns. With spinal dogs and cats, the male exhibits an erection of the penis on gentle manipulation of the skin of the thighs or the genitals. The same has been reported in the spinal monkey. Ejaculation, also, may be brought about in the same way. In the spinal dog, manipulation of the genitalia causes the animal to assume a copulatory posture. With humans, in some cases in which there has been an injury breaking the spinal cord, it has been reported that both erection and ejaculation can occur.

Earlier observations on the copulatory posture of the male frog during the breeding season indicate that once the posture has been developed, actual decapitation of the frog does not disturb the pattern.

In view of the above evidence it is correct to conclude that the sexual behavior patterns of both sexes are organized in the subcortical regions of the nervous system. In this respect sexual responses are very similar to those of rage, startle, and other patterns.

The sexual behavior of man contains reflexive patterns of response that depend upon built-in neural mechanisms. The reflexive patterns of erection, copulatory movement, ejaculation, and uterine contractions, are fairly constant components of sexual activity in all times and places. In the complex sexual activities of civilized man however, these patterns are often modified or inhibited through custom and taboo. Esthetic and romantic interests color human behavior; ethical and practical considerations complicate it.

The Startle Pattern

All of us are familiar with the quick, muscular jerk or contraction that occurs when there is a sudden, unexpected sound such as the firing of a gun. This is the startle reaction. The response to a sudden and intense noise involves contractions of the skeletal muscles throughout the body.

The startle pattern is shown diagrammatically in Figure 76. The pattern includes blinking of the eyes, forward movement of the head, and a characteristic facial expression, the most noticeable feature of which is closing of the eyes. There is widening of the mouth as though in a grin. The head and neck are brought forward and down but the chin is tilted up so that the features are directed straight ahead. The muscles of the neck are tensed and stand out prominently. The shoulders are raised and drawn forward. There is abduction and pronation of the upper arms, flexion of the fingers, forward movement of the trunk, contraction of the abdomen, and bending of the knees.

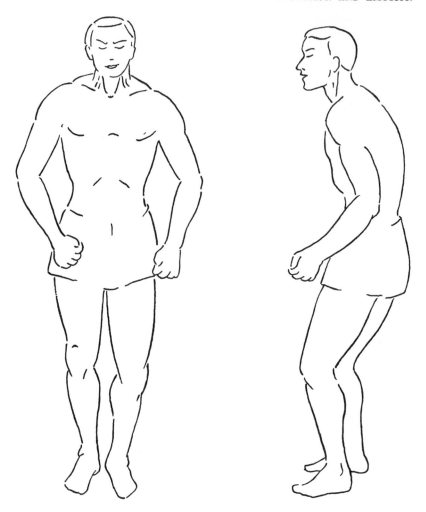

Figure 76. Schematic representation of the startle pattern. *After* Landis and Hunt (1939).

Not all of the elements of the startle pattern appear in every individual nor in the same individual every time he is startled. The eye-blink, however, always occurs, except with some epileptics. Usually, but not invariably, the startle pattern is symmetrical.

By means of superspeed motion picture cameras, taking as high as three hundred to three thousand exposures per second, Landis and

TABLE 2

SPREAD OF THE STARTLE PATTERN THROUGHOUT THE BODY

	Response Latency Range in Milliseconds
Eye blink	20–54
Widening of the mouth	52–140
Initiation of head movement	60–120
First neck-muscle movement	75–121
Beginning of shoulder movement	100–150
Beginning of arm movement	125–195
Beginning of hand movement	145–195
Beginning of knee movement	145–345

After Landis and Hunt (1939).

Hunt (1939) studied the spread of the startle pattern throughout the body. Some of their data are reproduced in Table 2. This table shows the time in milliseconds (1 millisecond = 0.001 second) required for a particular movement to begin after the firing of a revolver. The table presents the range of response latencies, for a group of subjects, for different components of the total startle reaction. It will be seen that the response starts in the head and spreads to the extremities.

Startle is produced not only by a loud noise but by other unexpected and intense stimulations. An electric shock or a jet of cold water, directed to hit between the shoulders, arouses the startle response. A sudden flash of light that is simultaneous with the sound increases the intensity of startle. Apparently an element of surprise is an important condition of startle.

If a gun is discharged at intervals of 1 or 2 minutes, habituation occurs. Habituation reduces not only the intensity of the response but its spread throughout the body. The habituation effect develops in a direction just the reverse of that shown in Table 2. Movements of the knees and legs drop out first, then those in the trunk and arms, then head movements; the eye blink is the last component of startle to disappear with habituation. The blink reflex and the facial changes were always present in the responses of trained marksmen in the New York Police Force, despite much habituation, when the men were practicing at the pistol range. Wide individual differences in the amount of habituation were found. For some subjects anticipation of the noise reduced the degree of startle; for others anticipation made little difference in the intensity of the reaction.

In man, the startle pattern is inflexibly patterned. The pattern is largely independent of the posture of the body at the time of sudden stimulation.

Tests for startle were made with animals at the Bronx Zoo. The startle pattern was not observed in reptiles and amphibia but it was clearly present in mammals. The most noticeable addition to the human pattern was flexion of the ears. The ears were commonly pressed back close to the skull. Also the flexion of startle sometimes resulted in a crouching posture with legs braced as if to spring—a postural response which suggests that startle may be a reflexive preparation for action.

The startle pattern was present with the sixteen non-human primates tested. In monkeys and chimpanzees the startle response was more widespread than with man; more elements were present. Laboratory tests upon five primates, after cortical extirpations, gave a positive result. Startle was always present; in no animal was the pattern modified. This finding indicates that startle is organized at subcortical levels.

Landis and Hunt regard startle as a skeletal reflex and not a true emotion because, for them, emotion involves visceral changes. Startle may be followed by increased blood pressure, increased heart rate, increased sweat secretion (as shown by the GSR), and other signs of visceralization; but these responses are not part of the startle pattern. The startle response is complete in the fraction of a second, well before visceral changes get under way. In man, startle may be followed by observant postures, defensive activity, flight, or just signs of annoyance. These are secondary reactions, however, and not part of the startle pattern as such.

The Disgust Pattern

Innately, nausea and vomiting are produced by the presence of irritating substances in the stomach. Later, through conditioning, the flavor, odor, appearance or even the thought of certain substances produces incipient or actual vomiting. To a sensitive individual, it is disgusting to find a fly in the milk or a hair in the butter. Disgust is bound up with the thought that these things contaminate the food or that they might be eaten.

In disgust, as described by Darwin, the mouth is rounded to a shape identical with that occurring in the act of vomiting. The upper lip is retracted, producing wrinkles beside the nose; there is retching or actual vomiting.

Disgust was studied experimentally by Brunswick (1924). He trained subjects to swallow a rubber tube with a small balloon tucked inside it. When the tube was in position the balloon was inflated through the tube so that it pressed against the walls of the stomach or duodenum. Changes in air pressure due to waves of gastrointestinal contraction were then graphically recorded.

To produce disgust, Brunswick used decaying rat flesh. A small piece of rat flesh was placed in a test tube which was corked and allowed to decay. At the proper time the experimenter produced the tube, uncorked it, and placed the open end directly under the subject's nose. After 10 to 15 seconds to give the subject time to respond to the stimulation, the experimenter announced: "This is a piece of rat flesh allowed to decay." The nature of the odor made the announcement plausible, and the statement often intensified the subject's disgust. After another 10 or 15 seconds the experimenter, with an intentionally shaky hand, allowed the end of the tube to touch the subject's nose. This seemingly accidental contact further increased the disgust.

The experiment showed an *increase*, during disgust, in gastrointestinal tone. In other emotional states involving startle and shock there was found to be a *decrease* of tone. Brunswick suggested that disgust involves two effects in combination. There is a specific "disgust effect" and a more general "unpleasantness effect." He assumed that contraction and relaxation occur simultaneously in different axes of the stomach, or in different groups or layers of muscle fibers, or in different parts of the gastric wall.

The question, *What disgusts us?* becomes: *What environmental conditions evoke the nausea-vomiting pattern of response?* Another important psychological question is: *How, through conditioning, does the innate response become modified and attached to situations not originally producing it?*

If we define *disgust* as a pattern of response associated with anti-peristalsis, the meaning of the term is definite and specific. Writers, however, use the term loosely with other meanings. The shuddering and revulsion against slimy contacts with worms, slugs, frogs, and the like, is sometimes called *disgust* but shuddering is very different from the anti-peristaltic pattern. Again, spitting out a substance that is bitter or too hot or peppery is a reaction of distaste; but this is not Darwinian disgust. A writer might state that it was "disgusting" to see a master beat a slave; but this is not true disgust unless the anti-peristaltic pattern is present.

The Facial Patterns of Crying and Laughing

Figure 77 illustrates two emotional patterns in the infant—crying and laughing. It is well known that frowning, crying, and screaming are innate expressions, being common to infants in all times and places. Similarly, smiling and laughing are inborn patterns of re-sponse that are common to infants the world over. Smiling and laughing mature somewhat later during early infancy than do crying and screaming.

Parents and other adults, without any instruction in psychology, take crying and screaming to be signs of distress, and smiling and laughing to be signs of delight. These are primitive innate patterns that mark the basic hedonic contrast between the negative and positive forms of response.

Patterns of Facial Expression in Man

Schlosberg (1941) studied patterns of facial expression by instruct-ing subjects to sort photographs on the basis of similarity and differ-ence. Seventy-two pictures of facial expressions were chosen from the Frois-Wittmann series. Three sets of these (a total of two hundred

Figure 77. Crying and laughing in the infant. *Courtesy* Dr. Nancy Bayley.

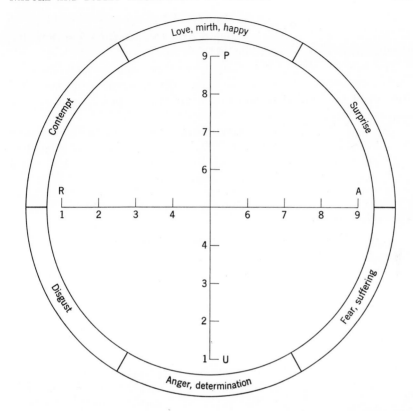

Figure 78. Frame of reference for scaling facial expressions. *Modified from* Schlosberg (1952).

and sixteen pictures) were shuffled and given to the subjects for sorting into seven bins.

The bins were arranged in a row and labelled, from left to right, with names of the six categories of facial expression used in Woodworth's scale: (1) love, happiness, mirth; (2) surprise; (3) fear, suffering; (4) anger, determination; (5) disgust; (6) contempt. The seventh bin, named "Scattering," was used for pictures that did not seem to belong in any of the other bins.

Analysis of scale values and overlapping of categories showed that Woodworth's scale is not a straight line but rather a circle with categories 1 and 6 near together. Figure 78, modified from Schlosberg (1952, 1954), shows the categories arranged in a circular series.

There are two scales in the center. The vertical scale is an hedonic continuum extending from pleasantness (P), through indifference, to unpleasantness (U). The horizontal scale extends from rejection (R), through neutrality, to attention (A).

The subjects readily placed all Frois-Wittmann pictures upon the surface determined by these two axes. The expressions did not cover the entire area but they fell within an oval-shaped area inside the circle.

The major dimension of facial expression is hedonic—expressing pleasantness or unpleasantness. The minor dimension is related to the fact that some facial expressions indicate attentive observation while others indicate rejection and avoidance.

Visceral Patterns

Following a suggestion of Knight Dunlap, Wenger (1950) identified emotion with visceralization. Emotions can be distinguished, he claimed, insofar as *patterns* of visceralization can be differentiated. The concept recalls a similar view held by the Danish physiologist, C. Lange.

The functioning of the autonomic nervous system, Wenger noted, is continuous and not limited to sporadic emotions. When a man is in dreamless sleep his vegetative processes continue without interruption. More than sixty times a minute the heart contracts and relaxes, pumping blood through the body. The lungs repeatedly expand and contract with rising and falling of the chest. The gastrointestinal and genito-urinary systems have rhythms of their own; there is an ebb and flow of changing contents. When a man is awake his blood pressure is constantly changing along with stretching and relaxing of the blood vessels. The glands of internal secretion have their independent rhythms, of long duration, that contribute to the ever-shifting visceral background of behavior. Thus there is continuous functioning of the viscera, night and day. During emotional disturbances there is a marked and heightened involvement of viscera in the total response. Emotional states *per se* can be distinguished from non-emotional only insofar as visceral changes occur.

In everday life the terms we use to name emotions are not directly applicable to visceral patterns because these terms refer to the external situations that induce emotions or to the overt responses or expressions —like laughing or weeping—rather than to internal physiological processes. Some of the words of daily life, however, recognize visceral processes. We speak of "cold feet" for cowardice and fear, of "being hot under the collar" and "red with anger" in referring to hostility and anger, of the "blush of embarrassment" and the "pallor of fear."

Patterns of visceralization assuredly exist. They have been observed in the laboratory and they differ from one emotional state to another. For example, Brunswick demonstrated that the gastrointestinal tract responds differently in disgust and in other unpleasant emotions such as startle and fear.

In sexual emotions there are several visceral patterns. There is a pleasure pattern that is present during the initial, or sacral, phase of sexual excitement. There is a different pleasure pattern occurring during and after ejaculation. The first pleasure pattern is appetitive. The second form of pleasure is akin to relief or relaxation; it is similar to the relief from tension that is experienced when noxious stimuli are removed.

The visceral patterns that appear during emotion are regulated by *both* divisions of the autonomic nervous system, responding conjointly. The work of Arnold, Kling, Gellhorn, and others, supports the statement that *both* divisions of the autonomic nervous system are excited during emotional behavior. (See pages 370–374.)

The visceral patterns differ from person to person. If completely described, they would probably not be recognized as the "emotions" of everyday life. But, Wenger argued, this does not matter. What we, as psychologists, want is an objectively correct and accurate account of the visceral patterns. We want to describe not only the degrees of visceralization but also the specific patterns of visceral response.

Wenger's view has an advantage to the investigator in that patterns of excitation really exist in the smooth muscles, glands, and nerves. These patterns can be observed objectively and studied experimentally. They can be analyzed in relation to the external situations that evoke them. Their development can be traced.

Most investigators would agree: (1) That emotions are characterized by patterns of visceral change that are controlled by the autonomic nervous system. (2) That primary emotions are dependent upon frustration, anticipation, satisfaction or anticipated satisfaction, of some motivation.

Conditioning of Visceral Processes

Conditioning undoubtedly plays a major role in the development of visceral patterns. Studies made in Russia, relying upon the methods of Pavlov, have extended the work upon conditioning to include important visceral structures.

Bykov (1957) has summarized this work. The post-Pavlovian experiments show, through the method of conditioning, that the cerebral cortex influences the functioning of endocrine glands, smooth muscles, and the metabolic processes generally. Different experiments were concerned with the influence of the cerebral cortex upon the kidneys, the liver, the heart and blood vessels, the respiratory apparatus, the digestive tract, and other structures.

Interoceptive as well as exteroceptive stimulation can produce conditioned responses in smooth muscles and glands. In other words, impulses arising in the *internal* organs may affect the visceral processes. These conditioned responses arising from the *internal* environment have an outer influence upon behavior as well as upon feelings, moods, and conscious emotions.

Since the organism functions as a whole it is difficult to separate sharply the visceral functions from the somatic. Both are integrated into a single pattern by the cerebral cortex. And the principle of conditioning applies equally to both components.

Difficulties with the Pattern-Response Definition of Emotion

In the foregoing sections we have considered some of the main patterns of response that appear in emotional behavior. Whether or not one holds to the pattern-response definition of emotion, he must faithfully describe and study these patterns that are observed. He must examine the conditions that elicit them, the way they develop, the neural mechanisms that control them, etc. The task of describing patterns of response is straightforward and scientifically important quite apart from any difficulties in defining emotion. Certainly no bias concerning the nature of emotion should interfere with the task of describing emotional patterns objectively. The patterns must be studied in their own right and in relation to the conditions that elicit them.

Despite these remarks I believe that the pattern-response concept does not adequately define emotion. There are several difficulties with the view of Watson, Bard, and others, that an emotion is an integrated pattern of response.

1. The pattern-response definition of emotion provides no criterion for distinguishing between emotional patterns and non-emotional reflexes. Coughing, sneezing, hiccoughing, sucking, swallowing, blinking,

etc., are well-integrated reflex patterns. They are not regarded as emotions. Why not? I do not know a satisfactory answer to this question. It is commonly assumed that emotional patterns involve visceral processes but visceral processes are also present in coughing, sneezing, sucking, and other simple reflexes. Again, the startle pattern was described above with the other patterns but Landis and Hunt regard startle as a general reflex of the skeletal muscles and not a true emotion. Startle is completed in the fraction of a second before visceral processes can get under way.

2. The pattern-response definition of emotion disregards the acute affective disorganization that is present in all emotions. Viewed from this angle, the pattern-response definition appears to be incomplete since it ignores important facts relating to acute disorganization at the level of the cerebral cortex. I prefer to speak of patterns of response that occur *in* or *during* emotional disturbances.

It may be that the cerebral disturbance *releases* the emotional patterns. If this is true, the emotional patterns differ in origin from simple reflexes which are responses to peripheral stimulation.

3. Another difficulty is that of specifying precisely the grouping of elements into emotional patterns. The patterns of response that are observed in the laboratory do not correspond to the forms of behavior that in everyday life are described as emotions. For example, Watson claimed that "fear" is an innate pattern of emotion; but his description of "fear" included more elementary patterns: crying, catching the breath, startle, possibly the Moro reflex, an impulse to crawl away, etc. Watson's "fear" is thus a complex of more elementary patterns.

Again, in everyday life we refer to pride, mother love, and the like, as "emotions"—but what reflexive patterns correspond to these complex affective states? Also we identify emotions by the forms of adaptive behavior that restore complacency. Flight reduces fear. Aggressive attack relieves anger. Sexual behavior follows the emotion of lust. The adaptive behavior is well integrated but can we define emotion as purposive activity? If we could, there would be no need for the concept of emotion.

EMOTION AND THE CENTRAL NERVOUS SYSTEM

A detailed study of the role of the central nervous system in emotion would take us into technical details that lie far beyond the scope of this book. But no study of emotion would be complete without at least some consideration of the relation between emotional disturbances and the functioning of the central nervous system.

A few points of general interest and importance are considered below.

Gross Anatomical Location of Centers which Coordinate Emotional Patterns

In its embryonic development, the nervous system of man presents something like a synopsis of early evolutionary history. The first appearance of the nervous system in the embryo is a neural groove which forms along the dorsal (back) side of the organism. With growth, this groove closes over, first near the middle of the body, and from this region the closure proceeds in both directions. A neural tube is thus formed.

During the first few weeks of development, bulges appear at the head end of the tube and there is a folding back of one part over another. One of these head regions (the pallium) becomes the cerebrum in the adult organism; this structure grows to such a size that eventually it covers over and hides from view all other portions of the brain.

A reconstruction of the brain of a human embryo at the age of 5 weeks is shown in Figure 79. The figure presents: a lateral view

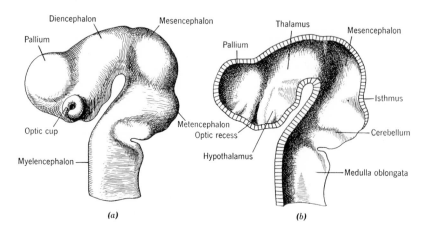

Figure 79. Reconstruction of the brain of a human embryo at the age of 5 weeks. (*Drawn by Mrs. K. H. Paul from the figure originally prepared for C. W. Prentiss, A Laboratory Manual and Text-Book of Embryology, 1915.*)

with some of the gross structures, marked *a*; a median sagital section, showing the original tubular structure, *b*. The human brain at this stage of development roughly resembles a vertebrate brain with cerebral hemispheres lacking. The similarity is due to the fact that the pallium has not yet grown. With growth, the different parts of the brain fold back upon each other and the pallium (cerebrum) covers the other structures.

In the adult brain the neural tube remains in the form of ventricles within the brain and as a minute neural canal within the spinal cord. In the adult brain, however, the external parts visible to the naked eye are largely the bulges and folds which conceal from view what is left of the embryonic neural tube.

Figure *a* shows the diencephalon, a general region of the nervous system, just behind the pallium. In this region are the thalamus and hypothalamus, represented in *b*. The hypothalamus of the adult brain contains coordinating centers for many of the patterns of response which appear during emotional disturbances.

From the point of view of development, it is interesting that the emotional patterns are coordinated in the diencephalon and lower centers. The cerebrum has other functions. In a way, the appearance of primitive emotional patterns is atavistic—a throw-back to the control by lower neural centers when cerebral dominance is weakened or lost.

Emotional Patterns and Activation

In a previous discussion of Lindsley's activation theory of emotion the point was made that this theory is more than an account of emotion. The theory of activation takes account of normal alertness, sleep, coma, and abnormal phenomena that are not ordinarily regarded as emotional processes. (See pages 182–185.)

I pointed out that one limitation of the activation theory is that it disregards the basic differences between positive and negative affectivity. Another limitation, now apparent, is that the theory does not show how specific emotional patterns are related to differences in the level of activation.

Since emotional patterns differ widely among themselves (compare, for example, crying, startle, and rage), it must be assumed that their neural mechanisms differ in locus and structure. There is no single center within the nervous system for "emotion" but there is a general region within which different emotional patterns are organized. This region is definitely below the level of the cerebral cortex. It includes the thalamus and hypothalamus and related neural structures.

Figure 33 in Chapter 5 shows schematically the functional interconnections of different parts within the central nervous system that are excited when various emotional patterns appear. The figure shows functional relations among the thalamus, hypothalamus, midbrain, medulla and cord. The pituitary body is also represented. The lines and arrows indicate neural interconnections among the centers. Arrows show the directions taken by neural impulses along pathways from one structure to another.

The cross-hatched region, extending up from the medulla through the midbrain, hypothalamus, and thalamus, is the reticular formation which provides a diffuse excitation to the cerebral cortex. Lindsley assumed that the central neural mechanisms which are known to produce the activation pattern in the EEG, are identical or nearly identical with the central neural mechanisms that are aroused during excited emotions. He stated that the activation pattern can be produced not only by external stimulation but also by direct electrical stimulation of points within the reticular formation.

Lindsley's work upon activation raises a question as to the relation between activation and specific emotional patterns.

The hypothalamus is a coordinating center for certain emotional patterns, like the rage pattern, but the hypothalamus also plays an important part in the causation ef emotional excitement. Hypothalamic stimulations yield discharges downward through the brainstem structures as well as upward to the cerebral cortex. Localized destruction within the hypothalamus produces sleep and lethargy—states which are opposed to high emotional excitement. Further, in the hypothalamus is a waking center which is constantly being bombarded by excitations from various somatic and proprioceptive and visceral receptors, keeping the subject awake. Reduction of this bombardment induces sleep. The hypothalamus thus serves an alerting, activating function as well as being the locus for coordination of certain emotional patterns.

Neural excitations from the receptors to the cerebral cortex take two routes: a direct route through the well-known pathways and an indirect route through the reticulum. Increased stimulation of any receptor increases the excitation along *both* routes. The two routes provide for the organization of specific emotional patterns and for differences in the level of general activation.

Role of the Hypothalamus in Emotion and Motivation

Bard (1950) demonstrated that after surgical removal of the cerebral cortex the cat and dog are capable of displaying a type of behavior that closely resembles rage in normal animals. The decerebrate animals are hypersensitive. Stroking the fur, which is indifferent or pleasurable to normal animals, may evoke displays of intense rage in decerebrate subjects. The facts suggest that the cerebral cortex normally inhibits the activity of the subcortical centers. When this inhibition is removed by surgical operation the animals become hypersensitive to stimuli eliciting rage.

In normal animals the cerebral cortex has more than an inhibitory function. A normal animal exhibits better coordination of muscles and better precision, in fighting, than does a decerebrate preparation. Further, the telencephalon increases the range of stimulations that produce rage. The intact animal responds with rage to visually perceived situations, such as the approach of a familiar enemy, but decerebrate animals are not aroused in this way. The telencephalon thus widens the range of conditions that are effective in producing rage and renders the behavior more effective in combat.

It is a fact of basic importance that the rage pattern is integrated within the hypothalamus. No one has produced a fully integrated expression of rage by stimulating any region of the brain other than the hypothalamus.

Stellar (1954) presented a physiological theory of motivation and emotion that emphasized the role of the hypothalamus. Stellar's theory gave a definite physiological and anatomical locus to Morgan's CMS (central motive state). (See pages 99–100.)

The activity of centers in the hypothalamus, Stellar pointed out, is dependent upon a large number of factors. These factors are of four main classes.

1. There are *excitatory and inhibitory centers* in the hypothalamus that regulate the appearance of innate patterns of response in highly motivated and emotional states. Such behavioral patterns as eating, drinking, copulating, sleeping, and the rage pattern, are known to be integrated by hypothalamic centers. The total evidence justifies the view that the neural centers regulating these fundamental forms of behavior are localized within the hypothalamus. Some centers excite and others inhibit the basic patterns.

2. The excitability of neural centers within the hypothalamus is

regulated by *sensory impulses* from receptors. With some forms of behavior no single sense organ has control; regulation is through various groups of sensory impulses. For example, sexual behavior is not dependent upon any single sensory channel since, with laboratory animals, any one of the senses can be removed without destroying mating behavior. It is the sum total of sensory impulses arriving at the hypothalamus that sets off sexual activity. Again, wakefulness depends upon the sum total of impulses arriving at a *waking* center in the posterior hypothalamus rather than upon any particular sensory system. Similarly, the patterns of eating and drinking depend upon a joint excitation from taste, tactile, temperature, and olfactory excitations. That is to say, the facts point to the joint operation of many stimuli in the regulation of basic forms of behavior.

3. *Chemical changes in the internal environment* exert both excitatory and inhibitory effects on the hypothalamus. The hypothalamus is the most richly vascular region of the central nervous system. It is also in direct contact with the cerebrospinal fluid in the third ventricle. There is thus ample opportunity for chemical factors of the internal environment to influence hypothalamic centers. For example, the hypothalamus is the most likely locus of action for sex hormones, since integrating centers for sexual behavior are known to exist in this region and since sexual patterns have been shown to depend upon hormones.

Stellar postulates that the activity of excitatory centers in the hypothalamus is regulated by the concentration of certain chemicals in the body fluids, by hormones, by changes in osmotic pressure, and by changes in blood pressure. Further, he assumed that consummatory behavior operates to produce satiation by arousing inhibitory centers which depress the excitatory centers.

4. The hypothalamus is functionally connected with *centers in the thalamus and in the cerebral cortex which exert both inhibitory and excitatory influences.* For example, there is evidence that the cortex can interfere with the arousal of sexual behavior or can facilitate it.

Regulation of hypothalamic centers by cortical activity provides for the fact that learning can influence the basic forms of behavior. The point is very important for human psychology.

In general, Stellar's theory provides a multifactor approach to the physiology of motivation and emotion. It takes account of sensory stimulations, chemical excitations, and the influences of the cerebral cortex upon behavior. It takes account, also, of both excitatory and inhibitory processes. The theory reads like a summary of what is actually known about the physiology of the hypothalamus. The gaps in our knowledge are clearly revealed by this kind of factual treatment.

Stellar's account is in line with the current tendency to treat the topic of emotion within the broader context of motivation. No lines of distinction are drawn between emotional and non-emotional patterns. For example, the rage pattern (emotional) is a response organized at the level of the hypothalamus. So also are the patterns of sleeping, eating, and drinking (non-emotional).

Stellar studiously avoided the term *drive*. Instead he spoke repeatedly of "motivated behavior." The phrase, however, implies that some behavior is *not* motivated. One wonders whether "motivated behavior" is limited to that which is organized on the hypothalamic level. If one postulates that *all* behavior is motivated (causally determined), there is little point in talking about "motivated behavior." (See pages 14–16.) According to the broader concept, the learned behavior of a well-trained rat in running the maze is motivated as truly as the animal's unlearned patterns of gnawing or fighting.

Physiological Conflict Theories of Emotion

Hodge (1935) pointed out that the brain can respond to a situation which confronts the organism: (1) through efferent visceral excitation *via* the general thalamic region; (2) with specific skeletal movements and postures that are patterned on the level of the cerebral cortex; or (3) by a combination of visceral and skeletal reactions determined in both the general thalamic and cerebral regions.

Emotion is aroused, Hodge argued, when the higher brain centers fail to provide an adequate response to the perceived situation or when some doubt, hesitation, or conflict is aroused as to one's ability to respond successfully. Thus: *"Emotional reactions are inversely proportional to the ability of the higher centers of the brain to meet a given situation."*

This statement agrees with the widely accepted view that visceral excitation is the earmark of emotional response but it adds to this an emphasis upon conflict at the level of the cerebral cortex. It is when the cerebrum *fails* to provide an adaptive response that emotion appears. Visceralization is characteristic of most highly motivated, well-integrated activities, as well as of emotion, but in emotion there is always some *failure* of integration at the level of the cerebral cortex.

Another physiological conflict theory of emotion is that of Darrow (1935). After reviewing the experimental evidence, Darrow pointed out that the centers which regulate *excited* emotion are located in the hypothalamus. This is evidenced by the fact that animals have a high capacity for emotional behavior after surgical removal of the cerebral cortex. When, however, there is destruction of a certain area within the hypothalamus, erstwhile wild animals change into docile ones.

The normal role of the cerebral cortex, Darrow stated, is: (1) that of differentiating patterns of stimulation, and (2) that of maintaining an appropriate inhibitory control over the subcortical mechanisms of excitatory response. Both roles are important in explaining emotional excitement.

If circumstances arise which involve a threat to the physical or intellectual equilibrium of the individual and which necessitate an active struggle, there is a release of the primitive (subcortical) mechanisms of *excited* emotion. An essential condition of excited emotion is that the cortical patterns precipitating the conflict shall be occasioned by a situation that demands action on the part of the individual.

Briefly, just as surgical decortication frees the lower centers from cortical control, so a dynamic conflict produces functional decortication, or "excortication," which weakens or largely removes cortical inhibition, in this way rendering the individual more excitable emotionally.

Darrow explained that his theory is limited to *excited* emotions. Another mechanism must be postulated to explain other emotional states like grief, sorrow, remorse, amusement, and embarrassment. In such emotions the cerebral cortex itself plays the major role for everything depends upon the subject's interpretation of the situation in which he finds himself.

Elsewhere Darrow (1950) pointed out that during normal emotional excitement there is feedback into the cerebral cortex from lower neural centers. This feedback, if excessive, can serve to release subcortical centers from cortical control. The feedback can produce a functional excortication similar in effect to that produced by surgical removal of the cortex.

The cerebral cortex plays a dominant role in the perception of environmental situations that produce emotions. The meaning of a situation depends upon an individual's past experience and, physiologically, upon the acquired neural organization that regulates the cognitive and affective aspects of response. When the cortical dominance is weakened, subcortical centers take over. Then patterns of emotional response appear in the stream of behavior.

There is, however, a constant interaction between cortical and sub-cortical centers.

CONCLUSION

An emotion is here defined as an acutely disturbed affective state of the individual that is psychological in origin and revealed in behavior, conscious experience, and visceral functioning. This definition has been extended to include persisting, relatively stable, states of disturbance within the individual which underlie repeated emotional outbreaks. Such persisting disturbances include states of conflict, expectations, incompatible attitudes, motives, and other conditions of emotional upset. The extended definition is useful when we consider emotional development and the dynamics of emotional behavior.

As a bodily event an emotion involves the organism as a whole. Well-integrated patterns of response appear during emotional disturbances. These patterns resemble reflexes but are more widespread and complex, involving the total body. Many of the patterns are organized in subcortical neural centers.

Visceral processes are invariably present during emotional upsets. The visceral changes indicate involvement of both divisions of the autonomic nervous system in emotional response.

The dominance and control of the cerebral cortex is weakened during emotion and the subcortical mechanisms take over more of the control. This weakening of cerebral dominance is associated with frustration, the clash of motives, painful stimulation, thwarted expectation, the release of tension, and other conditions which are direct determinants of emotional upset.

Reading Suggestions

The literature upon the nature and bodily mechanisms of emotion is extensive. The following works contain discussions and references to the voluminous literature: Ruckmick (1936), Lund (1939), Young (1943), Morgan and Stellar (1950), Lindsley (1951), Woodworth and Schlosberg (1954). The work of Cannon (1929) upon bodily changes in emotional excitement has had a profound influence upon physiological studies of emotion.

Anyone wishing to delve into the history of the subject should see the book by Gardiner et al. (1937), especially Chapter 11 on affective psychology in the twentieth century by J. G. Beebe-Center.

Gardiner, H. M., Metcalf, R. C., and Beebe-Center, J. G. *Feeling and emotion, a history of theories.* New York: American Book, 1937.

Cannon, W. B. *Bodily changes in pain, hunger, fear and rage; an account of recent researches into the function of emotional excitement,* 2nd ed. New York: Appleton-Century-Crofts, 1929.

Lindsley, D. B. Emotion. In S. S. Stevens (Ed.), *Handbook of experimental psychology.* New York: Wiley, 1951.

Lund, F. H. *Emotions; their psychological, physiological and educative implications.* New York: Ronald, 1939.

Morgan, C. T. and Stellar, E. *Physiological psychology.* New York: McGraw-Hill, 1950.

Ruckmick, C. A. *The psychology of feeling and emotion.* New York: McGraw-Hill, 1936.

Woodworth, R. S. and Schlosberg, H. *Experimental psychology.* New York: Holt, 1954.

Young, P. T. *Emotion in man and animal; its nature and relation to attitude and motive.* New York: Wiley, 1943.

10 DEVELOPMENT OF MOTIVES AND EMOTIONS

One finds that he needs to know about the past, not in order to predict the future, but in order to understand the present.

When Boring wrote the above sentence he was considering the reasons, sound and unsound, for studying the history of science. The statement stands, however, for the organism. To understand the present activities of an organism one must know something about its past. This is particularly true in the study of motives and emotions.

In this chapter we will consider the developmental, or temporal, aspect of the determinants of activity. The main topics are: (1) motivation and learning; (2) the physicochemical regulation of growth and behavior; (3) effects of early experience upon adult behavior; (4) emotional development; (5) emotional maturity and control; (6) the role of feeling and emotion in development.

Importance of a Developmental View in Identifying Emotions

A developmental view of the organism is ordinarily needed to recognize and name emotions consistently. This point was emphasized

411

by Hebb (1946b). He studied the diary records of thirty chimpanzees to discover how emotions are recognized and named by persons who have firsthand dealings with the animals. The records contained repeated references to emotional outbursts. (See pages 348–349.)

The chimpanzees had been under observation for periods of time varying from 6 to 19 years. Many of the records were based upon intimate knowledge of the subjects. An intimate and lengthy acquaintance with the animals is important, Hebb explained, because temperamental traits and specific emotions are recognized as deviations from the normal base of behavior rather than as momentary states. Hebb illustrated this point by considering the distinction between rage and hate.

The terms *rage* and *hate* apply to humans but they were used repeatedly by Hebb in describing the behavior of chimpanzees:

> Bimba, one of the chimpanzees of the colony, is said to be friendly to man, but quick-tempered; while another chimpanzee, Pati, is said to hate man. Bimba's anger, and Pati's hate, are actually manifested in attacks which cannot be reliably distinguished from one another. But when Bimba is not attacking an observer, she behaves very differently from Pati. She is always responsive to man, and acts in a way which promotes contact and petting by the attendants (except at the times when she is said to be angry), while Pati has a long history of vicious attacks with few efforts to be friendly. It is in this difference that the real distinction of rage and hate must lie.

Hebb questioned whether human emotions are recognized on the basis of conscious processes or specific patterns of motor and glandular activity. Early experiments by Landis, Sherman, and others, showed that we cannot consistently recognize emotions on the basis of photographs or momentary views of behavior. A long-time acquaintance with the subject, combined with a knowledge of the inducing situation, is required to identify and name emotions consistently. Furthermore, since human subjects tend to develop individual habits of expression, a long-time acquaintance is necessary to recognize these habitual marks of emotion.

In man, then, as in other animals, familiarity with the subject over long periods of time is necessary to furnish a sound basis for recognizing and naming emotions and temperamental traits. This is because emotions are deviations from habitual lines of behavior. Knowledge of past behavior, as well as observation of present reactions, affects our judgments.

The term *temperament* is generally used to designate relatively stable affective traits. Temperaments are said to be cheerful, gloomy, excitable, stable, moody, apathetic, vigorous, etc. Obviously, when we speak of temperaments we must have a view that extends over considerable periods of time. A long-term knowledge of the subject is necessary to identify and name specific emotional reactions with consistency and to distinguish one affective response from another.

Past Experience and Present Situation in the Causation of Fear

In the emotional reactions of fear, anger, love, jealousy, disgust, and others, past experience as well as the present situation play important roles. Hebb (1946a) illustrated this point by reference to the emotion of fear.

Hebb investigated the kinds of objects that elicit fear in chimpanzees. His method was to expose a test object for thirty seconds while observing the behavior of the animal in its presence. He tested thirty chimpanzees by presenting a variety of test objects.

The objects that most frequently excited fear were: a skull with moving jaw, a painted wax snake, the moving head of a monkey, plaster cast of a chimpanzee visage, a human head. It is well known that chimpanzees fear toy animals and snakes, but the fact is new that they avoid parts of the chimpanzee and human bodies. The sight of a clay chimpanzee head, when carried from cage to cage, produced an avoidance that was akin to panic in five or six of the thirty animals.

Several behavioral criteria were relied upon in determining the presence of fear: (1) Consistent withdrawing behavior that continues when the position of the test object is changed. If moving the test object produces a corresponding movement of the animal so that the animal keeps his distance from it, fear is judged to be present. (2) Withdrawing behavior appearing abruptly when the test object is suddenly presented. (3) Coincident excitation, such as erection of hair, screaming, threatening gestures directed at the test object, or continued orientation of the gaze at the object while the animal is moving directly away from it.

In analyzing results Hebb pointed out that fear arises spontaneously. The animals did not have to learn the fear response. The evidence indicates, in both man and chimpanzee, that fear occurs spontaneously when the subject is presented with mutilated and unresponsive bodies. Other investigators have shown that fear is produced by uncanny situations, i.e., by situations that are strange—partly familiar and partly new and not well understood. The fear of strangers, however, must be based upon some *experienced discrepancy* rather than upon a property of sensory excitation. This kind of fear is based upon the fact that certain perceptions have become habitual. A strange person produces a discrepancy relative to familiar patterns.

Hebb concluded that fears are a joint product of sensory and central processes and that no amount of analysis of the sensory processes alone (along the lines of Watson and others) can elucidate the nature of fear. Existing studies upon the causes of fear have failed to reveal any common psychological grounds for the fear response.

Fear can be produced by: (1) conflict, (2) sensory deficit (absence of usual and expected sensory patterns), (3) constitutional changes related to glandular function. These conditions point to a cerebral factor in the causation of fear.

Hebb argued that the fundamental source of both fear and rage is of the same kind: *a disruption of coordinated cerebral activity.* The question was left open as to whether there are different kinds of disruption, one kind leading to fear, the other to rage. Fear originates, Hebb believed, in the disruption of temporally and spatially organized cerebral activities. Fear can be distinguished from other emotions by the nature of the behavior that tends to restore cerebral equilibrium. In fear it is flight that tends to remove the disturbance.

The impossibility of flight accentuates the emotional disturbance. Consider, for example, the state of mind of people in an airplane when something goes wrong. It might be a misfiring engine or unusual turbulence of the air. In the early days of aviation a panic might spread through the passengers. Since the individual passenger can neither run away nor take charge of the threatening situation, he becomes the victim of anxiety. Today when the plane is in trouble the pilot tells the passengers through the loudspeaker just what the situation is and that it is not really serious (although actually it may be), that he knows exactly what to do, and that there is no occasion for anxiety. This usually has a quieting effect.

The sense of danger which elicits fear and anxiety is based upon past experience as well as present perception. An organism's knowledge or understanding of the present situation rests upon the past. Hence, as Hebb claimed, it is necessary to take a longitudinal view of the organism rather than a cross sectional view to understand the nature of emotional disturbances.

MOTIVATION AND LEARNING

In studying the growth of motives and habits psychologists are concerned with three kinds of processes that go on within the organism: (1) contemporary activity, (2) development, (3) dynamics.

Contemporary activity can be viewed and analyzed objectively or from the point of view of the experiencing individual. When viewed objectively, it is called *behavior*. The same objective view reveals *physiological processes:* events within the nerves and other bodily structures that can be described in physicochemical terms without reference to the external world. When contemporary activity is viewed subjectively, it is called *experience*. Individuals experience objects and events. They perceive, feel, desire, act, remember, imagine, think. Conscious experience is not a substance but a process or activity— *experiencing*.

The aspects of contemporary activity are very different. Each aspect can be studied without reference to the others. We have assumed, however, that the different aspects reveal a single real event which occurs here and now as a contemporary activity.

Development is a very different kind of process. Development is a more or less gradual change in the structural organization of individuals. Although developmental changes like cell division may be directly observed, development is usually inferred from changes noted on two or more occasions within the life cycle of an individual. Forms of psychological development include: maturation or physical growth, learning, adjustments to accidents and diseases, changes of structure due to function, etc.

There are, of course, forms of development that lie outside the scope of psychology because they extend beyond the life span of individuals, e.g., organic and cultural evolution. The psychologist is concerned with development within the life span of individuals that influences behavior and experience.

Dynamic processes are of special interest to the student of motivation and emotion. They imply developed interests, attitudes, intentions, goals, states of conflict, and the like. The study of psychodynamics is concerned with the interaction of the underlying determinants of activity.

In Chapter 12 we will consider the dynamics of emotional behavior. The present chapter is concerned with the development of motives and emotions. Our immediate concern is with the difficult but important problem of the relation between motivation and learning.

Motivation and Learning as Factors in Development

In a previous discussion of the functions of affective processes, I listed the following. Affective processes: (1) activate; (2) sustain and terminate; (3) regulate; (4) organize. (See pages 201–202.)

Since affective processes have an organizing function, they determine what neurobehavioral patterns will be learned and what will not be learned. They determine how well an organism will perform a learned act and under what conditions the learned act will appear, whether a learned act will be repeated or disappear, and so on. Hence affective processes are most intimately related to the development of behavior. But we must distinguish between the roles of affective processes and learning in development.

Young (1959) drew a distinction between: (1) reinforcement as a growth of habit strength through practice; and (2) reinforcement as a change in performance dependent upon affective processes. The first view regards reinforcement as a phenomenon of learning—a change in performance due to exercise (practice, drill, training). The second view regards reinforcement as a phenomenon of motivation. (See pages 237–241.)

Now if we define learning as a developmental change that is dependent upon exercise (practice, drill, training), it must mean just that and we are obliged to hold consistently to this definition. (I have mentioned practice, drill, and training specifically because some bodily changes due to exercise are not instances of learning. For example, the increase in the girth of a muscle with exercise is not to be identified with learning.)

According to this view, the *initial* organization of a neurobehavioral pattern is not an instance of learning. Learning is a *developmental* process and not a *behavioral* process. Two occasions are needed to prove that learning has occurred. If the neurobehavioral pattern is different on the second occasion from what it was on the first, and if the change is due to exercise, learning has occurred. Organizing and reorganizing a neurobehavioral pattern is a *behavioral* process and not an instance of learning.

Bindra (1959) defined the problem of motivation broadly as the study of conditions that determine the occurrence of certain forms of behavior. Within this broad definition of motivation he did not hesitate to consider habit strength as one of the basic determinants of performance. This way of looking at things brings the study of learning within the broad context of motivation as one of the major determinants of behavior. Learning is a *developmental* determinant.

Most students of learning, however, would hesitate to subordinate learning to motivation. They would prefer to regard motivation as a condition of learning. There is confusion here that goes back at least as far as Thorndike. Thorndike described two laws of "learning," the law of exercise and the law of effect. I have argued that the law of exercise includes everything that is properly called learning and that the law of effect is motivational since it deals with activating, sustaining, terminating, regulating, and organizing neurobehavioral patterns.

The confusion is due to definition of concepts. To clarify the picture it is necessary to recognize that both learning and motivation are determinants of development. And the concept of determinant, or cause, is broader than the concept of motivation.

There are broad and narrow views of learning. The view of learning that I have taken is definitely narrow: Learning is a change in neurobehavioral organization that is dependent upon exercise (practice, drill, training). A broad view of learning recognizes that individuals develop interests, attitudes, traits, and motives. In the growth of these determinants, a major role is played by factors other than exercise: affective processes, chemical sensitizers, external and internal stimuli, and other factors. Motivational factors influence performance apart from exercise.

The broad view of learning is useful but not very precise because the role of non-associative factors is poorly defined and specified. I have taken a narrow view of learning and a broad view of motivation. Others, e.g., Brown and Farber, have taken a narrow view of motivation and a broad view of learning. The basic facts of behavior and development are the same, of course, regardless of how one defines the concepts of learning and motivation.

Actually, it is difficult to separate learning and motivation sharply in considering psychological development. Psychologists agree that an organism learns only when it is active; a completely passive organism learns nothing. But if all activity is motivated (in the sense of being causally determined), some motivation is necessary for learning to occur. Motivation is thus the more fundamental concept.

Is Learning always Motivated?

This question has been asked repeatedly but it is misleading unless we know what we mean by motivation. The difficulty lies with the definition of motivation.

If we take a broad view and argue that all behavior is motivated (in the sense of being causally determined), then we must affirm that learning never occurs in the absence of motivation. Students of learning agree, as we have said, that learning does not occur in a completely passive organism. An organism must respond in some way for learning to occur; and since every response is an activity that is causally determined in some way or other, motivation is essential to learning.

If we take a narrow view and restrict the definition of motivation to the determination of behavior that is goal-directed or need-related or purposive, then we must state that "motivation" is *not* necessary for learning to occur. The facts clearly indicate that there is incidental learning, and learning without an intent or goal or will to learn. Further, emotional experiences which are aimless leave a trace that is well retained. Again, Maier argued that an organism learns patterns of abnormal behavior that are due to frustration and not to "motivation." In general, it must be recognized that much learning occurs apart from a will to learn or an intent or goal.

Habits and Motives

Farber (1955), in a useful review of studies upon verbal learning and performance, drew a clear distinction between motivation as an energizing, dynamogenic function and learning as an associative function. Thus electric shock, hunger, fear and failure are classified as motivational by virtue of their non-associative (drive) properties. Verbal habits are associative in nature; they are learned and can be adequately described in terms of stimulus and response.

Although motivation is a non-associative function, its effect upon learning and performance, in some situations, is best understood in terms of associative characteristics. Associative factors, rather than dynamogenic, explain many experimental results.

In conventional psychological usage, Farber pointed out, motives are assumed to have an associative as well as a dynamogenic aspect. The concept of drive refers to the *energizing* aspect and that of mechanism to the *regulative* aspect. Thus, for Shaffer, a motive involves both drive and mechanism. Drives arouse mass activity; mechanisms are acquired response tendencies. For Hull, all drives are able to sensitize all habits, but associated with every drive (D) is a characteristic drive stimulus (S_D). For Dollard and Miller, it is the drive aspect of stimuli that impels to action and the cue aspect that leads to differential response. Mechanisms are modified by learning and they are describable in terms of S-R associations.

Farber agrees with the view of Brown (1953), previously considered (See pages 104–106). Brown restricted the concepts of motive and motivation to an energizing function. He thus avoided a confusion between habits and motives that is implied in such concepts as "learnable drives" and "acquired drives." Drive, he said, is an *energizing* variable; habits are *directive and regulative* and are the result of learning.

Brown and Farber have clarified the picture by distinguishing sharply between an *energizing* function (drive) and a *regulative* function (habit). They are correct in pointing out that the usual concept of motive combines both functions.

Both motives and habits are learned. By common consent motives are recognized as acquired determinants of action. They develop during the life cycle of an individual; they have a certain duration or temporal course; they are terminated by goal responses.

How do motives differ from habits? I previously pointed out that the neural organization underlying a motive has the capacity to produce muscle tension and action; the neural organization underlying a habit lacks such a capacity. Contrast, for example, a motive such as my present intent to purchase a new battery for my automobile with the latent habit organization that makes it possible for me to recite the Greek alphabet. Since there is no intent to recite the Greek alphabet, this bit of neural (habit) organization is inert, latent. A motive may be latent, too, but there is this difference: a motive has the potential for building up muscle tension and instigating action. A second difference between motives and habits is this: The motive is terminated by a goal response but latent habit organization has no such terminal response. At present, for example, I have the latent neural organization requisite for reciting the Greek alphabet but I have no motive to recite it. If there were such a motive, it would be removed by completion of the task, by making of the final response, or goal response.

The above view places motivation in the context of development. Motives are learned; they regulate and direct behavior as well as energize it; they are located within the nervous system; they are dynamogenic; they may be latent but are potentially activating. A motive is a stable regulator and energizer as well as a determinant of contemporary behavior.

Affective Arousal and the Growth of Motives

McClelland et al. (1953) defined a motive as a learned determination to act in relation to a goal. The complete description of a motive, such as a need for achievement, requires specification in four dimensions: (1) The *quality* of a motive is its goal or direction. (2) The *extensity* of a motive is the variety of cues that elicit it—its generality to diverse situations. (3) The *intensity* of a motive is the strength of desire or interest. (4) The *dependability* of a motive is the probability that a given cue will elicit it.

In the growth of motives, according to McClelland et al., affective arousals play a basic role. "A motive is the learned result of pairing cues with affect or the conditions which produce affect." "A motive is the redintegration by a cue of a change in an affective situation." Thus motives are essentially redintegrated affective arousals.

The view of McClelland et al. that motives are affective arousals associated with environmental stimulus cues and redintegrated by those cues, requires several comments.

1. It is true that affective arousals become conditioned to environmental situations and that stimulus cues evoke affective processes previously conditioned to those cues. Objects and situations, through conditioning, acquire positive or negative incentive values.

2. Although motives, in the sense of McClelland et al., are learned, it must be recognized that affective arousals, apart from learning, are motivating. Affective processes, whether aroused innately or through conditioning, activate, sustain, and to some degree regulate behavior.

3. The affective arousal concept is not a sufficiently broad base to account for the origin and growth of all motives. Motives may be organized on a purely cognitive basis apart from affectivity. Verbal instructions, commands, and suggestions, can build up determinations to act quite apart from feelings. One can resolve, on coldly rational grounds, to act in the absence of feelings and even contrary to feelings. One can accept a command to act when the action is difficult, unpleasant, and contrary to one's best judgment.

It should be recognized, however, that affective arousals *are* of fundamental importance in the growth of motives in animals, children, and many adults; but we must not overgeneralize the principle. Non-affective (cognitive) factors, too, are important in the growth of motives.

4. An environmental stimulus cue redintegrates the total pattern of response including affective and non-affective components. It commonly happens that with repetition of a situation the affective component drops out and the response becomes indifferent, automatic, habitual. It is in the early stages of behavioral development that affective processes are of prime importance.

Active and Passive Neural Structures

In a discussion of the diversity of definitions of motivation and the difficulty of finding any single definition upon which psychologists can agree, Littman (1958) pointed out that terms which refer to motivation imply *activity*. Other psychological terms which do not refer to motivation imply *passivity*. The active-passive distinction thus seems to go to the heart of the motivational problem even though there is little agreement about other matters.

It is important to point out that the neural organization which regulates the processes of behaving and experiencing is latent, inactive, most of the time. A man may have acquired a lot of motor skills through practice and a lot of information through reading and study, and he may have lived through a lot of experiences during his life time —but most of this is hidden from view when he is asleep and when he is carrying out the routine activities of daily life. A man's acquired neural structure carries many systems of habit and experience. When a man moves from place to place he transports this neural organization with him but this is not evident on the surface.

Leeper (1935) drew an important distinction between the acquisition and utilization of habits. (See pages 132–134.) If a rat has acquired the habit of taking one path to food and another path to water, an organic state of hunger will activate the going-to-food pattern and an organic state of thirst will activate the going-to-water pattern. The acquired neural organization, however, remains latent when the animal is satiated.

The distinction between passive neural structure and activation applies to innumerable human situations. For example, if a child has memorized a poem, he will recite it when his parents ask him to do so. But most of the time the verbal associations—built into the nervous system by drill—remain idle, inert, passive. It is the demand of the present situation that activates the latent neural organization.

The concept of activation is exceedingly useful. It can apply to the arousal of specific bodily mechanisms as well as to the general level of neural activity.

Implicit and Explicit Activation of Neural Structures

When one remembers, imagines, thinks, plans, there are bits of neural organization that are aroused implicitly and covertly. The same bits of neural organization are aroused explicitly and overtly when one perceives and acts. There is a difference, for example, between mentally planning a trip to the beach and actually carrying out the plan. The same bits of neural organization may be involved in both activities.

By analogy the brain is like an automobile engine that continues to run when it is out of gear and does not move the car. The same engine when in gear is capable of producing overt action.

The neural structures which underlie our skills and knowledge may be completely latent, dormant, inactive. They may be activated implicitly in thinking, remembering, and in fantasy. They may be activated explicitly on the level of perception and overt action.

Transformation and Functional Autonomy of Motives

As an individual develops from infancy to maturity there is a constant transformation of motives. The behavior of the neonate is governed by organic states. He sleeps and wakes, cries when hungry, sucks nourishment at the breast, urinates and defecates, is responsive to external stimulations and again quiescent, breathes, and grows. His activity is physiologically determined.

As the child grows up he learns the ways of his group. He conforms more and more to the standards of society. From his social environment he acquires habits, attitudes, traits, and motives, that regulate his behavior. The bodily needs remain throughout the life cycle and these needs must be met within the framework of society. Behavior becomes increasingly determined by the social world into which the infant is born.

From birth to maturity there is a constant transformation of motives. The transformations continue throughout adult life. As an example of the transformation of motives on the adult level consider the following example, borrowed from Krech and Crutchfield (1948):

A man of great wealth finds that his ruthless business practices have made him an object of hatred and scorn in his country. He grows old, gets religion, and begins to worry about his soul. He needs social approval, and needs it desperately. On the advice of his friends he hires an eminent public-relations expert, who advises our millionaire to become a great philanthropist—to give large sums of money to churches, universities, research foundations, hospitals, libraries, etc. This is done, and gradually the name that was anathema to the public becomes highly respected. But the millionaire continues to give money to the support and expansion of these many institutions. Why? ... Our millionaire, in giving money to public institutions, has met theologians, scientists, philosophers, writers, doctors—people whom he had not known on intimate terms before. He may have become interested in new concepts; he has been exposed to new ideas, talked with men of strange enthusiasms. All this could very well have altered his cognitive structure, his range of appreciations, and even his personality structure in such ways as to invoke new needs and demands.

Human life is filled with less spectacular examples of the transformation of motives. The easiest way to understand them is in terms of the social experience of the person and its effect upon his dynamic structure.

Gordon Allport (1937) argued that the motives of an adult are infinitely varied, self-sustaining, contemporary systems, growing out of antecedent systems but functionally independent of them. The motives of a mature person, he stated, are so far removed from the original physiological drives that nothing can be gained by attributing the social behavior of an adult to primary physiological drives.

As the individual advances from infancy to maturity the character of his motivation alters so radically that adult motives may be said to have supplanted those of infancy. The dynamic pattern of each person is, in a sense, unique. The contemporary systems of motivation are functionally independent of the preceding systems. Just as a child grows up to become independent of his parents so human motives become autonomous in the sense that they are self-sustaining and independent of physiological drives.

To illustrate the functional autonomy of motives Allport cites the example of a sailor who has repeatedly gone to sea, driven by the necessity of making a living. The sailor becomes wealthy and retires. He continues to go to sea when it is no longer necessary. Going to sea has become a way of life with him. The dynamic pattern is autonomous—independent of economic motivation.

To the present writer it seems that Allport's account of the transformation and functional autonomy of motives is a clear statement of something important that actually occurs in the course of human development. Further examples of apparently self-sustained activities can readily be found.

Allport's doctrine of functional autonomy is a kind of declaration of independence from the enslavement to dominant biological drives. It provides a principle that is applicable to the numerous specific motivations that are apparent in social behavior.

The principle of functional autonomy, however, does not explain anything. When we state that an act is autonomous we have not answered the questions "Why?" and "How?". Why does the sailor continue to go to sea if there is no financial need for it? How did this pattern become autonomous?

The bare statement that an activity is functionally autonomous does not answer questions like these: How are the motivations of infancy transformed during the course of development? How, especially, does a child acquire social patterns? How does he come to conform to the ways of his group? What bodily mechanisms sustain interests and hobbies? What motivates a tic, a compulsive act, a perseverating process, an associative response?

The bare statement that these activities are functionally autonomous does not explain them. It would be better to admit our ignorance than to assume that the doctrine of functional autonomy of motives explains anything. Explanation may some day be found through the study of interests, values, and intrinsic motivations.

Allport's doctrine is a protest against the view that we must seek extrinsic motivation for every bit of behavior. Autonomous acts are self-motivated. They are like other natural movements. The moon goes around the earth and the earth around the sun without any external force pushing it. Activity, rather than passivity, is the normal state of affairs. Perhaps some such principle applies to behavior.

THE PHYSICOCHEMICAL REGULATION OF GROWTH AND BEHAVIOR

The following sections are intended to underscore the basic importance of chemical and physical determinants of growth and behavior. This emphasis is important in any study of development because many writers have regarded psychological development as primarily a matter of learning. The physicochemical determinants of behavior are *not* learned. They simply exist but they are of tremendous importance as determinants of behavior.

Regulation of Behavior in the Lower Organisms

In his classic analysis of behavior in the lower organisms, Jennings (1915) placed a heavy emphasis upon the importance of the physiological state as a determinant of behavior. He summarized a mass of data by the following general principles:

1. *Activity does not require present external stimulation.* The single-celled organisms exhibit a spontaneous activity which is, perhaps, the most important factor in their behavior.

2. *Activity may change without external cause.* When environmental conditions are constant behavior still varies.

3. *Changes in activity depend on changes in physiological state.* Specifically, such states as hunger or satiety regulate the behavior of unicellular organisms.

4. *Reactions to external agents depend on physiological states.* Whether an organism accepts a food particle or rejects it depends upon the stage of metabolic processes at the time of stimulation.

5. *The physiological state may be changed by progressive internal processes.* The supply of oxygen, for example, may be slowly exhausted and along with this are behavioral changes.

6. *The physiological state may be changed by the action of external agents.* For example, if stentor does not respond to the stimulus of carmine grains in the water, the continued stimulation from the grains changes the physiological state and eventually stentor does respond.

7. *The physiological state may be changed by the activity of the organism.* Movements such as turning, contracting or expanding, affect the internal state and thus the resulting behavior.

8. *External agents cause reaction by changing the physiological state of the organism.* The stimulus changes the physiological condition and the latter determines the response. This is a general principle implied by the above.

9. *The behavior of the organism at any moment depends upon its physiological state at that moment.* In both the spontaneous movements and the reactions to stimuli the behavior depends upon the physiological condition of the animal at the moment of response.

10. *Physiological states change in accordance with certain laws.* In particular, different states follow each other in sequence and the resolution of one state into another becomes easier and more rapid after it has taken place a number of times. This principle suggests a rudimentary form of learning in organisms that lack a nervous system.

11. *Behavior depends upon different factors.* At a given moment behavior may depend upon: the present external stimulus; former stimuli; former reactions of the organism; progressive internal changes such as those due to metabolic processes; and the laws according to which one physiological state is resolved into another.

On the basis of Jenning's analysis, it is obvious that the fundamental problems of motivation appear in the very simplest of unicellular organisms. Further, the physical and chemical state within the single cell is a major determinant of behavior.

A nervous system is not required for positive and negative reactions to food particles. Stimulus differentiation, varied patterns of behavior, and adaptive responses, all exist in the behavior of the simplest creatures. This point should be underscored because it is important to note that chemical motivation exists in the absence of a nervous system. Any attempt to limit the study of motivation to organisms that possess a nervous system, therefore, is likely to miss an important point.

Whether an organism possesses a nervous system or not, there are certain general characteristics of behavior which Jennings mentions:

1. Organisms have characteristic ways of acting, known as action systems, which are largely determined by bodily structure and which limit action under a variety of conditions.

2. Organisms, even the simplest forms, exhibit both positive and negative reactions to external stimulus conditions.

3. Organisms respond to situations by making varied, excessive movements and from these they select certain adaptive patterns.

4. The lower organisms show differential reactions to such stimulating conditions as temperature and the presence of chemical substances.

5. Behavior is adaptive in that it relieves the organism of unfavorable environmental conditions.

6. Reactions are localized in relation to the place of stimulation, the movement of the source of stimulation, and the position of a fixed stimulus object.

The Ontogenetic Priority of Chemical Motivation

Coghill (1936) has shown that organic movements appear in a developing embryo before sensory structures have matured to such a degree that they can function. For example, the embryo toadfish exhibits rhythmic, integrated, muscular contractions before sensory structures have become functional. These rhythmic movements are endogenous in origin. They are chemically motivated. They can be accelerated by an increase in the quantity of carbon dioxide present in the surrounding water. Coghill's observations are theoretically important because they establish, at least for one organism, the principle that chemical motivation is ontogenetically prior to neural function.

Coghill's demonstration that internal chemical motivation is present before sensory and neural channels can regulate behavior should be related to Jenning's demonstration that chemical motivation is present in lower organisms that have not evolved a nervous system. Thus ontogenetically as well as phylogenetically chemical motivation is basic and prior, functionally, to motivations that depend upon activation of neural structures.

Hormonal Regulation of Growth and Behavior

Hormones are substances produced in the cells of the body, especially in the ductless glands, that are circulated in the blood to all parts of the body. They regulate growth, metabolism, reproduction, activity and vigor. We have previously seen that hormones activate patterns of sexual behavior and other instinctive activities. (See pages 87–88.)

Especially important as determinants of growth and behavior are secretions from the gonads (reproductive glands) and the pituitary body. The testis of the male, in addition to forming sperm cells that carry the paternal chromosomes, secretes hormones directly into the blood. The ovary of the female, in addition to forming egg cells that carry the maternal chromosomes, pours out hormones into the blood stream. In general, male hormones are called *androgens* and female hormones *estrogens*. These hormones regulate growth as well as sexual behavior. The pituitary gland and the gonads act reciprocally; the secretions of the pituitary stimulate gonadal secretions which, in turn, act to check the pituitary secretion.

It has been shown in experiments with chicks that the testes and

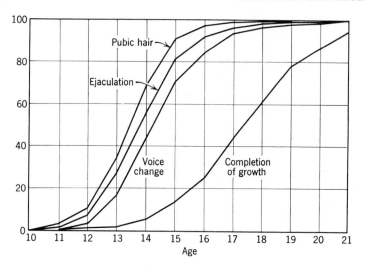

Figure 80. Physical developments in adolescence. The curves show physical developments in adolescence of the male: age at which pubic hair appears; age of first ejaculation; age of voice change; age upon completion of growth. *After* Kinsey et al. (1948).

ovaries can be successfully transplanted. A bird hatched as a female can have the ovaries removed and testes implanted. Then the body form and featheration of the rooster develop and along with this the typical copulatory behavior of the male. Similarly a bird hatched as a male can have the testes exchanged for ovaries. Then the body form and mating behavior of the hen develop. Thus the gland transplantation experiments have shown that both growth and behavior depend upon internal secretions from the gonads.

In human development the marked physical and mental changes that occur at adolescence are, in both sexes, associated with increased activity of the reproductive glands. Some of the changes that occur in the adolescent boy are shown graphically in Figure 80, which is based upon the report of Kinsey et al. (1948). Between the ages of 12 and 15 most boys go through a period of rapid growth. Pubic hair appears; the beard commences to grow; the voice lowers; there is rapid increase in stature. Sex interest and sex activity are stepped up until, within a few years, most young men reach their maximal rate of sexual activity.

Some Effects of Drugs

A rapidly expanding field of research is known as *psychopharmacology*. This professional speciality is concerned with the effects of drugs upon behavior, upon conscious experience and adjustments.

The medical and psychological literature on the effects of drugs is so extensive that no attempt will be made to survey it. This literature deals with many theoretically and practically important problems such as, for example, the nature and treatment of drug addiction.

Drug addictions. The drugs to which people become addicted are often called "habit-forming," but it would be more nearly correct to label them "appetite-forming." There is a difference between a simple food habit such as drinking milk for breakfast and an addiction, for example, to coffee. If the caffeine is removed, as with the commercial product Sanka, the flavor of coffee is still present. Although an addict may be fooled temporarily by the removal of the caffeine, he later knows that something is wrong—he may have a headache or other "abstinence" symptom. The absence of milk from the breakfast table, contrastingly, does not produce an after-effect even though the habitual milk drinker is equally well accustomed to the beverage.

Of course, if we are deprived of air or water we suffer severe after-effects, but it is not correct to say that we are addicted to air and water. These substances are necessary for the survival of everyone. The drugs to which people become addicted are not necessary for survival. Many drugs are harmful to health, and relatively few people become addicted to them.

The drugs to which people become addicted have been classified as stimulants and narcotics. Common stimulants are tea and coffee (both contain caffeine), tobacco (nicotine), and alcohol. Some of the better-known narcotics are opium, prepared from the juice of seeds of the poppy plant, and alkaloid derivatives—morphine, codeine, and heroin; cocaine, prepared from leaves of the coca tree; marijuana, known as *cannabis indica* or hashish; and barbiturates, with many trade names such as Amytal, Luminal, Nembutal, etc.

Spragg (1940) gave chimpanzees repeated injections of morphine until the animals developed a clear dependence upon the drug. Prior to receiving morphine the subjects were trained to cooperate voluntarily in receiving hypodermic injections of a physiological saline solution. The animals required from 3 weeks to 3 months to associate the injection of morphine with the drowsy state it created. When the animals had acquired the appetite they were deprived of the shots of morphine. The enforced abstinence produced unmistakable signs of an intense craving for the drug. A chimp might tug on the hand of the experimenter literally pulling him into the experimental room; he might get out the hypodermic needle and hand it to the experimenter and get up on the table thus communicating a wish very clearly without words. The appetite appeared when morphine was withheld. Incidentally, the addicted animals lost weight, their general food appetite was low, hair began to fall out, and there were other signs of ill health.

The human opium addict, although his health is impaired, enjoys momentarily a euphoric release from his troubles and unhappiness. It is tempting to argue that the euphoria is related to the development and persistence of the addiction. This may be true but it is also true that the addiction has a biochemical basis. Any neural habit is secondary to the biochemical determinants of the addiction.

Drugs in psychotherapy. During World War II, Doctors Grinker and Spiegel (1945) used sodium amytal and sodium pentothal to induce a drowsy state as an aid in psychotherapy. Following preliminary interviews the patient was placed in a darkened room and told that he would be given an injection to make him sleepy. He was then given an intravenous injection of sodium pentothal and asked to count backward from 100. When the counting became confused but before he was actually asleep the injection was discontinued. The device served to establish a satisfactory level of narcosis. Some patients began to talk spontaneously but others had to be stimulated by the therapist who began by describing whatever he knew about the traumatic situation.

In a condition of twilight consciousness, between sleep and waking, there is a dramatic reliving of the situation. When the patient recalls moments of supreme danger, such as during an explosion within the plane, the falling of a plane, the mutilation or death of a friend before the flyer's eyes, a terror is exhibited that is electrifying to watch. As the critical event approaches, the body becomes increasingly tense and rigid. The eyes widen; the pupils dilate; the skin becomes covered with fine perspiration. The hands move convulsively seeking a support, a protection, a weapon, or a friend to share the danger. Breathing becomes incredibly rapid and shallow. At times the intensity of emotion becomes more than can be borne, and there is a collapse. The individual falls back in bed and remains quiet for a few moments, usually to resume the story at a more neutral point. While the patient is under the influence of the drug the psychiatrist tries to relieve the tension and to help him work out a reorientation. This is called narcosynthesis.

The relation of drugs to moods. Vincent Nowlis (1953) reported an experiment (carried out in collaboration with Helen Nowlis, A. Riesen, and G. R. Wendt) upon the psychological effects of drugs. They selected several behaviorally potent drugs and administered them, under controlled conditions, to adult college students.

The interest of the investigators was in the effect of certain drugs upon affective responses. Affective responses were measured upon a rating scale that covered a wide range of affectivity and social behavior, including: anxiety, elation-depression, hostile aggression, cooperativeness, dominance, relaxation, organic symptoms, etc. In the experiments there were self-ratings, partner ratings, and observer ratings.

The subjects were observed behind a one-way vision screen. In addition to the ratings each subject indicated his present mood or conscious emotion by checking approximately twenty to forty adjectives in a carefully prepared list. A subject could go quickly through the list and check the items descriptive of his present mood.

A typical experimental session involved three consecutive hour-long blocks. Within each hour, 12-minute periods were assigned to separate tasks: (1) the French ball and spiral task, requiring a high degree of cooperation among four men; (2) a game in which the four men solved a problem involving the sequence in which four buttons must be pressed to light a panel of jewel lights; (3) discussion of a dilemma; (4) a free period; (5) a final 12-minute period of rating and checking the adjective list.

Medication was given at the half-way point of the first hour. With fast-acting agents they gave one pre- and two postmedication series of tests in the session. With slower-acting drugs there was only one postmedication series.

Definite, consistent, and repeatable changes in mood and social behavior were found with small doses of the medications employed. For example, a certain drug used to prevent motion sickness drastically reduced elation, social initiative, cooperativeness, surgency, affiliation and task involvement; this drug increased relaxation and organic symptoms. The adjectives checked before the medication but not after were: *businesslike, talkative, industrious, genial, sociable, ener-*

getic, cheerful, ambitious, friendly, cooperative, satisfied, intent, amiable, adaptable, warm-hearted, and *careful.* The adjectives checked after the medication but not before were: *tired, drowsy, detached, sluggish, disinterested, dull, lazy, retiring, withdrawn, dizzy, dreamy, drifting, hesitant, indifferent, irritable, lackadaisical, languid, closemouthed, gloomy, light-hearted,* and *quiet.*

All things considered, this work shows clearly that drugs have a profound effect upon moods. Nowlis is convinced that the study of affective processes by the method of checking adjectives, when used along with other methods, can yield very valuable information about the structure of motivational systems.

EFFECTS OF EARLY EXPERIENCE UPON ADULT BEHAVIOR

Early experience has a profound effect upon adult behavior. Several studies with mammalian species have shown that if the young are isolated they develop increased emotional responses to strange situations, poorer ability to solve problems, and poorer capacity for discriminative learning, than litter mates allowed a more stimulating infantile environment. Again, experiments upon mothering and gentling have demonstrated that stroking and petting the young animals affects their physical growth and behavior. When animals are petted and gentled during the early stages of development, they tend to become superior, physically and psychologically, to those that are ignored.

The following sections deal with the effects of early experience upon later behavior.*

The Effect of Infant Feeding Frustration upon Adult Hoarding

Psychoanalysts harbor the belief that experiences of infancy and early childhood determine personality traits of adults. Through the study of dreams and free associations they have arrived at the view that the early experiences of feeding, toilet training, genital behavior, and social conflict within the family, affect adult patterns of behavior.

---

* I am indebted to Dr. J. McV. Hunt for letting me see his unpublished manuscript dealing with the effects of early experience upon adult behavior. He is convinced that infantile experience has important effects upon the behavior of adults; but he discounts Freud's theory that infant traumata are of critical importance in development of personality.

Supporting evidence for the psychoanalytical view comes from studies of primitive cultures. Tribes using similar practices in nursing, weaning, toilet training, and care of the young, appear to develop similar personality traits even though they live in different geographic and economic environments. Where the infants are nursed affectionately and weaned late, and where little attention is paid to toilet training, the adults are optimistic; they do not hoard food even though famines repeatedly occur. Where the infants are reared without affection, nursed briefly, and treated harshly in other ways, the adults become competitive, arrogant, aggressive, quarrelsome.

This emphasis upon the importance of infantile experience and early training, however, is based upon casual observation and impression rather than upon any systematic array of scientific evidence. We would like to see data from controlled experiments upon infantile experience but such data do not exist. For social and humanitarian reasons valid data upon human subjects cannot be obtained. It is possible, however, to carry out controlled experiments with subhuman animals.

A pioneer experiment upon the problem of infant feeding frustration was carried out by Hunt (1941). He asked: Will feeding frustration during infancy alter the pattern of collecting food, or hoarding, in adulthood?

Hunt formed two equivalent groups of rats—experimental and control. At the time of weaning, the experimental animals were subjected to a 15-day period of feeding frustration. The frustration was produced by a competitive and unpredictable system of feeding. The animals were fed in groups so that each rat had to compete for his share of the available food. To minimize inanition, rats that lost weight were given extra individual feedings. The rats were fed for 10-minute periods at irregular intervals varying from 9 to 36 hours. The control animals were placed at the time of weaning upon an unrestricted diet of food and water; they were not subjected to feeding frustration.

Following the 15-day period of feeding frustration all of the rats were maintained for 5 months upon an unrestricted adequate diet.

As adults the proclivity for hoarding was tested. It was found that when the rats were satiated there was no difference between groups in hoarding behavior. That is to say, when an unlimited supply of food pellets was available the infantile feeding frustration had no apparent effect upon hoarding. But when the food supply was restricted a difference between the groups appeared.

The adult rats were placed on a subsistence diet for 5 days; then given a controlled test of hoarding. After this feeding frustration it was found that the experimental animals hoarded two and a half times as many food pellets as their litter-mate controls. In other words, the early feeding frustration made a significant difference in the amount of adult hoarding of food pellets. The difference appeared when the adult animals were frustrated in a feeding situation.

In another experiment Hunt et al. (1947) repeated and extended the study of the effects of infantile feeding frustration upon adult hoarding. In each of three repetitions of the original experiment it was found that the rats that had experienced infantile feeding frustration hoarded more food pellets than their litter-mate controls. The odds against such a series of results being obtained by chance are better than 1 in 1000. The *degree* of the effect, however, was less in the repeated experiments than in the original.

In general, it is reasonable to conclude that the amount of food hoarding exhibited by adult rats is dependent upon their early history. Rats that had to compete for food and were subjected to brief and unpredictable periods of feeding were, as adults, more prone to hoard food than their litter-mate controls that experienced no feeding frustration.

The Effect of Infant Sensory Deprivation upon Adult Behavior

We have seen that the deprivation of food during infancy has a marked effect upon adult behavior. There is a very different kind of deprivation that also has been shown to affect adult activity.

Wolf (1943) deprived young rats of their vision or hearing during the nursing period to study the effect of such sensory deprivation upon subsequent behavior. His general method of preventing sensory function was to seal off the eyes or ears of the young animals and later to remove the seals.

On the tenth day after birth the animals were etherized and the ears of one group were sealed off with cotton and paraffin. On the twelfth to fifteen days after birth the eyes of another group were sealed. Ears and eyes were not sealed until one day after these sense organs had begun to function. The young rats, therefore, had had some sensory experience prior to the sensory deprivation. The rats of a control group were not deprived of hearing or vision.

At the end of the nursing period, 25 days after birth, all seals were removed and the subjects were isolated in separate cages. At the age of 39 days, each rat was trained on the apparatus.

The apparatus consisted of a box with a door at one end that led to a food compartment. Above the door was a light that could be flashed and a buzzer that could be sounded as signals to go through the door to food. If a rat ran through the door *before* the signal (light or buzz) was given, he was shocked on the grill in front of the door. He had to learn to await the signal and then to dash across the grill into the food box.

In one series of tests all animals, following a 12-hour period of food deprivation, were trained to respond to a flashing light which was a signal of food. In another series the same animals were trained to respond to a sounding buzzer as a signal of food. The preliminary training was given individually, ten trials per day, for 20 days.

After preliminary training the animals were tested at first individually and then under competitive conditions. When tested individually it was found that the rats which had been subjected to sensory deprivation during infancy were quite able at maturity to respond adequately to the visual and auditory signals. There was an important difference, however, between the sight-deprived and the hearing-deprived rats that showed up when *competitive* tests were given.

In the competitive tests two rats were placed together in the box and the situation arranged so that the first animal to reach the door got all the food and the loser had none. In the competitive tests a rat previously deprived of vision was always paired with one previously deprived of hearing. Competitive tests were made first with a visual signal and then with an auditory signal. Each animal entered two hundred races for food and each race, for a given animal, was scored as won or lost.

Results of the competitive tests with a visual signal are presented in Table 3 for groups of fourteen animals. The figures give the number of races won by animals deprived of vision and by animals deprived of hearing when the signal for food was a flashing light.

It will be seen that the sight-deprived rats won fewer races than the hearing-deprived animals. The rats that had been deprived of vision during infancy won 37.9 percent of the races while those not deprived of vision won 62.1 percent. The figures show a consistent difference between the groups.

Similar tests with an auditory signal showed that the hearing-deprived rats were at a disadvantage. They usually lost the race to animals which had suffered no auditory deprivation.

The result is clear cut. The interpretation is somewhat uncertain. Wolf believes that all the rats revealed a normal capacity to respond

TABLE 3

NUMBER OF RACES FOR FOOD WON BY SENSORY-DEPRIVED
RATS FOLLOWING A VISUAL SIGNAL

Animals Deprived of Vision	Animals Deprived of Hearing
63	137
90	110
89	111
77	123
91	109
20	180
70	130
81	119
79	121
90	110
78	122
83	117
62	138
89	111
Average 75.9	124.1

Data from Wolf (1943).

to visual and auditory signals under non-competitive conditions. But under the stress of competition, he believes, the animals reverted to immature forms of behavior.

Another possible interpretation is that the winner of the race was aided by greater acuteness of sight or hearing than the loser. The early deprivation of experience may have done permanent damage to sensory functions. This damage, present all the time, showed up clearly when the level of motivation was raised by competition.

In any event, Wolf's interesting results demonstrate that sensory deprivation during infancy can have important effects upon adult behavior. They demonstrate that a change in motivation can bring to light a sensory handicap that is normally concealed.

What Is the Effect of Early Fright upon Adult Behavior?

Freud believed that the infant is easily traumatized by emotional experiences but where is the factual evidence to support this view?

Hall and Whiteman (1951) subjected a group of twenty-one infant mice to repeated stimulations with a loud, high-frequency bell. The mice were placed in a tub and, on four occasions, subjected to a 2-minute period of intense auditory stimulation. The twenty-one mice in a control group were *not* stimulated by the bell but otherwise they were treated like the experimental animals.

When the mice were between 30 and 40 days old all were given an open field test for fear. A month later, when the mice were between 70 and 80 days old, they were given Stone's stovepipe test in which the relative time spent in the starting box and in a stovepipe is the index of timidity.

In the open field test the animals were placed for ten successive trials in the *same* tub that had been used for stimulation. The number of animals defecating or urinating served as the measure of emotional responsiveness. The stovepipe apparatus was *new* to both groups.

Hall and Whiteman concluded that mice that had been exposed for four two-minute periods to an intense, high-frequency sound in early infancy were less stable emotionally in later life than the mice that had not received such auditory stimulation; and that, in general, "subjecting the infant organism to intense stimulation will result in emotional instability in later life."

Unfortunately, however, this experiment is not convincing. Since the same tub was used for initial sound stimulations and for the later open field tests that were conducted without sound, it is possible to explain the result in terms of simple conditioning. It is well known that autonomic responses can be conditioned to specific environmental situations and that such conditioned responses are remarkably stable. Hence the present experiment can be regarded as a good demonstration of the persistence from infancy to a later stage of development of conditioned autonomic responses. It would be gratuitous to assume any general change in the temperament of the mice.

Our explanation in terms of simple conditioning is confirmed by results of the stovepipe test. This test was unfamiliar to all mice. Results with the stovepipe test, as we might expect, were less decisive. Fifteen of the twenty-one mice behaved normally in the box-and-stovepipe situation; only six showed fright. These six might have been disturbed emotionally by stimulus cues from the experimenter or the room or from some other source that was previously associated with fright.

The experiment, therefore, can be interpreted in terms of the conditioning of autonomic responses. It is not necessary to assume a general change of temperament resulting from infantile fright. And Freud's emphasis upon the traumatic effect of early infantile fright remains to be proved.

Perhaps Professor John E. Anderson was correct when he voiced skepticism concerning the alleged effects of early traumata upon development of personality. He argued that the child has a substantial capacity to withstand stress and strain, and a good capacity for recovery, self-repair, and readjustment.

Emotional Development through Conditioning

Watson's pioneer work upon the beginnings of human emotions emphasized the fact that emotional patterns, like simple reflexes, can be conditioned and extinguished. The well-known example of emotional development through conditioning is the case of Albert, aged 9 months:

At first Albert showed no sign of fear when presented with a rat, rabbit, dog, monkey, masks with and without hair, cotton wool, a burning newspaper, and other objects. But when a loud noise was made near him, by striking a steel bar, Albert behaved emotionally. Response: the infant started violently; his breathing was temporarily stopped, arms were raised in a defensive manner. On the second stimulation the same thing occurred and, in addition, Albert's lips began to pucker and tremble. On the third stimulation he broke into a fit of crying.

At the age of eleven months and three days, the conditioning experiment was tried. A white rat was presented and, as before, there was no fear. The next time the rat was shown, a loud sound was produced by striking the steel bar. There was a definite fear response to the loud sound. On following days when the rat alone was presented, Albert began to cry. At the first test he not only cried but almost instantly turned sharply to the left, fell over on the left side, raised himself on all fours, and began to crawl away so rapidly that he was caught with difficulty before reaching the edge of the table. The fear reaction had become conditioned to a stimulus object not originally producing it.

The conditioned fear response was generalized. Albert now showed fear when presented with a rabbit and various other furry animals and objects resembling fur.

According to Watson, a conditioned emotional reaction can be extinguished by presenting the conditioned stimulus repeatedly, in favorable circumstances, without the unconditioned stimulus. For example, if a child is afraid of rabbits, a rabbit may be introduced at a considerable distance while the child is eating a palatable food. Very gradually, day by day, the rabbit is brought nearer until the child will tolerate the animal near by—petting it while eating. The extinction of fear by this method, however, must be handled with caution or the fear reaction will be transferred to the feeding situation and the child, in the situation, will not eat.

There is no doubt that visceral as well as somatic responses can be conditioned. Responses of glands, heart, blood vessels, and other internal structures, as well as responses of the skeletal muscles, can become conditioned so that they are produced by stimuli not originally eliciting them. There is much evidence for this. Through such conditioning, external situations can become visceralized.

Watson's account of emotional development through conditioning presupposes the pattern-response definition of emotion and has the limitations of that doctrine. We have elsewhere considered the limitations of the pattern-response definition of emotion and the inadequacy of Watson's description of the fear pattern. (See pages 400–401.)

EMOTIONAL DEVELOPMENT

The most useful accounts of emotional development take it for granted that everyone knows what the term *emotion* means. For example, Jersild (1954) has written in a clear and instructive way about the development of fear, anger and hostility, jealousy, affection, pleasure, sex behavior, laughter and humor, sympathy, etc., in children. He assumes, quite correctly, that his readers understand the meaning of these words. There is nothing theoretically profound about the account. The story is clear, practical, straightforward.

The psychological concept of emotion, however, is a bit fuzzy. It means different things to different psychologists. Obviously one's account of emotional development will be colored by what one means by emotion. We will later consider the different meanings of emotional development but first let us examine some of the basic facts.

Early Motor Development

Experimental studies upon the behavioral development of organisms, including the human infant, point to a few general principles of growth that will be stated briefly and dogmatically:

1. Motor development of the neonate is continuous with fetal development. The early patterns of behavior are determined by bodily structures that, in turn, are determined by the genes.

2. Motor development appears as the unrolling of patterns in sequence. The sequence is consistent from baby to baby, and to some extent the human sequence resembles that of the non-human animal. So regular is this sequence that schedules of normal behavioral development have been made. The uniformity and regularity of these sequences indicate their dependence upon biological laws of growth.

3. In the fetus the first responses to stimulation are diffuse mass activities. Later, reflexes and patterns of response are differentiated out of mass action. For example, the embryo salamander moves the trunk with limbs attached before it can move the limbs independently; it moves the limbs before the digits are moved separately.

4. The general course of development proceeds from head to foot and from proximal to distal segments. Movements of the lips and tongue lead in development, movements of eye muscles follow, then come response patterns in the neck, shoulders, arms, hands, fingers, trunk, legs and feet.

5. There are individual differences in the speed of behavioral development. Some infants are relatively accelerated and others are retarded. The explanation of these differences is not known.

6. Maturation and learning are closely interrelated factors in the process of development. Maturation implies the importance of heredity and the genes. Learning implies the importance of function (activity and experience) in development.

Early Emotional Development

In a comprehensive study, Bridges (1930, 1931, 1932) repeatedly observed and tested the emotional behavior of infants and young children. Her subjects were in the Montreal Foundling and Baby Hospital and in a nursery school. Because she approached the study without any bias concerning the nature of emotion, her observations are of special interest and value.

According to Bridges, the first emotional response of the infant is a general agitation or excitement produced by a great variety of stimulating conditions. This diffuse excitement is an innate emotional response—perhaps the only one. During emotional excitement in the young infant, the arm and hand muscles are tensed; the breath is quickened; the legs make jerky kicking movements; the eyes are opened as if gazing into the distance, and the upper lid is arched. The stimulations which produce such agitation or excitement are: direct sunlight in the infant's eyes, suddenly picking up the infant and putting him down on the bed, pulling the infant's arm through his dress sleeve, holding the arms tight to the sides, rapping the baby's knuckles, pressing the nipple of the bottle into the mouth, the noisy clatter of a tin basin thrown onto a metal table or radiator, and so on.

Bridges described diffuse excitement as follows:

Time after time on waking suddenly from sleep the infants were observed to wave their arms jerkily, kick, open and close their eyes, flush slightly, and breathe quickly and irregularly. Some grunted, some cried spasmodically for a moment or two, while others cried loudly for several minutes. The combined stimulation of light, of sounds, of damp or restricted bed clothes, and the change from sleeping to waking breathing-rate seemed to produce a temporary agitation and often distress. Waking apparently requires emotional adjustment.

The hungry child before feeding would often show restless activity, waving, squirming, mouthing and crying at intervals. The infant who had been lying in one position for a long time and the tired child before falling asleep would also show emotional agitation. Their breath would come jerkily, uttering staccato cries of "cu-cu-cu-ah," and they would thrust out their arms and legs in irregular movements. At the moment the nipple was put into the hungry baby's mouth he again breathed quickly, occasionally cried, waved the free arm, and kicked in excited agitation.

This diffuse emotional excitement can be differentiated from distress, or negative emotion, at an early age. It is difficult, Bridges writes, to distinguish between distress and general agitation in the newborn; but in a 3-week-old infant, *excitement* and *distress* are definitely distinguishable.

Bridges continues:

The cry of distress, recognizable in the *month-old* baby, is irregular. There are short intakes of breath and long cries on expiration. The eyes are "screwed up" tight, the face flushed, the fists often clenched, the arms tense, and legs still or kicking spasmodically. The mouth is open and square in shape or, more usually kidney-shaped with the corners pulled down. The pitch of the cry is high and somewhat discordant, and the sounds something like "ah, cu-ah, cu-ah, cu-æh."

Cries of distress were heard from month-old babies in the hospital on the following occasions; on waking suddenly from sleep, struggling to breathe through nostrils blocked with mucus, when the ears were discharging, when lying awake before feeding time, after staying long in the same position, lying on a wet diaper, when the child's buttocks were chafed, and when the fingers were rapped. The three main causes of distress at this age, therefore, seemed to be discomfort, pain, and hunger.

The emotion of *delight,* according to Bridges, is also recognizable at an early age. The main characteristics of delight are these: open eyes and expansion of the face into a smile as contrasted with the puckering of the forehead and closing of the eyes in distress; movements of incipient approach rather than withdrawal; audible inspirations and quickened breathing; soft vocalizations lower pitched than those of distress or excitement; more or less rhythmic arm and leg movements which are free from restraint; prolonged attention to the object of interest; cessation of crying.

Although the details of behavior vary from child to child and with age, delight can readily be recognized by certain characteristic activities. Free and rhythmic movements, welcoming and approaching gestures, and smiles and vocalizations of middle pitch are the commonest features.

Observes Bridges:

At *eight months* of age the child seems to take more delight than ever in self-initiated purposeful activity. He babbles and splutters and laughs to himself. Especially does he seem delighted with the noise he makes by banging spoons or other playthings on the table. Throwing things out of his crib is another favorite pastime. He waves, pats, and coos, drawing in long breaths, when familiar adults swing him or talk to him. He will watch the person who nurses him attentively, exploring her, patting gently, often smiling. Here are perhaps the earliest demonstrations of affection. The child will also pat and smile at his own mirror image. But his behavior is rather more aggressive and inquisitive than really affectionate.

According to Bridges, then, the first emotional behavior observable in the infant is a diffuse *excitement* that is dependent upon various kinds of stimulation. During the first few weeks *distress,* or negative emotional excitement, can be distinguished from the primal form of excitement and, somewhat later, *delight,* or primitive positive emotion, is recognizable.

These early forms of emotional behavior can be readily distinguished. In *distress* the infant cries, screams, wrinkles the brow, kicks and moves excitedly. In *delight* he smiles, laughs, coos and gurgles. In pure *excitement* there is a heightened level of general activity but without the complications of crying or smiling, etc.

These primitive forms of emotional behavior persist throughout life but the many specific forms of emotion that we recognize in adults are lacking in the neonate. These develop gradually. By the time an infant is 2 years old he has acquired a variety of emotional responses. In addition to general excitement, distress, and delight, the 2-year-old shows fear, disgust, anger, jealousy, joy, elation, affection for adults, and affection for children.

Figure 81 gives the approximate ages at which these different forms of emotional behavior develop. Bridges discussed in detail, and with many examples, the gradual growth of specific forms of emotional behavior out of the more primitive forms. The primitive forms of emotional behavior agree with the two basic dimensions of affectivity: the degree of excitement corresponds to the level of activation; distress and delight are obviously hedonic differences.

Bridges pointed out that emotional development and social development are intimately connected. In fact, she stated, emotional development might be treated as an aspect of social development. General characteristics of emotional development are: (1) decreasing

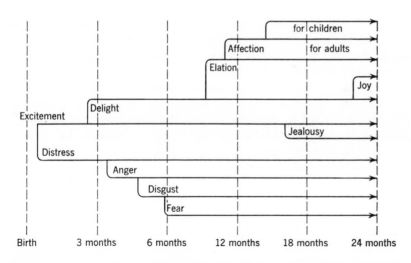

Figure 81. Early emotional development. The diagram shows the approximate ages at which the early forms of emotional behavior emerge from the more primitive forms. *Modified from* Bridges (1932).

frequency of intense emotional responses; (2) progressive transfer of emotional responses to situations which are socially approved; (3) gradual change in the nature of overt emotional responses in accordance with training and social pressures. Thus emotional and social development go along hand in hand.

Lack of Specificity in Early Behavior

The first emotional behavior of the newborn, as Bridges pointed out, is a diffuse, undifferentiated, rudimentary excitement. Reactions to stimuli are not at all specific and they present the picture of an overflow reaction from intense stimulation.

A specific reflex, like sucking, is normally elicited by stimulation of the lips, especially when the infant is hungry; but sucking movements in the hungry infant can be produced by stimulation of the cheeks, the eyes, the temperature senses, the senses of taste and smell. In short, many kinds of stimulation can evoke the sucking reflex.

The behavior of the neonate has been described as "mass action." It is general and diffuse. Activity is greatest in segments of the body near the region stimulated and it decreases in magnitude and frequency in rough proportion to the distance from the zone stimulated.

A good many specific reflexes, it is true, are present in workable fashion shortly after birth. Examples are swallowing, closing the eyes upon stimulation of the cornea, grasping a small stick placed in the hand. Sucking is present in nearly all infants after 24 hours; sometimes before this age sucking is difficult to elicit. Sneezing, the knee jerk, and the biceps and triceps reflexes, also, can be demonstrated in the newborn. The Babinski reflex (stretching upward and outward of the toes) is elicited by light pressure on the sole of the foot during the first few weeks. Stimulation of the larynx or pharynx produces a cough. The excretory processes are adequate at birth.

Despite these specific reflexive patterns, the gross behavior of the neonate is uncoordinated, undifferentiated, and non-adaptive. It is diffuse and general. For this reason it is extremely difficult to differentiate emotions.

If we limit ourselves to the most elementary terms and speak only of two primal responses—positive and negative—this distinction is still difficult to demonstrate in the neonate. The neonate does not smile or laugh; these patterns develop with maturation; he seems limited to expressions of negative emotion and neutral excitement. His counterpart of positive emotion is simply quiescence or the cessation of crying. The neonate, however, does show a primitive acceptance and rejection. He will swallow warm milk and other foods when placed in his mouth and he will reject some other substances. This primal acceptance and rejection is an indication of affectivity.

The earliest emotional expressions of the infant are crying, screaming, kicking, moving restlessly about, turning red, etc. We are probably justified in interpreting such behavior as marks of distress though, of course, we have no way of knowing what the infant consciously feels. One may assume that conditions, like hunger, thirst, pain from injury or sickness, lack of air, and extremes of heat and cold, inflict suffering. But this is, strictly speaking, only an inference and not a fact of objective observation.

Developmental Changes in Frequency and Causation of Crying

The reflex pattern of crying is present at birth. As a matter of fact the birth cry, incidental to the establishing of respiration, is about the first response that the infant makes to his new environment. Mothers universally regard the cry as a sign of distress but when viewed objectively it is just a reflex pattern.

Bayley (1932) gave sixty-one infants a variety of tests to determine the amount of crying during a test period of about an hour. She found that the percentage of time given to crying declined after the first month and reached its lowest point at about 4 months; after that the percentage of time given to crying increased with age up to 1 year. Subsequently there was a decrease in the frequency of crying to 18 months.

A partial explanation of these developmental changes lies in the fact that various factors which elicit crying vary independently in effectiveness as the child grows older. This is illustrated in Figure 82.

Bayley listed the causes of crying in infants from birth to 12 months as follows: specific test situations employed by the experimenter; continued handling; fatigue at the end of a test period; internal conditions such as colic pains, sleepiness, and hunger; strangeness of the place and persons; being put down; interference with play activities; postural discomfort; "spoiled" behavior; adverse conditioning.

In the early months of infant development, crying resulted mainly from internal organic conditions which yielded pains and discomforts.

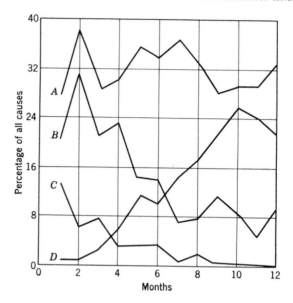

Figure 82. The causes of crying in infants. Developmental changes in four causes of crying are shown: *A*, Specific test situations. *B*, Fatigue at the end of a laboratory test. *C*, Colic pains. *D*, Strangeness of places and persons. *After* Bayley (1932).

These internal conditions were recognized in various ways. For example, a colic pain was recognized by its continuity, recurrence, and relief when gas was expelled. Later the external environment rather than internal conditions became increasingly potent as a source of crying. A strange situation, an unusual method of handling the infants, and other environmental factors, became increasingly important. It is likely that places and persons cannot be experienced as strange until, through previous experience, infants have learned to perceive things as familiar.

The form of crying changed gradually from infancy to childhood. The early cries of the infant were tearless; tears did not appear until the second or third month. The weeping and sobbing of older children is an emotional expression in which tears are plentiful. In sobbing, the vocalization is reduced to a minimum; but younger children do not inhibit the vocal element in their weeping. The inhibition develops as a result of social training and experience.

Development of the Smiling Response

The smiling response is absent at birth but normally develops during the third, fourth, fifth, and sixth months. Like other reflexes of the infant, the smiling pattern is not rigidly attached to a fixed stimulus-pattern but is elicited by a variety of stimulations.

By the age of 6 months the smile becomes a normal response to social stimulation and is utilized in communication. Some students of infant behavior (Charlotte Bühler) believe that the infant's smile is a social phenomenon from the start, that smiling is *the* specific response of an infant to social contacts, to the voice and glance of the human being. Others (Arnold Gesell) believe that the smile in response to the mother's face is a kind of conditioned reflex. Innately the smile is a mark of satisfaction from being fed and placed in a warm crib. Repeated satisfactions of this kind build up expectancies that are associated with the face, voice and actions of the mother. Through conditioning, the social stimulation comes to elicit a response that was originally elicited by a non-social satisfaction.

The development of smiling during the first year of life was carefully investigated by Spitz (1946). He made repeated observations upon two hundred and fifty-one infants. The infants came from different environments: nursery, private homes, a foundlings home, a hospital delivery clinic, an Indian village. The infants were of different races: White, Negro, Indian. The subjects were thus a heterogeneous, randomly selected group.

To elicit smiling Spitz applied several kinds of stimulations. In one set of experiments the investigator presented a smiling or nodding face as the stimulus. The experimenter turned *en face* to the infant so that both eyes and the smiling mouth could be seen simultaneously. If the infant responded with a smile the experimenter turned his (or her) face slowly into profile, continuing either to smile or nod. If the infant stopped smiling, the experimenter turned the face back to its original position and tried again to provoke a smile. This kind of stimulation was tried with both male and female investigators to check upon a possible sex factor in the stimulus.

Spitz found that the human face, presented in front view, elicited smiling, especially with infants aged 3 to 6 months. He next performed a series of experiments to discover whether the human face *in its human quality* was the stimulus that elicited a smiling response or whether the stimulus was some perceptual configuration *within* the human face. In these tests the human attributes were removed by using a black skull cap and a mask that retained only configurational factors such as eyes and mouth. The mask, of course, could not smile.

Previous observations had shown that movement of some kind must be present but movement of the smiling mouth could be replaced by movement of other facial muscles. Knowing this, the experimenter stuck out his tongue rhythmically through the mouth-slit of the mask. This stimulus pattern proved completely successful in provoking a smile from the babies. Then the experimenter, still retaining the mask, replaced tongue movements with nodding movements of the mask-covered head. The babies' reactions were the same: they smiled, laughed, crowed, according to the individual's inclination.

In another experiment a life-size puppet was presented as a stimulus object. This puppet was prepared by stuffing a bag roughly into the shape of a head, attaching a mask to it and covering the top with a skull cap. A body for the scarecrow was provided by hanging a dark shirt on a clothes hanger and fixing the artificial head to the collar of the shirt, so that it could be nodded. Spitz was surprised to find that the very first time the puppet was presented it had an effect identical with that of the experimenter himself bending over the baby and smiling. The babies greeted the nodding scarecrow by smiling, laughing, gurgling, or crowing exactly as they had responded to the experimenter's face. There were no signs of fear.

On the basis of many such observations Spitz concluded that it is not the human face, as such, that elicits smiling but a configuration of elements in the facial stimulus pattern. The configuration consists of two eyes presented *en face* and not in profile, combined with a factor of motion. The motion can be produced by various facial muscles other than those used in the normal smile or by a movement such as sticking the tongue through the mask or by nodding.

Spitz confirmed the findings of other investigators that the smile is absent during the first 20 days of life and rarely appears during the first 60 days. The pattern matures during the third, fourth, fifth, and sixth months. For some reason, smiling as a response to the above forms of stimulation, disappears after the sixth month. The disappearance is gradual but becomes complete by the end of the eighth month.

The appearance and subsequent disappearance of the smiling response during the first year of life is shown in Table 4 which is based on the findings of Spitz. The age limits of this table are zones that

TABLE 4

FREQUENCY OF SMILING AS RELATED TO AGE
OF THE INFANT

Age in days:	0–20	21–60	61–180	181–365
Smile present:	0	3	142	5
No smile:	54	141	3	142
Total subjects:	54	144	145	147

After Spitz (1946).

merge imperceptibly into each other. The smiling response does not suddenly disappear after the sixth month but gradually, varying from infant to infant.

The significance of this gradual reduction in the frequency of smiling raises a question of interpretation. During the first 6 months the infants smiled indiscriminately at every adult offering the appropriate pattern of stimulation, and at masks and scarecrows. The smile appeared to be reflexive. During the second half of the first year the infants discriminated, smiling at some persons and not at others.

Although the smiling pattern is innate and universal, being found in infants in all times and places, this pattern comes to be used as a signal of social recognition and approval. The smile becomes a basic form of social expression. It is used to communicate positive affectivity.

The failure of an infant to smile is a symptom of organic defect or of some marked abnormality in social relations. Spitz described a child detained in prison and raised from birth in the prison nursery. The child's mother was emotionally disturbed. The child reacted to the presence of the mother by screaming instead of smiling and reacted in the same manner to other adults. During the time that the mother was emotionally unbalanced, the approach of any grownup, elicited a "reversed smiling response," i.e., screaming with marked negative affectivity.

In this case the intervention of a matron relieved the mother from her emotional tension, and this resulted in a completely normal smiling reaction within 1 week. The child undoubtedly perceived and recognized her mother but the facial configuration did not elicit smiling. The smiling response, therefore, depended upon some discrimination among persons.

Development of Anger

The emotion of anger is associated with behavior that can be described as hostile, destructive, retaliative. Such behavior is a normal result of frustration.

In the small child retaliative behavior is frequently observed. Thus, a boy of 3 violently mussed his freshly combed hair with both hands when his mother refused to give him permission to go to a playmate's home. A boy of 7 whose mother insisted that he dress himself before coming to the table rushed violently to the table, caught hold of the tablecloth and jerked it to the floor, breaking dishes and glassware. A child of 2, when thwarted by removal of his play things, ran to the davenport, dragged off the cushions and flung them to the floor, screaming violently during the act. A boy of 3, although not an habitual thumb sucker, sucked his thumb conspicuously when frustrated by his mother. Apparently the act was retaliative since the mother had carefully trained him to avoid thumb sucking.

Such retaliative behavior is lacking in the newborn and rarely appears during the first few months of life. Retaliative behavior becomes more and more frequent as the child grows older.

In a careful study of the development of anger in young children, Goodenough (1931) first trained college-educated mothers to observe and record outbursts of anger in their own children. Attention was paid to the causes of anger, the manifestations, the duration, the time of occurrence, and other details. Altogether, forty-five children were observed. Their ages ranged from 7 months to 7 years and 10 months. A total of 2,124 outbursts of anger was recorded.

Percentages, based upon Goodenough's data, are shown in Table 5. The table gives the percentages of anger outbursts in which there was a display of random, undirected energy. It also shows the percentage of outbursts in which retaliative, aggressive behavior was definitely present.

The undirected energy displays were such as these: jumping up and down, holding the breath, stamping and kicking, throwing self on the floor, pouting, screaming, snarling, etc. The retaliative behavior took a good many forms: throwing objects, grabbing, pinching, biting, striking, calling names, arguing and insisting, etc.

The form of retaliative behavior was found to depend somewhat upon the age of the child. A small child may bite when frustrated; an older child may strike or throw something at the offender. Still

TABLE 5

DEVELOPMENT OF RETALIATIVE BEHAVIOR
AS RESPONSE TO FRUSTRATION

Age in years:	0–1	1–2	2–3	3–4	4–8
Percentage of outbursts with undirected energy					
Boys:	100.0	78.0	73.1	65.2	45.0
Girls:	86.9	78.7	83.3	29.6	29.0
Both:	88.9	78.4	75.1	59.9	36.3
Percentage of outbursts with retaliative behavior					
Boys:	0.0	9.4	10.4	25.7	30.0
Girls:	0.8	3.8	11.5	25.3	26.3
Both:	0.7	6.3	10.6	25.6	28.0

Data from Goodenough (1931).

older children retaliate verbally but the size and picturesqueness of a child's vocabulary varies with age and experience. A youth or adult may plot revenge; he seeks retributive justice—to get even.

The percentages in Table 5 show clearly that random, undirected energy displays become less frequent with advancing age, and behavior that is definitely retaliative and aggressive becomes more frequent. This transition from random emotional excitement to retaliative hostility marks the normal course of events in the development of anger in young children.

With older children and adults, anger is recognized and identified by the destructive, retaliative, hostile, aggressive actions directed against the frustrating person, object, or situation. With adults, however, hostility may be suppressed and not manifested openly as it is with small children.

Development of Fear

Jersild and Holmes (1935) studied the kinds of situations that elicit fear in children of different ages. They depended upon a variety of methods of gaining information about the fears of children: direct observations by parents and other adults; interviews with parents and teachers; interviews with the children concerning their fears; questionnaires to adults concerning present fears and fears of childhood; observations of children under controlled conditions; case studies. From the various sources they obtained a mass of information for analysis and interpretation.

A finding of general importance was that the relative frequency of specific fears varies markedly with age. This is illustrated, by a small sample of the data, in Figure 83.

The figure shows the relative frequency of fear in response to various situations at biyearly age levels. This figure is based upon records kept by parents over a 21-day period. In the study, nine hundred and fifty-three fear-inducing situations were recorded.

A brief description of the fear-inducing situations follows:

1. Noise, mechanical or vocal, and agents or objects associated with noise, plus instances of noise combined with movement.

2. Strange objects, unfamiliar persons or situations; queer, deformed or ancient persons; also unfamiliar variations in otherwise familiar objects and persons.

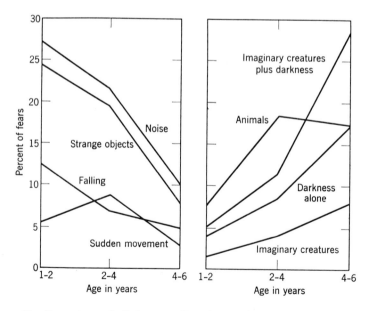

Figure 83. Percentage of all fears attributed to various situations as related to age. *After* Jersild and Holmes (1935).

3. Falling, loss of support, danger of falling, high or insecure places, or events associated with falling, danger, or loss of support.

4. Sudden, rapid, or unexpected movement, plus flashes, reflections, sudden disappearance of persons; also events combining noise with sudden, rapid, or unexpected motion.

5. Imaginary creatures, in connection with or apart from darkness or solitude, fear of ridicule, fears arising during dreams, fear of death, robbers, etc.

6. Animals, active or inactive, aggressive or passive.

7. Being alone in the dark, or darkness plus imaginary creatures.

8. Imaginary creatures, feared in connection with or apart from the factors of darkness or being alone.

Some of the above categories overlap. This is because the situations that elicited fear in children usually contained several factors in combination, such as darkness, noise, solitude.

A point that stands out clearly in the data is that the effectiveness of a given factor (or group of factors) in eliciting fear varies with age of the child. Some fear-inducing situations decrease in effectiveness with age; others increase; still others show at first an increase and then a decrease. There are fairly consistent developmental trends. Age and experience thus make a marked difference in the kind of situation that induces fear in children.

EMOTIONAL MATURITY AND CONTROL

The final product of emotional development, presumably, is emotional maturity. The mature individual is said to have control over his emotions. So let us consider what is meant by emotional maturity and emotional control, and how the mature differs from the immature individual emotionally.

Social and Emotional Development

Social and emotional development are aspects of a single process of growth. As a child grows up within his social environment he learns how to dress and act according to the standards of his group, how to speak the common language, and also how to express feelings and emotions according to conventional norms. He learns to conform.

Carney Landis was certainly correct in distinguishing between social expressions (which are learned and differ from group to group) and emotional expressions (which are biologically determined and common to all men). The shedding of tears, for example, is universal in weeping; but cultural factors determine the time, the place, the circumstances, and even the amount of weeping which is correct and proper. With us, a man is expected to refrain from tears and sobs in public places. A boy is taught that it is "sissy" to weep openly. In mid-Victorian England, however, a gentleman could weep quite openly and conspicuously at theatrical performances, during sermons and concerts; this was accepted as socially correct. Thus, a gentleman, upon hearing a rendition of Dickens' *The Old Curiosity Shop*, might take out his handkerchief and weep openly at the story of the death of Little Nell and no one in the audience would think anything of it. Today styles in weeping have changed somewhat!

Most people express joy by a smile or laugh, but among the Andaman Islanders there is no observable difference between their demonstrations of joy when meeting a long-absent relative and those of grief upon the death of one of their number. In both instances a stranger might suppose that a great sorrow had befallen them. But weeping is the socially correct form of greeting!

Whatever the expected pattern may be, the child learns to conform. A good deal of emotional development consists of suppressing biologically normal responses in the interests of conformity. Thus the child must learn *not* to smile and laugh at the misfortunes of others; *not* to show fear in the face of danger, but to act courageously; *not* to weep as an appeal for sympathy; *not* to show anger when frustrated, but to act within the bounds of correct manners; *not* to show love and hate indiscriminately and with bad taste; etc. In a word, the child must learn to inhibit many of his normal emotional responses.

The development of gestures and facial expressions, in communication, is another aspect of social development. At a tea we learn to put a smile on the face and say agreeable things. But this does not mean that there is a genuine affective arousal inside of us!

Contrast between Mature and Immature Emotional Behavior

As an individual advances from infancy to maturity his emotional behavior changes radically. One way to study emotional development is to contrast the emotional reactions of child and adult.

The phrase *emotional maturity* has been used loosely by psychologists and others, but Hollingworth (1928) and Morgan (1934) have attempted to give meaning to the phrase by describing the contrast between the emotional behavior of infants and young children, on the one hand, and that of adults, on the other.

The first important contrast between the emotional behavior of infant or young child and adult is in the *degree of frustration tolerance.* The infant is intolerant of discomfort and thwarting. Hunger pains, a bath that is too cold or too warm, the prick of a pin, restraint of free movement, uncanny sounds, a toy just out of reach—all these arouse an emotional display in the infant. The older child is more tolerant. Instead of crying like a baby at every mishap, he is able to withstand suffering and disappointment with fewer signs of disturbance.

A 2-year-old kicks and screams when refused a second helping of some desired food. Adults take this for granted, for, as they say, he is "just a baby and he behaves like one emotionally." If, however, a 6-year-old behaves in the same manner, he is regarded as "naughty." When a 9-year-old kicks and screams in this situation we say he is "spoiled." But such conduct from an adult would be regarded either as hysterical or as a sign of emotional immaturity. If an adult were to scream and kick when refused a second helping at dinner, a psychiatrist would be summoned!

In ancient pubertal ceremonies of a certain primitive people, physical and mental hardships were inflicted as an ordeal. If the youth refused to submit to the ordeal, or yielded with outcries of fear or distress, he failed in the initiation to adulthood. (Possibly some trace of this custom remains in the more modern fraternity initiation.) That the capacity to endure pain and to face danger with fortitude is a criterion of emotional maturity is implied in the pubertal ordeal.

A second contrast between the emotional behavior of child and adult is a *decrease in the frequency and intensity of emotional upset* as the individual grows up. An adult does not display outbursts of anger as frequently as a child nor does he weep so often. When the adult is emotionally aroused, his response is less intense than that of the child. If the adult pinches his finger, he does not scream as loudly as possible. If insulted, he does not fly into a towering rage but limits the degree of response, keeping it within bounds. If his hat is blown off, he does not bellow.

A third contrast between child and adult is a difference in the *impulsiveness or exposiveness of behavior.* The child "cannot wait" to express anger, joy, or fear. He must respond without delay. In anger, he strikes; in joy, he jumps up and down; in fear, he cries out or runs away; in pain, he screams. The adult, in contrast, is able to delay his response and manifests less impulsiveness.

A fourth difference between the emotional behavior of child and adult is found in the *attitudes of self-regard*. Injury to the human ego awakens in the child a self-pity which is out of all proportion to the pity felt by sympathetic onlookers and comforters. This solicitude for self is keenly felt by the injured person.

Writes Hollingworth:

> In childhood self-pity is unrestrained. The injury to the person strikes at the very center of the universe. The mature person approximates the "poor-you" attitudes in pitying his own injuries and mishaps. He tries to feel no sorrier for himself than others would feel for him, and strives against sinking into the "poor-me" attitude, with its childish appeal for a sympathy from others which they cannot sincerely give. The emotionally mature person does not prey upon the amiability of his fellow men.

This self-pity reflects the fact that the child is self-centered. As his knowledge of the world increases, he becomes less obviously ego-centric. This may be due to the fact that manifestations of self-interest are socially disapproved and that the signs of self-pity are suppressed more in adults than in children.

Finally, the child in contrast with the adult is *more overt* in his emotional manifestations. If an adult is grieved, he refrains from weeping; if angered, he controls the facial muscles which express anger and the impulse to attack; if afraid, he assumes the anti-fear attitude of courage.

Summing up the above points, we may say that the child in contrast with the adult is: (1) less tolerant of discomfort and thwarting; (2) given to more frequent and intense outbursts of emotion; (3) more impulsive, explosive in behavior, and with less capacity to delay his response; (4) more given to self-pity and egocentricity; (5) more overt, direct, frank in his emotional displays.

It is true that adults differ among themselves in these respects. Psychiatrists and clinical psychologists often speak of an adult as being "emotionally immature." By this is meant that his pattern of emotional behavior is more like that of a child than like that of an adult. In referring to temperamental differences in adults it would be well to keep in mind the contrast between the emotional behavior of the immature and the mature individual.

Diverse Meanings of Emotional Control

The phrase *emotional control* has several possible meanings. According to the commonest meaning, emotional control is the voluntary suppression of the outward expressions of emotion. The visceral processes are involuntary and may still be present. Thus, a man may control his words and actions but he blushes involuntarily, in embarrassment. Voluntary control is limited to the somatic mechanisms— facial expressions, vocalizations, gestures, and gross ways of acting.

The voluntary enactment of emotional behavior does not necessarily induce the associated visceral responses. Years ago William James interviewed actors asking them whether they *felt* the emotion they enacted on the stage. Testimony was sharply divided: some actors said they did and some that they did not *feel* the emotion they expressed. Perhaps some actors played the emotional role solely with their skeletal musculature; others threw themselves into the part, identifying themselves empathically with the situation and allowing behavior to become visceralized.

According to another meaning of *emotional control,* the total response, though highly visceralized, remains integrated and free from disturbance. For example, an airplane pilot, realizing that his plane is out of control, may act with utmost precision and skill to regain control. Although he is in great danger and there is a high degree of visceralization, the total behavior remains integrated. The behavior is highly motivated, well organized, and free from upset. Emotional disturbance does not arise. How such control of the total response can be achieved, of course, is another question.

One way to avoid emotional upset is to acquire skill in meeting a situation and to gain knowledge and understanding. To illustrate: A 5-year-old boy was afraid to go to bed at night. There were shadows moving on the wall of his bedroom. His father explained that the shadows were from branches of trees moving in front of a street lamp. The child was shown the branches moving in the wind. He was allowed to produce other shadows by moving the window curtains. When he understood the cause of the shadows and could control some of them the fear vanished. The fear came from lack of understanding and inability to meet the situation postively.

A possible (but rare) meaning of *emotional control* is the conscious avoiding of situations that produce emotion. Thus an adult may avoid dangerous occupations like auto racing and thus avoid anxiety; he may stay away from a dead animal that disgusts him; he may avoid public meetings where the speeches anger him; he may move out of town to avoid becoming infatuated with the wife of his friend, etc. In all such instances there is an active avoiding of situations that are known to arouse emotion. This is a yield-not-to-temptation kind of control. The situation is controlled so that emotion does not arise.

Some General Principles

John Anderson (1950) stated several general principles of emotional development that are worthy of record.

1. *With growth and development, the emotional life of the person becomes more differentiated.* Emotional development involves both an increase in the number of objects that elicit a particular emotional response and in the variety of emotional expressions. Both kinds of change are bound up with growth in understanding of the world and the self. This does not imply that the 5-year-old is more *intensely* emotional than the infant but only that there has been diversification in the conditions eliciting a particular kind of emotion and in the means of expressing it.

2. *With growth and development, changes in somatic processes within the organism affect and modify emotionality.* The clearest example of this principle is found in the physical changes of bodily structure that occur at the time of puberty.

3. *With growth and development, there are progressive changes in the sensitization of the organism that in the main reduce the effect of most stimulations but may increase the effect of some.* Emotionality is normally reduced by repetition of the inducing circumstances. Repetition, however, sometimes leads to increased emotional responsiveness.

4. *With growth and development, the organism successively masters situations and as he builds skill in meeting them gains control over his emotions.* A good many emotional upsets depend upon lack of skill or knowledge; the acquisition of such skill or knowledge is one form of gaining emotional control. When an individual is in control of the situation, emotion is less likely to arise.

5. *With social pressures and cultural demands, the pattern of emotion and the manner in which emotion is manifested vary widely.* Cultural factors sometimes suppress and inhibit emotional expressions; they sometimes facilitate or encourage particular emotional expressions; they sometimes modify the elements which make up the emotional pattern or change the relation of these elements.

THE ROLE OF FEELING AND EMOTION IN DEVELOPMENT

In Chapter 5 we considered the relation between motivation and the affective processes and in the next chapter we will consider the importance of feeling and emotion in the formation of attitudes. Here we will examine the role of affective processes in the development and shifting of interests and, in general, the part played by emotion in psychological development.

The Nature and Development of Interest

Interests have been defined as activities that are pleasant, that are carried on "for their own sake."

Many pleasant activities, upon repetition, become indifferent and are carried on automatically. The pleasantness appears to have an organizing and sustaining function but when an activity has become thoroughly learned it runs along of itself without a continuing affective process.

Because the feeling of pleasantness is a subjective experience which appears to be unnecessary to sustained activities, objective psychologists have defined interests in terms of behavior without reference to pleasantness. Viewed in this light, a man's interests are simply the things he does. If he spends time regularly playing golf, then he is interested in golf. Since, however, he spends time sleeping, eating, eliminating, working, etc., these, too, must be regarded as among his objective interests.

Hedonic motivation is obviously part of the story of the development of interests, attitudes, and motives, but only part. There are non-hedonic motivations. To illustrate the interaction of hedonic and non-hedonic factors consider the development of an objective interest in reading:

A small boy looks at the colored pictures in a book and finds them pleasing—interesting. Looking at pictures is entertaining, pleasing "for its own sake." Later the boy is taught to read about the pictures. Since reading is a grown-up activity, there is a satisfaction in reading which is more than the fun of looking at pictures.

When the boy is older, other motivations enter the stage. He becomes curious about the world in which he lives. He insists upon asking, "Why?" Some books satisfy this curiosity; these books are interesting because they answer his questions. This is a form of satisfaction. Other books take him into an imaginative world of magic and success; these are exciting, entertaining, interesting in their own right, quite apart from the pictures. This is another form of satisfaction.

On the adult level reading has many motivations. A college student will read a book that is dull, difficult, irksome, unpleasant. He does not enjoy the reading of it but he wants to pass a course in which the book has been assigned for study. He wants to be well thought of by his teachers and fellow students, but especially he wants to pass the course. So he reads a book for reasons other than enjoyment.

There are clearly non-hedonic motivations that underlie the student's activities and if we simply describe, objectively, what the student does, we lose sight of underlying motivations. An objective account of behavior disregards the distinction between hedonic and non-hedonic determinants. To speak more exactly, we can describe an individual's interests as the activities he *likes* and his aversions as the activities he *dislikes*. From this point of view it must be said that extrinsic motivations may lead a man to do something which he dislikes. Man is governed by considerations other than pleasantness and unpleasantness.

The Shifting of Interests

Observations upon the vocational interests of American boys and girls indicate that there are many shifts at the time of adolescence. For example, the desire to be a movie actor or actress usually declines with the onset of pubescence; interest in becoming a cowboy generally wanes at the same period. The interests of adults, by contrast, are relatively stable, but even here the changes of interests are more rapid between the ages of 25 and 35 than in succeeding decades of life.

Strong (1931) found that about 50 percent of the interests expressed by his subjects changed between the ages of 25 and 35, about 20 percent between 35 and 45, about 30 percent between 45 and 55. There was little fluctuation of interests between the ages of 55 and 65.

Figure 84 presents a sample of Strong's data to show certain fluctuations in interests between the ages of 25 and 55. Some of the items listed are liked at all ages, others are disliked at all ages. For example, the occupation of undertaker is generally disliked by young and old; the *National Geographic Magazine* is generally liked. The curves

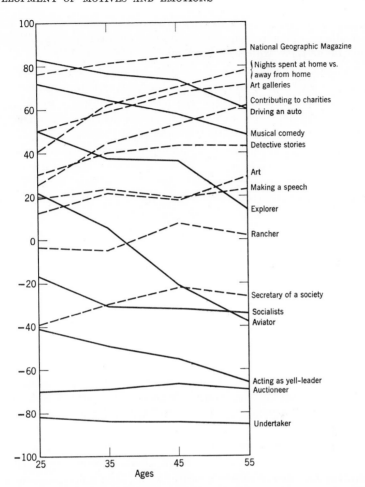

Figure 84. Change of interests with age. The curves are based upon a study of the interests of 2,340 men. The attitude index on the vertical at the left presents numerical differences between the percentage of a group liking and the percentage disliking the various items indicated at the right. Indifference, when expressed, is ignored in computing the attitude index. For example, at age 25, 88 percent like and 2 percent dislike driving an auto; the attitude index in this case is 86 percent. At age 25, 3 percent like and 84 percent dislike the occupation of undertaker; the attitude index is −81 percent. The solid lines represent interests which decrease with age or remain about constant; the dotted lines, those which increase. *After* Strong (1931).

show many interests which increase with age (dotted lines) and numerous others which remain about constant or decrease (solid lines). Fields of activity which demand marked physical skill and daring show pronounced changes in popularity with age. For example, the interest in such occupations as aviator and explorer declines with age, doubtless because the younger men are physically more fit for these vigorous activities. Older men, again, dislike items suggestive of change or interference with the established order.

In general, interest in all occupations, including one's own, shows a decline with advancing years. Interests in activities which involve reading manifest an increase with age, whereas those which involve talking or writing decline with advancing years. It is worth noting that older men prefer amusements pursued alone rather than group activities. Also, as men grow older they become more discriminating in their likes and dislikes for people, showing an increasing preference for those with traits which they regard as desirable, and a growing aversion for those with qualities which they consider unworthy.

There was no appreciable difference, Strong found, in the number of items liked or disliked at the ages of 25, 35, 45, and 55. At age 25, 35 percent of all items were liked; 30 percent were disliked. At age 55, 34 percent of all items were liked; 31 percent were disliked. The older men, therefore, had as many likes and dislikes as did the younger ones, or at least indicated as many on the test blanks. The older men did not develop more interests with increased age, as one might expect, nor were they more catholic in their interests than the younger men. The interests of the younger men were simply different from those of their elders. This means, in general, that the acquiring of new interests goes hand in hand with the abandonment of old ones. It is plain that this must of necessity be the case, unless one's waking hours are to become a hodgepodge of diversified activities shifting kaleidoscopically with increasing speed as age advances.

Instead of asking why an interesting activity continues with advancing age it might be more instructive to inquire why, in so many cases, it finally ceases. Why, for example, does a boy actively engaged in stamp collecting lose interest in this hobby and stop collecting? As a man of 40 he doubtless retains all the skills needed for stamp collecting, but the neural organization has become inert. There is no dynamic determination to call it into function.

A fading interest is somewhat like a perseverating experience that gradually disappears.

The Nature of Emotional Development

In the previous chapter we saw that psychologists do not agree concerning the definition of emotion. Since there are many definitions of emotion, it is to be expected that there will be equally many accounts of emotional development.

Emotional development is just an aspect of development in general. There is nothing sacrosanct or mysterious about it. Emotional development implies maturation. Reflexive patterns, like smiling, laughing, rage, and fear, appear during the normal growth of individuals. These patterns are modifiied through experience and training. Especially important is social learning which is part of development in general.

If we hold to the view that emotion is a chronic disturbed affective state, we can view emotional development in the light of this concept. Individuals develop persistent, relatively stable, states of disturbance: unsolved emotional conflicts and neuroses. A student of emotional development might well ask: How do stable states of emotional disturbance come into existence? What frustrations, conflicts, threats, expectations, and the like, underlie persisting emotional disturbances? What dynamic factors are involved?

The development of disturbances, however, is only one phase of emotional development. With or without the aid of counseling, individuals do solve problems, make adjustments, and escape from disorganized states. Emotional disturbances commonly result in the organization of attitudes, interests, goal orientations, sentiments, habits, and other determinants, within the individual.

Emotional upset may thus be an important determinant in the development of motives and attitudes. For example, it is said of Lincoln that when he saw slaves being sold on the New Orleans market he was greatly disturbed and resolved then and there to "hit that thing hard, if ever the opportunity came." Lincoln's emotional disturbance resulted in the formation of a fixed determination to fight slavery. The motive grew out of an emotional disturbance.

It is true that individuals develop attitudes, interests, goals, as well as motor skills, knowledge, and wisdom. One might well ask: What is the role of emotional disturbances in the development of well-organized patterns of action? And again: How do individuals develop techniques for managing emotional upsets? We can readily distinguish between mature and immature methods of handling frustrations and conflicts. For example, when an infant is frustrated he simply cries, screams, kicks, and makes restless movements; with older children frustration leads to retaliative behavior; with adults the impulse to strike may be inhibited.

It often happens that emotional upset is followed by purposive, adaptive behavior that removes the emotional turmoil. Fear is relieved by flight—escape or avoidance—which is a form of purposive activity. Anger is relieved by aggressive, hostile, retaliative acts. Lust is relieved by copulation. There are different forms of purposive behavior that relieve different kinds of emotional disturbances. Laughing and weeping lead to no particular purposive acts but they do release or reduce an underlying physiological tension.

In general, it is important to keep in mind that it is always the *individual* who develops and that he develops organized states (motives, interests, attitudes, etc.) as well as disorganized states (emotional conflicts, anxiety neuroses, etc.).

The above discussion has revealed two views of emotional development that appear when emotion is regarded as a relatively stable, persisting state of disorganization within the individual. First, emotional development is the growth of disorganized states of conflict, neurosis, and the like. A study of emotional development is a study of the causes of such disturbed states. Second, emotional development is the process of forming adaptive reactions to disturbing situations. As an individual develops he acquires attitudes, interests, traits, motives, sentiments, habits, and the like, as a means of reducing or removing affective disturbances. This second view implies that emotional development is an escape from emotional upset, or turbulence.

The two views are supplementary. Both are necessary. They can be combined into a single view of the nature of emotional development: *Emotional development is a growth process through which disturbed affective states are generated and a subsequent process through which adjustments are made to emotionally disturbing situations.* More broadly, perhaps: *Emotional development is the growth of techniques for dealing with frustrations, threats, and other causes of upset.*

CONCLUSION

When we consider emotional development it is necessary to take a longitudinal view, for development occurs within the life cycle of individuals.

Throughout most of the present book, motivation and emotion have been regarded as contemporary events or processes. All that we know about them, in fact, is based upon direct observation and experience of contemporary activities. But when we consider *development* a longitudinal, or temporal, view is necessary. We must postulate a certain stability and permanence in the determinants of activity.

The determinants of human action persist through time. When one speaks of interests and aversions, attitudes, sentiments, traits, habits, goal orientations, and other determinants, one is referring to constructs which have the attributes of duration, stability, and relative permanence. Such stable determinants are inferred, not directly observed. They develop, persist, and change within the life cycle of individuals.

When one speaks of an emotionally disturbed child or patient one refers to a persisting state of frustration, conflict, stress, anxiety, or neurosis. Emotional disturbances have important consequences for behavior and for mental health.

From one point of view, the story of emotional development is an account of the conditions that cause emotional disturbances. From another point of view, emotional development is seen as the acquisition of adaptive behavior that reduces, minimizes, escapes, avoids, emotional disturbances. Individuals solve problems and make adjustments through the acquisition of interests, attitudes, traits, motives, habits, and other determinants. More broadly: *Emotional development is the growth of techniques for dealing with frustrations, threats, and other causes of upset.*

Reading Suggestions

A useful empirical discussion of motivational development will be found in Chapter 4 of Bindra (1959). Further details of emotional development, and references, are in Chapter 4 of Young (1943).

Jersild (1954) refers to many studies of emotional development that are not considered in the present chapter. Chapter 9 deals with affection, joy, humor, and sex, Chapter 10 with fear and anxiety, Chapter 11 with anger and hostility. Jersild's work is very readable and matter-of-fact.

Educational psychologists are practically concerned with motivational and affective development. Prescott (1938) published a report of the committee on the relation of emotion to the educative process. Cronbach (1954) considers motivation and emotion in Parts D and E of his excellent textbook.

McClelland (1955) has published readings that deal with the biological origins of motives (Part Two) and social origins of motives and values (Part Three).

Bindra, D. *Motivation, a systematic reinterpretation.* New York: Ronald, 1959.

Cronbach, L. J. *Educational psychology.* New York: Harcourt, Brace, 1954.

Jersild, A. T. *Child psychology.* (4th ed.) Englewood Cliffs, N. J.: Prentice-Hall, 1954.

McClelland, D. C. *Studies in motivation.* New York: Appleton-Century-Crofts, 1955.

Prescott, D. A. *Emotion and the educative process.* Washington, D. C.: American Council on Education, 1938.

Young, P. T. *Emotion in man and animal; its nature and relation to attitude and motive.* New York: Wiley, 1943.

11 SOCIAL AND PERSONAL DETERMINANTS

The importance of sound knowledge as to how the motivation of an individual may be controlled by his social environment cannot be exaggerated. It is the problem of problems for psychology as applied to many practical fields of human endeavor.

JOHN FREDERICK DASHIELL

It is sometimes said that psychology deals with individuals and sociology with groups. The statement is misleading for two reasons. First, psychology is concerned with individuals who are members of groups and whose behavior cannot be understood apart from the social setting. A man's ways of acting, language habits, traits of personality, attitudes, motives, conflicts, neuroses—all developed within a social setting and cannot be correctly understood apart from that setting. A second reason why the statement is misleading is that some behavioral scientists prefer to study the group as a psychological unit rather than to study separate individuals. From the point of view of group dynamics it can be said that the group—for example, a football team—behaves as a unit within which the responses of one member influence the behavior of the group as a whole.

The human individual is an organism living in a sociocultural environment. His conduct is influenced both by the characteristics of protoplasm and by the characteristics of the cultural environment within which he lives. In other words, human behavior has both biological and social determinants—as we will see in the following pages.

The present chapter is broad in scope. The topics are diverse but all are related to the social and personal determinants of behavior. The main points of the chapter are centered around the following: (1) The biological and cultural determinants of behavior. (2) Individual and group dynamics. (3) Social motives and incentives. This section considers social incentives like the spoken word, praise and reproof, reward and punishment, competition and cooperation, and also social motives like the will to achieve and to conform. (4) Motivation as a personality variable. Needs, interests, attitudes, values, loyalties, and similar factors, have been tested by various techniques and statistical methods applied to test scores and measurements. (5) Orientation and attitude—dynamic factors of prime importance. (6) The dynamics of self-esteem, including the concept and role of the self. In general, the psychologist's task in studying social and personal determinants is an exceedingly complex one.

Biological Determinants within the Social Setting

There is little, if any, value in an artificial separation of biological and social determinants of behavior. Rather we should consider the biological determinants as operative within the social setting.

Festinger (1954) questioned the value of the distinction between biological and social motivations. He argued that the same motivations determine social and non-social patterns of behavior and that man's basic biological motivations usually operate under social conditions. To illustrate: a child might want to eat at a time when his parents ordinarily prohibit eating. Getting food presents a social problem because adults have power to control the gratification which a child seeks. A social situation can yield either satisfaction or dissatisfaction.

Festinger asked: Are there any unique social motivations? He thinks not but that the basic biological motivations operate within the social setting.

Some patterns of behavior that are clearly social are biologically determined by built-in mechanisms. Consider, for example, the response of a hungry infant to the mother's breast, the response of the mother to her crying infant, the sexual responses of males and females. Such responses are biologically determined but they are social in the sense that they involve interaction between two organisms. It is confusing to try to separate the biological and social aspects.

As another example, consider the responses of smiling and laughing. These patterns depend upon built-in mechanisms yet they are evoked by social situations. Men smile and laugh alike in all parts of the world, in all cultures, at all times. Men communicate in different tongues but they smile and laugh alike. The patterns are biologically determined but evoked by social situations.

It must be emphasized that social behavior cannot be defined on a purely physiological basis. It must be defined in terms of the social environment. Social motivation, with all its complexities, must be investigated from the standpoint of the sociocultural situation. In approaching a study of the determinants of social behavior the physiologist must take a fresh start from the rich and complicated details of human behavior in its concrete social setting.

An Example of Social Behavior—Indian Corn Dance

To illustrate the complexity of social behavior we will consider the Indian corn dance at Santo Domingo, New Mexico:*

On the great feast day in August, Indians at the pueblo of Santo Domingo, New Mexico, gather to celebrate an annual corn dance. Several hundred persons take part in the ceremony. In addition to the dancers and the chorus there are clown-like men painted to represent mythical beings; their almost naked bodies are painted with broad stripes of black and white, large red spots, or other conspicuous designs and their hair is smeared with mud and tied with corn husks. The ostensible purpose of these clowns is to make merry and to do what mischief they can. They are called "delight-takers." Actually they are the only persons who can conduct the gods of rain and fruitfulness into the village. Thus they occupy an important place in the religious life of the tribe.

In the early morning of the day set apart for the ceremony the dancers

* Discussion of the corn dance is based upon the writer's observation and upon information from the following works: H. J. Spinden, Indian dances of the southwest, *Amer. Museum J.*, 1915, 15, 103–115. L. A. White, The pueblo of Santo Domingo, New Mexico, *Memoirs Amer. Anthrop. Ass.*, 1935, No. 43, p. 210. L. Gilpin, *The Rio Grande, River of Destiny*, Duell, Sloan and Pearce, New York, 1949. The photograph in Figure 85 shows costumes worn at the corn dance of San Ildefonso Pueblo, New Mexico, since photography was prohibited at Santo Domingo.

and singers gather in the great subterranean kiva where secret rites are performed and dancers are robed in ceremonial costumes. At the start of the dance, about 11 o'clock, the dancers in single file climb up the great ladder and out of the kiva. They form two lines, men and women alternating. When they enter the plaza of the pueblo the dancers are preceded by the rain priest who holds the sacred emblem of the ceremony—a pole to which is attached a banner bearing symbols of the powers of earth and sky. A chorus of thirty or more singers takes its place at one side of the plaza and the dancers enter to the rhythmic beat of the tom-tom.

The women wear a simple black tunic of ancient weave, fastened diagonally over the right shoulder, leaving the left shoulder bare, as shown in Figure 85. A hand-woven belt of red is about the waist. Their feet are bare and move with slow and stately tread to the penetrating beat of the drum. Silver necklaces, strings of turquoise or coral or shell hang about their necks. Crowning their heads are *tablitas*—thin painted boards bearing the symbols of sun, moon, and clouds, with eagle feathers attached to the edges. In each hand the women carry branches of evergreen, symbolic of life. The men, also wearing and carrying the same symbol, mark the rhythm of the dance by shaking gourd rattles.

The men are more elaborately dressed. The upper part of their bodies is painted—sometimes black, sometimes earth color, orange, or turquoise—while the forearms are usually white. They wear embroidered kilts and about their waists are sashes whose deep-fringed ends symbolize rain. Attached to the

Figure 85. Indian Corn Dance. (Photograph by Laura Gilpin.)

top of their heads are bright orange parrot feathers, symbols of the sky. Fox skins hang from their belts in back, while about their waists and legs are sleighbells now replacing the ancient rattles of turtle shell and carved-out deer toes. Their feet are encased in moccasins and above the ankle is an encircling band of skunk skin to dispel evil.

Various dance steps are used; some are simple, others complicated, involving feet, arms and gross posture. Sometimes the two lines of dancers interweave, then separate.

All ages are included in the dance: very old men and women, the older men with hair in a braid down their back, braves and squaws in the prime of life, youths and young girls, all the way down to four-year-olds who like their elders rarely miss a step. The manner of all is one of impressive dignity, their faces grave and earnest.

The singing helps to bring out the meaning of the ceremony. It may start as a crooning monotone, then change to a tragic wailing expressing, perhaps, the troubles of drought years. Suddenly the singers burst into wild shrieks for a time, then quiet down to a cheerful repetitious monotone. The dance lasts till sundown, despite the usual intense heat, two groups of dancers relaying each other hourly all day long. At the end of the day the faces of the dancers still have a look of serenity.

To the casual onlooker this dance is just an interesting spectacle, a ceremonial drama. The dance, however, has a religious significance that is hidden from ordinary view. Throughout the ceremony are threaded prayers of supplication to insure rain and the preservation of crops. The ceremony dramatizes a system of religious beliefs concerning the natural and supernatural worlds in which they live.

To understand this corn dance one must study the cosmology of the people—their beliefs concerning their origin and the world, the gods of nature and the appropriate methods for dealing with them. One must understand their language, their daily lives, their dependence upon corn and other crops, their practices that relate to birth, death, healing, training the young, and other matters. This understanding is difficult to gain, for an Indian is severely treated if he tells the secrets of his tribe. An intrusion of the white man into their religion is most unwelcome. Great patience and tact are required to gain an understanding of the meaning of the dance to the dancers.

An adequate analysis of some bit of human behavior during the corn dance must take account of the cultural and social setting of the dance. The origin of the ceremony is lost in the remote past. A child growing up in the community acquires the beliefs, attitudes, and ways of the group. He becomes like the others.

If we ignore the cultural and social background of the dance, how far can we go in explaining the behavior of individuals during the ceremony? We know that muscles contract in rhythmic patterns, that sense organs are excited, and that such bodily processes as respiration, circulation, and digestion, continue in the dancers throughout the ceremony. But the knowledge of a physiologist is not enough. To understanding some bit of this behavior we must know something about the social and cultural determinants of the activity and the developmental history of individuals growing up within the Santo Domingo community. Human behavior is *socially* determined.

Lines of Approach to Study of Social Behavior

The cultural, or institutional, approach to the study of social behavior is characteristic of sociology and cultural anthropology. It lies outside of psychology. Within social psychology there are three main lines of approach: *differential, interactional,* and *genetic.*

Differential social psychology is the study of individuals collectively by means of psychological techniques. It is possible to test and measure the abilities, interests, aptitudes, motor skills, traits of personality, knowledge, attitudes, adjustments, and goals of individuals in different groups and classes. The test scores can be correlated and factor analyzed to discover uniformities and covariations.

Differential social psychology is concerned with differences that are *psychological* in nature regardless of how individuals and groups are defined. Individuals may be classified on the basis of some *social* criterion such as economic status, occupation, nationality. *Biological* criteria may also be used: age, sex, height, weight, skin color. Whether the basis for classification is social or biological the psychologist is interested in *psychological* comparisions.

Interactional social psychology is directly concerned with interpersonal relations that involve actual energy changes in the tissues. It is concerned with functional relations that might be called dynamic.

When two people meet in a face-to-face situation there is interstimulation and response. The two, in a very genuine sense, are interacting. Social interaction can be illustrated by a fist fight between two boys, a mother kissing her child, or two persons engaged in a telephone conversation. Each person in the pair influences the other and there are reciprocal interactions between the persons concerned. The dyadic relation may be symbolized as follows:

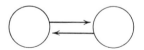

When three or more persons interact there is greater complexity of dynamic relationships:

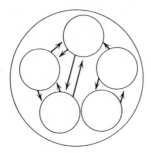

Groups, also, may interact. Illustrations are: two basketball teams playing a game, two debating teams holding a public debate, a group of workers striking for more pay, two nations at war:

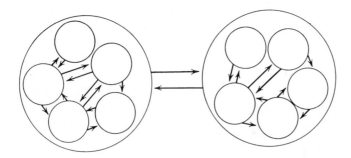

When we attempt to analyze dynamic interactions we encounter such relationships as competition and cooperation, leadership and followership, conflict and the processes of accommodation. It has been shown that groups differ in degree of integration, they differ in morale, in effectiveness, in stability of goals, and in various other ways. These are matters studied in the field of group dynamics.

Genetic social psychology is a third avenue of approach. In general, genetic psychology is concerned with growth and development. It is an attempt to trace out the principles through which an individual acquires the ways of his group. As an individual develops he acquires the language patterns, attitudes, interests, motives and states of conflict of his group. A genetic approach is not opposed to the differential and interactional; it is a supplement which takes account of the total course of development.

CULTURAL DETERMINANTS OF BEHAVIOR

To understand a bit of complex human behavior, such as that of the men and women participating in the Indian corn dance, it is necessary to go beyond psychology to a study of culture. The detailed investigation of culture is a concern of anthropology, sociology, and other social sciences.

A cultural pattern has an objective existence which outlives the individuals of a society. Although cultural patterns are the product of evolution and subject to constant change, they still have a degree of objective stability.

In general, culture has been described as that aspect or part of the world which is the creation of man. There are both physical and behavioral aspects of culture.

The Transmission of Culture

How are cultural patterns carried from generation to generation? There are two main forms of transmission: physical and psychological.

Culture is transmitted physically through the persistence of artifacts —buildings, machines, tools, books and manuscripts, drawings, pottery, clothing, basketry, and the like. For example, a book preserves the knowledge of a people for anyone who can understand the printed words. It may remain unopened in an attic or the stacks of a library for a century. Still it preserves the knowledge and experience of the past.

An archaeologist while excavating a prehistoric ruin uncovers an eolith—a stone that was chipped by human hand. If it were only a stone, eroded by water and weather, it would have little interest but as an implement used by primitive man the stone is an important record of the past. It is a physical carrier of culture. The archaeologist finds hieroglyphic writings, wall paintings, objects of unknown origin and utility. These things are bearers of culture even when their significance is lost in prehistory.

Culture is transmitted psychologically. By word of mouth and example and formal training the child learns the ways of his group. From birth till death the individual adjusts to his sociocultural environment. The language he happens to speak is dependent upon the place of birth—whether in New York, Berlin, Paris, Moscow,

Shanghai, or Timbuktu. The accident of birth also determines his manner of dress, the ethical and religious codes to which he sub- scribes, his food habits, hobbies and sports, manner of earning a living, his beliefs, attitudes, and forms of emotional expression.

What we learn (the content) is specific to a cultural situation, but the way in which we learn is common to all. The psychologist has discovered laws of learning in the laboratory. These laws have a general validity; they can be tested with specific instances of social learning such as learning to eat with chopsticks or with knife, fork, and spoon.

In general, cultural patterns are transmitted from generation to gen- eration through the preservation of material objects—artifacts and symbols—that are the products of human activity, and through learn- ing by individuals who have contacts with other persons and with physical objects.

Cultural Change

The sociocultural world into which an individual is born may appear to be stable. Actually it is undergoing continual, sometimes im- perceptible, change. One way to appreciate this change is to contrast the manner of life in a country at different periods of time.

Krout (1942), for example, has described America as it was in the decade 1790–1800:

The whipping post and the pillory were still standing in Boston and New York. There was not a single public library in the United States. An old copper mine in Connecticut was being used as a prison. The prairie schooner creaked across the nation, and only two stagecoaches carried passengers be- tween New York and Boston. There was one hat factory in the entire land, and it made cocked hats. Almost all the furniture was made in England and imported for the use of a few select families. Beef, pork, salt fish, potatoes, and hominy were the staple diet not only at breakfast but for most meals throughout the year. Leather breeches, a checked shirt, a red flannel jacket, and a cocked hat formed the dress of the artisan. Buttons were scarce and expensive, and trousers were fastened with either pegs or laces. Every gen- tleman wore a queue and powdered his hair. The hairdress worn by ladies of taste more closely resembled that of Kaffir Africans than of the well- dressed woman of today. A day laborer considered himself well paid if he earned a dollar a day. Anyone criticizing a sermon was arrested and fined. . . .

The ways of life in America are markedly different today. They have changed with expansion of the population into a new land. The present writer, within a single life span, has witnessed the appearance of the electric light, telegraph, telephone, radio, television, motion picture, automobile, airplane, rockets and satellites, atomic and hydrogen bombs, and other marvels.

Cultural changes are produced by expansion of population, by migration, by invention and discovery, by revolution and war, and other conditions.

To the individual the cultural pattern may appear to be relatively stable. This is because many changes occur gradually but there are, of course, sudden and radical changes. Cultural evolution is a continuing process that outlasts the life span of individuals. Individuals are born and die, but there is a continuing extraorganic evolution.

The Common Denominator of Cultures

Although patterns of behavior differ widely from one human group to another and the components of different cultures are highly divergent, there is nevertheless a common denominator to all cultures that have been studied. Cultural anthropologists have paid close attention to those differences that are immediately obvious but the recognition of points that are similar in all cultures has been less common. The early reports of peoples lacking language or fire, morals or religion, marriage or government, have been proved to be erroneous in every instance. Cultures have many universal, common features.

The anthropologist G. P. Murdock (1945) has prepared a list of items that are common to all cultures. He writes:

The following is a partial list of items, arranged in alphabetical order to emphasize their variety, which occur, so far as the author's knowledge goes, in every culture known to history or ethnography: age-grading, athletic sports, bodily adornment, calendar, cleanliness training, community organization, cooking, cooperative labor, cosmology, courtship, dancing, decorative art, divination, division of labor, dream interpretation, education, eschatology, ethics, ethnobotany, etiquette, faith healing, family, feasting, fire making, folklore, food taboos, funeral rites, games, gestures, gift giving, government, greetings, hair styles, hospitality, housing, hygiene, incest taboos, inheritance rules, joking, kin-groups, kinship nomenclature, language, law, luck, superstitions, magic, marriage, mealtimes, medicine, modesty concerning natural functions, mourning, music, mythology, numerals, obstetrics, penal sanctions, personal names, population policy, postnatal care, pregnancy usages, property rights, propitiation of supernatural beings, puberty customs, religious ritual, residence rules, sexual restrictions, soul concepts, status differentiation, surgery, tool making, trade, visiting, weaning, and weather control.

Rarely, if ever, Murdock points out, do the universal similarities represent identities of specific cultural content. They are similarities in the *classification* of the cultural elements rather than in actual content. The elements of culture are diverse, but competent observers feel compelled to classify them together. For example, the actual behavior exhibited in acquiring a spouse, teaching a child, or treating a sick person differs enormously from one society to another; but few would hesitate in grouping the divergent acts under the unifying categories of marriage, education, and medicine. Thus the divergent elements of cultures resolve themselves, as we have seen, into a series of generally recognized categories. There is a universal culture pattern. Cultures appear to be constructed according to a single fundamental plan.

One indication of this common denominator is the fact that any one language can be translated into another. Although word forms differ widely, translation is possible because there are common meanings. Of course, some of the meanings of one culture may be foreign to another. For example, the Eskimos have several words that refer to hunting seal on the ice. These words would be impossible to translate without awkward phrases or sentences. It is said that the Arabs have about six hundred words and phrases that refer to the camel. This is understandable since the camel plays a central role in Arabian life as does the seal in the life of the Eskimos. Our American culture is built around the automobile and other machines. Words like *park, motel, freeway, garage, service station,* etc., could not readily be translated into the language of a primitive group where the automobile is unknown. But despite these difficulties there is enough in common from culture to culture to make translation possible.

Attempts to explain this universality of cultural factors have generally started from the physiological and psychological uniformities of man. There are universal and basic processes: ingestion of food as related to hunger; intake of water as related to thirst; inhalation of air; excretion as found in urination, defecation, exhalation, sexual emission, and lactation; avoidance of pain, heat, and cold; activity as shown in exercise, play, fatigue, rest, and sleep. To these must be added hostile and aggressive behavior when one is frustrated; anxiety or fear in the presence of danger or threat; laughing, weeping, and other reactions that are common to mankind everywhere.

In all times and places there are common sources of distress, common forms of relief, common enjoyments. In a word, human nature does present striking psychological uniformities that transcend cultural boundaries. In all societies, regardless of time and place, human existence is possible only because basic needs are met and basic satisfactions provided. In all societies there are common needs to be met in one way or another. The common factors in human nature explain why the elements of diverse cultures can be classified according to a single comprehensive plan and why one language can be translated into another.

Culture and the Individual

McClelland (1951) distinguished between cultural organization and individual organization that depends upon culture. He distinguished, in particular, between three main types of cultural pattern and three corresponding types of individual schemata. These distinctions are shown in Table 6.

TABLE 6

CULTURAL AND INDIVIDUAL ORGANIZATION

Cultural Organization		Individual Organization
Types of Social Institutions	Types of Cultural Patterns	Types of Individual Schemata
Family School Church Class etc.	1. Ideology 2. Role definitions 3. Socialization procedures	1. Ideas and values 2. Perception and performance of roles 3. Development and maintenance of conceptions, including motivation.

After McClelland (1951).

Within any given society there are types of institution such as the family, the school, the church, and the class. Each institution exists within the social structure and is represented by several different types of cultural pattern. First, the institution is characterized by a certain *ideology*, i.e., by ideas, beliefs, and values relating to the institution. Second, the society defines, for a given institution, the *roles* of individuals. For example, within the family the role of mother is clearly defined. Third, there are types of cultural patterns for socializing the individual. For example, there are cultural patterns for training the child, becoming an adult, controlling sex behavior, etc.

Corresponding to these three main types of cultural patterns are types of schemata within the organization of individuals. First, McClelland points out, a person gains ideas and values from his group. These are most closely related to the ideology of his society but other types of cultural pattern influence the formation of ideas, beliefs and evaluative attitudes. Second, the individual clearly perceives his roles within the group and is aware of himself as carrying out those roles. A man, for example, is aware of his role as doctor, huntsman, chief of the tribe, etc., and he plays his part. Third, the individual acquires schemata relating to the development and maintenance of conceptions that are characteristic of the group; and he derives certain goals and ideals from his cultural environment.

These types of individual schemata have obvious psychological significance in relation to cognition and motivation. McClelland emphasizes the correspondence between the schemata and cultural patterns. It would be equally possible to argue that these schemata correspond to neural organization, within the individual, that has been acquired from the sociocultural world.

The concept of role is highly important in social science because it bridges the gap between individual behavior and society. Roles are defined by the social system; they are, in a sense, embedded within the cultural pattern. Roles differ with the age, sex, occupation, parentage, belief and ability of individuals. Human behavior cannot be correctly interpreted apart from its concrete social setting and from the roles that are culturally defined for individuals to perform.

Newcomb (1950) put it this way: "Of all forms of human behavior, role taking is that in which we can most clearly see *both* the influence of protoplasm and the influence of society. In this sense, role patterns provide the meeting ground between protoplasm and society."

Role taking may be illustrated by the mother role in our American society. Our society prescribes that a mother provide her children with enough to eat and, less certainly, that she teach her children to be honest. The role of mother prohibits physical injury to children but not spanking them for lack of conformity. Telling lies to children is forbidden in the role of mother (but there is some difference of opinion on this point). The role of mother also prescribes ways of behaving towards husband, neighbors, teachers, grandparents, and other persons who come into contact with the children. There are, in fact, a good many things that are prescribed or permitted or forbidden to the mother.

Closely related to the concept of social role is that of status. Within a given group a man has a certain standing or position; this is his status. In the Army, for example, status is indicated by titles such as General, Major, Captain, Lieutenant, and Private. In a university faculty there are various titles that indicate the standing of individuals: President, Dean, Director, Department Head, Professor, Associate Professor, Assistant Professor, Instructor and Assistant— not to mention assorted classes of students! Such titles indicate status and they imply certain privileges and prerogatives; they also define certain roles.

In general, role and status are defined by society. The individual learns to play his part according to what is expected of him. The unique content in role playing is determined by society. The process of learning is much the same everywhere. A child growing up within a group learns according to known psychological principles. Uniqueness lies in the pattern of *what* he learns rather than in the learning process. Also in carrying out a role all psychological processes are involved. The individual perceives, remembers, thinks, feels, deliberates, decides and acts.

INDIVIDUAL AND GROUP DYNAMICS

Kurt Lewin's dynamic psychology takes account of the individual in relation to his perceived environment. It also takes account of interpersonal relations and thus illustrates the interactional approach to social psychology. Details are given below.

Lewin's Dynamic Field Theory

In the dynamic psychology of Kurt Lewin (1935, 1954) one of the basic concepts is that of the *life space* of the individual. The life space is the totality of facts and values which determine the behavior of an individual at a certain time. It is defined by the perceptions of an individual including the perceptions of goals, barriers, incentives, rewards and punishments, and means.

No two individuals have the same life space. Each individual's world is unique. The life space has a dimension of reality-unreality. An individual may choose to operate within a system of perceptions which corresponds quite closely to reality, or he may retreat to the less real level of daydreams or fantasy.

The life space includes the person who perceives as well as surrounding objects. At a given moment the general formula for behavior is:

$$B = f(P, E)$$

where B is behavior, P is the person, E is the psychological environment. P and E are mutually interdependent constituents of the psychological field. Behavior within the psychological field depends upon environmental conditions as well as internal personal factors.

Within the field there are goals, barriers, and means which are instrumental in locomotions to the goals. If, for example, a child and a piece of candy are in the same field, the child moves towards the candy. This fact is represented by placing a plus sign on the candy, and speaking of this as a positive valence. Just as the iron filings arrange themselves in relation to the poles of a magnet so the child orients himself (wherever he may be in the field) towards the candy. There is a field of force which corresponds to an inner tension system.

Specific forces within a field are represented by vectors which show both the direction of the force and its strength or intensity. Objects in the field have valence, or positive and negative incentive value. Objects and events which the person perceives as likely to contribute to need satisfaction are considered as exerting an attractive force and to have positive valence. Those perceived as reducing or interfering with need satisfaction are repellent and have negative valence. Valences are represented topographically by plus and minus signs. The valence of an object may change from time to time as indicated by the behavior of the person.

Within the field there are barriers and restraining forces. A barrier might be a physical condition as when a child sees a piece of candy out of reach on a high shelf. A parent holding a whip is a restraining force with negative valence. The barrier is something which the person perceives as standing in the way of achieving need satisfaction which is represented by the psychological goal.

A psychological incentive is any object, condition, or event, which provides a motivating force in the direction of performance or the mastery of a learning task. Psychological incentives include anticipated rewards and punishments. Lewin made it clear that many activities are carried on with intrinsic interest. Rewards and punishments are required only when the task is something different from what the learner prefers to do for its own sake. It may be unecessary or undesirable to depend upon rewards and punishments in motivating a child.

A motive is a state or an event within the individual which initiates or regulates behavior in relation to a goal. The state of desire or need to achieve the goal is motivation in its general sense. When a need exists there is a tension within the person that persistently motivates behavior. Lewin does not attempt to reduce tension to physical or physiological terms; he thinks of tension psychologically as a cause of action. For example, if a man in a conversation wishes to make a remark but restrains himself, there is an inner tension. To make the remark would relax the tension but if the remark is not made, the tension sooner or later disappears.

Motives are commonly opposed. During conflict both field forces may be positive as when an individual is determined to move towards two attractive goals in opposite directions. In another type of conflict two negative forces may be opposed. Figuratively, one may be caught between the devil and the deep blue sea. In still another type of conflict the goal object has something attractive and also something repulsive about it. There may be an equilibrium of the forces that lead to approach and to avoidance.

Very intense motivation, Lewin points out, leads to a state of high tension with the result that the person's efforts are less constructive than they would be under lower levels of tension. With a conflict of strong motives a person may escape from the field of conflict.

Lewin's dynamic field theory is important because, as a fact, it has generated a great deal of research in the area of motivation and emotion. The theory lies close to the psychology of common sense and perhaps for this reason it has been utilized in many practical researches. In the later years of his life Lewin extended his psychology into group dynamics and action research.

Group Dynamics

If one holds to the view that psychology is the study of individuals, social psychology may be viewed as that part of the science that deals with the social environment and its influence upon behavior and development. A good deal of research has been carried out from the *individual* point of view. This work contrasts the behavior of individuals working alone and working within a face-to-face group. The earlier work has been well summarized by Dashiell (1935).

Since the time of Dashiell's review, however, there has been a major development within social psychology. It is claimed that social psychology deals with the *group* as a unit. A group is a small social system—such as a basketball team—which functions as a unit and is more than the sum of its parts. A group can solve problems, engage in activities, conflict with other groups, etc. In studies of group dynamics an emphasis has been placed upon the internal structure of the group—communication structure, degree of cohesiveness of the group, power structure, group effectiveness, and the like.

Group dynamics, under the influence of Lewin, has become a broad area of research. There have been field studies, especially by anthropologists and sociologists, as well as experimental investigations.

Studies in the area of group dynamics have been reviewed by Horwitz (1953). He distinguished three main kinds of systems within each of which there are important variables. First, there is the *individual* system. This is the traditional psychological system. The individual is a natural unit. Psychological events occur within this system during the individual's life cycle and these events are influenced by factors in the other systems. Second, there is the *group* system. This is the system studied in the field of group dynamics. The group *as a group* is a functional unit and group behavior depends upon factors within the group as well as factors in the other systems. Third, both the individual and the group systems operate within a wider *institutional* or societal system. The institutional system has a degree of independence of the other systems.

Horwitz states that in explaining social behavior one must consider the effect of variation in one of the systems upon some variable factor in the same or in another system. He formed a matrix of nine cells which is based upon the three systems—individual, social, institutional. The matrix is shown in Table 7. Explanation consists in demonstrating the effect of varying a factor in one system upon some factor in the same or a different system. There are thus three kinds of variables to be considered in explaining social behavior and a matrix of interrelations among these variables.

The matrix shows the complexity of possible interrelations among the determinants of social behavior. The complexity is so great that the social psychologist must necessarily limit his view to certain of the possible relationships.

Group dynamics is concerned primarily with the *group* system and especially with the internal dynamics of this system. We will now consider briefly some of the main aspects of the group system:

TABLE 7

LEVELS AND INTERRELATIONS OF VARIABLES USED IN
EXPLAINING SOCIAL BEHAVIOR

| | Effects of Variables in the: | | |
	Individual System	Group System	Institutional System
upon Variables in the:	*Variables* 1 2 . . . n	*Variables* 1 2 . . . n	*Variables* 1 2 . . . n
Individual System			
Group System	*Variables* 1 2 . . . n	*Variables* 1 2 . . . n	*Variables* 1 2 . . . n
Institutional System	*Variables* 1 2 . . . n	*Variables* 1 2 . . . n	*Variables* 1 2 . . . n

After Horowitz (1953).

First, there are *group goals*. A goal is a state of affairs in the external environment toward which activites are directed, and which,
if reached, terminates the sequence of activities. Just as with the
individual system, so group goals are dependent on possibilities existing
in the environment and are influenced by environmental demands, e.g.,
by institutional imperatives.

Within a group there are internal processes which influence the
selection of goals. One view is that disequilibria occur in relationships

among the parts of a group, which then operate "homeostatically" to influence the selection of group goals.

The goals of a group markedly influence the motivation of the individual members. Group goals can induce tension systems in individuals, and whether or not the group achieves its goal determines whether or not these individual tension systems will be reduced.

Second, there are *group activities*. In moving toward a goal, the group—more obviously than an individual—must provide for adequate working relationships and coordination among its members. Group activities present diverse aspects to the observer: (1) *Group locomotion*. If the members fail to be steered by group goals, the group locomotion is adversely affected by this failure. Cooperation is required for a group to achieve its ends. (2) *Group maintenance*. Since the activities of a group may continue for an indefinite period of time, there must be provisions for replacements and for stability in group action. (3) *Personal goals of members*. The individuals in a group may or may not accept the group goals, but group activities can change a person's position with respect to his own goals even though the individual is quiescent. Group activity has an effect on individual activity.

Third, there is *group structure*. There are different types of group structure and different ways of describing structure. Some of the basic concepts are the following.

1. *Functional roles*. In most groups, if not all, there is division of labor. Individuals differ in abilities and temperament, and these differences influence their functional roles within the group.

A topic of considerable importance, in this connection, is leadership. In the popular view there is one leader for a group. But in most current researches leadership is said to be exerted when individuals perform necessary group functions. According to this usage all the members of a group may be leaders. Cattell stated that leadership exists to the extent that properties of the group (syntality) are modified by the individual's presence. Designated group leaders assume certain functions such as "analyzing the situation" and "initiating action."

2. *Communication structure*. Groups possess or develop well-defined channels of communication. In the army, for example, orders are given along recognized channels from the top of the system downward.

3. *Power structure*. Power refers to the ability of certain individuals to influence the behavior of others or the activities of the group.

There are two main modes of influence, direct and by contagion. In large groups there are coalitions that have power and that may conflict with each other. Power structure is thus based on influence on dynamic interpersonal relationships.

4. *Sociometric structure.* Within a group there are relations based upon attraction and repulsion among individuals. Some choices are positive and others negative. These friendship relations underlie the structure revealed by sociometric methods. The structure is one based upon personal liking and disliking and may, therefore, be considered as a kind of affective or value structure.

5. *Group standards.* The members of a group develop expectations which apply to the behavior, attitudes, and beliefs of all members of the group, irrespective of their roles. Codes of conduct, ethical standards, develop within the group.

6. *Group cohesiveness.* Some groups hold together better than others; they are more cohesive. There are forces that tend to move individuals into or out of a group or to restrain such movement.

7. *Group effectiveness.* Questions arise concerning the effectiveness, or efficiency, of groups and the factors that influence group effectiveness. For example, Fiedler (1958) studied the relation between interpersonal perception and group effectiveness. He found that for effective group action (as in team work) the leader must be acceptable to his followers and the leader must maintain a certain psychological distance from his men, especially from his key subordinates.

The above survey, in general, only indicates the complexity and variety of work accomplished in the broad area of group dynamics. The indication, however, is sufficient to reveal a certain point of view.

SOCIAL MOTIVES AND INCENTIVES

The social environment is obviously the source of many motives and incentives. The goals that an individual accepts are established within a social setting; and the social environment also provides innumerable spurs and checks to action.

Human performance depends upon: understanding the task to be accomplished; having knowledge of the results of previous work; the subject's attitude towards his task; the nature and magnitude of the task; the subject's interest in the task; eagerness or zest to perform and effort exerted; social incentives such as rewards, prizes, praise, encouragement, competition; having a specific goal, etc. In addition to these factors, human performance depends upon environmental conditions such as sharpness or dullness of tools, temperature, humidity, movement of air, illumination, distraction, music, etc.; and upon organic conditions such as fatigue, sleepiness, illness; and upon conditions determined by the taking of alcohol, tobacco, coffee, sedatives, and other substances.

In the following sections a small sample of the *social* motives and incentives that influence performance will be considered.

The Influence of Words

Words influence behavior in several ways:

It is obvious that the verbal instructions of a parent or teacher regulate the behavior of a child. If a parent asks a child to go on a specific errand, the verbal request organizes the child's neural machinery in such a way that the child generally carries out the instructions. The child understands the instructions, maintains a mental set, and acts according to the instructions. The formal instructions in psychological experiments illustrate the same principle.

The following incident, described by H. S. Tuttle (1941), shows how words can control behavior:

In a department store during the Christmas rush a small child climbed on to a rocking horse. When his mother was ready to move on, he was not. He sat and rocked. The crowds watched with amusement while the mother vainly tried to persuade the child to leave the toy and go with her. Seeing the mother's predicament, some of the customers tried their arts of persuasion; but in vain. The boy still sat and rocked. Salesgirls tried their skill with no better effect. Finally a salesman stepped up to the child, whispering something in his ear. The child hopped off the horse and followed his mother. None heard what the salesman said, but whatever it was, it reversed the child's behavior.

The incident raises a question: How do words influence action? How can a few words change the course of behavior? It is quite clear that suggestions, instructions, orders and commands, do influence the course of human activity.

Words influence behavior by building up feelings. Contrast the feelings aroused by such words as *stink* and *moonlight*. Consider the feeling tone of words like *bright* and *dull, beautiful* and *ugly, life* and *death*. The words, through associations, arouse feelings, and the feelings are evocative.

Words affect the morale of workers. On the New York Post Office the following sentence is carved in stone: "Neither snow nor rain nor heat nor gloom of night stays these couriers from the swift completion of their appointed rounds." Of course, all this means is that the mails will be delivered despite bad weather. Yet if the material should be translated in this way, it would not only spoil the building but also would fail to support the morale of the postmen. A postman gets a sense of importance from the inscription—I am a "courier"; I will do my duty come snow, rain, heat, or gloom of night!

Words communicate ideas. To follow up this point we would have to launch forth upon a sea of fact. There is the social psychology of language, semantics, the emotional appeal of words, propaganda, etc., etc. Where would we stop?

Clearly, words have a profound and varied influence upon behavior. This influence is in part rational and logical. To a high degree, however, the influence of words is irrational and emotional.

Praise and Reproof as Incentives

A question is sometimes asked by parents and teachers: Which is more effective in motivating the child, praise or blame? Schmidt (1941) has shown that the question cannot be answered categorically. A final answer concerning the relative effectiveness of praise and blame, as incentives, is impossible because the effect of these incentives varies from individual to individual and with the social setting. In some teacher-pupil relationships praise is more effective than reproof; in others the reverse is true. The personality of the teacher as well as that of the child are factors that must be considered in answering the question. These factors vary widely.

In general, children who feel inferior are more highly motivated by praise than by blame. Self-confident children may be more highly motivated by reproof. Hence a discriminating use of praise and reproof is more effective than the blind and consistent praising of all children for all acts. If one had to choose, however, between consistent praise and consistent reproof, one would certainly make use of praise because this incentive is generally effective. Reproof, without the relief afforded by occasional approval, may develop attitudes of inferiority and lack of self-confidence.

An early evaluation of the relative effectiveness of praise and reproof, as incentives to school work, was made by Hurlock (1924, 1925). On the first day of her experiment the children were given a test in arithmetic and four equivalent groups were formed on the basis of the scores.

One group served as a *control*. The children in the *control* group worked in a separate classroom. They were instructed to add the figures as a class exercise; no comments were made about the quality of their work. The other groups worked together in the same room but under different incentive conditions. The children in one group were consistently praised for their excellent performance. Those in another group were consistently reproved for poor work. Those in another group heard the praise and the reproof but nothing was said to them about their work; they were entirely ignored.

On the second and following experimental days the names of the children in the *praised* group were read aloud and the children were asked to come to the front of the room and face the class. They were then praised for the excellence of their work on the preceding day as shown by improvement, and for their neatness and general superiority over other members of the class. They were encouraged to do even better, to try to avoid mistakes and to do even more problems in addition. After this the names of the children in the *reproved* group were called. They were severely reproved for poor work, careless mistakes, failures to improve, and for their general inferiority to the other members of the class. They were told that they would be given another chance. The youngsters in the *ignored* group, as we said, heard both the praise and the reproof but themselves received no recognition either favorable or unfavorable.

The relative performance of the different groups is presented graphically in Figure 86, plotted from Hurlock's data. On the basis of scores on the first day, the four groups were formed so that they would have the same average scores. On the second day the *praised* and *reproved* groups made about equal gains; both were superior to the *ignored* and *control* groups. On the third, fourth, and fifth days of the experiment the *praised* group continued to show improvement while the *reproved* group did not. At the close of the experiment the group that had been consistently praised was significantly superior to the other groups. The gains of the *reproved* and *ignored* groups, over and above the practice gains of the *control*, were not large enough to give high significance to the differences. The *praised* group was the only one that showed a consistent gain in proficiency from beginning to end of the experiment. Although the *ignored* group performed somewhat better than the *control*, it is probably bad from the point of view of mental hygiene to ignore the children. From this angle, it appears that some comment

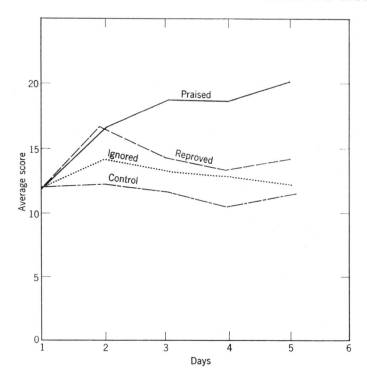

Figure 86. Average scores in addition tests given under different motivating conditions. *Plotted from* data in Hurlock (1924).

about their work—favorable or unfavorable—is better than no comment at all.

One must be careful not to over-generalize Hurlock's results. On the football field, for example, coaches sometimes reprove players for their errors, frequently in terms both forceful and picturesque. It may be that this kind of treatment tends to counteract the ovations players receive from the bleachers and in the newspapers, preventing the heroes from developing conceit. It is possible also that such reproof may engender anger that can be skillfully directed against an opposing team.

Reward and Punishment

What constitutes reward? To the small child: a toy, a piece of candy, a gold star placed after his name, a penny, the opportunity to play, permission to go to the circus—anything, in fact, which the child wants. To the adult the following are rewards: money, prizes, medals, degrees, titles, honors, decorations, invitations, and other recognitions of achievement. A reward is typically pleasant, satisfying; it is a positive incentive or spur to action. A reward is bestowed, in the training of children and animals, to motivate behavior.

What constitutes punishment? To the small child: a slap, a spanking, a verbal reproof, deprivation of something wanted such as money or time to play—most any deprivation or unpleasant experience, in fact, can serve as a punishment. To the adult punishments are inflicted by society: money fines, confinement to prison, hard labor, public ridicule, the stock, torture, even death—these constitute diverse forms of punishment. Punishments are typically unpleasant and often painful. They are inflicted by parents, teachers, society, to show disapproval of behavior and, presumably, to prevent the recurrence of the act that is punished. Sometimes punishments are inflicted "to get even," that is, for retribution.

With animal subjects a great many experiments have been performed upon reward and punishment. Some of them were considered in Chapter 6. Trainers of circus animals rely almost exclusively upon rewards and punishments. For the correct act the animal is rewarded by a lump of sugar or a word of approval. For the unskilled act he is punished by the stroke of a whip or a word of disapproval.

Thorndike (1935) carried out a series of experiments in which the words "right" and "wrong," spoken by the experimenter, were extensively employed for reward and punishment. On the basis of his findings Thorndike argued that reward, with as little punishment as possible, should be used in education. Punishment, he concluded, can disorganize the process of learning and lead the learner to make undesired responses. Reward, he argued, has a favorable effect upon learning which, moreover, spreads to responses both before and after the specific activity that is rewarded. This so-called "spread of effect" has been studied in other experiments but the matter remains controversial.

As the psychologist sees things, rewards are typically pleasant and punishments unpleasant. More exactly, a reward is an affective change in the positive direction and a punishment an affective change in the negative direction. A reward may be either a positive affective arousal or relief from a negative affective state. A punishment may be a negative affective arousal or reduction of a positive affective state.

In the social setting, however, the concepts of reward and punishment are normative. A reward is bestowed or a punishment inflicted to control the course and development of behavior. The concepts are definitely evaluative. Rewards are "good"; punishments are "bad." Rewards are bestowed to reinforce "correct" patterns of behavior. Punishments are inflicted to modify "incorrect" patterns.

But science deals with facts. Scientific explanation is factual, non-evaluative. The electric shock has been extensively used as an incentive to animal behavior. Electric shocks can be graded exactly and quantitatively; and the psychological effect of a shock varies with the intensity of the shock. The affective arousal from a shock is the same whether or not it is regarded as a punishment. Who can say whether the white rat regards the shock he receives as a punishment?

Again, a bear in the forest might get a taste of wild honey and find it delightful; but in getting the honey he is stung on the nose by a bee and this he finds unpleasant and painful. Is the taste of honey a reward and the sting a punishment? Perhaps so; but the facts of behavior are the same regardless of one's evaluation of them. One might philosophize that Nature has rewarded and punished the bear!

The basic fact about "reward" and "punishment" is the fact of affective arousal. Fundamental problems of reward and punishment center around the nature and role of affective processes in the regulation and organization of behavior.

The Effects of Punishment and Reward upon Discrimination of Visual Extents

Whether an incentive is a punishment or a reward depends not so much upon the physical characteristics of the stimulus as upon the conditions under which it is given. It is readily conceivable that under certain conditions an electric shock might be considered as a reward and that food might become a punishment.

In a well-devised experiment Hamilton (1929) planned conditions such that the sound of a bell would serve to one group of subjects as a reward and to another as a punishment. This plan assured that both kinds of incentive would have the same sensory basis.

The task of the subject was to discriminate and compare visual extents. The subject was seated before a modified Galton bar. The apparatus was arranged so that when the subject rotated a rod a black shield moved away from the central hair line, uncovering a white extent. The task of the subject was to move the shield so that the variable extent appeared to be twice the length of a standard extent of 120 millimeters. At the start of each trial the movable shield was placed at the center line and the subject was instructed to move it outward until the length of the variable was twice that of the standard length. When the subject was satisfied with his setting of the apparatus he pressed a button to signal to the experimenter that the task had been completed.

There were sixty subjects. On the first day each individual made fifty adjustments of the shield. From measurements based upon the data an average error was computed for each subject. On the second experimental day the first five trials were made under the same conditions as before. Then the subjects were divided into six groups and given different kinds of treatment as follows:

1. A *control* group completed the work of the second day with no additional incentive. The instruction and procedure were the same on the first and second days.

2. The members of a *punishment* group were told that a bell would ring, when they pressed the button at the end of each trial, if the length they estimated was *wrong*.

3. The members of a *reward* group were told that a bell would ring, when they pressed the button, if they had adjusted the length *correctly*.

4. The members of a *guess-with-punishment* group received the same treatment as those in the *punishment* group except that each subject was required to guess the direction of his error. He was not told whether his guess was right or wrong.

5. In a *told-with-punishment* group the subjects were treated like those in the *punishment* group, except that every subject was told the direction of his error.

6. A *knowledge* group heard the experimenter announce in a matter-of-fact voice "long," "short," "right." No bell was used.

The average errors computed from the data obtained on the first day gave a basis for determining whether an adjustment of the apparatus was "right" or "wrong." The apparatus was so constructed that an error would be signaled automatically if the setting were greater than the average error and that a correct setting would be signaled if the setting were less than the average error. This arrangement assured an equal number of "right" and "wrong" settings, in the long run, for every subject. Furthermore, on the second day a new average error was computed after every five trials and the apparatus was constantly adjusted to correspond to the lowered average error. The plan gave approximately equal numbers of rewards and punishments, with no possibility of changing the ratio by practice.

How much did the average errors decrease as a result of practice under the different incentive conditions? To answer this question the measure of the average error for a group on the first day was taken as a base (100 percent), and the average error for the last five trials was expressed as a percentage of this base. The values computed in this way are shown in the tabulation below:

Group	Percentage of Initial Error
Control	127
Punishment	24
Reward	26
Guess-with-punishment	15
Told-with-punishment	20
Knowledge	45

Results with the *control* group indicate that the continued estimations of visual extent in the absence of any feedback of information about the correctness of the setting and in the absence, too, of rewards and punishments, showed no improvement. Indeed, the finding of 127 percent of error suggests definitely that the subjects of the *control* group became increasingly indifferent and careless in carrying out their task. The remaining five groups, however, all exhibited a marked reduction in the average errors. The reduction was present in the results for each individual as well as for the group as a whole.

The results for *punishment* and *reward* groups are not significantly different. In regard to this Hamilton reminds us that physical aspects of punishment and reward were identical—the same bell rang for both—and the procedure for both groups did not vary. The only difference between punishment and reward was in the mental attitude of the subjects towards the bell. This difference, however, was a very genuine one. With punishment, the subjects sometimes swore at the bell, made faces when it rang, and adopted the attitude of trying to keep it from ringing. With reward, the spontaneous behavior of the subjects when the bell rang was quite the opposite. They gave exclamations of delight upon hearing the bell, sighed, and said, "What a relief," "That's better," etc.; and all appeared to be trying to make the bell ring as frequently as possible.

Such remarks were more common with the *punishment* and *reward* groups than with the *knowledge* group. This group received the most information of all, but the information was given in a matter-of-fact way. Knowledge of results alone reduced the average error to 45 percent of its initial measure. Contrastingly, punishment and reward when combined with less information effected greater reductions in the error scores.

Turning now to the *guess-with-punishment* group we are impressed by the fact that this group made the greatest reduction in average error (though not a reliably greater reduction than that of the *told-with-punishment* group). The subjects in the *guess-with-punishment* group were more active than the others. Although they were not informed as to the accuracy of their guessing, their additional activity gave them an advantage over the *told-with-punishment* group which merely received information passively. These results are in line with a well-known principle that we learn by reacting.

It would be interesting to know just how far the activity of guessing helped to make the *guess-with-punishment* group the most successful of them all. It seems likely that both the *guess-with-punishment* and the *told-with-punishment* groups were more constantly aware of the correctness or incorrectness of their settings than the groups with punishment or reward alone, and that this enforced emphasis upon results favored greater precision in the spatial discrimination.

After scrutinizing the different conditions of the experiment, I am convinced that several facilitating factors are present in the motivating conditions. There is an *information* factor that is present, to the highest degree, with the *knowledge* group. There is an *incentive* factor (to avoid negative and attain positive affectivity) that is present in all *reward* and *punishment* groups and probably to a less degree in the *knowledge* group. There is also an *activity* factor, present to the highest degree in the *guess-with-punishment* group.

An important conclusion to be drawn from this study is that the difference between reward and punishment lies in the subject's attitude and his understanding of the task. When a constant stimulus (bell) was used as an incentive "reward" and "punishment" were found to be equally effective.

It would be instructive to repeat the experiment varying only the physical characteristics of the reward-punishment stimulus. One might for example, use a voice, an electric shock, a perfume, a fire gong, etc., as the common incentive.

Among his more general conclusions Hamilton makes the arresting statement that special incentives yielded greater accuracy of visual discrimination of extent than had previously been attained in the well-known experiments with the Galton bar.

The Influences of Success and Failure

The experiences of success and failure are relative to a goal that has been set or to a system of values. Since there are diverse goals and values, there are various ways of estimating success and failure. If one is a musician, success or failure is estimated in terms of applause from the audience, press notices, professional recognitions, and the like. If one is a business man, achievement is measured in terms of a dollar standard of value. If one is a scientist, personal success may be rated in terms of objective contributions to the development of a particular science. If one is deeply religious, he may disclaim the dollar standard of success; he may think of success and failure in terms of salvation and sin—certainly not in terms of personal glory. In any event, success and failure are clearly relative to a goal or some system of values.

In an experiment dealing with success and failure, Sears (1937) forced his subjects to succeed or fail relative to their goal by falsifying scores on an experimental task. The subjects were instructed to sort playing cards into four piles according to suit.

The time required to sort a pack was measured with a stop watch but the actual times were falsified and true times not reported to the subjects. Half of the group were forced to fail and the other half to succeed, relative to the goals they had set, to their previous scores, and relative to the scores of other individuals in the group. The comments of the subjects indicated clearly, often in terms that were vivid and picturesque, that a genuine sense of success or failure had been aroused.

The subjects that were allowed to succeed made consistent gains in speed of sorting throughout the experiment. In the *success* group the subjects were distinctly superior, objectively, to those in the group that was forced to fail. On a given day the subjects in the *failure* group steadily slowed down from trial to trial. But on a day-to-day basis the *failure* group showed a definite practice effect. Their speed of card sorting increased appreciably. The *success* group, as I said, had a consistent advantage throughout the experiment.

The work supports the popular dictum that success breeds success and failure breeds failure. Success develops attitudes of self-confidence and a will to achieve. The principle has many practical applications.

Levels and Areas of Aspiration

Experiments stemming from the work of Kurt Lewin deal with what has come to be known as the *level of aspiration*. These experiments deal directly with the effects of success and failure upon the setting of goals. They have in common the following procedure: The subject is confronted with a task and asked how well he will do on the next trial; he then carries out the task and is informed of the result; knowing the result he again sets for himself a goal. For example, if the task is shooting at a target, the subject is asked to estimate how close he will come to the bull's-eye on the next shot. After the shot, knowing his score, he is again asked to estimate how well he will do on the following trial, and so on. The discrepancy between the goal which an individual sets for himself and his actual score on the following trial shows the influence of success and failure.

Rotter (1942) has pointed out that the goal an individual sets for himself is dependent upon two main factors. First, there is a wish to excel, to do better on the next trial, and to do better than other subjects. This desire for improvement tends to raise the level of aspiration. Second, there is a realistic estimate of one's ability that is based upon information concerning previous performance. The knowledge of previous performance tends to hold the level of aspiration down to a realistic level. Actually the goal that is set turns out to be a compromise between these two determinants.

Young and Yavitz (1946) suggested that studies upon the *level* of aspiration should be supplemented by work upon the *area* of aspiration. When a person succeeds in an activity he is likely to repeat it, to develop interest and an attitude of self-confidence along with increasing proficiency in that activity. When he fails he is likely to shift to some other area. For example, if a college student fails in a mathematics course, he may abandon this field of endeavor and go out for baseball. If his performance in baseball convinces him that he is only mediocre, he may then turn to social life in the hope of becoming a "good fellow well met" or just a "gentleman." These shifts from one area of activity to another protect the individual from a sense of failure and defeat. If an individual aspires to competence in one area of activity and then fails, he may make an adjustment by shifting to another area of professed competence. From the point of view of mental hygiene it is important that every person experience success in some line of activity.

Young and Yavitz instructed college students to list activities in which they obtained the experience of success and those in which they obtained the experience of failure. The subjects were asked also to list the activities in which they wished to be more successful.

A study of the 8,733 items listed by 558 college students resulted in a classification under the following headings: (1) Academic abilities, skills, achievements such as music, English literature, and mathematics. (2) Athletics, sports, games such as swimming and diving, tennis, and basketball. (3) Social skills and personality traits such as social dancing, public speaking, and leadership. (4) Professional and vocational activities such as clerical and office work, business, and finance. (5) Hobbies and collections such as photography and stamp collecting.

A correlational analysis of the data indicated that the experiences of success and failure tended to arise from the *same* activities, traits and abilities—presumably from the things with which the subjects were occupied and with which they were ego-involved. Of course, if the success-failure test had been given to other groups—businessmen, aged people, day laborers, etc.—different areas of aspiration would undoubtedly have been found. The areas reflect the activities of the subjects.

It was found, in general, that men and women experienced success and failure, and aspired to success, in the same areas of activity. There were, however, some areas of activity in which there were obvious sex differences such as football (masculine activity) and the study of home economics (feminine activity).

Although the study was aimed primarily at *areas of activity*, the subjects reported *traits of personality* and *social behavior* as important sources of the feelings of success and failure. In a follow-up study one might ask: What traits of personality give one a sense of success and what a sense of failure? What traits does one aspire to improve?

The study was exploratory. The coming of World War II made it impossible to investigate, as originally intended, the process of shifting from one area of aspiration to another during 4 years of college and the conditions that lead to a shift. It is hoped that this study will be completed and that further studies will be made.

The Achievement Motive

All of us wish to achieve something. Our ultimate goal may be economic security, wealth, health, fame, recognition, happiness, peace of mind, or something else. Whatever the goal may be, *achievement* is relative to that end.

The need to achieve something is related to the need for superiority. Most people have such a need. The strength of the need to achieve varies markedly from person to person and with circumstances.

McClelland et al. (1953) have produced a wealth of research upon the achievement motive. McClelland argued that the achievement motive, like other forms of human motivation, can best be studied in the realm of fantasy. Fantasy is "free" in the sense that conditions of testing do not place external constraints on the responses that are possible. The subject can think about anything—"about killing someone, committing suicide, touring the South Seas on a pogo stick, having an illegitimate child, and so forth. Anything is symbolically possible."

The study of human motivation in the realm of fantasy is widely recognized as sound and promising. Freud, as we know, believed that basic motivations are revealed in fantasy—in day dreams and night dreams. Projective tests, also, such as Murray's TAT and the Rorschach, depend upon imaginative content.

McClelland's technique for arousing fantasy was to flash a picture on the screen for 20 seconds. The subject was asked to write a story about it with the following instructions:

This is a test of your creative imagination. A number of pictures will be projected on the screen before you. You will have twenty seconds to look at the picture and then about four minutes to make up a story about it. Notice that there is one page for each picture. The same four questions are asked. They will guide your thinking and enable you to cover all the elements of a plot in the time allotted. Plan to spend about a minute on each question. I will keep time and tell you when it is about time to go on to the next question for each story. You will have a little time to finish your story before the next picture is shown.

Obviously there are no right or wrong answers, so you may feel free to make up any kind of a story about the pictures that you choose. Try to make them vivid and dramatic, for this is a test of *creative* imagination. Do not merely describe the picture you see. Tell a story about it. Work as fast as you can in order to finish in time. Make them interesting. Are there any questions? If you need more space for any question, use the reverse side.

Each sheet contained four questions approximately as follows:

1. What is happening? Who are the persons?
2. What has led up to this situation? That is, what has happened in the past?
3. What is being thought? What is wanted? By whom?
4. What will happen? What will be done?

The stories were scored for indications of achievement motivation. The scorer had first to decide whether the content of a story contained any reference to an "achievement goal." By an "achievement goal" is meant *success in competition with some standard of excellence.* For example, an individual in the story wanting to win an essay contest, or an apprentice wanting to show the master that he, too, can fix the machine, imply competition with a standard of excellence. This is what is meant by achievement motivation.

In scoring the imaginative stories the scorer referred to various subcategories of achievement motivation. The subcategories and, in fact, the entire scoring method developed gradually. The reliability of the scoring was checked by having two experienced judges rate the stories independently and by correlating their ratings on different occasions. The score-rescore reliability was high.

With a reliable index of the need for achievement, McClelland et al. carried out a variety of experiments. They studied the frequencies of different types of achievement imagery when the subjects were relaxed, when neutrally oriented, and again when they were oriented towards achievement. They studied, also, the effects of success and failure upon the imaginative stories.

In a summary of these investigations, at the close of *The Achievement Motive,* McClelland et al. write:

> In general, people with a high achievement imagery index score complete more tasks under achievement orientation, solve more simple arithmetic problems in a timed test, improve faster in their ability to do anagrams, tend to get better grades, use more future tenses and abstract nouns in talking about themselves, set a higher level of aspiration if reality factors are ruled out, tend to recall more incompleted tasks, score higher on the Interest Maturity scale of the Strong Vocational Interest Test, show a slight tendency to recognize achievement-related words faster, and so on. . . .

These are diverse findings. One wonders what they mean.

In another study McClelland (1955b) reported tests of some hypotheses arising from M. Weber's classic description of the nature and consequences of the protestant reformation. Weber had pointed out that the protestant revolt was a shift from reliance upon the Catholic church as an institution to greater reliance upon the self, so far as salvation was concerned. Weber's description of the kind of personality which the protestant reformation developed is strikingly similar to McClelland's picture of a person with a high level of achievement motivation.

Weber showed that the protestant reformation is associated with economic and technological developments. To explain this relation McClelland postulated a series of events relating to self-reliance:

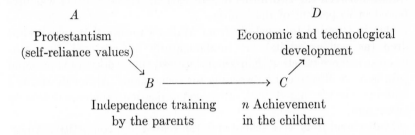

A

Protestantism
(self-reliance values)

D

Economic and technological
development

$B \longrightarrow C$

Independence training n Achievement
by the parents   in the children

Weber had been concerned mainly with the relation between A and D, but McClelland, assuming Weber to be factually correct, investigated the relations between A and B, B and C, and C and D. He concluded that the higher economic and technological development of protestant countries is dependent upon high achievement motivation in the citizens and that this motivation, in turn, rests upon independence training of the children in protestant homes. Thus the need to achieve has had important social consequences.

Competition and Cooperation

In a well-planned experiment, Maller (1929) contrasted working for personal gain (self-motivation) with working for the advantage of one's group (group-motivation). The former is egocentric and utilizes primarily the self-interest and self-seeking of individuals. The latter is social in the sense that the subject is required to work for the gain of a group to which he belongs. These two forms of motivation were compared separately and also when opposed to each other in a conflict situation.

Various groups of school children were formed comprising members of the same class, arbitrarily selected teams, voluntary partnerships, boys and girls. Different groups were made to compete against each other. The task was working problems in addition that were printed on sheets handed to the subjects. With *self-motivation* individuals competed for a prize. The score for an individual was the number of examples correctly added. With *group-motivation* prizes were awarded to the winning groups. The score was the total number of correct additions by the group.

In general, Maller found that the efficiency of work was consistently and significantly higher with *self-motivation* than with *group motivation*. Moreover, when conditions were arranged so that children could choose between the two forms of motivation, *self-motivation* was preferred in 75 percent of the choices.

One is tempted to conclude from Maller's results that school children (as well as adults) are fundamentally self-centered, that self-interest is more effective than group interest, that working for personal gain is more effective than working for social gain. Although Maller's findings clearly agree with this generalization, the conclusion is premature.

Maller's subjects were school children reared in a competitive American culture. Crafts et al. (1938), on the basis of anthropological studies, have pointed out that, in other cultures where cooperation is stressed, Maller's results might not be duplicated. The Zuñi Indians, for example, are a highly cooperative people with a pastoral culture. They pay little attention to property, although differences in wealth do exist. The ideal Zuñi is one who cooperates readily in the economic field and in religious ceremonials. Children are taught to be non-aggressive, sober, cooperative in all aspects of group life. Economic competition, as we know it, is frowned upon; greed, avarice, and stinginess are regarded as shameful and repulsive. In such a group *self-motivation* might not be found to be superior. In any event, Maller's conclusion must be regarded as relative to cultural conditions.

Various other experiments have shown that there are marked individual differences in the response to competition and rivalry. Some persons take competition seriously; they become overtense, overeager to win, and their performance is impaired. Other persons show an improved performance in the competitive situation; tension is increased but not to the point of impairment.

In general, a competitive situation has been found to level off the performance within a group. The slow workers tend to be speeded up by competitive attitudes but the fast workers tend to be retarded. Competition thus makes for uniformity of performance within a group of workers. For this reason educational psychologists have been reluctant to recommend rivalry as a suitable incentive for classroom work. Although it accelerates the work of some, it may be unfair to superior pupils by retarding their work.

Why do People Conform?

The individual accepts the ideology and ways of his group without questioning them. The small child believes what he is told; he does what others do. Unless something makes him doubt, the individual simply accepts the world surrounding him. People have a trait of "primitive credulity," as Alexander Bain called it many years ago.

A partial answer lies in the fact that children are taught to conform by parents, teachers, priests, playmates, and others. The system of education, in home and school and church, supports the moral code and the ways of the land. Further, people are influenced towards conformity by communications—through papers and books, radio and television, movies, and other channels—to act as most people do or as the "best" people do.

Rewards and punishments play an important part in training the individual to conform to his groups. A child is praised and given other social recognition for conformity; he is punished for lack of conformity. If a man breaks the laws of the land, he must face the consequences: a fine, an imprisonment, isolation from the group, and perhaps even the death penalty. If a man violates the moral code, he is ostracized or subjected to ridicule. If he defies the authority of the church, he wins the disfavor of believers; in earlier centuries he might have to face the inquisition as a heretic. In a word, conformity and obedience are rewarded; lack of conformity and disobedience are punished.

When an individual tests the social reality surrounding him he is made aware of the beliefs, opinions, attitudes, and motives, of others. He seeks to be accepted, recognized, appreciated by his groups. He wishes to affiliate himself with certain "good" or "best" groups. Consequently he is inclined to agree and conform.

Again, it is much easier to follow the beaten path than to strike out upon a new road; it is easier to believe than to doubt and think. To follow the accepted path involves less effort, less expenditure of energy, than to strike out on one's own. Although there are non-conformists in every society, the majority of people simply accept the norms of their group.

The question "Why do people conform?" can thus be answered in several ways. We are credulous by nature. We are taught to conform. We are rewarded for conformity and punished for lack of conformity. We conform because we wish to be accepted by a group. Conformity is easier, requires less effort, than non-conformity. There are doubtless other factors that lead people to conform to the social norms and patterns of their groups.

MOTIVATION AS A PERSONALITY VARIABLE

Personality factors are determined largely by the experiences of an individual who develops within a sociocultural world. Although these factors lie within the individual, they depend upon the sociocultural environment.

There are many phases and aspects of the study of motivation and personality. The complexity of the topic is revealed by the writings of Gordon Allport (1937), Murray (1938), McClelland (1951), Newcomb (1953), Guilford (1959), Cattell (1957), Atkinson (1958), and others.

It does not follow that, because students of personality and social behavior have introduced many words—*need, interest, erg, value, loyalty, attitude, motive,* etc.—there is a discrete psychological mechanism for each category. As a matter of fact these and related terms overlap in meaning and the question is still open as to how many separate categories are required by the facts. In so far as these terms imply something dynamic they belong within the broad area of motivation.

The following sections are concerned with several of these dynamic concepts.

Murray's System of Needs

Murray (1938) has made the concept of need (symbolized by *n*) one of central importance in his system of dynamics. His views were influenced by psychoanalysts (Freud, Jung, Adler) and by McDougall and Lewin; but details of his system are the result of his own extensive work and the work of associates.

Murray writes: "A need is a construct (a convenient fiction or hypothetical concept) which stands for a force (the physico-chemical nature of which is unknown) in the brain region, a force which organizes perception, apperception, intellection, conation and action in such a way as to transform in a certain direction an existing, unsatisfying situation."

He distinguished two kinds of needs: viscerogenic (primary) and psychogenic (secondary). The viscerogenic needs include the needs for air, water, food, sex, lactation, urination, and defecation—all of which have a known physiological basis. The need for food, Murray explains, could be broken down into separate needs for different kinds of foods. The viscerogenic needs also include harm avoidance, nox-avoidance, heat avoidance, cold avoidance, and sentience. The last (sentience) includes the needs for sensuous gratification as contact, taste sensation, tactile sensation, e.g., as seen in thumb sucking.

The viscerogenic needs can be grouped in a number of ways. The grouping in Table 8 calls for division of the need for air into two needs: the need for inspiration and the need for expiration.

TABLE 8

CLASSIFICATION OF VISCEROGENIC (PRIMARY) NEEDS

A. *Lacks* (leading to intakes)
  1. n Inspiration (oxygen)
  2. n Water
  3. n Food
  4. n Sentience
B. *Distensions* (leading to outputs)
  Secretion (life sources)
    5. n Sex
    6. n Lactation
	Positive

Excretion (waste)
  7. n Expiration (carbon dioxide)
  8. n Urination
  9. n Defecation
C. *Harms* (leading to retractions)
  10. n Noxavoidance
  11. n Heat avoidance
  12. n Cold avoidance
  13. n Harm avoidance
	Negative

After Murray (1938).

Murray also recognizes a need for passivity (not listed in the tab-ulation) which includes needs for relaxation, rest, and sleep.

Psychogenic needs, Murray states, are derived from the primary viscerogenic needs. The list is longer and the needs are more complex. Twenty-eight psychogenic, or secondary, needs are listed below with greatly abbreviated descriptions:

1. *n* Acquisition: to gain possessions and property; to grasp, snatch or steal things; to bargain or gamble; to work for money or goods.

2. *n* Conservance: to collect, repair, clean and preserve things; to protect against damage.

3. *n* Order: to arrange, organize, put away objects; to be tidy and clean; to be scrupulously precise.

4. *n* Retention: to retain possession of things; to refuse to give or lend; to hoard; to be frugal, economical and miserly.

5. *n* Construction: to organize and build.

6. *n* Superiority: what is commonly called ambition, will-to-power, desire for accomplishment and prestige. The following three needs are subordinate to or components of *n* Superiority:

> A. *n* Achievement: to overcome obstacles; to exercise power; to strive to do something difficult as well and as quickly as possible.
>
> B. *n* Recognition: to excite praise and commendation; to demand respect; to seek distinction, social prestige, honors or high office.
>
> C. *n* Exhibition: to attract attention; to excite, amuse, stir, shock, thrill others.

7. *n* Inviolacy: to prevent depreciation of self-respect; to be immune from criticism; to maintain psychological distance. The *n* Inviolacy has been broken into the following three needs:

> A. *n* Infavoidance: to avoid failure, shame, humiliation, ridicule; to conceal a disfigurement.
>
> B. *n* Defendence: to defend oneself against blame or belittlement; to justify one's actions; to offer excuses; to resist probing.
>
> C. *n* Counteraction: proudly to overcome defeat by restriving or retaliating; to defend one's honor in action.

8. *n* Dominance: to influence or control others; to persuade, prohibit, dictate; to lead and direct; to organize the behavior of a group.

9. *n* Deference: to admire and willingly follow a leader; to serve gladly.

10. *n* Similance: to empathize; to imitate or emulate; to identify with others; to agree and believe.

11. *n* Autonomy: to resist influence or coercion; to defy an authority or seek freedom in a new place; to strive for independence.

12. *n* Contrarience: to act differently from others; to be unique; to take the opposite side; to hold unconventional views.

13. *n* Aggression: to assault or injure another; to murder; to belittle, harm, blame, accuse or ridicule a person; to punish severely. Sadism.

14. *n* Abasement: to surrender; to comply and accept punishment; to apologize, confess, atone; to depreciate one's self. Masochism.

15. *n* Blameavoidance: to avoid blame, ostracism or punishment by inhibiting asocial or unconventional impulses; to be well-behaved and obey the law.

16. *n* Affiliation: to form friendships and associations; to greet, join, and live with others; to cooperate and converse sociably with others.

17. *n* Rejection: to snub, ignore, or exclude another; to remain aloof and indifferent; to be discriminating.

18. *n* Nurturance: to nourish, aid, or protect a helpless person; to express sympathy; to mother a child.

19. *n* Succorance: to seek aid, protection or sympathy; to cry for help; to plead for mercy; to adhere to a nurturant parent.

20. *n* Play: to relax, amuse oneself, seek diversion and entertainment; to play games, laugh, joke, and be merry.

21. *n* Cognizance: to explore; to look, listen, inspect; to satisfy curiosity; to ask questions and seek knowledge.

22. *n* Exposition: to point and demonstrate; to give information, explain, interpret, lecture.

One difficulty with Murray's elaborate system of needs is that it does not specify the criteria by means of which needs can be defined. We have previously pointed out (pages 124-125) that there are several possible criteria for defining organic needs objectively: homeostasis, survival, growth, reproduction, health (resistance to bacteria), etc. If the criterion is stated the need can be defined by reference to the criterion. An organism needs water *to maintain homeostasis*, needs oxygen *to survive*, needs vitamin D *for "normal" growth*, vitamin A *for "normal" vision*, vitamin E *for reproduction*, etc. But what are the criteria for defining personal and social needs?

One can think of possible criteria, such as: being accepted by the group, conforming to group ways, security within the group, recognition, etc. But these criteria are arbitrary and lack precise objective definition. It may be possible to define social needs objectively but this writer does not know how to do so.

Analysis of Human Interests

Interests are activities which one carries on repeatedly and consistently for their own sake. Apart from appetitive behavior, which is clearly determined by organic states, human beings manifest a wide variety of interests. There are interests in golfing, stamp collecting, dramatics, singing, gardening, social service, writing poetry, bridge, cabinet making, costume, perfume, and the like. The world is interesting, as Woodworth expressed it, not merely because it affords us food and shelter, but because we contain within ourselves adaptations to many of its objective characteristics. In dealing with these characteristics we are aroused to interesting activities, quite apart from the satisfaction of primary biological needs.

Aversions are negative interests. An aversion is accompanied by unpleasant feeling and a tendency to avoid an activity or object. For example, if one has an aversion to calculus, one will if possible avoid the solving of problems that involve calculus. The terms *like* and *dislike* refer to interests and aversions. They mark the positive and negative poles of an interest continuum.

Various tests of interest have been devised. They have been used extensively in vocational counseling and guidance. The better known are Strong's vocational interest test and the Kuder preference record.

Guilford et al. (1953, 1954) made an analysis of human interests with the method of factor analysis. They began by surveying general studies of motivation and formulating a tentative list of interests such as interests in adventure, esthetic expression, business, physical activity, science, thinking, and verbal expression. The original list proposed thirty-three hypothetical interests. It was a fairly comprehensive set of dimensions of interest within the wide domain of human motivation.

For each of the thirty-three hypothetical interests they listed subsidiary interests. For example, under "esthetic expression" they listed interests in drama, graphic arts, literature, and music. Then for each subsidiary interest they prepared a ten-item test.

The specific items of the test were of different general types. Some items required the examinee to state whether or not he would like to participate in a specific activity such as "hunt elk in Wyoming," "build a brick wall" or "operate a bulldozer." Other items were descriptive of personal traits. The examinee was asked whether he agrees or disagrees with such statements as "You avoid rough or dangerous games" or "You are usually one of the quiet ones when in a group." Still other items tested attitudes and beliefs. The examinee was asked to approve or disapprove such propositions as "Woman's place is only in the home" or "Children should be firmly disciplined when they disobey their parents."

Projective items were introduced wherever needed and appropriate. To illustrate, if we ask a person "Are you painstaking about your work?" he is likely to say "Yes," whether he is actually painstaking or not, because he wants to make a good impression. But if we ask, instead, "Do you admire people who are painstaking about their work?" he can readily say "No," without necessarily realizing that he has revealed something about himself.

The interest inventory was administered to four samples of Air Force personnel at the Lackland Air Force Base, including 600 airmen, 276 officer candidates, 257 AFROTC, and 187 air cadets. This was a large but selected group.

Not all of the original thirty-three hypothetical interest factors were verified by the factor analysis probably because there were not enough test items for some of them. The following fourteen were verified: mechanical interest; scientific interest; adventure vs. security; social welfare; esthetic appreciation; esthetic expression; diversion, need for; attention, need for; business interest; outdoor-work interest; physical drive; precision; thinking; orderliness vs. disorderliness.

It will be seen that some of the factors are bipolar, e.g., "adventure vs. security." An interest in adventure is opposed to an interest in security. Others are unipolar, e.g., "mechanical interest." There appear to be no activities that are opposite in kind to mechanical activity. This difference between bipolar and unipolar interests may be a statistical artifact because, obviously, there is a psychological continuum between the poles of liking and disliking mechanical, or any other, activity.

Probably the selection of test items for the inventory had a good deal to do with the factors discovered by the statistical analysis. For example, items relating to religious interest were intentionally omitted. As a result no factor of religious interest was discovered. The method of factor analysis takes out pretty much what the investigator puts in.

The interest analysis of Guilford et al. was not oriented towards specific vocational interests. It was, instead, quite general and comprehensive. Nevertheless some of the interest factors discovered are relevant to vocational and occupational pursuits. To test for vocational or other interests one must put pertinent and specific items into the inventory but this was not done in the present study. The structure of the interest domain can be pictured as having a large number of basic, generalized dimensions that cut across many vocational lines. Specific tests for vocational interests have, of course, been developed.

In the above list of factors some are more appropriately called *needs* than interests, e.g., the need for diversion and the need for attention. Others are more appropriately called *traits of personality*, e.g., physical drive, precision, orderliness vs. disorderliness. Since the original hypotheses were derived from a variety of sources (Cattell, Dunlap, McDougall, Murray, Thorndike, Young), it is not surprising to find diversity in the kinds of factors discovered by factor analysis. A very fundamental question can be raised as to how, in fact, interests are related to needs, traits of personality, attitudes, beliefs, and other psychological categories.

Ergs, Sentiments, Attitudes

Cattell (1957) speaks of ergs, sentiments, and attitudes.

Examples of ergic-drive structures are: sex erg, gregariousness, parental protectiveness, exploration (curiosity), escape (fear, need for security), self-assertion, narcissistic sex erg. These, in general, are somewhat similar to McDougall's instincts.

Examples of sentiments are: the sentiment for a specific profession (air force), sentiments for sports and games, the religious sentiment, mechanical sentiment or interest, material interest, the self-sentiment. In everyday language, sentiments refer to conscious feelings. In the psychology of Shand, McDougall, and others, sentiments refer to complex dispositions, acquired through individual experience, that underlie feelings and ideas.

Cattell's use of the term *attitude* includes the notion of *wanting*. This is shown in the following paradigm which defines an attitude:

"In these circumstances	I	want so much	to do this	with that."
(stimulus situation)	(organism)	(interest-need of a certain intensity)	(specific goal, *course of action*)	(object concerned in action)

The paradigm emphasizes the dynamic aspect of an attitude. It makes *attitude* equivalent to *motive* or *intention* to act. Intentions, of course, are individual determinants of action; they are innumerable and very specific. Attitudes, according to Thurstone, are pro or con; but intentions are not necessarily pro or con.

These motivations of human action were discovered by factor analysis. Writes Cattell: "It has taken many years of development of factor-analytic methods, adaptively applied to personality, together with conceptual advances in motivation measurement, to produce the evidence that drive patterns exist in man, and that they correspond with unmistakable parallelism to those intuited by clinicians like Freud and Murray, on the one hand, and naturalists like McDougall and Darwin on the other."

With all his fluency and mathematical analysis Cattell is not physiological. Bodily processes like muscle tonus can be observed; ergic tensions are inferred. Sex hormones and their effects upon behavior can be observed; a sex erg is inferred. Brain waves can be observed; sentiments and attitudes are inferred. For the physiologist, dynamic processes are energy transformations (physical) within the tissues of an organism. The *erg* is a dynamic concept but not a physiological process.

Cattell's dynamic traits of personality lack a bodily mechanism. Some day, perhaps, dynamic traits and bodily mechanisms will be brought into relation with each other; but this has not yet been accomplished.

I do not see any ultimate contradiction between physiological analysis and the factor analytical approach to the study of motivation; but the two are different. They are as different as roses and doughnuts—but both exist within the same world.

The Study of Values

If a person values something, he is willing to work and to spend money for it. He thinks it is worth while.

All of us have standards of evaluation. We judge things in terms of right or wrong, good or bad, true or false, beautiful or ugly, etc. We judge human conduct in terms of strength or weakness, morality or immorality, and we take account of such values as efficiency, power, safety, possessing goods, respect, heroism, mercy, loyalty, etc. Our standards of value are related to the goals of life. People value money, love, social position, advancement in a career, health, happiness, power, fame, reputation, prestige, rightness, religion, and other ends.

What a person *values* is not necessarily the same as what he *wants*. It has been said that a value is what a person *ought* to want and not necessarily what he actually wants. A person may fail to measure up to the norm of what he *ought* to be and to do.

Philosophers have written many volumes about value. Spranger (1928) argued that personality can best be known through a study of values. He described six main types of man, corresponding to six dominant values.

1. The *theoretical* man has a dominant interest in the discovery of truth for its own sake. He is an intellectual—a man of science or a philosopher.

2. The *economic* man is characteristically interested in what is useful and practical. He is interested in the business world—in production, distribution, and consumption of goods, and in the accumulation of wealth.

3. The *esthetic* man finds his highest value in beauty—in form and harmony. He may be a painter, a musician, a poet.

4. The *social* man values people. He has a love of people, which may be conjugal, filial, friendly, or philanthropic.

5. The *political* man places a high value upon power. He seeks to dominate others not necessarily in politics but in any and all human relations.

6. The *religious* man is a mystic who seeks to comprehend the unity of the cosmos; or he may be an ascetic who finds the experience of unity through meditation and self-denial.

No person is dominated by just one kind of value to the exclusion of the others; in everyone there is a mixture. Within a given person the above values have different weights, or relative influence.

Allport, Vernon, and Lindzey (1960) devised a test of values based upon Spranger's philosophical work. In taking the test the subject is instructed to choose between two items as in this example:

The main object of scientific research should be the discovery of pure truth rather than its practical applications. (*a*) Yes; (*b*) No.

If a person checks *Yes*, he has placed theoretical value ahead of economic. If he checks *No*, he has placed economic value ahead of theoretical. Of course, there is no objectively correct answer; it is all a matter of the subject's evaluation. The procedure forces the subject to make a choice but he may not be aware of the fact that his choice reveals relative values.

Consider this item (which is not in the test):

Should all of the water that goes over Niagara Falls be removed to generate electric power for the State of New York when this would destroy the beauty of Niagara? (*a*) Yes; (*b*) No.

Individuals who answer *Yes* have placed economic value ahead of esthetic; those who answer *No* have placed esthetic value first. The choice or preference reveals relative values.

With this type of item the Allport-Vernon-Lindzey test of values reveals, for each subject, a value profile which shows the relative importance of the main types of value for the individual. The test has been extensively used, criticized, and revised, but space will not permit further details.

Human values are acquired through experience. The individual learns to conform to society, to judge according to the standards of his group. He learns to discriminate between what is beneficial and harmful, useful and useless, practical and impractical, beautiful and ugly, true and false, right and wrong. He acquires these evaluative dispositions from his social world through a process of social learning.

A psychologist would like to discover how evaluative dispositions develop and upon what they rest. Chandler (1934) argued that most forms of esthetic value rest upon affective experience. The value of a painting rests upon the enjoyment of colors and forms. In music, pleasantness is derived from tones, harmonies, melodies and rhythms. In the dance, delight is from free rhythmic expression and graceful movement. In the culinary art, the value of food rests upon pleasing flavors (odors, tastes, tactual qualities). A primitive form of evaluation is simply expressing the attitude of liking or disliking the object evaluated.

On the level of animal behavior, repeated tests of preference show that foods arrange themselves in a hierarchy or transitive series from low to high palatability. This preferential series is a value system. We know from experiments that a rat's system of values is relatively stable provided dietary conditions are stable. Groups of rats maintained consistently upon the same diet tend to develop similar patterns of value. If the diet is disturbed by removal of an essential component, the value system gradually changes.

Philosophers have argued that science deals with facts and not with values; but if values, in some sense or other, are determinants of human behavior, the science of psychology must take account of them. Guilford (1959) regards the values that are revealed by the Allport-Vernon-Lindzey test as broad interest categories. If he is correct, we do not need two categories—value and interest—but only one.

Loyalties

Another closely related category is that of loyalty. Guetzkow (1955) defined a loyalty as: "An attitude predisposing its holder to respond toward an idea, person, or group with actions perceived by the holder to be supportive of, and/or with feelings which value the continued existence of, the object toward which the attitude is directed." Thus the patriotic citizen shows loyalty to his nation-state. The martyr shows loyalty to his religion. The ship's captain who goes down with the ship shows loyalty to a certain tradition.

The concept of loyalty is of major importance in dealing with problems of international tension. A person has multiple loyalties— simultaneous attitudes towards different objects. Thus, a citizen who is loyal to his nation-state is also loyal to an international order. It has been said that a man who is a loyal nationalist may become the best international civil servant because he has learned to support a social institution. As a member of the Secretariat of the United Nations he knows how to be loyal to the collective group.

Multiple loyalties may conflict. A man may be called upon to demonstrate his loyalty to his nation-state by abandoning his family. When loyalties conflict there are various ways of resolving the conflict. Guetzkow has noted the following:

1. *Non-perception.* When loyalties conflict within an individual a possible solution is simply not to see the contradiction. The history of ethics is full of tortuous attempts to untangle the implications of conflicting loyalties. For example, there have been controversies over loyalty to the church *versus* loyalty to the state. Moralists have pondered these contradictions but the average citizen fails to perceive inconsistencies between conflicting loyalties.

From the psychological point of view, it is clear that loyalty is determined by perception and not by objective reality. This explains why patriots in different nation-states are equally convinced of the appropriateness of their behavior when their conduct leads to war and disaster.

2. *Forming compartments.* When the contradictions in behavior demanded by conflicting loyalties are neither severe nor pervasive, the individual can place the loyalties in separate mental compartments. Thus, the average citizen is not greatly disturbed by the difference between the ethical principles which he teaches on Sunday and the principles which he applies in his business on Monday. Again, a war

profiteer is not inwardly tense when he attends a patriotic rally. The contradictions are not felt because they are not allowed to clash. There is functional dissociation.

3. *Narrowing of functions.* By conceiving the functions of conflicting groups as restricted, simultaneous loyalty roles may be perceived as not overlapping. For example, by defining his national group as properly functioning in the area of defense but not as legitimately concerned with the production of synthetic rubber, a citizen may be loyal to his nation-state and to his business of producing synthetic rubber.

4. *Redefinition.* By regarding the behavior demanded by one loyalty to be the same as that demanded by a conflicting loyalty, tension is reduced. Thus, an individual may define "being a good American" as identical with "being a good white man." Loyalty to America becomes identified with loyalty to the white racial group.

These devices help relieve the tension when loyalties conflict. But occasionally the conflict between loyalties becomes so severe that one must become dominant and the other necessarily abandoned. When a nation demands "supreme" loyalty from its citizens, that relieves the conflict with other loyalties by making national loyalty dominant. A religion may demand exclusive loyalty to God. The average citizen may solve the conflict between loyalty to state and loyalty to God by accepting loyalty to the state as "supreme". One loyalty must be abandoned or subordinated (in which event it is no longer "supreme").

Sociologists have long recognized in-groups and out-groups. The in-groups share a common loyalty to their organization and often a common hostility to some out-group. The mere recognition of an out-group may strengthen the loyalty and solidarity of the in-group. If we ask, "What is *loyalty* to a group?" the answer involves something more than an attitude. The individual is identified with the group to which he is loyal. There is an element of ego involvement. He has positive feelings towards his group.

Conclusion

Psychological tests and measurements of needs, interests, ergs, values, loyalties, attitudes, motives, and the like, do not reveal bodily mechanisms of motivation. They yield descriptive generalizations through the study of individual and group differences.

The physiologist, in contrast with the student of personality, deals directly with energy transformations within the tissues—with physical and chemical events. It must be admitted, however, that such energy transformations are purely physical. As such, they do not have any meaningful reference to objects and events in the socio-cultural environment. They have no reference to conscious experience but are purely physical events—nothing more. But needs, interests, ergs, values, loyalties, attitudes, motives, and the like, are described directly in external, situational, terms—not as energy transformations within the tissues.

The student of personality, therefore, has an approach to problems of motivation that is very different from that of the physiologist.

It can be argued that the study of personality traits through tests and measurements, combined with mathematical analysis, yields a descriptive psychology of human behavior within its concrete social setting. How do people act? How do they feel? What are their interests, value systems, goals? Such questions can be answered, as we have seen. But the answers are descriptive generalizations and not an account of truly dynamic mechanisms.

ORIENTATION AND ATTITUDE

If we are to understand the social behavior of man, we must under-stand not only the structure of the social world, as independently defined by the sociologist, but also the world as apprehended and comprehended by the individual. The problem of understanding social behavior becomes one of analyzing the *cognitive* and *affective* com-ponents of experience and the attitudes, or orientations, that underlie them.

Orientation and attitude are closely related concepts. Perhaps they are synonymous. They are intimately related to the direction and regulation of behavior within the social setting.

Orientation in a Social Setting

Newcomb (1953) believes that an adequate theory of social motiva-tion must take account of the great variety of interpersonal orienta-tions that are known to exist. There are orientations toward one's self, toward other persons, toward objects and social institutions. To inter-pret social behavior in relation to these diverse orientations is a basic task for social psychology.

There are various terms that designate orientation: *disposition, set, attitude,* and the like. They refer to some bit of organization, within the nervous system, that regulates action and experience. In social psychology, however, the regulative organization is not pictured in neural terms but rather in terms of the various persons and objects toward which the subject is oriented.

In the simplest social structure there are at least two individuals (*A, B*) in dynamic interaction. If *A* and *B* are communicating, for example, there is a common object (*X*) about which they are communicating. The interrelations can be diagrammed thus:

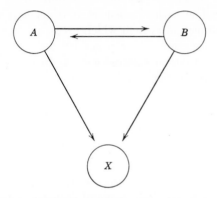

A has an orientation toward *B*, toward himself, and toward the object *X*. Similarly, *B* has an orientation toward *A*, toward himself, and toward the object *X*. It is necessary to understand these orientations toward one's self, toward another person, and toward the common object, for a sound grasp of the nature of motivation within the social context.

Prior to communication, *A* and *B* may have similar orientations toward *X*. After communication the orientation may change. The communication may lead to a change in the orientation of either individual toward *X* or toward the other person. During communication, *A* may change his orientation to agree with that of *B*; or *A* may change from a positive to a negative orientation toward *B* without changing his orientation toward *X*. *A* may refuse to consider *X* and thus "leave the field" by a process of cognitive dissociation.

Thus, Newcomb argues, social behavior can be analyzed, in detail and specifically, from the point of view of the interplay of orientations. The analysis is fundamental and important.

In all orientations, Newcomb points out, there are two basic aspects: *cognitive* and *cathectic*. The cognitive aspect is what we know or believe or imagine; such knowledge is based upon perception and upon past experience. The cathectic aspect refers to action—to arousal, or activation. An orientation includes always a readiness to do something with respect to the object.

The distinction between cognitive and cathectic aspects of orientation has been recognized by many psychologists. There is, moreover, an objective, physiological basis for the distinction. The cognitive aspect is based ultimately upon perception and depends upon sensory excitations from receptors through thalamic relay centers to the cerebral cortex. The cathectic aspect is dependent upon excitations *via* the diffuse projection system which excite the cortex without conveying usable information. (See pages 101-103.)

Newcomb states that no existing general theory of motivation has taken account of interpersonal relatedness. The implication is that to formulate an adequate theory of motivation one must start from analysis of dynamic interpersonal relations. If this can be done adequately, social psychology will have something to contribute to the general theory of motivation. The following gains might be expected from a study of orientation within the social setting:

1. A general theory of motivation, worked out from a social point of view, would add to our knowledge of *incentive variables*. There is much yet to be learned about incentive motivation, including such factors as social recognition, praise and reproof, rewards and punishments in the social setting, feedback of information, etc.

2. A study of social behavior can contribute a rich source of data upon *expectancies*. The development of expectancy theory is a prime task for contemporary psychology, Newcomb believes.

3. Newcomb suggests that a study of *coorientations* (similar orientations in different persons) should contribute much to a general theory of motivation. Coorientations can be studied in relation to the many problems of communication.

4. The study of *self-orientation* (self-regarding attitudes) should contribute to the general theory of motivation. Self-orientations are part and parcel of other-orientations. They are inextricable from the above triangle of self, other person, and common environmental object.

A general theory of motivation, when it becomes mature enough to include the interdependent orientations, will have borrowed from the special theory of motivation within the social setting, and the general theory will also help to establish the special theory.

The Nature of Attitudes

What Newcomb means by *orientation* is equivalent to what other social psychologists have meant by *attitude*. There are two words but only one set of neural machinery that regulates and directs behavior.

An attitude may be defined as a readiness of the individual to react toward or against a psychological object to a particular degree and in a certain pattern. The different points in this definition will be considered in detail.

1. An attitude is a readiness of the individual to react. This refers to a relatively permanent disposition that has been acquired through experience and that is regulative and directive.

2. The readiness to react is positive or negative in sign. Attitudes are toward or against, pro or con, approving or disapproving, accepting or rejecting, favorable or unfavorable, liking or disliking. This does not mean that attitudes are affective processes. Feelings and emotions play an important part in the organization of attitudes but are not to be confused with the attitudes themselves. An attitude is a disposition that may be aroused or remain latent; it is not a process.

3. The object of an attitude is something psychological—not a physical thing. An individual may have an attitude toward a specific person, a specific kind of food, a specific musical composition. In fact, an attitude may be assumed toward anything under heaven or earth. An individual may have an attitude toward a political idea, a system of government, a religion, a race, or any idea that can be expressed. This is what is meant by the phrase "psychological object."

4. Attitudes differ in degree, or intensity. One may approve weakly or disapprove strongly. One may love or hate intensely. There is thus a quantitative, or intensive, aspect of attitudes. It is this that makes possible the measurement of attitudes. Attitudes, of course, can be indifferent. They may be indifferent if the psychological object is of little personal importance and concern.

5. Attitudes differ in pattern or kind. The point is important but sometimes overlooked by those who would like to arrange attitudes along a continuum from extreme approval to extreme disapproval. There are attitudes of love and hate, of fear and courage (anti-fear),

of resentment, disgust, curiosity, amusement, friendliness and hostility, etc. These different kinds of attitudes can be pictured as different forms of orientation.

The psychoanalyst, Horney, once put it this way: We can react *towards* people with friendliness and love or *against* people with hostility and hatred or *away from* people with fear and anxiety. To this I might add that we can react *along with* people with cooperation and helpfulness. Perhaps the patterns of attitudes are based upon biologically primitive patterns of response: hostile attack, fear avoidance, sexual approach, hunger approach, disgust, observant approach, etc.

There are a few other points concerning the nature of attitudes that should be added:

6. Attitudes may be latent or activated. Suppose, for example, that a friend asks you a specific question: Do you approve of Communism? You unhesitatingly reply: "No." The question aroused in you a bit of neural organization that was previously quiescent. Your attitude against Communism remains latent for indefinite periods but it is revealed by a certain question. The question energizes you and the attitude—whether latent or activated—regulates and directs the response.

In one respect a latent attitude differs from a latent intention to act (motive). If I have determined to take a trip 1 week hence, this determination from time to time arouses tension within me and ultimately action. The latent attitude, by contrast, cannot be described as a plan for action. In this respect it is more like the latent habit organization that underlies acts of skill.

7. Social attitudes, like habit structures, are learned. They are acquired through experience. Thus, a white child growing up in the deep South may acquire anti-Negro attitudes from parents and playmates. A child growing up in the North is less likely to acquire anti-Negro attitudes.

8. Finally, attitude tests have made it possible to discover the extent to which a particular attitude is shared by members of a group and to investigate shifts in the attitudes of a group dependent upon some experience such as a bit of news, a radio broadcast, a motion picture film, or some factor in propaganda and advertising. The collective approach, of course, disregards the nature of attitude as a determinant within the individual.

Attitude Structure and Affectivity

It is generally agreed that an attitude has two main aspects—cognitive and affective. The cognitive component is defined as the set of beliefs (held by a person) about the value-attaining and value-blocking powers of the attitude object viewed as an instrumental agency. For example, in justifying his negative affect toward Negroes moving into white neighborhoods a man might contend that this would lead to discord and violence, would foster miscegenation and that it would lower the worth of property. The affective component is defined as the pattern of feeling regularly aroused by the presence of the psychological object. An example would be the complex of hate, anger, loathing, and condescension felt by a person when he reads, hears or thinks about Negroes moving into white neighborhoods.

An attitude has both positive and negative affective components. For example, a man believes that desegregation recognizes the equal rights of citizens. This he likes because he believes in democracy and fair play. But he also believes that if Negroes move into his neighborhood and send their children to school, he would lose status for he feels that white people are superior to Negroes. This belief that status would be lost has negative affectivity. The total attitude toward desegregation is thus a complex of intertangled meanings and feelings.

Peak (1955) has shown that disparity within an attitude may be cognitive or affective or both. When disparity exists there is a tendency toward consistency between the affective and cognitive components.

Abelson and Rosenberg (1958) classified the cognitive elements of attitudes into three categories: actors, means, ends. These categories may be illustrated from statements made by Yale students about the issue: "Having an honor system at Yale." The elements reflect a "thing-like" character:

Actors: myself, the Faculty, the Administration, the Student Body, a certain minority of students, the honest student....
Means: the honor system, other honor systems, the present examination system, cheating, reporting those who cheat, social pressure from other students....
Ends: the feeling of being trusted, mature moral standards, loyalty to friends, the University's reputation, having well-run examinations....

If such cognitive elements are arranged in the form of a matrix, the relation between any two of them can be expressed as: ArB, where A and B are elements and r is a relation. Many such sentences can be formed. The relation may be one of liking and approval (positive) or one of disliking and disapproval (negative) or one of indifference (null). Other relations also are possible. If the affective elements are entered in the matrix, the result is a representation of the cognitive and affective structure of an attitude. This is a psychological structure which may serve as a starting point for the mathematical analysis of attitudinal cognition.

In further studies, Rosenberg (personal communication) showed how attitude structures can be changed. A basic postulate is that when affective and cognitive components of an attitude are mutually consistent the attitude is in a stable state; but when affective and cognitive components are mutually inconsistent the attitude is in an unstable state and will undergo reorganization until there is affective-cognitive consistency. An attitude may be changed either by altering the cognitive structure or the affective elements of the structure. Cognitive structure may be changed by introducing new perceptions or knowledge. For example, if it can be demonstrated that property values will not necessarily decline when Negroes move into a neighborhood, then feelings about desegregation will change. To change the affective elements of an attitude Rosenberg relied upon hypnotic suggestion.

Under hypnosis subjects who were opposed to desegregation were given these instructions:

> When you awake you will be very much in favor of Negroes moving into white neighborhoods. The mere idea of Negroes moving into white neighborhoods will give you a happy, exhilarated feeling. You will have no memory of this suggestion having been made until the signal to remember is given.

The instruction conveyed no information. The subject was simply commanded to *feel* differently toward the object of his attitude. The post-hypnotic effect of this suggestion was tested and highly significant changes in feeling and belief were demonstrated. Beliefs about desegregation were changed to make them consistent with the new feeling.

The effect of hypnotic suggestion was tested with eleven subjects. In general, attitudinal affective-cognitive inconsistency was produced through the suggestion of affect reversal. The subjects showed significantly more change in their *beliefs* about the object of the attitude than did a control group not subjected to hypnotic suggestion.

THE DYNAMIC SELF-SYSTEM

One mental system of great psychological importance is the system of ideas and values that centers around the self. This system has developed from social interaction. In the social give and take there develop systems of belief and attitude that relate to the self and others. When we consider such topics as self-esteem, self-defense, self-assertion, self-display, self-abasement, self-reproach, self-consciousness, and the like, it becomes necessary to ask: What is meant by *self?* How do ideas about the self and attitudes towards the self develop? What part does the self-system play in behavior and experience?

Self-knowledge and Self-evaluation

Knowledge about one's self is similar to knowledge about other persons and things. Like all other cognitive systems the knowledge about one's self is a product of development. Self-knowledge is based upon perceptual discriminations, judgments, memories. The self-regarding perceptions, beliefs and attitudes develop and change with experience.

The ego is not a mysterious creature that hovers about the brain. It is an entity in the same sense that any system of experiences is an entity. When an infant is born into the world he does not possess an ego. He gradually develops a cognitive system that refers to himself.

During the early months of life the infant becomes acquainted with his surroundings. He learns to perceive objects—balls, blocks, furniture, toys, and various other things. He observes the size and arrangement of his crib, the kind and amount of nourishment he receives, the faces of people who care for him, the actions of others, and so on. He must learn to distinguish his own active body from other objects in the total milieu. He must learn, for example, to distinguish his foot from his shoe. He is aided by the fact that he moves as a physical unit. Other people regard him as an entity, an organism, and give him a distinctive name.

The growing child learns to evaluate himself in relation to other persons in his group. In the earliest years he sees and hears himself compared with others: John is bigger and stronger than you. He can fight better. He can knock you down. Harry can run faster. Dick can throw a ball farther. Jim has a finer house, a bigger yard, nicer clothes. Joe's folks drive a better car. Bill's father owns a store but your father is only a janitor. It may be the other way about: *You* are the biggest and strongest child in the group. *You* can fight better, run faster than the others. *You* have the bigger house, better car, nicer toys and play equipment. The process of comparison and evaluation goes on and on. In street fights, on the playground, in the class room, at home, this self-versus-other comparison continues endlessly.

An inevitable result is that the child builds up beliefs about himself and attitudes of self-regard. This process of self-knowledge and self-evaluation continues throughout life. Our beliefs and attitudes change with circumstances.

Transformations of the Self-system

The beliefs and attitudes of an adult concerning his own nature are by no means stable. They change with circumstances and there are wide differences, from time to time, in the self concept. Several illustrations of transformation in the self-system will underscore the fact that any definition of the self is arbitrary and relative to circumstances.

First, in all societies it is normal for a child to become an adolescent and grow into adult status. Not only does adolescence mark a transformation of the body of a child into that of an adult but the social roles and responsibilities of the adolescent become increasingly like those of an adult. The youth is forced to reformulate his beliefs concerning his nature and place in the group. The transformations in the concept of the self, at the time of adolescence, are so radical that it is correct to say that a new *self* has emerged from an old. There is a complete metamorphosis.

Second, in times of stress there are often radical changes in behavior, attitude, and personality, bound up with changes in self-evaluation. We sometimes say that a person "does not act like himself" or "a different self has appeared." For example, during World War II, prisoners arriving in German concentration camps attempted to preserve their independence and self-respect but this became impossible with the brutal treatment of the Gestapo. The prisoners were subjected to horrible experiences that completely altered their personality and their definition of the self. In time, people in these camps lost their old allegiances and identifications. In order to survive they gradually accepted new allegiances and identifications more in conformity with standards and practices of the Gestapo. The older prisoners regressed to a childlike relationship in which they cooperated with the Gestapo, took on their ideology, and continued an unhappy existence. Self-respect was gone; a new ego system emerged. There was radical change in perception and in belief and evaluation of the self. A record of the terrible conditions in these camps is preserved in first hand interviews and reports obtained by Boder (1949).

Further examples of transformation in the definition of self can be found in persons suffering some physical change, as in alcoholism, disease, or surgery. Under the influence of alcohol a man may become temporarily freed from his inhibitions. Normally he may be a controlled and serious individual but when drunk he becomes jovial, free and easy with his remarks, "a different person." Again, a patient suffering from a mental disease hears hallucinatory voices and sees visions; his behavior becomes so fragmented and bizarre that we commonly say he is "beside himself," "out of his mind," "unbalanced." Behavior and traits of personality are so radically altered, by the disease condition, that the man no longer acts like the same person. Finally, consider the effects of a surgical operation known as *prefrontal lobotomy*. In this operation connections are severed between the frontal association areas of the brain and lower neural centers. The operation reduces anxiety and leaves the patient more serene and less self-conscious. The operation changes the temperament of the individual to such an extent that he acts like a different person.

From the above illustrations it is clear that the definition and characteristics of the self are dependent upon physical, biological, psychological, and social conditions, and that the characteristics of the self can and sometimes do alter radically with change of circumstances.

Attitudes of Inferiority

If a child happens to have a physical defect—obesity, short stature, unsightly birthmark, crippled limb, deafness—other children make him painfully and repeatedly aware of it. An attitude of personal inferiority may thus be formed which persists indefinitely. The inferiority attitude is based upon frustration of a normal social impulse—to belong to the group, to participate in its activities, to find opportunity for self-expression, and to gain a sense of importance.

Alfred Adler pointed out that attitudes of inferiority may underlie a persistent will to achieve. History provides examples of well-known men with defects who, in compensating for their defects, have achieved greatly: Demosthenes, with a speech impediment, became a great orator; Lord Byron, who had a club foot, wrote immortal poetry; Steinmetz, a cripple, became a wizard of electricity; Kaiser Wilhelm, who had a withered arm, became a military leader, etc. But this is only part of the picture. Attitudes of inferiority can produce emotional disturbances and severe personal maladjustments. A sense of failure can build up an anxiety that is damaging to peace of mind and hampering to one's achievement.

Bagby (1928) made an inventory of the characteristics of people who have attitudes of inferiority. He pointed out that inferiority attitudes are revealed by extreme *sensitiveness to criticism* and especially to ridicule. A person with such an attitude resents any evaluation that puts him in an unfavorable light and he devotes much effort to self-defense. Again, the inferiority attitude is indicated by *ideas of reference*. The subject supposes that any whispered comment is a remark unfavorable to himself and that laughter, even that of strangers, has some personal reference. *Seclusiveness* is likely to be present. He hesitates to join a group, being convinced without evidence that his company is not wanted. Persons with attitudes of inferiority cross the street to avoid meeting people, and in other ways they avoid social contacts. Another manifestation of inferiority attitudes is an *expansive response to flattery*. Since there is need for feelings of adequacy and self-confidence, almost any praise or compliment will be met with a prompt response or over-response. The subject also shows a *peculiar reaction to competition*. Contests are entered with utmost seriousness as real tests of quality. He seeks to compete with persons he can easily defeat, or he may go to the opposite extreme of comparing himself with persons of renowned ability whom he could not possibly defeat. Finally, there is a marked *derogatory tendency*. The person who feels inferior points to the faults of other persons and tends to minimize his own defects. He is highly critical of others.

These symptoms are sometimes present in normal persons but when an abnormally intense attitude of inferiority is present, the above symptoms are exaggerated.

Opposed to attitudes of inferiority are attitudes of pride and conceit. A person may overrate his importance, ability or skill. He may live in a world with a better-than-thou attitude and with feelings of vainglory.

Somewhere between the attitudes of inferiority and conceit is an objective evaluation of one's traits, abilities and skills. The evaluation is based upon knowledge of what one can and cannot do, how one stands in a group, what one's relations are to other persons. It is possible to develop an attitude of self-confidence based upon factual knowledge and objective judgment.

Feelings of Guilt, Shame, Embarrassment

Feelings of guilt, remorse, self-reproach, shame, and embarrassment, involve an element of self-evaluation but the cause of these feelings lies in a discrepancy between the subject's conduct and his awareness of the social code.

If it is customary for the women of a tribe to conceal the face with a veil, a woman feels shame when caught with her face uncovered. Among many primitive peoples it is customary for female breasts to be uncovered and the women feel no shame at the exposure; but in societies that require the breasts to be concealed a feeling of shame is aroused when the breasts are inadvertently exposed. In some tribes the people wear no clothing and they experience no shame over exposure of the genital organs. Among civilized peoples the exposure of the genitals is felt to be indecent and a source of shame.

The clinical literature contains evidence that many a youth has feelings of guilt, remorse, and self-reproach over autoerotic practices and his inability to control the sexual impulses. The youth may have been taught that masturbation is a sin and that the practice is damaging physically, mentally, and morally. With such moral and religious teaching in his background the youth believes that he has sinned. He is filled with reproach for lack of self-control. There is a discrepancy between behavior and the moral code which the youth has accepted.

Among the people of an African tribe, the Monbutto, human flesh is bought and sold as if it were a staple article of food. These people do not feel depressed nor humiliated as a result of the practice. Since cannibalism is socially approved, there is no conscience about the matter. But with most civilized peoples cannibalism is strongly taboo. When the California pioneers were forced to eat human flesh to prevent starvation they averted their faces while eating the flesh thus indicating a sense of guilt.

Embarrassment arises when some social rule of conduct has been violated. Malinowski reports that among the Trobriand Islanders it is commonly believed that parents do not resemble their offspring and children of the same parents do not resemble each other. It is taboo even to hint that a child resembles its mother or any of its maternal kinsfolk. When Malinowski commented upon the striking likeness between two brothers, there was a hush over the assembly; the brother withdrew abruptly and the company was half-embarrassed, half-offended at the breach of etiquette. In this instance a taboo influenced the perception of similarity and difference. Feelings of embarrassment arose from violation of the taboo.

In the above and similar examples the negative self-feelings—guilt, shame, embarrassment—are bound up with social norms which the individual has internalized. There is a discrepancy between actual behavior and the socially "correct" patterns. This is the basis of conscience.

The Freudian View

The ego, or self, enters into psychology in many ways. Freud distinguished among the *id*, *ego*, and *superego*. For him the *id* consisted of blind, primitive impulses, especially the impulses of sex, hostility, and the like, that are unconscious. The *ego* is an agency that reconciles the claims of the *id* with reality, with environmental field forces, and with the *superego*. The *superego* acts as a conscience indicating what is right and wrong.

These agencies, according to Freud, are factors in human conflicts. The superego forces the ego to act in opposition to the id. The ego is thus subjected to pressure from both sides. The ego must reconcile the conflicting claims of id and superego. Beyond serving as umpire among the forces of the id, superego, and *environment*, the ego acts as an executive agent, setting goals, making and keeping promises, discharging obligations, avoiding catastrophic situations. Through the actions of the ego the individual becomes in some measure an effective, reliable, relatively autonomous, human being.

The Freudian terms appear to designate hypothetical (perhaps mythical) agents. Yet no one can question the existence of biological impulses such as sex, hostility, hunger, and thirst (id). Nor can anyone question the existence of social norms and standards of moral conduct. Standards of conduct are accepted, internalized, by the individual and serve as a basis of evaluation (superego). No one can question the existence of real and earnest conflicts between biological impulses and social ideals. Finally, there can be little doubt that to most individuals the self (ego) is about the most important thing in the world. This is true regardless of how psychologists define the self-concept.

Ego-involvement

During the second year of his life, when words begin to be used, the baby talks about himself in the third person: "Baby wants this" or "John wants that." It is later that words like *I, me,* and *mine* develop; the use of *we* comes later than *I.* References to the self and all personal pronouns are learned along with other words and by the same process of acquisition.

When a child first refers to something as *mine*—whether a toy, a pet, a piece of clothing, a parent, or a house—there is said to be ego-involvement. This manner of speech implies some knowledge of the individual as distinct from other individuals and things.

The child claims some place as his own. It may be a play yard or a room in the house or a bed. Even animals claim a territory as their own and defend it against intruders. Adults, too, recognize certain places as their own.

Sherif and Cantril (1947) have described the facts in this way:

The space may be some corner of a room where we have a favorite chair, it may be some glade in the woods to which we make recurrent visits, it may be a barrel in the woodshed we like to sit on in the evening after dinner. Whatever it is, we come to feel that that space is not only ours but it is a part of us. If it is pre-empted by someone else, destroyed, or intruded upon, *we* are annoyed, we feel that *our* privacy, *our* selves have been violated, injured or insulted.

In the normal adult, ego-involvement has developed very far. A man is ego-involved with his family, automobile, home town, profession, church, political party, with various goals and values, etc. He is ready to fight for his property, his rights, his beliefs and convictions. If he has taken a stand, a proposition becomes *his* to defend and he will be loyal to it.

Ego-involvement gives an emotional tinge to certain courses of action. It gives interest and zest to pieces of property, systems of belief, plans for action, or whatever it may be that the individual accepts as belonging to himself.

Ego-involvement is a form of identification. But *identification,* as a psychological concept, has at least three meanings: (1) In one sense a child is said to identify himself with his father or with an older boy or with some individual who serves as a model. Hero worship implies identification in this sense. (2) In another sense we identify ourselves with the characters on the stage or in a novel. We put ourselves in their place and experience their feelings. This has been called empathy. (3) Finally, identification means ego-involvement in the above sense. A man is identified with his clothing, his automobile, his home town, his club, etc. These are *his* things.

Concluding Statement

In general, the psychological self-system is similar to other systems of experience. It has a clear cognitive aspect that is shown in self-knowledge and self-evaluation. There is also a strong cathectic aspect. In ego-involvement and the various feelings of self-regard there is a marked cathectic factor. The self-system of experience is clearly a *dynamic* system.

CONCLUSION

The diverse materials surveyed in this chapter leave no doubt about one fact: A search for the determinants of human behavior may lead us far beyond the field of psychology into the fields of the various social sciences. To understand why we act as we do it is necessary to take account of the social and cultural determinants of behavior.

Biological determinants have a widespread influence upon human behavior—in all places, times, and cultures. But instead of placing biological and social determinants in opposition to each other, we must recognize that biological factors normally operate within the sociocultural system.

In the study of social and personal determinants there are three main points of view: differential, interactional, genetic. These three give supplementary pictures of social behavior and its determinants. The *differential* point of view reveals individual and group differences in the scores of psychological tests and measurements. Through the statistical and mathematical analyses of scores and measurements one discovers interests, values, attitudes, goals, traits, and other variables. The *interactional* view reveals the influence of persons and groups upon human behavior. This is seen in communication and other interpersonal relations. The studies of individual and group dynamics imply an interactional approach. The *genetic* view reveals the story of development of interests, attitudes and beliefs, goals, traits of personality, and other determinants, as well as the growth of abilities and motor skills. The genetic view was considered in the previous chapter. Personal motivations lie within the human organism. A highly important psychological system relates to attitudes and knowledge concerning the self. Self-regarding attitudes and beliefs play a tremendously important role as determinants of social behavior and emotional experience.

In general, the psychologist starts his study of behavior and experience with the analysis of psychological processes—perceiving, learning, remembering, believing, thinking, feeling, striving, acting, etc.—as they occur within the social setting as well as under laboratory conditions. Along with the analysis of these functions he seeks determinants. The determinants lie within the social and physical worlds as well as in the past experience of individuals.

The determinants discovered by correlational and factor analytical techniques are *descriptive* entities. They are *not physical determinants* that can be described in terms of energy transformations within the tissues of an organism.

Reading Suggestions

Instead of selecting specific works from the extensive literature of social psychology and personology we suggest a few general surveys.

The work edited by Parsons and Shils (1952) is an interdisciplinary study of action and its determinants. Four psychologists, three sociologists, and two anthropologists, have surveyed our knowledge of human conduct in the social context.

Kluckhohn (1954) has written a comprehensive chapter upon culture and behavior. The chapter on social motivation by Murphy (1954) is a helpful review.

On the work of Lewin the references cited in the text may be seen. In addition Deutsch (1954) has summarized the work upon field theory in social psychology.

Guilford (1959), in Chapter 17 entitled "Hormetic Dimensions," has considered needs, interests, and attitudes within personality.

Comprehensive reviews of the literature upon attitudes have been made by Allport (1935) and Stagner (1950).

Investigations on the assessment of human motives through analysis of content by the projective (T.A.T.) technique have been reported and summarized by Atkinson (1958). Materials from many investigators upon the various aspects of human motivation are considered.

Allport, G. W. Attitudes. In C. Murchison (Ed.), *A handbook of social psychology*. Worcester, Mass.: Clark University Press, 1935.

Atkinson, J. W. *Motives in fantasy, action, and society: a method of assessment and study*. Princeton, N. J.: Van Nostrand, 1958.

Deutsch, M. Field theory in social psychology. In G. Lindzey (Ed.), *Hand-*

book of social psychology. Vol. I. Cambridge, Mass.: Addison-Wesley, 1954.

Guilford, J. P. *Personality.* New York: McGraw-Hill, 1959.

Kluckhohn, C. Culture and behavior. In G. Lindzey (Ed.), *Handbook of social psychology.* Vol. II. Cambridge, Mass.: Addison-Wesley, 1954.

Murphy, G. Social motivation. In G. Lindzey (Ed.), *Handbook of social psychology.* Vol. II. Cambridge, Mass.: Addison-Wesley, 1954.

Parsons, T. and Shils, E. A. (Eds.) *Toward a general theory of action.* Cambridge, Mass.: Harvard University Press, 1952.

Stagner, R. Attitudes. In W. S. Monroe (Ed.), *Encyclopedia of educational research* (rev. ed.). New York: Macmillan, 1950.

12 DYNAMICS OF EMOTIONAL BEHAVIOR

The secret of health and happiness lies in successful adjustment to the ever-changing conditions on this globe; the penalties for failure in this great process of adaptation are disease and unhappiness.

HANS SELYE

The aim of the present chapter is to relate motivation and emotion, as these concepts have been developed in previous chapters, to the factors of frustration, stress, conflict, and to processes of adjustment.

It is important to know something about the conditions that determine emotion—frustration, stress, pain, conflict, sudden release of tension, expectation, etc. Emotion is a by-product of these conditions operating within a psychological situation. Emotion, however, is not only caused but is itself a causal factor. Emotion has an important influence upon health and happiness and human action. In this chapter we will examine some of these relationships.

The main topics of the chapter are: (1) Frustration and motivation. (2) Conflict and emotion. (3) Stress and neurosis. (4) Emotion and health. (5) Freudian dynamics. (6) The dynamics of adjustment.

FRUSTRATION AND MOTIVATION

Frustration is an occasional event. From time to time some activity is blocked by a barrier or obstruction. The meal is delayed, the highway presents a sign: DETOUR 20 MILES, one loses his watch. Such events are experienced as blocking of purposive behavior along with annoyance, aggressive and other impulses.

A great deal of human activity is free from frustration. Eating a meal, listening to enjoyable music, driving a car on the open highway —all can proceed without any interference. Many pleasant experiences are undisturbed. Human life also contains a good deal of purely automatic activity that runs its course habitually without outside interference—shaving in the morning, putting on a coat, walking to work, etc. But frustration does occur!

In reading the following sections it would be well to keep in mind questions like these: What are the forms of frustration? How are frustration and motivation related? In what sense is frustration a source of drive? In what ways does an individual adjust (or fail to adjust) to frustration?

Some Forms of Frustration

There are many forms of frustration. The typical forms vary from age to age, as Symonds (1946) has pointed out in the following list.

Restricting of exploratory behavior. The normal infant brings objects to his mouth; he grasps, touches, pulls, manipulates them. Parents find it necessary to restrict these activities to prevent injury, disease, fire. Inhibitions are imposed; these are frustrating to the normal exploratory activity of the infant.

Restriction of early sex experiences. The infant explores his world including different parts of his body; he finds that manipulation of the genital organs yields pleasant feelings. Parents, in our culture, are alert and vigorous in thwarting expressions of autoerotism. The frustrations centering around masturbation are reacted to with strong emotion, fantasy, and repression.

Rivalries within the family. When another baby is born the interest of the mother is diverted to the newcomer. The loss of attention and care is definitely frustrating to older children. Again, two children want to play with the same toy. One child (perhaps the youngest and weakest) must give it up, but this is frustrating.

Early feeding frustrations. Children brought into guidance clinics are frequently found to have had unsatisfactory nursing experiences. Perhaps they were weaned too soon or had unsatisfactory bottle feeding. Weaning is a prototype of later forms of frustration.

Loss of love and support. If the mother works or if the home is broken, there is a widespread frustration bound up with loss of love, security, and support. The frustrations from loss of love have a profound effect upon personality development of the child.

Cleanliness training. Toilet training is a frustration of early childhood. It is also frustrating to have to wash the hands, behind the ears, and generally to keep clean.

Lessening dependence on the parents. As a child grows up he is expected to do more and more things for himself, to require less attention and care. The child is definitely frustrated by being forced to depend upon his own resources rather than upon the care of parents.

Frustrations from the school. In the schoolroom the child is required to sit still, to refrain from speaking and even whispering, to refrain from temper displays, to take care of materials in an orderly and cleanly manner. In a word, he is regimented to fit into the school situation. In addition to these thwartings, he is frustrated by failure in his work, through competition with superior pupils, and in other ways.

Adolescent frustrations. The adolescent must abandon childhood dependence for adulthood. He must acquire skills and attitudes for work. He must adjust himself to members of the opposite sex and to companions of his own sex. These adjustments involve repeated frustrations.

Adult frustrations. Economic necessity requires that the male adult earn a living and support a family. In times of high taxes or economic depression this involves marked frustrations. The professional man or woman maintains a status within his profession, club, and community, but not without repeated frustrations. Again, there are deprivations from death, financial failure, and other losses, that are severely frustrating.

In other words, from the cradle to the grave, people experience repeated frustrations but their form and nature vary from one period of life to another. We do not escape frustration by growing up. We just grow into new and different kinds of frustration.

Maier's Distinction between Frustration and Motivation

Some psychologists define motivation in terms of goal-oriented, or purposive, behavior. Others take a broader view and define motivation as the causal determination of behavior in all of its aspects.

Maier (1949), holding to the narrower definition, thinks of motivation in terms of goal-oriented behavior. He contrasts motivated behavior with activity that lacks a goal. Many of the characteristics of abnormal and delinquent behavior, he states, must be attributed to the fact that the individual is frustrated, rather than to motivation.

He distinguishes between those characteristics of behavior that must be attributed to frustration and those attributed to motivation.

In contrasting motivated behavior with behavior instigated by frustration Maier makes, among others, the following points (paraphrased):

1. Motivated behavior is variable, plastic; it leads to adaptation. Behavior that is instigated by frustration is stereotyped, rigid, unchanging in pattern. Tics, stereotyped movements, and similar rigid patterns, are attributed to frustration rather than to motivation.

2. When a motivated pattern has been well learned it can be altered by rewards and punishments, but a response due to frustration cannot be altered readily by incentives. Frustration fixates whatever responses are in progress at the time the frustration occurs even though these responses are non-adaptive. Once established, the abnormal patterns cannot easily be changed.

3. In motivated behavior the separate responses appear as means to an end. They are instrumental acts that lead towards the goal-response. Frustration-induced responses, contrastingly, are not instrumental but appear as ends in themselves.

4. In motivated behavior, discrimination, choice, and selection are possible. Frustration-instigated behavior, by contrast, has a compulsive quality with no possibility of choice.

5. In motivated behavior the goal-response is adaptive and satisfying to the subject. The frustrated subject reduces the degree of frustration by emotional expressions whether or not they are adaptive.

6. Motivated behavior, on the whole, is constructive and results in the organization of adaptive patterns. Frustration-instigated behavior is non-constructive and often destructive. Frustration leads to disorganized, emotional, non-adaptive activity.

7. A motivated individual is influenced by anticipation of the consequences of his action but a frustrated person makes whatever responses are available with little or no foresight.

8. When behavior is motivated, learning takes place that permits an increased differentiation and discrimination. Under frustration, by contrast, there is dedifferentiation (regression) and sometimes compulsive or mass action.

9. Motivated behavior is characterized by zest and eagerness. Behavior determined by frustration is often marked by resignation—the opposite of zest.

These and other contrasts were made by Maier to support his distinction between the effects of motivation and the effects of frustration. Abnormal behavior, Maier states, is frustration-instigated, and its characteristics should be referred directly to the fact of frustration rather than to motivation.

Maier applied the distinction between motivation and frustration to the interpretation of delinquent behavior in children. The symptoms of delinquency can be referred either to a need state or to frustration. Consequently in the practical handling of such problems as stealing, lying, thumb-sucking, destructive behavior, whining, and the like, one must first determine how far such manifestations are due to a need and how far to frustration.

If the delinquent pattern has developed because it is satisfying, then the pattern should change when satisfaction fails or when dissatisfaction appears. If the delinquent pattern is an irrational manifestation of frustration, however, the behavior cannot be so readily modified. It will not be altered by the subject's realization of the consequences of his act. It is known that some delinquents repeat a non-adaptive pattern and are little changed by argument and awareness of the consequences of their behavior.

Thus there are two kinds of determinants of delinquent behavior. First, delinquent traits such as stealing, lying, destructiveness, lack of dependability, and the like, might reflect unfulfilled needs. Possibly there is a need to be accepted or to maintain prestige, a need for love and security, or a need for possessing things, etc. The blocking of a need can lead to antisocial behavior. Second, delinquent behavior may be the result of frustration. If the delinquent pattern is not changed by realization of the consequences of action, or by rewards and punishments, but remains stereotyped, rigid, compulsive, irrational, then the pattern is determined by frustration and reflects frustration rather than motivation.

To the present writer it seems that Maier is quite correct in attributing certain manifestations of abnormal behavior to the fact that the organism is frustrated and others to the motivation that is blocked. By analogy, if a train is wrecked, there is an abnormal state of affairs. The explanation lies as much in the frustrating situation (broken rail) as in the energy transformations that moved the locomotive down the track. Behavior, whether of man or machine, depends upon the total situation.

The only question that might be raised concerns the restricted definition of motivation. I have stated that *all* behavior is motivated, i.e., causally determined. Some of the determinants of behavior lie within the organism and others are within the environmental situation. All of the determinants and their interaction must be considered in explaining any bit of behavior. This broad view is more adequate, I believe, in the explanation of the total facts. With the broader view one can still take account of behavior that lacks a goal and of the effects of frustration.

Frustration as a Source of Drive

In psychological writings about frustration there is a double tradition. First, there is the tradition that frustration leads to improved performance and learning. For example, it is commonly stated that thinking is instigated by a problem. The problem is a frustrating condition that induces activity of the trial-and-error type. The result of thinking is solution of the problem. Second, there is the tradition that frustration leads to disorganization and impaired performance. For example, it is often affirmed that frustration is a condition that produces emotional disturbance.

Both traditions are psychologically sound. Under some conditions frustration leads to increased effort in carrying out a task, to greater impetus, to a higher level of performance, and to problem solving. Under other conditions frustration is extremely disturbing, even disruptive. It is commonly assumed that for a given activity there is an optimal degree of motivation and that the total energy liberated through frustration may yield a degree of motivation either above or below the optimum, depending upon conditions.

It is important to ask, as Child and Waterhouse (1953) pointed out: Under what conditions does frustration raise and lower the quality of performance?

The difference between improved and impaired performance is not solely a matter of the severity and persistence of frustration but it varies also with the situation. To illustrate: A man stubs his toe and swears! Here frustration is relatively minor and the result is an emotional outburst. Compare this with the behavior of a prisoner who has succeeded in carrying through his plan for escape. The prisoner's frustration from loss of freedom was a major thwarting, but behavior was well integrated, persistent, and efficiently executed.

Brown and Farber (1951) recognized both the emotional and the non-emotional aspects of frustration but they were especially concerned with the fact that frustration generates a drive. They modified the Hullian system by introducing frustration as an intervening variable that influences the vigor and pattern of response.

With a primary drive, such as hunger or thirst, deprivation creates a need. Stimuli arising from the need state are a source of persistent motivation. Frustration, however, produces an additional drive, one that is irrelevant to the basic need state. The irrelevant drive from frustration combines with a primary drive to produce a combined effective drive. That is to say, frustration produces an increment in motivation. The increment can be recognized in terms of improved performance.

Frustration not only produces an increment in drive but also a unique stimulus pattern. The stimuli from frustration evoke either an innate response or an acquired tendency to respond.

The drive from frustration differs from other drives in the nature of the conditions that reduce it. According to Brown and Farber, frustration is reduced by increasing the strength of the stronger tendency so that it dominates behavior, or by decreasing the strength of the weaker tendency, or by allowing fatigue to dissipate the conflict state, or in some similar way. The reduction of frustration is obviously different from drive reduction through removal of a bodily need.

That frustration produces an increment in the strength of drive has been demonstrated also by some experiments of Marx (1956). His work shows that frustration depends upon the interference or conflict of excitatory tendencies. The degree of frustration varies independently of the bodily need state.

In general, there is considerable evidence to show that frustration is a source of drive and that the drive from frustration combines with the drive from other sources. Whether the total drive facilitates or impedes performance depends upon the total level of motivation from all sources—need states as well as frustrations.

Frustration and Aggressive Behavior

It is the thesis of Dollard et al. (1939) that whenever aggressive behavior appears the aggressive individual is frustrated in some way. In other words, aggressive behavior is motivated by frustration. The converse of this proposition is not necessarily true for, as we shall see, frustration can lead to other types of adjustment than aggression.

Frustration can lead to regression or to resignation or to emotional upset without overt aggression.

The simplest and most direct form of aggressive behavior is a physical attack upon the frustrating object to destroy, injure, or remove it; but there are other forms of aggression. In polite society hostile aggression may take the form of a retaliative or derogatory remark. Words may be substituted for a direct attack on the tooth-and-claw level. Again, substitute aggression may take the form of burning in effigy or destruction of a symbol.

Two picturesque examples of the frustration-aggression relation are given below:

1. A college student was driving to a distant city to attend a football game. It was the Big Game of the season and represented an important event in the season's social festivities. He was accompanied by a girl whose good opinion he valued highly and whom he wished to impress with his extensive plans for a weekend of parties and amusement. They became very gay and hilarious during the course of the drive, and he was silently congratulating himself on the successful arrangements he had made. Suddenly a siren sounded behind him and, when he stopped, the traffic officer reprimanded him severely and in a very insulting manner for "driving like a high-school kid." The sound of the siren and the officer's intrusion immediately destroyed both his rapport with the girl and the happy anticipation he had had. As soon as he was permitted to drive ahead, he began berating the manners of the officer and telling the girl that the police in that state were notorious for their bullying methods. During the remainder of the drive he seemed to have difficulty with his car; he grated the gears frequently in shifting, refused to let other cars pass him, and made insulting comments about every policeman who came in sight (though, of course, slowing down whenever they appeared). The change in behavior here is not very baffling. The student was frustrated by being humiliated before his girl; his expectations of favorable response from her diminished. His behavior became aggressive because of his hostility toward the policeman, which he could not express directly and which kept bubbling up after the arrest.

2. A group of laborers . . . had gathered around a boarding-house table at six o'clock for dinner, as was their practice at the end of the day. On ordinary days they ate without much conversation but with a fair approximation of dignity and good manners. On the day in question, the group sat down at the usual hour but no waiters appeared. There were soon murmurs of protest to the general effect that, if the landlady were to stay home, dinner could be served on time; and threats were made that they might stop boarding at that house. Gradually the self-restraints usually governing behavior at the table disappeared and there was a rhythmic stamping of feet. Someone shouted, "We want food"—the rest took up the cry and produced a tremendous uproar. Hard rolls were seized from the table and thrown at the kitchen door, presumably in the direction of the landlady. Soon the object of their aggression appeared and explained the reason for the delay. Dinner was eventually

served, and the unusual behavior gradually died down, but with many threats and mutterings. Frustration was induced by the inability to continue those responses habitually connected with sitting down at a table, and aggressive acts assumed the form of the breaches of etiquette, vociferous demands, shouted threats, and bread throwing.

Aggressive behavior in its primitive form is a direct attack. A man may attack the enemy with his fists, kick with his feet, slap, bite, shoot a gun, strike with a club, throw a stone, or in some other way aim to injure or destroy. The enraged animal growls, shows his teeth, and in other ways expresses hostility. The human subject feels the anger and, if not expressed, there develops a resentment with determination to seek revenge, to retaliate, to "get even" with the offender in some way. There is a primitive kind of retributive justice—an eye for an eye, a tooth for a tooth.

If direct aggression is not possible, the hostile action may turn against some innocent object or person. Thus a man, frustrated in his office by the boss, puts on a smile and says nothing; but when he comes home at night he kicks the cat, spanks his child, or complains about the food. The following amusing incident, told by a psychologist to his colleagues at a meeting of the American Psychological Association, illustrates *displaced aggression:*

An Englishman was hurrying to catch a London subway train already standing in the station. He started to put a coin in the glass coin-box beside the gate. Then he noticed that the coin (still in his fingers) was a half-crown instead of a penny. He was in a dilemma that demanded immediate decision. He could drop the coin and catch the train or he could rescue the coin and risk missing the train. He took the latter course. Slowly and with difficulty he raised the coin from the coin-box, holding it tightly. Then the coin, nearly extricated, slipped between his fingers and fell back into the box. He had lost both the coin and the train! Doubly frustrated he walked down the platform. A short distance away was a man (a complete stranger), with one foot on a bench, trying his shoe. Impulsively and without pausing he gave the man a boot on the seat of the pants, saying, "Damn it, you are always tying your shoe!"

The remark was very bad logic—wholly irrational—but the action afforded a release of tension. The aggressive impulse, aroused by frustration, was directed against an innocent bystander. In a similar way a lynching mob, bent on violence, has been known to turn from one victim to another.

This is *displaced aggression.* The facts imply that when a man is frustrated there may be aroused a general hostility and readiness to attack or destroy. The man's hostile orientation may then be changed from one victim to another. We recognize this fact in daily life when we say that a man's ire is up, he is in an irascible mood, he is generally mad—so, look out! Hostility and aggression can be directed in this way or in that, by external circumstances.

Instances of displaced aggression imply that there is a general drive or tension produced by frustration and also an orienting factor that is directive and regulatory. When an individual is frustrated he must "let off steam" but the object of his aggression can be changed.

Frustration and Regression

Frustration, as we said, can also lead to regression. An example of regression due to frustration is found in a study by Barker, Dembo, and Lewin (1941) upon the play of children. They produced frustration by letting a child see but not play with some elegant toys.

Thirty children, ages 2 to 5 years, were given, individually, an opportunity to play with a standard set of toys. The toys were spread out on pieces of paper on the floor. Each toy was demonstrated to the child: "Look, here are some things to play with. Here is a teddy bear and a doll. Here is an iron to iron with, etc." All of the toys were shown. "You can play with everything. You can do whatever you like with the toys, and I'll sit down here and do my lesson."

One observer sat in the room and made notes on the play of the child. A second observer watched through a one-way screen while the child played for 30 minutes. The play was free, undirected.

In a *prefrustration* period all of the toys except crayons and paper were removed and incorporated into a more elaborate and attractive setting in another part of the room but concealed by a curtain. In the new setting was a big doll house, brightly painted and decorated. A child could enter the house through a doorway. Inside was a bed with a doll lying on it and a chair with a teddy bear sitting on it. An ironing board with an iron stood against one wall and a telephone, with dial and bell, was in the corner. Outside the house was a laundry line on which dolls' clothes hung. There was a rubber bunny near the entrance of the house and behind it a small truck and trailer. On the table were cups, saucers, dishes, spoons, forks, knives, an empty teapot and a large teapot with water in it.

When a child was shown the elaborate and attractive toys he immediately started to investigate them. Every child showed great interest in them; and every child was left free to explore and play as he wished.

In the *frustration* period the child was forced to play with the original, less attractive, set of toys and with the more desirable toys clearly visible behind a padlocked screen. After the child had played with the elegant toys, the experimenter collected in a basket all the materials that had been used in the original free-play period. He spread them out on pieces of paper on the floor as they had been placed at the start. He then approached the child and said, "And now let's play at the other end," pointing to the "old" part of the room. The child went or was led to the other end of the room and the experimenter then lowered a wire partition and fastened it by means of a large padlock. The part of the room that contained the elegant toys was now visible through a wire mesh netting but physically inaccessible.

In the frustration period the child played for 30 minutes in sight of inaccessible and desirable toys. This constituted the frustration. Incidentally, there was a *postfrustration* period in which the child was again allowed to play with the elegant toys; but this was to satisfy the child, and had no experimental purpose.

The records were rated for constructiveness of play. The constructiveness scores were found to be higher, on the average, during the free-play situation than during the frustration period. In other words, a background of frustration decreased the average constructiveness of play with accessible toys. The decrease in constructiveness was measured. For the younger children (28 to 41 months old) the constructiveness scores showed an average regression of 9.6 months of mental age. For the older children (42 to 61 months old) the constructiveness scores showed an average regression of 21.5 months of mental age. For all thirty children combined the average regression was 17.3 months of mental age. A few children were *more* constructive in play when frustrated, but most regressed to earlier levels of play constructiveness.

Frustration in the play situation also aroused moods and emotions that, for the most part, were negative in affective tone. Frustration produced restlessness, aggressive actions, and other signs of unhappiness.

Barker, Dembo, and Lewin recognized a distinction between *retrogression* and *regression*. Retrogression is a return to a type of behavior characteristic of a previous stage of life history of the individual. In retrogression the individual repeats an actual pattern of behavior that characterized an early stage of his life cycle. Regression, by contrast, is a change to a more primitive pattern of behavior, regardless of whether the behavior actually occurred previously within the life history of the individual. This kind of change has also been called *primitivization*.

From the Darwinian point of view, *primitivization* can be understood in terms of evolution. If a child is frustrated and shows the rage pattern, this is regression to a biologically primitive pattern. Frustration constitutes a block or interference typically on the cortical level. When this occurs, there is regression to a primitive pattern, i.e., *primitivization*.

Other Responses to Frustration

We have seen that when a man is frustrated he may become hostile and aggressive. If he cannot directly attack the frustrating object, he may show displaced aggression as when a man, insulted by his boss, comes home and kicks the cat. We have seen that a child when frustrated may regress to a more primitive biological pattern or retrogress to a form of behavior that was present in his earlier years. There are other responses to frustration. One of these is resignation.

Resignation is simply the unhappy or apathetic acceptance of a situation when nothing can be done to remedy it. Refugees persecuted under the Nazi regime or unemployed persons during an economic depression may become apathetic in their outlook. An attitude of resignation implies extreme limitation of needs, no plan for the future, no hopes that can be taken seriously. The frustrating situation, in fact, is accepted as hopeless. Aggression is blocked; regression is useless and retrogression impossible. The unhappy situation is simply taken for granted apathetically. The subject, as we say, is resigned to his fate.

Resignation is a form of adjustment that may reduce or remove emotional tension. Some persons, however, may remain in an emotional state of disturbance, when frustrated, without making any adjustment.

Since frustration implies a blocking of organized behavior, it is normally associated with the signs of disorganization. Under some circumstances frustration brings increased postural tension. Commonly there is emotional excitement or anger or anxiety. The level of activity may be either raised or lowered by frustration depending upon circumstances. Frustration may lead to an output of excessive energy as when the individual attempts to surmount a barrier; but in the frustration of grief there is often a lowered output of energy as shown by a drop in the level of activity. Sometimes when a man is frustrated there is hesitation—faltering, loitering on the job, postponing action, slowness in decision, reluctance to resume a task. Occasionally there are meaningless responses—excessive, random, incoordinated activities. A combination of these manifestations may be present when a man is frustrated and fails to make some kind of adjustment.

CONFLICT AND EMOTION

Conflict is a special form of frustration. A single motive may be frustrated but conflict implies two or more motives that are dynamically opposed.

According to the theoretical thinking of several psychologists, an emotion *is* a conflict state. In this connection see the previous discussion of physiological conflict theories of emotion. (See pages 407-409.)

Dewey's Conflict Theory of Emotion

In 1894-95, John Dewey published two articles upon the theory of emotion. For 30 years, these papers had a negligible effect upon psychological thinking. This was partly because the intricate style and speculative argument made them difficult to read, and partly because psychologists at the time were preoccupied with the James-Lange theory of emotion and other matters.

Angier (1927) restated Dewey's conflict theory of emotion in simpler terms and pointed out the psychological significance of the argument. Dewey's reasoning, essentially, was as follows.

Whenever a series of reactions, required by the purposive set of the organism, runs its course to completion, the result is satisfaction and abolishing of the purposive set. If other reactions can be integrated with the activity in progress, and do not impede it, there is no emotion; but if the extrinsic reactions are so inconsistent with the activity in progress that they cannot be integrated with it, an emotion arises. For example, a man riding a bicycle is hurrying to an important engagement. He passes a friend and waves a hearty greeting. Waving the hand does not interfere with the bicycle riding. But if the friend stops the rider and engages him in a lengthy conversation, the cyclist, concerned over reaching his destination on time, is thrown into conflict and becomes emotionally disturbed by the delay.

Emotion arises when there is a resistance, an interference with the activity in progress. *Without* a conflict, there is no emotion; *with* it, there is. Fundamentally, Dewey argues, an emotion is a state of conflict.

In his first paper, Dewey (1894) pointed out that the so-called expressions of emotion are in reality reduced movements and postures which originally were useful and which have persisted as bodily attitudes. Thus, as Darwin claimed, an angry man bares the canine teeth, leans forward, and clenches his fists. The complete biological act would be biting, striking, and other forms of hostile attack. If the "expression" were complete, it would be an act that is serviceable in the struggle for existence. Similarly, the "expressions" of romantic love are the beginnings of the complete sexual act.

The integrated reactions that lead an organism to some biologically useful goal normally include the vegetative processes. These latter reinforce and facilitate the activity in progress. If the purposive act is frustrated, however, the vegetative processes, instead of reinforcing a useful act and making it more efficient, now interfere. The awareness of these vegetative changes absorbs the subject's consciousness. In other words, the consciousness of an instinctive act is not an emotion but emotion arises and is *felt* when there is some blocking or interference with the instinctive behavior.

In his second paper, Dewey (1895) developed further the conflict theory of emotion, taking account of the dynamics and functional significance of the process. In addition to the upset or seizure, which is present in emotion, there are two other important phases. First, an emotion is a disposition towards some form of purposive behavior; it involves a purposive set or attitude. Thus, the emotional individual seeks to fight, to flee, to copulate, or to carry out some other purposive activity. Second, the emotional behavior is oriented towards some object. If one is angry, he is angry *at* someone or *on account of* something; if one is afraid, he is afraid *of* or *about* something. There is always an object *towards* or *against* which the individual is oriented. In pathological states of emotion which are objectless, such as certain anxieties and depressions, the individual, Dewey states, goes on at once to supply an object.

There is no reason to assume that biologically primitive acts (fighting, running from danger, etc.) and other purposive acts have a conscious emotional quality. When these acts are integrated and carried out without any blocking or interference, they are free from emotion. When there is interference with a purposive act there are organic repercussions and a feedback from the viscera to conscious states. Thus, the angry man becomes aware of his pounding heart, clenched fist, posture of attack. These are the conscious returns that symbolize a fight.

In summary: Dewey states that certain activities, formerly useful in themselves, have become reduced to mere action tendencies or bodily attitudes. As such, they serve to arouse useful actions and to realize ends. When a difficulty arises in adjusting the activity (represented by the attitude) to other activities, there is a temporary struggle, a partial inhibition of one or both activities, with visceral reverberations. The conflict state *is* or *constitutes* an emotion.

Critique of the conflict theory of emotion. Dewey virtually defines emotion as a state of conflict. Without a conflict, there is no emotion; when conflict is present, there is emotion. A state of conflict *is* or *constitutes* an emotion.

If we take these statements literally, they are open to several fairly obvious objections. In the first place, conflicts are known to exist that are relatively free from emotional disturbance. The blocking of motor impulses—as when one starts to answer the door bell and the telephone bell ringing at the same time or when one hesitates between taking the right or the left path—produces a momentary conflict that is not emotional. It seems necessary to distinguish between emotional and nonemotional conflicts. In the second place, conditions other than conflict are known to produce emotion.

In another connection (Young, 1943) I listed four main causes of emotion: (1) Emotion is produced by intense stimulation, especially by pain. If sufficiently intense, pain can disorganize any purposive activity and make the individual emotional. (2) Frustration, as we have seen above, can cause emotional upset. Conflict is a special form of frustration which involves the clash of two or more motives within the individual; but the thwarting of a single motive can produce emotion. (3) Conflict is undoubtedly one of the conditions that cause emotion but it is not the only one. (4) Emotional disturbance is produced by the sudden release of tension as in joy and laughter and triumph and sudden success in an undertaking. The release of tension is often, but not always, associated with a response that is hedonically positive. For example, a mother watching over the sickbed of a child may experience great anxiety tension; when the crisis has passed there is a letdown of tension—joy if the child lives, sorrow if he dies. The release from tension and conflict, no less than the conflict itself, produces emotional disturbance.

If the concept of conflict is extended from the immediately present behavior back into the life history of the individual, a significant relation appears between conflict and emotion. Unsolved conflicts and problems repeatedly and consistently produce emotional upsets. An emotion, in fact, may be taken as a sign of some persistent lack of adjustment. To understand the emotional upsets of an individual, the psychologist must take account of persistent attitudes, goals, interests, and sentiments, for these are basic determinants of feelings and emotions. Specific examples are found in the emotions of weeping and laughing.

Conflict and Release of Tension in Weeping and Laughing

To understand weeping and laughing one must take account of conflicts and their solution within the psychological situation.

A psychological situation involves both organism and environment in some kind of dynamic interaction. The situation may be perceived by the individual. It may be remembered. It may exist in fantasy. Social situations involve interpersonal relations but there are situations that involve a single individual and the physical world. The meaning of a situation depends upon an individual's past experience as well as his present surroundings.

The importance of a situational approach is realized when we ask: Why do we weep? Why do we laugh?

Lund (1930), with the help of his students, made a careful study of the situations that induce weeping. He found that weeping occurs in situations that involve conflict. States of pure dejection do not produce tears. The discharge of tears occurs typically when a depressing situation gains a redeeming feature, when the tension of an unpleasant situation is somewhat relieved or alleviated. For example, a wife whose husband had died 3 days previously was stunned by the blow but showed no outward signs of emotion other than extreme depression; she broke down in tears when a friend brought her a beautiful floral wreath. Again, the son of a physician had been run over in the street and the mangled body was taken to a hospital where an operation was performed. The boy died a few hours later. The physician wept for the first time when the boy's mother related a beautiful incident from the child's behavior that morning.

In these instances the tears began to flow when the distressing situation gained an alleviating feature that served to accentuate the conflict. At a funeral, the tears flow when the speaker eulogizes the deceased with remarks such as, "He was a fine father, a noble and big-hearted citizen." On the stage, Lund found, weeping was occasioned by a situation with some beneficent feature: the reunion of lovers after a harrowing experience or the generous remark of a poor cripple. In a word, weeping occurs in a conflict situation rather than one of pure dejection and loss.

The conflict that produces weeping may be persistent. *Grief*, as distinct from weeping, is a persistent state of disturbance within the individual. A bereaved widow may grieve for months or years while gradually making an adjustment to her loss. *Weeping* is a momentary bit of emotional behavior rather than a persisting emotional disturbance.

Why do we laugh? Many answers have been given. In an early review of the theories, Hayworth (1928) emphasized the *social* origin and function of laughter. The presence of another person or other persons, he said, is an important element in the situations that produce laughter. Laughing communicates good will, friendliness, that all is well. A man who laughs is not hostile.

Situations that induce laughter commonly release tension with a pleasant effect. A funny story, for example, commonly has a *point* at which we laugh. The clever story teller manages to build up a tension; then there is an unexpected turn of events with sudden release of this tension and a pleasant effect.

Ludicrous situations frequently involve an element of incongruity. Bad manners, unusual dress or antics, a dignified man slipping on a banana peel, a policeman in an awkward position—these are situations that tend to induce laughter. Children laugh in situations that are socially unacceptable to adults. Kicking a person, belching, and other manners that violate adult taboos, may be funny to the child.

There are other factors, also, that Hayworth considered. Children laugh when they are tickled. The tickler assumes the role of an attacker. He makes a thrust or lunge, and then, with a light touch, he stimulates sensitive parts of the body—the soles of the feet, armpits, ribs, the solar plexus. There are elements of threat, uncertainty, and surprise in situations that induce laughter through tickling. Again, with children, the element of motion is important in situations that elicit laughter. With the preschool child laughter occurs in situations that involve motion of the child himself or motion of other persons, as in various plays and games, or motion in toys. Finally, with adults, laughter occurs in situations that make one feel superior. Success in a game of cards, triumph over an enemy, unexpected good luck—are factors that tend to induce laughter.

It is difficult, if not impossible, to generalize the many factors in situations that induce laughter. The discussion, however, illustrates the nature of a situational approach to the determinants of emotion.

Hunt (1958) demonstrated that we commonly rely upon *situational* cues in distinguishing and naming such emotions as anger, fear, and sorrow. He assumed that these unpleasant emotions are based upon frustration. Cues for distinguishing among them have a temporal reference. *Fear* is named when the subject perceives a threat to his goal and some uncertainty about achieving it. *Sorrow* is named when the subject perceives his goal as irretrievably lost; concern is limited to the loss of the goal. *Anger* is named when the frustrating agent is central in the subject's present perception of a situation.

Dynamic Significance of Emotion

Emotion is an acute affective disturbance resulting from frustration, conflict, intense stimulation, the release of tension, or expectation.

It is not correct to regard emotion as a tense unpleasant state, as some writers have done, and to disregard pleasant states of upset. Joy, laughter, relief from anxiety, success, etc., are pleasant forms of emotional disturbance.

The dynamic significance of emotion is that it indicates a disturbance of integrated, smooth, goal-directed behavior. If the extended definition of emotion is accepted, an emotion is a persisting state of disturbance within the individual.

STRESS AND NEUROSIS

Hans Selye, as a young medical student, was impressed by the fact that most diseases are accompanied by nonspecific symptoms, such as fever. A specific disease has a specific syndrome but there is also a nonspecific syndrome that simply indicates that the individual is sick. The nonspecific syndrome can be studied independently of any specific disorder.

When some factor of stress is present the body reacts to it with a *general adaptation syndrome*. Writes Selye (1956): "I call this syndrome *general*, because it is produced only by agents which have a general effect upon large portions of the body. I call it *adaptive* because it stimulates defense and thereby helps the acquisition and maintenance of the stage of inurement. I call it a *syndrome* because its individual manifestations are coordinated and even partly dependent upon each other."

The general adaptation syndrome manifests itself in three ways: (1) There is enlargement of the adrenal cortex. (2) There is shrinkage of the thymus, the spleen, the lymph nodes and all other lymphatic structures in the body. (3) There is bleeding, and deep *ulcers* form in the lining of the stomach and uppermost part of the gut. There are further symptoms of the reaction to stress such as loss of body weight, alterations in the chemical composition of the body, etc.

The general adaptive reaction to factors of stress is a physiological unit, involving the pituitary gland, the adrenals, the thymus glands, the stomach and the white blood corpuscles. These structures provide a unitary defense of the body against the diverse forms of damage from stressor factors.

According to Selye, stress is a fundamental medical and biological concept that has broad practical and philosophical implications. Stress is related to the maintaining of homeostasis and to resistance of the body against disease—but stress cannot be identified with disturbed homeostasis nor with the power of the body to fight disease. Injury to the tissues, infections from the attacks of bacteria, fatigue, hunger, thirst, pain, and similar conditions, as well as frustrations and threats, are factors that produce stress.

If we analyze stress from the developmental point of view, three stages are revealed. There is, to begin with, a normal level of resistance when no special stressor is present. When some stressor appears there is an *alarm reaction*. This is similar to what Cannon called the emergency reaction—a reaction that occurs when the animal's life is threatened. The alarm reaction is followed by a prolonged stage of *resistance* to the stressor. Finally, there develops a stage of exhaustion. These three stages—alarm reaction, stage of resistance, stage of exhaustion—occur whether the stressor is forced muscular work, drugs, infections, exposure to cold, threat, frustration, or something else.

During stress the adrenal cortex produces two types of corticoid hormone. One is pro-inflammatory and the other is anti-inflammatory. If bacteria attack a specific organ, there is always inflammation—redness, swelling, heat, pain, and interference with function. This inflammation is the general reaction of the body to a stressor at some specific place. Also leucocytes attack the invading bacteria and form an insulating layer of pus around the invaders.

Stress is an organic process but it may originate in environmental conditions. If a local irritation exists, general stress from the environment may remove it or may make it worse. The curative property of environmental stress was demonstrated by producing a local irritation in the back of a rat and then frustrating the animal by restraint of free movements. If a rat is forcefully immobilized, so that he cannot run around freely, he struggles and becomes angry. Selye found that stress produced by forceful immobilization of movement influenced the reaction of the body to local irritants that were experimentally introduced. When the irritant was weak the general stress from frustration produced a cure. When the irritant was strong the general stress was damaging. Thus it was found that stress produced by environmental frustration could either cure or aggravate a disease. Of course, overwhelming stress (such as that produced by prolonged starvation, anxiety, great fatigue, cold, combined with frustration) is capable of breaking down the body's protective mechanisms.

Selye believes that each individual has a certain quantity of *adaptation energy*. This is not the same as caloric energy (usually considered to be the fuel of life) because exhaustion occurs even when ample food is available. He believes that "every living being has a certain innate amount of *adaptation energy* or vitality. This can be used slowly for a long and uneventful life, or rapidly during a shorter and more stressful, but often also, more colorful and enjoyable existence." We hear about burning the candle at both ends.

Selye writes, in summary: "The three most obvious lessons derived from research on stress are: (1) that our *body can meet the most diverse aggressions with the same adaptive-defensive mechanism;* (2) that we can *dissect this mechanism* so as to identify its ingredient parts in objectively measurable physical and chemical terms, such as changes in the structure of organs or in the production of certain hormones; (3) that we need this kind of information to lay the scientific foundations for a new type of treatment, whose essence is to *combat disease by strengthening the body's own defenses against stress.*"

Men under Stress

In times of war and other crises men may be called upon to endure hardship for long periods of time. A man may suffer from fatigue or exhaustion, hunger, loss of sleep, and pain, and also suffer persistent anxiety concerning the safety and security of others. Such factors may accumulate, producing acute stress.

During World War II two psychiatrists, Doctors Grinker and Spiegel (1945), examined the aviators in combat units who were called upon to fly in bombing missions. Their book, *Men under Stress*, gives a clear account of the stress of war conditions. The following illustrative materials are drawn from their account. The illustrations show

how stress arises within a compact group such as the members of a bomber crew.

Cohesion and integration of the combat unit group. When the individuals of a group are faced with a common task or a common danger, differences in belief, attitude, and motivation cease to have significance. The group as a whole becomes integrated for the task ahead and it shows great cohesion. The combat unit, for example, is made up of men who fly the same plane and fight the same enemy; this fact produces a high degree of group integration.

The impersonal threat of injury from the enemy, affecting all alike, produces such a high degree of cohesion throughout the unit that personal attachments become intensified. Friendships are easily formed by those who might never have been compatible at home, and these friendships are cemented under fire. Out of mutually shared hardships and dangers are born altruism and generosity that transcend ordinary individual selfish interests. So sweeping is this trend that the usual prejudices and divergences of background and outlook, which produce social distinction and dissension in civilian life, have little meaning to the group in combat. Religious, racial, class, schooling or sectional differences lose their power to divide men. What effect they may have is rather to lend spice to a relationship now based principally upon the need for mutual aid in the presence of enemy action. Such forces as anti-Semitism, anti-Catholicism, and differences between Northerners and Southerners, are not likely to disturb interpersonal relations in a combat crew.

Common danger and common anxiety. Men in a fighting crew are dependent upon each other for survival. An error on the part of one can bring disaster to all. There is thus a common danger and a common anxiety.

Although fear of the aircraft and of human inefficiency are a constant source of stress, the greatest fear is attached to enemy activity. The enemy has only two forms of defense against combat aircraft: fighter planes and flak. The enemy's fighter aircraft are efficient and highly respected by the combat crew members; but they are not as great a source of anxiety as flak. Enemy planes are objects that can be fought against. They can be shot down or outmaneuvered, but flak is impersonal, inexorable, and, as used by the Germans, deadly accurate. It is nothing that can be dealt with—a greasy black smudge in the sky until the burst is close. Then the flak is appreciated as gaping holes in the fuselage, fire in the engine, blood flowing from a wound, or the lurch of a ship as it slips out of control. Fear of enemy activity is seldom concrete until the flier has seen a convincing demonstration of what damage can be inflicted, and how little can be done to avoid it. After a series of such demonstrations, the men are fully aware of what can happen, and the expectation of a repetition produces fear that is difficult to shake off. This load of apprehension constitutes the chief emotional stress during combat. Almost everyone has to make a conscious effort to deal with it. The extent to which a man is able to control it determines his success as a combat crew member.

Common bereavement heightens common anxiety. Grinker and Spiegel point out that the men of the combat group have common grief. The loss of one of their buddies heightens a common anxiety.

The death of a buddy is felt as keenly as the loss of a brother. The men suffer not only from the sense of bereavement, but from having seen the anguish of a bloody and painful death. They cannot look away when a ship flying on their wing receives a direct flak hit and bursts into flame. The sight of their tentmates bailing out with burning parachutes, or exploded out of a disintegrating ship, becomes stamped upon their memory. Empty beds in the tent at night reflect this memory, which does not disappear with the sending home of their buddy's clothes and personal effects. The grief persists. It is dulled by time, but new losses may add to it. The loss of friends arouses increased anxiety. What happened to a buddy may well happen to one's self, since all are so much alike. This double load of grief and anxiety is part of the heritage of emotional stress that is incidental to combat.

Anxiety tension disturbs sleep. Combat service is fatiguing. Rest and sleep become of great importance but unfortunately the tension and anxiety of the situation carry over into the night. Insomnia is common on the night before a mission. Refreshing sleep becomes of greatest importance but sleep is often seriously disturbed.

The men are likely to be awakened in the middle of the night for briefings for early morning missions. Going to sleep may be difficult because of emotional tension from the previous day's mission, not yet worn off. Varying amounts of insomnia are routine among combat crews. It is possible to walk into any barracks or tent containing fliers supposedly asleep and find several pacing the floor or smoking cigarettes. Some give up entirely the idea of obtaining any sleep on the night before a mission and prefer gambling, drinking or talking to tossing in their bunks until it is time to get up. Others would like to sleep but are continually disturbed by slight noises or by their crewmates talking in their sleep. A restless sleep broken by dreams of combat occurs frequently among fliers who have been in combat for more than a few missions. It is not unusual for such dreams to be accompanied by vocal or physical activity. Frequently a man's tent-mates awaken the dreamer from a nightmare to quiet him so that the others can go to sleep. In this atmosphere of tension a long, refreshing sleep is a rarity and its absence increases the mounting fatigue. Only quick and short-acting sedatives are practical for fliers who need to be alert on the next day's missions. The anxiety thus carries over into the night and becomes relatively stable.

The problem of morale within the group. It is not surprising that under great emotional stress there should be a strong personal desire to escape and go home. Additional motivation is required to keep the men fighting. The morale of a group is more than the simple sum of individual motivations of the men before they entered combat. Morale is the resultant of interpersonal relationships. It is dependent upon the loyalty of men to each other, to their leader, to their group as a whole. The men are fighting for each other; guilt feelings develop if they let each other down. They seem to be fighting *for* each other or *for* someone rather than *against* an enemy. The personal fate of any one man becomes of secondary importance. The spirit of self sacrifice, so characteristic of the combat personality, is at the heart of good morale.

Leadership is important in the maintaining of the morale of the group. The leader must be technically competent, strong in character and decisive. There can be no question of his courage. He must have sound judgment concerning the limit of tolerance under conditions of combat, must hold the affection of his men, and must give every consideration to the creature comforts of those under his guidance.

War neuroses develop. It is not surprising that under prolonged stress, such as that experienced by fliers during the war, nervous breakdowns should occur. Combat stress results in psychological deficiencies from which no one is immune.

The unending strain eventually produces distress signals. Enthusiasm and eagerness give way to a weariness of battle, which is then endured because there is no way out. Transient fears turn into permanent apprehensions. Anxiety has a tendency to spread until it is continuous or is aroused by trivial sounds. Good muscular coordination is replaced by uncontrollable tremors, jerky manipulations and tension. Constant tension leads to restlessness that is intolerant of repose and never satisfied by activity. Sleep dwindles and gives way altogether to insomnia punctuated by fitful nightmares. Appetite is reduced and gastric difficulties appear. Although air sickness is rare, nausea and vomiting after meals, especially breakfast, are fairly common, as is a functional diarrhea. Frequency of urination, headache, and backache are common signs of the body's reaction to emotional stress. With the growing lack of control over mental and physical reactions come a grouchiness and irritability that interfere with good relations among the men. Some give way easily, and are always in a quarrel or argument. Others become depressed and seclusive, and stay away from their friends to avoid dissension, or because they feel ashamed. Thinking and behavior may become seriously altered. Forgetfulness, preoccupation, constant brooding over the loss of friends, and combat experiences impair purposeful activity. The behavior of the men becomes not only asocial but completely inappropriate and bizarre.

To avoid stigmatizing the flier these reactions are roughly grouped under the undiagnostic term of "operational fatigue." The symptoms merely reflect a struggle of the individual to cope with overwhelming anxieties and hostilities. The symptoms do not fall into clear-cut diagnostic categories. The most frequent symptoms of "operational fatigue" (war neuroses) in men who have returned to the U. S. A. are: restlessness, irritability and aggressive behavior, fatigue on arising and lethargy, difficulty in falling asleep, subjective anxiety, easy fatigue, exaggerated startle reaction, feelings of tension, depression, personality changes and memory disturbances, tremor and evidences of sympathetic overactivity, difficulty in concentrating and mental confusion, increased alcoholism, preoccupation with combat experiences, decreased appetite, nightmares and battle dreams, various psychosomatic symptoms, irrational fears (phobias), suspiciousness.

Some Factors Producing Stress

The above account shows both the complexity of the manifestations of stress and the close relation between the physical and psychological determinants. Some of the factors producing stress were described by Darrow and Henry (1949) in a study concerned with submarine personnel.

Suppose a man in a submarine awaits a depth bomb that can sink the ship. He senses danger but there is little to do about it. Anxiety develops. His heart rate increases, blood pressure rises, hormones from the adrenal glands are secreted into the blood, muscle tonus is heightened, sweating is accelerated, there is hyperglycemia, and other bodily changes occur which are characteristic of the alarm reaction.

If the submariner could engage in strenuous activity, these physiological changes would be useful; but the situation of awaiting a depth bomb in a submarine neither requires nor permits violent expenditure of energy. The internal processes are inappropriate and emotionally disturbing. The submariner may become irritable, disagree with a superior officer, develop nausea and loss of appetite (sometimes reported many days after a depth bombing), and other signs of "operational fatigue."

Physical stressors in the submarine situation include: oxygen deficiency, excessively high or low external temperatures, high or low humidity, mechanical vibrations, changes in air pressure, strong odors, dazzling or flickering lights, persistent loud sounds, etc. Such factors have physiological effects apart from anxiety and other psychological factors. Psychological stressors include: boredom, low morale, loss of interest in one's job, and especially anxiety. A persisting anxiety is a stressful factor that can exist even when the physical conditions of survival are satisfactory.

Some of the factors that produce stress have been studied in the laboratory. With animal subjects most of the work upon "experimental neurosis" has involved factors of stress. With human subjects it is obviously impossible to duplicate in the laboratory the stressful situations of real life.

Lazarus, Deese, and Osler (1951) reviewed research on the psychological effects of stress upon performance. They found that investigators produced stress in two main ways. First, stress has been produced by forcing subjects to fail in one way or another. The problem given to the subject may be one that has no solution; the subject may be interrupted before completion of his task; false norms, that indicate failure, may be used. Failure is a threat to the self-esteem of the subject and to the achievement of his goal. Second, stress has been produced by complicating the subject's task. Distractions in the form of shocks, noises, flashing lights, etc., as well as verbal disparagement, have been employed to make the task difficult and stressful.

One general result of these studies is that a moderate degree of stress may facilitate performance but a high degree is disruptive and damaging. This generalization agrees with the findings in many other experiments upon human and animal motivation. It also recalls the statement of Selye that mild stress has a curative property but intense stress is damaging to health.

Development of Neurosis in Animals

Neurotic behavior resembling that of human beings has been produced experimentally in dogs, cats, rats, sheep, pigs, goats, and chimpanzees. In all instances the neurotic behavior has been produced by a stressful situation involving the frustration of a basic motivation such as the need to escape from pain or from a terrifying situation.

The first reports of "experimental neurosis" were made by Pavlov (1927). He described three kinds of situations that produced neurotic behavior in dogs.

The first kind of situation was discovered accidentally. During the heavy floods in Leningrad, in 1924, water unexpectedly entered the living quarters of the dogs that were used as subjects in experiments upon conditioned reflexes. Before attendants could reach the scene, the water had risen to such a height that animals could keep their heads above it only with difficulty. To remove the animals through the low doors of their cells it was necessary for attendants to submerge the dogs' heads briefly. During the terrific storm—amid breaking waves, crashing trees, rising water against the walls of the laboratory —the animals had to be removed quickly by making them swim in small groups from their kennels into another laboratory about a quarter of a mile away. Here they were kept on the first floor, huddled together indiscriminately. The excitement strongly inhibited the animals. Most strikingly, they did not fight or quarrel; they remained quietly huddled together, which behavior is unusual with dogs in a group.

All of the animals were saved, but after the storm it was discovered that several of them had completely lost their conditioned reflexes to visual and auditory stimuli. The learned responses had been so thoroughly eliminated that only extensive training could restore them. One dog that seemed normal in behavior and that had not lost his conditioned reflexes, responded with intense fear when a loud bell (previously used in the experiments) was sounded near him. Pavlov believed that the loud sound produced an emotional disturbance equivalent to restoration of the flood experience. To test this hypothesis he produced a mock flood by letting water trickle under the door into the room where the dog, on a raised stand, could see it. When the animal noticed the stream of water trickling along the stone floor, it fell into extreme agitation—panting, yelping, trembling. The experiment ended with an impairment of behavior that Pavlov attributed to functional weakening of the nervous system through shock. There was produced an artificial or "experimental" neurosis.

In a second type of situation a neurosis was produced experimentally by placing the dog in a situation that required him to make a difficult discrimination. One of Pavlov's dogs was trained to discriminate between a luminous circle and an ellipse of about the same area projected on a screen. The circle was a positive signal for food and the ellipse a sign that no food would be given. At the start of the experiment discrimination was easy; the axes of the ellipse were in the ratio of 1:2. As training continued, the elliptical form was made more and more circular by changing the ratio of the axes progressively—from 2:3 to 3:4 to 4:5, and so on.

When the ratio of 8:9 was reached, the dog, that formerly stood quietly in the harness, began to struggle and howl, salivating profusely at the presentation of both circle and ellipse. It tore off with its teeth the apparatus used for mechanical stimulation of the skin and bit through the tubes connecting the animal room with that of the observer. It barked violently, contrary to usual custom. Importantly, the animal developed a fear of certain geometrical figures (phobia) and, to a less extent, of the experimental situation in which these figures had been encountered. The neurosis, in this situation, was produced by forcing the animal to discriminate up to the limit of his capacity and then giving him a task that was too difficult.

In a third type of situation that produced neurosis, pain was employed as a signal of food. Pavlov believed that a conditioned salivary response could be established to any kind of sensory stimulation, including pain from electric shock. In one experiment a weak shock was used as a signal of food. Conditioned salivation was established to the presentation of the shock; the dog showed no defense reaction against it. On the contrary, the animal responded by turning his head, licking his lips and salivating when the shock was given. For many months the conditioned response continued when the shock was strong. But there was a limit to the animal's tolerance. With repeated presentations of an intense shock there came an abrupt break in behavior. The conditioned salivary response vanished and no trace of it could be found. Instead there was a violent defense reaction against the painful stimulation. Even extremely weak currents were no longer effective in evoking the salivary CR.

A noteworthy feature of the neurosis produced by shock was the suddenness and completeness of the breakdown in behavior. Prior to a certain intensity of shock the animals showed no sign of fear; they appeared oblivious to the painful nature of the shock so long as it was a signal of food. Then, quite abruptly, the acquired reaction disappeared and pain-avoiding behavior dominated the animal instead.

Following Pavlov's pioneer work upon "experimental neurosis" other investigators have studied behavioral breakdowns in animals. Only a few of the many studies can be mentioned.

Maier (1939), in his work upon experimental neurosis in the rat, produced behavioral breakdowns by placing the animals in a situation that involved conflict. Using the Lashley technique, he forced rats to jump a gap to a goal box. There were two goal boxes, side by side, with geometrical figures on the doors. If the animal discriminated correctly, the door would be open and the animal could jump through it to a food reward; if the animal made an error, the door would be locked and the animal would receive a bump on the nose and a fall as punishment. When the problem was difficult or insoluble, many animals developed neuroses.

Maier demonstrated both active and passive phases of disordered behavior produced by conflict. During the active phase a rat rushes about violently, exhibiting convulsive movements and sometimes tics. He jumps in a curious manner. During the passive phase the rat is quiescent. His body can be rolled up into a ball or moulded into some posture which he maintains for several minutes. After the passive phase there is a return to a normal level of activity.

Liddell (1938), working in the laboratory barns at Cornell University, produced neuroses experimentally in sheep. Among other things, he found that neurotic behavior, once established, was relatively stable. One animal exhibited symptoms of neurosis during 9 years until its death at the age of 13.5 years. Two other animals remained in a neurotic state for 6 years. When the sheep were removed from the laboratory situation and from the painful shocks that had been used to produce neurotic behavior, they appeared to be normal in every respect. When they were returned to the laboratory and placed upon the threatening apparatus, their overreaction and other abnormalities of behavior developed within a few days of experimenting. In other words, the "rest cure" was effective so long as the animals were removed from the situation that produced the traumata but the neurotic symptoms returned when the animals were again placed in the apparatus.

Further studies, that have a bearing upon the therapy of neuroses, were carried out by Masserman (1947). He trained cats to close a switch that rang a bell or turned on a light and then dropped a pellet of food into the food box. When the cats learned to work the apparatus, they were subjected to sudden blasts of air at the moment of feeding. After several repetitions of the air blast, neurotic behavior developed and became well established. Various therapeutic procedures were then tested.

In one procedure the hungry cats were *forced to face the situation* by being placed in the apparatus and slowly pushed towards the food box by means of a movable partition. When the animals reached the scene of the former air blasts they went into an emotional state bordering on panic. Some of the cats, seeing the food in the box, made a dive for it and managed to eat; this put them on the road to recovery. Others were terrified, ate nothing, and left the apparatus in a state worse than that before the trials. In another procedure the cats were *retrained*. They were petted, stroked, and fed by hand when placed in the apparatus. When treated in this way they gradually learned to depress the switch, to tolerate the air blasts, and to eat in spite of it. If the retraining was hurried, the cats were thrown into neurotic excitement and further retraining became difficult. In still another method the animals were *left in the cage to work out their own solution.* They were in conflict between fear of the air blasts and hunger. As the hours went by, the cats became increasingly hungry and active. They would cautiously approach the switch and touch it lightly. When the bell sounded and the light flashed the cats would retreat, even when there was no air blast. As hunger became intense they grew bolder. Finally, being very hungry, they would eat the food. Reintroduction of the air blast sometimes renewed the neurotic behavior but with time the cats learned that even the blast of air was harmless and they would eat in spite of it.

The various studies of neurotic behavior in animals are important because they demonstrate the possibility of producing neuroses in the laboratory and the further possibility of investigating therapeutic techniques. Experiments that could not be performed with human subjects can be carried out with animals. Although the situations that produce behavioral breakdowns in man differ greatly from those employed in research with animals, the basic symptoms of neurosis are similar. Neurosis is produced in man and animal by conditions of stress, frustration and anxiety.

EMOTION AND HEALTH

In Chapter 9 an emotion was defined as an acute affective disturbance of the individual that is psychological in origin and revealed in behavior, conscious experience, and visceral functioning. According to this view, an emotion is a contemporary event—an occurrence felt and observed here and now. But a broader view of emotion was stated which is common within the literature of clinical psychology, psychiatry, psychoanalysis, and psychosomatic medicine. According to the broader view, an emotion is an inferred state of disturbance that persists within the individual.

The persisting disturbance (which is inferred) may be viewed as one main substratum of the observed emotional outbursts.

Emotion as a Persisting Disturbance

Emotion is commonly regarded as a persisting disturbance within the individual. (See pages 358-360.) When a clinical psychologist or psychiatrist speaks of an emotionally disturbed child or patient he implies that emotion is a disturbance of some kind that may endure for days, weeks, or even years. This view of emotion is especially characteristic of psychosomatic medicine.

The persisting disturbance might depend upon an unfulfilled need for security or love or recognition. The disturbance might be an unsolved personal problem. It might be a chronic anxiety as when one faces failure or disgrace or financial ruin or death from an incurable disease. The persisting disturbance might rest upon a frustrating or painful situation from which the individual sees no escape. As long as the situation continues, the individual remains in a disturbed emotional state.

Psychological literature is filled with illustrations of emotional disturbances that depend upon persisting external conditions. A single example of emotional disorganization will be taken from the work of Luria (1932) upon conflict.

In one of Luria's studies the subjects were students about to take a critical examination. It was in the spring of 1924 when the overcrowding of higher schools and universities, during the Russian revolution, made it necessary to cut down drastically the student enrollment. Every student had to appear before a commission that considered his academic activity. If the commission decided unfavorably, the candidate was expelled from the school and his plans for future education came to naught; if the decision was favorable, he could continue his academic career. Everything depended upon the outcome of the examination. It was no ordinary school exercise; it was called a "purge" or "cleansing."

Luria removed students from the waiting line and made psychological observations a few minutes before this all-important examination. His method combined the recording of muscular movement with verbal responses. Stimulus words were presented one at a time and the subject was instructed to respond with the first word that occurred to him. In the list of thirty stimulus words some were indifferent: *day, pillow, gold*. Others referred to the traumatic situation: *examination, cleansing, commission*. At the instant that the subject responded verbally he squeezed a bulb with the right hand and also attempted to hold a weight steady with the left. Graphic records were obtained of the pattern of voluntary contraction and of steadiness.

Luria found a blocking or obstruction of the associative processes. Verbal reaction times to indifferent words were lengthened if these words came in a period just after the critical words. Also the motor responses of right and left hands indicated disturbance of the normal patterns of motion. The gross behavior of a typical subject was described as follows: "Very excited, talking loudly, fidgeting in his chair, striking his hands on the table, continuously conversing in spite of being asked to keep quiet; scolding. He responds to the stimulus in fluctuating tones, sometimes in an ordinary voice and again very boisterously. Further investigations reveal a marked variability in the strength of the motor pressures; sometimes he strikes the dynamoscope. Toward the end of the experiment he says he cannot continue the experiment as he must wait his turn in the line."

Such emotional disorganization, according to Luria, is not a transient process. The individual is acutely disturbed but there is a chronic disorganization that outlasts the manifest emotion and that can be understood only in the light of the total situation.

Emotional Disturbances and Health

It is an interesting fact that within the English language there are two groups of words containing the same Greek root ($\pi\alpha\theta o\varsigma$). The one group of words refers to sickness and includes such forms as *pathology, pathogenic, psychopathic*, and the like. The other group refers to feeling and emotion; it includes *sympathy, apathy, empathy, pathetic,* etc. These two meanings—sickness and emotion—appear to converge in psychosomatic medicine where it is commonly recognized that persisting anxiety or depression may be the source of ill health and somatic symptoms. In any event, sickness and emotion are both *disturbances* of the organism; they may be interrelated disturbances.

How many bodily ailments that bring patients to the office of a general practitioner are based on emotional disturbances? There is no telling, but some conservative observers have put the estimate as high as fifty percent. In any event, the intimate relation between emotional disturbances and health is of practical importance to the physician as well as the clinical psychologist.

The old ideal of a sound mind in a sound body is changing. For one thing psychologists no longer regard the individual as a mind plus a body. They think of the individual as a single creature with physical, mental and social attributes. When there is ill health the physician must seek out all of the causes. It would be foolish to exaggerate the importance of psychogenic factors. A doctor would not diagnose a serious illness as psychogenic without first making thorough examinations and ruling out the presence of organic disease. If an organic explanation for ill health cannot be found, there is always the possibility of a psychogenic basis; even if an organic basis is present, there remains the possibility that the symptoms are exacerbated by psychogenic factors.

Several common forms of psychosomatic disorders are listed below:

Gastric ulcers. People in executive positions speak jokingly about a "two-ulcer" or a "ten-ulcer" job, implying that some kinds of employment and positions of responsibility may cause gastric ulcers.

It is not only anxiety and the responsibility of one's work that cause ulcers. Feelings of resentment, anger and hostility have been shown to increase the motility and acidity of the stomach, and these conditions, in turn, tend to produce ulcers. A man with a gastric fistula was observed to have increased motility and acidity in the lining of his stomach at those times in his life when he was dominated by feelings of anger and resentment. The symptoms were particularly acute when he was discharged from a job on grounds of inefficiency. Contrastingly, feelings of contentment and well-being reduced his stomach motility and acidity.

Essential hypertension. One of the important afflictions of American adults is high blood pressure, or hypertension. It is well recognized that this disorder can result from various organic conditions, especially diseases of the blood vessels and kidneys. Many cases of hypertension, however, are found to be free from organic causes. "Essential" hypertension is regarded as psychogenic in origin. It is presumed to be caused by continuing action of the sympathetic nerves which accelerate the heart and constrict the blood vessels. Since anger also involves speeding up of the heart and constriction of blood vessels, it is obviously important for persons with hypertension to avoid anger and resentment.

It has been observed that many individuals with essential hypertension are of a submissive nature and often very dependent upon others. They frequently have very domineering parents or bosses. A constant hostility or resentment occurs but, because of timidity, they rarely have outbursts of overt rebellion. Their blood pressures, usually high, are markedly lower following the relief that occasional periods of rebellion bring and rise when they again suppress their hostility. The relation between emotion and health is obvious in this condition.

Exophthalmic goiter. A serious thyroid disorder, exophthalmic goiter, sometimes appears to be caused by severe anxiety or at least to be exacerbated by it. A typical example is that of a stock broker who was in excellent health until his fortune was threatened by an economic depression and he finally failed in business. During the heavy strain, with its constant anxiety, he became increasingly nervous. Gradually he developed a pulsating enlargement of the thyroid gland, increased prominence of the eyes, palpitation of the heart, rapid respiration, and increased blood pressure. There were tremors in the fingers, a rapid loss of weight and strength, and a loss of control over impulses to act. He was broken in health as completely as in fortune. His symptoms were those of exophthalmic goiter.

In cases like this there are, in addition to the help from the physician's treatment, striking benefits derived from such things as success, happiness, and good luck; from a change of scene; from hunting and fishing; from optimistic friends.

Bronchial asthma. Another disorder sometimes attributed to psychogenic factors is bronchial asthma. Medical research has demonstrated that asthma is frequently caused by specific allergies to certain substances and can be cured by inoculation with these substances. When proper allergy tests have been found negative, climatic changes bring no relief, and the attacks of difficult breathing are regularly associated with certain emotional situations, then we are justified in assuming that the disorder may be caused or exacerbated by psychological conditions.

The factual basis of psychosomatic medicine is quite impressive. A leading clinical psychologist, R. W. White (1948), concludes:

Psychosomatic medicine opens up the area where mind and body overlap, where it is no longer possible to distinguish between them. The physician of the future, whether he be general practitioner, specialist, or research worker, must be a psychosomatic physician. He must be able to describe with equal precision the tissue changes in organs, the neural pathways, and the emotional constellations that may have sent traffic over the neural pathways. The physician will be forced more and more to take account of man's emotional nature. In this he is but a part of the great twentieth-century revulsion against purely mechanistic and materialistic thinking. Neither the disorders of the body nor the disorders of the world can be cured without reference to problems of emotional adjustment.

Anxiety as a Drive

Mowrer (1939) drew an important distinction between fear and anxiety. Fear is a built-in response of the organism to stimulating conditions. For example, when a dog barks at a cat the feline responds with the built-in pattern of piloerection, arching of the back, spitting, protrusion of the claws, growling, etc. The cat may fight her enemy (anger) or run for a tree (fear). The total pattern can be described in terms of stimulus-response relations. Some of these S-R relations are internal; others involve the organism as a whole in relation to its surroundings. As distinct from the built-in fear response, anxiety is definitely learned. Anxiety depends upon past experience and is anticipatory in nature. When a man anticipates failure in an enterprise or social disgrace or loss of love or imprisonment or pain or injury or death, he becomes anxious. The anxiety is a product of experience within his life situation.

Since anxiety is premonitory of injury or pain or other distress, the affective state has a cognitive aspect. There is an anticipation or expectation of harm that is based upon previous experience.

Mowrer pointed to the utility of anxiety in that it motivates an organism to deal with impending threats and dangers in advance of the occurrence of the traumatic events. The anxious organism can learn to avoid the threatening, dangerous situations. Clearly, however, a persisting state of anxiety can have harmful effects as Freud, Mowrer himself, Miller, and many others, have pointed out. Studies in psychosomatic medicine have shown that persisting anxiety interferes with sleep, digestion, and other vital processes, and may make for ill health and unhappiness. The damage to health and peace of mind caused by persisting anxiety should be considered when we talk about the adaptive utility of anticipating pain and injury. A mild anxiety may be beneficial and facilitating but an intense anxiety is disruptive.

Neal Miller (1951) agrees with Mowrer that anxiety is a drive. Anxiety is like other drives in that it motivates the organism to trial-and-error behavior, and instrumental acts that reduce anxiety are learned. A rat, for example, learns to press a bar or turn a wheel if these instrumental acts permit escape from a threatening compartment of the apparatus. (See pages 226-228.)

Farber (1954) considered the views of Mowrer, Miller, and others, and agreed that anxiety is a drive. He listed two criteria for recognizing drive states:

1. *The elimination or reduction of the drive is reinforcing.* For Farber "reinforcement" refers to a modification of performance rather than increase of habit strength or some physiological change. "Reinforcement" is an increment in the probability that a given stimulus will elicit a given response.

2. *The drive state is dynamogenic,* i.e., it instigates action, gives impetus to behavior. Just as the hungry organism seeks food and the thirsty organism seeks water so the anxious organism seeks escape from the situation that threatens its security. In this sense, anxiety is a drive.

Farber went on to consider another definition, in terms of the Taylor test, that also shows the dynamogenic effect of anxiety. Taylor (1953) developed a test for manifest anxiety in human subjects. In developing the test she selected fifty items from the Minnesota Multiphasic Personality Inventory that clinicians had judged to be indicative of chronic anxiety. These fifty items were supplemented by 225 additional items judged to be non-indicative of anxiety. The score on the critical items indicates the degree of manifest anxiety.

Figure 87 combines two graphs presented by Taylor. The solid-line graph shows the frequency distribution of scores for 1971 university students and the broken-line graph presents scores for 103 psychiatric patients. The difference between median scores of these two groups is highly significant and proves that the psychiatric patients show more manifest anxiety than college students.

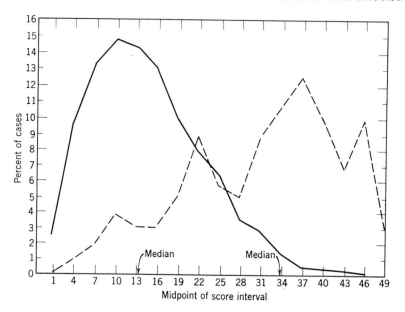

Figure 87. Frequency distribution of manifest anxiety scores. Solid line graph shows frequency polygon for 1971 university students. Broken line graph gives distribution of scores for 103 psychiatric patients. *After* Taylor (1953).

Since human anxiety, defined by the Taylor scale, has been found in several experimental studies to have a dynamogenic effect, anxiety meets at least the second of the above criteria for drive. Anxiety, Farber concludes, is a drive.

This conclusion raises a fundamental question: What is a drive? Since the definition of a drive has beeen considered in Chapter 3, there is no point in reviewing the discussion here. It will be recalled that *drive* has many meanings. Some of these definitions are incompatible with the view that anxiety is a drive. For example, Nissen argued that drive is an innate chemical sensitizer but since anxiety depends upon past experience it cannot, in this sense, be regarded as a drive.

A good many psychologists use the terms *drive* and *motivation* as if they were practically synonymous. I think everyone would agree that anxiety is a form of motivation and like other forms of motivation it may facilitate behavior at low intensities and become disruptive at higher levels. Also anxiety, as we experience it, is an affective state with a strong cognitive component. The investigations of anxiety can be regarded as further evidence of the great importance of affective processes in dynamic psychology.

For a further discussion of anxiety and drive see Woodsworth (1958).

Corrective Emotional Experience in Psychotherapy

The practical importance of emotion, in relation to health, is seen clearly in the field of psychotherapy. A man who is suffering from a persisting anxiety may be helped if he can freely express his feelings and emotions. The aim of psychotherapy is to aid him in expressing his emotions.

According to White (1948), psychotherapy is not an intellectual process. It has been wrongly said that the way to bring about readjustment is to help the individual understand his own problems. It is insufficient, however, merely to help him become aware of his motivations and frustrations on a cognitive level. There is a value in intellectual understanding but this is not enough to effect a cure.

Psychotherapy operates in the sphere of emotion. The main aim of psychotherapy is to provide corrective emotional experience by relaxing the subject's defenses and permitting him to reappraise his anxieties. In the major methods of psychotherapy the subject is encouraged to *feel*, to express his emotions.

This point will be illustrated by reference to three of the main forms of psychotherapy.

1. In *non-directive counseling* the counselor does not intervene by asking questions, by giving information or advice, or by directing the course of a conversation. He simply listens to what the client has to say, recognizes his feelings, and points them out. The counselor is constantly reacting to the feeling side of an interview rather than to the content. For example, if a student remarks that his study habits are bad and that he is not really so stupid as his grades indicate, it would be natural in a conversation to ask what the grades are. But in non-directive counseling the counselor might reply: "You are disappointed with your grades; you feel concerned lest they be taken as a true measure of your ability." If the client asks a direct question that shows anxiety, the counselor replies: "You feel anxious over a certain matter." If he asks for advice, the counselor replies that the client would like to have someone settle the question for him.

Non-directive counseling, as developed by Dr. Carl Rogers, takes it for granted that the client will grow in his own directions, that he will remove obstacles and make changes in his attitudes and motives, that will result in changed behavior. The counselor is not an all-knowing adviser but rather a sympathetic listener who lets the client take the lead in the corrective process and who simply points out feelings. When the counselor is successful in recognizing feelings the client expresses more and more feelings. The client has probably never in his life had a listener who paid so much attention to his feelings. As a result, it commonly happens that within a single hour the client discusses matters that have not been mentioned previously to anyone. He expresses and recognizes feelings, gets a release from tension, and of his own accord works toward a solution.

2. The goal of *psychoanalysis*, as developed by Freud and others, is the uncovering and resolving of major emotional difficulties that usually go back to the patient's childhood or infancy. This goal is reached through several stages and by the use of special techniques such as free association and dream analysis.

Psychoanalysis is distinguished from counseling by the technique of free association. The patient is made to relax upon a couch and told to report everything that occurs to him without change or omission. He is asked to assume a passive attitude toward his trains of thought, to eliminate conscious control over his mental processes and merely to report them. In this process there occur resistances and blockings, thoughts that are too unpleasant or too indecent to mention. The psychoanalyst notes these blockings and tries to get the patient to express his embarrassment and anxiety, and to explain the periods of silence. According to Freud, repressed memories and fantasies are strongly loaded with emotion. They are not easily expressed but may be expressed indirectly and in distorted form in dreams and fantasies.

The method of free association aims to reveal unconscious motivations and conflicts that underlie emotions. Freud interprets emotions to the patient and finds that troublesome problems, typically, date back to early emotional experiences. The problems involve repressed sexuality, hostility, or anxiety. These basic affects imply repression which has persisted, generating neurotic symptoms.

One feature of a complete psychoanalysis is known as the transference neurosis. In attempting to lift repressions and to make the patient aware of unconscious motivations Freud discovered an unexpected fact. The patient, instead of attending to his own conflicts and emotions, commonly began to manifest personal feelings toward the physician. He might show an interest in the doctor's affairs, becoming cordial, grateful, enthusiastic about the treatment; or there might develop a negative transference in which the patient would become hostile and uncooperative. The transference neurosis typically develops after the more superficial defenses have been relaxed. It is a stage through which the patient passes during the course of treatment. Before the psychoanalysis is complete, of course, the neurosis is removed and the patient prepared to face the world alone.

A complete psychoanalysis requires a considerable amount of time and hence is costly. The patient usually comes an hour a day, five days a week, for one, two or even three years. Because this is time consuming for the patient as well as the psychoanalyst there have been attempts to shorten the process.

3. The *abbreviated psychoanalysis*, as developed by Doctors Alexander and French, is based upon the need to shorten and simplify the complete method of Freud and to gain more flexibility. Instead of holding to a fixed procedure, Doctors Alexander and French have varied the techniques widely. They introduced a principle of flexibility that makes it possible to vary procedures according to the needs of the patient.

The psychoanalytic procedure, as pointed out above, requires the patient to relax upon a couch and to talk without restraint; free association then reveals the emotional blockings. In the brief method the therapist may depart from this procedure by engaging the patient in direct conversation, argument, or even making challenging interpretations, as demanded by the situation. Of course, this requires skill and experience to know what method should be used and when. The details of procedure are varied to suit the particular situation. In the briefer method, also, the transference relationship is controlled. Freud's method tends to develop a childlike dependence of the patient upon the analyst; the briefer method treats the patient as a grownup and discourages dependent relations. The transference neurosis may be discouraged and avoided, if that seems wise. In the briefer method, again, the analyst may encourage the patient to engage in activities outside of the analysis. It is important to keep in mind that the patient finally must solve his problems in the real world and that experiences gained in the transference relationship are only preparations and training for life's conflicts. In addition to encouraging the patient to take active steps of some kind, the therapist occasionally makes contact with his spouse, employer, or a friend. A change in their attitudes may aid in speeding up the patient's recovery.

In general, it can be said that all three of the above methods— non-directive counseling, complete psychoanalysis, abbreviated psychoanalysis—have certain features in common. All emphasize the

importance of corrective emotional experience in therapy. All require
the individual to express his feelings and emotions. All point to
affective experiences and aid the individual in recognizing and interpreting them. Again, in these basic forms of psychotherapy there is
always a unique personal relation between the individual and the
therapist. The therapist is permissive in the sense that he makes no
censorious judgments upon the patient's actions and feelings; he is
interested and friendly, and he is a source of encouragement. In this
personal relationship there develops a transference neurosis in which
the individual shows emotionalized attitudes—affection, hostility, fear
—toward the therapist. These attitudes are carefully handled and
treated so that the patient can face his problems alone when treatment
is terminated. Finally, all methods of psychotherapy aim at the development of new behavior. Emotional maladjustments and neuroses
are acquired through experience; they are learned. What was learned
in early life through traumatic experiences cannot be instantly changed.
Re-education, reorientation, change of attitude and habit, take time.
There is no radical intervention, like surgery, to produce a quick cure.

In addition to the above methods there are many technical aids to
psychotherapy: hypnosis, the use of drugs, re-education, the assign-
ment of tasks, play therapy, psychodrama, and other forms of group
therapy; but a consideration of these techniques is beyond the scope
of this book.

FREUDIAN DYNAMICS

There are two kinds of motivational psychology. First, there is a
comparative and physiological psychology of motivation that deals
empirically and experimentally with the determinants of human and
animal behavior. Second, there is a dynamic psychology which has
grown out of the work of Freud, Jung, Adler, and more recent psychoanalysts. Each kind of motivational psychology has its own terms,
methods, and concepts.

These two motivational psychologies, I believe, are merging but
they have not yet become integrated. The result is that most psychologists operate with two kinds of dynamic psychology. Despite
the valiant efforts of R. R. Sears, and others, the gap between experimental psychology and psychoanalysis still remains.

The terminology of psychoanalysis has penetrated so deeply into
general psychology that most students of elementary psychology are

familiar with the language. In discussing the mechanics of adjustment, Healy, Bronner, and Bowers (1931) listed the following seventeen "dynamisms" all of which originated within psychoanalysis, most of them with Freud: displacement, transference, symbolization, condensation, unconscious fantasy, repression, reaction formation, projection, isolation, undoing, conversion, introjection, identification, sublimation, rationalization, idealization, dream work.

The terms overlap in meaning and are difficult to define and distinguish. It is not my purpose to consider them here but rather to discuss several matters within the context of Freudian dynamics.

Repression and Dissociation

Modern psychoanalysis has been called "depth" psychology because it deals mainly with processes that are out of reach of conscious awareness, that originated in remote experiences of the individual. The term *preconscious* refers to an area of past experiences—ideas, feelings, wishes—that can readily be recalled. For example, one can recall his name and the conversation with a friend an hour ago. The term *unconscious* refers to a realm of past experiences where recall is impossible except with the aid of special techniques. This unconscious realm contains motivations, conflicts, and attitudes, that affect behavior in various ways.

Freud, as we all know, emphasized unconscious motivation. He taught that slips of the tongue, forgetting appointments, losing objects, breaking things seemingly by accident, awkward movements, and other phenomena of everyday life, are motivated by determinations of which the subject is not consciously aware. Even dreams, day dreams, and flights of fantasy, are causally determined by unconscious motivations.

We may voluntarily suppress or inhibit impulses and experiences that we regard as unworthy. Thus we refuse to think about a cutting remark that someone made or we inhibit an impulse to tell a dirty story. *Repression* is something different from simple suppression or inhibition. Repression places experiences beyond the awareness of the individual so that he cannot voluntarily recall them. Feelings of anxiety or guilt or impulses of hostility and sex may become repressed. The individual becomes unconscious of the nature of his basic motivations and emotional conflicts. He exhibits bizarre symptoms as long as their unconscious motivation is present.

Repression implies *dissociation*—a functional splitting or disintegration within the personality. Janet's classical case of dissociation (technically known as a somnambulism because it resembles ordinary sleepwalking) has been described by Bernard Hart (1937) in *The Psychology of Insanity:*

A French girl, Irène, had nursed her mother through a long illness that culminated in death. The trying experiences and painful events produced a profound shock upon the patient's mind. Then a somnambulism developed. Irène, engaged in sewing or in conversation at the moment, would suddenly cease her occupation and commence to live over again the painful scenes of her mother's death, enacting each detail with the power of an accomplished actress. While the drama was in progress she appeared to hear nothing that was said to her and to be oblivious of her environment. She was living in a world of fantasy. Quite suddenly Irène, seemingly unaware of the fact that anything unusual had happened, would return to her former occupation. After an interval of perhaps several days another somnambulism, similar in most respects to the previous ones, would abruptly appear and vanish. During the apparently normal intervals between somnambulisms the patient was unaware of what had occurred and, moreover, unable to recall the system of ideas and feelings connected with her mother's death. She remembered nothing of the illness nor of its tragic end. She discussed her mother's death without feeling and was reproached by relatives for her callous indifference.

In this and similar instances of dissociated functioning the usual explanation is that a psychological system of painful experiences, through repression, has become dissociated from the main mental system. There has been a functional splitting of experiences so that one mental system does not have memory access to the other. The repressed system asserts itself from time to time but between eruptions it remains unconscious. Dissociation and repression are nature's crude way of solving a conflict and freeing the individual from an intolerable situation.

The conditions that lead to repression and dissociation, according to Cameron and Magaret (1951), are these: (1) An unsolved personal conflict in which something of great importance is at stake. (2) Anxiety based upon the anticipation of punishment or misfortune. (3) A threat to one's self-esteem or prestige, i.e., an ego factor.

The Causation of Phobias, Obsessions, Compulsions

The principles of repression and dissociation have been used to explain abnormal phenomena such as phobias, obsessions, compulsions. A *phobia* is an irrational and persistent disposition to a fear-type of response. It dates back to an intense experience of fear followed by repression and dissociation. Typically guilt feelings are involved.

Many high-sounding names have been invented to describe phobias. Thus: *acrophobia* (fear of high places), *agoraphobia* (fear of open places), *hematophobia* (fear of blood), *misophobia* (fear of contamination), *achlophobia* (fear of crowds), *zoophobia* (fear of animals or of some particular kind of animal), etc. These words are useful for purposes of description. They give an air of profundity to the topic but they explain nothing.

An instance of phobia, examined by the writer, is the following: A woman was suddenly overcome with terror when the train on which she was riding went into a dark tunnel. The fear became intense and she could not explain it since there was no obvious reason for being frightened to this extent and she had previously ridden in subway trains without fear. A similar fear occurred in other shut-in places and especially when freedom of movement was restricted. If, for example, her head was held in a hair-drying machine at a beauty parlor so that immediate escape was impossible, this confinement was frightening. If a dentist put a clamp in her mouth so she could not close it, this brought fear with rapid pulse, sweating, and other symptoms. Also being enclosed in an elevator or other small place brought a reaction of intense fear, almost terror. Attempts to recall the origin of this phobia brought to light the following story: About 10 years before the examination this woman had been a medical missionary in central China. She became ill with a serious infection and for days had to be carried by coolies in a palanquin—a coffin-like conveyance—over winding mountain paths and finally down to the coast. She was enclosed in a nearly dark box unable to move about and to see out. Although the experience was terrifying, she did not complain. She tried to suppress signs of fear. It was unethical, she thought, for a doctor to show fear and complain under these circumstances.

When she was able to recall the original terrifying experience, on repeated occasions, and to relive the emotional events, the intensity of the claustrophobia was gradually reduced. This phobia did not entirely vanish but its strength was greatly diminished following the recall.

The main characteristics of phobias are these: (1) A phobia originates in an intense fear-producing experience, often an experience of early life. (2) The subject is usually unable to recall the original experience of fear unless aided by psychological techniques. He cannot say why he is afraid. (3) Typically there is a sense of guilt or shame connected with the original experience. (4) The phobia becomes generalized. Although originally induced by a specific situation, the phobia spreads to a class of objects or situations that are similar in some respect to the original situation. (5) Upon recall of the original emotional experience and reliving it, the phobia is lessened or removed. If the subject can recall the experience repeatedly, talk about it openly, and assimilate it, the phobia tends to vanish.

An *obsession* is a fixed idea that the subject cannot explain. For example, a patient complained of an idea that constantly recurred to her mind in spite of efforts to banish it. The patient was a young married woman who happened to look at another woman who was seated at a window across the street and who watched her most of the time. Quite suddenly the patient discovered that she could not get the thought of this other woman out of mind. She seemed forced to think of her but did not know why nor was she able to stop the thought. The obsession was accompanied by a sense of apprehension and depression that persisted for the greater part of the time during four years. No analysis of the obsession was made.

Obsessions are commonly associated with compulsive actions. A *compulsion* is an irrational impulse to carry out some act. Ordinarily the subject is unaware of the cause of his compulsion.

An example of compulsive action is discussed in Bernard Hart's, *The Psychology of Insanity:* A lady felt compelled to examine in the most careful manner the number of every bank note that came into her possession. She did not know why she acted in this way. She was distressed by this foolish behavior but the impulse was uncontrollable.

Freudian analysis revealed the following details of the patient's history: Some time previously the lady had fallen in love with a certain man whom she had met in a country hotel. One day she asked him to change a bill for her. He complied with her wish and, putting the bill in his pocket, remarked that he would never part with it. This remark aroused a hope that her affections were reciprocated, and she longed to know whether he would keep his word. The man departed, however, without making further advances, and the lady finally realized that her hopes were in vain. Money which came to her hands recalled the scene at the hotel and the feelings associated with it. The lady tried to forget the unhappy experiences and to banish the thoughts from her life. She was successful. After a while the painful experiences no longer affected her consciousness directly but there remained an exaggerated preoccupation with the numbers on bank notes.

The cure for obsessions and compulsions, according to Freud, rests upon the discovery of the unconscious motivation. The patient must, in some way, be made aware of the causal experiences and relive them emotionally. It may then be possible to work out a readjustment of attitudes and to integrate the dissociated systems.

Sublimation and Reorientation

Freud postulated a *libido*—a kind of free-floating psychosexual energy that can be channeled in this or that direction. If an individual's sexual urges are blocked, his libido may motivate creative work in art, religion, social welfare, science, philosophy, or other socially approved activity. An old maid, for example, may sublimate her libido by taking care of pets.

The difficulty with the concept of libido is that it is out of line with what is positively known about sexual motivation. There are no vital forces that flow through the nerves. The concept of a general energizing or alerting of the organism, however, is definitely tenable in the light of current physiology; but general activation cannot be identified with the Freudian libido.

It is obvious that one kind of activity can be substituted for another. For example, going to the movies may substitute for a glamorous and exciting life one would like to lead. Reading books about travel, exploration, and adventure may substitute for the real thing. Such substitutions do not imply any sublimation of the libido. They imply only a reorientation—a change of goal.

There are many instances of reorientation that can be described without recourse to Freudian terms. For example, a child reaches for his father's gold watch and starts to play with it. The father realizes that the watch is in danger, but knows that if he takes away the glittering object without substituting another, the child will cry. Instead of taking the watch, he offers the child a toy, demonstrating its merits and how it works. Playing with the toy becomes substituted for playing with the watch, without any sign of emotional disturbance. This redirecting of the child's activity implies a shift of set but there is no mysterious shifting of libido.

A question remains as to the nature of the energy or force that underlies all behavior. I have argued that the postulate of a single kind of energy—physical energy—is sufficient for psychological purposes. An organism may be bound, however, by the nature of its excitation, to some general kind of activity such as hostile attack, or sexual advance, or fear avoidance.

In the primary appetites—such as those for water, food, air, rest, sleep, elimination—the need and tension are specific. There is no evidence that a thirst for water can be quenched by writing poetry! Reading the best of poetry may temporarily distract one from the existence of a growing bodily need but it does not alter the primary motivation.

Sexual motivation is different from thirst in that sexual activity is not necessary for survival of the individual. It has significance, obviously, for survival of the species. Kinsey, Pomeroy, and Martin (1948) have shown that there are various kinds of sexual outlet. If one outlet is blocked, some other may be found. There is no scientific evidence, however, for a free-floating psychosexual energy, *libido*, that can be channeled in this way or in that.

Conscious and Unconscious Motivation

Freud, as pointed out above, emphasized unconscious motivation. It is important to note that unconscious motivation was conceived and described by him in terms of conscious experience. The unconscious motive was at one time conscious but it became repressed. Unconscious motives are outside of present awareness.

By conscious motivation one means simply that the goal or aim of behavior is known to the experiencing individual. Thus, if I have resolved to go to a show tonight and have made a date for the event, I am conscious of my intention. The motivation is clearly known and I am fully aware of it.

There are a good many meanings of *unconscious*. These are considered in the following section.

Meanings of "Unconscious"

For the sake of clarity it should be pointed out that *unconsciousness* has several meanings. Miller (1942) listed sixteen different meanings of the word and there are doubtless others. Several of the more important and distinctive meanings are these:

1. The basic meaning is *lack of awareness*. A man assumes that he is conscious when directly aware of some percept, memory image, feeling or desire. At other times he assumes that he is unconscious in the sense that awareness is lacking. There is no evidence that awareness exists during dreamless sleep, anesthesia and fainting. Hence it is the presence or absence of subjective awareness that distinguishes conscious from unconscious states.

2. Another meaning is the *absence of response to stimulation*. When a man has fainted, suffered brain concussion, or taken ether, or when he is in deep sleep, he does not respond to ordinary stimulations of the eye, ear or skin. This lack of response is an objective criterion of the unconscious state.

Similarly, if a local anesthetic has been used or a sensory nerve cut, stimulation of the skin by cutting or burning brings no response. In this sense there is a local unconsciousness even if the subject is wide awake and fully aware of his surroundings and responsive to other sensory stimulations. He is locally and specifically not responsive.

3. The word *unconscious* occasionally means *below the threshold of consciousness*. If the energy in the stimulus is below a critical value, the receptors fail to respond; or the receptors may respond too weakly to produce conscious awareness. In either event the subject is said to be unconscious of the subliminal stimulation.

4. *Unconscious* may refer to a bit of experience that is not noticed, *not attended to*. If a man is absorbed in his work, he may fail to notice the patter of rain upon the window even though the stimulation is definitely supraliminal. He may become aware of these sounds if he attends to them.

5. *Unconscious* may mean *not remembered*. To illustrate, the reader can recall the name of the city in which he lives or the appearance of his breakfast table this morning or the first line of "The Star Spangled Banner." A few minutes ago these items of past experience were not recalled. In a sense they were unconscious (out of conscious awareness).

6. Freud uses the term *preconscious* to designate the vast area of past experiences that can be voluntarily recalled and he reserves the term *unconscious* for systems of experience which, because of repression or dissociation, cannot be recalled unless special psychological techniques are employed.

Freud, as we pointed out above, has emphasized unconscious motivation. He thinks of the *Unconscious* (spelled with a capital) as a part of us that is dynamically active. Slips of the tongue, losing objects, forgetting appointments, breaking things we don't like, awkward movements, mistakes of all kinds, etc., are causally determined by unconscious motivations. Often we can discover why we acted as we did when, at the time, the true motivation was not apparent. Dreams, memories and fantasies are causally determined. A suppressed sexual wish or feeling of hostility may motivate the dream. Moreover, tics, amnesias, functional paralyses, and other neurotic symptoms, may rest upon some unconscious motivation.

7. An automatic action such as opening a door or buttoning a coat or a facial tic may be carried out without awareness. These automatic actions are sometimes said to be carried out unconsciously. In this sense of the word, *unconscious* means automatic, habitual, unthinking, functionally autonomous.

8. Occasionally we hear about *unconscious cerebration*. The phrase refers to solving problems, preparing speeches, and reaching decisions during sleep. For example, a mathematician is unable to solve a problem; he wakes up some fine morning clearly aware of the solution. Again, a man must make a speech in 2 weeks. He thinks for a while about the points to be made and then mentally drops the matter. When the time for his talk arrives the speech is prepared. The implication of such examples is that the brain works when the subject is not aware of its activity. There has been "unconscious cerebration."

The fact that these and other meanings of unconsciousness exist indicates the complexity of the topic. If we use the terms *conscious* and *unconscious*, we must define them.

I will use the terms *conscious* and *unconscious* to refer to physiological states of the organism. The conscious organism is alert and active. The unconscious organism is passive and unresponsive. I will use the term *awareness* for the subjective psychological state of a conscious individual.

Mental Causation

I have repeatedly asked students this question: "How many of you believe that your awareness of an intention, e.g., to return home for a vacation, has some influence upon your behavior?" The answer is clearly affirmative. Again: "How many of you believe that conscious feelings of pleasantness and unpleasantness influence what you do?" Most students answer affirmatively without knowledge of the complicated mind-body problem. Again: "How many of you believe that the perception of some event, such as the change in a traffic light from red to green, influences your actions?" Nearly all agree that perception influences action. The upshot of the matter is that *people commonly believe that their conscious experiences influence behavior.* They believe this without the benefit of philosophical study.

The psychologist, analyzing causation from the point of view of the individual, infers motives, perceptual dispositions, evaluative attitudes, personality traits, habit structures, abilities, and other determining factors. These are *inferred* determinants. They may be based upon observations and reports made from the individual, or subjective point of view.

By *mental causation* nothing more nor less is implied than the view of determination as experienced by the individual and as analyzed by the psychologist from the individual point of view. Here is an unusual and striking example of the kind of thing that is meant by mental causation. This is a true event as described by an Illinois newspaper:*

Staff Sergeant Martin Cookerow, 26, is recovering today in a Scott field hospital after jumping from a moving train near Odin several weeks ago. Sergeant Cookerow had just returned from Italy where he served as a gunner on a bomber.

Cookerow told relatives that, while he was sleeping on the train, the roar reminded him of a bomber. In his dreams, he was ordered to jump. Under the impression that his suitcase was a parachute pack, he leaped from the train. Both arms and legs were fractured.

There is little doubt that the young man was reliving vividly a war experience and that in a realistic dream he actually jumped from the moving train—with tragic result.

When a clinical psychologist or psychiatrist tries to understand the motivation of his client he probes the past experiences of the individual, especially the emotional and traumatic experiences. Through an anal-

* *The News-Gazette,* Champaign, Illinois, June 3, 1945.

ysis of the past he seeks to understand and to deal constructively with
the present problems. It is essential to look at motivation and conflicts from the point of view of the experiencing individual. This is a
valid approach to understanding of behavior. The world must be
viewed as it appears through the eyes of the experiencing individual.
This is what we mean by *mental*.

THE DYNAMICS OF ADJUSTMENT

There is a large literature upon the dynamics of human adjustment.
This literature deals with the ways in which human beings solve problems, meet threats and difficult situations. Adjustments may be made
by trial-and-error learning, by direct attack upon the frustrating object, by avoidance and escape, by substituting one goal or attitude for
another, or by a flight into fantasy and dreams. Some forms of adjustment are called *defense reactions* because they protect the self-
esteem of the individual. Rationalizations, projections of blame,
belittling others, are all means of self-defense; they are techniques
for saving one's face.

A study of the techniques of adjustment is beyond the scope of this
book. It will be worth while, however, to consider some of the theories
relating to the motivation that underlies the processes of adjustment.

Evaluative and Factual Views of Adjustment

The concept of adjustment can be evaluative or factual. According
to one definition, adjustment is a *"satisfactory relation of an organism
to its environment."* The meaning of this definition hinges upon the
evaluative word *satisfactory*. Again, adjustment has been defined as
an *"adaptation to the demands of reality."* *Adaptation*, implying an
element of fitness or suitability, is an evaluative term. A good adaptation favors survival; a poor adaptation interferes with survival of the
individual or species. According to another definition, adjustment is
an individual's *"relationship to his environment which is necessary for
him in order to live comfortably and without strain and conflict."* This
definition, like the others, is evaluative. All such definitions of adjustment imply some criterion—such as survival or health or happiness—
for judging whether an adjustment is good or bad. Whenever one
speaks of maladjustment he implies some standard of evaluation.

Clinical psychologists, psychiatrists, counselors, and others are interested practically in good and bad adjustments. They want to help people solve problems and to ameliorate human ills. The humanitarian urge is a worthy one. It is frankly recognized by the American Psychological Association in its statement of objectives: ". . . to advance psychology as a science, as a profession, and as a means of promoting human welfare."

It is possible, however, to view adjustment in a thoroughly scientific and matter-of-fact way. From a strictly scientific point of view, adjustment can be either: (1) a process somewhat akin to problem solving, or (2) a persisting state of affairs involving a relation between an organism and its environment. Adjustment, scientifically viewed, involves a dynamic relation or a change of relationship between an organism and an environment. For example, if a man leaves his community and takes up residence in another town to escape difficulties, he has made an adjustment by withdrawing from the environment. If he faces the difficult situation but changes his aims and evaluative attitudes, he has made an adjustment through internal modifications.

The second of the above meanings is implied when we speak of a person being chronically maladjusted. For example, a person who has been bereaved may require many months to become adjusted to his changed circumstances.

There are many ways in which adjustments are made but it will not be necessary to review them here. Adjustment has been described as a process of problem solving, restoring equilibrium, returning from disturbance to complacency, reducing drive, reducing tension, removing persistent stimulations, minimizing distress and maximizing enjoyment, etc. All these phrases imply that there is some factor of motivation underlying and regulating the processes of adjustment.

Homeostasis and Adjustment

The term *homeostasis* refers to a physicochemical state of the organism, to intraorganic conditions and events. When we take account of the environment another concept—adjustment—is needed.

Adjustment, as we said, implies a relation or change of relation between an organism and its environment. Non-adjustment is a disturbance of this relation. The disturbance can originate either within the organism (O) or within the environment (E). The E might present a problem—a block or threat or danger—and the O does something about it. Or the locus of disturbance might be internal—a griping empty stomach perhaps—and the O does something about it. The adjustment, as a process, is a change in the relation between O and E.

Underlying the process of adjustment are the dynamic events involved in frustration and conflict, opposed attitudes, cognitive disparity or dissonance. A dynamic disequilibrium, as described by a clinical psychologist, is not a disturbance of homeostasis but rather a condition that underlies a state of non-adjustment.

One point must be made clear: Homeostasis is a physiological steady state that can be described objectively. Disturbed homeostasis creates needs and drives that motivate behavior until there is restoration of homeostasis. The process of adjustment, by contrast, involves a changing relation between an organism and its environment. The environmental factor is always present when we consider adjustment. This factor distinguishes a psychological situation (O-E relation) from a purely physiological state. Disturbed adjustment, therefore, cannot be equated with disturbed homeostasis and *vice versa*. There are non-homeostatic motivations that call for adjustment. (See pages 141-142.)

Motivation as Disequilibrium

The organism is not a static, passive thing that merely responds to stimulations from the environment. It is in a constant state of dynamic interaction with its physical and social surroundings. Environmental changes produce behavior which in turn influences the environment.

The individual acts selectively upon the environment. This selectivity of response is well illustrated by the following example taken from a work of Ellis Freeman (1939):

A and *B* walk by a jewelry store in succession. The store and its window display is a constant, fixed characteristic of the environment of both. Yet it will affect both men, and they will affect it, differently and selectively in accordance with their personal differences. *A* is an unemployed laborer who had never possessed any jewelry. To him the significant fact about the window display is a small sign in the corner advertising a position for a porter. This is what he sees prominently, and this is what he responds to. His disequilibrium or motivation lies in the want of a job. He enters the store, gets the job, becomes a porter, and causes the removal of the sign. That is how he has been affected by the situation and how he has affected it. *B*, on the other hand, is a prosperous collector of rare stones. He notices the sign no more than the other had noticed the jewelry. But he does at once spot a rather unusual stone. He enters and purchases it, and thus alters the situation by its removal. That is how the motivation worked, arising from a different kind of want and disequilibrium. And that is how he affected the situation and was affected by it, but quite differently from the other individual. The point is that there was motivation for the behavior of each man and that this lay in the state of disequilibrium which he brought to the scene. The scene itself supplied a means of improving stability.

For Freeman, *motivation is the disequilibrium of the organism which leads to action for the restoration of stability.* It is an inner disturbance of the organism that motivates behavior.

Freeman explains that the stimulus motivates an individual only in so far as it arouses an inner disposition to respond. The object of desire does not motivate us directly but only by creating a disequilibrium. Before motivation is present there must be an inclination, at least a latent state of disequilibrium which the stimulus object can put into operation. In many instances the stimulus object need not be present at all. In a state of hunger, for example, the state of disequilibrium may develop spontaneously and this leads to the seeking of an appropriate goal object. It is the persisting disequilibrium that motivates behavior.

Freeman's position is based upon the earlier work of Raup (1925) who argued that the maintaining of equilibrium is the most basic principle of life. Equilibria are maintained at different levels: within the single cell, between groups of cells, between bodily organs, and between the organism as a whole and its environment. On all levels, Raup stated, the key to motivation is to be found in a state of disequilibrium and the tendency to restore equilibrium or dynamic balance—which he called a state of complacency.

Motivation from Disparity and Cognitive Dissonance

A current form of the disequilibrium theory of motivation has been developed by Peak (1955). She emphasized the importance of *disparity* as a motivating condition. Whenever the individual is motivated some disparity exists and long-sustained disparity underlies persistent motivations.

Peak illustrates the disparity concept by the following example: Two-year-old Annie observed that the plastic galoshes of a visitor collapsed when they were placed on the floor; Annie's boots and others she had seen did not collapse in this way. Here was a disparity within experience. After the observation Annie kept talking about "broken boots" whenever she met the visitor; this talk persisted for several months or more.

A disparity within experience is a disequilibrium that leaves the individual disturbed but also well motivated. A disparity may or may not be associated with affective processes, Peak explains. It may be largely cognitive.

The disparity view is closely related to the concept of cognitive dissonance as expressed by Festinger (1958). He postulates cognitive dissonance as a motivating state in human beings and goes on to explain his meaning:

> The word "dissonance" was not chosen arbitrarily to denote this motivating state. It was chosen because its ordinary meaning in the English language is close to the technical meaning I want to give it. The synonyms which the dictionary gives for the word "dissonant" are "harsh," "jarring," "grating," "unmelodious," "inharmonious," "inconsistent," "contradictory," "disagreeing," "incongruous," "discrepant." The word, in this ordinary meaning, specifies a relation between two things. In connection with musical tones, where it is usually used, the relation between the tones is such that they sound unpleasant together. In general, one might say that a dissonant relation exists between two things which occur together, if, in some way, they do not belong together or fit together.

Festinger states that cognitive dissonance refers to a relation between cognitions which exist simultaneously for a person. If, for example, a person knows that he is very intelligent and also that he meets with repeated failure, the two cognitions are dissonant—they do not fit together.

If two cognitions are dissonant with each other there will be a tendency for the person to attempt to change one of them so that they do fit together, thus reducing or eliminating the dissonance. A cognitive dissonance thus resembles a state of need and it has a motivating character.

Festinger's view fits in with a good many facts of everyday life. For example, one of my students told another that he was wrong. This other student, attempting to defend his views, made a vigorous search of sources in the library. It may be that an element of self-defense was involved in the motivation as well as the cognitive dissonance of opposed views. No one enjoys being shown that he was wrong!

In any event, cognitive dissonance seems to imply a negative affective arousal. The dissonance theory fits in well with other views that regard motivation as fundamentally an escape from distress.

Affective Arousal as Related to Adaptation Level

An attempt to combine the disequilibrium theory of motivation with the affective arousal theory has been made by McClelland et al. (1953). Unfortunately, however, the attempted combination produced certain gratuitous assumptions concerning the dependence of affectivity upon departures from the adaptation level.

McClelland et al. relied heavily upon Helson's concept of adaptation level. (See pages 319-320.)

They state: *"Positive affect is the result of smaller discrepancies of a sensory or perceptual event from the adaptation level of the organism; negative affect is the result of larger discrepancies."*

They assume that the hedonic effect is the same regardless of the direction of the discrepancy but small discrepancies are hedonically positive and larger discrepancies hedonically negative. A discrepancy, they state, must persist for a finite length of time before it gives rise to an hedonic response.

The view that small changes from the adaptation level are hedonically positive and large changes negative is not supported by empirical fact. Everyday experience would indicate that departures from the level of adaptation may be neutral or pleasant or unpleasant according to circumstances.

Actually, as we pointed out elsewhere, the concept of adaptation level is very broad and complex. Adaptation is of many kinds. Within psychology distinctions must be drawn among sensory, judgmental, and affective, adaptation. Before we can consider the relation of affective arousal to adaptation level we must agree upon some specific formulation of the AL.

In general, Helson's theory of the adaptation level appears to be related to the disequilibrium theories of motivation, but the relation of disequilibrium to affective arousal remains to be explored.

Limitations of Deficit-Tension Theories of Motivation

A common assumption underlying many theories of motivation is that the mainspring of human action lies in some *deficit* or *tension*. This assumption is implied in the writings of Hull, Miller and Dollard, Mowrer, Murray, and others. These writers speak of drive reduction, anxiety reduction, need satisfaction, tension reduction, etc.

The general pattern of the deficit-tension theories of motivation is that behavior moves from disequilibrium to equilibrium, from tension to tension reduction, from drive to drive reduction, from anxiety to anxiety reduction, from need to satisfaction, etc. The implication is that we are motivated by needs, tensions, irritants, frustrations, problems, annoyances, and the like.

This theoretical approach minimizes or ignores the positive side of motivation. Jersild (1954), in pointing out the limitations of the deficit-tension theories, writes that he is reminded of a certain mythical dog, Miltiades, who was never active except when he itched. Then the one compelling passion of his life was to scratch the itch so that he might return to a state of inactivity. Miltiades never had a yen to go places and do things of his own accord!

Jersild believes that in child development there is a positive striving. The child does not seek simply to achieve equilibrium. "The most significant developments do not consist solely in struggles to overcome a disturbed state, or to be rid of something, but also in strivings to gain something—to put potential abilities to use, to enter into experiences that utilize capacities for doing, thinking, and feeling, and for sharing with others. According to this view, it is natural to seek, to strive, to struggle toward a kind of self-fulfillment. Included in this view is the implication that life does not consist solely in getting away from something bad but that the highest good in life is the living of it."

The positive view of motivation, Jersild believes, is best suited to developmental psychology. There is a positive, forward impetus in growth which represents a kind of seeking and not simply a struggle for riddance, relief, and escape. The child, of course, cannot avoid dealing with irritants and coping with frustrations. In fact, he encounters considerable frustration, suffering and pain. But, to repeat, the main point is that there is a positive impetus in growth. The child seeks to be himself, to discover himself, to realize his resources, to stand on his own feet.

Moreover, there is a positive movement towards delight, enjoyment, pleasantness, when no distress is present. To ignore the positive aspect of motivation is to disregard half of the picture.

Deficit Motivation and Self-actualization

Maslow (1955), who is looking for a "humanly usable theory of human motivation," agrees with Jersild that the deficit theory of motivation is inadequate. He writes: "If the motivational life consists essentially of a defensive removal of irritating tensions, and if the only end product of tension reduction is a state of passive waiting for more unwelcome irritations to arise and in their turn, to be dispelled, then how does change, or development or movement or direction come about? Why do people improve? Get wiser? What does zest in living mean?"

As distinct from *deficit motivation* there is *growth motivation*. In itself growth is an exciting and rewarding process. There is positive motivation towards fulfilling ambitions, like being a good doctor, becoming a skilled violinist or carpenter. In any field of activity the development of creativeness is more than removing a deficiency. There is positive motivation towards understanding people, learning about the universe and about one's self. There is a positive ambition simply to be a good human being.

The highest form of positive motivation, Maslow (1954) states, is self-actualization. To understand what he means by this we must consider his view that human needs arrange themselves in a hierarchy.

On the lowest level of the hierarchy are physiological needs for food, water, oxygen, sex, etc. These basic needs are urgent and until they are met other needs are simply non-existent or they are pushed into the background. If the physiological needs are gratified, there then emerges a new set of needs—needs for safety.

The child needs a predictable, orderly world in which he can feel safe. In our society the normal adult is rarely motivated by a need for safety because in a peaceful, smoothly running society the members feel safe from wild animals, extremes of temperature, criminal assault, murder, tyranny, etc. The healthy adult is generally satisfied in his need for safety.

If both the physiological and safety needs are fairly well gratified, there will emerge higher order needs for love, affection and belonging. The man who is well fed and safe will keenly feel the absence of friends or sweetheart or wife or children. He will experience a need for affectionate relations with people in general. He will want to belong to certain groups and to hold a place of respect in them. Within our society, Maslow states, the core of much maladjustment is found in the failure of the situation to meet the needs for love, affection and belonging.

If all of the above needs are gratified, there develops another motivational cycle based upon the need for esteem. In our society there is a felt need for competence, mastery, adequacy, achievement, status, recognition, importance, appreciation, prestige. In other words, there is a need for the esteem of others.

Finally, when all of the above needs are met there often emerges a new kind of restlessness and discontent. There is a need for self-actualization. Very simply, this means that a man needs to do and to become what he is fitted for. A musician feels the need to make music; an artist must paint; a poet must write if he is to have peace of mind. A man *must* do what he *can* do. This is the need for self-actualization.

Maslow qualifies his need hierarchy hypothesis somewhat. He points out that there are other needs not placed in the hierarchy such as the need to know and the esthetic needs. He states that the need hierarchy is not the same for everyone. Nevertheless, needs do arrange themselves in a hierarchical order such that when one is satisfied another emerges. With the emergence of a new need there is another motivational cycle. And the highest need of all is self-actualization.

In contrasting deficiency motivation with growth motivation Maslow states that there is an important difference: In need gratification there is a climax, a consummatory goal response, which is followed by a period of relative freedom from the need. With growth motivation, contrastingly, this phenomenon is absent. The more one gets, the more one wants; the wanting of self-actualization is endless. The goal is never attained.

Self-actualization as Prime Human Motivation

Maslow's recognition that self-actualization is the highest need in the hierarchy of human motives is related to the postulates of Goldstein and Rogers.

Kurt Goldstein (1939, 1947) postulated that the organism is a unit which functions as a whole and that its motivation is unitary. The prime motivation of the human organism is *to realize its capacities.* The impression that there are special drives or motives appears only when one considers the activities of the organism as isolated from their relation to total behavior. Goldstein writes: "Any explanation is doomed to failure which attempts to reduce human motivation to a number of *isolable factors,* capacities, drives, etc., to *separate* forces which interact only secondarily with each other."

The basic trend of the organism to realize its capacities, as much as possible, is seen in both normal and abnormal persons. As a single example of the trend consider patients suffering from hemianopsia—a total blindness of corresponding halves of the visual field in both eyes due to lesions in the occipital lobe of the brain. The everyday behavior of patients with hemianopsia often fails to reveal that they are blind in half of the visual field. Patients with hemianopsia are subjectively aware of impaired vision but they see objects in their entirety and not only halves of them. Their visual field is arranged around a center as it is with normal people. The region of clearest vision lies *within* this field—not (as one might assume) on the margin of the preserved half of the field that corresponds to the location of the fovea. If such a patient wants to see an object, he deviates the direction of his eyes a little to bring the object into the center of the preserved field of vision. This is the only way that he can recognize objects. The object must be placed in a field and surrounded by other parts of the total field containing other objects.

The apparent goal of the organism, in hemianopsia, is to have vision as good as possible, to realize the capacities that already exist. This trend towards realization of capacities is a tendency shown by the organism as a whole. It is shown by many other forms of behavior— normal and abnormal.

A view similar to that of Goldstein was expressed by Carl Rogers (1951), whose name is associated with the technique of client-centered therapy. He agrees that the organism has one basic tendency and striving—to actualize, maintain, and enhance the experiencing organism. Behavior moves in the direction of greater independence or self-responsibility—of increasing self-government, self-regulation. As Rogers puts it: *"The organism has one basic tendency and striving— to actualize, maintain, and enhance the experiencing organism."*

This tendency to self-actualization occurs, as with all behavior, within a world perceived and known by the individual, i.e., within a psychological world. Self-actualization, Rogers states, is a prime human motivation.

SUMMARY AND CONCLUSION

If we think about motivation narrowly in terms of goal-oriented behavior, then frustration is a form of interference with purposive activity, a blocking of goal-directed action. Frustration can increase the degree of motivation and in this sense frustration is a source of drive, but if motivation is strong and frustration rigid, the frustration may produce emotional disruption through overactivation. Persistent frustration of a strong and stable motive commonly disorganizes the individual emotionally.

Stress includes much more than frustration. Organic states of hunger, fatigue, and sickness, are factors in stress. Frustration, of course, may combine with these factors to produce unpleasant states. The factors of stress predispose an individual to emotional upset but do not necessarily cause emotion. Intense stimulation, especially when painful, causes emotional disturbance. There is a limit to the amount of pain and frustration an individual can tolerate without emotional disruption.

In addition to the factors of frustration, stress, painful stimulation, and the like, emotion is produced by conflict. Persisting conflict is a form of frustration involving two or more motives. We cannot define emotion as a conflict state, however, because there are other exciting causes of emotion. The relief from tension, as in success and triumph, and satisfied expectations, are conditions that evoke emotional upsets.

Emotion arises within a *psychological* situation, i.e., one involving an environmental factor, present or past. The importance of the psychological situation is apparent in the analysis of weeping and laughing. In these emotions the release of tension is the main cause of emotional disturbance.

When we regard emotion as a persistent disturbance within the individual we have broadened the base of our definition. From the point of view of clinical psychology this broadened definition is justified. We cannot, however, identify emotion with neurosis.

A neurosis is a persistent disorganization of the organism that is revealed by various symptoms: tics, hyper- and hypoactivity, amnesia, insomnia, chronic changes in the vegetative processes, as well as by repeated outbreaks of emotion. Emotional behavior is thus only one of the manifestations of neurotic disorganization.

When emotion is viewed as a persisting disorganization within the organism it is intimately related to health. The whole area of psychosomatic medicine recognizes the view that physical and psychological determinants may have like effects. They become indistinguishable as factors influencing health. Especially important in psychosomatic medicine is the factor of anxiety. In mild degree anxiety is motivating. Worry causes us to do things to relieve or reduce the worry; but if anxiety is intense and persisting, it may damage the individual's health.

The Freudian concepts of repression and dissociation must be considered in relation to adjustment and to emotion. Repression and dissociation result from intolerable conflicts. These dynamic processes explain phobias, obsessions, compulsions, amnesias, functional anesthesias, and other phenomena.

The Freudian psychology has developed a rich terminology that is applicable to the study of motivation, adjustment, and emotion. But there is presently a gap: There are two kinds of motivational psychology—a human psychology of motivation that is stated in terms stemming from psychoanalysis, and a biologically-oriented psychology of motivation that originated in the laboratory and especially in experiments with animals. I believe that these two psychologies of motivation will eventually fuse into one and that a single psychology of motivation and emotion, well-grounded upon physiology and human experience, will emerge.

Current non-Freudian theories of motivation explain behavior in terms of disequilibrium, disparity, cognitive dissonance, deficit, tension, self-actualization, and the like. These current views account for only a part of the general problem of motivation.

Reading Suggestions

There is a great wealth of literature relating to the dynamics of emotional behavior and adjustment. For general orientation see: Symonds (1946), Shaffer and Shoben (1956), and White (1956). For a comprehensive survey of the history of medical psychology the work by Zilboorg and Henry (1941) is excellent.

Shaffer, L. F. and Shoben, E. J., Jr. *The psychology of adjustment.* (2nd ed.) Boston: Houghton Mifflin, 1956.

Symonds, P. M. *The dynamics of human adjustment.* New York: Appleton-Century, 1946.

White, R. W. *The abnormal personality; a textbook.* (2nd ed.) New York: Ronald, 1956.

Zilboorg, G. and Henry, G. W. *A history of medical psychology.* New York: Norton, 1941.

GENERAL
CONCLUSION

The aim of this book has been to search for the fundamental determinants of human and animal activity. The search has revealed many kinds of determinants—physical, social, cultural, psychological, and other. Motives, in the usual sense of the word, are only one variety. The survey of fundamental determinants has extended beyond the bounds of psychology.

The quest is timely and urgent. Modern man finds himself at the crossroads of civilization and barbarism. Obviously the understanding and control of human behavior is a matter of paramount importance. Modern man might soliloquize after the manner of Hamlet:

To survive or not to survive (war and peace, genicide);
To eat or not to eat (famine, starvation);
To mate or not to mate (sex, marriage, divorce);
To reproduce or not to reproduce (eugenics, population explosion, hereditary diseases);
To fear, to love, to hate, to play, to sleep, or *not* (emotional adjustments, mental health, anxiety neuroses).
These are the questions.

The dynamic psychology of motivation and emotion is relevant to the solution of these problems but alone cannot give all the answers.

Complexity of Motivational Psychology

We live in a world that is perceived directly through the senses. It is a world of experience in which thoughts, fantasies, feelings, and de-

594

sires play a part. The world we live in has been described as a molar world that exists at a level somewhere between the molecular world of the chemist and the stellar universe of the astronomer. Within this world are innumerable objects and events—among them the diverse phenomena with which dynamic psychology is concerned.

The field of dynamic psychology is exceedingly complex. The human brain is the most complex object known to science; but the brain is only one of the determinants of human behavior. There are determinants outside the organism.

Reasons for the complexity of motivational psychology are not hard to find.

First, motivational psychology is concerned with different kinds of processes. One kind of process is a contemporary event that is observed in several aspects. *Behavior* is observed as a contemporary event—a dynamic relation between organism and environment. Internal *bodily processes* are contemporaneous with overt behavior. They are observed by the physiologist as a separate aspect of the total process. The *conscious experience* of individuals constitutes another aspect of the contemporary event. Thus there are three aspects to the contemporary psychological process: behavior, bodily processes, experiencing.

A very different kind of process with which motivational psychology deals is growth, or development. This is typically a gradual change that takes place within the organism. Growth processes include maturing, learning, the development of attitudes, motives and habit structures, the development of conflict states and the making of adjustments. Growth processes go on within the life cycle of individuals.

Still another kind of process with which motivational psychology deals is the dynamic interaction of determinants. The clash of motives, the interaction of attitudes and perceptions, the repression of wishes, the formation of neuroses—these are dynamic events. They presuppose the existence of developed determinants.

In general, it can be said that contemporary processes are *observed*. Developmental processes and dynamic interactions are usually *inferred* from the facts of experience.

A second reason for the complexity of motivational psychology lies in the fact that the concept of determination has different meanings. "To determine" might mean to activate through brain action, chemical sensitization, external stimulation, or other means. Again, "to determine" might mean to regulate and direct behavior, actively or passively. Neural structures passively limit and restrict the patterns of behavior. Mental sets and postures and internal preparations actively direct behavior by maintaining a goal orientation. Again, "to determine" might mean to organize or reorganize patterns of activity. With these and still other meanings it may not be entirely clear what we mean by a search for the "determinants" of behavior.

Motives, in the usual sense of the word, are determinants of action but it is obvious that there are other forms of determining factors. Motives direct behavior persistently towards a goal; they also have a dynamogenic function; they also organize and reorganize activity. These different meanings of determination complicate the psychologist's problem.

A third reason for the complexity of motivational psychology lies in the fact that there are different models for analyzing motivation. Human and animal behavior has been explained in terms of homeostasis and the homeostatic drives, the concept of need, stimulus and response, the concept of central neural activation, affective arousal, the concepts of set, tension, feedback, and expectancy. Then in social psychology there are various concepts like attitude, orientation, interest, motive, personality need, value, loyalty. Some of the concepts can be combined, e.g., activation and affective arousal, homeostasis and organic needs or drives. Others are supplementary to the above, e.g., the concept of set.

Since there are many limited hypotheses and points of view, and since there is no general, integrating principle, a multifactor approach to the analysis of determination is clearly indicated. A general, all-inclusive theory of motivation does not exist.

A fourth reason for the complexity of motivational psychology lies in its historical origins. Current dynamic psychology has had a dual origin. First, the work of Freud and other psychoanalysts has yielded a rich vocabulary that is useful in understanding and interpreting human conduct. Second, the work of the laboratories for several decades has produced a wealth of fact and principle relating to human and animal motives and incentives. There are two historical trends. They are merging but have not yet coalesced.

Finally, in view of this complexity it is easy to understand why "motivation" means all things to all men. The diverse topics of the Nebraska Symposia, indeed, reveal many points of view, partial theories, along with a wealth of fact. It seems that almost any psychologist can discuss almost any topic and bring it within the broad context of "motivation."

Everyone approves of "motivation" but there is little agreement concerning its nature. Professor Littman, in a light and somewhat cynical vein, pointed this out in a paper presented in the Nebraska Symposium on Motivation. He wrote: "Hence motivational phenomena are like oranges, pussycats, chairs, kites, and genes; they can all be viewed as capable of doing something, but they all do it in different ways, and for different reasons."

Thus, as we have seen, there is great complexity and diversity of fact, principle, and concept within motivational psychology. There are: (1) different kinds of processes with which the psychologist must deal, (2) different meanings of "determination," (3) different models for explanation and no all-inclusive theory, and (4) different vocabularies with different historical origins. In view of this complexity we can easily understand why "motivation" means all things to all men.

The Pendulum Swings

Drive theory has pretty much dominated the motivational stage for several decades. Drive theory places the emphasis on internal organic conditions; it is tied up with the doctrine of homeostasis. But the emphasis has changed from internal organic conditions to external incentives.

Current studies of exteroceptive motivation (under the headings of curiosity, manipulation, exploration) emphasize the environmental determinants of behavior. But experiments upon sensory deprivation, deprivation of activity, and related topics, indicate that there may be an internal, bodily need for stimulation and activity. Permanent damage can be done by depriving an organism of sensory stimulation, of activity, and play.

Thus the pendulum swings from internal drives to external conditions and back again from exteroceptive motivation to the primary internal determinants. A complete theory, we believe, must embrace both internal and external determinants in interaction.

Emotion Enters the Picture

The concept of emotion is somewhat clearer than that of motivation but it is difficult, if not impossible, to find a definition upon which all psychologists will agree. Some psychologists would equate emotion with affectivity but others (including the writer) define emotion as a specific variety of affective process that is characterized by disturbance, disorganization.

An emotion may be defined as a strongly visceralized, affective disturbance, originating within the psychological situation, and revealing itself in bodily changes, in behavior, and in conscious experience.

This definition may be extended to include the conditions that determine emotion. When, for instance, we speak of an emotionally disturbed child we imply a persisting state of disturbance within the individual.

This extended definition has utility in studies of emotional development. It is useful in considering questions like these: What produces emotional disturbances? What is their influence upon behavior? How does an individual make adjustment to emotional conflicts? What is the end result of emotional disturbance in terms of adjustment and development?

The extended definition is also useful in the field of psychodynamics. Here a distinction must be drawn between the phenomena of emotion and underlying dynamics. As a phenomenon, emotion is initiated by perception, memory, fantasy, expectation, or other psychological event; it is *psychological* in origin. So far as we can observe or feel an emotion it is a contemporary event. In terms of the underlying dynamics (which we infer), an emotion is produced by frustration, conflict, painful stimulation and by factors of stress, expectation, release of tension, and related conditions.

Within the broad context of the present study, an emotion, as process, is both cause and effect, both a determinant and an event that is determined. The emotional process is determined by a variety of conditions and circumstances. As students of motivation we must search for these determinants. They are found in the dynamic interplay of motivating conditions. The emotional process is also a causal factor in the organization of attitudes, motives, sentiments, traits of personality, and the like.

The emotional process is thus a central figure in the total picture of motivation. Motivation is the broader concept. We have argued that all behavior is motivated in the sense of being causally determined but no one has argued that all behavior is emotionally disturbed!

Confusion and Turmoil

The present state of motivational psychology reflects a more general condition within psychology as a whole. Psychology itself is in an emotionally disturbed state and in need of some kind of reorientation.

Psychology is in a state of turmoil and confusion. There has been a revolution (or series of revolutions) and the outcome is not yet clear.

During the early decades of the twentieth century, schools of psychology flourished: introspectionism, behaviorism, gestaltism, and others. Then limited theoretical systems appeared: those of Hull, Tolman, Guthrie, Skinner, Spence, and others. Within motivational psychology, as we noted above, there have been limited explanatory theories but nowhere a complete and fully adequate account of the determination of human action.

Psychoanalysis developed along an independent path. The merging of psychoanalytical concepts with those derived from comparative, physiological, and experimental human psychology, has not clarified the situation.

Psychology is something like a ship drifting in a storm. It needs to anchor to a solid base. Psychological theory might be anchored to the physical world, to physiological processes, to the sociocultural environment, to individual conscious experience. Perhaps the ship would be more secure with several anchors.

Or, to use a different analogy, psychology is like a building that is being constructed by many workers. The general plan of the structure is not yet clear; the architects have different ideas. Many of the stones that will be used as building blocks have been examined in the present survey but they need to be fitted together properly in the structure that is being built.

Suggestions and Recommendations

In view of this confusion and turmoil and lack of agreement, what positive suggestions and recommendations can be made? A few tentative answers are considered:

First, the student of motivation and emotion would be well advised to define his task sharply and narrowly. There are various ways in which the study can be restricted. For one thing, the study might be limited to *psychological* determinants. Other forms of causation—physicial, social, biological—can be disregarded. The psychological determinants include goal orientations, attitudes, habit organizations, interests, sentiments, and the like.

Again, the task might be limited to some phase of determination such as: (1) the activating and energizing of behavior, or (2) the regulation and direction of activity, particularly goal-directed activity, or (3) the organization and reorganization of patterns of behavior in developing organisms. Since "determination" and "causation" have various meanings, the student would be well advised to state his aims precisely.

Again, it seems reasonable to restrict one's study to a single kind of event. As we have seen, psychologists deal with at least three different kinds of interrelated events: (1) contemporary psychological activities, (2) development that occurs within the life cycle of individuals, (3) the dynamic interaction of acquired determinants.

The student should recognize his specific interests and biases. This writer has not attempted to conceal his bias towards physiological psychology. One justification for this bias is that the physiological facts are so intimately related to the facts of behavior and experience that they can scarcely be disentangled. If all sciences are unitary and present a single body of knowledge, the physiological facts must be related to the phenomena of psychology.

Therefore, in any concrete study of motivation and emotion it is suggested that the student restrict his task, limiting it, if possible, to some phase of determination and to a single kind of event, and that he recognize his specific interests and biases.

Second, the student of motivation and emotion would be well advised to take account of the principle of psychological relativity. This principle was considered in Chapter 1, and several ways of dealing with it were examined. One might hold rigidly to a fixed point of view and thus restrict his task or one might shift viewpoints, as the eclectic does, thus gaining a certain amount of freedom from biases. But other courses are possible:

One can start from the basic fact that man is the kind of a creature who can shift his viewpoint; he can analyze different aspects and phases of complex situations. Certain questions arise: What is a point of view (orientation) in terms of the organism? How do points of view develop and how can they be changed? How do they operate to select, organize, and restrict human activity? These are straightforward questions and they can serve as points of departure in the psychological study of determinants.

Another way to deal with psychological relativity is to search for determinants that are *independent* of points of view. The physical universe proceeds along its course regardless of how men view it, what they believe about it, whether or not they understand it. Physical reality, in fact, is independent of the subject's shifting points of view. But within psychology there are distinctions that can be drawn from all points of view and that are independent of any particular point of view. Examples of such distinctions are these: the distinction between the individual and the world within which he lives; the distinction between latent neural structure and its arousal; the distinction between organization and disorganization; the distinction among different kinds of events—contemporary events, development, dynamic interaction. Formulations that are independent of all points of view can be sought.

Third, the student of motivation and emotion could simplify his task by rejecting all dynamic concepts like drive, motive, force, and other forms of impetus, and limiting himself to a purely descriptive psychology. In Chapter 2 it was pointed out that descriptive psychology deals with terms and relations, with graphs and equations, with co-variation, correlation, and factor analysis; and does not need the concept of causation, much less the concept of psychic force.

A descriptive psychology, to be adequate, must take account of determining conditions. One can argue that explanation is simply a more complete description of the conditions that surround the event to be explained. If a student settles for pure description, however, he has sold out dynamic psychology. He may be unwilling to do this.

Fourth, the student of motivation and emotion should realize that what psychology needs is a fully adequate account of the psychological organism. This organism develops through a cycle starting at conception and ending at death. It is a true unit for psychological science. All of the activities and processes that the psychologist studies occur within the psychological organism, or individual.

We have postulated a biological monism. There are not two organisms—body and mind—but only one. To this organism we impute attributes that make it fully adequate as a basis for explaining psychological phenomena.

Fifth, in view of the confusion, turmoil and lack of agreement within motivational psychology, we should recognize the validity of a *multifactor* view of determination. If we ask "Why is human experience as it is?" we will find partial answers in the different sciences.

For partial answers we can turn to the physical sciences—physics, chemistry, astronomy, and geology—and to biological sciences including physiology and the objective science of behavior. For other partial answers we can turn to the social sciences—to anthropology, sociology, history, government, and other disciplines that deal with the social environment. We can also turn to psychology which has a unique interest in the experience of individuals.

The psychologist is interested in the development of individuals through maturing and learning, in the organization of habit structures and attitudes, in development of personality traits including goal orientations, evaluative dispositions, interests, and the like. The psychologist is also interested in basic processes like perceiving, remembering, and thinking; in conflict, stress, and adjustment; and in the dynamic interaction of motives, attitudes, and habits. A *multifactor* view of determination is clearly indicated. This multifactor view is especially important because the search for determinants extends beyond psychology into the physical and social sciences, and because, within psychology itself, the search for salient determinants is made in all areas and related to all psychological functions and processes.

Finally, in view of the diversity and complexity within psychology as a whole, as well as within the area of motivation and emotion, a firm recommendation must be—tolerance.

QUESTIONS AND EXERCISES

These questions and exercises are designed to aid the student in study and review of the materials in the different chapters. They may also serve as aids to discussion.

Chapter 1. Orientation

1. Describe several situations in everyday life that call for an understanding of motivation.
2. Distinguish between broad and narrow definitions of motivation.
3. How would you define the psychological problem of motivation?
4. What is meant by *explanation* of behavior? What is the nature of scientific explanation?
5. If the common-sense concept of causation is set aside, is it possible to have a dynamic psychology?
6. Is it possible to reconcile scientific motivational psychology with a doctrine of free will?
7. What is psychological relativity?
8. What is your opinion concerning the nature and value of eclecticism?
9. What is a cause? A condition? A determinant?
10. Most people believe that conscious feelings and desires influence their actions. What do you think about this belief?

Chapter 2. Forms and Determinants of Activity

1. What is the difference between sleeping and waking? Is sleeping a habit?
2. Can a doctrine of mental energy be formulated so that there are no objections to it?

3. What endocrine glands influence the level of general activity?
4. Describe a behavioral trend such as manipulative or exploratory behavior. How can such a trend be explained?
5. If we had a completely adequate descriptive psychology, would we need a theory of motivation?
6. Is goal-directed behavior a fact of observation or an inference?
7. Briefly describe: Woodworth's behavior-primacy theory, competence and effectance, functional autonomy of motives, hedonism.
8. Is it necessary to postulate extrinsic motivation to explain behavior?

Chapter 3. Instinctive Behavior and Drive

1. Define and distinguish: reflex, instinct, tropism, taxis.
2. Is instinct a descriptive label or an explanatory concept? Justify your answer. Give an example of instinctive behavior.
3. Describe several examples of sexual behavior in animals and show what conditions determine it.
4. List the main views concerning nature of the drive and show how they can be related to each other.
5. How would you distinguish among drive, habit, and motive?
6. Do you believe that the concept of drive should be dropped from scientific psychology? If the concept of drive is dropped, could we dispense with the concept of motivation?

Chapter 4. Homeostasis, Need, and Behavior

1. Define homeostasis and give several specific examples.
2. Discuss the evolution of homeostatic mechanisms.
3. What are the limitations of the doctrine of homeostasis as a general theory of motivation?
4. Contrast the concepts of homeostasis and adjustment.
5. What criteria can be used in defining needs objectively?
6. Distinguish between need and drive.
7. Is it possible to define personality needs and social needs objectively?
8. Describe the experiments of Hull and Leeper on the control of behavior by organic states of hunger and thirst.
9. What did Anderson mean by the externalization of drive?

Chapter 5. Affective Arousal and Activation

1. Describe: The empirical law of effect, beneception and nociception, the hedonic continuum.
2. Can affective processes be defined objectively? If so, how?

3. Give objective evidence for the distinction between palatabiltiy and appetite.
4. How are affective processes related to the organization of attitudes and motives?
5. What is activation as viewed by the physiologist?
6. Give psychological evidence for existence of both positive and negative affective arousals.
7. What are the main functions of affective arousal in behavior and development?

Chapter 6.   Incentive Motivation

1. What is the difference between drive and incentive?   Give examples to show how drive and incentive differ and how they are related.
2. What is meant by secondary reinforcement?   Under what conditions does secondary reinforcement develop?
3. What is symbolic reward?   Describe an experiment to illustrate symbolic reward.
4. What is a negative incentive?   How can negative incentives be studied in the laboratory?
5. Describe N. Miller's experiment upon "fear as an acquired drive." How would you interpret his findings?
6. Describe the psychological effects of weak, moderate, and strong electric shocks.
7. State several views concerning the nature of reinforcement and extinction. Criticize the view that reinforcement comes solely from the reduction of a drive.

Chapter 7.   Direction and Regulation

1. Do you believe that all goal-directed behavior is learned?   How about the moth flying into a flame?   Clarify.
2. What is a goal gradient?   Give an example.
3. Cite original examples of pregoal and postgoal behavior.
4. What are the most important psychological meanings of *set?*
5. How is *set* related to attention?   To will?   To perception?
6. Describe Courts' experiment upon degree of muscular tension and efficiency of memorizing.   How is muscular tension related to efficiency of performance?
7. State Zipf's law of least effort.   What limitations and restrictions do you see to this principle?
8. What is feedback?   Give examples of visual, auditory, and proprioceptive feedback, and show the role of feedback in regulation of behavior.

Chapter 8. Cognition and Motivation

1. What is perception, as viewed physically and psychologically?
2. Describe experiments to show what is meant by the directive-state theory of perception. How do needs and values influence perception?
3. What is the role of perception in the instigation of emotion?
4. Distinguish between affective arousal and the evaluation of experience.
5. What does Helson mean by adaption level (AL)?
6. What experimental evidence did Tolman advance to prove that rats form cognitive maps of their environments?
7. What does F. Allport mean by the cyclical structure of events? Does Allport's concept of psychological structure agree with what is known about neural structure and function?
8. Recall some past experience persistently until the main details are present. Then show the relation of these details to each other in terms of a cyclical structure. How well does the cyclical format work in diagramming the structure of remembered events?
9. Distinguish between intrinsic and extrinsic motivation. Illustrate the difference.
10. Under what conditions are beliefs influenced by desires more than by reason?

Chapter 9. Nature and Bodily Mechanisms of Emotion

1. How, in everyday life, do we recognize and distinguish emotions?
2. Why is there so much confusion about the definition of emotion?
3. If emotional behavior is a useless disturbance, would we be better off without any emotions?
4. Do you believe that all affective processes should be called "emotional" processes?
5. Is a strictly scientific definition of emotion possible—one that is factual and not evaluative?
6. What physiological events distinguish emotional from non-emotional states? Be specific.
7. Describe the main anatomical and physiological features of the autonomic nervous system.
8. State Cannon's emergency theory of emotion and review the criticisms that have been raised against it.
9. What is the psychological and physiological basis of lie detecting?
10. Describe several typical patterns of response that appear in emotional behavior.
11. What are the advantages and disadvantages of the pattern-response definition of emotion as compared with the disruption concept?

12. Where, anatomically, are the neural centers that coordinate patterns of emotional response?

13. From the point of view of physiology describe how conflict and frustration are related to emotional disturbances.

Chapter 10. Development of Motives and Emotions

1. Why is it necessary to know about the past of an organism to identify emotional states? In what sense does the past determine present behavior?

2. Can one distinguish between learning and motivation as independent factors in performance? If so, how?

3. What is the functional autonomy of motives? Would it 'be better to speak of the functional autonomy of habits?

4. Give an example of chemical motivation.

5. Discuss the roles of maturation, early experience, and social regulation, in emotional development.

6. Describe an experiment upon the physiological effects of drugs.

7. Describe an experiment with animals that shows the influence of early experience upon adult behavior.

8. How, in general, can one best describe emotional development?

9. What is meant by emotional maturity? emotional control? What is the role of social pressure in emotional control?

10. Comment upon the view that emotional development is the growth of techniques for dealing with frustrations, threats, and other causes of upset.

Chapter 11. Social and Personal Determinants

1. Can a sharp distinction be drawn between the biological and social determinants of behavior?

2. Distinguish among differential, interactional, and genetic points of view in the analysis of social behavior.

3. What is culture? How do cultural factors influence individual action?

4. In what sense can we speak of the group as a psychological unit?

5. What is field theory? Group dynamics?

6. Distinguish between social motives and social incentives giving examples of each.

7. Describe an experiment upon one of the following: praise and reproof, reward and punishment, success and failure, competition and cooperation.

8. What is meant by level of aspiration, area of aspiration, achievement motive?

9. Define: need, interest, attitude, value, loyalty. Are all these concepts required to describe motivation as a personality variable?

10. Contrast the cognitive and affective aspects of attitude. Illustrate the relation between cognitive and affective aspects of attitude.
11. What is the self, or ego, psychologically considered?
12. How did Freud distinguish among ego, superego, and id?

Chapter 12. Dynamics of Emotional Behavior

1. Define frustration. How do frustrating circumstances vary with age of the individual?
2. Describe several types of behavior that result from frustration.
3. State and evaluate Dewey's conflict theory of emotion.
4. In what way does stress differ from frustration?
5. How can emotion and neurosis be distinguished from each other?
6. What concept of emotion is implied when we affirm that emotional disturbances produce ill health?
7. In what sense is anxiety a drive? Under what conditions does anxiety impede behavior? How is the concept of anxiety related to motivation and emotions?
8. What conditions lead to repression and dissociation?
9. Define or describe: phobia, obsession, compulsion, sublimation.
10. What did Freud believe about unconscious motivation?
11. What is psychosomatic medicine? What is the systematic point of view of psychosomatic medicine upon the mind-body relation?
12. Distinguish between the evaluative and factual views of adjustment.
13. How is the maintaining of homeostasis related to the process of adjustment?
14. State the disparity theory of motivation.
15. What are the limitations of the deficit-tension theories of motivation?
16. What is self-actualization? How is self-actualization related to other forms of motivation?
17. To what extent is man a rational animal?

REFERENCES

Following is a list of works cited in the text. The pages on which citations occur are given in brackets.

Abelson, R. P., and Rosenberg, M. J. Symbolic psycho-logic: A model of attitudinal cognition. *Behaviorial Science*, 1958, **3**, 1–13. [521]

Allport, F. H. *Theories of perception and the concept of structure: a review and critical analysis with an introduction to a dynamic-structural theory of behavior.* New York: Wiley, 1955. [277, 296, 301, 329, 343]

Allport, G. W. Attitudes. In *A handbook of social psychology* (C. Murchison, Ed.). Worcester, Mass.: Clark University Press, 1935. [531]

—— *Personality, a psychological interpretation.* New York: Holt, 1937. [423, 504]

—— Scientific models and human morals. *Psychol. Rev.*, 1947, **54**, 182–192. [264]

——, Vernon, P. E., and Lindzey, G. *Study of values.* Boston: Houghton Mifflin, 1960. [512]

Anderson, E. E. The externalization of drive: I. Theoretical considerations. *Psychol. Rev.*, 1941a, **48**, 204–224. [134]

—— The externalization of drive: II. The effect of satiation and removal of reward at different stages in the learning process of the rat. *J. genet. Psychol.*, 1941b, **59**, 359–376. [134]

—— The externalization of drive: III. Maze learning by non-rewarded and by satiated rats. *J. genet. Psychol.*, 1941c, **59**, 397–426. [134]

—— The externalization of drive: IV. The effect of pre-feeding on the maze performance of hungry non-rewarded rats. *J. comp. Psychol.*, 1941d, **31**, 349–352. [134]

Anderson, J. E. Changes in emotional responses with age. In *Feelings and emotions: the Mooseheart symposium in cooperation with the University of Chicago* (M. L. Reymert, Ed.). New York: McGraw-Hill, 1950. [458]

Angier, R. P. The conflict theory of emotion. *Amer. J. Psychol.*, 1927, **39**, 390–401. [545]

Angyal, A. *Foundations for a science of personality.* New York: The Commonwealth Fund, 1941. [25]

609

Arnold, M. B. Physiological differentiation of emotional states. *Psychol. Rev.*, 1945, **52**, 35–48. [371]

Asdourian, D. *See* Young and Asdourian, 1957.

Ashley, W. R., Harper, R. S., and Runyon, D. L. The perceived size of coins in normal and hypnotically induced economic states. *Amer. J. Psychol.*, 1951, **64**, 564–572. [306]

Atkinson, J. W. *See* McClelland, Atkinson, Clark, and Lowell, 1953.

——— *Motives in fantasy, action, and society: a method of assessment and study.* Princeton, N. J.: Van Nostrand, 1958. [36, 504, 531]

Ausubel, D. P. Introduction to a threshold concept of primary drives. *J. gen. Psychol.*, 1956, **54**, 209–229. [97]

Backer, R. *See* Sheffield, Wulff, and Backer, 1951.

Bagby, E. *The psychology of personality, an analysis of common emotional disorders.* New York: Holt, 1928. [526]

Bard, P. The neurohumoral basis of emotional reactions. In *A handbook of general experimental psychology* (C. Murchison, Ed.). Worcester, Mass.: Clark University Press, 1934a. [355, 384]

——— An emotional expression after decortication with some remarks on certain theoretical views. *Psychol. Rev.*, 1934b, **41**, 309–329, 424–449. [384, 390]

——— Central nervous mechanisms for the expression of anger in animals. In *Feelings and emotions: the Mooseheart symposium in cooperation with the University of Chicago* (M. L. Reymert, Ed.). New York: McGraw-Hill, 1950. [197, 384, 405]

Bare, J. K. The specific hunger for sodium chloride in normal and adrenalectomized white rats. *J. comp. physiol. Psychol.*, 1949, **42**, 242–253. [155]

Barelare, B. *See* Richter, Holt, and Barelare, 1937.

Barker, A. N. *See* Hull, Livingston, Rouse, and Barker, 1951.

Barker, R., Dembo, T., and Lewin, K. Frustration and regression, an experiment with young children. *University of Iowa Studies: Studies in Child Welfare,* 1941, **18**, No. 386. [542]

Bayley, N. A study of the crying of infants during mental and physical tests. *J. genet. Psychol.*, 1932, **40**, 306–329. [445–446]

Beach, F. A. Effects of cortical lesions upon the copulatory behavior of male rats. *J. comp. Psychol.*, 1940, **29**, 193–239. [87]

——— Current concepts of play in animals. *Amer. Natur.*, 1945, **79**, 523–541. [49]

——— Instinctive behavior: Reproductive activities. In *Handbook of experimental psychology* (S. S. Stevens, Ed.). New York: Wiley, 1951. [71, 82, 86–87, 107–108]

——— Characteristics of masculine "sex drive." In *Nebraska symposium on motivation* (M. R. Jones, Ed.). Lincoln, Nebr.: University of Nebraska Press, 1956. [84, 88–89]

———, and Holz-Tucker, A. M. Effects of different concentrations of androgen upon sexual behavior in castrated male rats. *J. comp. physiol. Psychol.*, 1949, **42**, 433–453. [87]

Beebe-Center, J. G. The law of affective equilibrium. *Amer. J. Psychol.*, 1929, **41**, 54–69. [317]

Beebe-Center, J. G. *The psychology of pleasantness and unpleasantness.* Princeton, N. J.: Van Nostrand, 1932. [151, 204]

―――― *See* Gardiner, Metcalf, and Beebe-Center, 1937.

Berkum, M. *See* Kagan and Berkum, 1954.

Berlyne, D. E. Novelty and curiosity as determinants of exploratory behaviour. *Brit. J. Psychol.*, 1950, **41**, 68–80. [54]

―――― *Conflict, arousal, and curiosity.* New York: McGraw-Hill, 1960. [54]

Bernard, C. *Leçons sur les Propriétés physiologiques et les Altérations pathologiques des Liquides de l'organisme.∂* Paris: Baillière, 1859. [109]

―――― *Leçons sur les Phénomènes de la Vie communs aux Animaux et aux Végétaux.* Paris: Baillière, 1878. [109]

Bindra, D. *Motivation: A systematic reinterpretation.* New York: Ronald, 1959. [17, 29, 36, 58, 63, 67, 143, 187–188, 204, 256, 259, 296, 356, 416, 465–466]

Bitterman, M. E. *See* Ryan, Cottrell, and Bitterman, 1950.

Boder, D. P. *I did not interview the dead.* Urbana, Ill.: University of Illinois Press, 1949. [525]

Bond, N. A. *See* Guilford, Christensen, Bond, and Sutton, 1954.

Bowers, A. M. *See* Healy, Bronner, and Bowers, 1931.

Braun, H. W., Wedekind, C. E., and Smudski, J. F. The effect of an irrelevant drive on maze learning in the rat. *J. exper. Psychol.*, 1957, **54**, 148–152. [207]

Bridges, K. M. B. A genetic theory of the emotions. *J. genet. Psychol.*, 1930, **37**, 514–527. [440]

―――― *The social and emotional development of the pre-school child.* London: Kegan Paul, Trench, Trubner, 1931. [440]

―――― Emotional development in early infancy. *Child Devel.*, 1932, **3**, 324–341. [440–443]

Britt, S. H. *Social psychology of modern life.* New York: Rinehart, 1949. [339]

Bronner, A. F. *See* Healy, Bronner, and Bowers, 1931.

Brown, J. S. Problems presented by the concept of acquired drives. In *Current theory and research in motivation: a symposium.* Lincoln, Nebr.: University of Nebraska Press, 1953. [16, 95, 104, 172, 419]

―――――, and Farber, I. E. Emotions conceptualized as intervening variables—with suggestions toward a theory of frustration. *Psychol. Bull.*, 1951, **48**, 465–495. [351, 361, 538]

Bruner, J. S., and Goodman, C. C. Value and need as organizing factors in perception. *J. ab. and soc. Psychol.*, 1947, **42**, 33–44. [303–305]

Brunswick, D. The effects of emotional stimuli on the gastro-intestinal tone. *J. comp. Psychol.*, 1924, **4**, 19–79, 225–287. [395]

Brush, E. S. *See* Solomon and Brush, 1956.

Bugelski, R. Extinction with and without sub-goal reinforcement. *J. comp. Psychol.*, 1938, **26**, 121–133. [216]

Bykov, K. M. *The cerebral cortex and the internal organs* (trans. by W. Horsley Gantt). New York: Chemical, 1957. [400]

Cameron, N., and Magaret, A. *Behavior pathology.* Boston: Houghton Mifflin, 1951. [123, 362, 574]

Campbell, B. A. *See* Sheffield, Roby, and Campbell, 1954.

Campbell, B. A., and Sheffield, F. D. Relation of random activity to food deprivation. *J. comp. physiol. Psychol.*, 1953, **46**, 320–322. [97–98]

Cannon, W. B. *Bodily changes in pain, hunger, fear and rage: An account of recent researches into the function of emotional excitement* (2nd ed.). New York: Appleton-Century-Crofts, 1929. [369, 409–410]

———— *The wisdom of the body*. New York: Norton, 1932. [109, 143]

Cantril, H. *See* Sherif and Cantril, 1947.

Carper, J. W. A comparison of the reinforcing value of a nutritive and a nonnutritive substance under conditions of specific and general hunger. *Amer. J. Psychol.*, 1953, **66**, 270–277. [140]

Carr, H. A. *Psychology: A study of mental activity*. New York: Longmans, Green, 1925. [316]

Cattell, R. B. *Personality and motivation structure and measurement*. New York: Harcourt Brace-World, 1957. [504, 510]

Chandler, A. R. *Beauty and human nature: elements of psychological aesthetics.* New York: Appleton-Century-Crofts, 1934. [513]

Chaplin, J. P. *See* Young and Chaplin, 1945.

Child, I. L., and Waterhouse, I. K. Frustration and the quality of performance: I. A theoretical statement. *Psychol. Rev.*, 1953, **60**, 127–139. [538]

Christensen, P. R. *See* Guilford, Christensen, Bond, and Sutton, 1954.

Clark, R. A. *See* McClelland, Atkinson, Clark, and Lowell, 1953.

Clay, J. *See* Harris, Clay, Hargreaves, and Ward, 1933.

Cobb, S. *Borderlands of psychiatry*. Cambridge, Mass.: Harvard University Press, 1948. [10]

Coghill, G. E. *Anatomy and the problem of behaviour.* New York: Macmillan, 1929. [70]

———— Integration and motivation of behavior as problems of growth. *Pedagog. Sem.*, 1936, **48**, 3–19. [427]

Cole, L. E. *General psychology*. New York: McGraw-Hill, 1939. [276]

Cole, R. H. (Ed.) Consumer behavior and motivation: Marketing symposium, October 1955. *Univ. Ill. Bull.*, 1956, **53**, No. 45. Urbana, Ill.: University of Illinois Press, 1956. [2]

Combs, A. W., and Snygg, D. *Individual behavior: A perceptual approach to behavior* (rev. ed.). New York: Harper, 1959. [301, 343]

Compton, R. K., and Young, P. T. A study of organic set: Immediate reproduction of spatial patterns presented by successive points to different senses. *J. exper. Psychol.*, 1933, **16**, 775–797. [267–268]

Cottrell, C. L. *See* Ryan, Cottrell, and Bitterman, 1950.

Cotzin, M. *See* Supa, Cotzin, and Dallenbach, 1944.

Courts, F. A. Relations between experimentally induced muscular tension and memorization. *J. exper. Psychol.*, 1939, **25**, 235–256. [278–279]

———— The influence of practice on the dynamogenic effect of muscular tension. *J. exper. Psychol.*, 1942a, **30**, 504–511. [280]

———— Relations between muscular tension and performance. *Psychol. Bull.*, 1942b, **39**, 347–367. [280, 296]

Cowles, J. T. Food-tokens as incentives for learning by chimpanzees. *Comp. Psychol. Monog.*, 1937, **14**, No. 5. [220]

Crafts, L. W., Schneirla, T. C., Robinson, E. E., and Gilbert, R. W. *Recent experiments in psychology.* New York: McGraw-Hill, 1938. [502]

Craig, W. Appetites and aversions as constituents of instincts. *Biol. Bull.,* 1918, **34**, 91–107. [275]

Crespi, L. P. Quantitative variation of incentive and performance in the white rat. *Amer. J. Psychol.,* 1942, **55**, 467–517. [208–209]

———— Amount of reinforcement and level of performance. *Psychol. Rev.,* 1944, **51**, 341–357. [208]

Cronbach, L. J. Response sets and test validity. *Educ. and Psychol. Meas.,* 1946, **6**, 475–494. [273]

———— Further evidence on response sets and test design. *Educ. and Psychol. Meas.,* 1950, **10**, 3–31. [273]

———— *Educational psychology.* New York: Harcourt Brace-World, 1954. [465–466]

————, and Davis, B. Belief and desire in wartime. *J. ab. and soc. Psychol.,* 1944, **39**, 446–458. [340]

Crutchfield, R. S. *See* Krech and Crutchfield, 1948.

Dallenbach, K. M. *See* Supa, Cotzin, and Dallenbach, 1944.

Darrow, C. W. Emotion as relative functional decortication: the role of conflict. *Psychol. Rev.,* 1935, **42**, 566–578. [407]

———— A new frontier: Neurophysiological effects of emotion on the brain. In *Feelings and emotions: the Mooseheart symposium in cooperation with the University of Chicago* (M. L. Reymert, Ed.). New York: McGraw-Hill, 1950. [408]

————, and Henry, C. E. Psychophysiology of stress. In *Human factors in undersea warfare.* Washington, D. C.: National Research Council, 1949. [556]

Darwin, C. *The expression of the emotions in man and animals.* London: Murray, 1872. [349, 384, 388]

Dashiell, J. F. Experimental studies of the influence of social situations on the behavior of individual human adults. In *A handbook of social psychology* (C. Murchison, Ed.). Worcester, Mass.: Clark University Press, 1935. [482]

———— *Fundamentals of general psychology.* Boston: Houghton Mifflin, 1949. [276]

Davis, B. M. *See* Cronbach and Davis, 1944.

Davis, R. C. Methods of measuring muscular tension. *Psychol. Bull.,* 1942, **39**, 329–346. [296]

Deese, J. *See* Lazarus, Deese, and Osler, 1951.

Delgado, J. M. R., Roberts, W. W., and Miller, N. E. Learning motivated by electrical stimulation of the brain. *Amer. J. Physiol.,* 1954, **179**, 587–593. [195]

De Martino, M. F. *See* Stacey and De Martino, 1958.

Dembo, T. *See* Barker, Dembo, and Lewin, 1941.

Dempsey, E. W. Homeostasis. In *Handbook of experimental psychology* (S. S. Stevens, Ed.). New York: Wiley, 1951. [117, 143]

Deutsch, M. Field theory in social psychology. In *Handbook of social psychology.* Vol. I (G. Lindzey, Ed.). Cambridge, Mass.: Addison-Wesley, 1954. [531–532]

Dewey, J. The theory of emotion: I. Emotional attitudes. *Psychol. Rev.*, 1894, **1**, 553–569. [545]

―――― The theory of emotion: II. The significance of emotions. *Psychol. Rev.*, 1895, **2**, 13–32. [545–546]

Dollard, J., Doob, L. W., Miller, N. E., Mowrer, O. H., and Sears, R. R. *Frustration and aggression.* New Haven: Yale University Press, 1939. [539]

Doob, L. W. *See* Dollard, Doob, Miller, Mowrer, and Sears, 1939.

Duffy, E. An explanation of "emotional" phenomena without the use of the concept "emotion." *J. gen. Psychol.*, 1941, **25**, 283–293. [351]

―――― Leeper's "Motivational theory of emotion." *Psychol. Rev.*, 1948, **55**, 324–328. [351]

―――― The concept of energy mobilization. *Psychol. Rev.*, 1951, **58**, 30–40. [93]

―――― The psychological significance of the concept of "arousal" or "activation." *Psychol. Rev.*, 1957, **64**, 265–275. [360]

Dufort, R. H., and Kimble, G. A. Changes in response strength with changes in the amount of reinforcement. *J. exper. Psychol.*, 1956, **51**, 185–191. [240–241]

Dyal, J. A. Response strength as a function of magnitude of perceived incentive. *Perceptual and Motor Skills*, 1960, **10**, 35–38. [212]

Eckert, J. F. *See* Richter and Eckert, 1939.

Ellis, H. *Studies in the psychology of sex: III. Analysis of the sexual impulse.* Philadelphia: Davis, 1920. [90]

Elwell, J. L., and Grindley, G. C. The effect of knowledge of results on learning and performance: I. Co-ordinated movement of the two hands. *Brit. J. Psychol.*, 1938, **29**, 39–54. [288–290]

Eriksen, C. W. Subception: fact or artifact? *Psychol. Rev.*, 1956, **63**, 74–80. [312]

―――― Unconscious processes. In *Nebraska symposium on motivation* (M. R. Jones, Ed.). Lincoln, Nebr.: University of Nebraska Press, 1958. [309–310]

Estes, W. E. Generalization of secondary reinforcement from the primary drive. *J. comp. physiol. Psychol.*, 1949, **42**, 286–295. [247]

Falk, J. L. *See* O'Kelly and Falk, 1958.

―――― *See* Young and Falk, 1956a, 1956b.

Farber, I. E. *See* Brown and Farber, 1951.

―――― Anxiety as a drive state. In *Nebraska symposium on motivation* (M. R. Jones, Ed.). Lincoln, Nebr.: University of Nebraska Press, 1954. [567]

―――― The role of motivation in verbal learning and performance. *Psychol. Bull.*, 1955, **52**, 311–327. [16, 418]

Ferster, C. B., and Skinner, B. F. *Schedules of reinforcement.* New York: Appleton-Century-Crofts, 1957. [235]

Festinger, L. Motivations leading to social behavior. In *Nebraska symposium on motivation.* Lincoln, Nebr.: University of Nebraska Press, 1954. [468]

―――― The motivating effect of cognitive dissonance. In *Human motives* (G. Lindzey, Ed.). New York: Rinehart, 1958. [586]

Fiedler, F. E. *Leader attitudes and group effectiveness.* Urbana, Ill.: University of Illinois Press, 1958. [486]

Freeman, E. *Principles of general psychology.* New York: Holt, 1939. [584]

Freeman, G. L. The optimal muscular tensions for various performances. *Amer. J. Psychol.,* 1938, **51**, 146–150. [280]

────── The energetics of human behavior. Ithaca, N. Y.: Cornell University Press, 1948. [114–115]

Fryer, D. The measurement of interests, in relation to human adjustment. New York: Holt, 1931. [16]

Fulton, J. F. Physiology of the nervous system. New York: Oxford University Press, 1938. [390]

Galambos, R. *See* Griffin and Galambos, 1941, 1942.

Gardiner, H. M., Metcalf, R. C., and Beebe-Center, J. G. Feeling and emotion: a history of theories. New York: American Book, 1937. [409–410]

Gebhard, P. H. *See* Kinsey, Pomeroy, Martin, and Gebhard, 1953.

Gellhorn, E. Autonomic regulations: their significance for physiology, psychology and neuropsychiatry. New York: Interscience, 1943. [370]

Gibson, E. J. The role of shock in reinforcement. *J. comp. physiol. Psychol.,* 1952, **45**, 18–30. [233]

Gibson, J. J. A critical review of the concept of set in contemporary experimental psychology. *Psychol. Bull.,* 1941, **38**, 781–817. [264, 296]

────── The perception of the visual world. Boston: Houghton Mifflin, 1950. [299, 325]

Gilbert, R. W. *See* Crafts, Schneirla, Robinson, and Gilbert, 1938.

Gilchrist, J. C., and Nesberg, L. S. Need and perceptual change in need-related objects. *J. exper. Psychol.,* 1952, **44**, 369–376. [302–303]

Goldstein, K. The organism, a holistic approach to biology derived from pathological data in man. New York: American Book, 1939. [590]

────── Organismic approach to the problem of motivation. *Trans. New York Acad. Sci.,* 1947, **9**, 218–230. [590]

Goodenough, F. L. Anger in young children. *Univ. Minn., Institute of Child Welfare Monog. Series,* No. 9. Minneapolis, Minn.: University of Minnesota Press, 1931. [450–451]

Goodman, C. C. *See* Bruner and Goodman, 1947.

Grant, D. A., Hake, H. W., and Hornseth, J. P. Acquisition and extinction of a verbal conditioned response with differing percentages of reinforcement. *J. exper. Psychol.,* 1951, **42**, 1–5. [252–253]

Greene, J. T. *See* Young and Greene, 1953.

Grice, G. R. The relation of secondary reinforcement to delayed reward in visual discrimination learning. *J. exper. Psychol.,* 1948, **38**, 1–16. [246]

Griffin, D. R., and Galambos, R. The sensory basis of obstacle avoidance by flying bats. *J. exper. Zoöl.,* 1941, **86**, 481–506. [292]

────── Obstacle avoidance by flying bats: The cries of bats. *J. exper. Zoöl.,* 1942, **89**, 475–490. [292]

Grindley, G. C. *See* Elwell and Grindley, 1938.

Grinker, R. R., and Spiegel, J. P. Men under stress. Philadelphia: Blakiston, 1945. [430, 552]

Guetzkow, H. Multiple loyalties: Theoretical approach to a problem in international organization. Princeton, N. J.: Publication No. 4 of the Center for

Research on World Political Institutions, Princeton University Press, 1955. [514]

Guilford, J. P. *Personality.* New York: McGraw-Hill, 1959. [504, 513, 531–532]

——, Christensen, P. R., Bond, N. A., and Sutton, M. A. A factor analysis study of human interests. *Res. Bull.* 53–11, *Human Resources Res. Center, Lackland Air Force Base, San Antonio, Texas,* May 1953. Also published in *Psychol. Monogs.: General and Applied,* 1954, **68**, No. 4, Whole No. 375. [508]

Guthrie, E. R. *The psychology of human conflict: the clash of motives within the individual.* New York: Harper, 1938. [92]

—— Personality in terms of associated learning. In *Personality and the behavior disorders* (J. McV. Hunt, Ed.). New York: Ronald, 1944. [93]

Guttman, N. Operant conditioning, extinction, and periodic reinforcement in relation to concentration of sucrose used as reinforcing agent. *J. exper. Psychol.,* 1953, **46**, 213–224. [240]

Hake, H. W. *See* Grant, Hake, and Hornseth, 1951.

Hall, C. S., and Whiteman, P. H. The effects of infantile stimulation upon later emotional stability in the mouse. *J. comp. physiol. Psychol.,* 1951, **44**, 61–66. [437]

Hall, J. F. Studies in secondary reinforcement: I. Secondary reinforcement as a function of the frequency of primary reinforcement. *J. comp. physiol. Psychol.,* 1951a, **44**, 246–251. [213–215]

—— Studies in secondary reinforcement: II. Secondary reinforcement as a function of the strength of drive during primary reinforcement. *J. comp. physiol. Psychol.,* 1951b, **44**, 462–466. [214]

Hamilton, H. C. The effect of incentives on accuracy of discrimination measured on the Galton bar. *Arch. Psychol.,* 1929, **16**, No. 103. [492]

Hargreaves, F. J. *See* Harris, Clay, Hargreaves, and Ward, 1933.

Harlow, H. F. The formation of learning sets. *Psychol. Rev.,* 1949, **56**, 51–65. [271]

—— Motivation as a factor in the acquisition of new responses. In *Current theory and research in motivation: A symposium.* Lincoln, Nebr.: University of Nebraska Press, 1953. [53, 141]

——, Harlow, M. K., and Meyer, D. R. Learning motivated by a manipulative drive. *J. exper. Psychol.,* 1950, **40**, 228–234. [50]

Harlow, M. K. *See* Harlow, Harlow, and Meyer, 1950.

Harper, R. S. *See* Ashley, Harper, and Runyon, 1951.

Harris, L. J., Clay, J., Hargreaves, F. J., and Ward, A. Appetite and choice of diet: the ability of the vitamin B deficient rat to discriminate between diets containing and lacking the vitamin. *Proc. roy. Soc., London,* Series B, 1933, **113**, 161–190. [164, 176]

Hart, B. *The psychology of insanity* (4th ed.). New York: Macmillan, 1937. [574]

Hayworth, D. The social origin and function of laughter. *Psychol. Rev.,* 1928, **35**, 367–384. [549]

Healy, W., Bronner, A. F., and Bowers, A. M. *The structure and meaning of psychoanalysis, as related to personality and behavior.* New York: Knopf, 1931. [573]

Hebb, D. O. On the nature of fear. *Psychol. Rev.*, 1946a, **53**, 259–276. [348, 413]

—— Emotion in man and animal: an analysis of the intuitive processes of recognition. *Psychol. Rev.*, 1946b, **53**, 88–106. [348, 412]

—— *The organization of behavior: A neuropsychological theory.* New York: Wiley, 1949. [20, 101, 130, 236, 355]

—— Drives and the C. N. S. (Conceptual Nervous System). *Psychol. Rev.*, 1955, **62**, 243–254. [102]

Helson, H. Adaptation level theory. In *Psychology: a study of a science.* Vol. 1. (S. Koch, Ed.). New York: McGraw-Hill, 1959. [319]

Henry, C. E. *See* Darrow and Henry, 1949.

Henry, G. W. *See* Zilboorg and Henry, 1941.

Herrick, C. J. *An introduction to neurology.* Philadelphia: Saunders, 1915. [66]

Hilgard, E. R. *Introduction to psychology.* New York: Harcourt Brace-World, 1953. (Not included 1957, rev. ed.). [353]

Hill, J. H., and Stellar, E. An electronic drinkometer. *Science*, 1951, **114**, 43–44. [166]

Hill, W. F. Activity as an autonomous drive. *J. comp. physiol. Psychol.*, 1956, **49**, 15–19. [55]

Hodge, F. A. The emotions in a new role. *Psychol. Rev.*, 1935, **42**, 555–565. [407]

Hollingworth, L. S. *The psychology of the adolescent.* New York: Appleton-Century-Crofts, 1928. [454]

Holmes, F. B. *See* Jersild and Holmes, 1935.

Holt, E. B. *Animal drive and the learning process: an essay toward radical empiricism.* New York: Holt, 1931. [92, 202]

Holt, L. E. *See* Richter, Holt, and Barelare, 1937.

Holz-Tucker, A. M. *See* Beach and Holz-Tucker, 1949.

Hornseth, J. P. *See* Grant, Hake, and Hornseth, 1951.

Horwitz, M. The conceptual status of group dynamics. *Rev. Educ. Research*, 1953, **23**, 309–328. [483–484]

Hull, C. L. Differential habituation to internal stimuli in the albino rat. *J. comp. Psychol.*, 1933, **16**, 255–273. [132]

—— The rat's speed-of-locomotion gradient in the approach to food. *J. comp. Psychol.*, 1934, **17**, 393–422. [260–262]

—— *Principles of behavior: an introduction to behavior theory.* New York: Appleton-Century-Crofts, 1943. [20, 211, 245]

—— *Essentials of behavior.* New Haven, Conn.: Yale University Press, 1951. [211]

—— *A behavior system: an introduction to behavior theory concerning the individual organism.* New Haven, Conn.: Yale University Press, 1952. [212]

——, Livingston, J. R., Rouse, R. O., and Barker, A. N. True, sham, and esophageal feeding as reinforcements. *J. comp. physiol. Psychol.*, 1951, **44**, 236–245. [245]

Hunt, J. McV. The effects of infant feeding-frustration upon adult hoarding in the albino rat. *J. ab. soc. Psychol.*, 1941, **36**, 338–360. [433]

—— Situational cues distinguishing anger, fear, and sorrow. *Amer. J. Psychol.*, 1958, **71**, 136–151. [549]

——, Schlosberg, H., Solomon, R. L., and Stellar, E. Studies of the effects of infantile experience on adult behavior in rats: I. Effects of infantile feeding frustration on adult hoarding. *J. comp. physiol. Psychol.,* 1947, **40,** 291–304. [434]

Hunt, W. A. *See* Landis and Hunt, 1939.

Hunter, W. S. The delayed reaction in animals and children. *Behav. Monog.,* 1913, 2, No. 6. [266]

Hurlock, E. B. The value of praise and reproof as incentives for children. *Arch. Psychol.,* 1924, **11,** No. 71. [488–490]

―――― An evaluation of certain incentives used in school work. *J. educ. Psychol.,* 1925, **16,** 145–159. [488]

Hyman, R. *See* Stellar, Hyman, and Samet, 1954.

Inbau, F. E. *Lie detection and criminal interrogation.* Baltimore: Williams and Wilkins, 1942. [383]

Jenkins, W. O. A temporal gradient of derived reinforcement. *Amer. J. Psychol.,* 1950, **63,** 237–243. [216–217]

Jennings, H. S. *Behavior of the lower organisms.* New York: Columbia University Press, 1915. [425]

Jersild, A. T. *Child psychology* (Fourth edition). Englewood Cliffs, N. J.: Prentice-Hall, 1954. [439, 465–466, 588]

――――, and Holmes, F. B. Children's fears. *Child Devel. Monog.,* 1935, No. 20. [451–452]

Jones, M. R. (Ed.) *Nebraska symposium on motivation.* Lincoln, Nebr.: University of Nebraska Press, 1953― ――――. [36]

Kagan, J., and Berkum, M. The reward value of running activity. *J. comp. physiol. Psychol.,* 1954, **47,** 108. [55]

Karwoski, T. F. *See* Stagner and Karwoski, 1952.

Kellogg, W. N. Echo ranging in the porpoise: perception of objects by reflected sound is demonstrated for the first time in a marine animal. *Science,* 1958, **128,** 982–988. [292]

―――― Auditory perception of submerged objects by porpoises. *J. Acoustical Soc. Amer.,* 1959a, **31,** 1–6. [292]

―――― Size discrimination by reflected sound in a bottle-nose porpoise. *J. comp. physiol. Psychol.,* 1959b, **52,** 509–514. [292]

Kelly, G. A. Man's construction of his alternatives. In *Assessment of human motives* (G. Lindzey, Ed.). New York: Rinehart, 1958. [8, 343]

Kempf, E. J. *Psychopathology.* St. Louis, Mo.: C. V. Mosby, 1920. [364]

Kendler, H. H. The influence of simultaneous hunger and thirst drives upon the learning of two opposed spatial responses of the white rat. *J. exper. Psychol.,* 1946, **36,** 212–220. [136]

―――― An investigation of latent learning in a T-maze. *J. comp. physiol. Psychol.,* 1947, **40,** 265–270. [136]

Kimble, G. A. *See* Dufort and Kimble, 1956.

Kinsey, A. C., Pomeroy, W. B., and Martin, C. E. *Sexual behavior in the human male.* Philadelphia: Saunders, 1948. [107–108, 428, 578]

Kinsey, A. C., Pomeroy, W. B., Martin, C. E., and Gebhard, P. H. *Sexual behavior in the human female.* Philadelphia: Saunders, 1953. [107–108]

Klein, G. S. Need and regulation. In *Nebraska symposium on motivation* (M. R. Jones, Ed.). Lincoln, Nebr.: University of Nebraska Press, 1954. [123]

―――― Cognitive control and motivation. In *Assessment of human motives* (G. Lindzey, Ed.). New York: Rinehart, 1958. [334]

Kleitman, N. Sleep and wakefulness. Chicago: Chicago University Press, 1939. [42]

Kling, C. The role of the parasympathetics in emotions. *Psychol. Rev.,* 1933, **40,** 368–380. [371]

Kluckhohn, C. *Mirror for man, the relation of anthropology to modern life.* New York: McGraw-Hill, 1949. [21]

―――― Culture and behavior. In *Handbook of social psychology* (G. Lindzey, Ed.). Cambridge, Mass.: Addison-Wesley, 954. [531–532]

Kniep, E. H., Morgan, W. L., and Young, P. T. Studies in affective psychology. *Amer. J. Psychol.,* 1931, **43,** 406–421. [150]

Koch, S. Behavior as "intrinsically" regulated: work notes towards a pre-theory of phenomena called "motivational." In *Nebraska symposium on motivation* (M. R. Jones, Ed.). Lincoln, Nebr.: University of Nebraska Press, 1956. [171, 335]

Krech, D., and Crutchfield, R. S. *Theory and problems of social psychology.* New York: McGraw-Hill, 1948. [423]

Krout, M. H. *Introduction to social psychology.* New York: Harper, 1942. [475]

Landis, C. Studies of emotional reactions: II. General behavior and facial expression. *J. comp. Psychol.,* 1924, **4,** 447–501. [347]

―――― , and Hunt, W. A. *The startle pattern.* New York: Farrar and Rinehart, 1939. [392–393]

Larson, J. A. *Lying and its detection: a study of deception and deception tests.* Chicago: University of Chicago Press, 1932. [383]

Lashley, K. S. Experimental analysis of instinctive behavior. *Psychol. Rev.,* 1938, **45,** 445–471. [76–77, 94]

Lauer, D. W. (Personal communication). [232]

Lazarus, R. S., Deese, J., and Osler, S. F. Review of research on effects of psychological stress upon performance. *Research Bull. 51–28, Human Resources Research Center, Lackland Air Force Base, San Antonio, Texas,* December 1951. [557]

―――― , and McCleary, R. A. Autonomic discrimination without awareness: A study of subception. *Psychol. Rev.,* 1951, **58,** 113–122. [311]

Leeper, R. W. The role of motivation in learning: a study of the phenomena of differential motivational control of the utilization of habits. *J. genet. Psychol.,* 1935, **46,** 3–40. [132, 421]

―――― A motivational theory of emotion to replace "emotion as disorganized response." *Psychol. Rev.,* 1948, **55,** 5–21. [351, 355]

Lewin, K. *Gesetz und Experiment in der Psychologie.* Berlin-Schlachtensee: Weltkreis verlag, 1927. [9]

Lewin, K. *A dynamic theory of personality: selected papers* (trans. by D. K. Adams and K. E. Zener). New York: McGraw-Hill, 1935. [480]

—— Behavior and development as a function of the total situation. In *Manual of child psychology* (2nd. ed.; L. Carmichael, Ed.). New York: Wiley, 1954. [480]

—— *See* Barker, Dembo, and Lewin, 1941.

Liddell, H. S. The experimental neurosis and the problem of mental disorder. *Amer. J. Psychiat.*, 1938, **94**, 1035–1041. [560]

Lindsley, D. B. Emotion. In *Handbook of experimental psychology* (S. S. Stevens, Ed.). New York: Wiley, 1951. [182–186, 360, 367–368, 375, 409–410]

—— Psychophysiology and motivation. In *Nebraska symposium on motivation* (M. R. Jones, Ed.). Lincoln, Nebr.: University of Nebraska Press, 1957. [204]

Lindzey, G. *See* Allport, Vernon, and Lindzey, 1960.

Lippitt, R. *See* Spence and Lippitt, 1946.

Littman, R. A. Motives, history and causes. In *Nebraska symposium on motivation* (M. R. Jones, Ed.). Lincoln, Nebr.: University of Nebraska Press, 1958. [14, 421]

Livingston, J. R. *See* Hull, Livingston, Rouse, and Barker, 1951.

Lowell, E. L. *See* McClelland, Atkinson, Clark, and Lowell, 1953.

Lund, F. H. The psychology of belief. *J. ab. soc. Psychol.*, 1925–1926, **20**, 63–81, 174–196. [337]

—— Why do we weep? *J. soc. Psychol.*, 1930, **1**, 136–151. [548]

—— *Emotions, their psychological, physiological and educative implications.* New York: Ronald, 1939. [409–410]

Luria, A. R. *The nature of human conflicts, or emotion, conflict and will* (trans. by W. H. Gantt). New York: Liveright, 1932. [562]

MacKinnon, D. W. Motivation. In *Foundations of psychology* by Boring, E. G., Langfeld, H. S., and Weld, H. P. New York: Wiley, 1948. [123]

Magaret, A. *See* Cameron and Magaret, 1951.

Maier, N. R. F. *Studies of abnormal behavior in the rat: I. The neurotic pattern and an analysis of the situation which produces it.* New York: Harper, 1939. [560]

—— *Frustration: The study of behavior without a goal.* New York: McGraw-Hill, 1949. [15, 535]

Malinowski, B. *Sex and repression in savage society.* New York: Harcourt Brace-World, 1927. [91]

Maller, J. B. *Cooperation and competition: an experimental study in motivation. Columbia Univ. Contrib. to Educ.*, No. 384. New York: Columbia University, 1929. [501]

Martin, C. E. *See* Kinsey, Pomeroy, and Martin, 1948, *and* Kinsey, Pomeroy, Martin, and Gebhard, 1953.

Martineau, P. *Motivation in advertising.* New York: McGraw-Hill, 1957. [313, 339]

Marx, M. H. Some relations between frustration and drive. In *Nebraska symposium on motivation* (M. R. Jones, Ed.). Lincoln, Nebr.: University of Nebraska Press, 1956. [539]

Maslow, A. H. *Motivation and personality.* New York: Harper, 1954. [15, 589]
—— Deficiency motivation and growth motivation. In *Nebraska symposium on motivation* (M. R. Jones, Ed.). Lincoln, Nebr.: University of Nebraska Press, 1955. [588]
Mason, D. J. *The relation of quantity, quality, and probability of reward to reaction potential and secondary reinforcement.* Doctoral thesis in psychology, University of Illinois, Urbana, Ill., 1956. [175, 250]
Masserman, J. H. *Principles of dynamic psychiatry, including an integrative approach to abnormal and clinical psychology.* Philadelphia: Saunders, 1947. [561]
McCleary, R. A. *See* Lazarus and McCleary, 1951.
—— Taste and post-ingestion factors in specific-hunger behavior. *J. comp. physiol. Psychol.,* 1953, **46**, 411–421. [159]
McClelland, D. C. *Personality.* New York: William Sloane Associates, 1951. [36, 478, 504]
—— *Studies in motivation.* New York: Appleton-Century-Crofts, 1955a. [36, 107, 465–466]
—— Some social consequences of achievement motivation. In *Nebraska symposium on motivation* (M. R. Jones, Ed.). Lincoln, Nebr.: University of Nebraska Press, 1955b. [500]
——, Atkinson, J. W., Clark, R. A., and Lowell, E. L. *The achievement motive.* New York: Appleton-Century-Crofts, 1953. [420, 499, 587]
McDougall, W. *Outline of psychology.* New York: Scribner's, 1923. [14, 257]
McGeoch, J. A. *The psychology of human learning, an introduction.* New York: Longmans, Green, 1942. [145]
McGinnies, E. Emotionality and perceptual defense. *Psychol. Rev.,* 1949, **56**, 244–251. [306–308]
Meehl, P. E. On the circularity of the law of effect. *Psychol. Bull.,* 1950, **47**, 52–75. [147]
Metcalf, R. C. *See* Gardiner, Metcalf, and Beebe-Center, 1937.
Meyer, D. R. *See* Harlow, Harlow, and Meyer, 1950.
Miller, J. G. *Unconsciousness.* New York: Wiley, 1942. [579]
Miller, N. E. Studies of fear as an acquirable drive: I. Fear as motivation and fear-reduction as reinforcement in the learning of new responses. *J. exper. Psychol.,* 1948, **38**, 89–101. [226–227]
—— Learnable drives and rewards. In *Handbook of experimental psychology* (S. S. Stevens, Ed.). New York: Wiley, 1951. [229, 230–231, 567]
—— Effects of drugs on motivation: The value of using a variety of measures. *Annals New York Acad. Sci.,* 1956, **65**, 318–333. [168, 222]
—— Experiments on motivation: Studies combining psychological, physiological and pharmacological techniques. *Science,* 1957, **126**, 1271–1278. [197]
Miller, N. E. *See* Delgado, Roberts, and Miller, 1954, *and* Dollard, Doob, Miller, Mowrer, and Sears, 1939.
Milner, P. *See* Olds and Milner, 1954.
Montgomery, K. C. The effect of the hunger and thirst drives upon exploratory behavior. *J. comp. physiol. Psychol.,* 1953, **46**, 315–319. [52]
—— The role of the exploratory drive in learning. *J. comp. physiol. Psychol.,* 1954, **47**, 60–64. [52]

Morgan, C. T. Physiological mechanisms of motivation. In *Nebraska symposium on motivation* (M. R. Jones, Ed.). Lincoln, Nebr.: University of Nebraska Press, 1957. [99]

—— Physiological theory of drive. In *Psychology: a study of a science. Vol. I. Sensory, perceptual, and physiological formulations* (S. Koch, Ed.). New York: McGraw-Hill, 1959. [99, 108]

——, and Stellar, E. *Physiological psychology*. New York: McGraw-Hill, 1950. [67, 409–410]

Morgan, J. J. B. The overcoming of distraction and other resistances. *Arch. Psychol.*, 1916, **5**, No. 35. [283]

—— *Keeping a sound mind*. New York: Macmillan, 1934. [454]

Morgan, W. L. *See* Kniep, Morgan, and Young, 1931.

Morissey, P. D. *See* Scott, Verney, and Morissey, 1950.

Moss, F. A. Study of animal drives. *J. exper. Psychol.*, 1924, **7**, 165–185. [93]

Mowrer, O. H. A stimulus-response analysis of anxiety and its role as a reinforcing agent. *Psychol. Rev.*, 1939, **46**, 553–565. [566]

—— *See* Dollard, Doob, Miller, Mowrer, and Sears, 1939.

Muenzinger, K. F. Motivation in learning: I. Electric shock for correct response in the visual discrimination habit. *J. comp. Psychol.*, 1934, **17**, 267–277. [223–224]

——, and Wood, A. Motivation in learning: IV. The function of punishment as determined by its temporal relation to the act of choice in the visual discrimination habit. *J. comp. Psychol.*, 1935, **20**, 95–106. [223–225]

Murdock, G. P. The common denominator of cultures. In *The science of man in the world crisis* (R. Linton, Ed.). New York: Columbia University Press, 1945. [476]

Murphy, G. Social motivation. In *Handbook of social psychology*, Vol. II (G. Lindzey, Ed.). Cambridge, Mass.: Addison-Wesley, 1954. [531–532]

Murray, H. A. *Explorations in personality: A clinical and experimental study of fifty men of college age*. New York: Oxford University Press, 1938. [123, 143, 504–505]

Nafe, J. P. An experimental study of the affective qualities. *Amer. J. Psychol.*, 1924, **35**, 507–544. [149]

Nesberg, L. S. *See* Gilchrist and Nesberg, 1952.

Newcomb, T. M. *Social psychology*. New York: Dryden, 1950. [479]

—— Motivation in social behavior. In *Current theory and research in motivation: a symposium*. Lincoln, Nebr.: University of Nebraska Press, 1953. [504, 516]

Newman, E. B. Perception. In *Foundations of psychology* by Boring, E. G., Langfeld, H. S., and Weld, H. P. New York: Wiley, 1948. [276]

Nissen, H. W. Phylogenetic comparison. In *Handbook of experimental psychology* (S. S. Stevens, Ed.). New York: Wiley, 1951. [96]

—— The nature of the drive as innate determinant of behavioral organization. In *Nebraska symposium on motivation* (M. R. Jones, Ed.). Lincoln, Nebr.: University of Nebraska Press, 1954. [51, 95]

Nowlis, V. The development and modification of motivational systems in personality. In *Current theory and research in motivation: a symposium.* Lincoln, Nebr.: University of Nebraska Press, 1953. [431]

Nutrition Reviews, Editors of. Self-selection of diets. 1944, **2,** 199–203. [129]

O'Kelly, L. I., and Falk, J. L. Water regulation in the rat: II. The effects of preloads of water and sodium chloride on the bar-pressing performance of thirsty rats. *J. comp. physiol. Psychol.,* 1958, **51,** 22–25. [120–122]

Olds, J. Physiological mechanisms of reward. In *Nebraska symposium on motivation* (M. R. Jones, Ed.). Lincoln, Nebr.: University of Nebraska Press, 1955. [191, 204]

—— *The growth and structure of motives: psychological studies in the theory of action.* Glencoe, Ill.: Free Press, 1956. [256, 322]

——, and Milner, P. Positive reinforcement produced by electrical stimulation of septal area and other regions of rat brain. *J. comp. physiol. Psychol.,* 1954, **47,** 419–427. [193]

Osgood, C. E. The nature and measurement of meaning. *Psychol. Bull.,* 1952, **49,** 197–237. [320]

——, and Suci, G. J. Factor analysis of meaning. *J. exper. Psychol.,* 1955, **50,** 325–338. [320]

Osler, S. F. *See* Lazarus, Deese, and Osler, 1951.

Parsons, T., and Shils, E. A. (Eds.). *Toward a general theory of action.* Cambridge, Mass.: Harvard University Press, 1952. [531–532]

Pavlov, I. P. *Conditioned reflexes: an investigation of the physiological activity of the cerebral cortex* (trans. by G. V. Anrep). New York: Oxford University Press, 1927. [558]

Peak, H. Attitude and motivation. In *Nebraska symposium on motivation* (M. R. Jones, Ed.). Lincoln, Nebr.: University of Nebraska Press, 1955. [521, 585]

Perin, C. T. A quantitative investigation of the delay-of-reinforcement gradient. *J. exper. Psychol.,* 1943, **32,** 37–51, 95–109. [247]

Piéron, H. Emotions in animals and man. In *Wittenberg symposium on feelings and emotions* (C. Murchison and M. L. Reymert, Eds.). Worcester, Mass.: Clark University Press, 1928. [389]

Pomeroy, W. B. *See* Kinsey, Pomeroy, and Martin, 1948, *and* Kinsey, Pomeroy, Martin, and Gebhard, 1953.

Postman, L. The history and present status of the law of effect. *Psychol. Bull.,* 1947, **44,** 489–563. [147]

—— The experimental analysis of motivational factors in perception. In *Current theory and research in motivation: a symposium.* Lincoln, Nebr.: University of Nebraska Press, 1953. [343]

Pratt, C. H. *See* Schlosberg and Pratt, 1956.

Prescott, D. A. *Emotion and the educative process: a report of the committee on the relation of emotion to the educative process.* Washington, D. C.: Amer. Council on Education, 1938. [465–466]

Quint, E. *See* Scott and Quint, 1946.

Rapaport, D. *Emotions and memory*. New York: International Universities Press, 1950. [315, 354]

Raup, R. B. *Complacency: The foundation of human behavior*. New York: Macmillan, 1925. [585]

Razran, G. A note on the use of the terms *conditioning* and *reinforcement*. *Amer. Psychologist*, 1955, **10**, 173–174. [235]

Richey, H. W. *See* Young and Richey, 1952.

Richter, C. P. Animal behavior and internal drives. *Quart. Rev. Biol.*, 1927, **2**, 307–343. [40]

—— Biological foundations of personality differences. *Amer. J. Orthopsychiatry*, 1932, **2**, 345–354. [44–45, 47]

—— The effect of early gonadectomy on the gross body activity of rats. *Endocrinol.*, 1933, **17**, 445–450. [44, 46]

—— Increased salt appetite in adrenalectomized rats. *Amer. J. Physiol.*, 1936, **115**, 155–167. [113]

—— Salt taste thresholds of normal and adrenalectomized rats. *Endocrinol.*, 1939, **24**, 367–371. [113]

—— Total self regulatory functions in animals and human beings. *The Harvey Lectures Series*, 1942, **38**, 63–103. [112, 143]

—— The self-selection of diets. In *Essays in biology, in honor of Herbert M. Evans., written by his friends*. Berkeley, Calif.: University of California Press, 1943, 501–506. [128]

—— *See* Wilkins and Richter, 1940.

——, and Eckert, J. F. Mineral appetite of parathyroidectomized rats. *Amer. J. med. Sci.*, 1939, **198**, 9–16. [113]

——, Holt, L. E., and Barelare, B. Vitamin B_1 craving in rats. *Science*, 1937, **86**, 354–355. [177]

Ritchie, B. F. A logical and experimental analysis of the laws of motivation. In *Nebraska symposium on motivation* (M. R. Jones, Ed.). Lincoln, Nebr.: University of Nebraska Press, 1954. [8]

Roberts, W. W. *See* Delgado, Roberts, and Miller, 1954.

Robinson, E. E. *See* Crafts, Schneirla, Robinson, and Gilbert, 1938.

Roby, T. B. *See* Sheffield and Roby, 1950.

—— *See* Sheffield, Roby, and Campbell, 1954.

Rogers, C. R. *Client-centered therapy; its current practice, implications, and theory*. Boston: Houghton Mifflin, 1951. [356, 591]

Rosenberg, M. J. (Personal communication) [522]

—— *See* Abelson and Rosenberg, 1958.

Rotter, J. B. Level of aspiration as a method of studying personality: I. A critical review of methodology. *Psychol. Rev.*, 1942, **49**, 463–474. [497]

Rouse, R. O. *See* Hull, Livingston, Rouse, and Barker, 1951.

Ruckmick, C. A. *The psychology of feeling and emotion*. New York: McGraw-Hill, 1936. [409–410]

Runyon, D. L. *See* Ashley, Harper, and Runyon, 1951.

Russell, R. W., and Younger, J. The effects of avitaminosis-A on visual intensity difference thresholds in the rat. *J. exper. Psychol.*, 1943, **32**, 507–512. [125]

Ryan, T. A., Cottrell, C. L., and Bitterman, M. E. Muscular tension as an index of effort: The effect of glare and other disturbances in visual work. *Amer. J. Psychol.*, 1950, **63**, 317–341. [282]

Samet, S. *See* Stellar, Hyman, and Samet, 1954.

Samuels, I. Reticular mechanisms and behavior. *Psychol. Bull.*, 1959, **56**, 1–25. [204]

Schlosberg, H. A scale for the judgment of facial expressions. *J. exper. Psychol.*, 1941, **29**, 497–510. [396]

―――― The description of facial expressions in terms of two dimensions. *J. exper. Psychol.*, 1952, **44**, 229–237. [397]

―――― Three dimensions of emotion. *Psychol. Rev.*, 1954, **61**, 81–88. [397]

Schlosberg, H. *See* Hunt, Schlosberg, Solomon, and Stellar, 1947.

―――― *See* Woodworth and Schlosberg, 1954.

Schlosberg, H., and Pratt, C. H. The secondary reward value of inaccessible food for hungry and satiated rats. *J. comp. physiol. Psychol.*, 1956, **49**, 149–152. [170]

Schmidt, H. O. The effects of praise and blame as incentives to learning. *Psychol. Monog.*, 1941, **53**, No. 3. [488]

Schneirla, T. C. *See* Crafts, Schneirla, Robinson, and Gilbert, 1938.

―――― An evolutionary and developmental theory of biphasic processes underlying approach and withdrawal. In *Nebraska symposium on motivation* (M. R. Jones, Ed.). Lincoln, Nebr.: University of Nebraska Press, 1959. [156, 202, 204]

Scott, E. M., and Quint, E. Self selection of diet: III. Appetites for B vitamins. *J. Nutrition*, 1946, **32**, 285–292. [178]

―――― , and Verney, E. L. Self-selection of diets: VI. The nature of appetites for B vitamins. *J. Nutrition*, 1947, **34**, 471–480. [178]

―――― , Verney, E. L., and Morissey, P. D. Self selection of diet: XI, Appetites for calcium, magnesium and potassium. *J. Nutrition*, 1950, **41**, 187–201. [179]

Sears, R. R. Initiation of the repression sequence by experienced failure. *J. exper. Psychol.*, 1937, **20**, 570–580. [496]

―――― *See* Dollard, Doob, Miller, Mowrer, and Sears, 1939.

Selye, H. *The stress of life.* New York: McGraw-Hill, 1956. [374, 550]

Shaffer, L. F., and Shoben, E. J., Jr. *The psychology of adjustment* (2nd ed.). Boston: Houghton Mifflin, 1956. [593]

Sheard, N. M. *See* Wiesner and Sheard, 1933.

Sheffield, F. D. *See* Campbell and Sheffield, 1953.

―――― , and Roby, T. B. Reward value of a non-nutritive sweet taste. *J. comp. physiol. Psychol.*, 1950, **43**, 471–481. [140, 249]

―――― , Roby, T. B., and Campbell, B. A. Drive reduction versus consummatory behavior as determinants of reinforcement. *J. comp. physiol. Psychol.*, 1954, **47**, 349–354. [250]

―――― , Wulff, J. J. and Backer, R. Reward value of copulation without sex drive reduction. *J. comp. physiol. Psychol.*, 1951, **44**, 3–8. [248–249]

Sherif, M., and Cantril, H. *The psychology of ego-involvements, social attitudes and identifications.* New York: Wiley, 1947. [529]

Shils, E. A. *See* Parsons and Shils, 1952.

Shoben, E. J. *See* Shaffer and Shoben, 1956.

Shuford, E. H., Jr. Palatability and osmotic pressure of glucose and sucrose solutions as determinants of intake. *J. comp. physiol. Psychol.*, 1959, **52**, 150–153. [158, 160–161]

―――― *See* Young and Shuford, 1954.

Shurrager, P. S. (Personal communication) [221]

Skinner, B. F. *The behavior of organisms: an experimental analysis.* New York: Appleton-Century-Crofts, 1938. [20, 100, 243–244]

────── *See* Ferster and Skinner, 1957.

Smith, F. V. *The explanation of human behaviour.* London: Constable, 1951. [7]

Smudski, J. F. *See* Braun, Wedekind, and Smudski, 1957.

Snygg, D. *See* Combs and Snygg, 1959.

Solomon, R. L. *See* Hunt, Schlosberg, Solomon, and Stellar, 1947.

──────, and Brush, E. S. Experimentally derived conceptions of anxiety and aversion. In *Nebraska symposium on motivation* (M. R. Jones, Ed.). Lincoln, Nebr.: University of Nebraska Press, 1956. [232]

Sorokin, P. A. *Society, Culture, and Personality.* New York: Harper, 1947. [20]

Spence, K. W. The role of secondary reinforcement in delayed reward learning. *Psychol. Rev.,* 1947, **54,** 1–8. [246]

────── *Behavior theory and conditioning.* New Haven, Conn.: Yale University Press, 1956. [20, 235, 256]

──────, and Lippitt, R. An experimental test of the sign-gestalt theory of trial and error learning. *J. exper. Psychol.,* 1946, **36,** 491–502. [137]

Spiegel, J. P. *See* Grinker and Spiegel, 1945.

Spitz, R. A. The smiling response: A contribution to the ontogenesis of social relations. *Genet. Psychol. Monog.,* 1946, **34,** 57–125. [447–449]

Spragg, S. D. S. Morphine addiction in chimpanzees. *Comp. Psychol. Monog.,* 1940, **15,** No. 7. [429]

Spranger, E. *Types of men: The psychology and ethics of personality* (Trans. from 5th German edition by P. J. W. Pigors). Halle: Niemeyer, 1928. [512]

Stacey, C. L., and De Martino, M. F. *Understanding human motivation.* Cleveland, Ohio: Howard Allen, 1958. [343]

Stagner, R. Attitudes. In *Encyclopedia of educational research* (rev. ed., W. S. Monroe, Ed.). New York: Macmillan, 1950. [531–532]

────── Homeostasis as a unifying concept in personality theory. *Psychol. Rev.,* 1951, **58,** 5–17. [326]

──────, and Karwoski, T. F. *Psychology.* New York: McGraw-Hill, 1952. [326]

Stellar, E. The physiology of motivation. *Psychol. Rev.,* 1954, **61,** 5–22. [405]

────── *See* Hill and Stellar, 1951.

────── *See* Hunt, Schlosberg, Solomon, and Stellar, 1947, *and* Morgan, and Stellar, 1950.

──────, Hyman, R., and Samet, S. Gastric factors controlling water- and salt-solution-drinking. *J. comp. physiol. Psychol.,* 1954, **47,** 220–226. [119]

Stevens, S. S. Adaptation-level vs. the relativity of judgment. *Amer. J. Psychol.,* 1958, **71,** 633–646. [320]

Strong, E. K. *Change of interests with age.* Stanford, Calif.: Stanford University Press, 1931. [460–461]

Suci, G. J. *See* Osgood and Suci, 1955.

Supa, M., Cotzin, M., and Dallenbach, K. M. Facial vision: The perception of obstacles by the blind. *Amer. J. Psychol.,* 1944, **57,** 133–183. [291]

Sutton, M. A. *See* Guilford, Christensen, Bond, and Sutton, 1954.

Symonds, P. M. *The dynamics of human adjustment.* New York: Appleton-Century-Crofts, 1946. [36, 534, 593]

Symonds, P. M. *Dynamic psychology.* New York: Appleton-Century-Crofts, 1949. [36–37]

Taylor, J. A. A personality scale of manifest anxiety. *J. ab. soc. Psychol.,* 1953, **48,** 285–290. [567–568]

Thomas, W. F., and Young, P. T. A study of organic set: immediate reproduction, by different muscle groups, of patterns presented by successive visual flashes. *J. exper. Psychol.,* 1942, **30,** 347–367. [269–271]

Thorndike, E. L. Animal intelligence: an experimental study of the associative processes in animals. *Psychol. Rev. Monog. Suppl.,* 1898, **2,** No. 4. [144]

—— *Animal intelligence, experimental studies.* New York: Macmillan Co., 1911. [145]

—— *The psychology of wants, interests and attitudes.* New York: Appleton-Century-Crofts, 1935. [251, 491]

Tinbergen, N. Social releasers and the experimental method required for their study. *Wilson Bulletin,* 1948, **60,** 6–51. [78]

—— *The study of instinct.* Oxford, England: Clarendon Press, 1951. [72–75, 107–108]

Titchener, E. B. *A textbook of psychology.* New York: Macmillan, 1921. [149, 275]

Tolman, E. C. A behavioristic account of the emotions. *Psychol. Rev.,* 1923, **30,** 217–227. [348]

—— Purpose and cognition: The determiners of animal learning. *Psychol. Rev.,* 1925, **32,** 285–297. [258]

—— *Purposive behavior in animals and men.* New York: Appleton-Century-Crofts, 1932. [296]

—— Cognitive maps in rats and men. *Psychol. Rev.,* 1948, **55,** 189-208. [326]

Troland, L. T. *The fundamentals of human motivation.* Princeton, N. J.: Van Nostrand, 1928. [5, 36–37, 147]

Tsai, L. S. The laws of minimum effort and maximum satisfaction in animal behavior. *Psychol. Abstracts,* 1932, **6,** No. 4329. [286]

Tuttle, H. S. *How motives are educated.* Ann Arbor, Mich.: Edwards Brothers, 1941. [487]

Verney, E. L. *See* Scott and Verney, 1947.

—— *See* Scott, Verney, and Morissey, 1950.

Vernon, P. E. *See* Allport, Vernon, and Lindzey, 1960.

Wang, G. H. Relation between "spontaneous" activity and oestrus cycle in the white rat. *Comp. Psychol. Monog.,* 1923, **2,** No. 6. [40]

Ward, A. *See* Harris, Clay, Hargreaves, and Ward, 1933.

Warden, C. J. *Animal motivation: Experimental studies on the albino rat.* New York: Columbia University Press, 1931. [101]

Waterhouse, I. K. *See* Child and Waterhouse, 1953.

Watson, J. B. *Behavior, an introduction to comparative psychology.* New York: Holt, 1914. [150, 384]

Watson, J. B. A schematic outline of the emotions. *Psychol. Rev.,* 1919, **26,** 165–196. [355]

Webb, W. B. "A motivational theory of emotions . . ." *Psychol. Rev.,* 1948, **55,** 329–335. [351]

Wedekind, C. E. *See* Braun, Wedekind, and Smudski, 1957.

Wenger, M. A. Emotion as visceral action: An extension of Lange's theory. In *Feelings and emotions: the Mooseheart symposium in cooperation with the University of Chicago* (M. L. Reymert, Ed.). New York: McGraw-Hill, 1950. [398]

Wertheimer, M. *Productive thinking.* New York: Harper, 1945. [324]

White, R. W. *The abnormal personality.* New York: Ronald, 1948. [566, 569]

——— *The abnormal personality: a textbook.* (2nd ed.) New York: Ronald, 1956. [593]

——— Motivation reconsidered: the concept of competence. *Psychol. Rev.,* 1959, **66,** 297–333. [60, 62, 67]

Whiteman, P. H. *See* Hall and Whiteman, 1951.

Wiesner, B. P., and Sheard, N. M. *Maternal behaviour in the rat.* Edinburgh: Oliver and Boyd, 1933. [74]

Wilkins, L., and Richter, C. P. A great craving for salt by a child with cortico-adrenal insufficiency. *J. Amer. Med. Asso.,* 1940, **114,** 866–868. [128]

Wolf, A. The dynamics of the selective inhibition of specific functions in neurosis: A preliminary report. In *Contemporary Psychopathology* (S. S. Tomkins, Ed.). Cambridge, Mass.: Harvard University Press, 1943. [434–436]

Wolfe, J. B. Effectiveness of token-rewards for chimpanzees. *Comp. Psychol. Monog.,* 1936, **12,** No. 5. [217, 247]

Wood, A. *See* Muenzinger and Wood, 1935.

Woodworth, R. S. *Dynamic psychology.* New York: Columbia University Press, 1918. [92]

——— Reenforcement of perception. *Amer. J. Psychol.,* 1947, **60,** 119–124. [95]

——— *Dynamics of behavior.* New York: Holt, 1958. [36–37, 59, 67, 569]

———, and Schlosberg, H. *Experimental psychology.* New York: Holt, 1954. [36–37, 185, 204, 409–410]

Wulff, J. J. *See* Sheffield, Wulff, and Backer, 1951.

Yamaguchi, H. G. Drive (*D*) as a function of hours of hunger (*h*). *J. exper. Psychol.,* 1951, **42,** 108–117. [126–127]

Yavitz, J. A. *See* Young and Yavitz, 1946.

Young, P. T. *Motivation of behavior: The fundamental determinants of human and animal activity.* New York: Wiley, 1936. (Out of print.) [36–37, 67, 92, 206]

——— Reversal of food preferences of the white rat through controlled pre-feeding. *J. gen. Psychol.,* 1940, **22,** 33–66. [162]

——— *Emotion in man an animal: Its nature and relation to attitude and motive.* New York: Wiley, 1943. (Out of print.) [409–410, 465–466, 547]

——— Studies of food preference, appetite and dietary habit: IV. The balance between hunger and thirst. *J. comp. Psychol.,* 1945a, **38,** 135–174. [135]

——— Studies of food preference, appetite and dietary habit: V. Techniques for testing food preference and the significance of results obtained with different methods. *Comp. Psychol. Monog.,* 1945b, **19,** 1–58. [163]

Young, P. T. Studies of food preference, appetite and dietary habit: VII. Palatability in relation to learning and performance. *J. comp. physiol. Psychol.*, 1947, **40**, 37–72. [167, 172]

—— Emotion as disorganized response—a reply to Professor Leeper. *Psychol. Rev.*, 1949, **56**, 184–191. [351]

—— Motivation of animal behavior. In *Comparative psychology* (3rd ed.; C. P. Stone, Ed.). Englewood Cliffs, N. J.: Prentice-Hall, 1951. [36–37]

—— Continuous recording of the fluid intake of small animals. *Amer. J. Psychol.*, 1957, **70**, 295–298. [41]

—— The role of affective processes in learning and motivation. *Psychol. Rev.*, 1959, **66**, 104–125. [204, 256, 416]

—— *See:* Kniep, Morgan, and Young, 1931; Compton and Young, 1933; *and* Thomas and Young, 1942.

——, and Asdourian, D. Relative acceptability of sodium chloride and sucrose solutions. *J. comp. physiol. Psychol.*, 1957, **50**, 499–503. [155, 237–238]

Young, P. T., and Chaplin, J. P. Studies of food preference, appetite and dietary habit: III. Palatability and appetite in relation to bodily need. *Comp. Psychol. Monog.*, 1945, **18**, 1–45. [163]

Young, P. T., and Falk, J. L. The relative acceptability of sodium chloride solutions as a function of concentration and water need. *J. comp. physiol. Psychol.*, 1956a, **49**, 569–575. [155, 181]

——, and Falk, J. L. The acceptability of tap water and distilled water to non-thirsty rats. *J. comp. physiol. Psychol.*, 1956b, **49**, 336–338. [180]

——, and Greene, J. T. Quantity of food ingested as a measure of relative acceptability. *J. comp. physiol. Psychol.*, 1953, **46**, 288–294. [155, 157]

——, and Richey, H. W. Diurnal drinking patterns in the rat. *J. comp. physiol. Psychol.*, 1952, **45**, 80–89. [41]

——, and Shuford, E. H., Jr. Intensity, duration, and repetition of hedonic processes as related to acquisition of motives. *J. comp. physiol. Psychol.*, 1954, **47**, 298–305. [173–175]

——, and Yavitz, J. A. Activities in which college students experience success and failure and those in which they wish to be more successful. *J. soc. Psychol.*, 1946, **24**, 131–148. [497]

Younger, J. *See* Russell and Younger, 1943.

Zilboorg, G., and Henry, G. W. *A history of medical psychology.* New York: Norton, 1941. [593]

Zipf, G. K. *Human behavior and the principle of least effort: an introduction to human ecology.* Cambridge, Mass.: Addison-Wesley, 1949. [284]

INDEX

631

646

INDEX

Sensory organization and suprasensory,
323–325
Sensory processes and affective, 154–156
Sentiments, 510–511
Set, experiments on central, 267–270
difficulty in organizing, 267–270
learning to assume a, 271–273
meanings of, 264–265
of attention, 275–276
properties of determining, 276–278
regulation and direction by, 264–278
Sexual activation, hormones in, 87–88
mechanisms in, 89
Sexual appetite, hunger compared with,
84–86
organic need and, 84–86
Sexual behavior, of stickleback, 72–73
neural basis of, 86–87
Sexual exhaustion, 84–86
Sexual motivation, 82–91
human, 89–91
Sexual patterns, female and male, 389–
391
"Sham rage," 386–388
Shame, feelings of, 527–528
Sherrington, C. S., 344
Shifting of interests with age, 460–462
Shock, before and after choice, 222–226
effects of electric, 222–226
for right and wrong choices, 222–226
Signs of emotional disturbance, 345–
346, 375–380
Simultaneous recording of bodily
changes in emotion, 380–381
Situation, external, as source of emo-
tion, 346–347
present, in causation of fear, 413–414
Size of perceived reward as determi-
nant, 212–213
Skin sweating, 378
Skin temperature in emotion, 377
Skinner's account of reinforcement and
extinction, 242–244
Sleep and wakefulness, 42–44
Smiling in infants, conditions eliciting,
447–449
development of, 447–449

Social behavior, approaches to study of,
472–473
corn dance as example of, 469–472
determinants of, 482–486
Social conformity, reasons for, 503–504
Social determinants, 20–22
Social development and emotional,
443–444, 453–454
Social incentives, 486–504
Social motives, 486–504
Social point of view, 25–26
Social psychology, three main ap-
proaches to, 472–473
Social setting, biological determinants
in, 468–469
Somatic and visceral components of
emotional response, 362–363
Spatial orientation through auditory
feedback, 291–292
Specific patterns of activity, 38–39
Specificity, lack of, in early behavior,
444–445
Speed of locomotion and quantity of
reward, 208–211
Startle pattern, 391–394
Status and role, 479–480
Stress, anxiety during, 553–555
factors producing, 556–558
morale under, 555–556
neurosis and, 550–561
reactions to, 552–556
Stickleback, mating behavior of, 72–73
Stimulation, as motivation, 19
role of, in mating, 83–84
Stimulus-response psychology, limita-
tions of, 154–156
Structure as determinant of behavior,
64–66
Structure-function relation, 64–66
Study of values, 511–513
Subception, 312
Subjective point of view, 25, 28–29
Sublimation, reorientation and, 577–578
Success and failure, influences of, 496
Suggestions to student of motivation,
599–602
Suprasensory organization and sensory,
323–325